ROMAN LITERATURE
NERVA, TRAJAN AND

This volume is the first holistic investigation of Roman literature and literary culture under Nerva, Trajan and Hadrian (AD 96–138). With case studies from Frontinus, Juvenal, Martial, Pliny the Younger, Plutarch, Quintilian, Suetonius and Tacitus among others, the eighteen chapters offer not just innovative readings of literary (and some 'less literary') texts, but a collaborative enquiry into the networks and culture in which they are embedded. The book brings together established and novel methodologies to explore the connections, conversations and silences between these texts and their authors, both on and off the page. The scholarly dialogues that result not only shed fresh light on the dynamics of literary production and consumption in the 'High Roman Empire', but offer new provocations to students of intertextuality and interdiscursivity across classical literature. How can and should we read textual interactions in their social, literary and cultural contexts?

ALICE KÖNIG is Senior Lecturer in Classics at the University of St Andrews. Her research focuses on ancient technical literature and the history of science, and the relationship between politics, society and literature in the early principate. She is preparing a monograph on the author and statesman Sextus Julius Frontinus, and has published a series of articles on Vitruvius, Frontinus and Tacitus. She established the 'Literary Interactions' research project in 2011, and is co-editor also of its second volume (on cross-cultural interactions in the Roman Empire, AD 96–235).

CHRISTOPHER WHITTON is Senior Lecturer in Classical Literature at the University of Cambridge, and Fellow and Director of Studies in Classics at Emmanuel College. His publications include a commentary on Pliny *Epistles* 2 (Cambridge, 2013), and he is co-editor (with Roy Gibson) of *Oxford Readings in the Epistles of Pliny* (2016).

ROMAN LITERATURE UNDER NERVA, TRAJAN AND HADRIAN

Literary Interactions, AD *96–138*

EDITED BY

ALICE KÖNIG

University of St Andrews, Scotland

CHRISTOPHER WHITTON

University of Cambridge

CAMBRIDGE
UNIVERSITY PRESS

CAMBRIDGE
UNIVERSITY PRESS

University Printing House, Cambridge CB2 8BS, United Kingdom

One Liberty Plaza, 20th Floor, New York, NY 10006, USA

477 Williamstown Road, Port Melbourne, VIC 3207, Australia

314-321, 3rd Floor, Plot 3, Splendor Forum, Jasola District Centre, New Delhi - 110025, India

79 Anson Road, #06-04/06, Singapore 079906

Cambridge University Press is part of the University of Cambridge.

It furthers the University's mission by disseminating knowledge in the pursuit of
education, learning and research at the highest international levels of excellence.

www.cambridge.org
Information on this title: www.cambridge.org/9781108430531
DOI: 10.1017/9781108354813

© Cambridge University Press 2018

First published 2018
First paperback edition 2020

A catalogue record for this publication is available from the British Library

Library of Congress Cataloging in Publication data
Names: Khonig, Alice, 1977– editor. | Whitton, Christopher, 1979– editor.
Title: Roman literature under Nerva, Trajan and Hadrian : literary interactions,
AD 96-138 / edited by Alice Khonig, Christopher Whitton.
Description: Cambridge : Cambridge University Press, 2018. |
Includes bibliographical references and index.
Identifiers: LCCN 2017058239 | ISBN 9781108420594 (alk. paper)
Subjects: LCSH: Latin literature – History and criticism.
Classification: LCC PA6042 .R653   2018 | DDC 870.9/001 – dc23
LC record available at https://lccn.loc.gov/2017058239

ISBN 978-1-108-42059-4 Hardback
ISBN 978-1-108-43053-1 Paperback

for John Henderson

Contents

Figure

Contributors

RHIANNON ASH is Professor of Roman Historiography, Merton College, Oxford.

EMMA BUCKLEY is Senior Lecturer in Latin, University of St Andrews.

WILLIAM FITZGERALD is Professor of Latin Language and Literature, King's College London.

TOM GEUE is a British Academy Postdoctoral Fellow in Classics, University of St Andrews.

ROY GIBSON is Professor of Latin, University of Manchester.

JILL HARRIES is Professor emeritus of Ancient History, University of St Andrews.

JOHN HENDERSON is Professor emeritus of Latin, University of Cambridge, and Fellow of King's College.

GAVIN KELLY is Professor of Latin Literature and Roman History, University of Edinburgh.

ALICE KÖNIG is Senior Lecturer in Latin and Classical Studies, University of St Andrews.

REBECCA LANGLANDS is Professor of Classics, University of Exeter.

MYLES LAVAN is Senior Lecturer in Ancient History, University of St Andrews.

ILARIA MARCHESI is Professor of Comparative Literature, Languages, and Linguistics, Hofstra University.

RUTH MORELLO is Lecturer in Classics, University of Manchester.

SIGRID MRATSCHEK is Professor of Ancient History, Rostock University.

VICTORIA RIMELL is Associate Professor of Latin, University of Warwick.

PAUL ROCHE is Senior Lecturer in Latin, University of Sydney.

MATTHEW ROLLER is Professor of Classics, Johns Hopkins University.

JAMES UDEN is Associate Professor of Classical Studies, Boston University.

CHRISTOPHER WHITTON is Senior Lecturer in Classical Literature, University of Cambridge, and Fellow of Emmanuel College.

Preface

This volume arises out of a research project, 'Literary Interactions under Nerva, Trajan and Hadrian', directed by Alice König and based at St Andrews since 2011. We explain more about it in the Introduction; here we have the pleasant task of recording some debts of gratitude, starting with the several institutes and funding bodies which have supported the project so far: the British Academy/Leverhulme Small Research Grants Scheme, the Institute of Classical Studies, the School of Classics (University of St Andrews), Emmanuel College, Cambridge, and Exeter University; the Alexander von Humboldt-Stiftung, the Heinrich Schliemann-Institut für Altertumswissenschaften (University of Rostock) and the Rostocker Freunde der Altertumswissenschaften; and the Peter Paul Career Development Professorship (Boston University).

Now to people: several dozen scholars have taken part in the project so far, delivering and responding to workshop and conference papers and posting working papers online. Our warm thanks to all of these for contributing their expertise and energy, and building such rich, productive and (we trust) unfinished dialogues together. We are especially grateful to our seventeen fellow-contributors to this volume, both for their individual work and for joining enthusiastically in the spirit of communal endeavour that we hoped would mark it: our many interactions, literary and personal, have been rewarding indeed. For logistical support at the St Andrews and Rostock conferences in which this volume finds its origins, we thank Margaret Goudie, Josephine Kliebe and Anke Wegner; and we fondly recall the warm hospitality and unstinting support of Christiane Reitz. Sincere thanks too to Michael Sharp and his team at Cambridge University Press, to Ana Kotarcic for her efficient editorial work and to James Uden for suggesting the cover illustration. Finally, for ready advice and unending patience, we thank Jason König and Michael Squire.

ARK and CLW, 31.1.17

PS John Henderson didn't know we would dedicate this volume to him when he agreed to contribute to it. It's a small but heartfelt token of thanks for many hours, and many years, of support as supervisor, mentor and friend.

Abbreviations

Abbreviations for ancient authors and titles follow LSJ, *OLD* or other standard conventions; those for journals are adapted from *L'Année philologique*.

AE	*L'Année épigraphique*, Paris 1888–.
ANRW	*Aufstieg und Niedergang der römischen Welt*, Berlin 1972–.
CEL	P. Cugusi, ed., *Corpus epistularum Latinarum, papyris tabulis ostracis servatarum*, Florence 1992–2002.
CIL	*Corpus inscriptionum Latinarum*, Berlin 1863–.
Coll. Leg.	*Collatio legum Mosaicarum et Romanarum.*
GL	H. Keil, ed., *Grammatici Latini*, 7 vols., Leipzig 1855–80.
IGR	R. Cagnat, ed., *Inscriptiones Graecae ad res Romanas pertinentes*, 4 vols., Paris 1901–27.
ILS	H. Dessau, ed., *Inscriptiones Latinae selectae*, Berlin 1892–1916.
LSJ	H. G. Liddell, R. Scott and H. S. Jones, *Greek–English lexicon* (with revised supplement), 9th edn, Oxford 1996.
MAMA	*Monumenta Asiae Minoris antiqua*, Manchester and London 1928–.
OCD[4]	S. Hornblower, A. Spawforth and E. Eidenow, eds., *Oxford classical dictionary*, 4th edn, Oxford 2012.
OLD	P. W. Glare, ed., *Oxford Latin dictionary*, Oxford 1982 (2nd edn, 2012).
PIR[2]	*Prosopographia imperii Romani saec. I, II, III*, 2nd edn, Berlin 1933–2015.
PL	J.-P. Migne, ed., *Patrologia Latina*, Paris 1844–65.
RP	R. Syme, *Roman papers* (ed. E. Badian and A. R. Birley), 7 vols., Oxford 1979–91.
SEG	*Supplementum epigraphicum Graecum*, Amsterdam and Leiden 1923–.
TAM	*Tituli Asiae Minoris*, Vienna and Bonn 1901–.
TLL	*Thesaurus Linguae Latinae*, Leipzig 1900–.

Introduction

Alice König and Christopher Whitton

Among the Scrolls

Picture yourself in Rome around AD 115, standing in the new Forum of Trajan. Beside you is the great equestrian statue of the emperor, before you the vast Basilica Ulpia, crowded with the usual mêlée of jurists and scribes, officials and petitioners. High above its roof is another statue of Trajan, glinting down from the summit of his victory column. As you make your way further into the forum, your eye is caught by the colourful carvings on the column's shaft; but you can't help also being struck by the buildings that flank it, the two monumental wings of the Bibliotheca Ulpia.[1] One of them houses a copy of Trajan's *Dacian war*, a textual account of his Danubian victories to complement the triumphal scenes winding up the column outside.[2] What other scrolls you might have found in this double library is now a matter of speculation. Archival material for sure, such as the praetors' edicts that would one day be called up by Aulus Gellius;[3] but it is a fair bet that literary works featured too,[4] Greek and Latin.[5] If so, here was a building grandly proclaiming its imperial patron's investment in the written word, both documentary and literary, and in both world languages.[6] The Bibliotheca Ulpia was not a public library as we know them, with borrowing rights and hushed reading rooms for research.[7] As well as consulting the collection, visitors may have come to marvel at the statuary or attend

---

[1] For an architectural description of the library, see Packer 2001: 78–9; on its position, Packer 1995: 353–4.

[2] Or so we might assume: see e.g. Coarelli 2000: 11–14; Nasrallah 2010: 160. We know of this work only from Priscian, who cites *Traianus in I Dacicorum* (*GL* II 205.6; cf. Fein 1994: 24).

[3] Gell. *NA* 11.17.1; also *HA Aur.* 1.7, *Tac.* 8.1.

[4] As in Augustus' library on the Palatine (cf. schol. Juv. 1.128 *bibliothecam iuris ciuilis et liberalium studiorum*); Neudecker 2013 discusses the likely contents of imperial libraries.

[5] Perhaps divided between the two wings (but the point is moot: see Nicholls 2010).

[6] Libraries were included often enough within a larger complex (see Bowie 2013 for a survey of other imperial foundations), but this central positioning was novel.

[7] Modern reconstructions are all too often 'disquietingly' familiar (Johnson 2013a: 347).

public lectures, even, perhaps, for senatorial meetings or judicial proceedings that had spilled over from the nearby Basilica Ulpia:[8] like other Roman libraries (and there seems to have been a flurry of construction around the turn of the second century),[9] it had a range of functions which alert us to the interconnectedness of literary, administrative, legal, religious, political and social activity – in short, to the full range of elite Roman culture. Its position at the heart of the forum signals the centrality of the written word in Trajan's capital. And while this library may or may not have contained all the works that will feature in the present volume, its function as repository and hub, bringing together all manner of texts for readers to walk past, scroll through, and set beside each other, makes for a good way of visualising what *Literary Interactions* is all about.

The book in your hands (or on your screen) is concerned with the connections, conversations and silences between texts composed in the years just before and after Trajan's Forum was built, during the principates of Nerva, Trajan and Hadrian. Like the Bibliotheca Ulpia, many of these texts are grandiose in scope or ambition: not just the lofty histories of Tacitus, but Frontinus' account of an aqueduct network that puts the pyramids to shame, Juvenal's monstrous satires, Martial's 'twelve' books (that epic number) of epigrams, Pliny the Younger's claims on posterity in *Epistles* and *Panegyricus* alike – all these assert monumental status, in their different ways. But, behind the imposing façades, the literature of this period is also a fluid, organic space, site of a myriad of interactions between writers and readers, characters and discourses, the living and the dead. Then as now, libraries may have served not least as repositories of the arcane;[10] but they were also 'place[s] of encounter between living generations, as well as between authors of the past and present'.[11] The same is true of the broad corpus of Nervan, Trajanic and Hadrianic texts. Many of their

---

[8] See Nicholls 2013. Senatorial meetings are attested for the Palatine library in the first century (see Bowie 2013: 241; Petrain 2013: 341).

[9] Not just in Rome, with the rededicated Palatine library (Mart. *Epig.* 12.2.7–8) and others restored by Domitian (Suet. *Dom.* 20), perhaps including the one in the Temple of Peace (so Tucci 2013). Pliny founded a library in his hometown Comum around 96/7 (*Ep.* 1.8 with Dix 1996); one featured among the projects of Dio Chrysostom in his native Prusa fifteen years later (Plin. *Ep.* 10.81–2 with Jones 1978: 111–14). T. Flavius Pantainos dedicated a library at Athens *c.* 98–102 (Platthy 1968: 113 no. 37), as did Tiberius Julius Aquila Polemaenus, in honour of his father Celsus, at Ephesus *c.* 125–7 (Hueber and Strocka 1975; Sauron 2010). Hadrian built several libraries, private (at Tivoli) and public (in Athens and Rome). Some other private libraries are mentioned by Martial (*Epig.* 7.17, 9.pr., 14.190) and Pliny (*Ep.* 2.17.8, 4.28); even poor Cordus has his basket of books (Juv. *Sat.* 3.206–7). On the libraries of the Roman Empire, see especially Neudecker 2004; Dix and Houston 2006.

[10] Johnson 2013a: 354–6, 362; Zadorojnyi 2013: 396; Neudecker 2013: 328–9; cf. Tucci 2013: 303.

[11] Nicholls 2013: 264.

authors knew each other personally; some collaborated in literary production, attending recitals and exchanging drafts; several mention each other or converse intertextually, whether unilaterally or in dialogue. They are joined by a host of personal acquaintances and public figures who walk off the street and into their pages to mingle with literary characters, past and present, in what thus becomes a complex and multifaceted tangle of socio-literary intercourse.

Our volume sets out to probe those interactions and conversations, both as a literary-historical phenomenon and as an opportunity for methodological reflection. Some chapters consider dialogues between one contemporary author or text and another; others tackle more complex nexuses of three works or more. Several look beyond 'allusion', to set texts in conversation (with or without their authors' conniving), to explore 'extratextual' dialogue, or to confront head-on the challenges posed by *absent* dialogue. In unpicking interactions between very different kinds of texts – historical, epigrammatic, biographical, satirical, epistolary, philosophical, pedagogical, legal, technical, administrative . . . – we seek to embrace the full range of literary production, and indeed to expand it. We look beyond texts, too, at the spaces – recitations, dinner parties, the schoolroom, philosophical debates – in which literary interactions were generated and refracted; the interface between textual and personal encounters will be a particularly recurrent theme. Between them, our eighteen contributors offer new readings of a wide range of texts. Quintilian's *Institutio oratoria*, Frontinus' *De aquis*, lawyers' letters, imperial rescripts and an anonymous Greek treatise claim attention alongside Martial's *Epigrams*, Pliny's *Epistles* and *Panegyricus*, Plutarch's dialogues, Tacitus' 'major' and 'minor' works, Suetonius' *Lives* and Juvenal's *Satires*. In the process they explore some of the implications of the term 'interactions': the strengths and limits of inherited approaches to intertextuality; potential alternatives; how, in short, we can most productively study relationships which exist both on and off the page. The scholarly conversation that results, we hope, not only sheds fresh light on the dynamics of Nervan, Trajanic and Hadrianic literary culture as a whole, but offers new provocations and challenges to students of other periods too. How can and should we read textual interactions in the increasingly cosmopolitan world of the principate?

Nerva, Trajan and Hadrian

More on the ramifications of 'interactions' in a moment, along with a methodological case study of our own. But first a pressing question arises: *is* there such a thing as 'Nervan, Trajanic and Hadrianic literary culture'? Why stake out the years 96–138 as a discrete period?[12] Compared with convenient monikers such as 'Flavian' or 'Severan', it certainly makes for a mouthful. 'Ulpian' might be stretched to cover Nerva and Trajan, but hardly Hadrian too; it's too early for 'Antonine', and 'the adoptive principate' will run for several decades more; a negative designation like 'post-Flavian' is unsatisfactory, not just for its insistence on 96 as a watershed; and the world is doubtless a better one without 'Nerjadrianic'. But these problems of naming only point up an artifice of all conventional periodisations for imperial history and literature, constructed as they are around emperors or dynasties: our period is no different, except that it features three emperors whose successive extra-familial adoptions did not produce continuity of nomenclature. In staking out three reigns and four decades as a coherent object of literary study, we are certainly adopting a periodisation of convenience. But it is not an entirely arbitrary one, inspired as it is by the rich crop of writing that those years witnessed, and to which we still have access.

In political terms this is a distinctive period, especially at its outset.[13] The assassination of Domitian on 18 September 96 put a bloody end to nearly twenty-seven years of rule by imperial Rome's second dynastic family, Vespasian and his sons Titus and Domitian. An epigram attributed to Martial sums up the view of that trio widespread from the late 90s to the present day:[14]

> Flauia gens, quantum tibi tertius abstulit heres!
>   Paene fuit tanti non habuisse duos.

> Flavian race, how much the third heir took from you!
>   It would almost have been worth not having had the [sc. other] two.

Domitian's last years had been marked by difficult relations with the senate, to put it mildly, a reign of terror, to put it dramatically.[15] Within hours of his murder the senate had elected the new emperor Nerva, twice consul and now in his mid sixties; subsequently Domitian suffered *damnatio memoriae*, and Rome (so the story goes) breathed a sigh of relief. Nerva allegedly succeeded in combining 'things long immiscible, principate and freedom',[16] but that did not mean calm: settling of scores in the senate, the

---

[12] A problem with which editors of all such volumes as this must wrestle: see e.g. Boyle 2003, Dinter 2013b and Zissos 2016: 5–14. All dates here are AD unless signalled.

[13] For the historical context, see Griffin 2000, Bennett 2001 and Grainger 2003. Much speculative reconstruction is required, given the paucity of detail on Nerva and Trajan in the literary record. For biographical details on emperors, Kienast 2004 is invaluable.

[14] Preserved in the scholia to Juvenal (on *Sat.* 4.38).   [15] See especially Syme 1983.

[16] Tac. *Agr.* 3.1 *res olim dissociabilis, principatum ac libertatem.*

threat of a pretender in the provinces and a revolt by the praetorian guard at Rome made for a turbulent first year, settled only by the adoption of Trajan in October 97. Four months later Nerva died, and 'Nerva Trajan Augustus' became emperor at the age of forty-four; the year 98 thus joins (and jostles with) 96 as the great moment of avowed renewal. From perhaps unassuming beginnings, Trajan would win renown in the historical record for military success abroad and political stability at home.[17] Victories in Dacia and Parthia swelled the empire to its greatest extent; at Rome literature flourished, dignity was restored to the senate and courts, and the 'best of emperors' governed by authority and respect instead of savage domination.

Such at least is the rosy picture painted by many of our ancient sources, above all those from the first years of Trajan's principate: in the *Agricola*, probably completed in 98, Tacitus made his literary debut with a biography of his father-in-law which integrates praise of Nerva and Trajan into its barbed attack on Domitian;[18] some years later, he began his *Histories* with the famous claim that he could write his account of the Flavians (and defer a history of Nerva and Trajan) 'with the rare good fortune of an age when you are allowed to think what you like and say what you think'.[19] Pliny's speech of thanksgiving to Trajan as consul, delivered in autumn 100 and written up as his *Panegyricus*, tirelessly works a polarity between Domitian, worst of emperors, and Trajan, the ideal opposite: false praise to the slave-master can be forgotten, as we offer genuine tribute to the man who 'commands us to be free'.[20] His nine-book collection of *Epistles*, apparently written between late 96 – after Domitian's death – and around 109, starts with buoyant celebration of literary revival,[21] and (more discreetly) works the same dichotomy as the *Panegyricus*.[22] A book of letters to and from Trajan,

---

[17] Trajan's military career before his accession was apparently not so distinguished as many have assumed; see Eck 2002a: 213–16, especially p. 215 n. 16.

[18] For three contrasting readings of the *Agricola*, see Whitmarsh 2006b; Sailor 2008: 51–118; Woodman 2014.

[19] *Hist.* 1.1.4 *rara temporum felicitate ubi sentire quae uelis et quae sentias dicere licet* – a claim taken very differently by different readers.

[20] In the famous paradox of *Pan.* 66.4 *iubes esse liberos: erimus* ('you command us to be free: we shall be'). Rees 2012b is a convenient overview of recent work on the *Panegyricus* (probably called *Gratiarum actio* by Pliny); see especially Bartsch 1994: 148–87, the essays collected in Roche 2011, and Roche's chapter in this volume.

[21] Especially *Ep.* 1.10 and 1.13.1. See Hoffer 1999: 3 ('restoration propaganda') and *passim*; Gibson and Morello 2012: 25–6.

[22] See Whitton 2013: 7. The precise dates of *Epistles* 1–9 are a topic of debate: for some different views, see Sherwin-White 1966: 20–65; Murgia 1985; Whitton 2013: 15–19; Bodel 2015. On Pliny's Trajanic self-presentation, see at length Geisthardt 2015, who identifies an '*optimus princeps* discourse' running through all his works (and those of Tacitus).

known as *Epistles* 10, appears to confirm this impression, both for Trajan's first years in power and during Pliny's governorship of Bithynia–Pontus a decade or so later, *c.* 109–11.[23]

Together Pliny and Tacitus, especially in their earliest works, have contributed in large measure to the judgment of history on Domitian, and on Trajan.[24] Others joined in the chorus: Martial, one of the few extant writers who published both under Domitian and after him, celebrates the Nervan 'Saturnalia' in *Epigrams* 11 (apparently dating to late 96)[25] and welcomes Trajan, renouncing his former flatteries, in the revised version of Book 10 two years later;[26] compliments to both emperors feature in his twelfth book (*c.* 101), though Martial's retirement to Spain by then is seen by some as a sign of disenchantment.[27] Another writer to bridge the gap is Frontinus, who wrote a four-book military manual (*Strategemata*) under Domitian,[28] then an account of Rome's water supply and its maintenance (*De aquis*) under Nerva, an emperor whose 'care for the state' he duly applauds.[29] But both Martial and Frontinus were dead within a few years of Trajan's accession.[30] How well the enthusiasm of Pliny and Tacitus for his brave new world held up is harder to say: quite apart from the ambiguities of the *Dialogus*,[31] many modern readers have detected a 'darkening' in Tacitus' view of the principate refracted through the *Histories* and subsequently the *Annals*, written later in Trajan's reign and perhaps into Hadrian's;[32] the final instalments of Pliny's *Epistles*, which certainly nuance his initial celebration of Nervan Rome, may reveal shadows lengthening over Trajan

---

[23] For these dates (not certain), see Millar 2000. The recently reopened question, whether Pliny published *Epistles* 10 himself and how far it should be read as a 'literary', how far a 'documentary' text (see Whitton and Gibson 2016: 43–6), is central to the chapters of Harries and Lavan in this volume.

[24] Modern scholars have been sceptical about both the blackening of Domitian and the claim of a watershed in 96; see e.g. Waters 1969; Coleman 2000; Wilson 2003; Galimberti 2016.

[25] Especially *Epig.* 11.1–7 and 15; see e.g. Sullivan 1991: 44–51 (on Books 10 and 11); Hinds 2007; Rimell 2008: 162–80; Fitzgerald in this volume.

[26] See especially *Epig.* 10.72, mentioned by both Rimell and Fitzgerald in their chapters. Such professions have not convinced all; see e.g. Fearnley 2003; Merli 2006a; Rimell 2008: 65–82.

[27] Howell 1998; Fearnley 2003: 603–5; Kelly's chapter in this volume. On the lively world of Greek epigram in our period, see Bowie 1990: 53–66; Nisbet 2003; Whitmarsh 2013: 137–53.

[28] For Domitian's role in the *Strategemata*, see variously Turner 2007; Malloch 2015; König 2017.

[29] See especially *Aq.* 1–3 with A. König 2007.

[30] Martial perhaps in 101 (depending on the date of Pliny *Ep.* 3.21), Frontinus perhaps in 102 or 103 (*Ep.* 4.8.3 with Sherwin-White 1966: 79–80 and Birley 2000a: 16).

[31] Commonly seen as Tacitus' death notice for oratory in the principate (including Trajan's); for a revisionist reading see van den Berg 2014. On *Dialogus* as a response to Quintilian's *Institutio oratoria*, see Whitton's chapter.

[32] On Tacitean 'Verdüsterung' see e.g. Fraenkel 1964, Woodman 1997: 92–3 and Woodman 2009b: 41–3. Syme 1958: 219–20 was sceptical (he doubted that Tacitus was enthusiastic with Trajan to start with).

too.[33] Juvenal was apparently writing into the 130s,[34] but his earliest Satires are usually counted as Trajanic. Whether that means the 110s (as many think) or as early as 100, his first poems join in the Domitian-bashing with abandon – or is it mocking exaggeration?[35] Either way, his satirical spin on the 'indignation industry' neatly underlines perhaps the most salient common point among our Nervan and Trajanic writers, the vilification of Domitian and concomitant celebration of the present. That these complementary aspects seem to be concentrated in the first years after Domitian's death must reflect in part sheer chance: no epigrammatist takes over from Martial, and the presumed death of Pliny around 111 leaves us with no (explicit) contemporary literary reflections on Trajan's later years. His demise also marks an end, for us, of overt personal and literary interactions: the teens are marked rather by Tacitus' increasingly austere history of Julio-Claudian Rome and Juvenal's ongoing *Satires*, which, for all their quotidian, contemporary qualities, can seem as reluctant as the *Histories* and *Annals* to join in contemporary conversations.

If Trajan's later years leave a patchy literary and historical record, the circumstances of his death in 117 and the accession of his former ward Hadrian are even more opaque, with allegations of a falsified deathbed adoption and the bloody suppression of a suspected early plot.[36] Like his predecessor, Hadrian was slow to return to Rome as new emperor; he would spend over half of his principate absent from the capital, sometimes on campaign, more often on pacific travels, above all in the Greek east. After Trajan's expansionism, Hadrian was more cautious: 'uninterested in extending the empire',[37] he pulled back from newly won territory and preferred to consolidate, as witness the wall in Britain and renewed fortifications along the Danube and Rhine. Yet his relentless travelling meant that the imperial centre of gravity was as much on the peripheries of the empire as at Rome;[38] an emperor who wore his philhellenism on his face, he also

---

[33] Respectively Gibson and Morello 2012: 27–31 and Gibson 2015.

[34] *Sat.* 15.27 gives a *terminus post quem* of 127; Courtney 1980: 2 and 571 (on *Sat.* 14.99) sets a *terminus ante* in 132.

[35] Domitian features most heavily in *Sat.* 4 but his shadow hangs over *Sat.* 1–5; like Tacitus (*Annals*) and Pliny (*Ep.* 7.29 and 8.6), Juvenal later looks back further, to the Julio-Claudians (especially Nero in *Sat.* 8). For two different interpretations of Juvenal's assaults on Domitian, see Ramage 1989 and Freudenburg 2001: 209–41. On the dating of *Sat.* 1 (late for e.g. Syme 1979, but early for Uden 2015: 219–26), see Kelly's chapter in this volume.

[36] So Dio Xiph. 69.1–2; *HA Hadr.* 7. See again Griffin 2000; also Birley 1997 (esp. p. 77); Syme 1984: 31–4. Contemporary sources are even scarcer here than for the events of 96–8.

[37] Tac. *Ann.* 4.32.2 *proferendi imperi incuriosus* – explicitly, at least, describing Tiberius.

[38] Athens enjoyed particular attention, but see Boatwright 2000 on Hadrian's investment in many cities around the empire. Zissos 2016: 13–14 identifies (loose) parallels with Domitian.

made cultural and intellectual interaction between Greece and Rome more fashionable than ever.[39] Hadrian's reign ended with as many tensions as it had begun,[40] and Aelius Aristides would give a speech in Rome some years later which implicitly painted him as an inconsistent, irrational and violent ruler.[41] Of course Aristides (if the speech is his) had his own agenda, not least to ingratiate himself with Antoninus;[42] but his oration suggests that contemporaries – Greeks among them – did not look back on Hadrian's principate with wholehearted approval.[43]

One notable exception was Arrian, a historian writing in Greek who rose high in Roman government under Hadrian's patronage and who wrote warmly to and about him in some of his works.[44] Other literary responses are harder to trace. Ronald Syme's celebrated theory that Tiberius' unwholesome succession in *Annals* 1 is a meditation *à clef* on Hadrian's in 117 is tantalising but moot;[45] so too the questions whether Juvenal's seventh Satire celebrates a new, Hadrianic age of literary patronage,[46] and how his fifteenth Satire, on cannibals in Egypt, might resonate with Hadrian's famous sojourn there in 130–1.[47] As for Suetonius, the other (for us) central Hadrianic author, and himself a Palace secretary, his *Lives of the Caesars* dwell firmly in the years before 96, offering, like Tacitus' *Histories*, only brief explicit testimony to the 'happier and more blessed state of the republic' thereafter.[48] All in all, this is a more diffuse literary

---

[39] For a subtle account of Hadrian's philhellenism, see Syme 1985b. His reign saw the continued integration of 'Greeks' (i.e. easterners) into the senate (see Halfmann 1979: 71–81) and their appointment to positions of administrative responsibility (Syme 1982a).

[40] Not least around the succession (Hadrian adopted Antoninus late in the day); see Dio Xiph. 69.17; *HA Hadr.* 15, 23–5.

[41] *To the emperor (Or.* 35), dated to 144 by Jones 1972 (date and ascription are questionable: see de Blois 1986).

[42] A form of praise familiar, of course, from early Trajanic literature, but in this case not necessarily a good tactic: Antoninus professed pious loyalty to Hadrian in multiple spheres of government, if we can trust the *Historia Augusta (Hadr.* 27.1–2; *Ant. Pius* 5.1–2).

[43] Another apparently ambivalent Greek is Favorinus, who enjoyed a spell in Hadrian's inner circle but was later exiled (for this and other stories about Hadrian and Greek intellectuals, see Swain 1989). On Hadrian's unpopularity, including with the senate (which was reluctant to deify him), see also Dio Xiph. 69.23.2–3, *HA Hadr.* 27, and the careful words of Fronto *Ad M. Caes.* 2.1.4 = vdH² p. 25.2–9; for some holistic estimations, see Dio Xiph. 69.3–7; Syme 1984; Stertz 1993.

[44] On Arrian's career and relations with Hadrian, see especially Stadter 1980: 1–18; Syme 1982b.

[45] Syme 1958: 465–503, ruled out for those who date the first books, or even most, of the *Annals* under Trajan (e.g. Goodyear 1981: 387–93 and Bowersock 1993 respectively).

[46] Hardie 1997–8. More broadly on Hadrian and literary culture (including his own productions), see André 1993; Stertz 1993; Fein 1994 (also on Trajan); for a wider early imperial picture, Mratschek 1993: 13–40.

[47] For two different views see Uden 2015: 210–15 and Ash's chapter in this volume.

[48] Suet. *Dom.* 23.2 *beatiorem . . . laetioremque . . . rei publicae statum.* Whether any such comment appeared at the beginning of his *Lives of the Caesars* (now lost) is unknown. On Suetonius, see

scene than what we see around the turn of the century, and one lacking in the copious social glue provided by epigrams and epistles. Nevertheless, not just because both Tacitus (perhaps) and Juvenal and Suetonius (certainly) were writing under Hadrian, the emperor's death in 138 supplies us with an end-point of convenience.

Whether 96 really did inaugurate a literary revival, then, and how long it lasted, are questions we can hardly answer. Nor is our corpus easily 'packaged' through identification of a *Zeitgeist* or even common concerns or features, beyond those early claims that urgent social and political reconstruction was needed after Domitian.[49] The absence of clusters of texts from a single genre makes it harder to read works against each other than it is, for instance, in early Augustan or Flavian times, where elegists and epicists respectively rub shoulders: perhaps the more jumbled miscellany of Tiberian literature is a closer parallel. Nor did the literature of our period become a gold standard in the following generations, as Augustan literature had: like their Neronian and Flavian forebears, Nervan, Trajanic and Hadrianic authors generally get the silent treatment from classicising Antonines such as Fronto and Gellius.[50] Together, though, they represent a significant chapter in Latin literary history. This was a time of energetic generic reinvention – from epistolography to history, satire to biography – and the early days of the so-called Second Sophistic, a cultural momentum that transformed the literary landscape (not just in Greek) across the empire. Besides, whatever the impact of 'our' authors in the second and third centuries, their influence in later antiquity and again since the Renaissance has been great. More diffuse and heterogeneous than the bodies of literature from some other 'periods', their texts are nonetheless products of a relatively short span which between them have a great deal in common – and which sustain rather more dialogues, and types of dialogue, than we have tended to hear. Listening more closely to those dialogues is the goal of this volume.

Literary Interactions

Nervan, Trajanic and Hadrianic literature has been a lively area of growth in Latin scholarship, but the trend in large-scale publications has been

first Wallace-Hadrill 1983; Power and Gibson 2014; on his partly extant *De viris illustribus*, see Kaster 1995: xxi–xxix.
[49] An obvious contrast is Neronian literature, bound up for many readers by its recurrent themes of spectacle, excess and the grotesque (see Dinter 2013b: 6–12).
[50] See e.g. Cameron 2010: 399–405.

for author-specific work.[51] Among shorter studies there have, to be sure, been broader attempts to identify spirits of the age across multiple works, often with a focus on shared concerns rather than dynamic interactions,[52] but most articles and chapters deal with discrete pairs of texts and authors. Pliny's personal and (inter)textual relationship with Tacitus is a firm favourite,[53] followed by his epistolary interactions with Martial or Suetonius;[54] then there is Juvenal's engagement with Martial and Tacitus,[55] and that of Tacitus with Suetonius and Frontinus.[56] Much attention has been paid in the process to the workings of allusion and intertextuality in our corpus, most influentially by A. J. Woodman on Tacitus (joined more recently by Timothy Joseph and Christopher van den Berg) and Ilaria Marchesi on Pliny.[57] Together this work has made great strides in unpicking individual instances of interaction and reflecting on its modes; what the period still lacks, though, is a synoptic study of the sort familiar for Augustan, Neronian and now Flavian literature.[58]

This volume grows out of a project that was developed to address that gap. Its first inspiration was Frontinus – or rather, the network of social, political and literary relationships tying him to a host of contemporaries: names such as Silius Italicus, Martial, Pliny, Tacitus, Plutarch, Aelian and

---

[51] To mention some recent monographs, collections and commentaries in English alone (routinely, of course, situating their author in a cultural context): Fitzgerald 2007, Rimell 2008 and Henriksén 2012 on Martial; Marchesi 2008, Roche 2011, Gibson and Morello 2012, Whitton 2013, Marchesi 2015a and Gibson and Whitton 2016 on Pliny; Power and Gibson 2014 and Wardle 2014 on Suetonius; Ash 2007, Sailor 2008, Woodman 2009a, Joseph 2012, Malloch 2013, Pagán 2012b, van den Berg 2014 and Woodman 2014 on Tacitus; Watson and Watson 2014, Keane 2015, Uden 2015 and Larmour 2016 on Juvenal.

[52] E.g. Ramage 1989; Wilson 2003; Pagán 2012a: 119–24; Kuhn 2015. An exception is Syme 1979, who identifies allusions between Juvenal, Pliny and Tacitus in the service of relative dating. Social and literary interactions in one important region, the Transpadana, are central to Mratschek 1984 and 2003.

[53] Griffin 1999; Ash 2003; Dominik 2007; Marchesi 2008: 97–206; Rutledge 2009; Woodman 2009b; Whitton 2010, 2012, forthcoming a; Gibson and Morello 2012: 161–8.

[54] Martial: Adamik 1976; Pitcher 1999; Henderson 2001, 2002: 47–57; Marchesi 2008: 62–8, 2013, 2015b; Neger 2015. Suetonius: Power 2010; Gibson 2014.

[55] Martial: Anderson 1970; Bramble 1982; Colton 1991; Uden 2015: 219–26. Tacitus: Nappa 2010; Keane 2012.

[56] Suetonius: references in Power 2014 (himself sceptical that he had even read Tacitus). Frontinus: König 2013.

[57] See respectively (e.g.) Woodman 1998, 2009b and 2012 *passim*, Joseph 2012 (also Lauletta 1998) and van den Berg 2014; Marchesi 2008 (also 2013 and 2015a). See also e.g. Schenk 1999a (translated as Schenk 2016); Hinds 2007; Whitton 2010; Gibson and Morello 2012 *passim*. More on intertextuality below.

[58] Also Antonine (see Russell 1990a) and Severan (Swain, Harrison and Elsner 2007; Kemezis 2014). Flavian literature has been a particularly vibrant scholarly scene in recent years, especially in the 'Flavian epic network': published volumes arising out of this and other similar enterprises include Nauta, van Dam and Smolenaars 2006; Boyle and Dominik 2003; Manuwald and Voigt 2013; Augoustakis 2013, 2014; Zissos 2016.

Arrian make for a long list. Exploring these relationships, Alice König saw a wider opportunity to bring researchers on the whole range of contemporary authors and texts into dialogue to examine the literary dynamics of the period collectively, and in 2011 she established a research project entitled 'Literary Interactions under Nerva, Trajan and Hadrian', based at St Andrews University and with Roy Gibson, Rebecca Langlands, James Uden and Christopher Whitton as co-investigators. In part, the project has been virtual, with a website hosting an expanding series of working papers,[59] but it has also developed through a series of conferences, beginning with two days at St Andrews in June 2013. Conversations started there were continued at a second, more methodologically focused conference ('Intertextuality, society and literary production') organised by Christopher Whitton at Rostock University in June 2014. New contributors joined forces with project veterans at a third meeting ('Literary interactions across linguistic, cultural and religious boundaries') organised by James Uden at Boston University in June 2015, with a particular focus on interactions between Greek, Latin, Christian and other writing traditions; and a fourth ('Literary and cultural interactions in the Roman Empire, 96–235', directed by Rebecca Langlands), extending the chronological range of the project into the third century, was held at Exeter University in June 2016. The blend of continuity and change in participants and the organic evolution of the project have allowed for ongoing but shifting conversations and a range of methodological experiments far beyond what is possible at a single event.

Rather than producing 'proceedings' of each conference, we have preferred to watch the project develop and grow before bringing together this first volume on Latin literary interactions, which reunites several contributors to the St Andrews and Rostock conferences to take a broad view – or rather, a range of views – on the dynamic relationships between Martial, Pliny, Tacitus, Frontinus, Suetonius and other contemporaries. We focus on Latin literary interactions, sidelining the likes of Dio, Arrian and Favorinus, not least for a pragmatic reason: the quantity of Latin–Latin interaction in our period is abundant material for a volume in itself.[60] That said,

---

[59] http://arts.st-andrews.ac.uk/literaryinteractions/.

[60] Two recent challenges from each side of the Greek/Roman divide are Stadter 2015, reading Plutarch in his Roman cultural context, and Uden 2015, situating Juvenal's *Satires* against the productions of contemporary Greek sophists and philosophers. See also Pelling 2009 on Plutarch and Suetonius and J. König forthcoming on Plutarch and Pliny; on Josephus, see e.g. Chapman 2009; Mason 2016a; (within the broader terms of 'Flavian Greek literature') Kemezis 2016. On the putative engagement of Dio Chrysostom's *Kingship orations* with Pliny's *Panegyricus*, see Trisoglio 1972 and Fedeli 1989: 433–5 (with scepticism in e.g. Moles 1990: 301–2); Whitmarsh 2001: 156–67 and 181–216 is a sophisticated reading of those *Orations* in broader terms of Trajanic ideology. The so-called Second Sophistic

all of our contributors explore Latin literary interactivity as one subset of a wider network of cultural and cross-cultural interactions. And our two concluding chapters (James Uden on Quintilian, Juvenal and a text once attributed to Plutarch, and Roy Gibson on Pliny and Plutarch) pave the way to a second volume on interactions that cross linguistic, cultural and religious boundaries, by probing some stubborn silences between Greek and Latin and by testing new methodologies for reflecting on cross-cultural exchange.

At this point, a few more words on our title are in order. Why 'literary', and why 'interactions'? To start with the latter, the preference for 'interactions' over, say, 'intertextuality' reflects a desire to encourage fresh scrutiny of tralatitious models of reference and allusion, and to explore the areas which intertextuality, as understood by most Classicists today, can find difficult to reach.[61] Our toolkit for intertextual studies in Latin literature was developed more or less exclusively with reference to late Republican and Augustan verse; for all its similarities – and many of the texts that we consider here adopt practices of allusion and intertextuality that look very familiar – Nervan, Trajanic and Hadrianic literary culture evolved under different conditions and in different ways. Inherited models play an important role in the discussions that follow, both as tools and as objects of reflection; but we also ask whether these now standard paradigms are sufficient for exploring the different kinds of interactivity in our period, with regards to both verse and – especially – prose. How far are practices of allusion or reworking consistent among the texts under consideration, and how far do they vary between authors and genres? What metaphors of intertextuality best describe the interactions we see taking place – alluding, borrowing, rewriting, evoking (Whitton, Buckley, Kelly)? What ways can we find to talk about distinctive absences of dialogue – omission, occlusion, erasure, amnesia (Geue, Uden, Gibson)? Do close lexical overlaps work differently from more diffuse 'clouds' of allusion (Roche, Mratschek, Marchesi)? Where in relation to 'intertextuality' might we place 'interdiscursivity' or synchronic but seemingly independent convergences in theme and content (Rimell, Fitzgerald, Ash, Morello)? How can we account for 'elements in

---

has of course acquired a wealth of bibliography, much of which examines Greek responses to Rome (as a cultural and political phenomenon); there is rather less discussion of Greek responses to Latin literature, and very little that considers such responses in an interactive light, as a dynamic form of engagement/intertextuality. Russell 1990b is an important discussion of the bilingual background.

[61] Or, to put it another way, to restore some of the Kristevan breadth to 'intertextuality', a term used in practice by most Latinists as a synonym for 'allusion' (see n. 77).

the ether' or 'extratextuality', the shared tropes/memes/schemata floating between texts in the oral culture of the period (Langlands)? What ancient audiences and contexts do we envisage for these various forms of literary interaction (Roller, König, Harries)? And what criteria do we (and did they) apply when it comes to assessing the visibility and 'meaningfulness' of such interactions? The emphasis throughout is on opening debate and embracing plurality: this volume – intended as a sample and stimulus, not as a handbook – aims to showcase the viability and profitability of many different methodological approaches.

In addition to, and through, broaching such methodological questions, we look to extend the horizons of interactions off the page, and beyond the 'canon'. Certainly literary texts, as usually defined, constitute the primary focus of attention, but their sociocultural context also plays a prominent role. As contributors variously illustrate, literary interactions in this period cannot be considered in isolation from social and political activity (e.g. Fitzgerald, Marchesi, Gibson); indeed, prosopography (the study of individual careers and personal relationships) can be a particularly revealing partner to intertextual study (König, Mratschek) – and a refreshing angle from which to consider the role of the authorial voice. We also probe the limits of 'literary' to consider how far traditional models of intertextuality can illuminate interactions between 'literature' and those texts commonly classed as 'non-literary' or documentary: what can such dialogues tell us about different contexts of consumption and production, and about boundaries or overlaps between (what are often perceived as) discrete spheres of Roman life (Harries, Lavan, König)? In the process we ask how textual interactions were shaped by contemporary trends in cultural and intellectual activity: modes of literary consumption, for instance, oral culture and philosophical debate. Matthew Roller reminds us of the vital role of *recitatio* in our period,[62] and other contributors ask how methodologies of intertextuality might help probe wider dynamics of cultural exchange (e.g. Langlands, Marchesi, Uden). *Literary Interactions* thus seeks not only to ground readings of literary works in their historical context, but also to enrich our understanding of that context itself, and – if we may risk a cliché of our own times – to expand interdisciplinary dialogue between literary and sociohistorical studies of the High Empire.

---

[62] For broader and bolder claims about the oral consumption of literature in Rome, see Wiseman 2015.

The Politics of Periodisation (*Encore*)

In that measure, this volume takes a historicist (as well as New Historicist) approach to its literary subject – which brings us back to the thorny issue of periodisation. We have already indicated that, in offering the principates of Nerva, Trajan and Hadrian as an object of literary study, we are as committed to challenging any simplistic idea that this is a discrete period as we are to identifying common threads. Accordingly, we resist the temptation to isolate it (as its authors often encourage us to do) from what came immediately before or after. Chapters by Christopher Whitton (on Quintilian, Pliny and the *Dialogus*), Emma Buckley (on heroism, tyranny and civil war in Valerius Flaccus and Tacitus) and Rhiannon Ash (on 'marvels' in Martial, Pliny and Juvenal) consciously explore interactions across that notorious Flavian/'post-Flavian' borderline, for instance, probing its significance as a cultural caesura. Our common enterprise also refuses to flatten out differences across the period; even as we work towards a more holistic appreciation of contemporary modes of interaction, we remain attentive to variegations and idiosyncrasies, synchronic and diachronic alike. By the same token, the identification of tidy 'Nervan', 'Trajanic' or 'Hadrianic' units is not our aim, nor do we want to construct a teleological march through the period. Some contributors plot developmental trajectories (Ash again, or the 'diachronic dialogues' traced by Ilaria Marchesi), and within each of the volume's three sections there are hints of chronological progression which readers may follow up if they wish. But they remain hints; and other organisational features pull in different directions, pointing to patterns and discontinuities that cut across notions of periodisation.[63]

Chronology, of course, determines the direction of many literary interactions. However, Gavin Kelly's study of Martial's poem to Juvenal (*Epigrams* 12.18) reminds us not to jump to conclusions about relative datings, and analogous uncertainties over other pairs of texts (by Pliny and Martial, Pliny and Tacitus, Martial and Frontinus, Pliny and jurists) liberate contributors to think more broadly about literary interactivity as a multi-stage and multi-directional phenomenon. And, while Victoria Rimell (on the

---

[63] The potential hazards of 'periodised' interpretation are well illustrated by Petronius' *Satyrica*, a text central to modern views of Neronian literature, but whose dating is notoriously problematic: as scholars continue to stress, it may well be Flavian or later (Laird 2007; Jeffrey Henderson 2010; Völker and Rohmann 2011; Roth 2016). That raises interesting questions for our own 'period': if, say, a date around 100 ever sticks for the *Satyrica*, what 'new' contemporary interactions will it generate, and how will it affect our perceptions of Nervan, Trajanic and Hadrianic literature at large?

Agricola and Martial's tenth book of *Epigrams*), William Fitzgerald (on sincerity and self-deception in Martial and Pliny) and Alice König (on Frontinus in Martial) focus on parallelisms between texts that entered circulation perhaps within a few months of each other, Sigrid Mratschek (on interactions between *Epistles* and *Epigrams* pivoting around Domitius Apollinaris), Ilaria Marchesi (on a double textualising of Regulus and Lucan by Martial and Pliny) and Paul Roche (on a single intertext running from the 80s, through the 100s, to the 120s) explore literary interactivity in the longer *durée*.

It is often claimed that the principate saw a gradual depoliticising of literature, as authors retreated into the safer world of *otium*. Texts published in the first years after Domitian's death are a particularly stark exception, not least because of the ways in which they construct complementary (as well as competing) visions of political transformation. Accordingly, political lines of enquiry are indeed pursued in several chapters here. That pursuit is accompanied, though, by our shared sense that the tendency to privilege 'high' politics not only reinforces a potentially brittle periodisation, but can only tell one part of the sociohistorical story. Refreshingly (we hope), the chapters by Christopher Whitton and Roy Gibson that bookend the volume trace interactions that cross the double caesura of 96/98 while making scant reference to political events. To return to our opening analogy, emperors may have founded some of the iconic libraries of our era; they may even have influenced their contents and who had access; but their own visits in person were perhaps not frequent. Just so, the Palatine did not cast a shadow over every interaction that took place in Roman society, on or off the page.

At the other end of our period, in the more sparsely charted 120s and 130s, we face different challenges: interactions here, as we have seen, are outnumbered by gaps in dialogue – between our Latin authors, at any rate.[64] But these fissures and challenges have stimulated some of the most innovative aspects of our volume. So, in his chapter on 'literary amnesia', Tom Geue construes Juvenal's reluctance to engage with contemporary texts as a provocative act of interaction-by-forgetfulness, inverting the familiar trope of 'poetic memory' to produce a kind of 'anti-allusion' by occlusion. Paul Roche uses more traditional models of allusion but explores a chain of echoes including not just published texts, but an emperor's spoken words;

---

[64] On the later Latin context – and the sometimes livelier Greek scene of Favorinus and his contemporaries – see Holford-Strevens 2003, esp. pp. 98–130. Bowie 2002 provides a snapshot of Greek literary activity in Trajan's last years.

James Uden for his part examines allusion to Quintilian's *Institutio* by Juvenal and offers a new approach to the lack of dialogue between Quintilian and a contemporary Greek treatise on education. Rebecca Langlands' chapter on 'extratextuality', meanwhile, points us further beyond texts to the floating anecdotes of contemporary oral culture as sites of 'off-literary' interaction. And Roy Gibson's dialogue between Pliny and Plutarch offers a novel route out of the impasse we face when sociability in life is erased in the textual record. In tracing relationships between chronology and literary interactivity, we thus address a topic of central importance to all students of Latin literature, not just those with a particular interest in our period: in different ways, the case studies and methodological reflections in the collection seek to push at the boundaries of intertextuality studies.

Interactions in Brief: Pliny, *Epistles* 9.19

Before taking a closer look at the chapters to come, let us try to illustrate some of the range and implications of our methodological approaches with a brief reading of our own. Centred as it is on a letter of Pliny, it will profess due modesty in its ambitions; still, a practical example seems helpful for setting out some of what we mean by 'literary interactions'. The letter in question is *Epistles* 9.19.

C. PLINIVS RVSONI SVO S.

Significas legisse te in quadam epistula mea iussisse Verginium Rufum inscribi sepulcro suo:

> Hic situs est Rufus, pulso qui Vindice quondam
>   imperium asseruit non sibi sed patriae.

Reprehendis quod iusserit, addis etiam melius rectiusque Frontinum, quod uetuerit omnino monumentum sibi fieri, meque ad extremum quid de utroque sentiam consulis. (2) Vtrumque dilexi, miratus sum magis quem tu reprehendis, atque ita miratus ut non putarem satis umquam posse laudari, cuius nunc mihi subeunda defensio est. (3) Omnes ego qui magnum aliquid memorandumque fecerunt non modo uenia uerum etiam laude dignissimos iudico, si immortalitatem quam meruere sectantur uicturique nominis famam supremis etiam titulis prorogare nituntur. (4) Nec facile quemquam nisi Verginium inuenio, cuius tanta in praedicando uerecundia quanta gloria ex facto. (5) Ipse sum testis, familiariter ab eo dilectus probatusque, semel omnino me audiente prouectum ut de rebus suis hoc unum referret, ita secum aliquando Cluuium locutum: 'Scis, Vergini, quae historiae fides debeatur; proinde si quid in historiis meis legis aliter ac uelis, rogo ignoscas.' Ad hoc ille: 'Tune ignoras, Cluui, ideo me fecisse quod feci ut esset liberum uobis scribere quae libuisset?'

(6) Agedum, hunc ipsum Frontinum in hoc ipso in quo tibi parcior uidetur et pressior comparemus. Vetuit exstrui monumentum, sed quibus uerbis?

> Impensa monumenti superuacua est: memoria nostri durabit, si uita meruimus.

An restrictius arbitraris per orbem terrarum legendum dare duratu-ram memoriam suam quam uno in loco duobus uersiculis signare quod feceris? (7) Quamquam non habeo propositum illum repre-hendendi, sed hunc tuendi; cuius quae potest apud te iustior esse defensio quam ex collatione eius quem praetulisti? (8) Meo quidem iudicio neuter culpandus, quorum uterque ad gloriam pari cupidi-tate, diuerso itinere contendit, alter dum expetit debitos titulos, alter dum mauult uideri contempsisse.

Vale.

My dear Ruso,

You indicate that you read in a letter of mine how Verginius Rufus instructed the carving of these words on his tomb:

> Here lies Rufus, who once crushed Vindex. He claimed power not for himself, but for his country.

You criticise him for doing so, you further say that Frontinus acted better and more nobly in forbidding any monument to be set up for him, and finally you ask my view on each of them. (2) I loved both men, but I had the greater admiration for the one you criticise – such admiration, in fact, that I thought he could never be given praise enough, this man whose defence I must now take on. (3) I for my part judge that all those who have done something great and worthy of record fully deserve, not just pardon, but actually praise, if they pursue the immortality that they have earned and strive to extend the glory of an undying name even in their last inscriptions. (4) Nor can I easily think of anyone besides Verginius whose modesty in declaration is equal to the glory from his deed. (5) I myself am witness, having enjoyed his close affection and esteem, that only once in my hearing did he go so far as to recall this one detail from his acts – namely, that Cluvius had once said to him: 'You are aware, Verginius, what commitment to the truth history demands; so if you read anything in my histories which is not to your liking, please forgive me.' Verginius replied: 'Are you unaware, Cluvius, that I did what I did precisely so that you writers would be free to write what you wished?'

(6) Come, let us compare Frontinus himself on the very point in which you find him more sparing and modest. He forbade the building of a monument, but in what words?

> The expense of a monument is needless: my memory will endure, if I have earned it in life.

Do you judge it more austere to give out, for all the world to read, that one's memory will endure than to mark what you have done in one place, with two short verses? (7) Though my intention is not to criticise Frontinus, but to defend Verginius – and what fairer defence could I produce before you than by comparing him with the man you preferred? In my estimation neither man merits blame, since they each aim for glory with equal desire but by different routes – the one in requesting the inscription he is due, the other in preferring to seem to have scorned it.

Yours, Pliny.[65]

It was predictable enough that Pliny would play a leading role in this volume on *Literary Interactions*. After all, his *Epistles*, along with Martial's *Epigrams*, is the most obviously 'interactive' Latin work of our period: not to mention his epistolary engagement with over a hundred addressees, there are the windows onto turn-of-the-century social history, the cameos from fellow writers living and dead, and the more discreet intertextual strata which have been so lively a topic in recent work.[66] Sure enough, the *Epistles* features substantially in twelve of our chapters; each applying a different combination of prosopographical, sociological, intertextual and ideological analysis, they set Pliny in a variety of dialogues with contemporary or near-contemporary authors. It feels appropriate enough, then, to take one of his

---

[65] Text from Mynors 1963, with minor alterations; translation by CLW (most similarities to Lewis 1879 are accidental).

[66] One reader for the Press suggested the 'Age of Pliny' as a snappier term for the title, which it certainly is; but we were reluctant to submit so far to the *Epistles*' centripetal pull.

letters as a brief introductory case study. We do so not to foreground Pliny as *the* paradigm of contemporary literary culture, but as one way to adumbrate the multiplicity of voices and texts that were interacting with each other in Nervan, Trajanic and Hadrianic Rome, and to outline some of the approaches taken in the chapters to come. Needless to say, the reading that follows also testifies to a scholarly interaction of our own, the collaboration of two readers who, for different reasons, have each had their curiosity piqued by these lines.

Epistles 9.19 is a dense nexus of personal, social, verbal and textual exchanges, private and public, between correspondents and acquaintances, authors and statesmen, the living and the dead.[67] Lucius Verginius Rufus and Sextus Julius Frontinus, two of only a handful of men (emperors apart) who reached a third consulate in Pliny's lifetime, had died within a few years of each other.[68] Each makes precisely three posthumous appearances in the *Epistles*, and each is revealed as a patron of Pliny; here, finally, they sit side by side, and come head to head, in a letter penned by Verginius' former ward and addressed, perhaps, to a nephew of Frontinus.[69] Even by Pliny's standards, this makes for a striking combination of the high-political and intimately personal. Nor is the exchange solely between writer and addressee: the dialogue embraces quoted epitaphs, personal conversation, published histories and (as we shall see) at least one unexpected intertextual strand, raising a series of questions about genre, circulation, readership, and the boundaries or lack thereof between interactions on and off the page. *Epistles* 9.19 thus introduces *in nuce* some of the central characters, texts and themes with which the rest of this volume will be concerned.

The letter opens with an exceptional intratext. Ruso has been reading a letter of Pliny's – apparently *Epistles* 6.10, in which Pliny cited the epitaph of Verginius that he quotes again here. Since that letter was addressed to a different correspondent, this passage stands as a prime witness in debates over the circulation and publication of the *Epistles*. But it also – and surely not by accident – foregrounds that urgent theme of Pliny's ninth book in particular, *fama* after death. As readers of Book 6 may recall, the salient

---

[67] For recent comment on this letter see Marchesi 2008: 146–7, 159–60, 239–40; Lefèvre 2009: 33–6; Whitton 2012: 351–2; Gibson 2015: 199–201. Klodt 2015: 362–79 is a detailed close reading with extensive bibliography.

[68] Verginius in 97 (*Ep.* 2.1.4–6 with Whitton 2013: 71, 74–5), Frontinus a few years later (see n. 30). On their careers see respectively Eck 2002b and 1982. Both, like Pliny, were *homines noui* (see Mratschek 1993: 32, 35 n. 85).

[69] As (speculatively) suggested by Syme (see Birley 2000a: 47 and 54; Bodel 2015: 81 n. 182). Pliny as Verginius' ward: *Ep.* 2.1.8–9; as protégé of Frontinus too: *Ep.* 4.8.3. As with Corellius Rufus, another of Pliny's 'elders and betters', in *Ep.* 9.13, Pliny here nuances the unmitigatedly positive impressions of both men given in his earlier books (see Gibson and Morello 2012: 129–31; Gibson 2015: 194–201).

feature of Verginius' epitaph is that it had not been set in the stone for which it was intended: a full ten years after his death, the tomb remained unfinished. What progress has been made by the time of *Epistles* 9.19 is unclear, making Pliny's published work perhaps the only place to preserve Verginius' funeral epigram.[70] If the letter's explicit concern lies with the ethics of self-memorialisation, this opening also alerts us to another, equally important and equally self-reflexive focus: the centrality of (Pliny's) writing in establishing men's reputations.[71]

Centrality also bears a more literal weight in this short text. Pliny's syncrisis of Verginius and Frontinus is constructed around the two (non-)epitaphs that he cites and compares. But the heart of the letter is a miniature exchange between Verginius and Cluvius Rufus (§5), relayed by Verginius to Pliny and now by Pliny to Ruso. Purportedly the crowning exception to Verginius' reticence over 'his acts',[72] it both aggrandises those acts and opens a dialogue with that most monumental prose genre, histo-riography. Cluvius, evidently, had not given Verginius unqualified praise in his narrative of the year 68, and begs his indulgence. Verginius mag-nanimously grants the request by dismissing it as needless: Cluvius was exercising on the page the very freedom that he, Verginius, had fought to preserve. In this account, history, however monumental, does not get the last word: it becomes just one step in an ongoing series of exchanges on and off the page.

The loss of Cluvius' history makes it a mystery to us whether, and how, this anecdote relates to any published words. Any attempt to map ancient intertextuality must allow for large areas of uncharted territory between our coordinates: an observation axiomatic to the point of banal, but essential all the same – and positive motivation for several of the attempts to move 'beyond intertextuality' in the present volume. In this case, though, we might allow another historian to come to mind. When Verginius addressed Cluvius and his fellow historians (§5 *uobis*), Tacitus was probably too young to be counted in that plural. By the date of Pliny's letter, though, his *Histo-ries* was well underway – and his own less than adulatory take on Verginius' deeds in 68 may already have been on record.[73] Tacitus features promi-nently in the *Epistles*, not least in the first Verginius letter, *Epistles* 2.1.

---

[70] Knowledge of it reached Cassius Dio (Xiph. 68.2.4) and Justin (Trog. *Epit.* 6.8.5) – by whatever means (see Sherwin-White 1966: 366; Klodt 2015: 378–9).

[71] *Ep.* 9.19 is framed by a brace of notes (albeit two of many in Book 9) about Pliny's own writings.

[72] I.e. as readers of *Ep.* 2.1 and 6.10 will recall, his suppression in 68 of Julius Vindex' revolt (and refusal to claim the throne for himself).

[73] The familiar references are in Klodt 2015: 349–54.

The second, *Epistles* 6.10, immediately follows a note to him; is *Epistles* 9.19 a third and final instalment in an ongoing tussle over *fama*, *fides* and Verginian commemoration?[74]

In weighing up such a suggestion, much depends on your view of how meaning is constructed between texts – in other words, on your conceptions of intertextuality, but also, in the terms we have outlined, of 'interactivity'. Interactivity might be thought of as a superset of which intertextuality is just a part: it not only embraces those 'allusions' or 'references' that can be captured and displayed in specimen jars, but also seeks to give voice to the fuzzier echoes and dialogues between the lines of our texts, and to invoke the sociohistorical communication and exchange that went along with literary production. To take *Epistles* 9.19: is it notable, or just accident, that Cluvius and Verginius are paired here, towards the end of Pliny's collection, given that they make their first Tacitean appearance, also in close proximity, near the start of the *Histories* (1.8)? Or consider Verginius' sententious appeal to authorial 'freedom' (§5 *ut esset liberum uobis scribere quae libuisset*), which, though few would call it an 'allusion', might remind some of that famous claim for Trajanic freedom of speech that we have already cited once: *rara temporum felicitate ubi sentire quae uelis et quae sentias dicere licet* (*Hist.* 1.1.4). Does Pliny quote Verginius' own, historical words (predating those of Tacitus, if so), or did the epistolographer have a hand himself in crafting this tidy epigram (which would then postdate *Histories* 1)?[75] And what of the striking rhythm? Verginius' retort to Cluvius begins and ends in dactylic hexameter (*tune ignoras, Cluui, ideo me . . .* , and *uobis scribere quae libuisset*): coincidence, or a delicate hint of that notorious feature of historiographical openings?[76] Not that it would evoke Tacitus' *Histories* in particular (it is the *Annals* which begins hexametrically). Nonetheless, we might still think in the broader terms of 'generic interactions' considered by Geue: an allusion (so to speak) to historical writing at large?

Such questions – exploring what lies beyond the strictly 'demonstrable' – underlie a series of productive thought experiments in *Literary Interactions*, as when Buckley pairs Valerius Flaccus and Tacitus for their treatment of

---

[74] See Whitton 2012: 351–2 and 2013: 80–1. On the first instalment (*Ep.* 2.1) see also Marchesi 2008: 189–99.

[75] It is notable for its precise balance (15–16 syllables) and word-play (*fecisse quod feci* and the semantically pregnant *liberum . . . libuisset*, familiar from Sen. *Apoc.* 1.1–2); see also Klodt 2015: 369–70. The intertextual challenges posed by successive 'live' and scripted epigrams are the subject of Roche's chapter.

[76] Which, like Verginius' line here, feature prosody that would barely pass muster in epic. For this mannerism of Roman historians, see Woodman 2012: 188–90, 378–84.

silence under tyranny, or Mratschek explores corresponding underworld imagery in Martial and Pliny. Differently put, these are to some measure essays in 'intertextual' reading in the Kristevan sense, in which all texts are in dialogue, and authorial intention – such as has lurked in our own last paragraphs – is at best a second-order issue.[77] Other chapters draw on and/or interrogate the more familiar tools for intertextual analysis which have been developed by Classicists, and Latinists in particular, in the last half-century and more. 'Allusion' figures, for instance, in Kelly's treatment of Martial and Juvenal, in Roche's analysis of *Panegyricus* and Suetonius, and König's reading of Frontinus and Martial. Allusive interpretation, like all literary hermeneutics, is more a matter of consensus than science, but a familiar system of rules and measures helps enable (or police) it: allusive 'hooks' (often esoteric lexis), distinctive metre or syntax, 'variation in imitation', 'memory markers' such as *memini* or *fertur* (a trope provocatively extended by Geue to Juvenalian 'amnesia'): these are now everyday terms for Classicists.[78] Similarity of subject matter is an obvious consideration, as is genre: readers have generally been readier to recognise *imitatio* in epic than in epigram, in verse than in prose.[79] Of course the ground continues to shift, and prose intertextuality in particular, as we have said, has become a more familiar feature on the 'high-imperial' literary landscape (as it has for scholars of late antiquity).[80] But this last is still a relatively new topic of study: allusion beyond the bounds of poetry is far less thoroughly explored, and remains more contentious, than that between, say, Ovid and Virgil. One of the distinctive features of our period, by comparison with earlier imperial literature, is the centrality of prose within our canon: this forces a challenge to the tendency to concentrate on poetry in studies of this sort, and invites fresh consideration of what might count as literary interaction.

---

[77] For an extended application of this approach to Latin literature, see Edmunds 2001. Allen 2000: 8–60 is a helpful summary of Kristeva's approach and its origins in Saussure and Bakhtin; see also Clayton and Rothstein 1991 and Orr 2003: 20–32. Kristeva and other semioticians, of course, did not restrict 'text(e)' to written language.

[78] For a succinct guide to such 'formal features of allusion', see Wills 1996: 1–41. We do not attempt here to give a full bibliography on Latin intertextual studies: Hinds 1998 remains an excellent point of departure, as in smaller space do Barchiesi 1997 (translated as Barchiesi 2001) and Fowler 1997. See also (among many) Conte 1986; Edmunds 2001; Hutchinson 2013; and the papers collected in Baraz and van den Berg 2013.

[79] For 'imitation' as a (positive) critical term see West and Woodman 1979. For discussion of Roman literary *imitatio* see Russell 1979 and, at greater length, Reiff 1959 and Cizek 1994.

[80] On the latter Kelly 2008 stands out; see also many contributions in van Waarden and Kelly 2013. Historiography has prompted some especially interesting methodological debate (Levene 2010: 82–163; Pelling 2013; O'Gorman 2014; Elliott 2015); the novel is another popular site of intertextual study (e.g. Finkelpearl 1998; Doulamis 2011; ní Mheallaigh 2014; much of Harrison 2013).

Indeed, the line between 'allusion' and other forms of interaction, if ever it existed, is at best blurred. Our letter is case in point. However intangible the reflexes of Tacitus' *Histories*, his *Agricola* is a (subtly) distinct presence in Pliny's ruminations on self-commemoration (§§3–4).[81] The closest to a lexical hook is the short phrase *in praedicando uerecundia*, which resembles Agricola's quality as a legionary legate (*uerecundia in praedicando*) in *Agricola* 8.3. But the whole sentence bears comparison:

> Nec facile quemquam nisi Verginium inuenio, cuius tanta in praedicando uerecundia quanta gloria ex facto. (*Ep.* 9.19.4)

> Nec Agricola umquam in suam famam gestis exultauit . . . : ita uirtute in obsequendo, uerecundia in praedicando extra inuidiam nec extra gloriam erat. (*Agr.* 8.3)

> Nor did Agricola ever exult in his deeds for his own reputation's sake . . . : in this way, through valour in obedience and modesty in declaration he steered clear of envy, but not of glory.

In each case 'modesty in declaration' (i.e. not vaunting oneself) is contrasted with the *gloria* that accrued all the same; further formal correspondences combine to suggest that Pliny's sentence is a minute rewriting (and abbreviation) of Tacitus'.[82]

This discreet engagement seems to extend to the previous sentence. Rising to a grander tone, Pliny expansively declares that all those who 'have done something great and worthy of record' (*magnum aliquid memorandumque fecerunt*) merit not just 'pardon' (*uenia*) but praise if they 'pursue the immortality they have deserved' (*immortalitatem quam meruere sectantur*). The preface of the *Agricola* thematises the difficulty of literary commemoration. In former days autobiography (*ad prodendam uirtutis memoriam*) was a noble pursuit. Now biography is still tolerated, when 'some great and noble excellence' (*magna aliqua ac nobilis uirtus*) shines out; but even so, Tacitus' intervention on Agricola's behalf required 'pardon' (*uenia*). Here the formal parallels are less pressing: one identical word (*uenia*), and one rather similar phrase (*magnum aliquid memorandumque fecerunt* ~ *magna aliqua ac nobilis uirtus*). But the theme is the same: when Pliny undertakes a 'defence' of Verginius' planned self-memorialisation (§2), has he looked to Tacitus' apologetic preface for inspiration?

---

[81] The following paragraphs develop remarks in Whitton 2013: 81.

[82] The openings (*Nec facile quemquam* ~ *Nec Agricola umquam*) evince both 'sound allusion' and 'prosodic marking' (in the terms of Wills 1996: 19–20); Pliny's prepositions (*in . . . ex . . .*) echo in miniature those of Tacitus (*in . . . in . . . extra . . . extra . . .*).

Here we seem to be on firmer ground than with the *Histories*. But this nexus, too, exemplifies some of the dilemmas of prose intertextuality. Readers of Statius or Silius Italicus are well trained to detect traces of Virgil and Ovid. But how many readers of imperial prose are prepared to countenance allusion on the evidence here presented? And, even if we pursue it, what story should we tell about it? One plot would be source-critical: casting around for an angle in his 'defence' of Verginius, Pliny lights on the *Agricola*, a biography and multiple *apologia* which was well known to him, and selects a couple of choice moves.[83] Another might be allusive. 'Allusion' (with *ludus* at its heart) implies teasing and evasion, and that could certainly describe the reader's experience here. Our little analysis worked backwards, because it is the second sentence which more readily reveals its target: from the distinctive phrase *in praedicando uerecundia* we traced the further correspondences that a reader – one with a good memory of the *Agricola*, or (as the sceptic might see it) a 'reader-philologist' at her computer – might detect.[84] Only then might she even begin to contemplate reading what precedes in the light of Tacitus' preface.[85] Allusion also (axiomatically) entails transformation. In this case Pliny simplifies both form and content, but he also contradicts. Where Tacitus agonises about 'pardon', Pliny's more forthright view is that self-commemoration deserves not just pardon but praise. And if Agricola set the standard for glory without self-seeking, Pliny for his part can think of no better candidate than Verginius (*Nec facile quemquam . . .*): the very sentence that looks to the *Agricola* erases Agricola himself as a point of reference. **Verg**inius is the better fit for ***uerecundia***, or so it might seem to those who countenance such word-play. Read in these terms, the *imitatio* is starting to look rather less passive and more playful, perhaps even aggressive, certainly revisionist. In the para-eulogy of *Epistles* 2.1 Pliny joins, or even ousts, Tacitus as the man who has the last word on Verginius. For the reader prepared to listen carefully, that tussle appears to run right through to *Epistles* 9.19.

Not by chance, this increasingly 'allusive' interpretation has also taken us full circle to the bigger social and personal picture. Tacitus, like Pliny, was a first-generation consular in middle age, a colleague (so Pliny attests) in *negotia* and in *studia*: intertextuality in this case (and in how many more?) can be only one part of the interactions happening on and off the page, and in between. Of course Pliny and Tacitus are one of those exceptional pairs, like Cicero and Caesar or Horace and Virgil, for whom we can

---

[83] Pliny certainly knew *Agricola* well (see Whitton 2010, 2013: 80–1 and forthcoming a).

[84] For the sceptical view see Edmunds 2001: 39–62 (starring Richard Thomas as 'reader-philologist').

[85] Further instances of this pattern appear in Whitton's chapter.

even begin to piece together the fragments of a double portrait. But inter-activity, we can be sure, extended far further in the society and literature of which we have such scant traces. Frontinus in this letter makes a good example.

As we have noted, *Epistles* 9.19 is not only Pliny's third and final epis-tolary instalment on Verginius Rufus; it is also the climax in a triptych of letters featuring Julius Frontinus. If that name evokes for us a military and political heavyweight and the author of two extant prose works (*Stratege-mata* and *De aquis*),[86] *Epistles* 4.8 and 5.1 present him only as a distinguished elder statesman. Indeed, the earlier letter draws a distinction between Fron-tinus, whom Pliny succeeds as augur, and Cicero, who was not just an augur but also (unlike Frontinus, we gather) an author to be emulated. Confir-mation that Pliny shared the common view, now coming under fire from several scholars, that 'technical' writing like *De aquis* does not occupy the same plain as 'literature' (whatever *that* means)?[87] Or, in styling Frontinus a *princeps uir* (*Ep.* 4.8.3), does he (pointedly?) honour him with precisely the status he assumes in his written work, that of an exemplary statesman, one of the *principes uiri* who have been entrusted with the office of *curator aquarum* (*Aq.* 1)?[88] Here is the moment, perhaps, to recall that Frontinus had also featured on Tacitus' page as *magnus uir, quantum licebat* – in the *Agricola* of all places.[89]

Epistles 9.19, by contrast, honours Frontinus with a direct quotation, as Pliny interrogates his anti-epitaph, *Impensa monumenti superuacua est: memoria nostri durabit, si uita meruimus.* Quite how Frontinus 'gave out' or 'consigned' this grand utterance 'for all the world to read' is unclear.[90] Unlike Verginius, though, he was successful in promulgating it, need-ing no help from Pliny to acquire readers and renown. Or so the letter

---

[86] His earlier *De re militari* is known only from *Strat.* 1.pr.1.

[87] See König's chapter. On the generic distinctiveness (or not) of 'technical' writing, see especially Asper 2007: 35–53 and (taking a different view) Fögen 2009: 9–66. For a representative range of views on different 'literary' features of ancient technical and scientific writing, see J. König and Whitmarsh 2007; Taub and Doody 2009; J. König and Woolf 2017.

[88] On Frontinus' self-presentation and self-promotion in the *De aquis*, see especially DeLaine 1995 and A. König 2007. In his *Tactical theory*, written not much later, Aelian also foregrounds Frontinus' social and political status and downplays his reputation as an author (*pr.*3); as Alice König will argue in the second *Literary Interactions* volume, Aelian's glossing over of Frontinus' literary activities is motivated in part by his desire to present the military writing tradition as (still) the preserve of Greek authors.

[89] *Agr.* 17.2 with König 2013.

[90] Perhaps in a lost work (so Marchesi 2008: 159–60), more likely in his will (e.g. Sherwin-White 1966: 503; Champlin 1991: 170), in which case Pliny is indulging in tendentious advocacy (cf. *per orbem terrarum legendum*). For a fuller *Forschungsbericht*, see Klodt 2015: 376–7. We might also ask: is Pliny quoting Frontinus precisely? The sentiment is exactly equal in length to that of Verginius.

claims: in fact the preservation of Frontinus' sentiment, as perhaps that of Verginius', is indebted wholly to the *Epistles*. Verginius laid claim to fame, but only on his tomb; Frontinus scorned a monument, but in words addressed to the whole world, and which thus end up as a distinctly grand *monumentum*[91] . . . until Pliny starts chipping away at the façade. This is a letter that fiercely instantiates its own subject, and on several levels – not just the fight for memory and survival, but the centrality to that fight of literary interactivity itself.

Do we also encounter Frontinus the author in this letter? Readers familiar with *De aquis* may recall the early, spirited outburst where Frontinus compares aqueducts, that marvel of practical Roman engineering, with the vain display of pyramids and famous but 'useless' Greek buildings (*Aq.* 16).[92] Others, thinking of Frontinian '*monumenta*', would find that word in two places, once in the preface to *Strategemata* (1.*pr.*2),[93] once near the end of *De aquis*, in the senatorial decree that forbids the building of tombs, amongst other things, in the vicinity of an aqueduct (*Aq.* 127). Here the sort of close formal echoes we found with *Agricola* are absent; still, there is a certain aptness to the resonance, as Frontinus in death spurns just the sort of tomb which he was concerned, in his capacity as *curator aquarum*, to keep clear of the buildings that really mattered. Does this lightest of hints invite us to compare his public service and the text that celebrated it with this last, very public (or even published) comment? If so, how favourable does the comparison turn out to be? Or do such questions simply show up the potential fallacy of overdetermination? As both Geue and König underline in their chapters, there is always the risk that circumstantial knowledge of social networks encourages ever more tenuous intertextual readings. Clearly any move from the hermeneutic safety of 'certifiable' intertextuality entails hazards. But high stakes should not always deter a gamble.

Indeed, we might positively emphasise the silences which surround Frontinus' work – and his career. If Pliny ignores *De aquis* and *Strategemata*, that might be a useful reminder, akin to his trivialising comment on Silius Italicus' *Punica*,[94] that individuals now known to us as 'authors' may not have seen themselves or have been seen by their contemporaries as primarily, even significantly, invested in literary production. Alongside the

---

[91] Frontinus' grandeur bears comparison with Horace *Odes* 2.20.23–4 *sepulcri | mitte superuacuos honores*, as commentators have noted (Gierig 1800–2: II, 32; Nisbet and Hubbard 1978: 348).

[92] As does Klodt 2015: 376.

[93] Referring to literary works. On Frontinus' (lack of) self-monumentalising in the *Strategemata*, and possible political motives, see n. 28.

[94] *Ep.* 3.7.5 *Scribebat carmina maiore cura quam ingenio* ('he wrote poetry with more care than talent').

questions of 'technicality' raised above, Jill Harries' and Myles Lavan's chapters in particular apply some New Historicist pressure to the still familiar sorting of material as 'literary' and 'non-literary': one burden of this volume is to test how far that boundary can and should be blurred. Or does the absence of Frontinus' published work, like the partial appearance of Martial's in *Epistles* 3.21, (rather/also) show one text, the *Epistles*, wresting control over, rather than reflecting, authorial status and canons?

There may be a political side to this too, and a sharper silence. After all, Frontinus has arguably as much claim as Verginius to be remembered as someone who had safeguarded the state in a time of crisis. Verginius' refusal of *imperium* in 68 was one stage in that messy sequence of events from Nero's fall to the eventual accession of Vespasian. For Frontinus we must extrapolate, but his remarkable pair of consulates in 98 and 100, both held jointly with Trajan, leaves no doubt that he played a significant role in that emperor's adoption by Nerva, and so in securing the new regime fêted by Pliny and so many others.[95] Yet Pliny breathes not a word. Indeed, although Frontinus features (unnamed) in the *Panegyricus* as Trajan's fellow consul,[96] he earns mention in *Epistles* only after his death. Thanks above all to the proem of Tacitus' *Agricola*, silence and erasure are strongly associated with the political moment of the late 90s. Often that means the silence of tyranny and its survivors (Buckley), but it also extends to the erasures that might – must? – have accompanied the scrambling for position that followed Domitian's death (Rimell, Mratschek). Does Pliny's reticence over Frontinus reveal, by design or not, the delicacy of those backstage scenes – and the years that followed? We might even – speculatively, to be sure – try pinpointing a more specific historical moment in *Epistles* 9, a decade or so on from the outburst of Nervan and Trajanic accession rhetoric in which Frontinus, Tacitus and Pliny had all taken part. Does Pliny's readiness to criticise Frontinus here, in the last book of his 'private' collection, cast new shadows on those uncertain years – interacting, therefore, not just with the *Agricola* and (perhaps) *De aquis*, but also with his own, earlier textualisation of the 90s in his first books of *Epistles*?

With that ring-composed return to intratextuality (a suitably Plinian conceit) we take our leave of *Epistles* 9.19, a short but polyphonic disquisition on self-memorialisation and interaction which itself energetically

---

[95] See Eck 2002a: 219–26; for a possible modification, Grainger 2003: 13–14. Of course Frontinus was not alone; among our dramatic *personae*, Verginius' third consulate followed hard on Nerva's accession, and Tacitus (consul in the last two months of 97) may have been party or witness to Trajan's adoption in October (Syme 1958: 129–30). Another key player was evidently Frontinus' son-in-law Sosius Senecio (Eck 2002a: 220–1), who features in Gibson's chapter here.

[96] *Pan.* 61–2.

(re)calibrates a whole series of personal, political and literary relationships. Not every line of Nervan, Trajanic and Hadrianic literature might prove quite so intensely interactive, and we have offered (we hope) more questions than answers; but such are some of the approaches that this project on *Literary Interactions* sets out to test.

Literary Interactions in Brief

Interaction has been hardwired into this project from the beginning, with scholarly dialogue on paper, online and around the seminar table serving as an essential corollary of individual work. The eighteen chapters of the present volume accordingly offer themselves to be read as a network of dialogues, implicit and explicit, and we actively encourage you to 'choose your own adventure'. The titles, and the summaries we offer here, should make for easy raiding by those hunting contributions on any given author, genre or theme, or simply by the impatient.[97] But even such excerptors, we hope, will be struck both by the interchange between chapters and by the diversity of approach: this volume, to repeat, is intended as a lively conversation and prompt, not a methodological manifesto. It *does* have a manifesto, but one in which plurality plays a double role: *Literary Interactions* is a call to work harder at reading high-imperial texts in their mutual context, and to attend to their dialogues (and lacks thereof) in as many ways as may be profitable.

In that spirit, the sequence of chapters offers only one path through this volume, and a necessarily arbitrary one at that. We have not observed strict chronological order, though that claim, as so often, is disingenuous:[98] each section does move roughly through time, and there are vestiges too of a progression across the volume as a whole – even if (not quite by chance) the closing dialogue between Pliny and Plutarch is staged *before* 'our' period gets underway. In some cases, chapters are juxtaposed for similarities of material (as with Harries and Lavan, two contrasting interventions on *Epistles* 10) or method (as with Mratschek and König, intertextual readings in which prosopography plays a central role): but in these pairs, as throughout, variety rules: nowhere, we hope, will both manner and matter turn out to be the same.

Part 1, 'Bridging Divides: Literary Interactions from Quintilian to Juvenal', takes an initial sweep through four decades of Latin literature, examining a variety of interactions across prose and verse, and looking repeatedly towards the double caesura of 96/98 – both to give due voice to

---

[97] Cf. Mart. 10.1.1–2.   [98] Cf. Plin. *Ep.* 1.1.1.

a particularly concentrated moment of textual production, and to ask how firmly that Flavian door can be kept shut. **Christopher Whitton** opens with 'Quintilian, Pliny, Tacitus', a summary triangulation of three prose authors writing across the chronological divide. Both Tacitus' *Dialogus* and Pliny's *Epistles*, he argues, respond not just *grosso modo* to Quintilian's *Institutio oratoria*, but are defined by textual engagement of a remarkable, and perhaps unprecedented, minuteness and extent. Such prose–prose intertextuality is often considered hard to pin down as 'allusions'; in response, Whitton tries to find a critical discourse beyond the brittleness of binary 'all or nothing' interpretations – and asks quite how 'public' these intimate dialogues may be.

Another of Tacitus' 'minor' works features in **Victoria Rimell**'s chapter, 'I Will Survive (You): Martial and Tacitus on Regime Change'. The *Agricola* is rarely considered in the same breath as Martial's revised tenth book of *Epigrams*. But these two productions of (probably) 98 make stimulating material for comparative reading. Where Whitton focuses on author-generated allusion, Rimell combines that with a more capacious sense of reader-determined intertextuality to sound out some striking resonances, as Tacitus and Martial each confront the 'silence' of the Domitianic past and the challenge of literary re-creation facing its survivors.

Tacitus and taciturnity also loom large in 'Flavian Epic and Trajanic Historiography: Speaking into the Silence' by **Emma Buckley**. She too addresses two texts rarely mentioned together, Valerius Flaccus' *Argonautica* and Tacitus' *Agricola* and *Histories*, using a form of 'reverse reception' to probe that political caesura which so firmly sets Valerius in the Flavian camp, Tacitus in the Trajanic. Both *Argonautica* and *Agricola* emerge from this account as ambivalent reflections on heroism under a tyrant; responses to Lucan in Valerius' epic and Tacitus' *Histories* make for a second intriguing syncrisis. Attention to 'periodic interactions' such as these, Buckley shows, can teach us a good deal about the works of both authors, about interdiscursivity, and about (the limits of) literary interactivity.

William Fitzgerald's chapter, 'Pliny and Martial: Dupes and Non-Dupes in the Early Empire', is the first of three pieces on this most interactive pair. Fitzgerald is concerned less with intertextuality per se than with a comparative reading of two corpora in which 'sincerity, flattery, free speech and self-deception' (those inescapable themes of our period) play so prominent a role. Ranging through Martial's (Flavian) *De spectaculis*, (Nervan) *Epigrams* 11 and (Trajanic) *Epigrams* 10, as well as Pliny's confidently post-Flavian prose, this chapter holds up the 'booster' and 'debunker' for joint inspection, finding contrasts, to be sure – but also some notable commonalities.

Rhiannon Ash also covers a wide span, from *De spectaculis* via Pliny (*Epistles* 8.20, on Lake Vadimon) to Juvenal (the Egyptian cannibals of Satire 15). Her chapter, 'Paradoxography and Marvels in Post-Domitianic Literature: "An Extraordinary Affair, Even in the Hearing!"', approaches this novel trio with two different hermeneutic models of interactivity. One is a concept of 'tacit' allusion, which sees one author (Pliny) silently vying with another (Martial). The other looks to the more expansive view of intertextuality adumbrated by Rimell, Buckley, Fitzgerald and others, but combines it with a strong diachronic element, as Ash considers how thematically resonant but formally unrelated texts can be set in dialogue to reveal shared – and shifting – responses to emperors in Flavian and post-Flavian Rome.

Paul Roche sustains the political theme in 'Pliny and Suetonius on Giving and Returning Imperial Power', a case study which advocates a more 'allusive' approach to the prose of both authors. Trajan's accession in the *Panegyricus* and Domitian's as reported by Suetonius are marked by a surprisingly similar epigram. Roche traces this *sententia* from an original declaration by Domitian himself, through reappropriation by Pliny in his speech, to a Suetonian 'correction' of the *Panegyricus*. The result, besides a new insight into Pliny's earliest reception history, is an intriguing 'window allusion' in which dialogue is sustained on and off the page – and which edits history in the process.

This first part of the volume ends with another allusive case study, now in verse and off the high-political stage. In 'From Martial to Juvenal (*Epigrams* 12.18)', **Gavin Kelly** probes a textual and personal nexus which finds its most intense expression in one late poem of Martial, remarkable as an address to Juvenal which also shows strong similarities to Juvenal's first Satire. Most scholars take Juvenal to be the 'imitator'; following Uden's recent intervention,[99] Kelly considers the consequences of a revised dating which makes Martial, not Juvenal, the respondent in this poetic exchange. *Epigrams* 12.18 thus emerges as an elegant intertextual homage to a fellow author, and Martial and Juvenal as an altogether more 'interactive' pair of poets than usually assumed.

Our second part, 'Interactions on and off the Page', pursues in more depth a theme touched on several times in the first: the overlap and interplay between textual and personal, literary and social. We begin with the most obvious instantiation of that interplay, the *recitatio*. The centrality of literary recitations to, and in, the texts of our period is well known;

---

[99] Uden 2015: 219–26.

how they functioned is a less straightforward question. In 'Amicable and Hostile Exchange in the Culture of Recitation', **Matthew Roller** analyses a wide range of texts, foregrounding the societal role of recitation – and its implications for our understanding of literary as well as socio-literary interactions. Recitation emerges from his account as a notionally semi-private form of aristocratic exchange whose blend of competition and cooperation is in fact as uneasy as it is elegant.

Intertextual agonistics, that is to say, are just one part of a larger social picture. That insight is also central to the next two chapters, both of which demonstrate the value of combining prosopographical and intertextual approaches. **Sigrid Mratschek**'s study, 'Images of Domitius Apollinaris in Pliny and Martial: Intertextual Discourses as Aspects of Self-Definition and Differentiation', explores the personal and textual bonds tying Apollinaris, consul of 97, to those two miniaturists, in the context of the 'competitive ranking games' that played out on the elite cultural stage. Teasing out the semiotics of visualisation on the one hand (as the political instability of a new regime is encoded through loaded imagery of Hades), ecphrastic villa descriptions on the other, Mratschek shows how interlocking images of Apollinaris are deployed for muscular ethical and political self-definition, by Martial and Pliny both.

That privileged political moment of the late 90s is also central to **Alice König**'s chapter, 'Reading Frontinus in Martial's *Epigrams*', which explores another collision of personal and textual interaction through a figure familiar from our introduction. Julius Frontinus features twice in *Epigrams* 10; König considers how both poems, for all their apolitical veneer, can be read as provocative reflections on the new, Trajanic regime. She also examines possible echoes of Frontinus' *De aquis* in Martial, challenging assumptions that poetry and 'technical' treatises are poles apart amid so dense a personal and literary network.

Questions over 'technical' literature are equally live in a pair of chapters which take us into the latter half of Trajan's principate, and to Pliny's tenth book of *Epistles*. **Jill Harries**' 'Saturninus the Helmsman, Pliny and Friends: Legal and Literary Letter Collections' introduces an often overlooked production of our period, the epistles of legal experts. The epistles in question were collections of 'questions and answers', such as Javolenus Priscus' discussion of one Saturninus, a helmsman in the British fleet. This submerged genre makes a stimulating comparandum with the more familiar output of Pliny, in particular *Epistles* 10. Itself a collection of working correspondence, it serves in Harries' reading not just to advertise Pliny's friendship with Trajan, but to administer some sharp elbowing to the 'competition' – further demonstration, then, of the 'competitive ranking games' to which Roller and Mratschek draw our attention.

Myles Lavan sustains the prompt to look beyond the 'literary' canon in 'Pliny's *Epistles* 10 and Imperial Correspondence: The Empire of Letters'. Recent years have seen vigorous debate over the question whether *Epistles* 10 was edited and published by Pliny himself,[100] and that debate continues here: while Harries votes 'yes', Lavan prefers to problematise. Invoking the traces of imperial correspondence preserved in inscriptions, papyri and the jurists, he argues that *Epistles* 10 displays not (necessarily) so much the hallmarks of Plinian editing as typical features of imperial communications in general. Not that we need resist reading *Epistles* 10 as literature: rather, he suggests, we should start taking a more 'literary' view of other material too – while trying harder to read our 'literary' texts in their wider discursive context.

Another complementary pair of chapters rounds off Part II, this time with a shared thematic interest in exemplarity. In 'Traditional *Exempla* and Nerva's New Modernity: Making Fabricius Take the Cash', **Ruth Morello** considers counterexemplarity through a pair of case studies from Martial (*Epigrams* 11.5) and Pliny (*Epistles* 7.29). Both invoke heroes of old not as models, but to produce hyperbolic counterfactuals involving one new emperor (Nerva) and one imperial freedman of times past (Pallas). How much pressure can these inverted *exempla* bear? Is their exemplary status itself brought into question? And what emerges out of them, within the broader discourse of early imperial exemplarity? Counterfactuality, Morello suggests, is a distinctly post-Caesarian phenomenon, shot through with political tensions.

Rebecca Langlands pursues related questions in 'Extratextuality: Literary Interactions with Oral Culture and Exemplary Ethics'. Here too *exempla* are the focus, this time positive, and in war. Tacitus' *Histories* and Suetonius' life of Otho each feature the noble suicide of a soldier-messenger – essentially the same episode, but attached to different emperors and with different narrative outcomes. Faced with this curiosity, Langlands puts source-criticism aside and offers a new model of 'extratextuality', the idea that texts interact not just with each other, but also intermedially with the 'floating anecdotes' (a term owed, interactively enough, to Rhiannon Ash) familiar in oral culture.

Langlands' invitation to look beyond textual and intertextual approaches made an immediate impact when first issued in Rostock, and leads us here

---

[100] See n. 23.

into the volume's third and final part ('Into the Silence: The Limits of Interaction'), which offers four quite different approaches to the challenges posed by gaps, fissures and silences among our texts. **Ilaria Marchesi**'s chapter, 'The Regulus Connection: Displacing Lucan between Martial and Pliny', offers a contrastive reading of how *Epigrams* and *Epistles* handle one contemporary figure (Regulus) and one author of a previous generation (Lucan). A combination of surprises – Lucan's presence in Martial and absence from Pliny's pages – and 'pulviscular allusions' (delicate intertextual 'clouds') produces a striking case study, as Marchesi explores what this might tell us, not just *about* contemporary readings of Lucan's notorious proem, but about *how* such interpretations may have developed, and considers what political stakes attended literary interpretation and production on both sides of the Flavian divide.

Tom Geue carries us further into the second century, and back to verse–prose dialogue, in 'Forgetting the Juvenalien in Our Midst: Literary Amnesia in the *Satires*'. In an important interrogation of the terms of this volume, he squares up to some difficulties of 'interactions' as a model, both in general (do reconstructions of social networking threaten to overdetermine intertextual readings?) and in one problem case, Juvenal's apparently antisocial *Satires*. Both in Satire 2, with its notorious reference (if it is that) to Tacitus' *Histories*, and in Satire 8, (in)distinctly reminiscent of a letter of Pliny, Juvenal challenges 'allusive' readers. Geue's response is twofold: on the one hand, to think in terms of more broadly defined 'generic interactions'; on the other, he floats the idea of 'anti-allusion', in which the *Satires* pointedly *fails* to interact with an ideological antitype.

James Uden's chapter, 'Childhood Education and the Boundaries of Interaction: [Plutarch], Quintilian, Juvenal', also explores both Juvenalian intertextuality and more capacious models of 'interaction' – now applied to the silences between Greek and Latin literature of our period. The tract *On educating children* once attributed to Plutarch, the first book of Quintilian's *Institutio* and Juvenal's fourteenth Satire share a culturally urgent theme (infant pedagogy); how, and how far, can they be put in dialogue? Faced with allusions by Juvenal to Quintilian on the one hand, a distinct lack of conversation between them and the pseudo-Plutarchan tract on the other, Uden lays out a methodology for exploring the 'broader and largely extratextual exchange of images and ideas' of which intertextuality can be only one part.

Finally, **Roy Gibson** signals another response to the stubborn silences between Greek and Latin in 'Pliny and Plutarch's Practical Ethics: A Newly Rediscovered Dialogue'. The rediscovered dialogue in question is a fragment in which Pliny and Plutarch are found conversing in the early 90s. Gibson's translation is accompanied by an introduction and notes revealing remarkable similarities with the published works of Pliny and Plutarch. In fact the two authors betray no hint in their own writings that they even know of each other. Such silence across the Greek–Latin divide is not unusual, but it is made especially poignant in this case by the many overlaps in their circles of acquaintance: here is a pair 'who really ought to have met, but for whose actual encounter there is only slim or contestable evidence' – making for a fascinating but conventionally frustrating scholarly dead-end. Their exchange of views on ethics thus proves to be a serendipitous opportunity to reflect on 'the silences, omissions and exclusions inflicted by contemporary texts on each other' through imaginative engagement: with it Gibson offers, in all seriousness, a novel approach to the dynamics of literary and personal interactions which constitute the variegated threads of this volume.

With this final evanescent dialogue our volume of *Literary Interactions* reaches its own end. But that, **John Henderson** ('ENVOI/VENIO') calls in to say, is where the interactions really begin.

Bridging Divides
Literary Interactions from Quintilian to Juvenal

CHAPTER I

Quintilian, Pliny, Tacitus

Christopher Whitton

Quite a pretentious title, to be sure. This single chapter can hardly hope to do justice to its theme, namely – as you've guessed from my allusion to a classic paper (*have* you?) – an interpersonal and intertextual triangle of rare intensity. Each of its sides (QT, QP, PT) represents a certain, abundant and (very? barely?) audible textual relationship; at its apices are the three most prolific extant prose writers of their age(s), connected, in at least two cases, by sure personal acquaintance. For all that, my trigonometry here can be no more than exploratory.[1] To lessen the absurdity, focus will be restricted to one work of each author. Easy enough in Quintilian's case, since we have only *Institutio oratoria*, his monumental *Gesamtredekunstwerk* of the early to mid 90s. Pliny will be represented by *Epistles*, a more discreetly monumental vision of Roman elite virtue produced between the late 90s and around 110, Tacitus by *Dialogus de oratoribus*, that challenging miniature masterpiece written – well, *there's* a question![2] – written, at all events, within the fifteen-odd years (*grande spatium...*) covered by Pliny's *Epistles*. We thus have (*i*) sure diachronic engagement (QT and QP), as two orator-consulars respond to a blockbuster by Rome's master of rhetoric – or, if we prefer to politicise, two (one-way) conversations across the notorious Flavian‖Nerļanic divide, between self-styling men of a new age and Domitian's pet professor. We also have (*ii*) the more or less synchronic interaction of PT in that new age. In sketching an account of this triad, my goals are four. First, to show that Quintilian's text (not just his lore) was the target of extensive and minute engagement by both Tacitus and Pliny. Second, to administer some experimental shots to the chronic debate over the relationship of *Epistles* and *Dialogus*. Third, to challenge any lurking assumptions that intertextual *intensity* must be matched by *visibility*.

---

[1] I try a fuller survey, focused on QP, in Whitton forthcoming b.

[2] E.g. Syme 1958: 670–3 (AD 102 or *c.* 106); Murgia 1980 and 1985 (before mid 97 and before *Ep.* 1); Brink 1994 (99–103); Woodman 2009b: 32–3 (after *Ep.* 1); van den Berg 2014: 32 (suspending judgment).

Much of the manoeuvring we shall observe is subtle to the point of imperceptible – hermeneutically untidy, to be sure, but not (I submit) reason to shut our ears to it. Finally, and most ambitiously, to grope towards a comparative reading of these three relationships in their *modes* of interaction: how like, or unlike, each other are P and T as intertextual artists?

One last question before we begin. Though I shan't try to prove it comparatively, each side of this triangle strikes me as a sustained intertextual dialogue of unprecedented intensity, and a useful reminder that intertextual studies in our period are far from exhausted. What lies beyond QPT?

QT

In some ways the relationship of *Institutio* and *Dialogus* is the most straightforward side of our triangle. The two works share an obvious theme (oratory at Rome); the relative dating is now secure (Quintilian first); several intertextual nodes have been hunted out and shaken down:[3] already a luxurious situation compared with what awaits us in *Epistles*. At another level it is the trickiest: here, as always, any estimate of intertextual minutiae must go hand in hand with a broader view of how Tacitus engages with Quintilian – and thus that most contentious question, what the *Dialogus* 'says' about oratory in Flavian and post-Flavian Rome. A holistic interpretation in a few pages is a tall order, so you'll have to forgive some cursory joining of dots. Still, I hope a brief survey of the landscape will prove helpful – not least in staking the importance of 'mere detail' in weighing up Tacitus' creative response to the *Institutio*.[4] *Dialogus*, we should recognise, engages with the text of Quintilian as intensely as with any of Cicero's dialogues – and as pregnantly.[5]

That Tacitus is intertextually alert will not surprise;[6] in *Dialogus* the sustained and complex engagement with Cicero's dialogues in particular should be familiar.[7] To take just one instance, Maternus' celebrated description of oratory as a 'nursling of licence . . . which does not come into being

---

[3] Primarily in the service of a protracted debate over the relative chronology (Güngerich 1951 was decisive) and a concomitant one about the authorship of *Dialogus*.

[4] The dismissive words from Brink 1989: 488 (in a signal analysis of QT, to be sure).

[5] For 'intensity', see Pfister 1985: 26–9, with his very useful six gradations of intertextuality (modelled for modern poetry and fiction).

[6] On *Hist.* and *Ann.*, see first the work of A. J. Woodman (e.g. Woodman 1998 *passim*, 2009a: 1–14, 2012, esp. pp. 384–94) and Joseph 2012. Woodman 2014 explores *passim* the rich and variegated intertextual underlay to *Agricola*.

[7] Quite *what* Tacitus is doing with or to Cicero is less agreed. See first Hass-von Reitzenstein 1970 and van den Berg 2014: 39–41, 208–40.

in well-ordered states' virtuosically – and archly – combines and recon-
figures passages from three separate dialogues in a single sentence:[8] evidently Tacitus was working *very closely indeed* with his Ciceronian material. Should we hesitate to suppose the same for Quintilian? Many do. I
have often encountered reluctance, both in print and around the seminar
table, to treat *Institutio* as a likely object of allusion, and why else should
the index to Roland Mayer's efficient commentary have fifty-five references
under 'Cicero: his writings evoked, imitated or referred to', but not a word
for Quintilian?[9]

Such reluctance surely reflects in part scholarly marginalisation of *Institutio* (admired from afar, but how many career Classicists have actually
read it through?) and a concomitant sense that Quintilian's twelve bulky
rolls are too massive, too technical, too *uncanonical* to be a plausible intertextual target. Misplaced preconceptions, in my view. Not to mention the
abundant reflexes we shall see in the texts of *Dialogus* and *Epistles*, Quintilian was a household name,[10] his *Institutio* went straight into the mass
distribution of its day,[11] and at least two other contemporaries show signs
of close reading.[12] Not that every part was studied with equal attention.
To judge from their intertextual habits, Tacitus and Pliny share with each
other (and with most modern readers) a marked preference for Books 10
and 12, with Books 1 and 2 the next favourites; the most technical parts,
with their enthymemes and status-theory, are lucky to be noticed at all.[13]
Not twelve bulky rolls, then, at least for repeated consultation, but a selection of highlights most interesting to the mature reader, and notable for

---

[8] *Dial.* 40.2 ~ *De or.* 2.35, *Rep.* 1.68, *Brut.* 45, rarely analysed with all three passages in view. Translations are mine unless noted.

[9] Mayer 2001. Much keen judgment underpins individual references to *Inst.* in the notes, but synthesis is hard to find (fleeting mention on p. 23). Güngerich 1980 is more detailed and explicit (as you
would expect: cf. Güngerich 1951 and 1955), but Quintilian is underplayed in the 'Nachwort' supplied by Heubner (pp. 201–2, 207). For an indiscriminate but handy list of parallels, see Gruenwald
1883; for a spectacularly unhelpful one, Dienel 1915: 252 n. 1.

[10] Implied by Mart. 2.90.2 (*c.* AD 86) (on which see Lorenz 2014); Pliny *Ep.* 2.14.9 *Quintiliano prae-
ceptore meo* (a proud declaration, with the single name anticipating recognition); Juv. 6.75, 279–80,
7.186–98 (with the sometimes questionable analysis of Anderson 1961).

[11] So to speak. *Institutio* is prefaced with a letter to the bookseller Trypho, who also dealt in Martial:
not just an address for rhetoric buffs, then. Cf. White 2009: 278–9.

[12] Whoever wrote *Minor declamations*, if not Quintilian (cf. Winterbottom 1984: xiv–xix); also, though
the traces are more sparing, Juvenal (see Uden's chapter in this volume, with further references). The
importance of intertextuality has been sorely underestimated in tracing Quintilian's early reception
history (e.g. Adamietz 1986: 2265–6).

[13] Books 1, 2, 10 and 12 are the four equipped with modern commentaries in English, at any rate
(respectively Colson 1924; Reinhardt and Winterbottom 2006; Peterson 1891; Austin 1948).

their ethical focus: in short, a less massive, less technical, more canonical and entirely plausible intertextual target.

Neither *Institutio* nor its author is named in *Dialogus*.[14] But Quintilian's work is audible from the very first line – or so let me claim. Fabius Justus often asks Tacitus why it is that, whereas earlier ages blossomed with talent and glory (*cum . . . ingeniis gloriaque floruerint*), our own age in particular (*nostra potissimum aetas*) is so barren and bereft (*deserta et laude eloquentiae orbata*) that it barely still knows the word 'orator'. Among the Ciceronian polyphony here, *Brutus* sings through loudest (330 *orbae eloquentiae*): a programmatic echo, no doubt, as Tacitus picks up where that gloomy close left off.[15] But what of another, more recent historical survey? Quintilian ends his monumental reading list (*Inst.* 10.1) with upbeat talk of the present: 'today there are talents of the highest order (*summa ingenia*) lighting up the forum . . . ' (*Inst.* 10.1.122).[16] Quite a contrast to Justus' relegation of great *ingenia* to the past. A couple of pages on, he urges his view that *imitatio* means growth and development, not stale repetition – 'unless, that is (*nisi forte*), we condemn our own times in particular (*nostra potissimum tempora*) to the unique misery of being the first period in which nothing grows' (*Inst.* 10.2.8).[17] Quintilian, of course, is being ironic (*nisi forte*); Justus' condemnation of *nostra potissimum aetas* seems quite straight. A piquant outcome: the *Dialogus* opens with a double inversion of Quintilian – on contemporary talent and imitation of all topics. Wry homage, or all-out (undercover) assault?

Let me start with 'undercover': I chose this passage not just as Tacitus' opening, nor for an intertextual tease of my own:[18] it also well illustrates that old dilemma, the indeterminacy of intertextuality. Quite apart from

---

[14] *Institutio* could hardly feature in the debate itself (*Dial.* 3.2–41.2), which takes place in the 70s. That did not preclude mention of Quintilian (then a practising orator and rhetor), had Tacitus wanted it – and if Quintilian was dead when *Dialogus* was composed. On Quintilian's life and death, see Kaster 1995: 333–6; Whitton 2013: 209.

[15] Gowing 2005: 111–12; cf. van den Berg 2014: 243. Later (*Dial.* 30.3), uniquely and remarkably, *Brutus* is actually named (cf. Woodman and Martin 1996: 298 on 'encoding' in the *Annals*, 'alerting readers to decode an intertextual reference'), in a sentence beginning *notus est* to boot (see n. 74 on memory markers).

[16] Tacitus seems to return to these words, and/or *erant clara et nuper ingenia* nearby (*Inst.* 10.1.118), in his own praise of Aper and Secundus, *celeberrima tum ingenia fori nostri* (*Dial.* 2.1; Murgia 1985: 186). Warm words – or rather lukewarm: *celeberrima tum* falls well short of *summa* or *clara* (we will see later how Pliny, perhaps, responds). With Q's 'lighting up the forum' (*illustratur forum*), should we compare Aper's appeal, *illustrate saeculum suum* (*Dial.* 23.5)?

[17] Translated after Russell 2001b. Justus' *floruerint* resonates with Quintilian's *crescat*, though I hear *De or.* 1.1 *cum . . . gloria florerent* more distinctly.

[18] Did you suspect that I would disguise my debt to (and variation from) my friend Chris van den Berg (2014: 244–5)?

the problem, whether Justus' words encode Tacitus' views,[19] how many readers *would* think of two fairly proximate phrases deep within *Institutio* 10? Will a duplicated idea about oratorical talent (*ingenia*) and a pair of time expressions containing *potissimum* catch the eye of anyone but a 'reader-philologist'? How ready are *you* to sniff out specifics among the topical and call this allusion? Questions often asked, I know (*saepe ... requiris*), and the shipwrecked really ought to have found some driftwood by now. But the *Dialogus* remains a good – and still underexploited – laboratory for extending such experiments to prose.[20] I for one am convinced that Quintilian is a crucial point of reference, both great and small. Not that every similarity can be nailed down as allusion, but that says as much about rigid hermeneutics as about Tacitus (or any intertextual artistry),[21] and in any case, enough can be nailed to satisfy anyone, I think, that *Institutio* is much in mind, and close to hand.[22] That being so, we might be surprised *not* to find traces in the opening lines. But I gladly confess it is one of those intertexts that resist being caught, stuffed and mounted – because that is a telling fact in itself.

Having made that claim, I'll try an easier tack, skipping forward to the area of loudest Quintilianic intertextuality. It concerns Messalla, the central but controversial figure in modern debate over Quintilian and *Dialogus*. Does his obsession with Cicero, and his focus on education, make him a 'Messalla–Quintilian', set up to be knocked down by 'Maternus–Tacitus'? Should we rather stress the differences? Is he a *semi*-Quintilian, partially restating and fatally undermining his cause? Or is none of these sufficient?[23] One thing is sure, and worth restating: whatever the role here of Quintilian's lost *De causis corruptae eloquentiae*,[24] Messalla's contribution

---

[19] See van den Berg 2014: 101–8 for both sides. Tacitus characteristically makes a point of *not* proffering his own opinion (*Dial.* 1.2), but I find it hard not to see relative (if not total) decline as a premise of *Dialogus* as a whole.

[20] Echoes of Edmunds 2001 (esp. pp. 42–3), Hinds 1998 and Barchiesi 1997 surely need no acknowledgement. Very helpful remarks on *Dialogus* and intertextuality in van den Berg 2014: 212–15.

[21] Consider, e.g., *Dial.* 6.6 extemporalis audaciae atque ipsius temeritatis ~ *Inst.* 10.6.6 extemporalem temeritatem; the athlete Nicostratus in *Dial.* 10.5 and *Inst.* 2.8.14 (nowhere else in extant Latin); Ovid's *Medea* and Varius' *Thyestes* in *Dial.* 12.6 and *Inst.* 10.1.98 (both passages otherwise name only authors, not works). The longer the list (and it is long), the less one is minded to put any one of these down to chance, but none can be 'proved' a conscious echo: a good reminder that intertextuality is more of an art than a science (cf. Barchiesi 1997: 211–12; Hinds 1998: 17–51). See also n. 64.

[22] As you will hopefully agree after a loop round the hermeneutic circle (since of course 'detecting an allusion is a process of reading that depends on one's overall view of a given work or tradition', Wills 1996: 16).

[23] See respectively Barwick 1954 (esp. pp. 19–20); Heldmann 1980; Brink 1989, esp. pp. 484–91 (also Alberte González 1993); van den Berg 2014: 83–90.

[24] Brink 1989. Messalla's first words drop a clear hint (*Dial.* 15.2 causas ... quas mecum ipse plerumque conquiro; cf. 27.1 and 28.1).

is heavily engaged with *Institutio*, and well illustrates the *personal* element that attaches to *textual* imitation.[25] A first, short speech on style (*Dial.* 25–6) casts oblique glances at Quintilian's late, great chapter on that topic (*Inst.* 12.10).[26] When Messalla gets into his stride (*Dial.* 28–32, 33.4–35), his argument has a double structure, combining syncrisis of ancient and modern with a narrative of the orator's upbringing up to *tirocinium fori* and declamation. Already the biological organisation nods to *Institutio*, especially Books 1 (infancy) and 2.1–13 (the rhetor's school, and declamation), with several points of detail to match: a 'window allusion' to *Brutus* through *Institutio* 1, for instance;[27] another to *De oratore* through *Institutio* 2.[28] But Messalla ranges more widely, as far as *Inst.* 10.5 (more declamation and *tirocinium fori*),[29] 12.2 (the value of philosophy)[30] and 12.6 (the debut in court).[31] None of the drier central tomes, to be sure;[32] but this speech adds up, I'd say, to a virtuosic (if severely partial) miniaturisation of the *Institutio*. Structural allusion, that is to say, is an important part of the story here.

But 'partial' is important: Messalla by no means emerges as an ersatz-Quintilian. This is, rather, a quintessentially *dialogic* engagement, in which

---

[25] 'Imitation' in the strong sense, as a 'dynamic law' of ancient literature (West and Woodman 1979: ix). Compare Quintilian's call to imitate not just *uerba* but the *res atque personae* of one's models (*Inst.* 10.2.27), and Clauss 1997 (esp. pp. 184–5) on character-*imitatio*.

[26] Best traced through the notes of Güngerich 1980. Messalla is led there, in fact, by Aper (*Dial.* 23.3 ~ *Inst.* 12.10.13–15; note also *Dial.* 18.4–5 ~ *Inst.* 12.10.12–16). The salient intertext is *Dial.* 26.1 *hirta toga* 'shaggy toga' (cf. *Inst.* 12.10.47), but that is only the tip of a mushy iceberg. With *Dial.* 26.4 (on the 'brawler' Cassius Severus) cf. *Inst.* 2.1.12 and 10.1.116–17 (on Severus) *and* 11.1.29–30 (on 'brawlers').

[27] *Dial.* 28.4–29.1 ~ *Inst.* 1.1.6 ~ *Brut.* 211 (Murgia 1980: 105–6). For the term 'window allusion', see e.g. Hinds 1998: 31 ('two-tier allusion') and Thomas 1986: 188–9 ('window reference'). It is (evidently) a particularly intense form of intertextuality.

[28] *Dial.* 35.1 ~ *Inst.* 2.4.42 ~ *De or.* 3.93–4, discussed below.

[29] Most closely *Dial.* 34.1–2 ~ *Inst.* 10.5.19–20 on *tirocinium fori* (Brink 1989: 487 n. 59). When Messalla sets out to discuss exercises but is sidetracked onto flogging the declamation horse, is that a parody of *Inst.* 10.5?

[30] Coming up shortly.

[31] Let me give a flavour of the (unnoted) extent of Tacitean reworking here: *Dial.* 34.3 *Magnus ex hoc usus, multum constantiae, plurimum iudici iuuenibus statim contingebat in media luce studentibus atque inter ipsa discrimina, ubi nemo impune stulte aliquid aut contrarie dicit quominus et iudex respuat et aduersarius exprobet, ipsi denique aduocati aspernentur* ~ *Inst.* 12.6.4–5 *alia lux, alia ueri discriminis facies, plusque, si separes, usus sine doctrina quam citra usum doctrina ualeat . . . At illic et iudex tacet et aduersarius obstrepit et nihil temere dictum perit.* From his model Messalla develops topic, structure (the tricolon beginning *et iudex . . .*) and a key idea (foolish remarks get no mercy); compare also the *lux/discrimen* pairs and *plus . . . usus* (Q) ~ *magnus . . . usus, multum . . . plurimum . . .* (T). But much has been altered (including a suitably Messallan upgrade of *tacet* to *respuat*), reordered and redeployed: delicate traces indeed.

[32] See Brink 1989: 488 '[Messalla] must not look professional, let alone professorial' – but see also above at n. 13.

the 'dialectic between resemblance and difference' tells the most.[33] In plainer terms, Messalla's arguments and his persona are closer to a caricature than a replica, recognisable but heavily exaggerated. Take declamation: Quintilian values it highly, but often inveighs against its degenerate manifestations; Messalla simply damns it outright. More broadly, where Quintilian by turns attacks (elements of) modern practice and style and evangelises for his neo-Ciceronian corrective, Messalla goes heavy on the moralising, light on positive suggestions for remedy.[34] Not that caricature need mean (cruel) parody: in itself, the *ethopoeia* is potentially as much comment on Messalla as on Quintilian.[35] But Messalla – or is it Tacitus? – lands some more direct hits. Most telling, I think, are the window allusions in which he 'corrects' Quintilian on citations of Cicero. Here is Cicero on rhetoric vs philosophy, in the proem to *Orator*:

> Fateor me oratorem, si modo sim aut etiam quicumque sim, **non** ex rhetorum **officinis sed** ex Academiae spatiis exstitisse. (*Or.* 12)

> I confess that I won eminence as an orator, if I am one, or however much of one I am, thanks **not** to the **workshops** of rhetors **but** to the porticoes of the Academy.

Here is Quintilian's version:

> Nam M. Tullius **non tantum** se debere **scholis** rhetorum **quantum** Academiae spatiis frequenter ipse testatus est. (*Inst.* 12.2.23)

> For Marcus Tullius frequently attested himself that he did **not** owe **as much** to the **schools** of rhetors **as** to the porticoes of the Academy.

And now Messalla's:

> Et Cicero **his, ut opinor, uerbis** refert, quicquid in eloquentia effecerit, id se **non** rhetorum <**officinis**> **sed** Academiae spatîs consecutum. (*Dial.* 32.6)

> And Cicero reports – **in these words, I think** – that whatever he accomplished in eloquence, he achieved **not** in the <**workshops**> of rhetors **but** in the porticoes of the Academy.

Quintilian – hardly disinterested when it comes to teachers of rhetoric – takes the edge off *Orator* in citation: the rhetors' 'workshops' become their 'schools', and Cicero owes *some* debt to them (*non tantum . . . quantum*) rather than none at all (*non . . . sed*); the amendment is eased by a genteel

---

[33] See Pfister 1985: 29 (harnessing Bakthin's 'dialogicity' for intertextual intensity); Fowler 1997: 18.

[34] For Brink 1989 he has no such suggestions at all; but see Luce 1993: 34 n. 72 and van den Berg 2014: 83.

[35] See, however, Brink 1989: 493–4.

(or better disingenuous?) vagueness over the source of his quotation (*frequenter testatus est*). The aristocratic Messalla – who damns rhetors outright and is distinctly more enthusiastic about philosophy – restores at least one, probably both, details, administering some pert gentility of his own (*his, ut opinor, uerbis*): with *ut opinor* (i.e. 'I think you'll find'), that is, Quintilian's silent erasure is registered and wryly exposed.[36]

If you suspected 'overinterpretation' just then, consider what immediately precedes in each text:

> ... it is agreed (***constat***) that Demosthenes, chief among all the orators of Greece, paid attention to Plato (***dedisse operam Platoni***). (*Inst.* 12.2.22)

> If witnesses are required, which of the Greeks shall I name before Demosthenes, who was *a most devoted student of Plato* (***studiosissimum Platonis auditorem fuisse***), as tradition records (***memoriae proditum est***)? (*Dial.* 32.5)

Messalla improves on Quintilian's lukewarm *dedisse operam* with help from Cicero,[37] and expands *constat* into a grander – and, it now seems, pointed – affirmation of authority (*memoriae proditum est*).[38] So too, a little later, with the rhetors' schools at Rome: Quintilian reports, with Cicero as his source, their existence already in the time of Crassus; Messalla, on the same authority, adds what Quintilian preferred to omit, that Crassus damned those schools as a *ludus impudentiae*.[39] If two or three such examples is company, Aper makes a crowd, likewise lifting a Quintilianic veil, and with

---

[36] My account extends Dienel 1915: 262 and Güngerich 1951: 163 (*pace* Döpp 1985: 163 n. 14). The claim to greater precision is also (approximately) justified by Messalla's *quicquid ... effecerit* (for *si ego ...*, omitted by Q). Alas, Tacitus' *officinis* is a conjecture, making interpretation partly circular (Smiraglia 1955: 163–4), but that is only one detail among several, and the coming examples add ballast. For a similar use of *opinor* compare *Inst.* 2.13.13, where Quintilian identifies (with the Elder Pliny's help) *pictor ille* of Cic. *Or.* 74 – not twitting Cicero, I think, but with a little more edge, I think, than Reinhardt and Winterbottom 2006: 211 suggest ('being modest or cautious').

[37] He 'neatly combines' (Mayer) and inflates *De or.* 1.89 *Platonis studiosus* and *Or.* 15 *Platonis auditor*.

[38] The argumentative move is also the same: with Messalla's *si testes desiderantur* compare the start of Quintilian's sentence, *Haec si ratione manifesta non essent, exemplis tamen crederemus ...* Messalla had earlier contradicted Quintilian directly on Epicurus (*Dial.* 31.6 ~ *Inst.* 12.2.24; Güngerich 1955: 441), following it up with the tart *Dial.* 31.7 *neque enim sapientem informamus* (cf. *Inst.* 12.2.7 *ego illum quem instituo Romanum quendam uelim esse sapientem*).

[39] *Dial.* 35.1 (including *ut ait Cicero*) ~ *Inst.* 2.4.42 ~ *De or.* 3.93–4 (Dienel 1915: 261, Güngerich 1951: 163; *contra* Smiraglia 1955: 164–5, Reinhardt and Winterbottom 2006: 119). When Messalla further claims that Crassus had the schools closed down, he appears to misunderstand Cicero. Whether that is a slip by Tacitus, or tendentious 'misreading' (as by Aper in *Dial.* 20.1: details in n. 43) or historical 'forgetfulness' (as again by Aper, now with the *Verrines*, also in *Dial.* 20.1) on Messalla's part, is hard to say. On this nexus see also van den Berg 2014: 79–81.

a discreet marker of intertextual sparring (*ut ipsius uerbis utar*).[40] Delicate hints, to be sure, as scepticism in some learned quarters confirms;[41] you need to know *both* your Cicero *and* your Quintilian pretty well to spot them; and the story is complicated by the fact that Messalla and Aper each have their individual axes to grind. Still, once we are attuned, it is clear from this medley that someone is making mischief; and, with two different speakers now involved, that someone is starting to look, to me at least, like Tacitus.[42]

If Messalla is a partial caricature of Quintilian, Aper is something at once similar and different. He too is capable of tendentious borrowing from Quintilian, as notoriously on the 'infirmity' of Messalla Corvinus,[43] and of the sparring we have just seen. But he also displays a deep – and deeply compromised – Quintilianic streak, in his energetic advocacy of modernity and of oratory as a career choice. In schematic terms, if Messalla (over)plays Quintilian the moralist, Aper (over)plays Quintilian the modernist: here, if you like, is the other 'semi-Quintilian'.[44] This role-play starts and peaks in his lively opening *suasoria*, pressing Maternus to return to oratory (*Dial.* 4.3–10) – a speech which looks to me like a blow-up of the great *suasoria* that closes the *Institutio* (12.11.8–31).[45] More precisely, Aper homes in on a few lines in which Quintilian sets aside his idealistic tenor (we have little hope of becoming perfect orators, but should try all the same) and advertises in semi-*praeteritio* the benefits that even lesser practitioners can

---

[40] *Inst.* 12.10.12 paraphrases a (lost) letter of Brutus criticising Cicero's style; Aper (*Dial.* 18.5) borrows from the same letter, restoring with relish the word apparently skirted by Quintilian, *elumbis* – 'lacking balls' (cf. Q's paraphrase, *uiro molliorem*), rather than 'with a dislocated hip' (*OLD*, Mayer).

[41] Nor *must* such phrases signify correction; at least, no one has suggested it of Maternus in *Dial.* 13.5 *me uero dulces, ut Vergilius ait, Musae*... (*Georg.* 2.475; see Joseph 2012: 19–22). For a long bet, I might look to *Inst.* 10.3.22–30 (Quintilian on countryside composition and urban hubbub): those lines have been in the air since *Dial.* 9.6 (see Murgia 1985: 178, also (?) Mayer's enigmatic 'cf.' at *Dial.* 12.1). When Quintilian parodies those who fetishise *siluarum amoenitas et praeterlabentia flumina* etc. (10.3.24), might Maternus/Tacitus have heard Virgil in the background (*Georg.* 2.456 *flumina amem siluasque inglorius* etc.)?

[42] On the difficulty of deciding whether intertexts are 'owned' by individual speakers or corporately by the *Dialogus*, see van den Berg 2014: 239–40. For another interpretative mode again, see Mayer on *Dial.* 21.9 (a Ciceronian intertext, evidently attributed to Tacitus, 'subtly undermines' Aper's own position).

[43] *Dial.* 20.1 ~ *Inst.* 4.1.8, the flagship proof since Güngerich 1951: 159–60 that Tacitus knows and alludes to Quintilian. Aper 'mistakes' Quintilian's *infirmus* 'inadequate (as a speaker)' for '(physically) ill', turning precept into farce. Murgia 1980: 100 n. 10 (misrepresenting Güngerich) and Barnes 1986: 229 think Tacitus made the error; Jeffreys 1987 and Zwierlein 1997 surely miss the joke.

[44] Cf. Dienel 1915: 254 'die Zuweisung der Stellungnahme Quintilians... an zwei gegnerische Personen, Aper und Messalla...' and even (p. 253) 'Aper-Quintilian'. This point has been much understated amid the focus on Messalla as 'the' Quintilian(ic) figure (some hints in Brink 1989: 295 and van den Berg 2014: 260).

[45] Again cf. (broadly) Dienel 1915: 255–7.

enjoy (12.11.29). Were anyone to measure oratory in terms of utility alone (*utilitate sola*), writes Quintilian at the last, it is clear what advantages – *opes honores amicitias, laudem praesentem futuram* – accrue to the orator; but this would be a poor way of thinking: we should aim for virtues, not the pleasures (*uoluptates*) they may bring. When Aper produces an entire speech on the division *utilitas, uoluptas, dignitas* (cf. Q's *opes honores amicitias*) and renown (*fama* and *notitia*; cf. Q's *laudem praesentem futuram*), he precisely and spectacularly violates that last injunction.[46] Not that *Institutio* lurks in his every line by any means; but it seems (quietly) eloquent that the peroration of Aper's little speech features the very 'citadel of eloquence' motif used by Quintilian just one sentence previously.[47]

This *first* speech of the *Dialogus*, in other words, literally incorporates its own dialogic partner, as Aper keys into Quintilian's finale and turns it inside out, replacing high-minded ethics with unadorned self-interest. As in Messalla's case, the minutiae only affirm character traits one might otherwise detect. But does his intertextual violence say something about *Institutio* too? That Aper is worlds apart from Quintilian in taste and ethics is clear enough: as a 'naturalist' he has little truck with rhetorical theory; he merrily swims with the stylistic tide of modernity; and he takes as his exemplars 'delators' *par excellence*.[48] Above all, he positively revels in what Quintilian so rarely mentions: the imperial (Flavian) context. A delicate intertext may underline the point. When Aper calls Vibius Crispus and Eprius Marcellus *principes fori* (*Dial.* 8.3), compare Quintilian – still in *Institutio* 12.11 – on Domitius Afer, *quem principem fuisse quondam fori non erat dubium* (*Inst.* 12.11.3). Quintilian has only the highest praise for Afer, as he does (and doubtless must) for Crispus.[49] Tacitus' dim view of Afer,

---

[46] *Dial.* 5.4 (where *uoluptas* depends on an editorial supplement, but not a contentious one). A more specific nexus is faintly audible at *Dial.* 9.4 ~ *Inst.* 12.11.29 (Woytek 2006: 133).

[47] *Dial.* 10.5 *Sed tecum mihi, Materne, res est, quod, cum natura tua in ipsam arcem eloquentiae ferat, errare mauis et summa adept<ur>us in leuioribus subsistis*; cf. *Inst.* 12.11.28 *Cicerone arcem tenente eloquentiae*. Not only the 'citadel' is Quintilianic: straining for the heights (*summa*) is a favourite image of his, and Aper comes particularly close (as Gudeman 1914: 255 saw) to *Inst.* 1.pr.20 *quod si non contingat, altius tamen ibunt qui ad summa nitentur quam qui praesumpta desperatione quo uelint euadendi* [cf. *summa adept<ur>us*] *protinus circa ima substiterint* – uniting, if so, opening and close of the *Institutio* in his invocation. For the suggestion of a comparable 'miniaturisation' in Pliny *Ep.* 2.5, see Whitton 2015b: 131–8.

[48] On all this, see first Winterbottom 1964: his Aper stands for the mindset Quintilian set out to combat. Aper's remarks on textbooks (*Dial.* 19.3 *aridissimis Hermagorae et Apollodori libris*) certainly cut close to the bone (Mayer). You'll notice I'm sceptical of those who would 'redeem' Aper altogether (for the lively recent debate see e.g. Dominik 2007: 30–4 with references; van den Berg 2014: 65–6 and *passim*).

[49] Afer often, Crispus four times; they are two of the five outstanding orators whom Quintilian professes to have met himself (*Inst.* 10.1.118–22). Marcellus (disgraced in 79) was presumably a name not to be mentioned.

Crispus and Marcellus is clear:[50] it is a safe bet that he read Quintilian's lines as cynically as he wrote Aper's. Consider too how Aper develops the motif: *donec libuit, principes fori, nunc principes in Caesaris amicitia.* Quintilian proclaimed forensic eloquence the highest goal. Aper, with a cynicism all too familiar from *Histories* and *Annals*, points out the real apex in the principate: not the courts, but the Court.[51]

'All parody refunctions existing text(s) and/or discourse(s), so it can be said that these verbal structures are called to the readers' minds and then placed under erasure' (R. Phiddian).[52] In Aper's case even more than Messalla's, this seems an apt definition. How far Quintilian is 'called to the readers' minds' is debatable: the details I have laboured demand as intense a reading as they must reflect intense composition.[53] But 'placed under erasure' well captures the devastating effect of Aper's cynical 'imperialising' of Quintilian's ideals. This seems to operate at a higher level than his own dubious ethics (a point of *ethopoeia* which, as in Messalla's case, need per se have no ramifications for Quintilian),[54] since Aper's emphasis on the autocratic context – and his implausible whitewashing of it[55] – paves the way for Maternus' climactic intervention, the most incendiary answer in *Dialogus* to the question of oratory in the principate. We might even care to invert 'placed under erasure', since what Aper does is graphically *unerase* the Flavian context (Domitianic for Quintilian, Vespasianic for him) of which Quintilian so rarely speaks. At all events, *Tacitus'* engagement with Quintilian, as performed through Aper, looks to fit Phiddian's account of parody all too well.

All this is borne out, finally, in that last intervention of Maternus. For our purposes the most striking feature of his closing speech, the finale of *Dialogus* (36–41), is its apparent *lack* of engagement with *Institutio.* Just one famous – but loose – nexus demands attention: Maternus' climactic, fourfold declaration that oratory is redundant in the utopian monarchy

---

[50] *Ann.* 4.52.4 (Afer); *Hist.* 2.10 etc. (Crispus); *Hist.* 2.95.3, *Ann.* 16.28–9 etc. (Marcellus).

[51] Cf. Lana 1973: 52–7. On a harder (and freer) reading, Aper might expose Quintilian himself as Flavian stooge: Crispus and Marcellus rose beyond oratory to become *principes* in the court of Vespasian; Quintilian, for all the fine words about *orandi maiestas* (*Inst.* 12.11.30), achieved his own highest *dignitas* as palace tutor (*Inst.* 4.pr., of which more below) and honorary consul (Auson. *Grat. act.* 7).

[52] Phiddian 1995: 13.

[53] If my own exposition, footnotes and all, is less than easy going, that may not be by chance.

[54] Though it might (n. 51).

[55] E.g. *Dial.* 7.1 *apud principem ipsos illos libertos et procuratores principum tueri et defendere* (for of course imperial servants can do no wrong); 8.3. Unlike Bartsch 1994: 115 I take Aper – like any Tacitean 'insider' – to be as knowingly cynical in his account of Vespasianic bliss as is the 'outsider' Maternus.

he professes to inhabit (*Dial.* 41.4)[56] finds an analogy in Quintilian's sole explicit reference to the changed constitution ('in our day, when all things, relying as they do on the care and protection of one man (*curae tutelaeque unius innixa*), can be endangered by no judicial outcome', *Inst.* 6.1.35).[57] Call it irony, call it doublespeak; one thing must be clear: Maternus' words stretch the public transcript – the only transcript Quintilian could ever voice – well beyond breaking point.[58] Perverse as it may seem (I did say the nexus is loose), this seems to me the ultimate explosion of *Institutio* – and one where Tacitus cannot be too far from the fuse.

Here, though, I step back from the brink,[59] since I have been less concerned to pin down quite *what* Tacitus' reply to Quintilian is than to argue that minute intertextuality plays an integral and essential role in the construction of that reply. At one level, we find a serial system of 'adjustment in imitation', both textual and personal: Messalla and Aper substantially, Maternus at most selectively, have each drawn on their model for ethics and argument, but made him more than their own, adapting – and exposing – the *Institutio* freely, and with a distinct lack of deference. It seems equally hard not to sum up the *Dialogus* as a cynical, not to say antagonistic, response to Quintilian – a *Paradebeispiel*, on the smallest and the largest scales, of 'opposition in imitation'.

You'll have noticed by now that I'm working with a 'hard' model of allusion, in which meaning is produced for the reader who detects and interprets intertextual nodes. In fact, I have positively argued for its validity. Enough proof, I hope, has been in the pudding to sustain my opening claim, that *Dialogus* itself is grounds to posit a contemporary readership sufficiently sensitive to prose allusion, and sufficiently familiar with the *Institutio*, to trace its intertexture – or least some of it: as in all composition, no individual detail need be savoured by even a single recipient for it to *mean*.[60] At all events, a softer proposition, that several of Tacitus'

---

[56] Too long to quote; in summary: the monarch (*unus*) is wise (*sapientissimus*) and always merciful (*clementia cognoscentis*); his advisers, the senate, quickly agree on what is right (*cito consentiant*); citizens are not driven to crime (*tam raro et tam parce peccetur*).

[57] Brink 1993: 347; Goldberg 1999: 236–7; van den Berg 2014: 300 n. 15 (not all necessarily thinking of 'allusion').

[58] See Köhnken 1973 for irony; Bartsch 1994: 98–125 for doublespeak; Scott 1990 (brought into play by Bartsch) for 'public transcript'.

[59] I hesitate to call anything clear in Maternus' speech (cf. *Dial.* 42.1 *et si qua tibi obscura in hoc meo sermone uisa sunt, de iis rursus conferamus . . .*). But elsewhere Tacitus *in propria persona* leaves little room to share Quintilian's optimism so far as Domitianic Rome is concerned: cf. *Agr.* 39.2 *studia fori et ciuilium artium decus in silentium acta* (notionally in 84), 2.2 *omni bona arta in exsilium acta* (in 93/4), 3.1 *ingenia studiaque oppresseris . . .* 3.2 *silentium* (all fifteen years) – rhetorically driven claims, of course, but not easily neutralised altogether.

[60] How many of *you* knew that the article to which my title alludes has a personal relevance for me in its date? (You all know Syme 1979, of course . . . (cf. *Dial.* 30.3).)

first readers would catch some or even most of the intertextual drift, is not implausible. Not necessarily from the outset and at first reading: in fact, we can loosely chart a gradual shift in intertextual intelligibility, from the barely perceptible node in the opening sentence through Aper's highly selective first speech through to the heavy colouring of Messalla (and back into silence with Maternus). But – if you'll forgive the *petitio principî* – the *Dialogus*, as much as any ancient prose or poetry, could hardly reveal all its depth at first reading. We might even think of Tacitus' work itself as a process of education, in intertextuality as in other things: after all, I can think of no prose written with quite such allusive intensity before it. Unless, that is, Pliny's *Epistles* was under way.

QP

At first sight, *Epistles* has little to do with *Institutio* in genre, style and topic. Even if we see past the differences and recognise both works as holistic, ethical interventions in the definition of a Roman elite life, there is the second point, that Quintilian's text is far more selectively invoked than in *Dialogus*. The nine books of (the 'private') *Epistles* amount to several times the length of Tacitus' short text and range far more broadly in topic, in manner, and in mode of intertextuality; the average density of engagement, measured in pounds of Quintilian per square inch, is much lower. Two reasons that readers may well be forgiven for missing it altogether, even in this age of intertextual fervour.[61] But we should not underestimate the extent of that engagement, or its variety.[62] On a scale of 'fleeting to sustained', it ranges from scores of passing miniature borrowings (a neat *iunctura*, a pertinent idea) to (at least) two letters composed with close and persistent reference to a few pages of *Institutio*. On another scale, 'unmarked to marked', the range is equally broad: often Quintilian's text (and it is not special in this regard) is silently incorporated into Pliny's, as a discreetly digested object of *imitatio*; elsewhere, the reworking seems to be performed with just 'the teasing play . . . between revelation and concealment' that defines allusion.[63] *Mutatis mutandis*, a picture not dissimilar

---

[61] On Plinian intertextuality see especially Schenk 1999a (translated as Schenk 2016) and the important work of Marchesi 2008; also Marchesi 2013 and e.g. Henderson 2002; Gibson and Morello 2012; Whitton 2010, 2013 *passim*.

[62] As with QT, doctrinal positioning vis-à-vis Quintilian will be of secondary interest here. There is a large Italian bibliography on the subject (see Mastrorosa 2010, with references), if scarce agreement: for Picone 1978 Pliny is a faithful disciple, for Boccuto 1990 he is an independent one; Cova 2003 sees *Epistles* as an outright attack on Quintilian. It is remarkable that even these detailed studies can include statements that Pliny may not have had the text of *Institutio* in mind (e.g. Cova 1966: 203 and 2003: 84, 88, echoed in Mastrorosa 2010: 126 'ascoltati dalla viva voce').

[63] Hinds 1998: 23.

from that of *Dialogus*, with its numerous small echoes but also larger-scale structural imitation (Messalla's topped and tailed *Institutio*, Aper's *suasoria* remixed), many unmarked reworkings but also distinctly (if discreetly) ludic ones too.[64] In another way, too, QP shows interesting similarity to and difference from QT. Quintilian could be seen as a constituent part of all three protagonists of *Dialogus*, a core ingredient – in different ways and degrees – of their positions and *personae*. Textual *imitatio*, that is, goes hand in hand with *ethopoeia*.[65] So too with Pliny, who makes Quintilian a constituent part of his epistolary self, and with no less freedom and creativity – if (I think) with rather less violence. But in his case author and persona are (to be crude) one and the same.

Let me try to substantiate these claims a little. Here I will be even more cursory than before, partly in response to the sporadic intertextuality of QP, partly to spare ink.[66] And I'll begin with a provocation, or an irritation. Leaving aside the two passages where Pliny famously names Quintilian (*Ep.* 2.14.9, 6.6.3), let me try a question. When Murgia tells us that the first words of Pliny's first letter –

> **Frequenter hortatus es**[A] *ut epistulas*, si *quas* paulo curatius *scripsissem*,[B] **colligerem publicaremque**.[C]

> You have often urged me to collect and publish any letters which I write with a little more care than usual.

– are modelled on the opening of Quintilian's prefatory letter to Trypho –

> **Efflagitasti cotidiano conuicio**[A] *ut libros quos* ad Marcellum meum de institutione oratoria *scripseram*[B] **iam emittere inciperem**.[C]

> You have demanded with daily and noisy reproof that I finally start publishing the books that I wrote to my friend Marcellus on 'The Orator's Education'.

---

[64] In leaning on the latter, I catered to (or revealed my anxieties about) the need to 'justify' intertexts as more than arbitrary speculation or Kristevan freedom. A proper need, in my view, for any historicist criticism; but one in tension with the fuzziness of so much ancient intertextuality. See also n. 21.

[65] Compare West and Woodman 1979: 198–9 on the blurring of literature and life in Horace. Here, as with *Dialogus*, disregard for the surrounding polyphony (above all Cicero) is of course a temporary hermeneutic convenience.

[66] A broader synopsis in Whitton forthcoming b, where fuller arguments and references will be found. I leave *Pan.* out of the count here with regret, since it presents a material contrast, à propos of both QP (if there is any substantive Quintilianic intertextuality, I have yet to see it) and PT: *Pan.* does seem to draw on *Dial.* for phrasing (Brink 1994: 266–7), but far more rarely than it does on *Agr.*, and with scant substantive engagement (on 'aesthetic' borrowings see below).

– will we believe him?[67] The claim might seem outlandish: lexis shows little similarity, the prefatory topos complicates such identifications, and, besides (a question Murgia did not ask), why should *Epistles* invoke *Institutio* anyway? There again, he was right that the sentences are particularly close in structure; Quintilian's intimation of sequential publication (*emittere incipiam*) finds an exaggerated match at the end of Pliny's letter (*si quas addidero non supprimam*); and then there is the letter 'M/C' beginning each of their superscriptions . . . I must be joking – or is that one more evanescent marker of intertextual intent lurking in Pliny's preface?[68] *Paulo curatius* indeed, if so. With *Dialogus* I argued my way out of the dilemma with the help of the hermeneutic circle: the reader who has learned to see the Quintilian lurking between the lines later may, one day, catch the hint here. If that will wash in this case too (let's see . . .), here may be a declaration, programmatically prominent and barely visible, that *Institutio* will play a very (subtly) significant role indeed in *Epistles* to come.

At the least spectacular end of the scale are many similarities that might be more safely – but I think misleadingly – neutralised as ('mere') 'parallels' or 'reverberation'.[69] Quintilian's history of oratory includes an exuberant harvest metaphor, 'let the great crop (*prouentus*) of orators blossom [before our eyes]' (*Inst.* 12.10.11); Pliny buoyantly declares 'this year has brought a large crop (*prouentum*) of poets' (*Ep.* 1.13.1). Quintilian advises reading the best authors 'diligently and with almost as much care as we give to writing' (*prope ad scribendi sollicitudinem, Inst.* 10.1.20); Pliny asks Lupercus to read over a speech of his with 'the concentration of a writer' (*intentionem scribentis, Ep.* 2.5.2). Again, Quintilian warns that revision must have limits, 'so that the file polishes the work rather than wearing it away' (*ut opus poliat lima, non exterat, Inst.* 10.4.4); Pliny urges Suetonius to get on and publish: 'the work is finished and complete: it is no longer gaining sheen from the file, but is being worn down' (*opus . . . nec iam splendescit lima sed atteritur, Ep.* 5.10.3).[70] With little by way of lexical or syntactical hooks, no obvious markers of allusion, and scant 'dialogism' to speak of, these typify (in my view) an important compositional aspect of the *Epistles* which risks

---

[67] Murgia 1980: 125 ('closely followed') and 1985: 121; pedantic details mine.

[68] *M. Fabius Quintilianus Tryphoni suo s.* ~ *C. Plinius Romano suo s.* Not quite as silly as it sounds: inclusion of the author's *praenomen* is otherwise rare in lettered Latin (see Whitton 2013: 66). 'One more': other targets (may) include Ovid *Ex Ponto* 3.9.53 (references in Whitton 2013: 12), Cicero's *Ad Atticum* (via Nepos: Gibson and Morello 2012: 83–4), Sen. *Ep.* 1.1 (Whitton 2010: 130 n. 74) – and, who knows, *Dialogus* (below)?

[69] For the terms, see Thomas 1986: 174; Woodman 2012: 385–7. On the problems of any binary system ('meaningful/interpretable' vs 'accidental/incidental'), see Hinds 1998: 17–51.

[70] These three parallels were already adduced in Gierig's excellent, neglected commentary (1800–2).

being frozen out in the new intertextual orthodoxy: the incorporation of a neat idea or phrase not by accident, but not necessarily in 'strong' allusion either – rather, *for its own aesthetic sake*. That is no Plinian peculiarity. On the contrary, it is the bread and butter of imperial *imitatio* – and does not, in my view, require an 'allusive' interpretation to rescue it from the jaws of (supposedly) disparaging *Quellenforscher*.[71]

At the other end of the scale are *Epistles* 1.20 and 7.9. The first of those is extensively but freely modelled on part of Quintilian's great chapter on style (*Inst.* 12.10), transforming (*inter alia*) Quintilian's endorsement of the 'grand style' into an out-and-out claim for oratorical length.[72] The second crafts out of Quintilian's precepts on writing exercises for the mature student (*Inst.* 10.5) what strikes me as the most intertextually intense letter of the whole collection, as Pliny not only tells young Fuscus Salinator how to study on vacation, but demonstrates his own exceptionally close reading and rewriting of *Institutio* in the process.[73] In these long letters, too, the aesthetic motivation should not be downplayed. But *Epistles* 7.9 in particular shows signs of a more ludic intent. I'll save my favourite for a few pages, since it will involve Tacitus too. For now, consider Pliny's playful coda. Having finished his precepts, he feigns an afterthought: he's quite forgotten to tell Fuscus what to read! No need: let him just remember (*memineris*) to seek out the best in each relevant genre: *aiunt enim multum legendum esse, non multa* ('read a lot, not lots, as they say'); who these are is too well known to need setting out (*Ep.* 7.9.15–16). Commentators have duly registered a parallel with Quintilian's advice that 'the mind should be trained by a lot of reading rather than reading a lot [sc. of different things/authors]' (*multa magis quam multorum lectione formanda mens, Inst.* 10.1.59). But this is more than a parallel. Pliny's tautly turned *sententia* has all the usual markers of *variatio* and *aemulatio in imitando*, the whole letter has been brimming with *Institutio*, specifically the tenth book – half of which, of course, is given over to a monumental reading list (*Inst.* 10.1) – and we even have a memory marker (*memineris*).[74] The conclusion is surely clear: *aiunt* is not marking a proverb,[75] but disguising (and thus, by ludic rules, flagging up) a specific reworking. Almost Alexandrian, you might say – but with a twist: Pliny has *not* departed from the source he 'fails' to signal. He has (arguably)

---

[71] Or priority critics, also prone to associate 'later' with 'inferior' (clear tendencies of this, for instance, in Murgia 1980, 1985; Woytek 2006). The aesthetic stakes and modes of declamation culture are relevant here.

[72] Most broadly, *Ep.* 1.20.3–17 is constructed after *Inst.* 12.10.48–57, *Ep.* 1.20.18–22 from *Inst.* 12.10.64–5. See (roughly) Cugusi 2003.

[73] Gierig 1800–2 ad loc., Boccuto 1991 and Keeline 2013 uncover a good part of the story.

[74] On memory markers who could forget Conte 1986: 57–69? See also Wills 1996: 31; Hinds 1998: 3–4.

[75] Otto 1890: 232. Certainly it *can* mark a proverb (e.g. *Ep.* 4.5.1, *Inst.* 12.11.9).

improved on the *form*, yes; but the content remains precisely the same. A rather different form of irony, this, from what we saw in *Dialogus*.

QP, if I read it right, features a wide range of 'structurality' (from fleeting to sustained engagement) and of markedness, motivated by both aesthetic and ludic concerns. That makes getting a grip on any individual node tricky. Pliny's famous *recusatio* of historiography, for instance, includes a highly wrought syncrisis of history and oratory (*Ep.* 5.8.9–11), in which two flourishes are modelled on *flosculi* in Quintilian's equivalent syncrisis (*Inst.* 10.1.31–4). Is this silent borrowing? Formal emulation? Pointed correction? When Pliny states that *plurimum refert, ut Thucydides ait,* κτῆμα *sit an* ἀγώνισμα, *quorum alterum oratio, alterum historia est* ('there is a great difference, as Thucydides said, between a *ktema* and an *agonisma*, of which oratory is one, history the other'), he is evidently prompted by Quintilian's own reworking (*Inst.* 10.1.31) of Thucydides' celebrated comparison of showy and useful modes of history (1.22.4). Does *ut Thucydides ait* show Pliny hauling Quintilian up for imprecision, as we found Messalla and Aper doing in *Dialogus*? I have my doubts, and not just because Pliny both agrees and disagrees with him.[76] Besides, this time Quintilian's own intertextuality seems qualitatively different: in the passages we saw earlier, he cited his sources but silently erased unwelcome details; here he does not name Thucydides (i.e. is more 'allusive'), and ironically turns the historian's judgment into an insistence that *oratory*, not history, is superior. In other words, if Pliny is having fun here, he may be smiling with, as much as at, Quintilian. But which it may be is much harder to specify than with *Dialogus*.[77]

The same is true when it comes to politics. If situating oratory in (Flavian) imperial Rome was arguably (inevitably?) the most urgent point of the dialectic in QT, such concerns rarely surface in QP. When they do, Pliny's version of the public transcript can be very similar to Quintilian's.[78] But is Quintilian, for Pliny, tainted by his Domitianic associations? There is no sign of that either time Pliny names him (*Ep.* 2.14.9, 6.6.3), though he is caught elsewhere by the sharp tail of an epigram on cruel Fortune, who (under Domitian) 'makes senators into professors, and professors into

---

[76] P and Q agree, against Thucydides, in appropriating ἀγώνισμα for 'oratory'. But, where Q makes that the greater good, P restores the Thucydidean hierarchy, in which κτῆμα (now 'history') reigns supreme.

[77] To sample the long and often confused debate on these lines, see Cova 1975: 135–8; Baier 2003; Woodman 2012: 238. I address the passage (and the others mentioned here) at proper length in Whitton forthcoming b.

[78] *Ep.* 3.20.12 *Sunt . . . cuncta sub unius arbitrio, qui . . . solus omnium curas laboresque suscepit* ~ *Inst.* 6.1.35 (met earlier) *omnia curae tutelaeque unius innixa* (freely interpreted by Cova 2003: 93–4).

senators'.[79] And what should we make of *Epistles* 2.9? Canvassing for Erucius Clarus as tribune of the plebs, Pliny professes anxiety over his own reputation: should Clarus fail in the election, Pliny will seem to have 'deceived'
the emperor in recommending him; accordingly he must persuade everyone that Clarus is the sort of man Trajan has believed him to be (*Ep.*
2.9.1–3). Remarkably (but quietly) enough, these opening lines are closely
modelled on the preface to *Institutio* 4, where Quintilian advertises his
appointment as tutor to the royal princes. He is anxious over his reputation: now that Domitian has shown such confidence in him, he must
not prove inadequate and so seem to have 'deceived' the emperor; he prays
to all the gods, chief among them Domitian himself, to make Quintilian
the sort of man he (Domitian) has believed him to be (*Inst.* 4.*pr.*1–5).[80] In
stripping out the divinity and shifting the context from Palatine patronage
to a senatorial election, Pliny updates Flavian cravenness for a new civic
age, and in an apt spot: *Epistles* 2.9 is the first letter to feature his personal
dealings with the emperor, and is also (probably) Trajan's first appearance
in the collection. A pointed transformation, then? Yet neither the intertext
nor that observation about Trajan leaps off the page:[81] if this passage distances Pliny from Quintilian, it does so in deeply submerged – hitherto
empirically unfathomable – fashion.

Let me end this selective survey with a brace of intertexts which take
us to the beating heart of *Epistles*. Pliny's first letter to Tacitus begins with
famous banter about catching boar ('you'll laugh . . .') and proceeds to a
striking proposition about the merits of writing while hunting (*Ep.* 1.6.2):

> Non est quod contemnas hoc studendi genus: mirum est ut animus agita-
> tione motuque corporis excitetur; iam undique siluae et solitudo ipsumque
> illud silentium quod uenationi datur magna cogitationis incitamenta sunt.

> You needn't scorn this sort of composing: it is remarkable how the mind is
> stimulated by physical exercise and movement. What is more, the woods all
> around, the solitude and that very silence that is accorded to hunting are
> great spurs to thought.

---

[79] *Ep.* 4.11.2, a *sententia* of Licinianus (exiled under Domitian) which Pliny quotes with admiration.
The reference is to Quintilian's honorary consulate (n. 51).

[80] Schematically put, both passages proceed 'anxiety' > 'reputation' > 'deceiving the emperor'
(P. *ne decepisse Caesarem uidear* ~ Q. *ne fefellisse in iis uidear principem*) > 'the sort of man . . .'
(P. *. . . qualem esse princeps mihi credidit* ~ Q. *. . . me qualem esse credidit*). Only gradually does the
intertext become lexically visible (compare *Dial.* 34.3 in n. 31) – as, on the large scale, the Quintilianic intertextuality in both *Dial.* and *Ep.* unfolds from the most discreet beginnings. I noted just
part of the story in Whitton 2013: 144.

[81] You need first to work out that *princeps/Caesar* in *Ep.* 2.1.3 and 2.7.1 refer to Nerva, then that *Caesar*
here means Trajan (see Whitton 2013: 143) – all of which (if it is right) requires extensive contextual
knowledge not supplied by Pliny. Further on the social context of *Ep.* 2.9 and its addressee Domitius
Apollinaris, see Mratschek in this volume.

Amid much debate over an alleged reflex of *Dialogus*,[82] we have all been slow to see that *Epistles* engages here closely and precisely with *Institutio* 10. Specifically, in advocating his novel mode of composition, Pliny enters into dialogue with Quintilian's precepts on how, when and where to compose (*Inst.* 10.3). That passage includes a warning against dictation: amongst other things, the presence of a slave impedes 'those movements which accompany profounder thoughts (*animi motum*) and which themselves, in a certain way, spur on the mind (*animum quodam modo concitant*)' (10.3.21); Quintilian returns to his insight (cf. *quodam modo*) at the end of the same book, when he mentions 'the movement of the body, which (as I said) in itself stimulates the orator' (*motum corporis, qui et ipse (ut dixi) excitat oratorem*, 10.7.26). Solitude is better, then; but let us not heed those who fetishise rural inspiration: 'pleasant woods, flowing streams' and such delights only distract us, 'so that in my view that so-called pleasure takes the focus off one's thought rather than sharpening it' (*ut mihi remittere potius uoluptas ista uideatur cogitationem quam intendere*, 10.3.24).

Pliny's letter shows him accepting and rejecting Quintilian's views in equal measure. His insight (*mirum est . . .*) about physical movement (in his case, striding or riding around his estate) restates Quintilian's, apparently in both its statements,[83] while his claims for sylvan solitude (. . . *magna cogitationis incitamenta*) precisely invert Quintilian's invective against the 'ruralists' (. . . *cogitationem quam intendere*)[84] – with a perfectly Quintilianic argument: far from celebrating the idle pleasures of natural beauty, Pliny focuses on the solitude ('woods all around', not 'woods') and the concentrating power of silence.[85] It is a curious, contorted effect, honouring the letter of the text even as he contradicts the spirit. Not to mention the ethos of *Epistles* 1.6 as a whole, a professedly languid portrait (cf. §1 *inertia et quies*) that hardly befits the iron discipline of Quintilian's ideal pupil.

---

[82] According to Murgia 1985: 171–81 (building on Bruère 1954: 166–8), Pliny's *motuque corporis excitetur* can be explained solely as a reflex of *Dial.* 36.1 *motibus excitatur* and thus proves *Dial.* to pre-date *Ep.* 1, a claim variously pursued by Edwards 2008: 41–2; Marchesi 2008: 118–35; Whitton 2012: 357–9. The Quintilianic underlay shows it false (for earlier scepticism, Brink 1994: 256–64; Woodman 2009b: 32–3) – though it need not follow that *Dial.* is absent (below, nn. 96–7).

[83] *Inst.* 10.3 is clearly in view (to judge from the next point), but *Inst.* 10.7 is most proximate in form (Q. *motum corporis . . . excitat* ~ P. *motuque corporis excitetur*): Pliny put Quintilian's cross-reference there (*ut dixi*) to good use. More than an indeterminate possibility, then (cf. Woodman 2009b: 33, omitting *ut dixi*).

[84] The latter contrast has been well observed, from Cataneaus 1506 ad loc. to Cova 2003: 92. But I have not seen it read as a verbal intertext, or put together with the *animi motus* that precedes.

[85] The more striking given Pliny's great emphasis on views in *Ep.* 2.17 and 5.6 *passim*, especially 2.17.21 on the vistas from his favourite study. Equally, Quintilian's explicit warning against *uenandi uoluptas* (*Inst.* 12.1.6) is nowhere in sight.

Once again (recall *Dial.* 1.1) we find two adjacent passages from *Institutio* 10 being deployed in close proximity, now with a third (*Inst.* 10.7.26) thrown into the mix. This time the stakes are very different, but high in their way: not questions over the decline of oratory, but the core of Pliny's *ethopoeia*. *Epistles* 1.6 is an important early still life in his suite of self-portraits, cutting to the heart of Pliny's projected ideal as leisured man of *studia*. (Or are these the same stakes after all, as Pliny (in good Quintilianic fashion) indirectly answers the 'decline' question by validating the good orator – himself – as literary and social exemplar?)[86] But if *Dialogus* (or at least Justus) inverted Quintilian's claims, here the picture is more variegated. Are we witnessing pointed transformation, or a more delicate negotiation between Pliny and the ghost of his old teacher? As Plinian liaisons go, this one is nicely suspended between marked and unmarked: the intertextual reader might now recognise a second level to *non est quod contemnas* (' . . . given/despite Quintilian's views'), and a certain irony in *mirum est*, casually claiming possession of borrowed acumen;[87] others can remain oblivious to the Quintilianic underlay, and take Pliny's claim to insight straight.

The plot really thickens, though, when we leaf forward to Pliny's final, climactic portrait, the 'day-in-a-life' *Epistles* 9.36 – because this letter begins with recourse to the very same passage of *Institutio* 10. Pliny spends the early hours at his villa mentally composing in the dark, then dictating the results to a secretary. As William Johnson has brought (back) to light, this solitary *cubiculum* scene is written with reference to Quintilian's description – just after his comments on rural composition – of Demosthenes meditating in his darkened cave.[88] Besides the implied invitation to read Pliny as a *Demosthenes redivivus*, the intertext shows him once again both breaching Quintilian's advice (by dictating) and honouring it (by first meditating in the dark, just like Quintilian's specified exemplar).[89] This brief engagement combines with *Epistles* 1.6 to tell a remarkable tale: Pliny's nine-book study in self-representation is framed by precise, discreet and – shall we

---

[86] So essentially Riggsby 1995 on *Ep.* 1.20.

[87] This last feature strikes me as piquant, the more so because it recurs frequently: see e.g. *Ep.* 9.26.1 (recasting an epigram from *Inst.* 2.4.9 as a witticism in Pliny's own mouth) with Whitton 2015c: 224–6. When Pliny takes so little trouble to advertise his *imitatio*, is that at some level inevitably disingenuous?

[88] *Inst.* 10.3.25 with Johnson 2013b; see already Gesner 1738 on *Inst.* 10.3.25 and Gierig 1800–2 on *Ep.* 9.36.

[89] And thus respecting, or neutralising, Quintilian's concerns about dictation (by keeping the slave out of the room while actually composing); cf. Johnson 2013b: 667–8.

say? – polemical reference to Quintilian's precepts on dictation.[90] Not only the very process of writing is inscribed into Pliny's self-portraiture from (more or less) beginning to end, then, but also the intertextual act of self-fashioning – and a Quintilianic intertextuality at that.[91]

There's much more to be said, but we have seen enough, I hope, to suspect that *Institutio* takes a very real role in Pliny's self-construction as orator, theorist and man of letters; enough too, perhaps, to find meaning as well as plausibility in that first alleged intertext (*frequenter hortatus es . . .*) after all. Measured across the *Epistles* as a whole, Quintilian's role is more sporadic than we saw with *Dialogus*, but as an integral element of Pliny's persona, it is coopted into a dialogue which is no less intense. In both cases *ethopoeia* plays a central part alongside argument; but where Tacitus creates (parody-)characters, Pliny constructs his *own* person – a person for which Quintilian is by no means the only genetic donor, but (we now start to see) one of the most important. And where Tacitus seems to me unambiguously sharp in his intertextual dealings with *Institutio*, the situation with Pliny is less clear-cut. Certainly he is no craven imitator of his old teacher, and his manner can often be called ludic; but I find it harder here to pin down the differences and adaptations, as he makes what he finds best in Quintilian his own,[92] on a scale from pious to parricidal. One thing, though, should be clear: in *Epistles*, as in *Dialogus*, engagement with Quintilian (and, we might extrapolate, prose–prose intertextuality more broadly) is an important and, dare I say (for *some* readers, at least), an essential component of the textual weave.[93]

PT (coda)

The third side of my triangle will be the sketchiest, a few gestures at best. It is, however, as important as it is tantalising – both for dating the *Dialogus*, and as an intertextual dialogue in itself. It will also reveal, for a third time, a dialectical relationship which is at once intimate, muscular and ludic.

---

[90] Do they resonate too in his curiously worded paean to the Laurentine villa, *quam multa inuenitis, quam multa dictatis* (*Ep.* 1.9.6)?

[91] Let me underline that my exclusion of other points of reference (Cicero, Horace, al.) is a temporary convenience, not an argument.

[92] Cf. *Inst.* 10.2.4 *prudentis est quod in quoque optimum est, si possit, suum facere.*

[93] I am less sure, then, than Ilaria Marchesi (justly a *doyenne* of Plinian intertextuality) that allusion to prose is categorically different from allusion to verse (Marchesi 2008: 244–5), or that verse is the preferred allusive target in the *Epistles* and beyond (Marchesi 2013: 101–2).

Pliny's quotation of *Dialogus* in *Epistles* 9.10 is well known.[94] But it isn't the first. When Pliny begins a letter (*Ep.* 6.21.1) –

> Sum ex iis qui **mirer antiquos**,[A] non tamen (*ut quidam*) **temporum nostrorum**[B] **ingenia despicio**[C] . . .

> I am one of those who admire the ancients, not that (like some) I despise the talents of our own times . . .

– one of the *quidam* to whom he refers can be precisely identified, if we recall some words of Aper to Messalla (*Dial.* 15.1):

> Tum Aper, 'non desinis, Messalla, **uetera** tantum **et antiqua mirari**,[A] **nostrorum** autem **temporum**[B] **studia irridere atque contemnere**.'[C]

> Then Aper said, 'Messalla, you don't desist from admiring only what is old and ancient, while you mock and condemn the literary culture of our own times.'

If the (exceptional) proximity of lexis, thought and sequence left any doubt, it should soon dissipate: this Plinian opening immediately follows the second 'Vesuvius' letter – addressed to Tacitus.[95]

Surely, then, *Dialogus* was known to Pliny by the time of *Epistles* 6. Can we push further back into the earlier books? Murgia was convinced we could, with *Epistles* 1.6 as his key witness. But he underestimated the import of Quintilian there, a consideration which leaves it possible, but rather less certain, that *Dialogus* is in the air.[96] In fact I'm sure there *is* intertextual contact between that letter and Tacitus – but I'm not yet ready to

---

[94] *Ep.* 9.10.2 *poemata . . . quae tu inter nemora et lucos commodissime perfici putas*, all but quoting Aper (*Dial.* 9.6 *poetis . . . ut* (*que*) *ipsi dicunt, in nemora et lucos . . . recedendum est*) and – secondarily, I would say – Maternus (*Dial.* 12.1 *nemora uero et luci . . .*). Scholarly debate since Lange 1832: 5–8 (orig. 1811) can be traced through Murgia 1985: 176 n. 16 and Marchesi 2008: 132 n. 51; good remarks also in Häußler 1986: 72.

[95] The link was rediscovered by Roy Gibson in 2011, before either of us had noticed Gierig 1800–2 ad loc. My remarks on *Epistles* 6 are informed by Roy's work in progress (towards Gibson forthcoming), and may perhaps inform it too: how . . . interactive.

[96] For Woodman 2009b: 33, *Dial.* cannot precede *Ep.* 1.6 because Pliny would hardly claim novelty for his writing practice if Tacitus had 'expressed, in a work of his own, the view that the countryside was conducive to literary composition'; but *Dial.* nowhere couples *hunting* and writing (a distinctly Plinian habit: *Ep.* 2.8.1, 5.18.2). On the other hand, arguments in favour of *Dial.* > *Ep.* 1 (n. 82) fall short of proof, to use that dirty word. I try some additional ones in Whitton forthcoming b.

pronounce on the direction of influence:[97] I only flag the teasing prospect that *non seruato temporis ordine* in Pliny's first letter (*Ep.* 1.1.1) could be yet one more clue to the rich intertextuality to come (cf. *Dial.* 1.3 *seruato ordine disputationis*).[98] Perhaps we will get further by pressing more substantive nodes like that between *Epistles* 4.22 (delators and dinner *chez* Nerva) and *Dialogus* 12.2 (Maternus on delators),[99] though here too pinning down priority is no easy business. If and when we do make progress, interesting prospects await: when Tacitus' disputants resemble Pliny, what is the direction of ethical *imitatio*? Pliny and Aper, for instance, each talk enthusiastically of provincials seeking out celebrities in Rome.[100] We glimpse both Pliny and Messalla entering declamation halls and hearing the students' chatter.[101] Pliny, in fact, has several striking resemblances with both Aper the 'modernist' and Messalla the 'traditionalist' (as he himself makes clear in *Epistles* 6.21.1) – a further marker, if one were needed, of his ethical proximity to Quintilian. But who is being modelled on whom is in this case a trickier question.[102] And beyond it lurks a greater question still. Tacitus and Pliny, I have suggested, each engage in prose intertextuality of unprecedented intensity, and both do so with Quintilian. If that is true, how far did *Dialogus* prompt *Epistles*, or vice versa?

I end, for now, with an easier theme. In *Epistles* 6–9, at least, we have a clear direction of travel: how does Pliny handle *Dialogus*? With explicit reference, as we have seen (*Ep.* 6.21, 9.10); but not only that. Look back to *Epistles* 7.9, the miniature rewrite of *Institutio* 10.5. One of their precepts

---

[97] There must, I think, be some evanescent contact, given the import of *Inst.* 10.3 to both *Ep.* 1.6 and the exchange of views about poetic retreat in *Dial.* 9–12 (n. 41) – an exchange picked up in *Ep.* 9.10 (n. 94). Such contact shows Pliny's self-imagination as *homo studiosus* (and one who *combines* the duties of civic participation with the pleasures of *secessus*) deeply implicated not just with *Institutio* but in the submerged dialogue of *Epistles* and *Dialogus*. A firmer attempt to pronounce, again, in Whitton forthcoming b.

[98] Murgia 1985: 181 (not pressed).

[99] Most obviously *Ep.* 4.22.6 *de huius nequitia sanguinariisque sententiis* ~ *Dial.* 12.2 *lucrosae huius et sanguinantis eloquentiae*, and the idea of *delatio/delator* as weapon (see Güngerich 1980 ad loc.); also the proximate talk of spreading *uitia* and *mores*. *Dial.* 12.2 includes a cross-reference (*ut tu dicebas*) to *Dial.* 5.6, where Aper called eloquence *praesidium simul ac telum quo* . . . (compare *Ep.* 4.22.5 *non secus ac tela quae* . . .).

[100] *Ep.* 2.3.8 ~ *Dial.* 7.4, 8.1 (see Syme 1958: 672). On Pliny and Aper, see also Whitton 2013: 33.

[101] *Ep.* 2.18.2 ~ *Dial.* 29.3.

[102] One I hope to pursue elsewhere, tied up as it is with dating *Pan.* and *Hist.* The clarity of *Ep.* 6.21.1 (above), the more discreet insistence of *Ep.* 6.11 (below) and further signs of *Dial.* in Book 6 (see Gibson forthcoming) might suggest that *Dial.* is freshly out – sending us back to a date of c. 106, then (Syme 1958: 671; cf. Brink 1994: 271–2)? There again, Pliny's fullest reworking by far of *Agricola* (AD 98) comes only in Book 8 (*Ep.* 8.14 with Whitton 2010; for *Agr.* elsewhere in *Ep.* see Whitton 2013: 80–1).

concerns the genres an orator should practise for variety's sake. Quintilian prescribes history and dialogues (*Inst.* 10.5.15). Pliny (closely tracking
Quintilian) prefers history and epistles, on the grounds that *pressus sermo
purusque ex epistulis petitur* ('straightforward and simple language is learned
from letters', *Ep.* 7.9.8). Compare those words with Tacitus' comment on
his former mentor, Julius Secundus: *Secundo purus et pressus et, in quantum satis erat, profluens sermo non defuit* ('Secundus did not lack straight-
foward, simple and – so far as was necessary – abundant speech', *Dial.* 2.2).
Pliny follows Tacitus not just in qualifying *sermo* with the adjectives *purus*
and *pressus*, he even imitates (and improves on) the striking *p* alliteration.
When you notice that his model text concerns another man called Secundus – and that his phrase replaces a Quintilianic precept about dialogues
of all things – it should be clear that this cute moment of self-reference
extends to a wry intertextual game, featuring both *Institutio* and *Dialogus*,
and smartly reframing Tacitus' words as praise of Pliny *avant la lettre*.[103]

　　Having digested that, we might take a fresh look at *Epistles* 7.20.[104] Murgia found this letter particularly resonant of *Dialogus*.[105] He may not have
been wrong. Consider the famous lines at its heart (§4):

> For my part I desired as a young man, when you were already blossoming
> in fame and glory (*cum iam tu fama gloriaque floreres*), to follow you, to be
> and be considered 'a long way off, but second still' [*Aen.* 5.320]. And there
> were many very distinguished talents (*erant multa clarissima ingenia*); but
> you seemed to me (so the similarity of our nature drew us) the one most
> fit for imitation – who most *had* to be imitated (*maxime imitabilis, maxime
> imitandus*).

Erant multa clarissima ingenia, writes Pliny, describing his youth. Tacitus
had described Secundus and Aper as *celeberrima tum ingenia fori nostri*
(*Dial.* 2.2). Has Pliny seen Tacitus' point of departure in Quintilian,
describing the time of his own youth (*erant clara et nuper ingenia*, *Inst.*
10.1.118) and/or his time of writing (*sunt enim summa hodie quibus illustratur forum ingenia*, 10.1.122)?[106] If so, he restores both Quintilian's
adjective *clarus* and the emphatic claim that those were great times for
forensic talent. We are in gossamer realm again, but while we are there:
does Pliny's **cum** *iam tu* **fama gloriaque floreres** remind anyone of the first
sentence of *Dialogus*, **cum** *priora saecula tot eminentium oratorum* **ingeniis**

---

[103] The lexical parallel is well known. Tony Woodman made me think about 'Secundus', Chris van
　　den Berg about the alliteration.
[104] On which see also Marchesi 2008: 135–43 (focused on Virgil, and a different *secundus* pun).
[105] Murgia 1985: 185–7.　　[106] Ibid. 186.

gloriaque floruerint (*Dial.* 1.1)?[107] Another subtle node, but 'imitation' may be scripted into this letter at more than one level. More than that, Pliny makes a spirited reply to the very premise of *Dialogus*, as expressed in Justus' opening question, that Flavian Rome was bereft of talent. We may hardly be surprised to find Pliny being more enthusiastic in outlook than Tacitus; but this dialogue turns out to be 'stringent' indeed.[108]

To fade out, three (more) potentially spectacular triple collisions of QPT. The first comes back in *Epistles* 6.11, a short but weighty letter marking Pliny's progression to oratorical patron. As Roy Gibson will point out in his commentary, Pliny's enthusiasm over the splendid young Fuscus and Quadratus is expressed in tones reminiscent both of Aper in *Dialogus*[109] and of Quintilian in *Institutio* 10.[110] Nor is it just any passage of *Institutio* 10: Pliny reaffirms Quintilian's buoyancy with precisely the line that Justus apparently inverted at the opening of *Dialogus*.

Second, the well-known anecdote in which Tacitus' neighbour at the circus counts Pliny and Tacitus the two great names of letters (*Epistles* 9.23). 'I cannot express how delighted I am,' says Pliny, 'that our names are being ascribed to literature as if they belong to literature, not people (. . . *quod nomina nostra quasi litterarum propria, non hominum, litteris redduntur*)' (*Ep.* 9.23.3). High praise indeed – and surely taking its cue from a climactic plaudit for Cicero (*Inst.* 10.1.112): the great orator achieved such fame in afterlife 'that Cicero is now held to be the name not of a person, but of eloquence' (*ut Cicero iam non hominis nomen sed eloquentiae habeatur*).[111] Pliny and Tacitus thus emerge as two Ciceros of their age, and more (they achieve in lifetime what Cicero did in death). And how piquant to find the author of *Dialogus* – a work staged, we recall, in an age which

---

[107] If so, the replacement of (*priora saecula*) *tot eminentium oratorum* with (*iam*) *tu* smartly contradicts through compliment. There was also, you recall, *De or.* 1.1 (*cum* [sc. *uiri*] *et honoribus et rerum gestarum gloria florerent*).

[108] Marchesi 2008: 97.

[109] *Ep.* 6.11.3 *audiui ex diuerso agentes summae spei summae indolis iuuenes . . .* ~ *Dial.* 7.3 *iuuenes uacuos et adulescentis quibus modo recta indoles est et bona spes sui.* With that in mind, Pliny's opening *O diem laetum!* (§1) must have a ring of Aper about it too (*Dial.* 7.1 *Equidem . . . non eum diem laetiorem egi . . .*), with allusive pointing in his reprise (§3 *O diem (repetam enim) laetum*).

[110] *Ep.* 6.11.3 *Quid enim . . . mihi optatius quam me ad recta tendentibus quasi exemplar esse propositum* ~ *Inst.* 10.1.122 'mature advocates rival (*aemulantur*, NB) the ancients, and the efforts of the young men striving in the best direction (*ad optima tendentium*) imitate and follow them'. Pliny had been one of the 'young men' in the 80s; now he takes the place of 'mature advocate'.

[111] Cf. Cortius and Longolius 1734 and Gierig 1800–2 ad loc.; Alfonsi 1962. There is a(n unobtrusive) lexical core (*nomina . . . non hominum* ~ *non hominis nomen*) as well as the similarity of thought. The shift from *eloquentia* to *litterae* eases the anecdote in a typically Plinian direction, from oratory to literature in general.

uix nomen ipsum oratoris retineat (*Dial.* 1.1) – treated to a paroxysm of, precisely, Quintilianic praise.

More intangible, and perhaps most revealing of all: Pliny's last letter to Tacitus (*Ep.* 9.14) is a brief *suasoria* to literary eternity. Is Quintilian's ringing final *suasoria*, so familiar to us from that first speech of Aper, resonating in the distance?[112] If so, it adds yet another closural touch to Book 9, sealing too a remarkable – and still mysterious – ring of *Dialogus* and *Epistles*. How pleased would Tacitus have been with this Quintilianic whisper, as he fades back into the silence? I start to wonder.[113]

One of the goals of this volume is to look 'beyond intertextuality' in measuring up literary interactions of the High Empire. Several chapters do just that, and with stimulating results. Others demonstrate that intertextual studies are far from exhausted; and I hope this chapter can be counted one of them. I promised only exploratory trigonometry, and don't claim to have squared any circles yet. I hope I have succeeded, though, in intimating how minutely *Dialogus* and *Epistles* are intricated with *Institutio* and with each other – and how challenging it must be even to start untangling the threads. What those threads reveal (and to whom) remains, well, quite a tricky problem.

---

[112] Note the non-committal comment of Trisoglio 1973 ad loc. ('Con un analogo ammonimento si conchiude l'*Institutio oratoria* di Quintiliano'), but I would push harder, and annotate more rebarbatively: *Ep.* 9.14 . . . <u>*Pergamus*</u>[A] *modo itinere instituto,* QVOD VT <u>*paucos in* {**lucem** *famamque*}</u>[B] <u>*prouexit, ita* **multos** *e tenebris et silentio protulit*</u>[C] ~ *Inst.* 12.11.30 (Quintilian's last sentence proper) *Ipsam igitur orandi maiestatem . . . qua remota muta sunt omnia et* {**luce** *praesenti ac memoria posteritatis*}[B] *carent, toto animo* <u>*petamus nitamurque*</u>[A] *semper ad optima;* QVOD *facientes* <u>AVT *euademus in summum*</u> AVT <u>*certe* **multos** *infra nos uidebimus.*</u>[C] Or am I (are we) starting to see double in the fog?

[113] The dialogue here is with Whitton 2012: 364.

CHAPTER 2

I Will Survive (You)
Martial and Tacitus on Regime Change

Victoria Rimell

res olim dissociabiles miscuerit . . .

(Agricola 3.1)

I

One of the (perhaps surprising, or not altogether foreseen) revelations of this volume, I predict, will be that a minor poet – or writer of 'minor' poetry – who debuted in AD 80 under Titus and was on his way out in 98, should loom large in so many of our chapters on Nervan, Trajanic and Hadrianic literary networking. Discussion of Martial and his take on the heady, mixed-up years of 96–8 peppers this book from start to finish, reminding us not only that the epigrammatist, as he hastens in his re-issued tenth *libellus* to advertise links with rising Trajanic stars Pliny and Frontinus, is the *elder* of these statesmen, but also that when it comes to modishly reinventing the tropes of memory and forgetting, monumental-isation and iconoclasm in response to the double regime change of 96/98, Martial trumps all his fellow jostlers for fame in experience and proven success.[1] In many ways his ubiquity in such a project should not surprise us. When it comes to variegation, to the performance and observation of interactivity, to the poetics of deniability, to recontextualisation and moving with the times, Martial – *pace* Pliny – sets the bar. By the time Trajan becomes emperor, Martial has been selling his fans cultural authority as portability, survivability and social blending for decades. Yet his ongoing presence seems testimony not only to his ingenious pre-modelling of post-96 social interplay as enacted and engineered through literary texts, but also therefore to a sense of urgency in defining the new age, and in self-defining, *against* Flavian (or more to the point, Domitianic) epigrammatic

---

[1] Martial features in the chapters by Ash, Fitzgerald, Geue, König, Marchesi, Morello, Mratschek and Roller in this volume.

strategies. As Pliny shows in his much analysed Epistle 3.21, the trick is to
cut down or partially delete Martial while saving what can be recycled of
his idiom of reciprocity and wryly self-deprecating (self-protecting) mechanisms of memorialisation.[2] As soon-to-be-retired, Domitianic hanger-on
bound to infect all newcomers with his ebullient interactivity (those *lusus*
are catchy: *Epig.* 6.85.9), Martial becomes the poetic icon that 'moderate'
Pliny and Tacitus, first and foremost, must go beyond – just as the editors
of this volume are motivated to frame as outdated the previous generation's
intellectual mono-focus on Augustan–Neronian texts and on concomitant
'models' of intertextuality.[3]

   In other words, the epigrammatist's consistency from one 'new era' to the
next[4] is arguably an unspoken *problem,* not just for Martial himself, as he
apparently produces a new edition of *Epigrams* 10 in response to the *damnatio* of Domitian in 97–8, but also for the vanguard wanting to associate
themselves with Nerva's, and then Trajan's, 'clean slate'. Martial, however,
offers a ready-made template (with inbuilt critique) for future attempts to
erase or rewrite him, teaching us – alongside Freudian psychoanalysis and
modern memory theory – that forgetting and remembering are never simply opposites.[5] Thus Pliny's barbed and self-promoting obituary of Martial
(*Ep.* 3.21) must mime his predecessor's own trademarked *damnatio memoriae*, as inflicted on his latest collection of monumental inscriptions (*Epigrams* 10, first edition).[6] As Pliny slices *Epigrams* 10.21 in two and discards
the first half, he is also no doubt well aware that Martial's empowered readers must now be experts in scanning a pared-down page for what is or *might
be* missing – silent sarcasm or subversion, less than obvious puns lurking in
final lines, jokes drummed but never spelled out in the disconnect between
jolly metre and sober content . . .[7] 'Forgetting' Martial, in short, inevitably
conjures up the poet's own sleight of hand, as well as his cheerful embrace of
the indifferent and disrespectful reader (*iam dudum quasi neglegenter audis,*

[2] See Henderson 2001; Marchesi 2013.   [3] See pp. 12–13.
[4] See especially Lorenz 2002: 219–31, who emphasises the continued implicit presence of Domitian
     in Book 10, and speaks of 'unverkennbare Kontinuität' rather than change between Books 1–9 and
     Book 10 (p. 210).
[5] See e.g. Caruth 1995 on trauma, and Billig 1999 on Freudian repression and remembering to forget.
     Cf. Sailor 2008: 111 on *Agricola.*
[6] See Henderson 2004: 68–70, and Hardie 2012: 329 on Mart. 10.3 ('The skulking poet may be Martial
     himself'); cf. Rimell 2008: 71–6.
[7] Cf. Elsner 2003 with Hedrick 2000: xi–xii, 100, 109–10, on the extent to which *damnatio memoriae*
     is predicated on remembering as well as forgetting what is erased, and Flower 2006: 234–62 on ways
     sanctions against Domitian might have reflected 'long term difficulties in dealing with the memory of
     previous disgraced emperors' (237). Cf. Derrida's concepts of 'trace' and (after Heidegger) of 'rature'
     or erasure (e.g. Derrida 1976, esp. pp. xv–xviii, 1978).

6.42.23): Juvenal's wilful forgetting will in turn pay covert homage to this barely-there satire, as Tom Geue will show towards the end of this volume.

It is with all this in mind that I turn to Martial *Epigrams* 10, and to its unlikely, erasable partnership with a text published in the same year, Tacitus' *Agricola*. Tacitus apparently wrote the preface to the *Agricola* between October 97 and January 98, in the months after Domitian's death and Nerva's ascent to power; he was completing the whole text after Trajan became emperor in 98. Martial, meanwhile, initially published the tenth volume of his *Epigrams* in 95, followed swiftly by Book 11 in 96; Book 10 was then withdrawn and rewritten (some poems 'polished up' but most 'new', 10.2.3–4) after Domitian's assassination on 18 September 96, and the second, new-era-friendly version published in 98. While Martial is rebooting his career, Tacitus is publishing what looks to be his first book belatedly, after many possible virtual editions.[8] Yet both face the same Catch-22: how to reinvent themselves anew without cancelling out, or overly implicating themselves in, 'The Domitian Years', when all the time *they were there*, climbing ladders and avoiding trouble? How to gloss over the problematic aspects of (their role in) the past, while also memorialising the life of a man who lived through it (a father-in-law, or in the case of Martial, the author himself)? Both these synchronal, regime-change *libelli* are concerned with the awkwardness of *silentium* and of self-censorship under Domitian and in the wake of his assassination, and with the fundamental question of the extent to which an author can exert control over (ungovernable) *fama*, or over representation:[9] they deal in strikingly similar (complementary or competing) ways with how we might think about the past, alongside these writers' relaunched identities, from the new vantage point of the post-Domitianic present, yet their surface incompatibilities are such that they have yet to be read in detail side by side. This chapter is an open-ended and all too brief experiment in seeing what might emerge – and how we might perceive both authors/works differently in the social-literary climate of 98 – when we analyse the texts in juxtaposition, or even envisage them as (mutely) interacting.[10]

---

[8] The critical consensus puts *Agricola* first, but see Murgia 1980 and Beck 1998 on the possibility that the *Dialogus* and *Germania* were written slightly before the *Agricola*. In any case, as Sailor (2004: 161) puts it, 'the *Agricola* presents itself as the first step down a particular path'.

[9] Cf. Hardie 2012: 273–84, 321–9, dealing separately with Tacitus and Martial on *fama*; Sailor 2008: 51–117.

[10] Cf. Marchesi 2013 on Pliny's selective silencing of Martial in the letters, with Geue in this volume on Juvenal and Pliny. The chapters by Fitzgerald, König and Mratschek also discuss the transition from Nerva to Trajan in 98.

II

It is clear why it would seem on the face of it counterintuitive, even perverse, to twin *Epigrams* 10 and *Agricola* in this way. What would serious, politically engaged, monumental history commemorating the life of one aristocrat-general with an eye on the past and the future have to say to a miscellaneous collection of flippant, satirical poems cataloguing random and often seedy episodes in Rome's ephemeral present, or indeed vice versa? On the face of it Tacitus has the more to lose from any such synergy, particularly if we concur with Dylan Sailor's and Philip Hardie's readings of the *Agricola* as 'correcting' the crime of Domitian's 'perversion of representation' according to which great men like Agricola were treated with envy, intolerance and suspicion rather than granted the honour they deserved (such 'correction' is predicated on a canny delimitation and resolution of the complex textual struggles traced by Tim Whitmarsh and epitomised, crucially, by Martial's jostling epigram book, where vulnerability to the vagaries of *fama* is overtly thematised).[11] Might then the (prose-heavy) intermeshing of literary genres and registers in our period extend this far? Would Taciturn Statesman Tacitus – whose name advertises grim subtlety – want to associate himself with scurrilous comedian Martial, particularly as he makes his 'spectacular' long-awaited debut[12] (politically tainted Martial, meanwhile, struggles to reach his final *meta* in the second edition of Book 10, which strictly speaking is the twelfth book, a fitting 'end' to the camp epic edifice of *Epigrams*)? In short, will the pressure to make these texts converse throw up no more than clunky, handbook-style oppositions? It sometimes looks as though Martial, at least, went out of his way to avoid Tacitus: the friendship between Tacitus and Pliny the Younger is well attested, as is the edgy rapport between Pliny and Martial.[13] But why are there no epigrams mentioning the equally distinguished Tacitus (forty years old in 98, an experienced orator who had been made suffect consul in the previous year), especially if, as some have conjectured, he was almost a fellow Spaniard?[14] Given the opacity, guardedness and silencing strategies of both works as they announce a new freedom to speak openly, is an apparent absence of interaction in itself significant?

---

[11] Sailor 2008: 51–117; Hardie 2012: 273–84; Whitmarsh 2006b.

[12] Woodman 2014: 35: 'Few historians can have made such a spectacular debut.'

[13] See p. 10 nn. 53–4.

[14] The possibly Spanish origin of the Fabius Justus to whom Tacitus dedicates the *Dialogus* has suggested to some a family connection to Hispania. He was most likely from Gallia Narbonensis, which had a border with northern Hispania, although some scholars have suggested Trier in Gallia Belgica as an alternative. See Birley 2000b.

Working from apparent silence prompts us to reset our critical approaches (as Tom Geue's chapter also underlines). If we move cautiously from the general to the specific, we might start by noticing that the two authors have more than a little in common. Tacitus layers satire into his coruscating histories, and like Martial has a marked taste for violent metaphor, concision and *inconcinnitas* – the incongruous or weird. His turn of phrase, much in evidence already in the *Agricola*, often lends itself to citation as a series of (epigrammatic) sound-bites – what do we remember of the *Agricola* (a text all about *how* we remember, as well as about how the right kind of remembering is contingent on a select forgetting) if not the bitter opening slogan *sicut uetus aetas uidit quid ultimum in libertate esset, ita nos quid in seruitute* (*Agr.* 2.3), and Calgacus' magnificent definition of imperialist hypocrisy (*auferre, trucidare, rapere falsis nominibus imperium, atque, ubi solitudinem faciunt, pacem appellant, Agr.* 30.5)?[15] Both, as far as we can tell, are monogeneric writers: Tacitus dedicates his entire writing career to historical prose, echoing his older colleague Martial's total dedication to the genre of epigram. Other writers working in the same elite community, like Statius (who died in 96, but was perhaps no more than six to ten years Tacitus' elder),[16] Silius Italicus (who we know wrote philosophical dialogues and speeches as well as the *Punica*)[17] and Pliny (Tacitus' coeval, friend and ally, and Martial's patron) were much more conventionally wide-ranging in their literary output: Pliny produced the *Panegyricus* and ten books of letters, a Greek tragedy, plus elegiac poems, an epic (*Ep.* 7.4.2–3), and poetry in the manner of Catullus. Nevertheless, the *Agricola* also shares epigram's core feature of, as Sailor puts it, wearing 'its variety on its face'. Critics invariably comment on 'the multiplicity of generic claims that can be made for the book', and the *Agricola* has been read as an attempt to synthesise the assorted 'voices' and modes of representation suppressed under Domitian.[18] Yet despite the work's 'uniqueness', the extent to which this description also fits the polyphonic epigram book, and Martial's Book 10 in particular, is striking.

Arguably, Tacitus and Martial end up, each in their chosen genre, undertaking what might be construed as analogous projects. Well before Tacitus published his *Annals*, Martial styled himself as annalistic 'one book a

---

[15] It is commonplace to note the 'epigrammatic' aspects of Tacitus' language, yet earlier historians, rather than epigrammatists like Martial, are usually mentioned as models (e.g. Sailor 2012: 37).

[16] Cf. Juvenal 7.82ff.

[17] Silius was well known to Pliny, Tacitus and Martial, as evidenced for example at Mart. 7.63, 6.64, 4.14, Tac. *Hist.* 3.65, Plin. *Ep.* 3.7.

[18] Sailor 2008: 116.

year' historian of the random, the everyday, the absurd: in 10.70, he complains he's so busy, hardly one of his books comes out in a single year (*quod mihi uix unus toto liber exeat anno*, 10.70.1), which is turned round into an achievement (Martial did, roughly, publish one book a year between *c.* 86 and *c.* 101), and gives another nod to the extra work and delay involved in editing and reissuing volume number 10, *lima rasa recenti* (he *would* have been the perfect annalistic epigrammatist, if politics had not intervened . . .).[19] While Martial's *libellus* (10.1.2) writes the life of everyman (*hoc lege, quod possit dicere uita 'meum est'*, 10.4.8), as well as the final chapter of his own Odyssean autobiography, Tacitus' *liber* (*Agr.* 3.3) dedicates itself to a single *uita* of a man who died in 93, who comes to exemplify the public figures whose careers can and should now be celebrated in an age which promises to revive a love of virtue (proving 'that even under evil emperors there can be great men', *posse etiam sub malis principibus magnos uiros esse*, *Agr.* 42.4). At the same time, as many have recognised, the account of Agricola's career allows Tacitus to promote a subtle, silent defence of his own trajectory under Domitian: the palimpsestic nature of *Agricola* is hinted at already in this chapter's nostalgia for times when self-respecting men could write their *own* lives (*ipsi uitam narrare*, 1.3).

Both works begin by claiming their authors' noble 'survival' and 'rebirth' after an era that seemed bent on killing them off, and forced them to experience a 'living death': Tacitus' (Rome's) 'body' has escaped physical torture but still needs time to heal after resuscitation, while Martial imagines a post-Augustan 'afterlife' and re-embodiment through his readers, rewriting his own epitaph in the virtual monument of 10.2 while simultaneously returning his faithful public to the ironic tombstone publicising his 'always already posthumous fame' in 1.1.[20] In terms of structure, each work shows off exemplary ring-composition. As commentators observe, the *Agricola* is framed by a three-chapter preface and conclusion which echo one another in message and vocabulary, while the middle sections on Britain (10–17, 29–38), almost identical in length and working over the same themes, sandwich the centrepiece cataloguing events in Britain in the years 77–83.[21] Meanwhile Martial's book develops an especially elaborate frame which itself promotes the larger plot of circularity and return (to the now revised *editio prima*, to *Epigrams* Book 1, to poetic beginnings, to the poet's Spanish

---

[19] 10.2.3 *nota leges quaedam sed lima rasa recenti.*

[20] The first edition *elapsum manibus* at 10.2.2, where *manibus* ('from my hands') also puns on the ablative of *manes*, 'shades of the dead': the volume is reborn. On *Epig.* 1.1 as an epitaph to the poet himself, see Citroni 1975: 14–15; Howell 1980: 102–3.

[21] See Woodman 2014: 2–3; Whitmarsh 2006b: 305: 'The architecture of the text is eloquent'. Also see Sailor 2008: 84, 106–8.

origins, to Augustan monumentality, and to an idealised past suggestively captured by *alta Bilbilis*). In a chiastic pattern, 10.1 and 10.2 deal with the *libellus* and the *lector* respectively, while 10.103 and 10.104 address Spanish audiences and finally the book itself as it boards the ship to Spain, a finale-rebeginning to match 10.2's dense concentrate of allusions to Augustan poetic endings (more on this below).[22] In each case the book performs and trains readers in remembering (the text they have just read), so that the political courage of not-forgetting becomes inseparable from honouring the literary lives of Tacitus/Agricola and Martial themselves, as they assert their power to memorialise, or to avoid oblivion ('we would have lost our memory as well as our voice, had it been as much in our power to forget as it was to remain silent', *memoriam quoque ipsam cum uoce perdidissemus, si tam in nostra potestate esset obliuisci quam tacere*, *Agr.* 2.3; cf. Martial 10.2.7–8).

<h3 style="text-align:center">III</h3>

Whether Tacitus and Martial interacted in the period in which they were writing *Agricola* and *Epigrams* 10 side by side, we cannot know for sure. But the symbiotic nature of their subject matter is itself fascinating, and Tacitus' self-serving claim at *Agricola* 3.1 that the Domitian years saw the extinguishing of *ingenia studiaque* (which we might translate more vaguely as 'men's spirits and enthusiasm', or more specifically as 'literary talents and devotion to study') seems actively to bait the robust reaction of an ingenious career poet like Martial. Both works are of similar length and both straddle eras – Martial's book because it is, so self-consciously and thematically, a second edition, and Tacitus' *Agricola* because it deals with a life and events in Britain that belong to the Domitianic past, from the perspective of the Trajanic present. Both are dyadic texts that thematise doubling and take as their structural underpinning the then and the now, the then vs the now, the then in the now. Indeed Tacitus seems to evoke – and perhaps also harness – the bustling variety of Martial's book, with its energising strategies of juxtaposition (or *putting two together*), when he writes that Nerva has already 'mixed up things that were once incompatible: the principate and liberty' (*res olim dissociabiles miscuerit, principatum ac libertatem*, 3.1), an image redeployed by Pliny in his *Panegyricus* (*iunxisti enim ac miscuisti res diuersissimas, securitatem olim imperantis et incipientis pudorem*, 'you have

---

[22] Sullivan 1991: 48, 50 refers to the 'superiority' of Book 10 and defines it as 'carefully crafted'. On 10.103 and 104, see Buongiovanni 2012 ad loc.

joined and blended very different things, the security of a governor and the modesty of a beginner', 42.1). Tacitus' motto seems to capture a (Martial's) connection between epigrammatic poetics and the social and political worlds epigram represents and remakes. We might be tempted to infer that epigram's poetics of miscellany is destined to come of age under Trajan, especially if we extend the rhetorical, philosophical and political models of diachronic contrast and synchronic synthesis proposed and performed by the *Agricola* itself to include interrelationships between this and other texts written at the same time.[23]

While *Epigrams* 10 reaches out towards Spain, the *Agricola* encompasses Britain (as Tacitus writes in *Agricola* 11, the two countries were imagined to lie opposite each other, and the Silures, especially, look Spanish).[24] Likewise, in both texts we inhabit an empire that has recently brought all within its grasp and whose outer margins are *known* (not least by these writers), an empire in which, as Martial puts it at 10.13.10, 'any place can be Rome for the two of us' (*in quocumque loco Roma duobus erit*).[25] The question to what extent both Bilbilis and Britain do not just 'belong' to Rome but also represent a Rome lost in the idealised past is provoked by both texts, split as they are not just between geographies and ethnic/cultural identities, but also between times.[26] While Tacitus' Britain has 'not yet' (*nondum, Agr.* 11.5) been 'softened' by luxury, and is portrayed as the last bastion of rugged manliness (or primitive *ferocia*, depending on where and how we look), Martial's return to Spain in Book 10 will allow him to turn away from effeminate *urbanitas* and to rediscover a macho, anti-elegiac aesthetic, in apparent defence against *otium*'s connotations of political impotence and compliance (Tacitus will mount a parallel defence of Agricola's *tranquillitas* and *otium* on his return to Rome, in *Agr.* 40.4–42.3). In 10.65, for example, the poet aggressively dismisses a depilated, lisping Greek who persists in calling him 'brother', asserting his own impenetrability and physical difference ('You go around all spruced up with your hair in curls, mine is stubborn and Spanish', *Tu flexa nitidus coma uagaris,* | *Hispanis ego contumax capillis*, 10.65.7–8), where the adjective *contumax* ('stubborn') also

---

[23] On miscellany and poetic-as-social interaction in the *Epigrams*, see Fitzgerald 2007 and Rimell 2008, *passim*; cf. Whitton 2010: 120 on the 'inextricability of literature and governance in the Trajanic senatorial elite'.

[24] *Agr.* 11.2 *Silurum colorati uultus, torti plerumque crines et posita contra Hispania Hiberos ueteres traiecisse easque sedes occupasse fidem faciunt.*

[25] See Clarke 2001 and Sailor 2008: 89–92 on why Britain as it comes to be not just conquered but known is the ideal location for the *res gestae* of Agricola and the ambitions of *Agricola*.

[26] On Rome vs Bilbilis in Martial 10, see Merli 2006b: 338–40. On competing times as represented in *Agricola*, see Ludolph 1997: 82–8; Hardie 2012: 277–84.

signals a Calgacus-like irreverence in the face of all that *domina Roma* has become.[27] Yet whereas Tacitus' Britain will be violently, brutally subdued into a state of 'civilised' *quies et otium* (*Agr.* 21.1)[28] which begins with the eerie silence of devastation (*solitudinem faciunt*, 30.5; *uastum ubique silentium*, 38.2), Martial represents Bilbilis as a dignified, philosophically winning 'citadel' (*arces*, 10.104.4; *altam Bilbilin . . . uidebis*, 10.104.6–7), a town that retains its own identity despite a far longer history of Romanisation. His rustic idyll (10.96) stands for the noble non-paradox of 'luxury' to be enjoyed in 'small means' (*tenues luxuriantur opes*, 10.96.6): there is no contradiction, he insists, in the virtuous, masculine poet enjoying well-earned leisure time – a point Agricola's supporters may or may not have wanted to carry over into Tacitus' *libellus*.

IV

The *Agricola*, as critics have observed, is shaped around a series of antitheses, or what turn out to be pairs, chiasmata, or double perspectives:[29] Tacitus and Agricola themselves in tandem, first of all, as the quiet success stories of Domitianic tyranny, giving rise to the troubling, latent pairs Tacitus–Domitian, Agricola–Domitian, and to the uncertain oppositions Tacitus + Agricola vs the brave or possibly reckless biographers and their subjects (Rusticus Arulenus, Thrasea Paetus, Herennius Senecio, Helvidius Priscus),[30] together with Agricola vs Domitian, and Calgacus vs Domitian, where Calgacus stands for the heroic outspokenness oppressed and killed off by Domitianic tyranny. The antagonistic pair Rome and Britain reproduces this specular dynamic in a global perspective (where Britain now belongs to Rome, while figuring an old Rome, glimpsed only to be destroyed anew). General Agricola is also set in parallel with/opposed to barbarian leader Calgacus, who looks at times more Roman than his counterpart, at least until we reach chapters 33–5 of Tacitus' text, where the two internal audiences react to a duet of speeches, and we are

---

[27] Despite continuing to write in elegiac couplets, Martial rejects the quasi-Ovidian 'elegisation' of his poetic identity: his body is the inverse of that of the effeminate *puella compta comas* (cf. Ov. *Am.* 1.1.20). We spy traces, too, of Ovid's hirsute exilic book with its messed-up hair at *Tr.* 1.1.11–12, an icon at once of slave-like vulnerability and of poetic individuality, and specifically of the reinvention of a standard elegiac aesthetic.

[28] We are, as many have noted, prompted to recall the use of the same phrase in the ablative at *Agr.* 6.3 (*quiete et otio*), where it describes the 'quiet and retirement' of Agricola's life between his quaestorship and his tribunate of the plebs. See Woodman 2014 ad loc.

[29] See McGing 1982; Whitmarsh 2006b.

[30] Sailor 2008: 115 also suggests that 'Tacitus in a way equates him [i.e. Agricola] with the martyrs'.

invited to prefer surging enthusiasm (*Agr.* 35.1) to wild barbarian uproar (33.1).[31]

As Whitmarsh observes, the upshot of this nexus of similarities and differences in the *Agricola* is that any secure interpretative and ethical position for the Roman reader is necessarily destabilised to a degree. Like the book itself, we find ourselves on the fence, hopefully transitioning into better times but still fully immersed – as far as the world of *Agricola* goes, at least – in an anxious culture of *dissimulatio*. The less than concrete if not overtly ambivalent commitment to the ideology of quietism that emerges in the course of our reading has us scouring the work for all the clarifying pointers, all the answers to our questions, that are inevitably absent – as if they were rendered mute in the (embittered?) spirit of quietism itself. By its very intricacy, Sailor's impressive articulation of the *Agricola* as representing (or enacting, through its virtuous readers) the solution to an imperial crisis of signification in which 'words no longer correspond to things' reveals the truth of Whitmarsh's account. Yet, in part because of the irony that the virtuous reader of *Agricola* coincides perfectly with the old-school philologist determined to assert a single 'correct' (Sailor's much-repeated adjective) meaning of a text, neither scholar can afford to admit that their positions are not in fact mutually exclusive. There can be little doubt – as Whitmarsh argues – that *Agricola* is rhetorically ambiguous and 'profoundly troubling',[32] but arguably Tacitus must force his readers to (re-)experience the confusions, challenges and risks of interpreting in such (unspecified) *tempora*, in order to identify the arduous process of trying to find a true and honest path through the fog (a process Sailor performs in exemplary style) with the valour worthy of Agricola, and of *Agricola*.[33]

One of the strongest points of Sailor's reading of *Agricola* is his emphasis on this text becoming a cultural and political *deed* through the active embodied memories (and I would add, determinedly lucid and courageous articulations) of its readers. It is interesting, then, that Martial spells out – not for the first time but now with overt political weight – the power of readers to decide his fate, at 10.1 and 10.2: indeed the trope of the active reader who embodies *libelli* and saves them from their all too evident

---

[31] See Whitmarsh 2006b: 317.   [32] Whitmarsh 2006b: 306.

[33] In an introductory footnote, Hardie 2012: 273 states that Whitmarsh 2006b locates more ambiguity than he himself will 'allow' in his reading of *Agricola*, yet 'allow' is an apt verb, suggesting the discipline involved in refusing to let this text's internal struggles and tensions – and the trauma, disappointment and uneasy compromises they potentially bring to the surface – lead to critical paralysis. My only criticism of Sailor 2008 and Hardie 2012 is that they locate 'correction' within the text itself rather than in the reader's interaction with it, and do not really acknowledge or analyse the fraught, politically, ethically and philosophically loaded process of this interaction.

materiality has Martial's fingerprints all over it. Like the *Agricola*, more-over, Martial's revised tenth book performs the shift between epochs, the contrast and interplay between memory and forgetting, between heroic outspokenness and cautious or guilty silence, and between the old and new Rome, or Rome and elsewhere, through and by means of the trope of twoness. In many ways there is nothing new here: as William Fitzgerald reminds us, individual epigrams regularly 'manipulate puns, zeugma, antithesis and double entendre to put things wittily together'.[34] Yet overtly, now, the secondariness of Martial's 'second edition' establishes a bivalency that both defines and haunts the volume, so that it is itself reminiscent (rather more blatantly than usual) of the anthology 'at odds with itself' produced by a plagiarist who mixes stolen poems with his own, at 10.100 (*Quid, stulte, nostris uersibus tuos misces?* | *Cum litigante quid tibi, miser, libro?* 'Idiot, why do you mix your verses with mine? What do you want, you wretch, with a book that argues with itself?'). As well as recalling and updating the witty and self-implicating riff on plagiarism from Martial's own 'first book' (see especially 1.53.12 *stat contra dicitque tibi tua pagina 'fur es'*), Book 10's novel evocation of epigrammatic miscellany doubles up as a description of the book we are reading, a blend of old, updated poems with new epigrams, which presumably replace the now silenced, unacceptably 'Domitianic' poems. The final lines of 10.100 compare the plagiarist's *liber*, a blend of Martial's stellar poems and the poetaster's own pathetic efforts, to a 'silly' man trying to run with a wooden leg (*inepte, frustra crure ligneo curres*, 10.100.6), yet the verb *curres* itself stumbles at the end of Martial's unbalanced scazons, raising a double laugh: that which is by definition excluded from the new, improved Book 10 perhaps still lingers, after all, emerging in a series of metrical – if not political – limps.[35]

While the *Agricola* looks to the future by reviving the 'old custom' of biography (1.1), and by remembering a particular version of the past, the test (and parlour game) for Martial's sharp-nosed reader-critics is to try to pick out which poems look newly inserted and which look recycled. Inge-niously, the poet's ploy is to get us to linger, to read harder. As John Hen-derson puts it, we are made to feel the undecidability of the instruction *utrique faue* ('favour both [editions]', 10.2.4),[36] an experience that might now extend both to the *Agricola* and to the antagonisms of its reception: our reading is lured to participate enthusiastically in the *Zeitgeist* of historical-political liminality. Martial conveniently grants his audience all the power to decide what vision of the Nervan–Trajanic age they want to project onto

[34] Fitzgerald 2007: 4.   [35] Cf. Lorenz 2002: 219–31.   [36] Henderson 2001: 81.

the book, which – they are told – they can make as brief as they like (10.1.1–2). Yet the challenge of ambidexterity seems an impossible or entrapping one from the start, or perhaps, to put it another way, readers given free rein to remake this book get little or no help (or interference from the poet) in making decisions. There are some *apparent* giveaways, as Hannah Fearnley notes, such as 10.72, which announces that there is no place any more in Rome for an emperor who demands to be called *Dominus Deusque*, that this new era signals the return of truth. But we're tripped up by the barbed final verses, which make today's 'freedom of speech' sound rather like yesterday's censorship in a different guise: 'under this ruler, Rome, beware – if you are wise – of speaking the language of earlier days' (*hoc sub principe, si sapis, caueto,* | *uerbis, Roma, prioribus loquaris,* 10.72.12–13).[37] Likewise, in the metaphorical dinner party of 10.48, which, as Alice König points out in Chapter 10, seems to celebrate the end of torture and anxiety, *libertas* amounts to being able to chat freely about chariot races[38] – hardly the radical reassertion of civil liberties we have been waiting for. Unless talk of the circus is always already a politically sensitive topic in which tensions between political factions were mirrored and played out: given that according to the epitome of Book 68 of Cassius Dio's histories Nerva abolished many horse races and other spectacles in an attempt to reduce expenditures,[39] is the emphasis on circus gossip emblematic of how Nervan *moderatio,* rather than (or as well as) Domitianic tyranny, put a dampener on plebeian pleasures? The bothness of edition 10(2) is always complicated by the in-between role of the never rewritten Book 11, dedicated to assassin Parthenius and buzzing with newly licensed Saturnalian festivity: Nervan licence is subtly but perceptibly dampened in the new Book 10, yet we are also lured to enquire how many 'Nervan' epigrams survived the edit.

Every time we feel we've got Martial cornered, his book finds a way to escape. The *Agricola* projects a similar, politically necessary/opportune slipperiness, as many have noted, and Tacitus' virtuous readers might well find a side order of *Epigrams* 10 cathartic, before they get back to being noble. Yet, as we pore over the two *libelli* side by side, Tacitean amphibology can also take shape, and firm up, in relation to the 'other' of Martial *Epigrams* 10, and alongside epigram's dizzying fragmentation of experience. Where Martial stands for ungovernable *fama* (although, he might counter, there is

---

[37] Fearnley 2003: 626–7. Also see Lorenz 2002: 225–7.   [38] See pp. 244–5.

[39] Later in the epitome (68.7), it is reported that Trajan enlarged and embellished the circus, which had crumbled away in places, again implying that this aspect of Roman social life was neglected or suppressed by Nerva.

no such thing as bad publicity),[40] Tacitus – as Philip Hardie argues – asserts the urgent ethical necessity of making subtle but fundamental distinctions between decent *fama* and its corrupt imperial calque.[41] At the same time, through a radically different generic filter, Martial's new edition (its precious reader now the dedicatee of the book in place of the all-powerful Domitian) can offer a more ludic and less painful model for such 'correction': both authors, for overlapping reasons, are banking on your *fides* (cf. *citra fidem, Agr.* 1.2).

V

Readers of Tacitus and Martial face different but overlapping versions of the challenge of how to interpret these works' fudging of (Domitianic–Trajanic/Nervan–Trajanic) *tempora,* a key word in both texts. Epigram's investment in the evening of diurnal time (at 10.20, the *libellus* is told to wait until nightfall before daring to knock on day-jobbing Pliny's eloquent door; before that is not its 'time': *tempore non tuo,* 12) can now perhaps be recast in 10.48 as an aptitude for 'cooler' and more civilised times (after Neronian midday heat and Flavian afternoon steam) under Trajan.[42] Martial, not austere Pliny, leads the way to the party in 10.20, if that doesn't come across as a little too *Nervan* (there are anxieties to be repressed here, too, about epigram's timing and Bacchic propensities now seeming inappropriate). The old age of the poet himself, or the notion that his time is finally up,[43] also gets airbrushed in epigram's suggestive vision of historical-as-diurnal time: this is just another 'daily' cycle, and epigram's evening will surely come round again (leaving aside the possibility of tyranny's return, at the next Neronian sunrise). Tacitus is just as canny in spinning *tempora* to suit the threshold-politics of his book. He repeats the word *tempora* thrice in the opening chapter, which takes us from *nostris temporibus* (1.1) to *tempora* (the final word, at 1.4). Indeed, at Pliny *Epistles* 3.21.3, the phrase *nostris temporibus* appears to become a bookmark linking Martial Book 10 with *Agricola,* where Pliny states, 'but in our day, this was one of the first things to fall out of fashion, along with other fine and honourable things' (***nostris uero temporibus*** *ut alia speciosa et egregia, ita hoc in primis exoleuit*). Whereas Pliny ends his book by bringing praise back into vogue (the object

---

[40] Cf. Sailor 2008: 91 on *Agr.* 5.3 (under Nero 'good *fama* was as dangerous as bad').

[41] Hardie 2012: 273–84.

[42] Cf. König in this volume (pp. 236–47) on 10.48's apparent allegory of imperial time.

[43] Cf. the anxiety about managing to leave Rome in time in the final line of 10.104 (*nauem, scis puto, non moratur unus*).

of praise is Martial, who will ironically be 'rewarded' by being paid to pack his bags, as his time's up – the *first* line of the edited *Epig.* 10.20 now tells him *ne tempore non tuo . . . | pulses . . . ianuam, uideto*), Tacitus begins his *liber* by making precisely the same claim for Agricola (biographies honouring great men are no longer in vogue, but what you are reading will show you such practices still belong *nostris temporibus*). Tacitus, like Pliny, is conspicuously imprecise about the exact 'times' to which he refers: a little further on, the concluding line to chapter 1 (*tam saeua et infesta uirtutibus tempora*, 1.4) is near-impossible to translate as it lacks (or has silenced) the verb *esse*, so that readers must speak up and infer the tense (*erant*, or *sunt*?):[44] Tacitus' final *narratus* (46.4), counterbalancing the initial future participle *narraturo* (1.4), which refers to some unspecified, to be inferred point in the past or present (*isdem temporibus . . . nunc*, 1.3), will ensure Agricola's *fama* in a (now positively open-ended) 'eternity of times' (*aeternitate temporum*, 46.4). Both texts – as Pliny may well have noticed – mould their own temporal and historical specificity while miming their liminal and still-uncertain place in time.

What's new in *Epigrams* 10 is that the doublespeak implicit in Martial's basic satirical technique (epigram's final punch relies on the pun) is now flooded with political potential. In synch with the 'bamboozling'[45] *Agricola*, Martial's forked meanings put us on the spot: what kind of cultural-political climate do we think we're living in? Are we, paradoxically, going to have to censor dissident voices, put on our political blinkers, in order to believe in real change? Doubleness, or the concept of two in one, is developed in a characteristic medley of ways in Book 10, trumping even the *Agricola*'s puzzle of pairs. Leading off from the trope of virtual monuments and human memory trumping the monumental power of actual marble (*marmora Messallae findit caprificus*, 10.2.9; cf. *quae marmore aut aere finguntur . . . simulacra uultus imbecilla ac mortalia sunt*, *Agr.* 46.3), Martial gives us the hybrid book (*lector, utrique faue*, 10.2.4). Martial's putative 'response' to the *Agricola* (Book 10 begins with the same tight knot of allusions to Augustan *fama* with which *Agricola* ends) is perhaps also to be

---

[44] See Woodman 2014 ad loc., and also on the preceding sentence in 1.4 (*at nunc narraturo mihi uitam defuncti hominis uenia opus fuit quam non petissem incusaturus*), the subject of ongoing controversy not least because it is unclear what period of time Tacitus is referring to in *fuit* – Domitian's reign or Nerva's – and therefore whether or not he is explicitly saying that he attempted to write the *Agricola* under Domitian. Woodman understands it as meaning that Tacitus had fully intended to write the biography but, when he heard in 93 that Rusticus and Senecio had been executed, felt compelled to delay. Cf. Sailor 2008: 115 on the 'ambiguous chronology' of Agricola's life following his return to Rome.

[45] Whitmarsh 2006b: 305.

spied in his uncharacteristically perfectionistic *nota leges... sed lima rasa recenti* (10.2.3), after Tacitus' mock-amateur posing at *Agr.* 3.3 (*non tamen pigebit uel <u>incondita ac rudi uoce</u> memoriam prioris seruitutis ac testimonium praesentium bonorum composuisse*). We are encouraged to enthuse over the double-act of poet-reader, where it is the *lector* who will ensure an illustrious 'I will survive' duet over time with Horace and Ovid (*et meliore tui parte superstes eris*, 10.2.8, cf. *fama superstes*, Horace *Odes* 2.2.8; *non omnis moriar multaque pars mei | uitabit Libitinam*, *Odes* 3.30.6–7; *pars mei multa superstes erit*, Ovid *Amores* 1.15.41, alongside *Am.* 3.15.20; *fama superstes erit*, *Tr.* 3.7.50; *parte tamen meliore mei... ferar*, *Met.* 15.875–6).[46] Lines 47–50 of *Tristia* 3.7 potentially tinge this ever-evolving stemma with Ovid's assertion of the poet's superior control (vis-à-vis the emperor) over his own *fama* ('Caesar could have no power over that', Ovid writes at v. 48). However, the 'thefts' (*furta*) that will not harm paper at 10.2.11 are immediately brought to life in the twin-set of 10.3 and 10.5, where Martial's anonymous, shadowy enemy-double, imitating Ovid's Ibis, is threatening not just to smear Martial's PR stunt of 'positive', 'memorialising', 'personalised' *damnatio memoriae* as performed in 10.2, but also to recreate his own nasty, inharmonious version of Martial's 'two books in one', allowing us to sneer at the split monument, the *nigra fama*, that was once far removed from the polished, politically correct *libellus* presented in 10.2.[47] Martial will be renowned for his (own highly controlled spin on) self-deprecation and self-exposure, which wouldn't serve Tacitus in the slightest – unless it can be called on to stand for the useful option of 'inconsequentiality'.[48]

While post-Ovidian games with the shapes and rhythms of the elegiac couplet (the most popular metre in the *Epigrams*) are par for the course for seasoned readers of Martial, in Book 10 they are set up to retrace the Ovidianised political manoeuvrings of the opening two poems. 10.1 and 10.2 tinge Martial's playful, 'young' rebirth in 98 with the sprightly equilibration of the epigram fronting Ovid's updated, twenty-something juvenilia – the *Amores*:

> Si nimius uideor seraque coronide longus
>   esse liber, legito pauca: libellus ero.
> Terque quaterque mihi finitur carmine parua
>   pagina: fac tibi me quam cupis ipse breuem.
>   (Martial *Epig.* 10.1)

---

[46] Cf. Rimell 2008: 65–71; Hardie 2012: 327.   [47] Cf. Rimell 2008: 71–6.

[48] See Sailor 2012, who argues that the *Agricola*'s prologue is at pains to maintain for the work the option to be important or to be inconsequential: Martial's poetics of paradox can encode this doubleness.

If I seem too large and long a book whose colophon arrives
too late, just read a few: I'll then be a little book.
Again and again my small page ends with the end of a poem:
so make me as short for yourself as you desire.

Qui modo Nasonis fueramus quinque libelli
    tres sumus; hoc illi praetulit auctor opus.
Vt iam nulla tibi nos sit legisse uoluptas,
    at leuior demptis poena duobus erit.
                    (Ovid *Amores, epigramma ipsius*)

We, who previously were five little books of Naso,
now are three; the poet preferred this work to that.
You may now take no pleasure in reading us,
Yet – two books down – the pain will be lighter.

Do we glimpse already here an agonistic response to Tacitus' debut? Traces
of Ovid's youthful, career-boosting second edition in *Epigrams* 10 might
also bear with them Ovid's agonistic self-fashioning via allusion to the
hexameter 'epigram' attached in some editions to Virgil's *Aeneid*:[49] while
Virgil's epic was 'updated' to advertise the great poet's career only after
his death, Ovid – and Martial after him – remake their works themselves,
while still very much alive, or in Martial's case, brought back from the dead.
Any bifocal allusion to Ovid's career incipit + Virgil's career apex would,
we have to admit, capture the all-encompassing genius of Martial's tenth
volume perfectly. Especially if we were to hear echoing through Tacitus'
hoarse, mock-humble opening (*incondita ac rudi uoce*, *Agr.* 3.3) the voice
of novice Corydon in Virgil's first opus, hurling *haec incondita* into the
woods (*Ecl.* 2.4). While Tacitus begins, Martial begins and ends, ends and
begins again, *climactically*: what kind of contest is this?

'Survival' is cannily appropriated (and rebranded) by Martial as always
already the epigram's speciality. In the *Agricola*, meanwhile, the term is
heavy with loss and tinged with guilt, and belongs to the stammering new
vocabulary of *now*. Those who survive (*superstites sumus*) at *Agricola* 3.2 bear
the scars of trauma, so much so that they have 'outlived' themselves. Like
tempora, the word *superstes* frames both texts, and here the points of contact
(whether they were fully intended by one or both authors) seem designed
to tease. Martial's Horatian–Ovidian *et meliore tui parte* **superstes eris** ('you
will survive in the better part of yourself', 10.2.8) appears to echo and recast

---

[49] *Ille ego qui quondam gracili modulatus auena | carmen, et egressus siluis uicina coegi | ut quamuis auido
parerent arua colono, | gratum opus agricolis, at nunc horrentia Martis . . .* Cf. Conte 1974: 63–4.

the final words of the *Agricola*, **superstes erit**, 'he will survive' (*Agr.* 46.4),
or vice versa. Commentators on Tacitus' text recognise that *superstes erit* 'is
an Ovidian tag',[50] yet don't point out that it becomes such in part *through*
Martial's undeletable epigrammatisation of Ovid (whichever direction we
imagine allusion working in here).[51] It's a salutary reminder for a volume interested in the distinctiveness – or otherwise – of Nervan–Trajanic–
Hadrianic interactions that epoch-spanning Martial has already restyled
Augustan intertextual strategies for post-96 literary culture. Tacitean terse-
ness is perhaps bound to look as if it is inspired (tainted?) by epigram's snide
laconics, whether that is the intention or not. The brevity of Woodman's
comments on what he calls an Ovidian tag at *Agricola* 46.4 is indicative
of a reluctance among scholars to pursue markers of Tacitus' engagement
with small-scale poetry (epigram, lyric, elegy):[52] we should not underestimate this engagement, but more precisely, juxtaposing Martial and Tacitus
allows us to see that both authors employ a density of hyperlinks (coded as
Augustan) to frame their own context-specific assertions of the longevity
and influence of winged words. *Superstes* comes to stand not just for *spes* and
fides at this delicate historical moment, but also for a traceable poetic *stirps*
that has redefined survival – through Ovid in particular – as the endless,
playful reinvention of the same, and in terms of quasi-biological memory
embodied in and transformed by readers. Rome's weakened body (*Agr.* 3.1)
draws *animus*, potentially, from that.

VI

Yet how might we measure the (playful) risk implicit in the mere inkling
of an *Agricola–Epigrams* 10 duo? We might note that one way for Martial to diffuse the political contradictions of epigrammatic monumentality
(rewritten as a *damnatio memoriae* of the Domitianic book that must be at
once a forgetting and a remembering) is by allowing the heavily political
concept of the double volume to mutate within the sociopolitical laboratory of the *libellus* itself. Hence in the elegiac 10.71, the two-books-in-one
premise is hinted at yet also painted over by the image of two bodies on a
single pyre (*arserunt uno funera bina rogo*, 6), where memorialising noble

---

[50] Woodman's term (2014 ad loc.). His commentary does not develop nuanced discussion of the nexus
of allusions in the final chapter of *Agricola* in Smith 2002, Harrison 2007a and Hardie 2012: 282–4:
no scholar, however, mentions Martial.

[51] See Hinds 2007 and Rimell 2008 on Martial's reception of Ovid generally.

[52] Austin's comments (1939) on the 'feel of lyric' in the *Agricola* epilogue are highly suggestive.

lives is subtly linked not with *saeua et infesta tempora* but with happy endings, as well as with pleasing the reader of epitaphs alongside the empowered reader of short-as-you-like *libelli* (*breuem titulum marmoris huius ama*,
10.71.2; cf. *fac tibi me quam cupis esse breuem*, 10.1.4). Once the poet has
taken the edge off *bothness*, he can deliver an epigram like 10.81, which
remakes the imperative *utrique faue* of 10.2.4 as the prostitute Phyllis' trick
of satisfying two customers simultaneously, taking them both inside her
singular, versatile body:[53] note how the tag *utrique faue* is reshuffled at the
end of both the first pentameter and the second hexameter of the poem,
and how the engine of embodied elegiac rhythms (Phyllis' *pes* lifted at the
final caesura) propels us back to the sexually passive book open to readers'
desire, at 10.1:

> Cum duo uenissent ad Phyllida mane fututum
>   et nudam cuperet sumere **uterque prior**,
> promisit pariter se Phyllis **utrique daturam**,
>   et dedit: ille pedem sustulit, hic tunicam.
>   (*Epig.* 10.81)

> When two had come to Phyllis for a morning fuck
> and each yearned to take her naked first,
> Phyllis promised to give to both at once, and
> gave: one lifted her feet, the other her skirt.

After barely a distraction from 10.82 (if we are reading the book straight
through), the trope of the double *opus* or textual/human corpus returns at
10.83, a skit in hendecasyllables featuring a man named Marinus whose
comb-over tends to flip over in the wind to reveal a bald pate, so that
he ends up being not one man but two (now bald, now not, an oxy-
moronic *caluus comatus*). Nothing is *turpius* than this (10.83.11), though
we have heard Martial advocate 'simplicity' before (*absit a iocorum nostrorum simplicitate malignus interpres*, *Epig.* 1.*pr.*8; cf. *uis tu simplicius senem
fateri*, 10.83.9), and been tempted to read that as an invitation to read suspiciously from the outset. Might Marinus' cover-up, or double-act, which
relies on exploiting *tempora comata* (long-haired temples), hint at the tight-
rope act of the double book, at Martial's canny exploitation of the *tempora*
he finds himself in, and their association with renewal and rejuvenation,
as he attempts to engineer his own makeover in the same old genre? How
could it possibly? How could it possibly not?

---

[53] Compare 10.62, the epitaph to a matron who had ten children but only knew one cock.

Likewise, the string of epigrams about looking back in time in Martial's revised tenth book revisit the memorialising spiel and uncanny rebirth or afterlife of the poet in 10.2. In 10.23 we admire the ironically named Antonius Primus, seventy-five years old but able to reminisce about those long years, about which we do not (specifically) talk, with neither guilt, nor horror, but pure pleasure (this epigram's twin, 10.32, pictures the same man looking back with joy at an image of his younger self): *hoc est | uiuere bis, uita posse priore frui*, Martial concludes ('to be able to enjoy former life is to live twice over' 10.23.8), just like (or perhaps just unlike) this book, which is shady about its own past life under a now vilified regime. This is followed by an epigram marking Martial's own birthday (10.24): again, any mention of the trauma of looking back – so central to Tacitus' opening chapters – is conspicuously absent. Poem 10.38, the hendecasyllable partner to 10.35 (about Calenus' wife Sulpicia, herself a personification of doubleness) is also about remembering the past fifteen years (*quindecim . . . annos*, 1–3) which just happens to be the exact length of Domitian's rule, as marked by Tacitus at 3.2.[54] Yet this time is now recalled as unadulterated domestic bliss. In fact, Calenus reckons his life *began* when he married: the years 81–96, or (if we are to imagine this is one of the 'new' poems) 83–98,[55] have been the best of his life. It is as if Martial were facetiously overwriting Tacitus' key statement on the Domitian years, surreptitiously codifying epigram's distinctive and (newly) provocative *Weltanschauung*.

> Quid si per **quindecim annos**, grande mortalis aeui spatium, multi fortuitis casibus, promptissimus quisque saeuitia principis interciderunt, pauci et (ut ita dixerim) non modo aliorum sed etiam nostri **superstites sumus**, exemptis e media uita tot annis, quibus iuuenes ad senectutem, senes prope ad ipsos exactae aetatis terminos per silentium uenimus? (*Agr.* 3.2)

> For if, over a period of fifteen years, a large span of human life, many of us perished by chance events, while others, each one showing great spirit, died by the emperor's ferocity, we few who remain have survived not just our neighbours but also, so to speak, ourselves. For so many years have been stolen from the prime of our lives, during which young men reached old age, and old men came to the very outer limits of a spent life, and all in silence.

It is perhaps inevitably less entertaining to flip this inference around, and to read Tacitus both subtly erasing Martial's vulgar diffusion of perspectives on the recent past, and taking back *quindecim annos* for himself. In

---

[54] On 10.35 see Buongiovanni 2012: 124–82.
[55] And if so, with no distinction to be made between the 'Domitian years' and 96–8.

the world of epigram, meanwhile, immersed as it is in synthesising and repackaging the minutiae of social life, those fifteen years have not (necessarily) been a living hell. For Sulpicia and Calenus – whether we are to judge them as politically apathetic lovers who like all good elegiac couples reject the harsh reality of Roman public life and inhabit their own little utopia, or as heroes in a political resistance determined to remake Roman *tempora* within peaceful and only mock-bellicose domestic space – every hour of those years was worth counting, relishing, and thanking the gods for: *indulsit deus*, 'a god bestowed [this]', 10.38.3. Though we are naturally *not* thinking of *dominum deumque*, titles now unutterable in a Rome that has risen from the Styx (cf. 10.72). Tacitus, presumably, would file Sulpicia and Calenus under *desidia* and *inertiae dulcedo*, that sensual laziness that *some* people came to love under Domitian (*amatur*, *Agr.* 3.1). Yet in silent dialogue with *Agricola* 3.2, Martial can reinvent the powerful tension animating his trademark epigram book, a 'virtual society' that is both permeable to the surrounding world and at the same time separate from or fenced off from it. Those 'fifteen years' were Rome's years, Domitian's years, yet they also belong to a poet empowered to remodel urban environments and political landscapes, to carve out his own spaces, and to hone a (now not just self-interested but defensive, defiant, even *triumphant*) 'art of survival'.[56] Tacitus' speech seems to underpin Martial's provocations, which – to put it mildly – now offer another angle on Tacitean quietism.

VII

Martial's *libellus* celebrates the survival of the book-as-poet into a new age, and the ability of epigram and the epigrammatist to thrive in any environment, to constantly elude incriminating political 'seriousness' and to reinvent itself as necessary. Meanwhile, the notoriously difficult *Agricola* vaunts the survival of one man's memory in the minds of Tacitus' readers, and aspires to ensure the future survivability of Tacitus himself, who like Martial from *Epigrams* 10 onward, will enjoy the Nervan-Trajanic 'afterlife' without dying. It is perhaps significant, then, that Martial was an almost exact contemporary of Agricola (who was born in AD 40). Unlike Tacitus' father-in-law, however, who did not live to see the happy event of Trajan's accession (*Agr.* 44.5), this poet has *literally* survived: he celebrates the fact in a birthday poem at 10.24, where he asks to be allowed to live another

---

[56] Cf. Fitzgerald 2007: 9, 12: 'Martial . . . adopts the persona of the struggling dependant not to give voice to the resentment of the unrewarded but to explore the art of survival' . . . 'The epigram becomes the art of survival as Martial dishes the dirt, takes revenge, enlists allies, and solicits friends.'

18 years, bringing him up to a perfect $15 \times 5 = 75$, matching the grand age of Antonius Primus in the previous epigram. Whereas the first edition of *Epigrams* 10 was published in the spirit of *festinata cura* (10.2.1) but has been born again, Agricola's end, though *festinata* ('premature', 'hurried', *Agr.* 44.5), was terminal. Martial, in short, is already well-placed – were there to be such a reckoning – to trump Tacitus' powers of monumentalisation (his biography can't, after all, bring back Agricola from the grave): Pliny affirms this even as he underscores the end of Martial's life and 'time' in his implicit alignment of Martial-Agricola as objects of praise (*Ep.* 3.21). Yet if we begin to envisage Martial interacting with Tacitus, such dialogues can only help both parties endure. Moreover, if we were to read into *Epigrams* 10 a subtle analogy between the poet and Agricola, we might sense Martial's bid to attach himself to Tacitus' astute recuperation of his father-in-law's *gloria*, which on the one hand was stifled by Domitian (Agricola is forced to lie low and to 'drink deep' of politically compliant *otium* when he returns to Rome in *Agr.* 40.4, just as Martial fights to make the best of his 'retirement' to otiose yet dignified Bilbilis) but on the other is proven to be unsilenceable.[57] Through *Agricola*, and by outliving Agricola, Martial can potentially refashion a paradoxical (that is, quintessentially epigrammatic) role for himself as humble, downtrodden poet who is as much a victim of Domitian as anyone else but who is also wildly, undeniably successful, and who deserves to play a part in Tacitus–Pliny's creation of a new political order.

Yet Martial, whose second edition reminds us that he always does the same thing (at least) twice (*bis*, cf. 1.44.3), cannot resist spinning out rather more grotesque afterlives around the ennobling and now Tacitean maxim *superstes erit*. In 10.67, Plutia – presumably a prostitute, or a matrona who liked to take multiple lovers – has outlived 'all the crows' (*iam cornicibus omnibus* **superstes**, 10.67.5), and even in her grave she itches (*prurit*) with lust: epigram's unquashable love of *uariatio* is captured and sullied here in this nymphomaniac body, which must also figure the rebellious materiality of Martial's poetic monuments. Earlier at 10.48, Martial and his poet friends look forward to a miscellaneous feast fit for epigram's table, featuring a mix of classy dishes, peasant food, and leftovers, including a prosciutto that has already 'survived' three dinners (*cenis tribus iam perna* **superstes**, 10.48.17). Martial is perhaps regurgitating memories of Trimalchian tyranny better left behind in the boiling midday heat of Nero's baths: we recall the scene at *Satyricon* 40–1, where a roast boar is carried

---

[57] Cf. Sailor 2008: 99.

into the dining room wearing a cap of freedom. Trimalchio explains that
the boar had been 'freed', that is declined by the guests, in a previous dinner, so now it returns as a *libertus*. But how much (of the past, of Petronius' text) are we meant to remember here? To what extent are we invited
to recall the facetious creativity of the Neronian tyrant presenting itself as
'freedom'? Martial is also presumably jesting around the Ennian-Augustan
trope of poetry 'surviving on the mouths of men': epigram's dishes survive
(although, necessarily, not for long) in the *actual* mouths of guests/readers,
who consume them physically and come back for more.

   This inaugural dinner promotes the familiar 'piatto unico' of epigram as
perfectly situated to unify old and new times: early greens and just-ripe fruit
announcing the new spring next to good honest fare like workman's beans
and a young goat snatched from the jaws of a tyrannical-sounding wolf,
with remnants of past dinners and vintage wine thrown in too. But will
this *cenula unā mensā*, evocative of other epigrammatic dinners in which
the joke is on the diners, repeat on us? 10.48 promises jokes without bile
(*sine felle*, 21), the licence to speak without wishing later that you had been
silent. Any possible satirical epigrammatisations of *Agricola* must surely be
received in the spirit of festive free speech – who wouldn't cheer Martial on,
given the occasion? Still, we don't need Pliny's response to Book 10 in *Epistles* 3.21 to tell us that *sine felle ioci* are themselves, in all likelihood, a joke,
coming from a poet who had *plurimum . . . salis . . . et fellis* ('a lot of salty
wit and bile', *Ep.* 3.21.1).[58] In the spirit of recalling the ingenious exchange
between Martial and Pliny, are we already also remembering Tacitus' mon-
umentalising *libellus*, and licensing Martial to blast new life into all those
decrepit, embittered 'survivor' bodies of *Agricola* 3? Which *remedium* do the
public prefer – the paradigm of survival as reinvention, as quasi-biological
process, one that celebrates the instant detox of burps and bowel-loosening
(10.48.7–10), or the cautious *tardiora remedia* (*Agr.* 3.1) prescribed in historical prose? Miscellany as jostling urban bodies and Saturnalian lucky
dips (Martial), or as the rhetorical and philosophical method required to
temper enthusiasm and to 'combine the advantageous with the honourable'
(Tacitus)?[59] This is a test of virtue if ever there was one: Martial's reinvented
epigram entices us to believe that if we chose the former, now *that's libertas*.

---

[58] Cf. *Ep.* 7.25.3, and 10.45 (denying the sharp, vinegary taste of this smoothed-out book).
[59] *Agr.* 8.1 *Temperauit Agricola uim suam ardoremque compescuit, ne incresceret, peritus obsequi erudi-
      tusque utilia honestis miscere.* As Woodman (2014 ad loc.) notes, the terms employed here are famil-
      iar from philosophy, and especially from Cicero. Whereas the conventional moral stance consists
      in preferring *honestum* to *utile* (cf. Cic. *Off.* 1 and 2, Hor. *Carm.* 4.9.40–1), Agricola combines the
      two, implicitly politicising the aesthetic principle advocated by Horace at *Ars poetica* 343 (*omne tulit
      punctum, qui miscuit utile dulci*). Also see Whitmarsh 2006b: 319.

At the same time, Tacitus' (soon to be reinforced by Pliny's) appropriation of epigrammatic mixing as the new recipe for *pax Romana* could well make Martial's quick-fix menu look like yesteryear's tat.

VIII

How to conclude? In the face of silence, there can be no doubt that *we* – the empowered readers on whose memories Tacitus–Agricola and Martial rely – are making these potential interactions happen: the scope of this chapter has been to turn up the volume, to get silence to speak (orate, hiss). As a result it has become harder than ever to overestimate the extent of Martial's polish and ambition in Book 10, and likewise much harder to 'correct' *Agricola*, at least not without immersing ourselves self-consciously in that process, under the spotlight of timely, culturally and politically specific interrelation. And when we do, we find excitement, risk, contamination, humour with the power to lighten, cut down and upturn, plus a sense of striving towards firm self-definition in the awareness that this striving is bound never quite to succeed, that singular distinction blurs in *tempora* that have yet to come into focus, in a climate of exchange and commutuality. The key function of both *Epigrams* 10 and *Agricola* is to create and consolidate old and new relationships in a community of readers and listeners: but they also invite us to participate in that venture, to put our tired bodies and jaded minds into it, to access this live, drawn-out historical moment for the opportunities it offers for reading (that is, *living, doing*) differently.

CHAPTER 3

Flavian Epic and Trajanic Historiography
Speaking into the Silence

Emma Buckley

Introduction

This volume celebrates the bustling connectedness of the Nervan–Trajanic–Hadrianic period, an ostentatiously new cultural milieu celebrating the freedom to interact. Its authors grasp this opportunity not only by constructing intimate reciprocal literary relationships and wide-sweeping socio-literary networks, but also by generating meaning through conspicuously *absent* forms of literary engagement which operate beyond conventional horizons of critical expectation, via 'silenced' intertexts, postures of cultural isolation, and paraded alienation.[1] The intense noise of this age, together with its attraction to oblivion, is at least partly a reaction to the voice-stopping *seruitus* of Domitianic Rome, or so Tacitus famously claims in the preface to *Agricola*: the Flavian past there is not just a literary 'Dark Age' but also an era to be acknowledged only with discomfort by those surviving into the Nervan–Trajanic present. Yet while critics have begun to turn their gaze upon continuities between Flavian past and post-Flavian present, above all in the epoch-spanning careers of Juvenal, Tacitus, Pliny, Frontinus and Martial, the notion that Flavian epic might cast its shadow on the Nervan–Trajanic period has received less attention.

This is hardly surprising. Aided by the malicious critique of Juvenal's first Satire, Flavian epic has long been regarded as a retreat into the hackneyed world of myth, actively in flight from the dangerous category of 'relevance'.[2] Critics have always been interested in the recovery of allusions to specific historical events in individual epics, and modern readers have

---

I would like to thank the editors, Tim Stover and Salvador Bartera for their very helpful comments, and Jessica Blum and Tim Stover for sharing their unpublished but forthcoming work with me.

[1] On 'silenced intertexts', see Marchiesi 2013b; for alienation and cultural isolation, see Geue and Uden in this volume.

[2] *Sat.* 1.1–11. On Juvenal's possible sideswipe at Valerius Flaccus in particular (*Sat.* 1.6–11), see Henderson 1995: 108–11 and Geue in this volume (p. 369).

been alert to the 'politics' of Flavian epic poetics, uncovering contemporary political and social nuance in Flavian epic. But Donald T. McGuire's 1997 monograph on the themes of suicide, tyranny and civil war in Flavian epic – a set of texts, which, McGuire argues, investigate modes of political behaviour, the workings of monarchy and authorial voice under authoritarian rule in ways which refract contemporary Rome – is still the only general treatment of the politics and poetics of Flavian epic. And his discussion of these texts, conditioned by the hostile periodisation of Pliny and Tacitus, and modelled after Soviet writing strategies of the 1930s, makes 'dissidence', 'subversion' and 'resistance' central to his reading of Flavian epic (as much other work on the politics of Flavian (and Neronian) literature has also done).[3]

Both in literary-critical value judgment and in the political framing of the poems, then, modern critics have read Flavian epic with the grain of Nervan–Trajanic judgment, for the most part treating this poetry as a distinctly self-contained entity. Intertextual analysis and citation studies have done something to break down such divisions, 'proving', for example, that Tacitus has read Valerius, Statius and Silius.[4] But potentially more fruitful are the insights of recent work on epic and historiography more generally: in parallel readings of individual psychology and group behaviour, investigations of the shared intellectual backgrounds of history and epic, and analysis of similar approaches to causation and motivation, approaches to the literary interaction of historiography and epic have expanded beyond allusive influence.[5]

This chapter will stretch such interactivity further, aiming to look again at periodisation and literary interactivity between two particular authors, Valerius Flaccus and Tacitus, through the prism of a reader-response 'reverse reception'. Focusing first on the *Argonautica* and a Tacitean text that has not been read in close contact with Flavian epic, the *Agricola*, I will

---

[3] This chapter, while attempting to escape such 'totalitarian' framing, acknowledges the importance of and works closely with McGuire 1997. Other important political readings are (for Statius) Dominik 1994, Braund 2006, McNelis 2007; (for Silius) Liebeschuetz 1979: 167–80, Ripoll 1998, Marks 2005; (for Valerius Flaccus) Burck 1971, 1981, Hershkowitz 1998, Zissos 2009, Bernstein 2013. The classic discussion of the politics of Flavian literature is Ahl 1984; cf. Bartsch 1994, Rudich 1997 on Neronian 'dissidence' and 'doublespeak'.

[4] See especially Woodman 2009b: 36–7. On Tacitus/Silius, Jacobs 2010, Manolaraki and Augoustakis 2012; on Tacitus/Valerius Flaccus, Syme 1929, Stover forthcoming. Significant intertextual studies of earlier epic include (on Virgil and Sallust) Ash 2002: 257–66; (on Virgil and Livy) Rossi 2004; (on Lucan and Livy) Radicke 2004; (on Tacitus and Virgil/Lucan) Joseph 2010, 2012.

[5] See e.g. Leigh 2007; the edited collections of Kraus, Marincola and Pelling 2010, and Miller and Woodman 2010, include contributions reaching beyond intertextuality in Hardie 2010, Gibson 2010, Jacobs 2010.

argue that a reading of Valerius' text through Tacitus' biography – a biography that places an individual hero within a corrupt, tyrannical system, within a frame juxtaposing a new imperial 'golden age' with the tyranny of Domitian – will help readers to negotiate the problematic periodisation of the Flavian epic, often seen as *either* an 'optimistic' Vespasianic poem of the 70s *or* a 'pessimistic' Domitianic work of the 80s and early 90s. Such reverse reception is of course the result of circular reading – Valerius 'feels' Tacitean because we have read the *Argonautica* through Tacitus.[6] But a more nuanced awareness of the 'impossible' affinities between Tacitus and Valerius in this reverse reception should prompt new reflections on Tacitus' own problematic separation of past and present and support readings that perceive an ideological instability in *Agricola*. Moving from the individual in history to broader notions of Roman identity, I will then attempt to reverse the trend, showing how Valerius' panoramic view of warfare at Colchis can in turn open up new insights into the imperialism of Tacitus' *Agricola* and beyond. Though I will not claim that Tacitus has been directly 'influenced' by Valerius, I will conclude that a reader-response-oriented reading of the Flavian epic alongside Tacitus is evidence of a much broader, distinctly post-Julio-Claudian and obviously shared cultural discourse in these texts, one seeking to examine anew the nature of elite Roman identity through war after civil discord.[7]

Reversing Reception: a Tacitean *Argonautica*?

> et sicut uetus aetas uidit quid ultimum in libertate esset, ita nos quid in seruitute, adempto per inquisitiones etiam loquendi audiendique commercio. Memoriam quoque ipsam cum uoce perdidissemus, si tam in nostra potestate esset obliuisci quam tacere. (*Agr.* 2.3)

> and just as a previous age saw liberty at its most extreme, so we saw an extreme of slavery, with informers taking from us even the interaction of conversation. We would have lost memory itself along with our power of speech, if it had been equally in our power to forget as to be silent.

At first glance Tacitus' *Agricola*, with its stark picture of late Flavian Rome as a 'silenced generation', inhabits a very different world from Valerius Flaccus' *Argonautica*, the first Flavian epic, and one which promises from the start

---

[6] McGuire 1997, esp. pp. 147–54, does not argue for explicit intertextual 'interactivity' with Tacitus, instead reading the epics 'in conjunction' with posthumous descriptions of Domitianic tyranny. McGuire suggests that Flavian epic offers 'indirect commentary' on what is nevertheless a distinctive new characterisation of tyranny.

[7] Cf. Rimell in this volume, reading Martial and *Agricola* in synchronic dialogue.

the bold primacy of the voyage, the heroic status of its participants, and a newly assertive, uncomplicated authorial voice.[8] Valerius' proem fuses the recuperation of a traditional epic form with the fortunes of the new ruling dynasty: catasterism of Argo is the ultimate *telos* of the poem and the poet predicts that Vespasian himself, an emperor famed for his own great nautical exploits, will eventually take his place in the sky too (*Arg.* 1.1–21). And when Valerius' Jupiter promises – in a prophecy that previews the course of history – his sons the chance of apotheosis through epic endeavour (*labor*), the epicist frames the journey as origin not only for individual heroes, but also for the progress of the universe itself.[9] No wonder, then, that critics have interpreted the *Argonautica* as, in essence, an *Aeneid* for Vespasian, Argo's civilising journey as a truly suggestive model for the exploration-conquest and peace-bringing exploits of the new Flavian regime.[10]

A very different strand of critical interpretation, concentrating instead on the evocation of a contemporary social climate, has argued that Valerius' *Argonautica* is a poem of the 80s and early 90s, engaged in pessimistic analysis of contemporary Rome, even if written through the Greek mythological lens.[11] In addition to potential allusions to historical events after 79, McGuire stresses Valerius' constant evocation of the oppressive tyrannical milieu of Tacitus' imperial Rome, featuring in Pelias and Aeetes (kings of Thessaly and Colchis) brooding, deceptive and wrathful rulers who prefigure Tacitus' Tiberius and Domitian.[12] Andrew Zissos' contribution to the

---

[8] As Conte 1994: 489–90 summarises, 'Valerius [sc. exhibits] . . . a reactionary poetics. The subject is mythological, the divine apparatus omnipresent, the moral approach unquestionably edifying.' Important readings of the 'rehabilitated' epic voice of *Argonautica* are Feeney 1991: 316–34 and Hershkowitz 1998; the strongest and most recent 'optimistic' reading of a 'Vespasianic' *Argonautica* is Stover 2012, who at pp. 7–26 argues for a completion date not long after AD 79. Cf. Ehlers 1980, who argues that the epic was mostly finished by AD 80, with 'allusions' to later contemporary events being emendations of a second published edition.

[9] Jupiter will go on specifically to connect Argo's journey and this *labor* to a series of shifts in empires, which, he strongly hints, will culminate with the eventual domination of Rome (*Arg.* 1.558–60): this opening, together with the poem's depiction of the rape of Medea in Herodotean terms in Book 8 (*Arg.* 8.395–6; cf. *Hist.* 1.1–2) frames the poem as between myth and history after the Virgilian model: see Hershkowitz 1998: 236; Zissos 2008: xli; Gibson 2010: 31 for more on the Herodotean framing.

[10] On the important self-presentation of the Flavians as conquerors, restorers of the state, 'bringers of peace', and figures for continuity in the aftermath of the civil wars of AD 69 (also markedly inspired by Augustan models), see for coinage e.g. Rosso 2009; Hurlet 2016; in statuary and portraiture, e.g. Hannestad 1986: 117–21; Kleiner 1992: 173–89; on the Temple of Peace, begun in AD 71, Darwall-Smith 1996: 55–68.

[11] Syme 1929; Preiswerk 1934; Liberman 1997; Kleywegt 2005; Zissos 2008 see allusions to events of the early 90s. While the proem praises a living Vespasian, the only secure 'datable' moment in the poem is a reference to the eruption of Vesuvius (*Arg.* 4.507–11). On the problems of dating the work through its proem, see Syme 1929; Lefèvre 1971; Otte 1992: 1–9.

[12] McGuire 1997: 185–97. See also Preiswerk 1934: 439–40; Burck 1971: 29, 48; Hershkowitz 1998: 246.

'politics' of *Argonautica* provides a more cautious and nuanced approach
to the same question, pointing to the epic's interest in interrogating 'socio-
cultural and political givens' and arguing that in addition to the contem-
porising themes of civil war, tyranny and suicide, the *Argonautica* betrays a
more specific interest in the role of heroic aristocracy, together with a distinct nostalgia for the republican past, which amounts to the inclusion of
a subtle 'oppositional perspective'.[13]

The problem, then, for readers of Valerius, is that we have two seemingly
incompatible *Argonauticas*. The optimistic, forward-looking epic of the
70s, written through close contact with Virgil, celebrates the new regime
in uncomplicated, confident voice: but this voice is in hostile competition
with the brooding, 'oppositional' and more nebulously Tacitean study of
the 80s and early 90s. Such readings have resulted in critical *impasse*: Zissos
has concluded that the *Argonautica* is a fundamentally fractured epic capable of only the most aporetic ideological perspective.[14] But readers of Tacitus' *Agricola* will already be familiar with the challenges of heroism (and of
writing about heroism) in an age hostile to virtue, of writing quest and conquest against a backdrop of tyranny, and of framing 'dark' tyranny against
the dawn of a new golden age.[15] And while Tacitus pits glorious foreign
conquest against servitude at Rome, and champions Agricola's exemplary
heroism, he also provides a powerful internal critique of such conquest,
implicating both Romans and barbarian-Britons in a mutually debilitating
enslavement, acknowledging the complexities and perhaps compromises
of Agricola's behaviour, and potentially even obscuring the line between
Flavian past and Nervan present.

To my knowledge, *Agricola* and *Argonautica* have not been read together
before.[16] But in their framing they are strikingly similar. *Agricola*'s main
theme is, of course, 'how a man can become great even under a bad
emperor' (*Agr.* 42.4), and Jason's mission too is one undertaken in the
shadow of oppressive tyranny. Jason finds himself trapped by a hopeless
political situation at home, in a socio-cultural constellation that anticipates
the kind of bind which Tacitus visualises for Agricola under Domitian:[17]

---

[13] Zissos 2009.

[14] Zissos 2006, 2009. Cf. Blum 2015, who sees a pervading moral *aporia* in the *Argonautica*, structured
through the struggle characters have with their 'exemplary' metapoetic and mythological histories.

[15] On the complex characterisation, imperialism and periodisation of *Agricola*, see e.g. Bastomsky 1985;
James 2000; Clarke 2001; Evans 2003b; Whitmarsh 2006b; Sailor 2008; Lavan 2011, 2013: 127–42.

[16] Though McGuire 1997: 147–8 compares the situations of Agricola and Jason as part of larger reflections on the Domitianic character of Valerian tyranny: see below.

[17] McGuire 1997: 169 and Zissos 2006: 671–2 (also 2009: 354–9) note the Romanising language here,
with its division between the 'people' (*populus*), elders/senators (*patres*), and tyrant (*tyrannus*).

Mox taciti patuere doli nec uellera curae
esse uiro, sed sese odiis immania cogi
in freta. . . .
Heu quid agat? **Populum**ne leuem ueterique **tyranno**
infensum atque olim miserantes Aesona **patres**
aduocet an socia Iunone et Pallade fretus
armisona sperat magis et freta iussa capessat,
siqua operis tanti domito consurgere ponto
fama queat? Tu sola animos mentemque peruris,
Gloria: te uiridem uidet immunemque senectae
Phasidis in ripa stantem iuuenesque uocantem.

(*Arg.* 1.64–6, 71–8)

Soon Pelias' silent trap lay open: the Fleece was not really the hero's task, but
he was being forced onto the vast seas through his uncle's hatred . . . But what
could he do? Call upon a fickle *populus*, hostile to the old tyrant? *Patres*, who
had long pitied Aeson? Or, putting his faith in comrade Juno and Pallas of
the clashing armour, should he hope for more and take to the sea as ordered,
and see if any fame could arise from the taming of the ocean, such a great
undertaking? You alone inflame hearts and minds, Glory: Jason sees you,
youthful and untouched by old age, standing on the bank of Phasis, calling
young men.

Nor does Valerius' Jason simply contemplate rebellion in terms which look
both Roman and proto-Tacitean. He also sets the individual hero's quest for
glory (cf. *Arg.* 1.77) against an overarching frame of tyrannical oppression,
precisely the conditions Tacitus will figure for Agricola, also the possessor
of an ardent nature (*incensum ac flagrantem animum*, *Agr.* 4.3) who must
balance his strong instinct to gain glory with a wise moderation. Indeed,
when Pelias sends Jason on his way 'gazing on him calmly, with an unthreat-
ening expression' (*tranquilla tuens nec fronte timendus*, *Arg.* 1.38) he closely
anticipates the Domitian of *Agricola*, who receives news of Agricola's deeds
fronte laetus, pectore anxius ('with a happy expression and uneasy heart', *Agr.*
22.4).[18] Read in interaction with Tacitus' *Agricola*, Jason is Roman not just
in his predicament but also in his decision to seek success and fulfilment in
the attainment of glory abroad, though robbed of the same opportunities
at home.

---

[18] McGuire 1997: 147–8. *Agr.* 41 once again returns to Domitian's hostility to Agricola, sparked by
the man's glory: *Causa periculi . . . infensus uirtutibus princeps et gloria uiri . . . Sic Agricola simul suis
uirtutibus, simul uitiis aliorum in ipsa gloria praeceps agebatur* ('Agricola's peril came from a *princeps* hostile to virtue and his own glory . . . Thus in the midst of his very glory he was being hurled
headlong, both by his own virtues and by others' vices'). On the special role of *gloria* in Valerius'
Argonautica, see Ripoll 1998: 196–213; Stover 2012: 58, 300. Blum 2015: 70–3 provides further discussion of the generic and ethical context of this passage.

Tacitus' encomiastic account of Agricola is, however, notoriously not without ambiguity. In an age whose hostility to merit made even Agricola's desire for a soldier's renown (*militaris gloriae cupido*, *Agr.* 5) a perilous thing, Tacitus creates a 'quietist' hero who rejects the futile glory of suicidal resistance in favour of a policy of 'heroic moderation'. But Tacitus allows Agricola's moderation to come uncomfortably close to complicity with the subjugation he is both enforcing on the Britons and apparently escaping at Rome.[19] At first sight we might think that the position of Valerius' Jason is far less ambiguous: he has the opportunity for 'epic' glory guaranteed not only by the protection of Juno and Pallas but also, apparently, by an explicit vision of *Gloria*.[20] Yet it is important to point out that Valerius offers a similarly complex mix of motivations here. Indeed, it could be argued that Jason is self-consciously refusing to confront reality by *deciding* to interpret his mission as route to glory. He certainly does not trust his fellow sailors with the truth, encouraging his fellow Argonauts to embark with him by framing the voyage as divinely ordained epic rather than tyrannical trap:

> 'Superum quando consulta uidetis,
> o socii, quantisque datur spes maxima coeptis,
> uos quoque nunc uires animosque afferte paternos.
> Non mihi Thessalici pietas culpanda tyranni
> suspectiue doli: deus haec, deus omine dextro
> imperat; **ipse suo uoluit commercia mundo**
> **Iuppiter** et tantos hominum miscere labores.
> Ite, uiri, mecum dubiisque euincite rebus
> quae meminisse iuuet nostrisque nepotibus instent.'
>   (*Arg.* 1.241–9)

'Since you see heaven's decision, comrades, and the great hope granted to so great an enterprise, summon now your strength and ancestral courage. I will not blame the criminal piety of the Thessalian tyrant, or suspect a plot: it is god – god – who orders this voyage with propitious omen. Jupiter himself has willed interaction for his world, and has wanted to stir up such great

---

[19] See especially *Agr.* 5.3 and 39.2 on Agricola and martial glory. While Sailor 2008: 72–118 argues that Britain offers opportunities for engagement with *labor et periculum* (*Agr.* 18.5) not possible at Rome (see esp. p. 80, 'Tacitus' marking off Britain . . . lets Tacitus show a system of glory operating with full freedom from the distorting pull of Rome's center of gravity'), he is not able to fully escape servitude at Rome: Lavan 2013b: 139–41 rightly points to the uncomfortable way in which Agricola's heroic *obsequium* and *modestia* at Rome echoes the language of senatorial enslavement elsewhere in *Agricola*. Cf. Whitmarsh 2006b: 305–7.

[20] Zissos 2008 ad loc. rightly notes Valerius' return here to a distinctly Homeric *kleos*-code. Blum 2015: 72–3, noting the similarity of the description of *Gloria* to Homer's Sirens, reads Jason as potentially 'seduced' by glory here.

human labours.²¹ Go, men, and with me win in adversity that which will be a pleasure to remember, things that will spur on our descendants.'

From this point of view, Jason's own vision of glory is less divine epiphany than acute understanding of human nature, offering the right kind of motivation for his young crew. His speech to his fellow Argonauts certainly advocates a rhetoric of heroic optimism that at the same time points up its own deceptiveness, in the same kind of self-critiquing approach to heroism with which Tacitus' *Agricola* will later struggle. Jason's appeal to historicising exemplarity taps into the very tradition of heroic memory *Agricola* will later be designed to perpetuate. And Jason's confidence in the divine backing of his mission is 'guaranteed' by his casting as the new Aeneas, his speech peppered with obvious borrowings from Aeneas' famously exhortatory speech after shipwreck in Libya (*Aen.* 1.198–203).²² Yet we know that Jason is in fact lying to his men at this point when he makes Jupiter, not Pelias, responsible for the mission: while his *representation* of the voyage is 'epic', the reality is that it has been instigated by the jealousy of a monarch.²³ While Agricola and Jason inhabit different generic worlds, their motivation to fashion a new kind of heroism, to say nothing of the uncomfortable fit that representation of heroism may have with 'reality', shares significant similarities.

Indeed Valerius compounds the pressure to read this way when he has his hero declare that *commercia mundo* is the purpose of Argo's voyage. *Commercium* is famously rejected in the *Aeneid*: the single instance occurs when the enraged Aeneas refuses to engage in what he disparagingly terms 'trading in war' (*Aen.* 10.532). Instead, Jason's words appeal to a different conceptual world: he evokes not merely 'human interchange' but more specifically the business of imperialism, evoking, for example, the Elder Pliny's stress on the interdependent role of Roman empire and commerce: *Quis enim non communicato orbe terrarum maiestate Romani imperi profecisse uitam putet commercio rerum ac societate festae pacis . . . ?* ('Who would not admit that intercommunication has been established throughout the world through the majesty of the Roman Empire, life has advanced through the interchange of commodities and the partnership of joyful peace . . . ?',

---

²¹ Kleywegt 2005: 150 notes the zeugma (cf. *TLL* VIII 1058.33) produced when both *labores* and *commercia* are dependent on *miscere* (with *commercia* = 'exchange' (*OLD* 10), 'stir up' (*OLD* 13); with *labores* = 'combine efforts', *OLD* 9).

²² See Zissos 2008 ad loc.

²³ Note that Jason's self-serving appeal to heroic exemplarity echoes Pelias (*Arg.* 1.140–57), who in addition to family duty appeals to Jason's 'manly spirit' and dares him to deem himself worthy of danger.

NH 14.1).[24] Again, this may frame Jason as a new 'Flavian' Aeneas, on a mission of exploration, conquest and civilisation, mouthpiece and symbol for an up-to-date positivist narrative of foreign imperialist expansion. Yet there is a sting in the tail to Pliny's vision of the benefits of expansive Roman *imperium*, for he goes on to argue that such expansion has corrupted later generations;[25] and such negative imperial expansion is hinted at in Jason's own words, which allusively echo Seneca's worries about *commercium* and empire in the *Natural questions* (5.18.4–6):

> Quid quod omnibus inter se populis **commercium** dedit et gentes dissipatas locis **miscuit**? Ingens naturae beneficium, si illud in iniuriam suam non uertat hominum furor! . . . (6) Non in hoc prouidentia ac dispositor ille mundi deus aera uentis exercendum dedit et illos ab omni parte ne quid esset situ squalidum effudit, ut nos classes partem freti occupaturas compleremus milite armato et hostem in mari aut post mare quaereremus. Quae nos dementia exagitat et in mutuum componit exitium?

> Just think how wind has given all nations communications with each other and brought together peoples separated by geography! An enormous kindness of nature's, if the folly of humans did not pervert it to their own harm! . . . (6) It was not for this that providence and the god who manages the world gave the winds the task of keeping the air moving and poured out winds from all directions to prevent anything becoming desolate through neglect – it was not so we could cram armed soldiers into fleets that would take control of a large part of the sea, nor so that we could search for the enemy on the sea or beyond the sea. What madness drives us on and sets us against each other to our mutual destruction?[26]

Valerius' interdiscursive appeal to more pessimistic assessments of the cost of progress from historiography and natural philosophy – set within a context that self-consciously destabilises the heroic nature of Jason's epic endeavour – anticipates the ambivalence of the broader imperialist vision

---

[24] All translations of Pliny are from Rackham 1938, sometimes adapted. *Natural history* was published in AD 77: on its composition dates, see Baldwin 1995. In historiography, natural history and natural philosophy, the language of *commercium* in the sense of 'human exchange' (of conversation, business, relationships) is common, but (with the important exception of Lucan, who is also interested in the relationship between Rome's expansion and war – see below) the term *commercium* is very rare in epic pre-Valerius. On *commercium* and civilisation, see e.g. Woolf 1998: 67; on *commercia* in Valerius, see Zissos 2008: 204; Stover 2012: 54–5, 81 (a more positive reading of the passage).

[25] *Posteris laxitas mundi et rerum amplitudo damno fuit . . . pessum iere uitae pretia omnesque a maximo bono liberales dictae artes in contrarium cecidere ac seruitute sola profici coeptum* ('The expansion of the world and our wealth of resources was detrimental to later generations . . . The true prizes of life have gone to ruin, and all the arts called "liberal" from liberty, the supreme good, have fallen into the opposite class, and slavery alone began to be the sole means of advancement', *NH* 14.5.1).

[26] Trans. Hine 2010. Both Kleywegt 2005 and Zissos 2008 note this parallel.

of *Agricola*, in which the heroism of Agricola is challenged and undermined by the broader unease about the direction and effects of empire.[27]

Perhaps the most obvious interaction between *Agricola* and *Argonautica* occurs in the aftermath of Argo's embarkation. Here, the important distinction Tacitus makes between the *gloria* achieved by Agricola and the fundamentally useless *gloria* attained by the Stoic martyrs at the cost of their lives but with no benefit to Rome (*Agr.* 42.5) finds anticipatory expression in the suicides of Jason's parents. Jason's decision to induce Pelias' son Acastus to join the voyage (backed by what he again *interprets* to be an omen from Jupiter (*Arg.* 1.156–62)) has a disastrous outcome, for Pelias' *saeuitia* is unleashed. Aeson too must now contemplate action, in words which closely recall Jason's earlier deliberations (*Arg.* 1.759–61);[28] his final decision, however, is to display precisely the kind of futile defiance which Tacitus both provocatively deprecates in *Agricola* and repeatedly celebrates in his later historiography: the choice to commit suicide.

McGuire has already noted the close parallels in the depiction of the death of Aeson and the exemplary suicides of the *Annals*, which include standard features – the emperor's death-sentence, the decision of the wife to co-suicide, the arrival of the emperor's troops at the house of the condemned – together with the ambition to serve as heroic example for his son Promachus, in whom he wishes to embed the memory of his death together with his greatness of heart and brave action (*Arg.* 1.771–3).[29] Of course,

---

[27] Indeed, a final 'intertextual' interaction might confirm this suspicion. It is surely no accident that Jason unwittingly evokes the single epic precedent for the collocation *commercia mundo* here, the far-more troubling *commercium* found in Lucan's assessment of the 'world interaction' of the Nasamones. These people, Lucan tells us, live off salvage: the wealth that comes from shipwrecks is their interaction with the whole world (*sic cum toto commercia mundo* | *naufragiis Nasamones habent, BC* 9.443–4). To cast the shadow of shipwreck over the speech with which Jason launches his voyage, and to evoke what Neil Coffee calls the 'corrupt trade' of the Nasamones in this optimistic appeal for human interaction, is to problematise any simple 'epic-imperialist' interpretation of the *Argonautica*: precisely the strategy of Tacitus' superficially straightforward encomium of *Agricola*. On this 'commerce' in Lucan, see Coffee 2009: 214.

[28] *Sic curae subiere ducem, ferrumne capessat* | *imbelle atque aeui senior gestamina primi* | *an patres regnique acuat mutabile uulgus* ('Thus anxiety oppresses the leader: should he grasp an unthreatening sword and the accoutrements of a warrior in his prime, though an old man? Or should he provoke the *patres* and the kingdom's fickle mob?', *Arg.* 1.759–61). One of the few 'specific' linguistic citations from Valerius may be found in Tacitus' own *uulgus mutabile, Hist.* 1.69.7: Valerius himself has borrowed from historiography and Livy's *mutabiles uolgi animi* (2.7.5) here, though of course this is a popular conceit: see e.g. Cic. *RP* 2.65; Sen. *De ira* 2.8.1–3. For Domitian's characteristic *saeuitia* (cf. Pelias' explicit association with *saeuitia*, see *Arg.* 1.700, 748, 818), see e.g. Kapust 2011: 165–6; Woodman 2014: 21–2, 75–6.

[29] *Est etiam ante oculos aeuum rudis altera proles,* | *ingentes animos et fortia discere facta* | *quem uelit atque olim leti meminisse paterni* ('There is too before his eyes his other son, just a young boy, whom he wished to teach greatness of spirit and brave deeds, and who would remember his father's death'). These lines form an obvious double to Jason's speech at the outset of the epic. On the framing of the suicide through heroism and *memoria*, see McGuire 1997: 193–4.

Tacitus was not the only author to memorialise the Stoic martyrs of the early Empire: as Dylan Sailor points out, Tacitus' generation was immersed in the experience of heroic death, with an entire genre of laudatory biography existing to commemorate the heroic suicides of the victims of Nero and Domitian.[30] But Tacitus' own famously complicated attitude to the Stoic martyrs in *Agricola* – his accusation that (unlike Agricola) these men sought fame and fate (*famam fatumque*, *Agr.* 42.3) in an empty display of *libertas* – is not unique, for Aeson's own expectations of a worthy fate (*fata . . . digna*) and a great death (*magnos obitus*, *Arg.* 1.768–9) are themselves tragically undermined. Aeson's expectation that his death should serve as *memoria* for his son is short-lived: his last sight is of the king's soldiers bursting in and ripping his son's body to shreds, and it is the horrified spirit-Aeson who is left to bear away the memory of Promachus' death (*Arg.* 1.823–6). Valerius sets Aeson's own glorious translation to the skies alongside the petty and pointless of death of the boy whose only action in the whole *Argonautica* is to die.[31]

It is not new to claim Valerius as a 'Tacitean' author, or at least as one whose *Argonautica* evokes a Tacitean pessimism, with its complex internal politics, dissimulating tyrants and political suicide. But by pressing the interaction of Tacitus' *Agricola* with Valerius' poem – a 'reverse reception' which highlights both texts' dynamic depiction of the role of a heroic protagonist trapped within a claustrophobically tyrannical regime – we can see that Valerius' epic is not incoherent or fundamentally fractured, but rather a response to the new complex negotiations that must take place whenever an imperial ideology has to start over. While *Agricola* deals with a 'real-world' problem – constructing a quietist heroism that is not subjugation – Valerius has already translated the issue into the world of epic. In framing Jason's heroism by tyranny, and in complicating his optimism in Jovian benevolence and the rewards of *labor* with a murkier vision of the costs of *commercia*, Valerius creates a new epic of empire which may be ambivalent but is hardly incoherent. Valerius instead exploits the gap between Jason's, to say nothing of the audience's, desire for a simple,

[30] Sailor 2008: 10–35 sets Tacitus' approach to the Stoic martyrs against the broader tradition, arguing that Tacitus' 'de-sanctifying' approach both speaks to the prevalence of a more uncritical tradition of appreciation and is part of the author's own ambition to provide alternative models of heroism.
[31] Cf. McGuire 1997: 185–97, 228–9 who (again perhaps influenced by Tacitus' singular approach) reads suicide throughout Flavian epic as problematically un-Stoic. Zissos 2009: 362–5 offers a more positive reading of Valerius' suicide episode, reading the Elysium scene following Aeson's death as a reconstructed ideal republican society.

teleological and optimistic epic for the new Flavian age – to *represent* and *interpret* Argo's quest in these terms – while simultaneously acknowledging the reality behind this new, post-Neronian, Flavian beginning. To this reader, the Tacitean, or more broadly 'Trajanic', ideological perspective – that is to say a perspective interested in the complexity of compromise and the difficulties of representation in negotiating past and present – makes more sense of the Flavian *Argonautica* than the mutually exclusive choices to read Valerius' epic as 'optimistic' poem for Vespasian or 'subversive' Domitianic text.

Anticipating Tacitus: *Argonautica, Agricola, Histories*

This awareness might encourage us in turn to look again at the sharp distinctions Tacitus himself attempts to forge between Flavian past and Nervan present in *Agricola*. For while Tacitus sets a tyrannical past against an idealised present, it has long been recognised that Tacitus also allows interpretative potential for the elision of that boundary-line, above all in the ambiguity of chronological reference in preface to the work.[32] The opening to *Agricola*, which both stresses a break with the past through a rhetoric of newness and acknowledges that this new beginning is a reiteration (*Nunc demum redit animus*, 3.1), is once again also repetition of the strategy of Valerius' own 'first' epic for the Flavian age, one that has employed the same tactics to stress the break with the Julio-Claudian past.[33] While the textual strategies of Valerius' epic and Tacitus' biography are clearly very different, they interact in their shared destabilisation of periodisation itself: both offer the promise of a new beginning, only to elide those boundaries,

---

[32] On the 'deceptively simple' then–now structure of *Agricola*'s preface and its susceptibility to deconstruction, see especially Sailor 2004: 153–8, 2008: 53–72. Lavan 2015: xliv–v, responding to the efforts of Woodman 2014: 65–7 (and especially his notes at 1.4, 2.1, 2.3) to close these chronological loopholes, reiterates the importance of the author's decision to make the reader arbiter of interpretation, and notes that the potential to see the present time as still one hostile to virtue (*Agr.* 1.4) need not be criticism of the new imperial regime.

[33] Whitmarsh 2006b: 310–13 well explores this 'reiterative' rhetoric of newness and *Agricola*'s mimicry of 'Trajanic propagandistic idiom'. Note especially the pleonastic *primo statim . . . ortu* to stress a new Trajanic *beatissimum saeculum* (*Agr.* 3.1). Valerius' *Argonautica* also obviously starts anew with a propagandist rhetoric of primacy that reiterates the strategies of previous imperial encomium: *Prima deum magnis canimus freta peruia natis | fatidicamque ratem . . .* ('Seas first crossed by the mighty sons of gods I sing, and the fate-speaking ship . . .', *Arg.* 1.1–2). *Arg.* 1.7–21, foregrounding Vespasian's role in the conquest of Britain, Titus' victorious generalship and Domitian's eminence in the arts, echoes closely the propagation of imperial image engineered at the outset of Vespasian's reign. On the proem, see Lefèvre 1971; Zissos 2008: 71–95; Stover 2012: 14–25, 62–70; on Flavian ideology more generally, Boyle and Dominik 2003; Kramer and Reitz 2010.

underscoring how tendentious and rhetorically framed any Roman imperial regime change will be.[34]

If readers of Valerius' *Argonautica* have tended to stress the voyage as a
retreat into myth, it has also been long recognised that when his Argonauts
arrive in Colchis and embark on war (in a sustained battle-narrative across
Books 5–7, another innovation on the Apollonian source), they have sailed
into territory that is at the forefront of contemporary Roman foreign policy. Nero's main military success had been in Armenia, but after Plautius
Silvanus' expedition into the south-western Crimea, the eastern Black Sea
coast had also come more directly under Roman control. Indeed, before
he lost power, Nero was preparing an expedition to the Caspian Gates,
creating a new legion for the task that would make for the Darial Pass
to secure the region from the Sarmatians and in particular to combat the
new threat from east Sarmatia, the marauding Alani. This area continued
to be of great concern to the Flavians: Vespasian, whose bid for imperial
power was secured by shifting legions from the east, made various deals
with Armenia and Parthia, the Iazyges and Suebi (see Tac. *Hist.* 3.5), while
the Dacians, Sarmatians and Rhoxolani all made attacks on the Empire,
aiming to capitalise on the civil war of AD 69.[35]

All these foreign enemies of Rome and more are then to be found not
just in the pages of Tacitus' *Histories* but also in the profoundly alien
tribes Valerius' Argonauts encounter in Colchis, in a consciously pre-Iliadic
battle-narrative that both paints the conflict as a traditional Homeric–
Virgilian war and at the same time revels in the barbarism and alien-ness
of its inhabitants.[36] Indeed, Valerius even offers some fresh ethnographical
detail about these new eastern foes that anticipates the later historiogra-
phers of the Flavian period. He gives the first accurate description of arms
and tactics of the Sarmatians (*Arg.* 6.160–2): their distinctive weapon, the
heavy lance (*contus*), their aversion to the bow, their distinctive yell: *fremi-
tus*, not *ululatus*.[37] His inclusion of the Parthian ambassador Myraces, at
court to make a treaty with Aeetes (*Arg.* 6.190–2), is also topical, given

[34] For other examples of uncomfortable rejection of and interaction with the Flavian past in this
volume, see König and Rimell in this volume; Saller 2000; for Martial, Rimell 2008; Marchesi 2013;
König 2013; for Pliny, Hoffer 1999, esp. pp. 141–59; for Pliny and Tacitus, Whitton 2012; for Tacitus
and Juvenal, Keane 2012; for Tacitus, Suetonius and Juvenal, Wilson 2003.

[35] See Wilkes 1983; Braund 2013.

[36] Valerius' up-to-date geopolitics includes a range of reference extending far beyond Scythia, to Egypt,
Persia, India and Germany, and incorporating many places still outside Roman control: see Shreeves
1978; Baier 2001.

[37] See Syme 1929.

the concerted diplomacy of both Nero and Vespasian in this region: the depiction of the Argonauts springing forth to fight those 'whom the Armenians, Iberians and Parthians cannot resist' may even recall the proposal of Vologases I of Parthia in AD 75 to launch a joint Roman–Parthian expedition against the Alani.[38] But right from the start, any 'clean' imperialist perspective of the war is undercut when Jason enters the tyrant Aeetes' court (itself again recognisably 'Roman'), reminds him of their kinship, and declares himself ready to intervene in Aeetes' civil war with his brother Perses.[39]

Allusively too this is a civil war, for the battle narrative of *Argonautica* consistently recalls Lucan's *Bellum ciuile*. Valerius' exotic collection of tribes and peoples draws from Lucan's own all-embracing vision of a Roman civil war played out on the world stage: responding to Lucan's own excursus on *Argo*, which makes this voyage the cause of eventual world war (*BC* 3.190–7) within the globe-spanning catalogue of Pompey's forces, Valerius embeds the Lucanian co-opting of the *orbis* into Rome's war in his own epic via a seam of imagery which consistently depicts the slaughter in Colchis – the Homeric–Virgilian duels, routs and massed clashes – in the words of *Bellum ciuile*.[40] Indeed, the Colchian impulse for death recalls closely Lucan's line that civil war is the slaughter of the world (*concurrunt ultroque ruunt in funera Colchi, Arg.* 6.242; *in funere mundi | mortibus innumeris, BC* 7.617–18).

There is a significant difference in Valerius' approach to writing 'Lucanian' civil war, though. When Valerius writes originary war as a confusing clash of *bellum externum* and *bellum internum*, he does not – as Lucan does – elide the kinds of distinctions between foreign and civil war the *Bellum ciuile* conspicuously tries to elide. Though Lucan's epic begins with the common lament that Romans have turned on themselves when so many

[38] *Arg.* 5.558–60 *Prosiliunt quos nec Rhipaea iuuentus | quos nec Hiber aut tota suis Aurora pharetris | sustineat*; see Hollis 1994: 211. See too *Arg.* 5.554–6, in which Castor identifies Aeetes as requesting help (*bello interea sed pressus iniquo | auxilium petit: armatos dux protinus omnes | accelerare iubet* ('under pressure of iniquitous war Aeetes seeks help: our general orders all men to hurry in arms at once'): while *auxilium petere* is a common phrase for military operations (e.g. Livy 8.1.10; 31.11.10, 32.39.11), the unusual sense of *accelerare*, of soldiers and with *iubeo*, is much rarer and may have inspired Tac. *Hist.* 2.100 (see Wijsman 1996: 254). Toohey 1993 argues for further 'Romanisation' of the Argonauts at *Arg.* 3.365 and 7.573. Statius' *Thebaid* also shows interest in this issue: the comparison of Thiodamas to a young Parthian succeeding to the throne (*Theb.* 8.286–93) also includes mention of the *Caspia limina* – a possible allusion to Pacorus II, who succeeded to the throne in AD 78: see Hollis 1994.

[39] Note too that Colchis appoints senators (cf. *Arg.* 5.464 *legit . . . patres*, with Wijsman 1996: 222).

[40] On Lucan's catalogue, see Radicke 2004: 244–5; for more on Lucan and Valerius Flaccus, see Buckley 2010, Stover 2013 and below.

foreign foes are left to fight, the typical strategy of the Neronian text is
to confuse the boundaries of identity and ethnicity in the creation of a
bellum ciuile on the world-scale.[41] *Bellum ciuile*, then, revels in the presentation of civil war as world war, the elision of *orbis* and *Vrbs*.[42] Valerius'
war in Colchis, on the other hand, is presented as both *bellum internum*
and *bellum externum*, fusing expansionist narrative of exploration, the kind
of 'clean' war stressed in the self-legitimising presentations of the Flavian
regime at its outset, with a much murkier kind of war: the kind of war, in
fact, that really put the dynasty in place and continued to rear its head into
the 80s and 90s under Domitian.[43]

Perhaps it should come as no surprise, then, that when Jason finally
escapes the claustrophobic court at Thessaly and finds himself in what
should be an uncomplicated foreign war, Valerius continues to exert destabilising pressure on his imperialising mission. Just as *Agricola*'s antagonist
Calgacus encodes defiance against Rome repeatedly as a defence of *libertas* (*Agr.* 30–2) in ways that reflect uncomfortably on Rome's own identity
under the principate, Valerius creates in Gesander, the chief of the Iazyges,
both an archetype of barbarism and a figure who is conspicuously, if problematically, proto-Roman. In a vaunting speech before he kills the Argo-
naut Canthus, Gesander boasts of a way of life that clearly fulfils standard
ethnographic stereotypes (a nomadic lifestyle based on warfare and plunder, a toughness inculcated by life in the frozen north, *Arg.* 6.323–9). But
his barbarism goes one step further: we have already learned, in a stirring
speech to incite his men to battle, that the custom of the Iazyges is to
euthanise their fathers before old age can make them weak (*Arg.* 6.278–
91). Yet this shocking barbarism is framed in a way that consistently makes
Gesander sound rather Roman himself. As he calls upon the spirit of his
father Voraptus to help him, he makes his father an example for the *parui
nepotes* that will follow (*Arg.* 6.291), before chiding an elderly opponent in
battle for the lack of *pietas* demonstrated by a son who had let him live (*Arg.*
6.311). And indeed, when Gesander boasts of his tribe's hardiness, he does
not just evoke the proto-Roman Italian identity of the *Aeneid*'s Numanus
Remulus in his words – he also ties that identity to the explicit notion of
both *patria* and freedom:

---

[41] This ambivalence is developed by post-Lucanian writers: see e.g. O'Gorman 1993 on Tacitus'
Germania.

[42] See e.g. Masters 1992; on Egypt, Reed 2011.

[43] See especially the presentation of victory in Judaea as 'foreign' conquest: on the importance of Judaea
in establishing Flavian *bona fides* and redirecting attention from their involvement in civil conflict,
see especially Mason 2016b: 3–59.

'Feror Arctois nunc liber in aruis
cuncta tenens; . . .
Numquam has hiemes, haec saxa relinquam,
Martis agros, ubi tam saeuo durauimus amne
progeniem natosque rudes, ubi copia leti
tanta uiris. Sic in patriis bellare pruinis
praedarique iuuat talemque hanc accipe dextram!'

(*Arg.* 6.330–1, 335–9)

'Now I am free as I roam the lands of the north with all my possessions . . . Never will I leave these wintry climes, these rocks – Mars' land –
where we have hardened our babies, our young sons, in such savage water,
where there is such an abundance of death for men. So it pleases us to make
war and plunder in our icy fatherland: receive such a right hand as this!'

Within the frame of reference provided by Tacitus' own complex
civilisation-narrative in *Agricola*, then, we might see Gesander as more than
simple blunt stereotype of the 'non-Roman'. Instead, this barbarian at the
furthest ends of the earth will serve as a conductor for Roman anxieties
about the costs of empire. Indeed, Gesander is not simply a 'primitive' in
the mould of Tacitus' Calgacus, a foil to Rome's own submission: his status as father-killer makes him both the antithesis of what it should be to be
Roman, but also only too fit for membership of a race ultimately headed
for *bellum ciuile*.[44]

There is no novelty in using a primitive to reflect on Roman identity
within a mythological epic, but Valerius takes a far more transgressive step
when he anachronistically and jarringly compares these 'foreign' barbarians
to the contemporary Roman soldier. Take Colaxes, a Scythian destined to
die in Jason's *aristeia*. This figure, introduced in a catalogue of 'enemy'
forces, clearly has a home in epic tradition – his mother is a nymph – but
even this ancestry has a precedent in historiography (Coloxais, forefather of
the Scythians: see Herodotus 4.5) and he is the commander of a Thracian
legion, which wears an emblem that, Valerius interjects, can be seen on the
shield of any Roman *miles* today:

Proxima Bisaltae legio ductorque Colaxes,
sanguis et ipse deum, Scythicis quem Iuppiter oris
progenuit uiridem Myracen Tibisenaque iuxta
ostia, semifero – dignum si credere – captus
corpore, nec nymphae geminos exhorruit angues.
Cuncta phalanx insigne Iouis caelataque gestat

---

[44] Cf. Buckley 2010: 16–21. For Tacitus' reflections on a more 'pure' primitive identity in the *Germania*,
see O'Gorman 1993.

tegmina dispersos trifidis ardoribus ignes;
nec primus radios, miles Romane, corusci
fulminis et rutilas scutis diffuderis alas.

(*Arg.* 6.48–56)

Next comes Bisalta's legion, and its commander Colaxes, himself of
divine bloodline. Jupiter fathered him on Scythian shores, next to green
Myrace and the mouth of the river Tibisis: bewitched, if we can believe it,
by the nymph's half-bestial body, he did not shudder at her twin snakes.
The whole phalanx bears the badge of Jupiter, shields engraved with the
scattered fires of the triple lightning-bolt: Roman soldier, you were not the
first to spread the rays of the gleaming lightning, with its red-golden wings,
on your shield.

This barbarian Colaxes is nothing less than a proto-Roman soldier, then,
regardless of whether (as some commentators suggest) his troops prefigure
in particular the Roman soldiers of the Twelfth Legion (Fulminata), or offer
a more generic Roman military identity.[45] Indeed, the very context of the
catalogue – drawing upon the aetiological framing of Virgil's Italian forces
in the *Aeneid*, who serve to link primitive past with contemporary Roman
present – forces us to consider not just whether the Roman soldier 'looks
like' an eastern barbarian, but also indeed whether that Roman soldier in
any sense 'comes from' this eastern barbarian.

   Thomas Baier paints Valerius' aetiological approach as artificial and
mannered, a barren 'decryption' (*Entschlüsselung*) and grotesque burlesque
of the *Aeneid*'s attempt to provide an aetiology for Roman character in
the age of Augustus.[46] But if we take seriously this jarring combination
of 'Roman' and 'other', centred via the figure of the Roman *miles*, then
we might see this comparison as rather more appropriate in the context of
Tacitus' later exploration of Roman identity in his *Histories*, which tackle
the civil wars of AD 69 as a confusing and confused series of battles and
switches of allegiance between armies which are in identity both Roman
and barbarian, even as the Empire is tested by attacks and incursions from
barbarian invaders.[47] Indeed Tacitus' *Histories* famously refuse to categorise
the conflicts of 69 and beyond as simply a question of civil war vs external
war (*Hist.* 1.2):

---

[45] Cf. Wijsman 2000: 38; Liberman 2002: 202. The Twelfth fought with Titus at the Fall of Jerusalem
   (see Tac. *Hist.* 5.1: Schenk 1999b: 184 n. 226), and may have been a particularly suitable comparison,
   given that they were posted by Domitian to the Caspian Sea (as an inscription dated between AD 83
   and 93 referring to a detachment of the legion – evidence of the most eastern base of any Roman
   legion – shows: see *AE* 1951, no. 262, and Grosso 1954: 117–18). However, other legions also carried
   the lightning flash emblem (including the Eleventh Claudian and the Fourteenth Gemina Martia
   Victrix, both part of the force Petillius Cerialis used to quell the Batavian revolt of AD 69).
[46] Baier 2001: 51–2.   [47] See especially Ash 2009.

Opus aggredior opimum casibus, atrox proeliis, discors seditionibus, ipsa etiam pace saeuum. Quattuor principes ferro interempti, trina bella ciuilia, plura externa ac plerumque permixta. Prosperae in Oriente, aduersae in Occidente res; turbatum Illyricum, Galliae nutantes, perdomita Britannia et statim omissa; coortae in nos Sarmatarum ac Sueborum gentes, nobilitatus cladibus mutuis Dacus, mota prope etiam Parthorum arma falsi Neronis ludibrio.

I embark on a history rich in catastrophe, fierce with battles, discordant in its rebellions, savage even in peace. Four emperors died by the sword: there were three civil wars, more foreign wars, and often wars containing both elements. Things went well in the East, badly in the West. The Balkans were disturbed, the allegiance of the Gallic provinces wavered, Britain was utterly subjugated and immediately lost. The Sarmatae and Suebi rose up against us; the Dacians won fame by disasters both inflicted and suffered; a laughable false Nero even nearly prompted the Parthians to war.

Tacitus distinguishes between three civil wars (the conflicts between Otho and Vitellius and between Vitellius and Vespasian in AD 69; and later, the AD 89 rebellion of Saturninus against Domitian) and more external wars, the conflicts ranging from Britain to North Africa, on the Rhine and Danube and along the Parthian border.[48] But crucially Tacitus also includes now a third category of war, *bella permixta*, and the events he goes on to relate in the *Histories* itself – the Illyrian uprising for Vespasian, the Batavian revolt supported by some of the Gallic provinces, which is simultaneously 'civil' and 'foreign' (*interno simul externoque bello, Hist.* 2.69.1) and has the mixed look of civil and external war (*mixta belli ciuilis externique facie, Hist.* 4.22.2) as well indeed as the rebellion of Saturninus – already re-order the paradigms of internal and external, fitting the bill as 'mixed' conflict.[49]

Valerius too is attempting to come up with a new way of addressing warfare that responds to the distinctly mixed conflict of the Empire after the death of Nero.[50] But it is not just in the creation a new category of war – the mixed conflict – that Valerius' own *bellum mixtum* in Colchis anticipates Tacitus. As Timothy Joseph has recently argued, Tacitus, just like Valerius, also writes the *Histories* as an 'epic successor', incorporating

[48] See Damon 2003: 83–4.
[49] Cf. Joseph 2012: 34–5, who notes the contrast with Josephus' (*BJ* 7.75–88) presentation of the Batavian uprising as *bellum externum* (and for more general reflections on the less pro-Flavian depiction of Tacitus, Keitel 1984; Ash 1999). For speculation about the Saturninus rebellion as repetition of the Batavian uprising under Vitellius, see Joseph 2012: 185–7; for the problems with the account of Timpe 2007, which seeks to separate foreign and domestic in *Histories* 4, see Whitton 2008.
[50] See A. König forthcoming for an important parallel reading of similar strategies dealing with foreign, civil and mixed conflicts in Frontinus' *Strategemata*.

into his own historiography the same kinds of patterns of repetition that fundamentally structure the *Aeneid* and Lucan's *Bellum ciuile*.[51] While Tacitus writes in a spirit emulative of Virgil, as Joseph shows, his approach to conflict is Lucanian: the *Histories* work as a series of destabilising and cumulatively reinforcing civil war conflicts, as the chaos of 68–9 returns again and again.[52] Indeed, Tacitus embeds this cycle of regression in the *Histories* at 1.50, when the *uulgus* reflect on Vitellius' rebellion in the context of the civil wars of the Republic, contrast the survival of the Empire under Caesar and Augustus with the guaranteed disaster at the success of either Vitellius or Otho, and anticipate the fresh horrors of another war to come with Vespasian (*Hist.* 1.50.2–4):

> Nec iam recentia saeuae pacis exempla sed repetita bellorum ciuilium memoria captam totiens suis exercitibus urbem, uastitatem Italiae, direptiones prouinciarum, Pharsaliam Philippos et Perusiam ac Mutinam, nota publicarum cladium nomina, loquebantur . . . Erant qui Vespasianum et arma Orientis augurarentur, et, ut potior utroque Vespasianus, ita bellum aliud atque alias cladis horrebant.

> Nor now did they recollect recent examples of the savage peace, but memories of the civil war: they spoke of Rome, so many times captured by its own armies; the devastation of Italy, the ransacking of the provinces; Pharsalia, Philippi, Perusia and Mutina, infamous names of public disaster . . . There were those who predicted Vespasian and eastern arms, and although Vespasian was preferable to either Otho or Vitellius, still they shuddered at another war, and other disasters.

As Joseph points out, Tacitus here does not simply borrow Lucan's common conflation of Pharsalus and Philippi in the *Bellum ciuile* and recycle the juxtaposition of Perusia and Mutina (something Lucan did at *BC* 1.41, *Perusina fames Mutinaeque labores*): he also repeats the narratological framing of Lucan's depiction of civil war, his *uulgus* recalling in AD 69 wars that go back to 49 BC, in the same way that the conflict of 49 BC is pitted in memory against the civil conflict of the Sullan era in *Bellum ciuile*.[53]

---

[51] Joseph 2012, drawing in particular on the work of Quint 1993, who argues that, whereas in Virgil the Trojan War gets played out again and again, *progressively*, until the Trojans can finally take on a role as victors and war in Italy cedes to the beginning of a new, integrated and coherent Roman personality, Lucan's *Bellum ciuile* instead writes the introduction of the principate as a *regressive* repetition of imperialist power-grabs that start with Romulus and Remus.

[52] On the repetitions of *Histories* see also the fundamental work of Ash 1999.

[53] On Pharsalia as Philippi in Lucan, see *BC* 1.680, 6.582, 7.872, 9.271; Lucan's 'recollection' comes via an unnamed old man (*BC* 2.67). For other negotiations of Lucan in this volume, see especially Marchesi.

Tacitus' approach to conflict, is, then, Lucanian both in its verbal texture and its construction of a narrative of regression, but in some ways distinctly non-Lucanian too. He is not interested in collapsing distinctions between centre and periphery entirely, instead shifting the focus of analysis to a different flashpoint for Roman identity, the categorisation of the rebellious legions, whose revolts against authority are both 'civil' and 'foreign' war. And once again, this approach has already been anticipated within the epic typology of Valerius' *Argonautica*, which positively demands that we read myth as history when the Scythian Ariasmenus, a warrior who has been achieving great destruction on the battlefield with his scythed chariots, is driven to self-destruction by the appearance of Pallas' aegis in a way that synthesises Lucanian aesthetic, barbarian identity, and Roman civil war:[54]

> . . . quam soli uidistis, equi. Pauor occupat ingens
> excussis in terga uiris diramque retorquent
> in socios non sponte luem. Tunc ensibus uncis
> implicat et trepidos lacerat Discordia currus.[55]
> Romanas ueluti saeuissima cum legiones
> Tisiphone regesque mouet, quorum agmina pilis,
> quorum aquilis utrimque micant eademque parentes
> rura colunt, idem lectos ex omnibus agris
> miserat infelix non haec ad proelia Thybris:
> sic modo concordes externaque fata petentes
> Palladii rapuere metus, sic in sua uersi
> funera concurrunt dominis reuocantibus axes.
>
> (*Arg.* 6.398–409)

You, horses, alone saw [Pallas' aegis]. Great terror overwhelms them and, having thrown their drivers out onto their backs the horses unwillingly turn a dreadful carnage upon their comrades. Then Discordia entangles the chariots with their hooked blades and cuts them to bits in their panic. Just as when Tisiphone at her most savage sets in motion Roman legions and their commanders and on both sides the battle lines gleam with javelins and standards: their parents work the same fields, and the same unhappy Tiber had sent these men, picked from the countryside, not for such battles as these. So had Pallas-induced terror seized the Scythians, men just now united and seeking to kill a foreign enemy: thus turned to their own self-destruction, the chariots clashed together as their drivers tried to hold them back.

---

[54] Specifically, this scene draws on *Il.* 18.202–31, where Achilles, adorned with the aegis of Pallas, has such a terrifying effect on the Trojans that twelve of them are killed by their own chariots. On Valerius' Ariasmenus, see Schenk 1999b: 307–8; Baier 2001: 77. On Greek myth and Roman relevance for Statius' *Thebaid*, see Henderson 1991; McNelis 2007.

[55] *Discordia* is the reading of Fucecchi 2006: *discordia* in Ehlers 1980.

In a passage which deconstructs that most Roman of cultural complexes, the concept of *metus hostilis*, Valerius offers a vision of warfare that colludes with the notion that *concordia* comes through *bellum externum* (cf. 6.407 *concordes externaque fata petentes*), only to turn that trope literally in on itself. As has long been recognised, Valerius' bold image of carnage, figured through the clashing legions, bears heavy traces of *Bellum ciuile*'s programme for civil war. And strikingly these echoes, which come from Lucan's proem (cf. especially *BC* 1.3 with *Arg.* 6.405; *BC* 1.8 with *Arg.* 6.390–1), from the most 'paradigmatic' moment for civil war, the Vulteian episode (cf. *BC* 4.463 with *Arg.* 6.406), and from the famous apostrophe to Thessaly at the battle of Pharsalus (*BC* 7.847; cf. *Arg.* 6.403), permeate both simile and narrative.[56]

Earlier critics of Valerius – sensing an unusual moment of historical specificity to cling to – have attempted to pin the simile's conflict down to a specific date, suggesting a dating-range from the civil war between Caesar and Pompey, to the conflict of AD 69, or even the later rebellion of Antonius Saturninus in AD 89.[57] But when read in anticipation of Tacitus, it becomes less necessary to find a specific time-frame for the legionary warfare we see in Valerius: for Tacitus too has recognised the value of writing each civil war as any and every Roman civil war. Rather, in its complex mixture of barbarian and Roman, civil and foreign war, the *Argonautica* offers a confused and at times bewildering battle-narrative that looks forward to the complex configuration of Roman and non-Roman identity explored via the troublingly similar picture of external and internal strife which will be the central theme of Tacitus' *Histories*.

Tacitus, Successor of Valerius?

For a long time, Valerius has been nebulously characterised as a 'Tacitean' author, imbuing his epic with a similar *Leidenspathos* to that of the world-views of the *Histories* and *Annals*. Such readings have been inevitably conditioned by Tacitus' depiction of a claustrophobic and tyrannical Rome, a picture clearly read back into the tyrants who inhabit the first Flavian epic. But this chapter has tried to develop that perspective, using 'reverse reception' not only as a means of confirming what we already

---

[56] See especially Río Torres-Murciano 2006 for more sustained discussion of the role of Lucan here.

[57] Preiswerk 1934, Ussani 1955 and Burck 1981 argue for AD 69; Syme 1929 for the rebellion of Antonius Saturninus; Wijsman 2000 for the Caesar–Pompey conflict. On the simile more generally, see Burck 1971; Cambier 1969: 196–213; McDonald 1970: 47–50; Shreeves 1978: 118–34; Otte 1992: 132–5; McGuire 1997: 58–9.

know about Valerius' *Argonautica* – that it presents oppressive tyranny in a 'Romanising', contemporary way – but also opening out in Valerius' epic a searching, ambivalent but not incoherent attempt at framing heroic epic from a necessarily ambivalent ideological perspective, revealing in *Argonautica*, as in *Agricola*, the complexities a world in which the conditions for traditional heroism do not exist. Tacitus might help us rehabilitate the 'ideological incoherence' of the *Argonautica*, then. But Valerius also provides a helpful interpretative steer for the difficult imperialism of *Histories*, providing – albeit through an epic lens – a clearly new contribution to distinctions between internal and external war which anticipates Tacitus' shifting 'Roman' and 'non-Roman' mixed conflicts of the Flavian period, written through a Lucanian poetics of 'repetitive regression'. Such a literary interaction is, of course, far less secure than Tacitus' relationship with Virgil or Lucan, authors who have left distinct intertextual traces on the historian's work. But the more indirect literary relationship I have argued for is equally important in its own way in terms of 'periodic interaction', highlighting as it does how tendentious the rhetoricisation of a Nervan–Trajanic 'new beginning' free of the Flavian past is. Tacitus, like other Trajanic authors, does all he can to compartmentalise and contain the literary production of the Flavian period. I hope to have shown that to assume – after the lead of Tacitus and Pliny – a conspicuous *absent* literary engagement with Flavian epic is to miss the shared intellectual preoccupations, ideological manoeuvring and even parallel allusive strategies shared between Valerius and Tacitus. More fundamentally, it is to fail to challenge or intervene in the story of 'irrelevance' created by Tacitus and others in the wake of the fall of the Flavian dynasty. 'Literary interaction' with Flavian epic might not be easy to find in Tacitus and other Trajanic writers: but this does not mean that Flavian epic cannot have a meaningful interactive relationship with the authors of the next age. The 'absent presence' of Flavian epic should perhaps be added to the category of 'silenced intertexts' which struggle to find a voice in the literature of the Trajanic age.

CHAPTER 4

Pliny and Martial
Dupes and Non-Dupes in the Early Empire

William Fitzgerald

We could, and often do, think of the Latin literary canon as a series of oppositions: Catullus and Cicero, Virgil and Lucan, Ovid's love poetry and Propertius', Horace's *Satires* and Juvenal's, and so on. Pliny and Martial, the booster and the debunker, might make another such pair, as my title suggests. It is rare that such oppositions are made or discussed without tendentiousness, even polemics. John Bramble's chapter on Juvenal and Martial in the *Cambridge history of classical literature* uses Juvenal as a stick with which to beat Martial, for instance, distinguishing between a satire that bites and one that gives no offence, a game that we all understand.[1] It is also rare that such oppositions don't run into difficulties: overlaps, smudgings and crossovers are common, turning oppositions into exchanges. But these pairings can be useful and stimulating ways of exploring a particular problematic, in the present case the important set of issues that cluster around sincerity, flattery, free speech and self-deception in the early Empire, issues that are particularly acute in the transition from one dynasty to another.

In the nineteenth and for most of the twentieth century the word that was most of all associated with Martial was 'nauseating',[2] and with Pliny, words such as 'gentleman' or 'humane'.[3] Things changed in the sceptical, deconstructive climate of the late twentieth century, in which Pliny's optimism has been unmasked as a defence against anxiety, even a form of denial,

---

[1] Bramble 1982.

[2] Most famously, Byron: 'And then what proper person could be partial / To all those nauseous epigrams of Martial' (*Don Juan* 1.43.7–8), though the passage goes on to mock the practice of expurgating Martial. Also Lord Macaulay: 'I wish he were less nauseous'; Revd. John Booth (after deploring the sexual epigrams): 'whilst his adulation of one of the most execrable of the Roman emperors is perfectly nauseating' (quoted Sullivan and Boyle 1996: xxxiii and xxxv respectively).

[3] Merrill 1903, for long the standard school text of Pliny, has this to say: 'Only his abounding good nature and tenderness of feeling saves him from being an aristocratic snob; only his real devotion to letters saves him from being a windbag. As it is, he is a charming gentleman – only a little too much given to form' (p. xxvi). Méthy 2007: 249 notes that Pliny's 'humanity' has been almost a commonplace. More on Pliny's reputation in Wolff 2003: 9–10.

that cardinal sin of our times,[4] while Martial's quotidian satire has been described as a form of 'getting real', as Victoria Rimell put it.[5] So the balance of sympathy has shifted somewhat from Pliny rather than Martial to Martial rather than Pliny. Above all, we postmoderns want to show that we are not fooled. In fact, the fear of being a dupe drove much of the French thought that dominated the Anglo-American intellectual scene of the second half of the twentieth century. Paul Ricoeur dubbed the line of thought that descends from Nietzsche, Marx and Freud 'the school of suspicion', and what has been called a 'hermeneutics of suspicion' became the default mode of cultural criticism.[6] Under this rubric we can include the principles that we should take nobody, least of all ourselves, at their word, and that the values which an author or culture claims are simply a mask for a particular group's self-interest. It came as something of a surprise, then, when Jacques Lacan proclaimed in 1973 that '*les non-dupes errent*' ('the non-dupes are wrong', with a pun on Lacan's formula for the role of the Oedipal, *le nom du père*). Slavoy Žižek unpacks Lacan's paradox as follows: 'those who do not let themselves be caught in the symbolic deception/fiction and continue to believe their eyes are the ones who err', pointing out that 'we behave AS IF we do not know that they [sc. our neighbours] smell badly, secrete excrement, etc. – a minimum of idealisation, of fetishising disavowal, is the basis of our coexistence' (Žižek's emphasis).[7] But I am not going to use this phrase for anything more than its most basic gesture, which is to question the 'rightness' of being a non-dupe. Pliny, I will argue, has his own version of why it would be wrong to aspire not to be a dupe. Classicists will note that Lacan was anticipated even earlier than Pliny by Gorgias, when he described tragedy as 'a deception in which the deceiver is more justly esteemed than the non-deceiver and the deceived is wiser than the non-deceived' (Plutarch, *On the fame of the Athenians* 348c). There are other analogies for this sentiment from the ancient world, but let us now turn to my subject, Pliny and Martial, the duped and the non-duped, as we might provisionally call them.[8]

---

[4] I am thinking primarily of Hoffer 1999, and particularly the remarks on pp. 227–8, but also Henderson 2002, focusing on what Hoffer (p. 228) calls Pliny's 'conscious and disingenuous attempt to shape his public image'.

[5] Rimell 2008: 2, with stimulating remarks on the coincidence of Martial's rise in critical fortunes in the post-postmodernist era.

[6] Scott-Baumann 2011: 59–77 discusses the term 'hermeneutics of suspicion', arguing that Ricoeur's use of the term has been exaggerated, though the term itself has become an important reference point for discussions of modernist and postmodernist thought.

[7] Žižek 1997.

[8] Another proponent of the value, or necessity, of (self-)deception would be Ovid (*Am.* 1.4.69–70).

Different though these two authors are, they address themselves to sim-ilar issues: how to praise an emperor; how to greet a new regime; how to model the imagined community of readers; how to distinguish between the welcome and unwelcome aspects of one's duties and pursuits; even how to situate oneself in relation to Catullus. They both write books that are self-consciously miscellaneous and varied, and their characteristic genres, letter and epigram respectively, are not dissimilar: if Pliny is not (and is) writing a history (see *Ep.* 1.1), Martial is not (and is) writing an epic, in twelve books. Their differences are manifold, but one that immediately springs to mind is what I have already alluded to: the opposition between Pliny's relentless boosterism and Martial's satirical, debunking spirit. Of course, Martial wrote his panegyrics too, but even there one senses a conspiratorial, winking non-sincerity, which contrasts with Pliny's pained attempts, at least in the *Panegyricus*, to convince his audience that he is sincere.

But let us begin with a more concrete interaction between these two authors. Among Pliny's obituaries of notable contemporaries is the last let-ter of Book 3, in which he announces the death of Martial. After a quick assessment of Martial's talents in the first sentence, distinguishing him for *sal* and *fel*, but also *candor*, Pliny turns to himself.[9] He had paid Martial's travel expenses when the latter left Rome to return to Spain. That much he owed to their *amicitia*, and more especially to the verses that Martial wrote in his honour. Before Pliny quotes the verses (in case we don't have a copy) he remarks that it used to be the custom to reward those who praised cities or individuals with money or honours. Now that we have ceased to do what is praiseworthy, we think that it's *ineptum* to be praised. Having quoted a cropped version of the relevant epigram, in which Martial sends his book to pay a reverent visit to the great Pliny, he asks his correspondent whether it was not right that he should support someone who wrote in this way about him, and grieve for him now that he is dead (*Ep.* 3.21.6):

---

[9] The tone of this letter has been variously interpreted. As Adamik 1976: 63–4 points out, both those who approve and those who disapprove of Martial as a poet cite Pliny's letter as evidence. The most sophisticated analysis of the relation between Martial's epigram and Pliny's letter is that of Henderson 2001, who sees a measure of aggression in Pliny's letter. Henderson notes that the qualities which Pliny approves in Martial, *fel*, *sal* and *candor*, echo the words of Martial 7.25 in which Martial berates another epigrammatist for his epigrams that are without a drop of *sal* or *fel* (salt or gall) in them. He comments: 'The very tussle to incorporate and re-animate the nasty squib [*Epig.* 7.25] in the nice letter, for this special occasion, makes Martial a sounding board for caring Pliny's fellow-feeling: we measure off epistolary manners by their all-encompassing elasticity. It's a mutually implicative conundrum: could Martial write nice? Can Pliny be nasty – when the occasion not suits, but actually *demands*? How best to show that you did (and do) care for Martial . . . if not to turn on him the way he would (and did) *take care of you*?' (p. 32, emphasis original).

Dedit enim mihi quantum potuit, daturus amplius si potuisset. Tametsi quid homini potest dari maius quam gloria et laus et aeternitas? At non erunt aeterna quae scripsit: non erunt fortasse, ille tamen scripsit tamquam essent futura. Vale.

He gave me of his best, and would have given more had he been able, though surely nothing more can be given a man than a tribute which will bring him fame and immortality. You may object that his verses will not be immortal; perhaps not, but he wrote them as though they would be. Farewell.

One suspects, then, that Pliny intimates, at the end of Book 3, that he is giving Martial the immortality that his poetry will not otherwise achieve. The words *tamquam essent futura* end the book. But let us not rest content to prove that we are not dupes, that we are well aware that Pliny is really lording it over Martial.

What did Pliny mean when he said that Martial wrote 'as though what he wrote would be eternal', even though it probably wouldn't? Perhaps we are to take this narrowly with the poem on Pliny: he wrote what he wrote on Pliny as though it was for the ages, expecting it to withstand the test of time. More broadly, he might have meant that Martial took his genre seriously, even though it is only the lowly epigram. Certainly the paradox of an ephemeral form which aspires to immortality is an important aspect of Martial's poetics (*Epig.* 10.2, for instance). Pliny's *tamquam* is worth dwelling on, because it is a characteristic locution of this author.[10] In some ways one could call Martial himself the poet of the *tamquam*: 'as if' in all its shades of meaning, including the modern vernacular (as *if*) for his satirical poems, and something more collusive for his panegyrical poems (let's behave *as if* Domitian were a god). But these senses are not applicable to Pliny's words on Martial.

Perhaps what is most striking about this passage is that Pliny applies to Martial a locution that he particularly associates with himself. In *Epistles* 1.23 Pliny answers a query from a friend of his about whether he should refrain from his activity in the courts for the period in which he is tribune. That depends, Pliny replies, on what you think of the tribunate: an empty shadow and a name without *honos*, or a sacrosanct power, not to be brought to order by anyone, even oneself (*Ep.* 1.23.1). Is it consonant with the dignity of the office, if such there be, to have to obey the rules and indignities of the courts? Not surprisingly, Pliny tells us what he did in these circumstances (*Ep.* 1.23.2):

---

[10] Compare Žižek's use of the phrase 'AS IF' in his explication of Lacan's '*les non-dupes errent*' (quoted above).

> Ipse cum tribunus essem, errauerim fortasse qui me esse aliquid putaui, sed
> tamquam essem abstinui causis agendis.

> When I was tribune myself, I may have been wrong in thinking that I was
> something, but as though I were I refrained from court work.

As with the passage on Martial, concession (*errauerim fortasse*; cf. *at non
erunt aeterna*, *Ep.* 3.21.6) is followed by the *tamquam* (*tamquam essem* (*aliquid*); cf. *tamquam essent aeterna*, *Ep.* 3.21.6). Pliny's 'as though I were something' (*errauerim fortasse qui* me esse aliquid putaui, 1.23.1) alludes unmis-
takably to Catullus *c.* 1.4 (*namque tu solebas* | meas esse aliquid putare
nugas). Catullus is encouraged by the urging of Nepos, who thinks that
Catullus' poems *are* something, and indeed this kind of encouragement
of literary endeavour and publication is central to Pliny's conception of a
mutually supportive literary circle, free from *inuidia*.[11] But, unlike Catullus, Pliny cannot point to any corroboration of his attitude to the tribunate.
Maybe he was wrong, but he persisted in acting out the charade. He made
a leap of faith and stuck to it. As he goes on to say to his correspondent,
you need to decide what persona you are going to adopt and then you must
take it on and carry it through to the bitter end. It is perhaps no coincidence that Pliny uses a Catullan phrase at this moment when he is speaking
about the persistence of a Republican institution.

Pliny's *tamquam* is one of a number of related locutions that are Pliny's
equivalent of Lacan's '*les non-dupes errent*'. For instance, answering complaints that Pliny praises his friends more than they deserve, he responds,
'Who are these people who know my friends better than me?' But then he
retreats to a fall-back position (*Ep.* 7.28.2):

> Qui sunt tamen isti qui amicos meos melius norint? Sed, ut norint, quid
> inuident mihi felicissimo errore? Vt enim non sint tales quales a me praedi-
> cantur, ego tamen beatus quod mihi uidentur.

> But who are these people who know my friends better than I do myself? And,
> even if they do, why begrudge me happiness in my delusion? My friends may
> not be all that I proclaim them to be, but I am lucky to think them so.

Compare *errore* here to *errauerim fortasse* in *Epistles* 1.23.2. Pliny's *error* is
felicissimus; he is *beatus* because he fools himself (*quod mihi uidentur*). One
notices the strategic importance of Pliny's bugbear *inuidia* (*quid inuident*

---

[11] Morello 2007; Hoffer 1999: 10–11.

mihi?), insinuating the reprehensible emotional roots of this criticism of Pliny: his felicity irks them.[12]

Error crops up again in an analogous formulation when Pliny is boasting about the reception of his hendecasyllables (*Ep.* 7.4.10):

> Sed quid ego tam gloriose? Quamquam poetis furere concessum est. Et tamen non de meo sed de aliorum iudicio loquor. Qui siue iudicant siue errant, me delectat. Vnum precor, ut posteri quoque aut errent similiter aut iudicent.

> But I must not boast (even though poets are allowed to talk wildly!), even if it is not my opinion I am quoting but other people's, which pleases me whether they are right or wrong. I only pray that posterity will be right or wrong in the same way.

The same hope, or confidence, that others will echo the (possibly misleading) reaction of some is expressed when Pliny reports the impressive attentiveness of the audience to his recitation of the *Panegyricus*, in which the plainest passages were particularly appreciated (*Ep.* 3.18.9):

> Memini quidem me non multis recitasse quod omnibus scripsi, nihilo minus tamen, *tamquam* sit eadem omnium futura sententia, hac seueritate aurium laetor.

> I am not forgetting that I recited to a few what I wrote for all, but nevertheless I rejoice in their chaste ears as if the judgment of all will be the same.

Even closer to the logic of Pliny's *tamquam* in *Epistles* 1.23 is a rather different, and very striking, sentence in *Epistles* 1.3, again rounding off a letter, where Pliny tells his addressee that if he thinks highly of himself others will too. But this is how he puts it:

> Tu modo enitere ut tibi sis tanti, quanti uideberis aliis si tibi fueris. (*Ep.* 1.3.5)

> See to it only that you have as much value in your own eyes as you will in those of others if you do in your own.

---

[12] When putting on display the quality of his casual intercourse with friends Pliny sometimes adopts a tone of mock resentment at an imagined or exaggerated slight (e.g. *Ep.* 1.15). In *Ep.* 2.2 he makes a joking use of the *tamquam* motif, acknowledging that he may be in the wrong, but claiming the right to act 'as though' he were justified in being very angry. Love, he says, can be cruel, headstrong or petulant, making a mountain out of a molehill (here Pliny turns to the Greek *mikraitios*). But his grudge really is a big one, he insists, though perhaps not just. Nevertheless, he reserves the right to be angry *as though* it were no less just than great (*Haec tamen causa magna est, nescio an iusta; sed ego, tamquam non minus iusta quam magna sit, grauiter irascor, Ep.* 2.2.1). Here the characteristic acknowledgement that his behaviour may not be justified is used to *criticise* a friend.

Caninius is to imagine how others will value him in order to value himself rightly, an interesting bootstrap operation which circles back on itself to emphasise that Caninius' self-valuation is a pure leap of faith with no prior external vindication (contrast Catullus' *meas esse aliquid putasti nugas*). The measure of Caninius' self-respect is to be what others *will* think of him, but only if he thinks highly of himself. Stanley Hoffer (1999: 43–4) refers to this strategy as the 'internalised friendly cycle of the self'. To put it in the terms of the twelve-step movement, we might say 'Fake it 'til you make it.' The whole process is suspended in air, or rather, concrete results will follow on mere imaginings: 'value yourself *as though* others valued you, which they will if you value yourself'.

So, to enunciate Pliny's implied principle: a necessary self-belief may require self-deception, or at least taking at face value what may not have been so meant. In some cases one may need to believe about oneself what has no external warrant, but fiction, even lies, may have real and beneficial results, as Pliny intimates. Pliny makes the same point when he declares that he is encouraged to publish something because the books he has already published are selling well (*Ep.* 1.2.6):

> Edendum autem ex pluribus causis, maxime quod libelli quos emisimus dicuntur in manibus esse, quamuis iam gratiam nouitatis exuerint; nisi tamen auribus nostris bibliopolae blandiuntur. Sed sane blandiantur, dum per hoc mendacium nobis studia nostra commendent.

> But I want to publish for several reasons, and above all because the books which I have already sent out into the world are still said to find readers, although they have lost the charm of novelty. Of course, the booksellers may be flattering me; well, let them, as long as their deception makes me think well of my own work.

Mendacium is a strong word, but it serves a crucial purpose: to make Pliny think well of his own work. He ends this letter with the words *dum . . . nobis studia nostra commendent*, a phrase which is equivalent to the words similarly stressed by their terminal position in *Epistles* 1.3, *si tibi fueris*. Pliny does not use *mendacium* in this context again, but *blandior* (*sed sane blandiantur*), a gentler word, does recur. In *Epistles* 8.3 Pliny expresses gratification that his addressee, Sparsus, liked the book he sent him. So does another very learned individual, he adds, leaving the anonymity of this judge to work on our imaginations (*Ep.* 8.3.2):

> Quo magis adducor ut neutrum falli putem, quia non est credibile utrumque falli, et quia tamen blandior mihi.

> This [sc. the fact that another learned individual agrees] leads me to think that neither of them is wrong, because it is scarcely credible that both of them are wrong, and because anyway I flatter myself.

Walsh (2006: 349) reads *etsi tamen* for *quia tamen* (i.e. 'even if I flatter myself' for 'and because I flatter myself'), which brings the passage into closer alignment with the end of *Epistles* 1.2, but either way Pliny here accepts that he may be flattering himself. He then admits that he always wants his latest work to be thought his best, so he is sending Sparsus a recent speech. But perhaps he has awakened too high an expectation, and Sparsus will be disappointed. He ends the letter with the words,

> Vereor ne destituat oratio mea in manus sumpta. Interim tamen tamquam placituram (et fortasse placebit) exspecta. Vale. (*Ep.* 8.3.3)

> I am afraid that the speech may disappoint when you take it up. But meanwhile wait for it as though you will like it (and perhaps you will). Farewell.

It is not clear whether Pliny is saying that Sparsus' expectation that he will approve (*tamquam placituram*) will be the cause of his approval or just that he may actually like the speech. But the familiar *tamquam* suggests that we are expected to entertain the former possibility, and that the logic of the endings of *Epistles* 1.2 and 1.3 is now being applied beyond the friendly circle of the self.

With flattery (*blandiuntur*) we touch on the territory of imperial panegyric, but it is not only the word *blandiuntur* that makes the connection, it is also the verb *commendent*, as we shall see. Before we turn to imperial panegyric we should consider the role of the 'as if' in imperial ideology more broadly. I have already cited above Pliny's determination, as tribune, to act 'as if' (*tamquam*) this republican magistracy still meant something. The same word crops up in a similar context in the *Panegyricus*, where Pliny praises Trajan for participating fully in his election to the consulship without expressing the contempt for the *appearance* of a free state (*liberae ciuitatis simulatio*, *Pan.* 63.5) that the behaviour of other emperors had evinced. Earlier emperors evidently thought that they would cease to be *principes* if they did anything *as* senators (*ut sibi uiderentur principes esse desinere si quid facerent* tamquam *senatores*, *Pan.* 63.6). But it is not only the machinery of elections and the continuance of republican magistracies, in short the simulation of a free state, that makes the early Empire the realm of the 'as if'. One could also point to legal fictions such as the *ius trium liberorum*, a privilege granted by the emperors which involved treating the recipient *as if* he were the father of three children, with all the legal privileges which that brought. Martial has a good deal of fun with this fiction.[13] Like Martial, Pliny does not directly draw attention to the fiction of the *ius*. However, in a passage in which he boasts that the *princeps* granted his plea for the *ius* on behalf of a friend he does use his favourite *tamquam* (*Ep.* 2.13.9):

> quod [sc. ius trium liberorum] quamquam parce et cum delectu daret, mihi tamen *tamquam* eligeret indulsit.

> Though he grants it [the 'right of three children'] sparingly and with discrimination, he indulged me as though he had made a free choice.

There are a number of interesting features of this particular usage. First, the *princeps* himself has been drawn into the circle of those who avail themselves of the 'as if'. The language, too, is striking, because Pliny has created a nexus of words related by sound in order to set off his *tamquam*, which balances *quamquam* and is immediately preceded by *tamen*: the aura of exceptionality is felt in the sonic texture of the sentence. Finally, this aura is well suited to the matter in question, which is the *ius trium liberorum*.

The *ius* brings us to a parallel use of *tamquam* that would have been well known to Pliny, and that is in the legal sphere. An important aspect of Roman legal practice was the principle of *fictio*, whereby a situation was considered to fall under a law for which it was not originally intended, on the principle that the situation amounted to the same thing as that for which the law was intended. The formula of *emancipatio*, by which a person's status was changed, for instance, involved a fictive 'sale' of the person who was being emancipated. Adoption, too, involved treating the person adopted 'as though' he were a son born from the same mother and father. Aulus Gellius gives us the formula as follows *Velitis, iubeatis, ut L. Valerius L. Titio tam iure legeque filius siet,* quam *si ex eo patre matreque familias natus esset* ('May you wish and command that L. Valerius be son to L. Titius in right and law as much as if he had been born from that father and mother', *Noctes Atticae* 5.19.9).[14]

Martial somewhat dangerously aligns the legal fiction of the *ius* to the extravagant flattery of imperial panegyric when he uses the verb *credo* in

---

[13] Martial 8.31 and 2.91–3 with Fitzgerald 2007: 136–8.

[14] Thanks to Professor Jill Harries for pointing out the relevance of *fictio* to Pliny's *tamquam*. See also Gaius *Inst.* 4.32–8 and, for a succinct introduction with bibliography, G. Schiemann in *Der neue Pauly*, s.v. *fictio*.

both connections in *Epigrams* 2.91: greeting Domitian as the guarantor of *salus*, through whose own preservation we come to believe that there are gods (*sospite quo magnos* credimus *esse deos*, 2.91.2) he asks the emperor to grant him the *ius trium liberorum*. But he phrases it so as to echo the opening lines (*Epig.* 2.91.5–6):

> quod fortuna uetat fieri, permitte uideri,
>   natorum genitor *credar* ut esse trium.

> let me seem what fortune forbids me to be, so I can be believed to be the father of three sons.

We will return to Martial's *credar* later, after we have confronted imperial panegyric more directly.

Can we apply the logic of Pliny's *tamquam* to imperial panegyric? On the face of it, certainly not. Shadi Bartsch's influential chapter on the *Panegyricus* (1994: 148–87) stressed Pliny's tortured attempts to convince (the emperor? his audience? himself?) that *this* time the flattery is true; in other words, it is not flattery. But Susanna Morton Braund (1998) has drawn our attention to panegyric's affinities with protreptic. Praise of the emperor becomes a form of manipulation: the emperor is presented with the virtues which he is expected to live up to ('behave as though these attributes were yours'). Gregory Hutchinson (2011: 137) has recently argued that Pliny's *Panegyricus* represents a version of the political sublime, referring both to the dominant style of the *Panegyricus* and to its content: 'The overall sublimity of impact is not a matter of endless straining for extremes, but a convergence of Trajan's unstrained nobility and Pliny's intelligent and unobvious praise.' The sublime, I would suggest, is a helpful concept here for another reason, namely because it aligns with a typical Plinian strategy: Longinus stresses that in confronting the sublime our soul is uplifted and filled with joy and pride, *as though* it had created what it has heard (*Subl.* 7.3 ὡς αὐτὴ γεννήσασα ὅπερ ἤκουσεν). This too might be the strategy of panegyric: not so much to flatter the addressee by showering him with virtues, as to create, for all listeners, the opportunity to confront something great that they can believe they have brought into being, by virtue of the fact that they are uplifted in the contemplation of it. The illusion is justified by its result. Sublime panegyric, then, doesn't so much reflect or describe a reality as produce one. Since we are by nature disposed to be uplifted by the sublime, we are filled with joy and pride *as though* we had brought it into being. It is an illusion, of course, but one which confirms our affinity with what is great and so, presumably, gives us the confidence to *be* great.

The circularity of this reasoning is not unlike the readiness to dupe himself into confidence which features so prominently in Pliny's letters, and in fact he does relate this strategy to the purpose of imperial panegyric, in a letter in which he defends his decision to publish his speech (*Ep.* 3.18). Here he echoes his statement that the flattery of the booksellers is fine provided it commends his *studia* to him (*dum per hoc mendacium nobis studia nostra commendarentur*, *Ep.* 1.2.6), but applies it to his own address to the emperor (*Ep.* 3.18.2):

> bono ciui conuenientissimum credidi eadem spatiosius et uberius uolumine amplecti, primum *ut imperatori nostro uirtutes suae ueris laudibus commendarentur*, deinde ut futuri principes non quasi a magistro sed tamen sub exemplo monerentur qua potissimum uia possent ad eandem gloriam niti.

> I thought it my proper duty as a loyal citizen to give the same subject a fuller and more elaborate treatment in a written version. I hope in the first place *to encourage our emperor in his virtues by a sincere tribute*, and, secondly, to show his successors what path to follow to win the same renown, not by offering instruction but by setting his example before them.

One of Pliny's purposes in the *Panegyricus*, then, was to give the emperor confidence to 'be himself' (as prescribed by Pliny).[15] Of course, Pliny insists that the praises are true. One suspects that *ueris laudibus* here protests against the *mendacium* and *blanditiae* that did the job perfectly well in the case of the booksellers (*Ep.* 1.2.6). But having borrowed from his own experience the notion that one needs to have one's virtues commended to oneself, and applied it to imperial panegyric, Pliny then raises anxieties about the sincerity of praise, ubiquitous in the *Panegyricus*, and applies them to what people think of *him*. He insists that invitees came to his recitation of the *Panegyricus* willingly, and in spite of the fact that he did not send them letters of invitation, but simply asked them to come 'if they had time and if it was convenient' (though, as he acknowledges, it's never convenient, and people are never free at Rome).[16] Pliny is anxious to prove here that the attendance of the audience at his reading of the *Panegyricus* was no mere lip service. They came and they asked for more! So we have a chiasmus: praise of the emperor serves the same purpose for the emperor as the flattery of the booksellers did for Pliny the author (it commends

---

[15] See also *Ep.* 1.8, about a speech in which Pliny praises his own munificence, self-praise which he justifies as a means of committing himself to his own generosity, eliminating any potential regret in a noble contempt for money.

[16] In giving his friends an 'out', Pliny also deprived them of the chance to perform an *officium*!

studia/uirtutes to the praised/flattered), while the flattering attendance of his friends at this recital of the *Panegyricus* is subjected to the same straining after a non-compelled truth as we see in the *Panegyricus* itself. Here, in connection with his recitation of the *Panegyricus* he does not say 'never mind if they really wanted to come or simply felt that they had to, their attendance was encouraging', but 'they really *did* want to come'. It is as though a certain strain of the *Panegyricus* has infected Pliny's friendly circle of the self.

I have said at the beginning of this chapter that issues of sincerity and freedom of speech were particularly acute at the beginning of new regimes. Tacitus and Pliny both coordinate the moment of transition between regimes with the beginning of an oeuvre. 'Now at last we can speak', as Tacitus puts it in the *Agricola* (*nunc demum redit animus*, 3.1), while Pliny associates the arrival of the new regime with the flourishing of letters (*Si quando urbs nostra liberalibus studiis floruit, nunc maxime floret, Ep.* 1.10.1; cf. 1.13.1 and 3.18.5). The circle of ungrudging, mutually supporting and admiring friends which Pliny builds up around the literary activity that has mushroomed at Nerva's accession is, as Hoffer (1999: 5–10) has shown, an image of a right-functioning polity. Pliny, like Tacitus, is able to coordinate the beginning of an oeuvre with the inauguration of a new regime. Martial can do this once, for the arrival of the Flavians. But when he welcomes a new imperial regime for the second time he must find a way to give a fresh inflection to a genre that has been compromised by its celebration of the last of the Flavians.[17]

Martial's equivalent of the *Panegyricus* is the *Liber spectaculorum* written to celebrate the opening of the Flavian Amphitheatre, and to usher in a new dynasty. Here too, as with the *Panegyricus*, the denigration of the final member of the last dynasty is an important factor in the praise (*Sp.* 2). But more important in this book is the close connection between the spectacles displayed in the arena and the power and virtues of the emperor. Martial's acclaim of the emperor is aligned with the need of an audience to suspend its disbelief, to believe in an illusion. The arena provides a series of wonders testifying to the divinity of an emperor who oversees it all. It is the site of illusion, in which the pleasures of the audience depend on a certain form of belief. Lacan's '*les non-dupes errent*' might apply here in the spirit of Gorgias' remark that tragedy is 'a deception in which the

---

[17] As though to mark this problem, in the seventeenth century a squib on Domitian, attributed to Martial by the scholiast to Juvenal *Sat.* 4.38, was appended to the *Liber spectaculorum*: *Flavia gens, quantum tibi tertius abstulit heres! | Paene fuit tanti non habuisse duos* (see Coleman 2006: xx–xxi).

deceiver is more justly esteemed than the non-deceiver, and the deceived is wiser than the non-deceived'. In Martial's *Liber spectaculorum* forms of the verb *credo* recur throughout, in protestations which are neither sincere nor insincere, in the same way as Coleridge's 'willing suspension of disbelief' (*Biographia literaria*)[18] is neither deluded nor open-eyed. 'Believe the wonders of myth,' says Martial, 'because something more wonderful has happened in the arena' (*Sp.* 14.8; 6.1); 'believe that Caesar possesses *numen*, because a beast hunted in the arena stopped at his feet' (*Sp.* 33.7–8). Perhaps most significantly, when a chorus of water-dancers mimed rowing in a boat, the spectacle elicits the cry *credidimus remum credidimusque ratem* ('we believed the oar, we believed the boat', *Sp.* 30.4). It is very difficult to say whether these elations are aesthetic or political, or how one could distinguish one from the other, and this is no small part of their ideological force. But here, as in the case of Pliny's *tamquams*, there is a pay-off to the self-deception acknowledged by the cry of *'credidimus'*. If for Pliny (unwarranted) belief may be a prerequisite for making it so, rather than just a device for hiding the ugly truth from ourselves, for Martial the belief is enough of a thrill in itself.

After the Flavian dynasty came to an end, greeting the new emperor was not such an easy proposition for Martial. The *Liber spectaculorum* had managed to align the epigram genre with a symbolic event in the institution of the Flavian dynasty, namely the inauguration of the amphitheatre. Epigram, Martial implicitly claims, is the right genre to celebrate such an event. But now that he has written ten books of epigrams, many of them in praise of an emperor who brought his dynasty to a shameful close, something must be done to make a fresh start, to give the genre a new inflection. In the *Panegyricus*, Pliny says that all citizens must make an effort to avoid saying of this emperor what they would have said of another (*Pan.* 2.1): since things are different now, we must say different things. Martial makes the same gesture when, in *Epigrams* 10, he tells *Blanditiae* to go away because they are not needed now:

> Frustra, Blanditiae, uenitis ad me
> attritis miserabiles labellis:
> dicturus dominum deumque non sum.
> Iam non est locus hac in urbe uobis;
> ad Parthos procul ite pilleatos
> et turpes humilesque supplicesque
> pictorum sola basiate regum.

---

[18] Coleridge 1817, ch. 14.

Non est hic dominus sed imperator,
sed iustissimus omnium senator,
per quem de Stygia domo reducta est
siccis rustica Veritas capillis.
Hoc sub principe, si sapis, caueto
uerbis, Roma, prioribus loquaris.

(Epig. 10.72)

Flatteries, you come to me in vain, you poor creatures with your worn-down lips. I am not about to speak of 'Lord and God'. There is no place for you any more in this city. Go away to turbaned Parthians and kiss the soles of gaudy monarchs – base, abject suppliants. There is no lord here, but a commander-in-chief and the most just of all senators, through whom rustic dry-haired Truth has been brought back from the house of Styx. Under this ruler, Rome, beware, if you are wise, of talking the language of earlier days. (trans. Shackleton Bailey 1993, slightly modified)

Like Pliny in the *Panegyricus*, Martial refuses to use the old expressions (*dominus et deus*, etc.) under the new emperor, and, like Pliny, he points to the good emperor's ability to be both senator and *princeps*. Unsophisticated truth (*rustica Veritas*) is instead to be dragged from her Stygian home. As in the *Panegyricus*, it is no longer appropriate to say what was said under the previous emperor (cf. *Pan.* 2.2: *Quare abeant et recedant uoces illae quas metus exprimebat*). What to say, then? Martial's solution is ingenious. In the fifth book he had associated the prominence of Domitian in that book with its respectful eschewing of sexual material. Now he associates the beginning of Nerva's reign with the return of Saturnalian freedom and the licence to use the obscenity that is appropriate to the genre. At last, the epigram is free to be itself! In *Epigrams* 8.1, under Domitian, he had declared, 'Away, naked Venus, this is not your book. Come to me instead, the emperor's own Pallas' (*Nuda recede Venus: non est tuus iste libellus; tu mihi, tu Pallas Caesariana, ueni*). Now he says:

Clamant ecce mei 'Io Saturnalia' uersus:
    et licet et sub te praeside, Nerua, libet.
Lectores tetrici salebrosum ediscite Santram:
    nil mihi uobiscum est: iste liber meus est.

(Epig. 11.2.5–8)

Look, my verses shout 'Hurrah for the Saturnalia!' Under your rule, Nerva, it's allowed, and it's our pleasure. You austere readers learn jerky Santra by heart. I am not concerned with you. This book is mine. (trans. Shackleton Bailey 1993)

Martial opportunistically uses the same motif he had used to express the book's deference to Domitian (obscenity), but from a different angle.[19] Obscenity is cast as uncensored straight-speaking, in good plain Latin. Book 11 several times makes the association of obscenity with good emperors/kings: Numa, who calls a *mentula* a *mentula* in *Epigrams* 11.15.10 and Augustus, whose obscene epigram against Fulvia is quoted in *Epigrams* 11.20, with the comment that Augustus, who knew how to speak *Romana simplicitate*, authorises Martial's *lepidos libellos*.

If Martial and Pliny approach each other as imperial panegyrists, my original polarity pitted them as opposites in a different area. Where Pliny insists on the value and utility of believing the best, however unwarranted it may be, Martial delights (us) in suspecting the worst. Virtue is to be unmasked as vice in disguise; the role of the epigrammatist is *not* to take anything at face value. Occasionally the two strains, imperial panegyric and satirical unmasking, converge. During Domitian's reign Martial celebrates the emperor's revival of Augustus' *lex Iulia de adulteriis coercendis*, which imposed penalties on adultery. Now, Martial exclaims, *Pudicitia* has been ordered into the Roman home; but the renewed law is scarcely ten months old and Telesilla has 'married' (*nubit, Epig.* 6.7.4–5) ten times. This is not marriage, it is legitimised adultery: *straightforward* adultery would be less offensive (*offendor moecha simpliciore minus*, 6). In *Epigrams* 11.7, a poem welcoming the new emperor to the detriment of Domitian, Martial gives us an example of an *adultera simplex*. We notice that *simplicitas* is the quality ascribed to Augustus' 'straight-speaking' obscenity in *Epigrams* 11.20, and indeed in *Epigrams* 11.7 our *moecha simplicior* does not shrink from a four-letter word:

> Iam certe stupido non dices, Paula, marito,
>   ad moechum quotiens longius ire uoles,
> 'Caesar in Albanum iussit me mane uenire,
>   Caesar Circeios.' Iam stropha talis abit.
> Penelopae licet esse tibi sub principe Nerua:
>   sed prohibet scabies ingeniumque uetus.
> Infelix, quid ages? Aegram simulabis amicam?
>   Haerebit dominae uir comes ipse suae,
> ibit et ad fratrem tecum matremque patremque.
>   Quas igitur fraudes ingeniosa paras?
> Diceret hystericam se forsitan altera moecha
>   in Sinuessano uelle sedere lacu.

---

[19] Lorenz 2002: 217–19.

Quanto tu melius, quotiens placet ire fututum,
  quae uerum mauis dicere, Paula, uiro!

(Epig. 11.7)

Now at least, Paula, you will not be saying to your dupe of a husband, whenever you want to go to a lover at a distance: 'Caesar has commanded me to
go to Alba tomorrow morning. Caesar has commanded me to go to Circeii.'
The day for such a ruse has gone by. Under Nerva's rule you can be Penelope, but your itch, your old bent, won't let you. What will you do, wretched
woman? Pretend a sick friend? Your husband himself will stick close to his
lady and accompany you to brother or mother or father. So, my clever one,
what fraud are you hatching? Perhaps another of your kind might say she
was hysterical and wanted to sit in the waters of Sinuessa. How much better you manage it, Paula! Whenever you have a mind to go for a fuck, you
prefer to tell your husband the truth. (trans. Shackleton Bailey 1993, slightly
modified)

Just as Pliny gives us the impression of a society working as it should,
immune to *inuidia*, as a reflection of the emperor's beneficent rule, so in
this epigram Martial notes how imperial morals 'trickle down' or, more
accurately, have a domino effect.[20] The chaste Nerva lets his female subjects be veritable Penelopes. So far, so good – Nerva is no Domitian, and
no husband is forced to collude with his wife's adultery. But Martial's epigram is as much concerned with free speech and truth as it is with the
emperor's sexual mores. Under Domitian, the adulterer had an excuse, or
cover, for her liaisons, and the cuckold could persuade himself that he had
no choice but to connive. Both could profess to act under compulsion,
and the disgraceful truth needed neither to be spoken nor heard. Now that
excuse is gone. The ending of this epigram has disturbed some commentators as undermining its panegyrical beginning. Lorenz (2002: 214) claims
that the emperor theme leaves the epigram at line 6, and Kay (1985: 81)
that Paula has always been straight-speaking, not that she changes under
Nerva.[21] Both commentators try to detach the ending from the welcoming
of the new regime. But I would place this poem among those others in this

---

[20] Compare 11.4.8 *moribus hic uiuat principis, ille suis*, a final line which contrasts interestingly with
the final line of 11.15, *mores non habet hic meos libellus*.

[21] Kay: 'It would have been a good excuse, just as feigning a sick friend etc., but Paula needs no excuse.'
Against this one can note that Martial specifically states that feigning a sick friend or a visit to father,
mother or brother won't work because her husband will accompany her (7–10). Only the excuse
of the emperor's summons would be infallible. It is true that Martial conjures up another excuse
that a lesser adulterer might make, namely the need for a curative bath in the waters of Sinuessa
(11–12). This pretext gives away (or conceals) the truth in a pun, for the woman who claims that,
as a hysteric, she needs to 'sit' (*sedere*) in the lake in Sinuessa also says that she wants to 'prostitute
herself' there (*sedere*, cf. Mart. 2.17.1 and 6.66.2; *OLD* 1c). Paula prefers obscenity to *double entendre*.

book that concern the return of straight-speaking under the new emperor, exemplified by the epigram's return to its native obscenity. Paula's *ingenium uetus* may be left over from the days of Domitian, but the obscenity with which it is described is consonant with the motif with which Martial's epigrammatic genre greets the accession of Nerva. Martial insists here on the value of truth (*uerum*) and transparency, which he claims for his genre.[22] Paula no longer has the motive, or indeed possibility, to mask her *ingenium uetus* ('old bent', 6) in concocting clever (*ingeniosa*, 10) pretexts, though she cannot shake off that *ingenium*. Playing off these two senses of *ingenium*, Martial suggests that it is her *ingenium uetus* that speaks in Paula's guilelessly ingenuous announcement to her husband. It is now Martial who is *ingeniosus* in the sense of the word that no longer applies to Paula, for the art of this epigram's denouement is exquisite. Obscenity is carefully *not* featured as the punchline, but tucked away in an adverbial clause in the penultimate line (*quotiens placet ire fututum*). The true punchline, Paula's own words '*placet ire fututum*', is not expressed at all. Under Martial's ostensible praise for Paula's laudable preference for the truth, expressed abstractly in the most innocuous of words, we readers supply the monstrous declaration that Paula makes to her husband. It consists in the same words that we have read in the previous line, now no longer the satirist's denunciation of Paula but her sovereign declaration of will. The same impersonal verb *placet*, which in the penultimate line implied the third person ('whenever *she* wants to go for a fuck') now expresses the first-person will of Paula ('*I* want to go for a fuck'). In the imperial context, Paula's imagined words (*placet ire fututum*) could be taken either as speaking truth to power, or as the reverse, an imperious gesture in which Paula's will is expressed with the conventional *sic placitum* of the tyrant (*quotiens placet ire fututum*).[23] It is as though two very different possibilities of straight-speaking, distributed across roles at opposite ends of the imperial scenario (unabashed subject and unrestrained tyrant), have been condensed into the words we must conjure up for Paula to speak to her husband.

If Pliny champions the beneficial effects of taking lies and flatteries at face value, and Martial (for the most part) plays happily with the emptiness of words and titles, and the deceptiveness of our pretensions to virtue, in this epigram Martial conjures up a monstrous phantom of spade-calling which is tied, in more than one way, to the phenomenon of imperial power.

[22] In the preface to his first book, Martial makes a programmatic contrast between a negatively valorised *ingeniosus* and a positively valued *ueritas* (*lasciuam uerborum ueritatem*, 1.*pr.*)

[23] Enhanced by the fact that Paula is the subject of the verb *futuo*, a position usually reserved for men, or for 'manly' Lesbians (Adams 1982: 121–2).

Just how much straight-speaking do we want? What happens when the bare truth is not only allowed, but cannot be avoided? Paula articulates the truth, partly because there's nowhere to hide under Nerva. No doubt her husband would have preferred to remain a dupe!

***

Martial's cynical versions of the advantages of being a dupe contrast sharply with Pliny's earnest quest for confidence. I have encouraged them to interact with each other not because I think that they are consciously engaged in a dialogue, but because the political circumstances which they share produce different but related responses in these two writers separated by genre, status and temperament. For us, swimming in a cultural and political environment permeated by non-sincerity of various kinds, it is appropriate to be interested in the full range of ways to manage such an environment, and to encourage them to speak to one another. When we address literary interactions, even in ancient Rome, we should include ourselves as interested parties.

CHAPTER 5

Paradoxography and Marvels in Post-Domitianic Literature
'An Extraordinary Affair, Even in the Hearing!'

Rhiannon Ash

Introduction

This chapter takes as its focal point for engaging with post-Domitianic literature the representation of marvels in the Roman world – an extraordinarily pervasive and enduring phenomenon.[1] Whether we think of Cybele transforming the Trojan ships into nymphs (Virg. *Aen.* 9.77–122) or Claudius' hippocentaur, brought from Egypt and preserved in honey (Plin. *NH* 7.35), *mirabilia* pepper and transcend all individual genres, captivating readers and viewers.[2] Yet while the Virgilian example exists solely in the text of the *Aeneid*, some marvels have an extratextual existence in the real world, as with the Claudian hippocentaur. Importantly, Pliny says that he saw this for himself (*uidimus*), and so his readers too could themselves potentially track down and view this strange creature. Indeed, interesting items given as gifts to emperors were often put on public display: 'Even on days when there were no games, whenever anything unusual and worth seeing (*quid inusitatum dignumque cognitu*) was brought to him [sc. Augustus], he would make a special display of it wherever he could: for example, a rhinoceros in the Saepta, a tiger on stage, a snake fifty cubits long in the Comitium' (Suet. *Aug.* 43.4, trans. Wardle). This practice (dating back to the republic) was an excellent way for emperors to demonstrate Rome's centripetal pull on her global empire and to advertise the diverse resources under her control.[3]

---

[1] Studies of ancient marvels and paradoxography include Pavlovskis 1973; Schepens and Delcroix 1996; Atherton 1998; Stramaglia 1999; Hardie 2009. Williams 2011 is a fascinating study of the phenomenon in the early modern period. The quotation in my title is from Dio 76.8.1.

[2] On the Virgilian example (modelled on Hom. *Od.* 13.125–64 and imitated by Ov. *Met.* 14.530–65), see Fantham 1990; Hardie 1994: 88–97. On the Plinian example, see Beagon 2005: 172.

[3] Wardle 2014: 329–30 notes precedents of L. Metellus exhibiting elephants in the Circus Maximus in 251 BC (Plin. *NH* 8.16), Pompey displaying the first rhinoceros in Rome in 55 BC (Plin. *NH* 8.71), and a snakeskin (120 feet long) sent to Rome after the creature was slaughtered by Regulus' troops in 256 BC (Val. Max. 1.8.*ext*.19; Sen. *Ep.* 82.24; Plin. *NH* 8.37; Sil. *Pun.* 6.140–293; Gell. 7.3, citing the *Histories* of Aelius Tubero; Livy also described it in Book 18).

One crucial consequence of authors recording marvels is the potential for reflecting and pinpointing shifting boundaries within broader cultural attitudes outside the texts. So, if an object or phenomenon is classed as *mirabile*, that categorisation itself must involve measurement against the yardstick of what is perceived as normal. We can thus gain insight into where the boundary between 'normal' and 'abnormal' is situated – and that can and does change over time. So, when Tacitus describes Nero's Golden House, in which jewels and gold were not so much a source of wonder, he glosses such features as *solita pridem et luxu uolgata*, 'items long familiar and made trite by luxurious living' (*Annals* 15.42.1). Nero must scale new heights to build a truly wondrous house. To consider such phenomena diachronically involves questions about different authors' views of continuity and discontinuity and about the wider collective sense of order and disorder which that perception reflects. For this reason, the category of 'marvels' is a particularly rich area to examine in this post-Domitianic Roman world, as a theme that can help chart developments in social, cultural, political and intellectual discourses across the period. What one era designates as abnormal can subsequently become normal and all too familiar, whether through better scientific understanding of causes or through jaded consumers needing increasingly extreme spectacles to provoke wonder – the fundamental yardstick of whether something is properly *mirabile*. As Hardie observes, paradox and the marvellous are potentially a compelling way of 'stimulating jaded palates', whatever the era.[4] One common feature of *mirabilia* (regardless of the timeframe) is that this sense of wonder is generally triggered through the visual sphere, whether in person, or vicariously through mediating authors using their literary skills to paint a picture which makes readers feel as if they are present.

Marvels are also richly expressive in terms of the 'literary interactions' which are the focus of this volume. I will argue that our authors' narrative techniques, when considered closely, show a pattern of post-Domitianic marvels sometimes being put back into their boxes and relocated to 'safe' zones (whether geographically or generically), or alternatively sometimes being released from the emperor's forceful domination and control. We can perhaps see reflections here of cautious collective optimism after Domitian's assassination in 96 (although this chapter will nonetheless be wary of underestimating differences between the Trajanic and Hadrianic eras and seeking purely political explanations – generally only one part of a complex range of factors in play when analysing post-Domitianic texts). This

---

[4] Hardie 2009: 2.

phenomenon involves authors either narrating safe and enjoyable domestic marvels in Italy, or displaying more shocking marvels pointedly moved
back to the imperial margins or to areas traditionally associated with the
bizarre, primarily Egypt, the topsy-turvy realm of reversal and the supreme
'land of inversion'.[5] Various overlaps and differences between how Domitianic and post-Domitianic authors present marvels also raise questions
about the nature of their awareness of and engagement with each other.
This is not so much a nexus linked by direct intertextuality, but authors
who move along similar intellectual trajectories as they reflect on the emerging post-Domitianic world around them.[6]

This chapter will offer close readings of three different authors to examine this general phenomenon in action. First I will take up a Flavian text
as a yardstick for my post-Domitianic examples. By considering how the
epigrams of Martial's *Liber spectaculorum* seek to inscribe the emperor as
the single source of uplifting marvels in the hierarchical setting of the
amphitheatre, I will argue that, beneath the dazzling surface of these poems,
the stage-managed *mirabilia* are essentially disturbing. The 'ownership' of
the marvels by the emperor is particularly pointed. In addition, by showing us a spectacular world where the abnormal essentially becomes normal,
predictable even, Martial devalues the relentlessly marvellous, rather in the
same way that the veteran guest at Trimalchio's dinner party is so certain
that he is about to be amazed (Petronius *Satyrica* 33.8). The second text is
a memorable and elegant letter of Pliny the Younger (*Epistles* 8.20) to his
friend Clusinius Gallus describing the remarkable Lake Vadimon, which
he has recently seen at his grandfather-in-law's property at Ameria. This
benign natural marvel is an expressive example of the marvellous made
wholesome and safe in a Trajanic context, but crucially without being stage-
managed by the emperor. Finally, the analysis will turn to an extraordinary
satire of Juvenal (Satire 15) outlining a shocking incident of cannibalism in
Egypt in 127. Juvenal here is not playing down this dark Hadrianic marvel, but he is at least containing it, reinforcing a sense of order by banishing
cannibalism to the margins, the appropriate locale. The only trouble is that
Hadrian too has plans to travel to Egypt, making the satire extremely topical. These three examples together show post-Domitianic authors actively
reclaiming and renegotiating the marvellous – a luxury afforded by the

---

[5] Plaza 2006: 318.

[6] Langlands in this volume introduces the useful concept of extratextuality to consider the interaction
between written texts and external, non-textual factors. Marvels attract talk and naturally lend themselves to 'intermediality' whereby written texts 'mobilise the special qualities of another medium that
has a separate existence outside the text' (p. 336).

more settled world of the principate in this era.[7] Together, they offer some fascinating insights not just into literary interactions across the period but also into the dynamic interaction between literature and society. *Inter alia*, this chapter will consider not simply the extent to which these texts were influenced by wider, off-the-page discourses but also the role they themselves played (both individually and collectively) in shaping them.

Martial: Staged Marvels in the Flavian Amphitheatre

Martial's *Liber spectaculorum* is an intriguing text.[8] The epigrams, addressed simply to 'Caesar' (11 times), recreate various extraordinary spectacles taking place in the Flavian amphitheatre and 'repeatedly stress the emperor's miraculous power over nature and his authority in the human realm'.[9] Indeed, the model of Caesar as god, even more powerful than Jupiter himself (*Sp.* 19.4), is a (perhaps *the*) distinctive feature of the collection (*Sp.* 20.4, 33.7), including dazzled animals spontaneously supplicating in deference to the emperor's divinity (*Sp.* 20, 33).[10] Opinion is divided about whether the poems derive from the principate of Titus and (perhaps) the inauguration of the Flavian amphitheatre in 80,[11] or whether they are Domitianic,[12] or indeed a mixture of the two. Yet they all cast the unnamed Flavian emperor as the controlling force for the marvels unfolding before our eyes. Even when the emperor's presence is not directly emphasised (e.g. *te praeside, Caesar*, 'with you as custodian, Caesar', *Sp.* 2.11), he is implicitly present within the *libellus* and frequently addressed by apostrophe, which constantly reminds us of his presence. The spectacles themselves, set against a worldwide backdrop which pales into insignificance compared with the *unum . . . opus* of the amphitheatrical stage (*Sp.* 1.8), draw in a global audience (*Sp.* 3). As Fitzgerald neatly puts it, 'the amphitheater has no

[7] In more unsettled times, marvels can be cast as darker phenomena, projected as portents indicating impending troubles. It is not so much the marvels which change, but how they are presented and interpreted.

[8] Yet it 'has come down in mutilated and truncated form' and 'less than half the volume that Martial had hastily issued to celebrate the historic games has survived' (Sullivan 1991: 8). On the transmission of the text, see Coleman 2006: xxi–xxv.

[9] Coleman 2006: xliii.

[10] The numbering of the epigrams is from Coleman 2006, who follows Carratello 1981.

[11] See too Suet. *Titus* 7 and Dio 66.25.

[12] Coleman 2006: xlv–lxiv cautiously sees the book as a composite, compiled from material involving both Titus and Domitian. She also acknowledges the possibility that not naming the emperor is deliberate, casting him instead as 'an idealised abstraction, above identification' (p. lxiv). Buttrey 2007 strongly prefers a Domitianic context for the whole book, drawing on the evidence of a rhinoceros depicted on a Domitianic *quadrans* (dated 83–5), which is an unprecedented image on a low-value coin designed to circulate widely.

outside'.[13] These visitors will soon be awestruck as they gaze on the parade of *delatores* facing imminent exile (*Sp.* 4, 5), the mythological re-enactments (*Sp.* 6, 9, 10, 24, 25, 28, 29), the female gladiators and a nocturnal dance troupe of Nereids (*Sp.* 7, 8, 30), exotic rhinoceroses (*Sp.* 11, 26), an acrobatic bear (*Sp.* 13), a pregnant sow fatally wounded but miraculously giving birth (*Sp.* 14, 15, 16), the exploits of the talented *bestiarius* Carpophorus (*Sp.* 17, 32), a levitating bull (*Sp.* 18, 19), and an elephant and a doe spontaneously kneeling in supplication before Caesar (*Sp.* 20, 33).[14] This is a miraculous, paradoxical space, where land can suddenly turn into sea (*Sp.* 27) and where individual animals take on anthropomorphic traits (e.g. the suppliant doe, *Sp.* 33). The language of wonder is present (*miramur*, 2.7; *mirandaque silua*, 24.3), as is the lexical register of the visual dimension (*uidet*, 2.1; *spectator*, 3.2; *uidimus*, 6.2, 8.4; *spectandum*, 17.5; *spectasse*, 24.1; *spectator*, 27.1; *specta*, 27.5; *uidit*, 34.3, 34.5; *spectator*, 34.9).[15] So too there is emphasis on these events (and the emperor) as talking-points now and in the future (*Fama loquetur*, 1.8; *uox diuersa*, 3.11; *Fama*, 19.3), while the use of deictic pronouns and adverbs creates immediacy (*hic ubi*, 2.1, 2.5, 2.7), as if Martial acts (on the surface, at least) as a benign tour-guide. The trope of apostrophe sees Martial addressing various figures, including Rome herself, but above all, Caesar (*Caesar*, 2.11, 3.1, 6.3, 7.2, 8.3, 11.1, 20.1, 24.2, 31.11, 32.1, 35.2; *Roma*, 9.10; *Daedalus*, 10.1; *Lucina*, 14.4; *Meleager*, 17.1; *Fama*, 19.3; *turba*, 26.12; *Leander*, 28.1). All these narrative techniques together cumulatively build up vividness and contribute to a reader's sensation of being part of the jubilant global audience. Yet whether readers readily join or warily detach themselves from these internal spectators is an intriguing question: post-Flavian responses may well differ from those of contemporary readers under Titus and Domitian.

Various positive qualities are ascribed to the emperor: Coleman highlights his accessibility, beneficent influence, *ciuilitas*, compassion, divinity, *liberalitas*, power over nature, *prouidentia*, speed, superhuman efficiency, and sympathy.[16] The carefully demarcated space also serves as the locale for the emperor's conspicuous delivery of reassuringly clear-cut justice (*Sp.* 4, 5, 9, 12), however brutal the punishments. As Sullivan observes, 'the

---

[13] Fitzgerald 2007: 43.

[14] Elephants 'seem to have impressed ancient writers as creatures especially endowed with spiritual sensibilities' (Newmyer 2003: 121, citing Plin. *NH* 8.1–3, Plut. *Mor.* 972B and Ael. *NA* 7.4 on the religiosity of elephants).

[15] Coleman 2006: 66 discusses Martial's appeals to the collective experience of autopsy for verification of an incident, 'harnessed as irrefutable proof of something that inherently beggars belief'.

[16] Coleman 2006: 312.

emperor's ingenious justice . . . extends even to the lowest social classes such as gladiators'.[17] This magical amphitheatrical space becomes the focal point for successive wonders, emphatically cast as spontaneous and pointedly *not* created through artifice (whatever the reality).[18] So we have the levitating bull: *non fuit hoc artis, sed pietatis opus* ('This was a creation not of ingenuity, but of devotion', *Sp.* 18.2). Also, an elephant kneels before the emperor: *non facit hoc iussus nulloque docente magistro*, 'He does this not by command, nor because a trainer instructs this' (*Sp.* 20.3). It may be that Martial, by insistently articulating the point about spontaneity, anticipates that his audience's capacity to believe is under strain, but on the surface, the device underscores the point that we are privileged spectators in a uniquely magical space. There are no tricks here!

Even so, amidst all this frenetic panegyric and showmanship, we can detect odd signs of tension. One epigram (*Sp.* 12) describes a performing lion which has unexpectedly savaged its trainer and is swiftly killed on the emperor's orders. That prompts Martial to exclaim, *Quos decet esse hominum tali sub principe mores,* | *qui iubet ingenium mitius esse feris!* ('What conduct of men is fitting under such an emperor who commands wild beasts' nature to be more mild!', *Sp.* 12.5–6). This exclamation, underscoring the emperor's power of life and death over all his subjects, has an oppressive edge to it and deftly reminds us that, actually, there is life outside the arena. Another epigram describes a tigress savagely mauling a lion – something which Martial claims would not happen in the wild: *postquam inter nos est, plus feritatis habet* ('now that she is in our midst, she has more savagery', *Sp.* 21.6).[19] The impact of this creature's contact with Roman civilisation is to make her more wild than she would be naturally. If this is the novel consequence of the tigress being imported into the fabulous space of Caesar's arena, then Martial makes a disquieting point about the corrosive impact of interaction with Romans.[20] We could compare here Sallust's Jugurtha, rapidly transformed from noble barbarian to tarnished anti-hero through his contact with the Romans (*BJ* 6–9).

What are we to make of this curious display of Flavian marvels? Despite the darker tones identified above, I do not want to suggest that Martial is

---

[17] Sullivan 1991: 11.

[18] Fitzgerald 2007: 46: 'Martial is not interested in celebrating technological miracles.'

[19] Cf. Juvenal, illustrating the peacefulness of the animal kingdom relative to the destructive nature of humans: *Indica tigris agit rabida cum tigride pacem* | *perpetuam* ('The Indian tigress lives with wild tigress in everlasting peace', *Sat.* 15.163–4).

[20] Epplett 2001 discusses the practical infrastructures for removing animals from the wild to the arena.

being covertly subversive in his *Liber spectaculorum*. Nonetheless, as a cultural artefact, this little book and its marvels are still revealing about the atmosphere of Flavian Rome as a precursor to the principates of Nerva, Trajan, and Hadrian. From a modern perspective, Martial's unique creation has the claustrophobic feel of a gilded cage, where orchestrated displays inside the arena trigger collective wonder which quickly effaces the spectators' individual identities. There is no room for dissent. So, when the diverse visitors from around the world assemble in the amphitheatre, their polyglot backgrounds evaporate and instead become a single, linguistically homogeneous entity: *Vox diuersa sonat populorum, tum tamen una est,* | *cum uerus patriae diceris esse pater* ('The peoples' speech sounds different and yet, when you are hailed as the true father of the fatherland, then they all speak as one', *Sp.* 3.11–12). The capacity of an emperor to bring unity is certainly a positive attribute (and one intended to be seen as such here), but in other settings the lack of dissenting voices can be dangerous for a *princeps*, who finds himself surrounded by people telling him exactly what (they think) he wants to hear.[21] Moreover, this is a place where the all-powerful imperial god controls everything around him and becomes the dominant focal point. Even the amphitheatre itself is personified and deferentially offers its spectacles to the presiding Caesar: *quicquid Fama canit, praestat harena tibi* ('whatever Legend sings about, the arena offers to you', *Sp.* 6.4). As Coleman observes, 'Frequently the arena . . . is said to "offer" the spectacle to the emperor.'[22] It is striking too that Martial blurs the boundaries between the marvellous displays within the amphitheatre and the physical structure of the amphitheatre, itself a marvel which pointedly overshadows 'the more pedestrian Wonders of the World':[23] *Omnis Caesareo cedit labor amphitheatro:* | *unum pro cunctis Fama loquetur opus* ('All labour yields to Caesar's amphitheatre: Legend will tell of one work in place of them all', *Sp.* 1.7–8).[24] The future tense of *loquetur* effectively closes down any scope for future wonders to impress, now that the Flavian amphitheatre exists, no

---

[21] Cf. Tac. *Hist.* 1.15.4, contrasting 'the continuous effort required in giving good advice and the ease of simply saying yes' (Damon 2003: 139): *nam suadere principi quod oporteat multi laboris, assentatio erga quemcumque principem sine affectu peragitur* ('For it takes much effort to advise an emperor what he should do, but flattering agreement with him regardless of his character can be delivered even in the absence of affection').

[22] Coleman 2006: 68, citing too *Sp.* 24.1–2, 34.9–10 (both featuring the all-encompassing *quicquid* periphrasis as the object of the main verb).

[23] Buttrey 2007: 106.

[24] Fitzgerald 2007: 38 sees ambiguity in *unum pro cunctis* as both 'one in place of all others' and 'one on behalf of all others', so that the amphitheatre 'will come to stand for all wonders, not so much eclipsing as representing them. The amphitheater is not just one wonder among others, the seventh and newest; it also replaces all others as the very medium of wonder.'

matter how hard people toil.[25] This dominant man-made structure seems to have a total monopoly on the marvellous, as the extraordinary displays unfolding unceasingly in its arena leave no room for *mirabilia* to take place elsewhere (either spatially or temporally). The marvels effectively become a 'currency' which the emperor owns completely. Beneath the dazzling surface of these poems, the *mirabilia* have a troubling edge to them.

Pliny the Younger: The Delight of Domestic Marvels in Trajanic Italy

Keeping Martial in mind, let us turn now to a case-study of a very different kind of post-Domitianic marvel presented in a memorable and elegant letter of Pliny the Younger (*Epistles* 8.20), dated by Sherwin-White (1966 ad loc.) to perhaps the summer of 107:[26]

C. PLINIVS GALLO SVO S.

Ad quae noscenda iter ingredi, transmittere mare solemus, ea **sub oculis** posita neglegimus, seu quia ita natura comparatum, ut proximorum incuriosi longinqua sectemur, seu quod omnium rerum cupido languescit, cum facilis occasio, seu quod differimus tamquam saepe **uisuri**, quod datur **uidere** quotiens uelis **cernere**. (2) Quacumque de causa, permulta in urbe nostra iuxtaque urbem non **oculis** modo sed ne auribus quidem nouimus, quae si tulisset Achaia Aegyptos Asia aliaue quaelibet miraculorum ferax commendatrixque terra, audita perlecta **lustrata** haberemus.

(3) Ipse certe nuper, quod nec audieram ante nec **uideram**, audiui pariter et **uidi**. Exegerat prosocer meus, ut Amerina praedia sua **inspicerem**. Haec perambulanti mihi ostenditur subiacens lacus nomine Vadimonis; simul quaedam incredibilia narrantur. (4) Perueni ad ipsum. Lacus est in similitudinem iacentis rotae circumscriptus et undique aequalis: nullus sinus, obliquitas nulla, omnia dimensa paria, et quasi artificis manu cauata et excisa. Color caerulo albidior, uiridior et pressior; sulpuris odor saporque medicatus; uis qua fracta solidantur. Spatium modicum, quod tamen sentiat uentos, et fluctibus intumescat. (5) Nulla in hoc nauis (sacer enim), sed innatant insulae, herbidae omnes harundine et iunco, quaeque alia fecundior palus ipsaque illa extremitas lacus effert. Sua cuique figura ut modus; cunctis margo derasus, quia frequenter uel litori uel sibi illisae terunt terunturque. Par omnibus altitudo, par leuitas; quippe in speciem carinae humili radice descendunt. (6) Haec ab omni latere **perspicitur**, eadem aqua

---

[25] There may be play with Virg. *Georg.* 1.145–6 *Labor omnia uicit | improbus*, 'relentless hard work has conquered everything'. Virgil's unrelenting (but ultimately fruitful) toil in the agricultural sphere becomes pointless toil in the architectural realm.

[26] On this letter, see Saylor 1982.

pariter suspensa et mersa. Interdum iunctae copulataeque et continenti similes sunt, interdum discordantibus uentis digeruntur, non numquam des-
titutae tranquillitate singulae fluitant. (7) Saepe minores maioribus uelut
cumbulae onerariis adhaerescunt, saepe inter se maiores minoresque quasi
cursum certamenque desumunt; rursus omnes in eundem locum appulsae,
qua steterunt promouent terram, et modo hac modo illa lacum reddunt
auferuntque, ac tum demum cum medium tenuere non contrahunt. (8)
Constat pecora herbas secuta sic in insulas illas ut in extremam ripam pro-
cedere solere, nec prius intellegere mobile solum quam litori abrepta quasi
illata et imposita circumfusum undique lacum paueant; mox quo tulerit
uentus egressa, non magis se descendisse sentire, quam senserint ascendisse.
(9) Idem lacus in flumen egeritur, quod ubi se paulisper **oculis** dedit specu
mergitur alteque conditum meat ac, si quid antequam subduceretur accepit,
seruat et profert.

(10) Haec tibi scripsi, quia nec minus ignota quam mihi nec minus grata
credebam. Nam te quoque ut me nihil aeque ac naturae opera delectant.

Vale.

Pliny sends greetings to his friend Gallus:

We are accustomed to embark on a journey and to cross the sea in order to
get to know things which we neglect, if they are located in front of our very
eyes. Perhaps this is because it has been so arranged by nature that, although
we are indifferent to what is closest to hand, we are ready to pursue distant
goals; or because desire for everything fades when access is easy; or because
we often put off seeing something which it is possible to see whenever you
want. (2) For whatever reason, there are numerous attractions in our city
and the immediate vicinity which we have never seen nor even heard about,
although if they were to be found in Achaea, Egypt or any other land agreeable and suitable for marvels, we would have heard about them, read about
them, and seen them for ourselves.

(3) Certainly, I myself have recently heard about and at the same time
seen something which I had never before heard about nor seen. My wife's
grandfather had asked me to look at his property near Ameria. While I was
walking around this area, there was shown to me a low-lying lake called
Vadimon. At the same time, some incredible details about it were being
explained to me. (4) I went up to it. The lake is round, so that it looks like
a wheel lying on its side, and perfectly circular. There is no indentation,
no kink, all is regular and even, as if it had been hollowed and cut out by
the craftsman's hand. Its colour is pale blue verging on green, rather dull;
it smells of sulphur, tastes medicinal, and has the facility to heal fractures.
Its extent is moderate, but nonetheless it feels the winds and swells up with
waves. (5) There is no boat here (for it is sacred), but grassy islands bob up
and down on it, all covered with reeds and rushes, and whatever other plants
the rather fertile marsh and the borders of the lake produces. Each island has
its own shape and size, but the edges of all of them are eroded, because they

frequently wear and are worn down by colliding with the shore and with one another. They all have the same depth, the same buoyancy; for they taper downwards in a shallow base, in the manner of a ship's hull. (6) This 'hull' can be clearly seen from every angle and lies half above and half below the water. From time to time, the islands join and couple together, and resemble a single land mass; from time to time, they are dispersed by the conflicting winds; and sometimes, the water around them recedes because of the calm weather and they float around one by one. (7) Often, the smaller islands cling to the larger ones, just as small boats do to their cargo ships; often, the larger and smaller islands pick a fight with each other, as if engaging in a race or contest; then again, all driven towards the same place, they advance the shore where they take their stand, and now in this direction, now in that, they restore the lake or take an area away from it, only then failing to contract the space when they have taken position in the middle of the lake. (8) It is generally agreed that livestock, while going after the grass, habitually advance onto those islands as if advancing onto the very edge of the bank, and they do not understand that they are on moving ground until, carried away from the shore as if loaded and put on board a vessel, they panic that the lake has flowed around on all sides, but soon they 'disembark' wherever the wind brings them, being no more aware that they have disembarked than they were of having embarked. (9) The same lake empties into a river, which, when it has exposed itself to view for a little way, then sinks into a cavern and travels buried deep underground, and any object which is previously dropped in, it takes, keeps, and brings forth.

(10) I have written this account to you because I believed that it was just as unfamiliar and pleasing to you as it was to me. For nothing delights you so much as the works of nature, just as they do me too.

Goodbye.

It is hard to imagine a marvel apparently more different from Martial's sequence of spectacles in the urban arena than this one (even if, as we shall see, the *Liber spectaculorum* offers intriguing points of contact and comparison with the natural marvel described in this letter).[27] Whereas Martial's eager crowds of spectators are irresistibly drawn to the Flavian amphitheatre from around the world, Pliny (one solitary visitor, there for another purpose) has only now seen this remarkable jewel of a lake, even though it is conveniently located nearby on his grandfather-in-law's property at Ameria.[28] It is almost as if he blunders on it by chance. And while the

---

[27] The works of Martial and Pliny certainly intersect with one another explicitly (e.g. *Epistles* 3.21 on Martial's death; Martial 10.19 on Pliny). Marchesi 2013: 101 explores how their works 'interfere with one another in a dense cloud of subtler allusions extending to wider areas of their collections' and posits (p. 102) 'intertextual "clouds", that is, of areas of loosely connected texts, which may still bear interpretive weight and may be shown to have interdependent meaning'.

[28] Ameria (mod. Amelia: *OCD*[4]) was an ancient hill-town in southern Umbria, about 46 miles (73 km) north of Rome.

spectacles of Martial's arena are triggered and orchestrated by the constant dominating presence of Caesar the god, Lake Vadimon is a quiet place, ripe for calm contemplation by oneself: certainly, it is a sacred locale (8.20.5), but its presiding divinity (unnamed) keeps a low profile and finds expression only in the uncanny strangeness of the perfect lake. That element of perfection also suggests *aemulatio* with the (elliptically shaped) Flavian amphitheatre. Lake Vadimon is even better, flawlessly circular, all regular and even, as if hollowed and cut out by the craftsman's hand (*quasi artificis manu cauata et excisa*). Yet the point is that it was not: this is a natural phenomenon as opposed to the man-made *unum . . . opus* of the amphitheatre (*Sp.* 1.8).[29]

It is intriguing that aspects of Pliny's description deftly play with Martial's *Liber spectaculorum* in other ways. One distinctive cycle within the epigrams involves a series describing fabulous aquatic displays and naval clashes within the arena (*Sp.* 27–30, 34). So Martial celebrates the miracle of a venue rapidly converted from land to water and then back again: *hic modo terra fuit . . . | parua mora est, dices 'hic modo pontus erat'* ('here just now there was land . . . After a brief delay you will say, "Here just now there was sea"', *Sp.* 27.5, 7). Yet compared with this finite double conversion of the arena, the wonderful Lake Vadimon is constantly in flux, as land becomes water and vice versa in unceasing and endlessly varying patterns: *modo hac modo illa lacum reddunt auferuntque* ('now in this direction, now in that, they [sc. the islands] restore the lake or take an area away from it', 8.20.7). Certain features of Pliny's imagery strongly hint that making comparisons with the Flavian amphitheatre is a valid way to read the letter. Not only are the floating islands compared with ships[30] (obviously suggestive of an amphitheatrical *naumachia*), but the trope of competition also features explicitly: *saepe inter se maiores minoresque quasi cursum certamenque desumunt* ('often, the larger and smaller islands pick a fight with each other, as if engaging in a race or contest', 8.20.7). And where animals are a focal point for spectators in Martial's arena, so too they feature memorably on Lake Vadimon as unwitting sailors. Two epigrams celebrate a bull miraculously hoisted into the air during some kind of mythological re-enactment (*Sp.* 18.1

---

[29] Clarke 2015: 41 observes how in Herodotus 'creating islands is in itself a recurring theme in the *Histories*, and one with strongly negative connotations'. This is in contrast with landscapes peppered 'with naturally amazing islands' such as the floating island of Chemmis (2.156.1) or the formerly wandering island of Delos/Ortygia on which Leto gave birth to Artemis and Apollo (Pindar fr. 33d.1; Callim. *Del.* 35–40). See further Nishimura-Jensen 2000.

[30] *Quippe in speciem carinae humili radice descendunt*, 'for they taper downwards in a shallow base, in the manner of a ship's hull' (8.20.5); *saepe minores maioribus uelut cumbulae onerariis adhaerescunt*, 'often, the smaller islands cling to the larger ones, just as small boats do to their cargo ships' (8.20.7).

Raptus abit media . . . taurus harena, 'a bull, snatched out of the middle of the arena, departed'; *Sp.* 19.1: a bull carries Europa *per aequora*).[31] It is tempting to see a connection here with Pliny's hapless cattle, finding themselves on *mobile solum*, 'moving ground', and *litori abrepta*, 'carried away from the shore' (8.20.8).[32] Impressive though the action inside the monumental Flavian amphitheatre undoubtedly was, comparison with Pliny's natural marvel of Lake Vadimon seems to cast it as trumping and outdoing that earlier man-made wonder. This instance of literary interaction suggests that Pliny uses Martial's text to engage in good-natured *aemulatio*: although readers do not have to compare Martial's *Liber spectaculorum* to admire the benign natural landscape of this marvellous lake (reassuringly situated in the timeless present), their appreciation of its qualities will be heightened if they do.[33]

We can see too that Pliny uses narrative techniques typically associated with representing *mirabilia*. So, like Martial, he repeatedly accentuates the visual dimension, particularly at the opening of the letter (*sub oculis, uisuri, uidere, cernere, oculis, lustrata, uideram, uidi, inspicerem* . . .), thereby opening up the register of vicarious autopsy for his addressee Gallus. Pliny also offers us an intriguing didactic 'hook' for the whole description, namely that although we are prepared to make long journeys overseas to seek out the sights, we so often overlook incredible features available locally under our very eyes.[34] Martial's international spectators, all drawn from the margins towards the amphitheatre in Rome, would arguably offer a good illustration of this point. Pliny's message is that there is simply no need to go overseas to have your senses stimulated by marvellous sights: wholesome and wonderful Italy has just as much to offer as the distant provinces. This is the exact opposite of the Herodotean notion that 'the most beautiful regions of the world are the furthest away' (3.106). Pliny's description of the natural wonder itself is extraordinary. In painting a picture of the perfectly round lake, Pliny stimulates our senses with his accentuation of its colour (the lake itself is *caerulo albidior, uiridior et pressior*), its

---

[31] The precise nature of the taurine spectacle has prompted different views: see Coleman 2006: 148–55.

[32] Saylor 1982 sees these cattle as an allegory for myopic human tourists who travel, but fail to appreciate their new surroundings.

[33] Rimell in this volume characterises some texts as '(mutely) interacting' (p. 65) and suggests that this is a particularly important concept for considering Pliny's relationship with Martial, which in the *Epistles* often sees the former selectively silencing the latter. The current (slightly different) case seems to involve Pliny tacitly trumping Martial.

[34] Nonetheless the phenomenon of 'floating islands' on Lake Vadimon is apparently not unique: cf. Sen. *NQ* 3.25.7–8 and Plin. *NH* 2.209 (lists of such lakes, including Vadimon). Shero 1933: 52 remarks: 'We may infer that other lakes were more famous for their floating islands, notably the lake at Cutiliae.'

smell (*sulpuris odor*), and the taste of its water (*sapor medicatus*). The series of comparisons between aspects of the lake and a sequence of man-made objects associated with travel and trade (wheel, ships) only underscore the essential natural serenity of Lake Vadimon. The sequence of naval imagery applied to the islands offers a nice twist on Pliny's opening picture of real sea journeys, ambitiously undertaken to visit distant places to see the sights (*transmittere mare solemus*, 'we are accustomed to cross the sea', 8.20.1).

What Pliny gives us in Lake Vadimon is a mischievous pastoral utopia, with an anthropomorphised land and waterscape playing innocent tricks on the livestock. There is something benign too about Vadimon's sulphurated waters, which have the power to heal fractures (*uis qua fracta solidantur*).[35] This becomes particularly tangible compared with the fragmented bodies littering Martial's arena, whether we think of Laureolus' 'mangled limbs' (*laceri . . . artus*, *Sp.* 9.5) after being attacked by a Scottish bear, or Orpheus, 'ripped apart by an unappreciative bear' (*ingrato . . . laceratus ab urso*, *Sp.* 24.7). And the islands themselves have a magical and alluring quality to them, generously offering grass to the grazing animals and bringing them back to dry land. Even if the boundary between land and water is sometimes confusingly fluid and shifting, there is clearly nothing malicious about this place (as there often is in liminal regions). It is striking too that Pliny has chosen to sidestep the detail that this lake was the site of real battles, first where the Romans fought against the Etruscans in 310 BC (Livy 9.39.4–11) and later in 283 BC (Polybius 2.20), another Roman victory against the Etruscans.[36] Instead we enter a pacific and playful *locus amoenus*. Readers who knew the area's martial history might feel uplifted by the transition from formative wars and struggles under the republic to the settled conditions of the present day. What is arguably most striking, however, is the location of this incredible place in Italy, not in some far-flung exotic locale on the margins. Pliny offers us here a particularly expressive example of the marvellous made safe in a Trajanic context (but totally decoupled from the figure of the emperor himself), where a kind of utopian landscape has been transported to the imperial centre.[37] As Evans has observed, 'locations of desire in

---

[35] Cf. Sen. *NQ* 3.25.8 on Lake Vadimon: *aquae grauitas medicatae* ('the weight of the medicinal water').

[36] Oakley 2005: 497–500 discusses a notorious textual *crux* and the curious doublet involving Lake Vadimon as the site of both battles, although the second one was much better known (Broughton 1950: I, 189).

[37] Trajan himself had only been sporadically present in Rome since being appointed emperor in January 98: 'Upon returning in June 107, he would then be continuously present in Italy until the Parthian war of September 113' (Gibson 2015: 221).

Greco-Roman antiquity are similarly isolated, often as islands, always situated on the periphery'.[38] Yet here we see an idealised inversion, with wholesome natural marvels in central Italy visible for anyone to enjoy, if they care to visit Ameria.

We should also make one final point about this letter. Whether or not my suggestion that Pliny actively works with Martial's *Liber spectaculorum* proves compelling, he is surely engaging with another Flavian author who inscribes and compartmentalises marvels within a massive monumental structure – namely Pliny the Elder and his *Historia naturalis*, dedicated to the emperor Titus.[39] Pliny the Younger's beautiful picture of a simple natural wonder manifests the kind of elegant literary miniaturisation of his uncle's grand project that is ideally facilitated by the more modest format of his letter collection.[40] Instead of the *princeps*, Pliny the Younger addresses his friend and fellow enthusiast, Clusinius Gallus ('an obscure figure').[41] Lake Vadimon, rather like one of its own floating islands, is pointedly decoupled from the imperialism which forms the bedrock of Pliny the Elder's ambitious encyclopedia. Where Pliny the Elder assembles a little catalogue of lakes around the world with floating islands (*NH* 2.209, including Lake Vadimon), paratactic and unelaborated, Pliny the Younger instead describes only one, but in some detail and exquisitely, simply because his addressee takes delight in *naturae opera* ('works of nature', 8.20.10). Where Pliny the Elder and Martial both wrote works which were, in their different ways, inextricably entwined with the Flavian dynasty, Pliny the Younger (an author who insistently distances himself from the Domitianic past, though see *Ep.* 8.14.8–9) energetically supports Trajan (see *Panegyricus*, *Epistles* 10), but without making him the centre of attention in *Epistles* 1–9 – itself a stance which reflects positively on Trajan.[42]

---

[38] Evans 2003a: 294.

[39] Cf. Murphy 2004: 194: 'As with the building of any other kind of monument, publishing an encyclopedia in Flavian Rome had certain ideological implications. Like other monuments, the *Natural history* is an instrument for communicating the power of its creator. Assembling knowledge from all the fields of Roman dominion, the book displays its contents to be witnessed by a literate elite, as a textual embodiment of an empire known and ruled.'

[40] Cf. Ash 2003 on the similar practice of Pliny embedding *exitus* narratives in his letter collection.

[41] Sherwin-White 1966: 471. Yet he is probably also the addressee of *Ep.* 2.17, one of Pliny's famous villa letters (a man-made marvel), explicitly articulated in terms of wonder (*miraris . . . mirari*, 2.17.1) and thus allowing constructive 'dialogue' between the two letters.

[42] Gibson 2015 rightly notes darker tones of Pliny's letters from Books 7–9, but 8.20 appears to be an exception. In Book 8, Trajan only features twice (*Ep.* 8.4 on his military triumph in Dacia; *Ep.* 8.17.2 on the failure of his attempts to alleviate flooding in Rome). The 'fading' of Trajan from view in Books 7–9 is a noticeable feature (Gibson 2015: 207).

His portrait of the benign wonders of Lake Vadimon is a good example of that dynamic in action.[43]

Juvenal: Restoring Dangerous *Mirabilia* to the Margins under Hadrian

Let us turn now to a very different marvel, namely Juvenal's extraordinary Satire 15, outlining a shocking incident of cannibalism which took place in Egypt in 127. This poem pointedly differs from the previous two case studies, first because of the location of the cannibalism outside Italy and second because of the dark and disturbing subject matter. Juvenal as a writer spans the principates of Trajan and Hadrian, but his fifth and final book (Satires 13–16) is securely Hadrianic.[44] What Satire 15 showcases is an account of recent mob murder inspired by deep-seated religious hatred between two Egyptian towns, Ombi and Tentyra, located about ten miles apart from one another.[45] The graphic subject matter pulls strongly against the grandeur of the hexameters through which it is relayed, and the satire itself is carefully constructed. After an introduction, addressed to a man named Volusius, outlining the bizarre tendency of the Egyptians to worship animal gods and deploring the fact that eating human flesh is allowed,[46] Juvenal ventriloquises an unnamed critic objecting to the plausibility of Odysseus' story to Alcinous about cannibalism (i.e. the Cyclopes and the Laestrygonians). Juvenal then intervenes in his own person announcing a recent event, which illustrates that such things can happen (15.1–32). He narrates the premeditated and escalating attack of one Egyptian town on the other during a religious festival (intriguingly without specifying which one was the aggressor), culminating in an act of cannibalism (15.33–92).[47] Juvenal then cites other cases of cannibalism, particularly one involving a Spanish tribe, the Vascones, driven to cannibalism during a siege in

---

[43] Later Pliny invites Trajan to win personal prestige associated with man-made aquatic projects by constructing a canal linking Lake Sophon in Nicomedia with the Sea of Marmara (*Ep.* 10.41, 61). Trajan initially seems interested if cautious (*Ep.* 10.42), but later backs down (*Ep.* 10.62).

[44] Braund 1996: 16. Courtney 1980: 2 dates the book to 130 (with 15.27 as a *terminus post quem* of 127 and 14.99 as a *terminus ante quem* of 132).

[45] Cf. Tac. *Hist.* 1.11.1 on the potential for trouble to erupt in mercurial Egypt because of the inhabitants' religious beliefs: *superstitione ac lasciuia discordem et mobilem*, 'in turmoil and volatile through superstition and unruliness'.

[46] On Egyptian animal worship see Smelik and Hemelrijk 1984. Herodotus 2.50.1 suggests that Greek gods originated in Egypt. Rosati 2009: 275–6 discusses this passage, as well as the rival idea that Greek gods fled to Egypt disguised as animals while fleeing from Typhon (Ov. *Met.* 5.318–31). The rival theories reflect a 'cultural battle' (Rosati 2009: 276).

[47] Courtney 1980: 598 suggests that the aggressors were from Tentyra, since the battle happened closer to Ombi, but the evidence is thin, as Anderson 1988: 207 emphasises.

72 BC, but he argues that the Egyptian incident is far worse because it was voluntary (15.93–131). Finally, he distinguishes between mankind and animals because, normally, mankind has compassion, whereas the Egyptian incident has shown that even snakes have more *concordia* than these contemporary cannibals (15.131–74).[48] All this feels a long way from Martial's miraculous arena or Pliny's benign floating islands.

Is it fair even to categorise this cannibalism as a marvel? After all, there were grim and relatively recent precedents, such as the Jews at Cyrene (AD 117) allegedly eating the flesh of Greeks and Romans and making clothes from their victims' skins (Dio 68.32.1).[49] Yet Juvenal in presenting the Egyptian cannibalism pointedly deploys language which recalls central techniques of Martial and Pliny in portraying their *mirabilia*. Firstly, Juvenal carefully categorises the event as a (dark) marvel and uses vocabulary associated with such phenomena elsewhere: *nos **miranda** quidem sed nuper consule Iunco | gesta super calidae referemus moenia Copti* ('I will relate deeds which are **to be wondered at**, but which happened recently during the consulship of Juncus beyond the walls of baking Coptus', 15.27–8).[50] Secondly, Juvenal also deploys visual language. He uses a second-person generalising subjunctive to say that you could *see* men's mangled faces (*aspiceres*, 15.56; cf. *aspicimus*, 15.169), prompting his readers to imagine themselves present. He also speculates what Pythagoras would say if he 'saw' (*uideret*, 15.172) such *monstra*. As Hardie remarks, 'Wonder and amazement are most immediately invoked through things seen.'[51] Juvenal may not have seen the cannibalism himself, but at strategic points he deploys the vocabulary of the visual so strongly associated with marvels.[52] Thirdly, he highlights the notion of witnessing events: after conceding how Odysseus told his story *nullo sub teste* ('without any witness corroborating', 15.26), Juvenal in the main account of the cannibalism interjects in the first person about the Egyptians' tendency to indulge in *luxuria*, adding *quantum ipse notaui* ('as far as I myself have noted', 15.45). Juvenal thus stakes a claim to personal knowledge of Egypt.

---

[48] A similar motif (man being worse than animals) features in the declamation schools (e.g. Papirius Fabianus: *neque feris inter se bella sunt*, 'wild animals do not have wars between themselves', Sen. *Contr.* 2.1.10) and elsewhere (Cic. *Sex. Rosc.* 63, Hor. *Epod.* 7.11–12 with Watson 2003: 278, Plin. *NH* 7.5).

[49] Ash 2010 discusses cannibalism amongst the Usipi, though that was forced upon them (Tac. *Agr.* 28).

[50] Juvenal has already called the Egyptian animal gods *portenta* (15.2) and at the close he speculates about how Pythagoras would react if he saw such *monstra* (15.172). His language recalls Seneca's humorously precise dating at *Apoc.* 1.1.

[51] Hardie 2009: 4.

[52] Singleton 1983: 199 tentatively suggests that Juvenal may have been a witness.

The crucial incident comes when a man from Tentyra slips while fleeing and his pursuers from Ombi pounce (15.78–83):

> . . . capiturque. Ast illum in plurima sectum
> frusta et particulas, ut multis mortuus unus
> sufficeret, totum corrosis ossibus edit
> uictrix turba, nec ardenti decoxit aeno
> aut ueribus, longum usque adeo tardumque putauit
> expectare focos, contenta cadauere crudo.

> He is caught. As for him, chopped into many chunks and little pieces, so that one corpse sufficed for many consumers – the victorious mob completely ate him up, gnawing on his bones. They did not cook him in a seething cauldron or on skewers and thought it too long and slow to wait for a hearth: they were content with the uncooked carcass.

The swift movement from the victim's capture to his dismemberment reflects the intense savagery of this rampaging mob. This is a frenzy, not premeditated butchery, as the bizarre *enumeratio* of rejected cooking methods shows, but the alliterative culmination of the passage casting the victorious mob as *contenta cadauere crudo* is especially jarring because it introduces the incongruous concept of happiness. This is the crucial reason why Juvenal categorises this cannibalism within *miranda . . . gesta* (15.27–8). It is not simply consuming human flesh which makes this a *scelus*, but the pleasure gained by the perpetrators: *Sed qui mordere cadauer | sustinuit nil umquam hac carne **libentius** edit* ('But nobody who has endured chewing on a carcass ever ate anything **with more relish** than this meat', 15.87–8; cf. *uoluptatem*, 15.90). Unlike besieged people, who only desperately resort to such food when all else has failed, these Egyptians actively enjoy human flesh. One man even draws his fingers over the ground to taste the blood when the cadaver has been eaten (15.93) – a chilling detail.

What is at stake here? Juvenal certainly goes to great efforts to mark off this barbaric act as shocking and boundary-breaking. As he summarises towards the satire's end: *aspicimus populos quorum non sufficit irae | occidisse aliquem, sed pectora, bracchia, uoltum | crediderunt genus esse cibi* ('We are looking at peoples whose anger is not sated by killing someone, but who think torsos, arms, faces are a kind of food', 15.169–71). That sort of sensationalising language sounds like a strong warning to fellow Romans about Egyptian barbarism and an attempt to foster xenophobia. Not all critics agree, however. Singleton argues that 'it is not the Ombites whom Juvenal wishes to condemn so much as the cruelty of men in general'.[53] Certainly there is an element of general condemnation in the satire (e.g. *Ast homini*

---

[53] Singleton 1983: 206.

ferrum letale incude nefanda | produxisse parum est ('For mankind it is not enough to have beaten out lethal steel on the wicked anvil', 15.165–6). Yet this generalising view misses something: for the Egyptian setting is absolutely central and surely cannot be explained away so readily. As Juvenal emphasises towards the end of the satire, we are looking at angry people who do not just kill victims, but consume their bodies (15.169–71). Anti-Egyptian feeling lies at the heart of this satire. Other critics acknowledge this, but respond differently. Anderson suggests that the satirical speaker is deliberately exaggerated to become 'a character so bigoted, racist, and extremist Roman . . . that he alienates his audience'.[54] That is possible, but Juvenal's consistently anti-Egyptian stance elsewhere in the *Satires* undermines this reading. Alternatively, Alston speculates that one intention of the satire is 'to mock the large number of his contemporaries afflicted by Egyptomania'.[55] This possibility can be pushed further. For it raises intriguing possibilities about this satire's relationship to its contemporary context, particularly the mysterious death of Antinous in Egypt in October 130, while Hadrian and his entourage were sailing down the Nile after restoring the monument to Pompey at Pelusium.[56] Preparations for this trip to Egypt were already being made well in advance, as we are reminded by one mutilated papyrus describing an oath sworn at Hermopolis in case Hadrian stayed there.[57] Even if Satire 15 pre-dates Hadrian's tour, the projected trip was probably widely known about. In that context, the satire could be seen as ringing a note of anxiety about Egypt as an unpredictable and alien place, where dangerous things could happen, and where an emperor needed to take care: Egypt certainly proved deadly to Antinous.[58] Birley sees a broad connection: 'It is difficult not to wonder whether the old poet had not chosen to write up this gruesome traveller's tale precisely because Hadrian was in Egypt or on his way there.'[59] By isolating the Egyptian cannibals from the rest of humanity (even other cannibals!) and anchoring them firmly in Egypt, Juvenal on the one hand restricts this darkly disturbing wonder within appropriate terrain, Egypt – a place which has a long track-record

---

[54] Anderson 1988: 211.   [55] Alston 1996: 101.

[56] On the restoration see Appian *BC* 2.86, *Syriaca* 50; *HA Hadr.* 14.4; Dio 69.11.1.

[57] Sijpesteijn 1991. See too Sijpesteijn 1969 for a papyrus concerning requisitions in connection with Hadrian's visit to Egypt: 'preparations were already being made long before Hadrian's visit' (p. 116).

[58] It is intriguing that Juvenal addresses the satire to *Volusi Bithynice* (15.1). Volusius (otherwise unknown) may be identical with Martial's addressee, Bithynicus (2.26.3, 6.50.5, 9.8.1, 3, 12.78.1). 'Bithynicus' may also reflect Volusius' provenance. Hadrian's favourite, Antinous, was also from Bithynia, as Dio (another Bithynian!) tells us (69.11.1). Perhaps Volusius had some connection with Antinous and therefore a special interest in Egypt as his destination (or death-place, depending on the date of this satire). Bithynia continued to celebrate its connection with the imperial favourite long afterwards by 'putting Antinous on the reverse of its coins commemorating Commodus and Caracalla' (Vout 2005: 93).

[59] Birley 1997: 235.

in ancient cultural perceptions as the location par excellence of the strange and impossible.[60] As Beagon has observed, 'In the world of Rome, wonders were transported from the margins to the centre of empire, to the enhancement of imperial omnipotence and the amazement of the masses.'[61] Here, Juvenal reverses that polarity in no uncertain terms, hurling the monstrous incident back to Egypt, a land which stirs both fascination and fear in Roman minds. At the same time, Hadrian's extended trip to this dangerous country is troubling (particularly since he had no obvious heir, and the succession was not resolved until 138).[62] The tone and subject matter of the satire may also reflect general anxieties about Hadrian's extended absences from Rome.

Conclusion

Although this diachronic study involves authors who differ markedly in their choices of genre and subject matter and who straddle principates from Titus and Domitian to Hadrian, nonetheless the three disparate texts are interconnected and in dialogue with each other through the presence of the marvellous. Where Martial 'captures' marvels in the magical space of the arena and anchors them at the imperial centre as a direct reflection of the emperor's global dominance, Pliny reacts against such a model. Instead he celebrates a simple natural marvel located in the Italian countryside and decoupled from any direct influence of the *princeps* but nonetheless indirectly casting a positive light on the fruitfulness (or 'clean slate', as Rimell puts it on p. 64) of Trajan's principate. Within Pliny's memorable and uplifting portrait of Lake Vadimon, 'Flavian' Martial's miraculous arena may even be an expressive 'invisible presence' in the imagery of the text, quietly trumped as 'Trajanic' Pliny reinstates the superiority of simple natural wonders as opposed to elaborate man-made marvels. Not only that, but Pliny also celebrates the simple and accessible pleasure of enjoying wonders by oneself in the countryside – so much better than the orchestrated collective awe of spectators in the demarcated and politically charged space of the arena. Pliny's readers perhaps appreciated the wholesome marvel of Lake Vadimon all the more sharply both through intertextual interaction with Martial and through extratextual interaction with the original amphitheatrical spectacles (or those like them) which underlie the *Liber spectaculorum*. Readers' real experiences as well as the world of texts are relevant here.

---

[60] Herodotus' Egypt is programmatic here. See Rosati 2009: 280.
[61] Beagon 2009: 309.   [62] Birley 1997: 289–96.

In these readings of Pliny and Martial, we can make a fairly strong case for Pliny's portrait of the marvellous Lake Vadimon being sharpened and enhanced by direct engagement with Martial's text. Yet even without positing that sort of authorial interaction, Pliny's readers could still draw on their own knowledge of the *Liber spectaculorum* to *Epistles* 8.20 and thereby appreciate the superiority of the liberating natural marvel at Lake Vadimon by comparing it with Martial's amphitheatrical marvels. That alternative analytical model, putting the author on the back burner, points the spotlight more directly towards the readers. This is important when considering the case of Juvenal. His dark and disturbing marvel (pointedly located on the distant imperial margins) superficially seems very different from the examples in Martial and Pliny. Since the shocking marvel of Juvenal's grotesque cannibals shows no direct intertextual interaction with Pliny's and Martial's texts, what sort of interaction is in play here? I suggest that Juvenal's Hadrianic readers engaging with the cannibals are likely to be enacting an (indirect) interactive triangulation between themselves as readers and these (and other) earlier texts about marvels. Despite Lake Vadimon (uplifting) and the Egyptian cannibals (frightening) being situated at opposite ends of the spectrum of marvels, the same impulses and shared cultural values which prompted Pliny's readers to admire Lake Vadimon would have led Juvenal's readers to condemn the prodigy of the cannibals. Each of our authors in different ways exploits the shared values of their readers to sharpen what is distinctive about their own categorisation of the marvellous.

Marvels by their very nature are defined in relative terms as individual phenomena which stand out as distinctive from what is (has been, or even will be) 'normal'. As such they demand contextualisation and comparison with previous marvels (whether real, textual, or both) and lend themselves to dialogic readings which transcend textual and temporal boundaries – and therefore they offer ideal material for the interactive strategies of analysis which are the cornerstone of this volume. They are naturally situated in the sphere of the superlative, but gain traction from comparative modes of reading. Both authors and audiences knew this and were primed to shape and consume marvels against earlier instances. In that sense they offer perfect material for diachronic analysis, even when apparently situated in a timeless narrative present. This interactive impulse for those enjoying marvels was always a feature of ancient *mirabilia*, regardless of era, but in a post-Domitianic setting, the layers of past marvels were increasingly rich, and our authors had considerable scope for mining them creatively.

CHAPTER 6

Pliny and Suetonius on Giving and Returning Imperial Power

Paul Roche

Introduction

The *Panegyricus* may seem an unlikely repository of textual interactivity. One may instinctively baulk at the notion that a speech delivered in the senate (or that this speech in particular) expects its audience to catch lexical echoes from the literary past. Recent studies seeking to engage with the speech on its own terms have looked for broader contexts with which to rehabilitate it: the sublime, contemporary encomiastic contexts, antithesis, periodisation, self-representation.[1] However, it is also viable to read the *Panegyricus* as possessed of the full allusive apparatus of any carefully composed literary artefact. It was Pliny's intention that his revised speeches be read and contemplated as literature by contemporaries and by posterity. He tells us as much in *Epistles* 3.13 to Voconius Romanus. In that letter, the revised *Panegyricus* is now referred to as a *liber* (*librum, quo nuper optimo principi consul gratias egi*, 'the book with which I, as consul, recently offered thanks to the best of emperors', 3.13.1). So too, in *Epistles* 3.18 to Vibius Severus, Pliny describes the speech as a *uolumen* (*conuenientissimum credidi eadem illa spatiosius et uberius uolumine amplecti*, 'I believed that it was most appropriate to cover the same material more expansively and more copiously in a book', 3.18.1–2). The substitution *liber* ('book') for *oratio* ('speech') is not generally uncommon for orations sent by letters (*TLL* VII.2 1274.81–4, as at *Ep.* 1.2.2), but Pliny's own usage in this regard is quite varied:[2] in describing the *Panegyricus* as a *liber*, and in commencing *Epistles*

---

[1] See e.g. Rees 2012b, esp. pp. 41–3 on the critical reception of the speech. Key studies are Morford 1992 on liberty; Bartsch 1994: 148–87 on sincerity and anxiety; Braund 1998 on the *Panegyricus* as recommending *humanitas* and *ciuilitas* for the new emperor; Rees 2001 on paradox and antithesis; Gowing 2005 on cultural memory; Manolaraki 2008 on political and didactic metaphors. More recently, see the studies in Roche 2011, particularly Hutchinson on the sublime, Gibson on late-Flavian/Trajanic contexts of praise, Henderson on historical exemplarity and Noreña on self-representation.

[2] At *Ep.* 1.8.2 the revised speech he sends to Pompeius Saturninus is called a *sermo*; at *Ep.* 2.5.1 he sends an *actio* to Lupercus; at *Ep.* 1.16.3 he refers to Pompeius Saturninus' published speeches as *orationes*

3.13 with the word *librum*, one may hear in the choice a programmatic allusion to the speech's transformation from performance into literature.

It was moreover Pliny's professed aim for his revised speeches to garner more praise by a reading audience than by those present at a recital (*Ep.* 7.17.7 *Nec uero ego dum recito laudari, sed dum legor cupio. Itaque nullum emendandi genus omitto*, 'Nor do I desire to be praised when I recite, but when I am read; and so I omit no form of correction'). In *Epistles* 3.13 Pliny describes the delights of the newly revised *Panegyricus* for a leisured reader at peace (*lectorem . . . otiosus securusque lector*, 3.13.2): one who can devote himself to its mode of expression (*elocutio*, 3.13.2) and is willing to pay careful attention to its structure, transitions and figures (*ordo . . . transitus . . . figurae*, 3.13.3). These last, he declares, are denied to all but the erudite (*nisi eruditis negatum est*, 3.13.3). A sophisticated author, then, and writing for an exacting readership. We further know with unusual clarity (courtesy of *Ep.* 3.13 and 18) of the laborious process of recital and revision preceding its circulation. These points, no less than the quality of the published oration itself, prompt us to accept the implicit challenge of *Epistles* 3.13: to consider this text as literature and to imagine for it not just a listening audience in September 100, but an attentive, engaged and reflective reading audience thereafter.

To this end, I shall in this chapter consider two aspects of the 'interactive' nature of the *Panegyricus*. I shall first consider Pliny's account of the praetorian mutiny under Nerva in 97. I shall argue that he overlays his treatment of this crisis with allusions to earlier texts that bring with them significant nuances of meaning. I shall then consider whether his client, colleague and friend, Suetonius, may be understood as alluding to and correcting the most tendentious of Pliny's allusions to the Flavian past. This second proposition is not without complicating factors. On the one hand, the nature of their personal relationship, their shared literary milieu, the scope, themes, approaches and preoccupations of their major surviving works, as well as the basic philological evidence that is usually adduced to justify an allusive relationship, will suggest strongly Suetonius' use of the *Panegyricus*. Moreover, the *a priori* case for their interaction is as solid as can be. Pliny's letters attest to their respectful friendship over three decades. We glimpse the two men consulting on matters of rhetoric (*Ep.* 1.18). We observe Pliny reading Suetonius' work, and urging him to

---

(*cum orationes eius in manus sumpseris* 'when you take up his speeches in your hand'; cf. *Ep.* 2.3.10); at *Ep.* 2.19.1 his own revised speech is an *oratio*. Note also that in *Ep.* 3.18 Pliny is not sending the *Panegyricus*, here also called a *liber* (3.18.4), to Vibius Severus.

publish (*Ep.* 5.10). We are made privy to Pliny seeking advice from Suetonius about the etiquette of recitation (*Ep.* 9.34); and of Pliny's regard for
the biographer as scholar (*Ep.* 10.94–5). It would be surprising, then, had
Suetonius not been familiar with Pliny's speeches. On the other hand, the
nature of Suetonius' style in the last of his imperial biographies, which are
characterised by a tendency to compression, summation and an extreme
reluctance to narrate or elaborate, are but one factor that makes it difficult
to establish unequivocally the nature of his engagement with Pliny's speech
to Trajan. I shall return to this issue in the second half of my discussion.

Pliny on Giving and Returning Power in 97

In chapter 6 of the *Panegyricus*, Pliny recounts to his emperor the great
disgrace of his age and the terrible wound inflicted upon the republic. This was the revolt of Nerva's praetorian guard against him in the
autumn of 97.[3] The *Panegyricus* is by far the most detailed source for the
mutiny; and it is contemporary. Apart from a half sentence in Suetonius
(*Dom.* 23.1), the other ancient accounts are in Cassius Dio (68.3.3) and
in the epitome of the fourth-century *De Caesaribus* (12.6–8). The guard,
incited by its prefect Casperius Aelianus, was clamouring for the execution
of Domitian's assassins. According to Pliny, the revolt took place in the
palace: at *Panegyricus* 6.1 he declares that Nerva was *obsessus captus inclusus*
('besieged, captured, contained'). Like so many of the major political
events in the wake of Domitian's assassination, it was concealed from
public view. It remained so until its very public sequel in the thanks that
Nerva was compelled to render up in a speech before the people to his own
mutinous guard because 'they had killed the worst and most wicked of
all mortal men' (*quia pessimos nefandosque omnium mortalium peremissent*,
Epit. de Caes. 12.8). Pliny adverts to this obscurity at *Panegyricus* 5.9, when
he claims that god conceals the *semina* ('seeds') of adversity and prosperity
under the mask of their opposites.

  Pliny thus had considerable freedom in his treatment of this event to
which few were privy, and he naturally shapes his rendition to suit the
themes and agendas at play in his thanksgiving. His choice was to pass
swiftly over what little about the event was already known in a tableau
of almost static, emotive images: a disgrace; a kindly old man robbed of
his authority, defrauded of his autonomy, compelled unwillingly to inflict

---

[3] For the coup and its historical contexts, see Syme 1958: 10–11; Schwarte 1979; Jones 1996: 153; Birley
   1997: 36–9; Griffin 2000: 94–6; Berriman and Todd 2001: 312–31; Eck 2002a; Grainger 2003: 94–6;
   Collins 2009.

capital punishment (*Pan.* 6.1–2). These are then elaborated by a lengthier meditation on the paradoxically providential nature of the crisis, in that it brought Trajan to power (6.3–5). Both the images of the crisis themselves and the exposition of their beneficial outcome are enhanced by a sequence of allusions to earlier texts that present the crisis of 97 and its outcome in terms suggesting earlier civil conflicts.

Pliny's register elevates in his grand opening image of a *magnum . . . saeclo dedecus* ('[that] great disgrace upon the age', 6.1). *Saeclum* as a modifier of *dedecus* is unique in extant Latin; its ready variant *aeuum* ('an age') is only attested twice. The choice phrase may suggest an earlier source; one thinks of the long-standing infamy of the Crassi unavenged and of Parthia's possession of Roman military standards, rectified at last by Augustus in Ovid's *Fasti*:

> Ille notas ueteres et **longi dedecus aeui**
>   sustulit: agnorunt signa recepta suos.
> (Ov. Fast. 5.589–90)

> That man took away those long-standing marks of censure and that **disgrace of a whole age**: the standards, recaptured, recognised their own men.

Closer thematically are the outrages of Gaius Marius' vengeance against his enemies in Lucan's epic:

> Degener o populus, **uix saecula longa decorum**
> sic meruisse uiris, nedum breue **dedecus aeui**
> et uitam dum Sulla redit.
> (Lucan 2.114–16)

> O degenerate people, **hardly was it fitting** for men to have merited **long ages in this way**, let alone this fleeting **disgrace of time** and life while Sulla was returning.

In each case the context as well as the vocabulary and image may be deemed compatible. Trajan fleetingly plays Ovid's Augustus: sweeping away the disgrace of the mutiny of 97, recapturing the praetorian standards for their own master. Or one might see subtle shadings of the Marian anarchy of 87 BC further deepening Pliny's rhetoric of crisis and abetting his image of an emperor who could only assume the burden of empire in order to put a stop to such outrages.[4] Pliny follows with the image of a wound impressed upon the republic: *magnum rei publicae uulnus impressum est*

---

[4] E.g. *Si tamen haec sola erat ratio quae te publicae salutis gubernaculis admoueret, prope est ut exclamem tanti fuisse* ('Nevertheless, if this was the only means to move you towards the helm of public safety, it is almost the case that I should cry out that it was worth so great a price', *Pan.* 6.2).

(6.1). Although this conceit was not exclusive to Cicero,[5] it was so monop-
olised by Pliny's model in both epistolography and rhetoric[6] that one might
hear behind the phrase the damage inflicted upon the commonwealth by
the acquittal of Clodius in 60 BC (*tanto imposito rei publicae uulnere*, 'such a
great wound inflicted upon the republic', *Att.* 1.16.7); or the ruinous scandal that was the consulship of Gabinius and Piso in 58 BC (*scelera uulneraque
inusta rei publicae*, 'crimes and wounds branded upon the republic', *Sest.* 17;
cf. 31); or the destruction meditated for the state by Gaius Gracchus (*quae
hic rei publicae uulnera imponebat, eadem ille sanabat*, 'the wounds that the
former [Gracchus] was inflicting upon the republic, the latter [Drusus] was
attempting to heal', *Fin.* 4.66); or the calamity of Trasimene (*C. Flaminium
Caelius religione neglecta cecidisse apud Transumenum scribit cum magno rei
publicae uulnere*, 'Caelius writes that Gaius Flaminius, after ignoring the
claims of religion, fell at Trasimene with a great wound for the republic',
ND 2.8). All of these events had been described as great wounds inflicted
or branded upon the republic in texts to which Pliny had access.

In such moments it is fair to see the speech assembling behind itself
a complex sequence of allusions that import deeper layers of nuance or
meaning to its surface narrative. However, in this particular section of the
speech the most explicitly marked, the least missable and in many ways the
most challenging of his earlier allusions is not to a literary predecessor at
all, but to Pliny's bête noire, Domitian. At the climax of the passage we
find this (*Pan.* 6.4):

> Imploratus adoptione et accitus es, ut olim duces magni a peregrinis
> externisque bellis ad opem patriae ferendam reuocari solebant. Ita filius ac
> parens uno eodemque momento rem maximam inuicem praestitistis: **ille
> tibi imperium dedit, tu illi reddidisti**.

> You were entreated by adoption and summoned home, as previously great
> generals used to be recalled from foreign wars abroad to bring help to their
> fatherland. Thus it was that father and son together, at one and the same
> moment, you bestowed on each other the greatest of all gifts: **he gave you
> supreme power, and you returned it to him**.

My main concern will be with Pliny's apophthegm on giving and returning
imperium. But we should attend also to the sentences leading up to it, for
they contextualise his closing phrase and well illustrate some of the speech's

---

[5] The only other example is Val. Max. 2.8.7 *uulnera rei publicae*, used of civil conflicts from the Gracchi
to Sulla.

[6] See e.g. Riggsby 1995; Marchesi 2008: 207–40, 252–7; Gibson and Morello 2012: 74–9; Whitton
2013: 2–3.

most prominent strategies of alluding to its past and of performing political memory. The identity of the *duces magni* ('great generals') to whom Trajan is compared has caused some consternation. As John Henderson has put the matter, 'no names pilfer limelight',[7] and Alain Gowing has shown that Pliny's overall tendency in the speech is to avoid naming names other than Trajan's.[8] Who were these generals? Marcel Durry preserves the venerable suggestion that 'they' are Hannibal,[9] while Henderson has entertained the notion of Agesilaus or Camillus, before returning to Hannibal.[10] I suggest rather that Pliny's *olim* does not look that far back in time,[11] and that the *duces magni* recalled from foreign wars abroad to bring aid to their fatherland are Vespasian and Titus, figuratively recalled from the Judaean War in order to restabilise the principate in the wake of the civil wars of 68–9. One of the earliest attempts by the Flavians to legitimise their bid for power in 69 was the circulation of a letter that Vespasian was supposed to have received from the doomed emperor Otho.[12] His death in mid April will put Vespasian in the midst of a 'foreign war abroad' such as Pliny describes (cf. Jos. *BJ* 4.548–51).[13] In that letter, Otho is purported to have begged Vespasian to avenge his death 'and to come to the aid of the republic' (*et ut rei p. subueniret*, Suet. *Vesp.* 6.4). We need not ascribe the notion of recalling Vespasian to assist the republic exclusively to this document; the recasting of a coup as answering the call of a beleaguered state was time-honoured,[14] and the notion of bringing aid to one's *patria* is a leitmotif of early Flavian public imagery. Vespasian initially claimed that he needed forty thousand million sesterces 'so that the state might stand again' (*ut res publica stare posset*, Suet. *Vesp.* 16.3). Suetonius further claims that 'during the whole period of his rule he made it his chief concern . . . to stabilise a republic that was close to ruin and on the verge of collapse' (*per totum imperi tempus nihil habuit antiquius quam prope afflictam nutantemque rem p. stabilire*, *Vesp.* 8.1).

The status of Vespasian and Titus as great generals (*duces magni*) was assured, and provided a useful contemporary foil to the military ineptitude

---

[7] Henderson 2011: 149.   [8] Gowing 2005: 122.

[9] Durry 1938: 93. The conjecture that either Sulla or Hannibal is meant is present as early as the 1676 edition of De la Baume, the latter on the basis of Liv. 30.9 (viz. 3–9); Sulla is dropped by the 1738 edition of Aerntzen.

[10] Henderson 2011: 149.

[11] That is, that Pliny uses it to mean 'formerly' (*OLD* s.v. 1a), not specifically 'a long time ago' (*OLD* s.v. 2a), although the twenty-eight-year difference between autumn 97 and summer 69 might arguably satisfy the latter definition: cf. Cic. *Arch.* 19 *olim*, referring in 62 BC to events that post-date 100 BC.

[12] On the letter, see Ferrill 1965; Levick 1999: 72.   [13] Levick 1999: 38–9.

[14] E.g. Cic. *Phil.* 5.43 *subuenit enim rei publicae* ('for he came to the aid of the republic'), comparing the 'assistance' of Octavian in 44 with that of Pompey in 83 BC: see Manuwald 2007 ad loc.

of Nero.[15] Tacitus points to a tradition of comparing Vespasian with the generals of old, presumably those of the republic: he was considered *antiquis ducibus par* ('a match for our ancient generals', *Hist.* 2.5.1). One may compare Pliny's Trajan, who at *Panegyricus* 12.1 is *Romanum ducem unum ex illis ueteribus et priscis* ('one Roman general from those famous generals of old').[16] Titus had been presented as a spectacular and daring general.[17] In Judaea, his horse had been killed under him mid-siege (either at Taricheae or Gamala, Suet. *Titus* 4.3). When he returned to Rome in mid 71 he was the conqueror of Jerusalem, and the partner of his father's triumph; later he would star in Josephus' *Bellum Judaicum*, in which Titus' personal intervention, his prowess in battle and his acumen as general would often be presented as the difference between victory and defeat.[18]

I suggest that Pliny's point was that Trajan, like Vespasian and Titus before him, was bringing stability to a republic whose crisis was thus likened to the civil anarchy of 69. It is well known that the difficulties besetting Nerva's principate and their resolution in the adoption of Trajan brought to contemporary minds the principate of Galba and that emperor's failure to avert catastrophe in the adoption of Piso at Rome. As Syme framed the matter, 'nobody could ignore or evade the parallel'.[19] However, for Pliny the analogy was not something to ignore or evade; on the contrary, it offered him a valuable rhetorical opportunity. The connection between 97 and 69 plays an important role in the early sections of the speech where his priority is to establish the notion that Trajan's unwillingness to assume authority was overcome only by the extremity of the crisis afflicting the state (e.g. *Pan.* 5.6, 6.2, 7.3–4, 10.1).

In light of the above, when Pliny drew out the moral of his simile and capped it with the epigrammatic tag *ille tibi imperium dedit, tu illi reddidisti* ('he gave you supreme power, and you returned it to him'), one wonders what the reaction in the senate was – and what the later impact upon a reflective readership could have been – given that this unmistakably alludes to a famous utterance made by the emperor Domitian in reference to the same civil war of 69. Suetonius tells us that

> Principatum uero adeptus neque in senatu iactare dubitauit et **patri se et fratri imperium dedisse, illos sibi reddidisse** ... (*Dom.* 13.1)

[15] Jones 1984: 347.   [16] Ash 2007: 88.   [17] See Jones 1984: 41–4, 47–55.   [18] Paul 1993.
[19] Syme 1958: 130, adducing *Pan.* 8.5 *oblitine sumus ut nuper post adoptionem non desierit seditio sed coeperit?* ('Have we forgotten that recently after an adoption rebellion did not cease but actually began?').

> When he became emperor, he did not hesitate to boast in the senate that **he had conferred their power on both his father and his brother, and that they had but returned him his own**.

This is conveyed to us in chapter 13 of the biographer's life of Domitian, which contains examples of that emperor's arrogance. The Latin clearly suggests that Pliny's summation of Trajan's shared authority is cut from the same cloth as Domitian's own claim to be the arbiter of Flavian power. Only in these two passages, of all surviving Latin, is the notion of giving and returning *imperium* so plainly stated.[20] The context of the allusion is also of a piece with what we have seen to be Pliny's allusive strategy when treating the mutiny against Nerva. Trajan, cast in the role of Vespasian and Titus, is given power by Nerva, who is cast in the role of Domitian, only to return it. The allusion also furthers Pliny's strategy of equating the mutiny of 97 with the civil of war of 69. The logic of Domitian's claim about his own distribution of Flavian power turns on his presence as an eighteen-year-old in Rome in the closing months of 69; his salutation as Caesar by the Flavian army who had besieged the city (Tac. *Hist.* 3.86); and his figurehead role as the representative of Vespasian's authority in the capital before his return in the summer of 70.[21]

Pliny's allusion would damn the credibility of both Nerva and Domitian as donators of power.[22] In the crisis of December 69, Domitian – so far from securing *imperium* ('power') to hand over to his father – was under the protection of Vespasian's brother, Flavius Sabinus (Tac. *Hist.* 3.70–2). He had further secured an ignominious flight from the besieged Capitol – *obsessus captus inclusus* ('besieged, captured, contained', *Pan.* 6.1) just as Nerva would be in 97 – by dressing as a priest of Isis and mingling with other priests (Tac. *Hist.* 3.74; Suet. *Dom.* 1.2). In Tacitus' account, Domitian only emerged from hiding after all threat of violence had passed (*postquam nihil hostile metuebatur, Hist.* 3.86). He then watched Flavian power pass from the hands of Antonius Primus in December to those of Mucianus in January. He himself remained a figurehead: *eius nomen epistulis edictisque praeponebatur, uis penes Mucianum erat* ('his name now stood at the head of all dispatches and edicts, but the real authority remained with Mucianus', *Hist.* 4.39). His indefatigable zeal as Caesar in the capital prior to his father's return was famously ridiculed by Vespasian. In a letter that

---

[20] Such phrases as 'surviving Latin' rely upon resources such as *TLL* and the Packard Humanities Institute's corpus of 'classical Latin texts' (at http://latin.packhum.org).

[21] On this period of Domitian's career, see Jones 1992: 14–18; for the broader political context of this period, see Levick 1999: 79–94.

[22] On Pliny's handling of Nerva in the *Panegyricus*, see Roche 2002.

was circulated publicly he thanked his son for allowing him to retain his own post as emperor and he expressed surprise that Domitian had not yet appointed him a successor (Cass. Dio 65(66).2.3). Upon Vespasian's return, Domitian was relegated to third place.[23]

One of Pliny's most pressing ostensible agendas in the *Panegyricus*, the one for which it is perhaps best known and the one that may self-destruct most easily, is the creation of a watershed moment in the assassination of Domitian or in the accession of Trajan in order to safely relegate to the past his own and a broader senatorial compliance in an oppressive regime. Pliny is explicit in his ambition to separate Trajan from the recent imperial past (*Pan.* 2.1–2):

> Equidem non consuli modo sed omnibus ciuibus enitendum reor, ne quid de principe nostro ita dicant, ut idem illud de alio dici potuisse uideatur . . . Nihil quale ante dicamus, nihil enim quale antea patimur . . .

> For my part I am convinced that not only the consul but all citizens must strive to say nothing about our emperor that could possibly have been said about another . . . Let us say nothing such as we did previously; for we suffer nothing such as we did previously . . .

However, in the period 97–100, anyone with eyes to see and the inclination to contemplate so many portrait-busts of Domitian being recarved and reconstituted into images of Nerva and Trajan could have objected that the past was not so easily relegated.[24] In his application to Trajan of the accession rhetoric of Domitian, Pliny seems emphatically to have transgressed his own rhetorical watershed. And more is at stake, I think, than merely denigrating Nerva or associating the crisis of 97 with that of 69. For Domitian's claim was not simply a relic from 81 made famous by his detractors after his death. Nor was it so easily cordoned off in that earliest phase of his principate when, in the assessment of many modern historians and in Pliny's own reconstruction, a more palatable relationship with the senate was on offer.[25] Pliny is in fact quite careful to delineate an earlier, more acceptable phase of Domitian's rule during which his own career advanced, before the emperor 'avowed his hatred for good men' (*ante quam profiteretur odium bonorum*, *Pan.* 95.3). After that, the consul claims that his career slowed.

Domitian's accession sentiments had been re-echoed by Martial in *Epigrams* 9.101, the longest and final political piece in that book, and

[23] See Jones 1992: 19–21.
[24] For Domitianic portraits recarved as Nerva and Trajan, see Varner 2004: 115–23.
[25] See e.g. Eck 1980: 55; Syme 1991b: 560.

an epigram that had become by the time of Pliny's consulship Martial's valedictory statement on Flavian power.[26] Book 9 was published in 94: that is to say after the death of Agricola and at the beginning of a period of tension that was to last until Domitian's death and was marked by a cluster of consular executions.[27] Looking back to the beginning of Domitian's reign Martial writes (*Epig.* 9.101.13–16):

> Asseruit possessa malis Palatia regnis,
>   prima suo gessit pro Ioue bella puer;
> solus Iuleas cum iam retineret habenas,
>   tradidit inque suo tertius orbe fuit.

> He freed the Palatine held under evil dominion, and in boyhood waged his first war for his Jupiter; though he alone already held the Julian reins, he gave them up and became third in the world that was his own.

Martial was very much on Pliny's mind while the *Panegyricus* was undergoing revision and publication. Pliny records the death of the poet at *Epistles* 3.21, the letter that closes Book 3, in which we read of the revision and recital of our speech (*Ep.* 3.13 and 3.18).[28] In the final letter of the book Pliny incorporates *Epigrams* 10.19, in which he had been celebrated by Martial. Martial was, furthermore, not alone in echoing Domitian's apophthegm in the mid 90s. Quintilian, Pliny's teacher, had in the same period further reinvigorated the notion of Domitian's donation of power in 69. At *Institutio* 10.1.91 he alludes to it in the context of Domitian's literary endeavours:

> Quid tamen his ipsis eius operibus in quae **donato imperio** iuuenis secesserat sublimius, doctius, omnibus denique numeris praestantius?

> But what can be more sublime, more learned, more excellent in every detail than those works of his to which he had retired **after conferring imperium**?

The original context of the quotation by Domitian and its iteration by Martial and Quintilian thus effectively span the trajectory of Domitian's principate. Had Pliny's new emperor the inclination to reflect upon the various contexts of Domitian's claim, he might have been struck by the foreboding arrogance of the quote in 81 and its bitter sequel in the mid 90s, when the emperor's relationship with the senatorial aristocracy had deteriorated to the point of lethal dysfunctionality. There was in Pliny's

---

[26] On Mart. 9.101 see Henriksén 2012: 389–413, esp. his overview at pp. 390–6, and comments on our lines at pp. 405–7.

[27] Tac. *Agr.* 42–5; Suet. *Dom.* 10; Cass. Dio 67.13–14; Jones 1992: 182–8; Roche 2003.

[28] Martial's place in *Ep.* 3.21 is also discussed by Rimell, Fitzgerald and Mratschek (see Index locorum).

reapplication of this famous utterance a powerful negative *exemplum* for Trajan to contemplate in the context of his own newly acquired power.

Suetonian Allusion

Thus far Suetonius has been used only to provide objective historical context for Pliny's allusion. However, I contend that a compelling case may be made for the notion that Suetonius is at *Domitian* 13.1 making reference to Pliny's version of Domitian's saying at *Panegyricus* 6.4.[29] Recent scholarship on the imperial biographies has begun to identify and discuss allusions made by Suetonius to earlier literature, but the endeavour of establishing the range of texts co-opted by the biographer is still in its early stages.[30] On any textual criteria, the case to be made for *Domitian* 13.1 as an allusion to *Panegyricus* 6.4 is encouraging. As a useful taxonomy, Jeffrey Wills offers two key criteria for allusion: context and content, the latter being echoes of the text, whether verbal, positional or rhythmical.[31] In their application of the same phrase for a new emperor who claims authority after a crisis only to surrender it, Pliny and Suetonius clearly share context. They obviously have nearly identical content. Although the words used by our authors are each relatively quotidian, nowhere else in surviving Latin do we find the collocation *imperium* ('power'), *dare* ('to give') and *reddere* ('to return'), and especially not crafted into a neat paradox. Wills promotes such shared content as the single most important criterion. The less common such shared content, the more confident we can be in the allusion, provided that the uniqueness cannot be accounted for by an earlier source or *topos*.[32]

Suetonius' phrase does not merely resemble the formal elements of an allusion, it suggests new nuances of meaning in a manner that has come to be associated with such allusions. When one compares Suetonius' version to Pliny's as its original, the effect is to bring into focus a recognisable and common polemical dynamic between texts in allusive relationships, that of a window allusion. It will be instructive to consider Richard Thomas' definition of this phenomenon:

---

[29] On the issue of separating allusions to an historical event from its representation in literature, see Damon 2010; Pelling 2013: 3–4 with references; and Power 2014, esp. pp. 209–17, testing the difference in the case of Suetonius and Tacitus' *Annals*.

[30] See e.g. Power 2007: Suet. *Galba* 19.2–20.1 ~ Virg. *Aen.* 2.148–51; Power 2012: Suet. *Tib.* 57.2 ~ Virg. *Aen.* 2.535–50; Macrae 2015: Suet. *Tit.* 7.2 ~ Virg. *Aen.* 6.460 and Cat. 66.39–40.

[31] Wills 1996: 18. The elements of Wills' basic framework are naturally found in models of allusion by both historians and philologists before and after his formulation: cf. e.g. Syme 1958: 690; Morgan 1977: 3; Hinds 1998: 26–7; Kelly 2008: 166–9. Wills' taxonomy has been applied to test Suetonian allusion by Power 2007: 792 and 2014: 209.

[32] I shall address this proviso shortly.

It consists of the very close adaptation of a model, noticeably interrupted in order to allow reference back to the source of that model: the intermediate model thus serves as a sort of window onto the ultimate source, whose version is otherwise not visible. In the process the immediate, or chief, model is in some fashion 'corrected'.[33]

Each point in Thomas' definition can be mapped onto Suetonius. He very closely adapts Pliny as his model; the adaptation is interrupted by the reattribution of the phrase to Domitian; this allows reference back to Pliny's model in Domitian; and Suetonius has corrected Pliny's use of his model. I suggest that the Suetonian detail at 13.1 *in senatu* not only adds an august location for Domitian's shameless distortion of the truth, but offers a guarantee of the authority of his own claim to recontextualise Pliny's use, in that it is potentially verifiable and on record.[34]

One objection to such a thesis would be that these are, as it were, parallel lines leading back to Domitian as source. That is, that the correspondence of vocabulary points not to an interaction, but to the *ipsissima uerba* of the emperor. However, there is no guarantee that Suetonius is reflecting Domitian's precise words, and some evidence to indicate the variety of phraseology and vocabulary that could evoke Domitian's famous saying. In the first instance, Suetonius does not quote Domitian's remark directly, but reports it in indirect speech. He does this despite the fact that he liberally quotes Domitian in direct speech in the life (there are eleven examples in the *Domitian* including an instance in chapter 13).[35] Moreover, we can see that in the mid 90s, the same utterance had been invoked in both prose and verse using varying expressions. The phrases utilised by Martial, *retineret habenas,* | *tradidit* ('he held the reins, he gave them up'), and by Quintilian, *donato imperio* ('when power had been conferred'), depart considerably from the formulation found in Pliny and in Suetonius. Note also that both Flavian authors could easily have used the vocabulary found in Pliny and Suetonius had they wished to get closer to a purported Domitianic original. The key words in Pliny's rendering were perfectly amenable to elegiac verse and Martial shows no reticence towards using *imperium* or the perfect tense

---

[33] Thomas 1986: 188–9; cf. Wills 1996: 284.

[34] That is, that arbitration on the matter might be found either in contemporary witnesses, their descendants or in the *acta senatus*, 'a highly detailed record with verbatim accounts of senatorial debates, speeches, and formal correspondence with the senate', Wardle 2014: 20; Ryan 1998: 18 n. 41 doubts that they were a verbatim record. On the *acta senatus* see Talbert 1984: 308–34 (and cf. Talbert 1988: 137–47). This is not to suggest that the *acta* was necessarily Suetonius' original source for the saying; cf. Jones 1996: xii 'oral testimony was available in abundance'. Feldherr 2013 considers a comparable example of a window allusion between prose texts to a 'real-life' source (Catiline).

[35] Suet. *Dom.* 9.1, 9.3, 11.1, 11.3, 12.3, 13.2, 15.2, 16.2, 18.2 (twice), 20.

of *dare* and *reddere* elsewhere in this metre.[36] Naturally, Quintilian was free to cast Domitian's saying in any vocabulary he wished, but it bears pointing out that the terms found in Pliny and Suetonius are used multiple times elsewhere in his work.[37] We might finally note that getting closer to the original words used by Domitian could be constructed as more of a priority for two Flavian authors, who might have hoped for the emperor who originally uttered them as a reader of their works.

A further objection might be that the section of Tacitus' *Histories* in which the historian treated the accession of Domitian is no longer extant and that its survival to us may have demonstrated Suetonius reacting not to Pliny but to Tacitus' treatment of the same scene. But no such consistent correlation in detail in reportage of the same senatorial speech in the surviving works of Tacitus and Suetonius would encourage such a belief. Consider the disparity of detail – rhetorical and otherwise – attending their respective accounts of Tiberius' first senatorial speech at *Annals* 1.11–14 and *Tiberius* 23–4, or Nero's accession speech in the senate in *Annals* 13.4 and *Nero* 8. From our extant evidence, from what we can see and compare, it would on odds seem likelier that Suetonius would pointedly avoid rather than emulate so specific a detail, were he to find it in Tacitus; and modern scholarship has more than once asserted that it would be unlikely for Suetonius to consult Tacitus in any case.[38]

Finally, one might object to the anonymity of Suetonius' 'correction' of Pliny, but Suetonius does not mention any written sources of information for his life of Domitian.[39] The content relevant for various parts of the biography overlaps with material treated in Tacitus' *Histories*, Plutarch's biographies of Galba and Otho, Pliny the Elder's *Continuation of Aufidius Bassus*, as well as in the works of Claudius Pollio, Fabius Rusticus, Pompeius Planta, Cluvius Rufus, Vipstanus Messalla, Titinius Capito and Gaius Fannius.[40] Suetonius names no one. In sum, a 'tacit' correction would be completely consistent with Suetonius' aversion to naming sources in his *Domitian*.

---

[36] First occurrence noted only: *imperium*: *Epig.* 6.61.4; *dedi*: 1.58.2; *reddidi*: 6.89.6.

[37] First occurrence noted only: *imperium*: *Inst.* 9.2.67; *dedi*: 9.2.74; *reddidi*: 9.3.23.

[38] Syme 1980: 111 'The *Historiae* of Cornelius Tacitus no man of the time could ignore. Suetonius decided to write as though that masterpiece did not exist. Demonstrating his independence, he went back to the sources employed by the eloquent consular. The biographer made his own selection, for purposes of his own'; Power 2014: 218 on the *Annals*: Suetonius seems 'entirely ignorant of Tacitus' writing'.

[39] On this pattern in the latter lives, see Townend 1959: 288–9; Cornell 2013: 128–9.

[40] See Jones 1996: xi.

Conclusion

In this chapter I have attempted to demonstrate and interpret some of the allusive potential of the *Panegyricus*. I have suggested that Suetonius was familiar with Pliny's speech; that he recognised his misapplication of Domitian's tag about giving and receiving power; and that he corrected it by a window allusion through Pliny to his ultimate source in Domitian's utterance. I have also tried to contextualise this interaction against the style and tendencies of the later biographies in Suetonius' *Lives* and have attempted to meet such objections as might be made to reading their shared content and context as an allusion. I have opted to make a detailed case for one example because the notion of Suetonius as a reader of Pliny, and perhaps especially of the *Panegyricus*, is one that is yet to be established and accepted: as the matter has been put in the case of the *Epistles*, the present task is to separate common contemporary coin from intertextuality.[41] Here, I think, we have a defensible case of the latter. The notion of Suetonius citing Pliny is in itself significant. It suggests in Suetonius an engaged reader of Pliny's speech in a period in which his oeuvre seems to be slipping into obscurity.[42] Moreover, it implies a readership for Suetonius who can recognise an allusion to the *Panegyricus*. We may assume for example that Septicius Clarus, the dedicatee of both Pliny's letters and of Suetonius' biographies, was familiar with the work of both men and was in a position as reader to appreciate Suetonius' correction. To allude to a text is to give to it or recognise its cultural authority. In the act of correcting Pliny's application of Domitian's famous utterance, Suetonius marks the *Panegyricus* as a privileged repository of information about the imperial past. This was a destiny that Pliny nowhere explicitly dreams for his speech, but one with which he can hardly have been displeased.

[41] Whitton 2013: 35 n. 204.   [42] Rees 2011: 175–7; Whitton 2013: 35.

CHAPTER 7

*From Martial to Juvenal (*Epigrams *12.18)*

Gavin Kelly

Dum tu forsitan inquietus erras
clamosa, Iuuenalis, in Subura,
aut collem dominae teris Dianae;
dum per limina te potentiorum
sudatrix toga uentilat uagumque   5
maior Caelius et minor fatigant:
me multos repetita post Decembres
accepit mea rusticumque fecit
auro Bilbilis et superba ferro.
Hic pigri colimus labore dulci   10
Boterdum Plateamque – Celtiberis
haec sunt nomina crassiora terris –:
ingenti fruor improboque somno,
quem nec tertia saepe rumpit hora,
et totum mihi nunc repono, quicquid   15
ter denos uigilaueram per annos.
Ignota est toga, sed datur petenti
rupta proxima uestis a cathedra.
Surgentem focus excipit superba
uicini strue cultus iliceti,   20
multa uilica quem coronat olla.
Venator sequitur, sed ille quem tu
secreta cupias habere silua;
dispensat pueris rogatque longos
leuis ponere uilicus capillos.   25
Sic me uiuere, sic iuuat perire.

While you perhaps, Juvenal, wander restlessly in noisy Subura or tread Lady
Diana's hill, while your sweating toga fans you as you cross the thresholds of

My thanks to the editors of this book, who have taught me much, to Sam Hayes, who offered valuable
suggestions, and to James Uden for collegially sharing a section of his book on Juvenal in advance of
publication. The chapter was completed in Munich, where I was supported by a fellowship from the
Alexander von Humboldt Foundation.

the powerful and the Greater and Lesser Caelian tire you with wandering: me my Bilbilis, proud of her gold and iron, revisited after many Decembers, has received and made a rustic. Here in idleness I exert myself pleasantly to visit Boterdus and Platea (such are the uncouth names in Celtiberian lands). I enjoy an enormous, indecent amount of sleep, often unbroken even past the third hour, and pay myself back in full now for my vigils of thirty years. The toga is unknown, but when I ask I am handed the nearest garment to hand from a broken chair. When I get up, a fireplace welcomes me, stocked with a proud pile of logs from an adjacent oak wood and crowned by the *uilica* with many a pot. The huntsman comes next, but one that you would like to have in a secret grove. The smooth-skinned *uilicus* gives the boys their rations and asks me to let him make a dedication of his long hair. So it pleases me to live, and so to die.[1]

This chapter takes a single, well-known epigram, addressed by Martial from his Spanish retirement to his younger contemporary Juvenal in Rome, as a focal point for exploring the interaction between the two poets afresh. The poem shows not only a textual but a personal interaction between two authors normally seen as belonging to different generations: Martial is thought of as a Flavian poet and a toady of Domitian, leaving Rome for Spain in about the year 98, not long after the new regime established itself, and dying about five years later; Juvenal, though obsessed with Domitian, is normally thought to have begun publishing in the second half of Trajan's reign. This poem, published shortly before Martial's death in the last of his fifteen books of epigrams, would by the standard view pre-date all five books of Juvenal's *Satires*.[2]

In extant Latin literature, there are few relationships between authors writing in different generic traditions that are as strikingly close as that between Martial and Juvenal.[3] It is natural enough that scoptic epigram and satire should be seen as closely aligned. Both genres deal expressly and frankly with human foibles as opposed to higher ideals or the gods and heroes of epic or tragedy. Martial came up with the motto *hominem pagina nostra sapit* ('my page has the flavour of *man*', *Epig.* 10.4.10), while in an equally programmatic passage Juvenal described the ingredients of his

---

[1] Martial 12.18, translated by Shackleton Bailey 1993, with some modifications.

[2] That is, Books 1–12 of Martial's *Epigrams*, plus the earlier collections *De spectaculis*, *Xenia* and *Apophoreta*, the latter two of which are labelled editorially as Books 13 and 14. On the suggestion that Book 12 was posthumously published, see n. 20.

[3] Contrast the much greater distance involved in the interactions traced between Martial and Tacitus by Rimell in this volume, and those between Martial and Pliny traced by Fitzgerald and Mratschek.

work: *quicquid agunt homines, uotum, timor, ira, uoluptas, | gaudia, discursus, nostri farrago libelli est* ('whatever people do – their prayers, their fears, their anger, their pleasure, their joys, their exchanges – is the mishmash of my book', *Sat.* 1.85–6). Their choices of subject matter, traditional as they are, overlap to a remarkable degree: arrivistes and effeminates, foreigners and women, the rich and the poor, legacy-hunters and bad writers are all mocked, from the viewpoint of a middle-ranking, middle-aged Roman male citizen-poet. Moreover, both poets relentlessly set their scene in the city of Rome (scenes outside Rome are always imagined in comparison to Rome) and address a primary audience there.[4] However, we are dealing not simply with a similarity of themes but with a powerful and wide-ranging intertextual relationship: 'Martial's influence on Juvenal is massive', as a commentator remarks.[5] A good deal has been published on individual intertexts,[6] but the point can be made powerfully enough by remarking on how some of Martial's epigrams seem to prefigure entire satires of Juvenal. The obnoxious party host Zoilus in *Epigrams* 3.82, subjecting his guests to inferior foods while he gorges himself on luxury products, resembles the Virro of Juvenal's fifth Satire. An epigram of Martial's first book, presenting a serious and hirsute philosopher, before revealing his role as a bride in a wedding ceremony, recalls in its details and could almost serve as a summary *avant la lettre* of the second Satire.[7]

Of course the comparison needs to be qualified in some ways. The likeness is greatest of all between Martial and the earlier, angrier satires of Juvenal, the first two books or perhaps the first three.[8] Martial's flattering attentions to a diverse range of wealthy patrons contrasts with the absence of any patron figure in Juvenal: although his individual satires may have ostensible addressees, these are shadowy figures and definitely not patrons. For all that, the two poets are remarkably, unmistakably close. The same

---

[4] See e.g. Roman 2010.   [5] Williams 2004: 11.

[6] See Colton 1991 (I do not here mention Colton's numerous journal articles on this theme from the early 1960s onward, but the reader can consult *L'Année philologique*).

[7] Mart. 1.24 *Aspicis incomptis illum, Deciane, capillis, | cuius et ipse times triste supercilium, | qui loquitur Curios assertoresque Camillos? | Nolito fronti credere: nupsit heri* ('Do you see that fellow with the unkempt hair, Decianus, whose grim eyebrow daunts even you, who speaks of the Curii and Camilli, champions of liberty? Don't believe in appearance: he took a husband yesterday'); cf. Juvenal 2.3 *qui Curios simulant et Bacchanalia uiuunt*; 8–9 *frontis nulla fides; quis enim non uicus abundat | tristibus obscenis?*; 15 *supercilio breuior coma*; 134 *nubit amicus* ('who pretend to be the Curii and live the Bacchanalia . . . There's no trust in appearances: what village is not overflowing with the grim perverts? . . . hair shorter than their eyebrow . . . a friend is taking a husband'). For discussion of *Epig.* 1.24 and *Sat.* 2, and the related *Epig.* 12.42, see Anderson 1970: 24–8.

[8] That is, Satires 1–6 or 1–9. On anger as the defining feature of the early Juvenal, and the move away from it, see Braund 1988. For a summary of the influence of Martial on Juvenal's books see Anderson 1970: 5–6, and Colton 1991 for detailed coverage.

scholars have often treated both,[9] and they are often treated together:[10] a classic example is Bramble's chapter on the two poets in the *Cambridge History of Latin Literature*, which deals with the problem of Martial's profound influence on his younger contemporary by looking down on him. In recognition of the same problem, a distinguished Roman historian once remarked to me that one of the reasons he would not trust Juvenal as a source for Roman social history was that the content of the *Satires* seemed in effect a fantasia on themes of Martial.

I have remarked on the possibility of seeing both a personal and a literary (indeed, as we shall see, intertextual) interaction here. Martial's verse in general is addressed to and engages with many well-attested contemporaries. For Juvenal, by contrast, the poem under discussion and the other two seemingly addressed to him (*Epig.* 7.24 and 7.91) are the only definite contemporary mentions of him – and he can only really be identified as the addressee of the other two, which are much less informative, because of this one.[11] Indeed the poem is the only solid evidence for a close, non-hostile connection between him and an identifiable contemporary.[12] The greater difficulty with linking Juvenal to his contemporaries has, unsurprisingly, led to different styles of scholarship on the two poets. Martial's verse is interpreted as playing a function in patronage relationships, and biographical inferences about Martial from his work are treated in scholarship as a real possibility, for all the potential problems.[13] For Juvenal, by contrast, most scholarship would now identify the speaker of the satires as a literary persona with no certainty that any biographical inference at all is possible: and even if there has been a tendency to nuance and question persona theory in recent times, the dominant mood is utterly different from the positivism of Gilbert Highet's *Juvenal the Satirist* (1954).[14] Highet identified the speaker of the *Satires* fairly straightforwardly with the poet

---

[9] For example, the nineteenth-century commentaries of L. Friedländer (1886 on Martial and 1895 on Juvenal) and the twenty-first-century ones of L. and P. Watson (2003 on selected epigrams of Martial and 2014 on Juvenal 6).

[10] E.g. Anderson 1970; Bramble 1982.

[11] These two poems give much less impression of their addressee, who would perhaps not even be identified with the satirist, and certainly not with any assurance, were it not for the existence of 12.18. Galán Vioque 2002 ad 7.24 (p. 180) accepts the identification but points out that 'this *cognomen* is a common one'. Why we should think of the addressee of 12.18 as Juvenal the satirist will become apparent in the discussion that follows.

[12] This generalisation holds, I think, irrespective of whether Juvenal's claim at the end of the first Satire to attack only the dead (170–1) is taken seriously.

[13] Despite understandable caution, this is the basic assumption of such standard works as Sullivan 1991 (see e.g. pp. xxii–xxv), and can be found, for example, in many of the essays in Grewing 1998.

[14] For exemplary recent discussions see Watson and Watson 2014: 1–8, 35–48; Uden 2015: 3–8.

Juvenal; taking into account the other two epigrams addressed to a Iuvenalis, he infers a picture of their rocky relationship quite unlike anything
that anybody else has seen in the poem: a nice demonstration of the arbi-
trariness of his method.[15] To look at Martial and Juvenal together, then,
is also to contemplate the interaction of contrasting scholarly approaches.
Martial's busy and unending performance of social interactions through his
epigrams has shaped his scholarship so that prosopographical and chronological questions mingle with careful weighing of the balance between fantasy and joking on the one hand and *Realien* on the other; Juvenal's portrayal of himself in opposition to and isolation from his contemporaries, in
accordance with but going beyond the requirements of his genre, sets the
tone for scholarship much less imbued in the contemporary world.

In what follows, I first explore the poem's context in Martial's oeuvre,
its argument, and its generic affiliations, arguing for the importance of the
satiric genre and of previous epigrams of Martial, especially *Epigrams* 1.49:
this lays the necessary ground for looking specifically at the possibility that
Martial alludes to Juvenal in the poem, and the implications of that possibility. The brief section that follows adds to the discussion another, hitherto
seemingly unnoticed allusion to a contemporary, and its implications for
Martial's poetics.

The Poem's Place in the Collection and Its Argument

Before turning to the poem itself, it may be helpful first to say a word about
the way that scholars have found it increasingly profitable to interpret individual poems in the context of the collection as a whole. Of course, the
epigram book is a highly excerptible genre, and some of the poems appear
at least to have an origin in a particular occasion or to preface a private
collection of epigrams; still, Martial's books were organised with immense
care and much can be gained from the perspective of the book (which
is, after all, the medium in which the poems were transmitted: we cannot
always be sure that any earlier versions contained the same text).[16] Indeed, it
has been argued that the whole collection of twelve books, although bearing the traces of their separate publication, mostly on an annual basis at

[15] *Epig.* 12.18 is 'a letter in poetry which reads lightly and pleasantly but which is in fact rather
cruel ... It looks as though the two men had been estranged. In the earlier poems Martial protests
his ardent friendship and sends a gift. In this he stands aloof, without pity, almost with amusement'
(Highet 1954: 18). For his inferences from Martial's poems on Juvenal's homosexuality, see n. 49.

[16] For exploration of 'arrangement' within the oeuvre, see e.g. Fowler 1995; Scherf 2001; Holzberg
2002, 2004/5; Lorenz 2004; Maltby 2008.

Saturnalia, is designed as an oeuvre (twelve books being, of course, a canonical number since the *Aeneid*).[17] Now naturally the historical Martial cannot have known that he would die after twelve books, and we have no way of knowing that he would not have published more had he lived; but for a published poet of epigrams to issue his 'first book of epigrams' perhaps as much as two decades into his career is clearly indicative of design. This tension between reading by the book and seeing a carefully planned oeuvre on the one hand, and a fragmented historical analysis of the individual poems on the other, finds close parallels in other genres and above all in letter collections.[18] Pushed to an extreme, the two approaches can be incompatible, and the impression of incompatibility can be reinforced by the fact that these forms of interpretation tend to be practised by different scholars.[19] However, there is no reason why one cannot appreciate an aesthetic effect which might in historical terms be the result of a sequence of sometimes serendipitous decisions by the author over a period of years, nor to let such aesthetic effects blind one to powerful internal evidence for the corpus' composition.

The role of authorial design in Martial's twelfth and last book of epigrams is, in fact, controversial. From its prose preface and many of its poems it can be inferred that it was sent to Rome from Martial's retirement in Spain, probably at the end of 101, more than three years after the second edition of Book 10. However, scholars have found aspects of the organisation puzzling, and it is possible that the book in the form we have it is a posthumous collection.[20] For all that, it is possible to interpret

---

[17] See especially Holzberg 2002: 123–51.

[18] For the potential of reading by the book in our period, the closest analogue is naturally Pliny's letters: see Gibson and Morello 2012. For a good example of the two approaches in tension, see Gibson 2013 and Mathisen 2013 on Sidonius.

[19] I am sceptical of Holzberg's ingenious attempt (2004/5: 213–22, expanding on Holzberg 2002, esp. pp. 139–45) to evade the evidence that our version of Book 10 postdates Book 11: clearly this arises from historical contingency, specifically, the fall of Domitian. See Rimell in this volume.

[20] The date to be ascribed to Book 12 is complicated by the question as to whether the prefatory letter was written as the preface to the book as we have it or for a smaller collection sent to Priscus. If the former, the book seemingly belongs at the end of a year, given Instantius Rufus' arrival as a governor in Baetica (12.98), coincides with the consulate of Stella (12.2.10), who must be a suffect in 101 or 102, and comes after three years of idleness, a *triennium desidiae*, 12.*pr.* Given that the publication of the second version of Book 10 must belong to the year 98, the latter is a strong indication in favour of a date of 101. If the book is later than the preface, as has sometimes been thought (e.g. Friedländer 1886: 67), the most plausible date would be very soon afterwards, given the reuse of the preface, though it is not impossible that the book was assembled posthumously (for rejection of this suggestion and bibliography, see Lorenz 2002: 234–8, followed by Holzberg 2002: 145–7). Martial's death is attested in Pliny *Ep.* 3.21, in a book which otherwise records events before late 103 (Sherwin-White 1966: 31–2). For further discussions, see Sullivan 1991, 52–5; Howell 1998; Rimell 2008: 191–2; Craca 2011: 5–9.

chains of arrangement in this book as in others.[21] The opposition between
Spain and Rome is a running theme of the book from the preface onwards
(2, 9, 21, 31, 34, 62, 68); and there is also an ongoing and closely linked
opposition, similarly beginning in the preface, between rustic and urban
life, both in these poems and in others which lack a Spanish perspective:
for example, a number of poems on the pleasures of hunting (1, 14) or the
advantages of Martial's old villa in Nomentum over life in Rome (57, 60).[22]
Attitudes to his homeland vary in Book 12. To give some examples, in the
preface, addressed to Priscus as he arrives in Spain, Martial talks of missing his Roman audience and of the problem of small-town jealousies, and
worries that he sends to Rome a book not just from Spain but Spanish
(*non Hispaniensem librum . . . sed Hispanum*). Poem 2 imagines his book
going to Rome, and seems to answer the preface's concerns by imagining
his book's welcome despite its status as a non-Roman, a *peregrinus* (12.2.2):
if the focus is on Rome, the model in Ovid's exile poetry may not reflect
well on his feelings about Spain.[23] In 12.31 he praises the house and land
given to him by Marcella in idealistic terms, casting himself as a returning
Ulysses, against which in 12.21 the highest compliment that can be paid to
his provincial patroness is that she would fit in like a native daughter at
Rome and in her own person mitigates his longing for the city. Along with
12.31, poem 18 is notable within the book for showing a clear preference for
Spain; it sits at one extreme of a range of views on the nature of absence
from Rome, and is the most explicitly distant from Martial's former life
and art.[24]

Idealising visions of his Spanish homeland had also occurred in Martial's
earlier books, published before his return.[25] The letter to Juvenal reprises
various elements from such poems, in particular those in praise of Bilbilis.
Above all we can see a recasting of a poem in the very first book, with a
pleasing symmetry – and this is not, as we shall see below, the only way
in which the poem presents closural qualities. *Epigrams* 1.49 is addressed
to the poet's friend Licinianus, who is about to travel to Spain. It praises
Bilbilis for its situation and natural resources (1.49.3–6; cf. 12.18.9), as well

---

[21] E.g. Rimell 2008: 195; cf. n. 23. Of course, that meaning can be extracted is no guarantee of arrangement by the author himself: cf. Lavan's stimulating reflections on Pliny's Book 10 in this volume.

[22] There are many poems which have a purely Roman perspective: a natural assumption is that they
were written earlier and fitted into this book, though that is unknowable from the book as we have
it.

[23] On this intertextual relationship, see Hinds 2007: 133–4; on intertextuality with the exile poetry
more broadly, 129–36.

[24] See Hinds 2007: 133 n. 58.   [25] Dolç 1953.

as nearby sites including Boterdus (1.49.7 ~ 12.18.11),[26] and describes the possibilities for swimming and hunting (1.49.9–26), before imagining a domestic scene with a friendly gamekeeper, much as in the letter to Juvenal (1.49.29–30 ~ 12.18.22–3). Then, in implicit contrast to Rome, the advantages of country life are listed, many of which are repeated in 12.18: the absence of the toga (which for Licinianus is a purple-striped senatorial one, 1.49.31–2 ~ 12.18.17), clients, widows, defendants (1.49.33–5) – and the resulting possibility of sleeping all morning (1.49.36 ~ 12.18.13–16). In accordance with the change in the status of the addressee in poem 12.18, the annoyance of having clients is changed to the annoyance of being a client; interestingly, Martial will pick up on both 1.49 and 12.18 later in Book 12, in a poem where the narrator complains at being woken by his own client: this was why he left Rome (*urbis mihi causa relictae*, 12.68.1), and if he has to lose sleep here as well, he might as well go back (*redeo, si uigilatur et hic*, 12.68.6).[27] 1.49 ends with a two-line summary on how best to spend one's life (41–2), matching the one-line conclusion of the letter to Juvenal (12.18.26).

Epigrams 1.49 is notable for a striking indebtedness to the satirical mode, and Horace in particular; arguably the same can be said of 12.18. At base, the town/country dichotomy is not particularly typical of Roman epigram, and Martial's deployment of it owes much to Roman satire.[28] The presence of intertextuality with Horace is particularly dense in 1.49, and much discussed.[29] The sententious closing lines of both poems, in place of the joke that Martial normally favours, seems to set a seal on their close relationship, resembling as they do the conclusions of a number of Horace's *Satires* (for example, 1.3, 1.6, 2.2, 2.6).[30] Horace's second Epode can be seen as a primary model for 1.49, which follows it in its metre (alternating iambic trimeters and dimeters), even if Horace's ironic final twist – that the conventional praises of country life turn out to be the words of a cynical urban moneylender – is absent. The same poem is also the object of clear allusion early in 12.18 (*dum per limina te potentiorum*, 4 ~ *Epodes*

---

[26] The specific comment on the outlandish sounds of Spanish names (12.18.12) echoes a second poem about Bilbilis, which like 1.49 is addressed to Licinianus: 4.55.9 *nostrae nomina duriora terrae* ('our land's harsh names'), a few lines after which Platea is named (4.55.13 ~ 12.18.11).

[27] Of course, still other poems in Book 12 will remark not on *imperia uiduarum*, the commands of widows, but a generous, and as far as we know unmarried, patroness, Marcella (12.21, 12.31), who is alone capable of making him feel as if he is in Rome again (*Romam tu mihi sola facis*, 12.21.10). The connection is reinforced by Martial's fondness in Book 12 for casting Rome through the metonymy of its Subura district: we move from it as the district of Stella's house (12.2.9), to the location of the wandering client Juvenal (12.18.2), to the place where Marcella might have been born (12.21.9).

[28] Merli 2006a.   [29] Salemme 1976: 86–92.   [30] See Craca 2011: 139.

2.7–8 *forumque uitat et superba ciuium | potentiorum limina*).[31] The satirical patina, of course, is still more appropriate in 12.18, a poem addressed to a satirical poet, than in 1.49; further satirical intertexts can be identified in the poem, as we shall see below.

In contrast to 1.49, where references to the disadvantageous aspects of urban life are embedded within a description of a Spanish rural idyll, *Epigrams* 12.18 makes the town/country divide much more explicit in its structure: first, in lines 1–6 the poem summons up the drudgery of Juvenal's imagined life in Rome, and then in stark contrast it depicts the idyll of Martial's life in Spain in the last twenty lines. This opposition is also linked with the poem's epistolary mode and emphasis on the distance between speaker and addressee: in contrasting the misery of the addressee's life, which was previously the author's, with the pleasant situation of the author now, the poem has been compared to a holiday postcard[32] (one can also see the potential cruelty of the 'wish you were here' cliché in Martial's emphasis on how much Juvenal would like his gamekeeper, 22–3).

The situation of Juvenal is directly opposed to Martial's by the chiastic arrangement of persons and cases across the first ten lines, with the second person in subject and object mirrored by first-person object and subject (*dum tu* (1), . . . *dum . . . te* (4), *me . . .* (7), *hic colimus* (10)). Roman topography, in the names of Subura, the Aventine (expressed through metonymy) and the Caelian hills (2–6), is balanced in 9–11 with the exotic names of Bilbilis, Boterdus and Platea. Martial's new habit of sleeping in is explicitly presented as payback for his thirty years of wakefulness in Rome (15–16). And Juvenal is currently suffering from lack of sleep in Rome as well, as we learn both explicitly (*inquietus*, 1) and indirectly through reference to the noise of Subura (*clamosa*, 2) and to the toga-clad Juvenal entering the thresholds of powerful patrons for the morning *salutatio* (4–5): we know from elsewhere of the need for the client to rise before dawn, and the lack of sleep that that entails. Juvenal's tiredness (*teris* (3), *fatigant* (6)) is contrasted with Martial's idleness (*pigri . . . labore dulci*, 10) and his restlessness (*erras* (1), *teris* (3), *uagum* (5)) with Martial's gloriously immobile morning routine (17–21). Indeed that routine is described in pointed opposition to the situation of a Roman client. He does not get up early. The toga (17), which elsewhere in Martial is the worst thing about Rome and a metonymy for early morning *salutatio*, is unknown. Instead, he asks for and receives the nearest piece of clothing from a broken chair (17–18). The words used

---

[31] 'While over the thresholds of the powerful . . .' ~ 'and avoids the forum and proud thresholds of the powerful'.

[32] Neger 2012: 258.

to describe this, *sed datur petenti* ('but one is given on asking...'), may perhaps evoke the *sportula* given to the client at the patron's house.

A contrast is also made between the types of company that Juvenal and Martial keep. While Juvenal treads the threshold of the powerful as a client, Martial rises late to be greeted by his household slaves. After asking for and receiving his simple clothes, he descends to a roaring hearth, another marker of the country in opposition to Rome, on which the *uilica* is cooking. Mention of her leads into mention of his other slaves. The *uenator*, the gamekeeper, has been seen before in 1.49, where he was a dinner guest – a sign of rustic equality. In this instance, he is transformed into an object of sexual desire: *uenator sequitur, sed ille quem tu | secreta cupias habere silua*, 22–3. One Italian scholar explains that the *secreta silua* would be where the better game was found,[33] whether from naïveté or the disingenuousness appropriate to a school edition; however, the euphemistic sexual sense of *habere* is well attested ('wohl *ad paedicandum*', as Friedländer remarks), *sed* implies that the huntsman has qualities other than his professional skills, and the monosyllable *tu* is emphatic at the line end.[34]

The point is repeated for the *uilicus*, the steward (24–5):

> dispensat pueris rogatque longos
> leuis ponere uilicus capillos.

The interpretation of the lines has provoked unaccountable problems for some interpreters, though the meaning is quite clear.[35] A passage of Columella expressing the view that a *uilicus* should be a mature slave is often cited (*RR* 11.1.3);[36] but while the slave here performs the essential duties of a *uilicus* in giving the other slaves (and here *pueri* need not imply that these slaves are all boys)[37] their rations, he is also clearly far from this ideal age. He is, however, the ideal age for a sexual fantasy, a youth at the peak of his attractiveness, as indicated by the fact that he is *lēuis*, beardless, and by his possession of the locks of a *puer capillatus*. The prospect of him removing his hair refers to the rite of passage in which long-haired boys cut off their locks as a sign of adulthood – and thereby also remove the indication

---

[33] Serafini 1947: 51.

[34] Friedländer 1886 ad loc. acknowledges that this interpretation derives from his correspondence with Walther Gilbert; see also Howell 1998: 178.

[35] It is rightly understood, for example, by Friedländer 1886 (who again cites his correspondence with Walther Gilbert for his interpretation); Shackleton Bailey 1993; Obermayer 1998: 112–13; Howell 1998: 178–9; Watson and Watson 2003; Neger 2012: 258–60.

[36] E.g. Tränkle 1996: 143; but Watson and Watson 2003 ad loc. and Neger 2012: 259 rightly realise that this is relevant only to portraying the scene as a fantasy.

[37] Cf. e.g. Virg. *Ecl.* 1.45; see *TLL* s.v. *puer* 2Bb.

and presumption of their availability as sex objects. Attempts to argue that the haircut is to be given to others (the *pueri*, or their hippyish master[38]) seem often to arise from prudishness;[39] they founder on the fact that there are no parallels for (*de*)*ponere capillos* or *crinem* referring to cutting somebody else's hair. While *ponere capillos* can refer simply to arrangement of hair,[40] the commonest sense, exemplified several times in Martial, is that of dedicating one's hair when it has been cut.[41] Domitian's eunuch favourite Earinus 'dedicated his sweet hair' (*dulcis . . . capillos . . . posuit*, 9.16.1–2), and in another poem inspired Ganymede himself to ask for a haircut, 'once he'd dedicated his lock' (*posito modo crine*, 9.36.1). Later in Book 12, a pretty boy asks to spoil his hair (*uiolare capillos*), but the paradoxical result is that he seems even more attractive having dedicated his locks (*positis . . . crinibus*). In these cases one suspects that, given the common sense of *ponere* as 'remove' and the comparable usage *deponere capillos*, the formal sense of *ponere capillos*, making a dedication of one's own hair, could easily merge into the simpler sense 'cutting', so translators who write that the *uilicus* wants to get his long hair cut are more or less right.[42] There are a number of similar passages in Martial in which masters choose to grant the request of their young slaves to cut their long hair: a painful choice but also an exercise of the master's sexual authority.[43]

How does the last line, *sic me uiuere, sic iuuat perire*, cap the poem? As we have already seen, it can be understood in the context of the debate on the *uita beata*, about whether the town life or the country life is best. It has the same function as the similar ending did in 1.49 and a number of Horatian satires before it: a decided answer in favour of the ideal *otium* of a simple country life. Of course in this poem, unlike those predecessors, it follows a description in which Martial's portrayal of his country property

---

[38] For Martial's own hair, see Curchin 2003: 222, misinterpreting (*de*)*ponere capillos* as 'give a haircut'. For the other slaves' hair, see e.g. Craca 2011: 139 and n. 47, understanding *lēuis* as bald and similarly misinterpreting *pono*: she cites *OLD* s.v. *pono* 6b ('to have . . . cut') as meaning 'tagliare', without realising that all cases refer to individuals dedicating or cutting their own hair; so too Tränkle 1996: 143–4, who, however, understands the meaning of *ponere capillos* and so perversely reads *lēuis* as accusative: the steward asks that the beardless boys should cut their own long hair.

[39] Tränkle 1996: 144, for example, wonders what the *uilica* of line 21 would think of her husband being treated as a sex-object of the master. But if she is indeed intended as the *uilicus*' spouse, this is not the only place where Martial remarks on the sexual attractiveness and availability of heterosexually partnered male slaves: cf. 2.48.5– 6 *et grandem puerum diuque leuem | et caram puero meo puellam* ('and a large boy, long keeping his cheeks smooth, and the girl who is dear to my boy').

[40] Especially in Ovid: *Am.* 1.7.68, 2.81; *Met.* 1.477 (a line deleted by Tarrant, however); cf. also Manil. 5.147.

[41] Varro fr. Non. p. 94, 18, Ov. *Met.* 3.506, Stat. *Theb.* 6.517, Martial 9.16.2 (cited in the text).

[42] Tibullus 2.1.48, Martial 5.48.6, Petronius 104.5; sometimes it refers to trees 'shedding their locks' (Ov. *Ars* 3.38, Stat. *Theb.* 9.596). Exceptionally at Juvenal 3.186 it means 'dedicate'.

[43] See, for example, the Earinus poems (9.16, 9.17, 9.36), as well as 1.31, 5.48, 12.82. For an interpretation of the passage along these lines, see Obermayer 1998: 112–14.

has gone well beyond the vaguely idealised Spanish countryside that was presented in 1.49: with all these handsome young slaves his home is also a pederast's paradise, which is surely to be understood as the reason why the poet's environment is so pleasing. Moreover, when Martial speaks not only of his ideal life but also of his ideal death, *perire*, it has been suggested plausibly that one can see not only an allusion to his advanced years, but also an implied reference to sexual climax: a jokey ending after all.[44] I would like to canvas a third possibility: it does not contradict the other two, and Martial's poetry can surely carry multiple meanings and operate on multiple emotional levels. This would be to understand the line as showing empathy with the boy-*uilicus*' wish to remove the long hair that associates him with sexual passivity. The condition of the client, in which Martial had once existed and Juvenal still does in the poem, is often compared to servitude by Martial; taken a step further, could it be seen as equivalent to sexual passivity? Does the *uilicus*' wish to give up his long hair match Martial's pleasure in giving up clientship and Rome? This would bring a degree of unity to the poem.

To summarise, the poem can be interpreted through its echoes of a number of other themes of Martial's corpus and of the satirical genre. A traditional debate between the desirability of town and country living is heightened by the greater distance between speaker and addressee. One can illustrate by the contrast to 1.49, where Martial addresses a *propemptikon* to a fellow Spaniard who will be returning to their homeland, characterised in passing as an advocate and as senator (lines 32–3). In 12.18 the opposition between town and country is heightened, as is the closely linked opposition between Rome and Spain, by being in letter form, written from Spain to an addressee in Rome. The addressee is more strongly characterised and associated with Rome as a client, and the country is idealised as the opposite of Rome. Martial also supplements his earlier idealisation of country life with an air of sexual fantasy and innuendo.

The Intertextual Relationship of Martial and Juvenal

So far I have purposely held back both from asking what difference the addressee makes to this poem and from treating the intertextual relationship between the poem and the satires of Juvenal. If one assumes that the

---

[44] Neger 2012: 259–60, citing Adams 1982: 159 and Poiss 2001: 262–3. This interpretation is arguably helped by the present tense of *iuuat*, although it need not be literally taken as meaning that he is dying at this moment. For all that, the sexual subtext seems to me likely but not quite certain: the metaphor of orgasm as *petite mort* is perhaps more associated with modern European languages and neither Adams' nor Poiss' examples offer a case with *perire* or anything very similar. For the 'advanced years' explanation, see Watson and Watson 2003 ad loc.

Iuvenalis here addressed is the same as in 7.24 and 7.91, one could observe that sexual innuendo and ribbing is present in all three poems,[45] which would argue for the identification of the addressee as the same. But this poem stands out from the other two, in that it seems patent that the addressee is Juvenal the satirist. The image of Juvenal in lines 1–6 seems inescapably redolent of Juvenal's oeuvre, and in particular the portrayal of the miserable client in his first book, where the first Satire is focalised around the client in his daily routine, the third centres on the emigration from Rome of the disappointed Umbricius, and the fifth imagines the humiliating reality of Trebius' longed-for invitation to dinner. The contrast between city and country made in the rest of the epigram is of course, as we have seen, a traditional opposition in Roman literature, but it is particularly reminiscent of the central poem of Juvenal's first book, Satire 3. As James Uden has remarked, in this poem 'Juvenal's character is suddenly recognisable.'[46]

This is clearly one of the reasons why this poem has fascinated readers: alongside the two epigrams in Book 7, it is our only contemporary mention of Juvenal outside his own work.[47] So the portrayal of Juvenal's clientship could clearly be seen, by those who are inclined to see the narrator of the satires as a self-portrait, as a simple reflection of the lifestyle that Juvenal had in Rome, and that Martial had had before his move to Spain.[48] This is the attitude of Highet's *Juvenal the Satirist*: indeed Highet went further and adduced the tone of *Epigrams* 12.18.22–3 as evidence for Juvenal's homosexuality, in terms that now seem amusing.[49] Of course, whether Martial and Juvenal actually had such a lifestyle is open to question. Martial often speaks in the persona of a client performing *salutatio*, collecting the *sportula*, hoping for dinner invitations, but he also ironises it, as in *Epigrams* 1.70 and 1.108, where his poem performs his *salutatio* in his place. A reasonable middle ground would be that, even if Martial was dependent on the financial support of a range of patrons and sometimes needed to join in the traditional rites of *clientela* and to swell a procession or two, the status of a poor client paying morning calls on the powerful is at the very least a simplification of his lifestyle. In the case of Juvenal, of course, the modern trend is reasonable scepticism about the very

---

[45] Pointed out by Highet 1954: 18.   [46] Uden 2015: 221.

[47] Indeed, to the best of my knowledge, in surviving texts only Martial mentions Juvenal before Lactantius (*Div. inst.* 3.29.17) in the early fourth century.

[48] See, for example, Romano 1987: 25 n. 1.

[49] 'It looks then as though Juvenal had begun his life with normal instincts, and had then been so disgusted by women that he turned to active homosexuality' (Highet 1954: 279 n. 17).

possibility of biographical reconstruction from the evasive and perhaps contradictory narrator of the satires – and yet this poem could be used as a testimony for a Juvenal who is not so distant from the angry narrator of Book 1.[50]

Purely biographical readings of the poem cannot in themselves be disproved, but for a number of readers, including myself, the poem has seemed to offer more than merely a biographical connection: it also offers a literary homage to Juvenal the satirist, and an intertextual connection with his first book. Craca has defined the poem as 'an act of homage . . . with subtle allusions to the work of his literary friend'.[51] Rimell remarks (more or less in passing) that the poem may allude to Juvenal's third Satire.[52] Neither comments on the problem of literary history thus raised, which is that the generally accepted date for Juvenal's first book of *Satires* is *c.* 110, nearly a decade after the last date, 101, when Martial can plausibly have composed this poem.[53] Others have perceived a problem: Pasoli argued in a little noticed article that, since Martial appears to allude to Juvenal, at the very least individual poems of Juvenal's first book must be earlier than thought.[54] Following in Pasoli's footsteps, James Uden makes a forceful case that the epigram is a response to the publication of Juvenal's first book, playfully characterising Juvenal as resembling the characters in his own work in the manner that Virgil had done with Gallus, or Martial with Stella.[55] Furthermore, he successfully demonstrates that, although the reference to the trial of Marius Priscus (1.49–50) gives a *terminus post quem* for Book 1 of the year 100, the *termini* that have been used to take the book a decade later are feeble (principally, the suggestion that *Sat.* 2.102 refers to the *Histories* of Tacitus).[56]

---

[50] For references, see nn. 13 and 14.

[51] 'Un atto di omaggio . . . raffinate allusioni all'opera dell'amico letterato' (Craca 2011: 130).

[52] Rimell 2008: 194.

[53] In Rimell's (2008: 193) case, she has just remarked that Juvenal 'began publishing his *Satires* around AD 100', which is not the normal view.

[54] Pasoli 1974.

[55] Virg. *Ecl.* 10; Martial 6.21 with Watson and Watson 2003 ad loc. (p. 119); Uden 2015: 219–26. I am most grateful to James Uden for sharing with me the relevant section of his manuscript in advance of publication, at the time of the St Andrews conference in 2013. His conclusions were considerably more developed than my suspicions. We had both spotted the most important intertext, Mart. 12.18.4–6 ~ Juv. 1.26–9, and the likely direction of imitation; we both realised, independently of Pasoli, that this created a problem. It is worth noting, however, that Pasoli, unlike Uden, does not think that the whole of *Satires* Book 1 was necessarily known to Martial and, following Highet, sees the letter as unsympathetic to Juvenal, rather than celebrating him.

[56] One might of course feel, as Uden himself acknowledges (2015: 225), that his suggestion puts a notably long gap between the publication of Juvenal's first book in 100 or 101 and that of Book 2 in about 116. On Uden's redating see also Geue (this volume), pp. 367 and 371.

How solid, then, are the intertextual links between the passages? Martial's image of Juvenal as client paying calls is reminiscent of Juvenal's own characterisation of his speaker in 1.100, of Umbricius in 3.124, and of Trebius in 5.20.[57] The whole concept of Martial's poem can be seen as taking up that of Juvenal's third Satire, where Umbricius leaves Rome for a life of rural quiet, though the speaker of the poem stays behind: the setting of Juvenal's morning calls in the Subura (2) matches the speaker's claim in *Satires* 3.5, sympathising with Umbricius, to rate even the backwater island of Procida above Subura (*ego uel Prochytam praepono Suburae*),[58] while the noise and sleeplessness of Rome evoked by *inquietus* and *clamosa* in 1–2 (and by opposition in the description of Martial's lie-in, 13–16) resemble Umbricius' description of Rome's noisy sleeplessness (*Sat.* 3.232–8); Martial's pleasure in that the toga is unknown (17, in contrast to 5) matches Umbricius' declaration that in much of Italy no one wears the toga except when dead (*Sat.* 3.171–2). Of course, it must be acknowledged that none of these similarities demands Martial's echoing of Juvenal rather than Juvenal's exploitation of themes from Martial. Given that escape from the noise of Rome and the absence of the toga are proclaimed as advantages of Bilbilis in Martial's closely related poem 1.49, and that Subura as a geographical marker or metonymy for Rome as a whole is found elsewhere in Martial, especially in Book 12, nothing can be proven from reference to Satire 3.[59]

The link to Satire 1 is much more compelling (*Epig.* 12.18.4–6 ~ *Sat.* 1.26–30):[60]

> Dum per limina te potentiorum
> **sudatrix** toga **uentilat** uagumque
> maior Caelius et minor fatigant . . .
>
> . . . cum uerna Canopi,
> Crispinus Tyrias umero reuocante lacernas
> **uentilet** aestiuum digitis **sudantibus** aurum
> nec sufferre queat maioris pondera gemmae,
> difficile est saturam non scribere.

---

[57] Craca 2011: 131.

[58] Ibid. 130; so too Bowie 1989: 102 (he argues that Martial clearly knows of Juvenal as a poet, and may allude to him here, but that the literary chronology is simply unknowable, particularly bearing in mind publication practices of the time; I am grateful to Abigail Buglass for consulting this unpublished thesis for me). Colton 1991: 86–7 had suggested that it was Juvenal imitating Martial: 'it is not unreasonable to believe that Juvenal is replying angrily to the tasteless words which the carefree Martial wrote him from Spain' (cf. the interpretation of Colton's doctoral supervisor, Highet, quoted in n. 15).

[59] See above, pp. 166–7.

[60] Pasoli 1974: 351; Uden 2015: 223–4. Uden also suggests (p. 224) a connection between the use of the financial metaphor *repono* in *Sat.* 1.1 and *Epig.* 12.18.15.

> While your sweating toga fans you as you cross the thresholds of the powerful and the Greater and Lesser Caelian tire you with wandering...

> ... when the slave from Canopus, Crispinus, his shoulder tugging back his Tyrian cloaks, is fanning a summer ring on sweating fingers and cannot bear the weight of a larger jewel, it is hard not to write satire.

The situations are quite different, though the Latinity is bold in both cases:[61] the Egyptian fop Crispinus airs his lighter summer ring on his sweating fingers and Juvenal flaps his sweat-drenched toga to cool himself as he makes his calls. But the verbal similarity with *sudantibus* ~ *sudatrix* and *uentilet* ~ *uentilat* is very striking, not paralleled to my knowledge elsewhere in classical Latin, and appears here in authors known to each other and writing within a very short space of time from each other (Uden notes also the less striking coincidence *maior* ~ *maioris*; Pasoli that between *toga* and *lacernas*).[62] For various reasons, the allusion works better as Martial's to Juvenal: the inventive form *sudatrix* and its equally daring usage in the nominative, seemingly capping Juvenal;[63] the prominent programmatic place in Juvenal's first Satire; and the unlikelihood of Juvenal reusing words that had been chosen to characterise himself in order to characterise a vile parvenu.[64]

If the intertextual relationship between the works is real (and I think it would be perverse to deny it), there are only two ways to evade Uden's conclusion. The first would be to argue that similarities owe to Juvenal's

---

[61] In Juvenal I prefer the scholiast's interpretation, that *aestiuum* designates a particular type of ring, to the banal adverbial usage 'in summer'. For the question of the authenticity of line 29, see e.g. Nisbet 1988: 86–8 and Uden 2015: 223 n. 11; my own inclination is to think it an (excellent) interpolation.

[62] The Library of Latin Texts database shows the combination of the verb *uentilo* with *sudo* or *sudor* nowhere else before Claudian *Carm. min.* 25.4, a very different context.

[63] Uden 2015: 224.

[64] Pasoli 1974: 151–2. Crispinus of course also appears as a subject of mockery in *Sat.* 4, and can be identified with a figure named several times in Martial and mocked in *Epig.* 8.48, to which *Sat.* 1.26–9 clearly alludes: *Nescit cui dederit Tyriam Crispinus abollam, | dum mutat cultus induiturque togam. | Quisquis habes, umeris sua munera redde, precamur | (non hoc Crispinus te sed abolla rogat)* ('Crispinus doesn't know who he gave his purple cloak to, while changing clothes and putting on his toga. Whoever has it, give his shoulders back their gift, please (it's not Crispinus that asks this, but the cloak)', *Epig.* 8.48.1–4). The similarity is unquestionable, with the epigram's conceit lying in its transformation from an apparent advertisement for lost property into mockery of Crispinus' dandyism. Of course it is perfectly possible either that Juvenal combined two passages from Martial (the more economical solution), or that Martial imitated a passage of Juvenal in which Juvenal had imitated Martial (the more interesting one). Nor is either possibility eliminated either by the intriguing suggestion of Schöffel 2002: 411–12 that Crispinus might in fact be a fiction of Martial's adopted by Juvenal. This suggestion, prompted by the problem of Martial's sharpness towards a prominent courtier of Domitian's, might soften the problem of Juvenal adopting his own characterisation in *Epig.* 12.18 for the depiction of a villain, or equally, if 12.18 imitates Juvenal's first book, create a teasing acknowledgement by Martial of Juvenal's own indebtedness to his earlier epigrams. I thank Chris Whitton for pointing out the potential significance of this allusion.

imitation of Martial, which would of course be entirely consistent with the rest of the oeuvre, and in particular in line with (though certainly not compelled by) the fact that there is a blatant allusion to an epigram of Martial's eighth book within the Juvenal passage.[65] This is, as we have seen, a possibility: in particular most of the similarities with Satire 3 are already seen in Martial 1.49, which is certainly earlier. The second way out would be to posit that Martial was aware of Juvenal's work through recitals or private exchange before publication.[66] The phenomenon of authors' holding on to literary work before publication is certainly well attested in this period and cannot be disproved in this case (though even if it were true, it would still mean that the description of Juvenal in Rome could be read as an attempt to make him a character in his own writings). Uden's argument on the date of Juvenal's first book is therefore not fully proven.

What he proposes is, however, attractive and plausible. We have seen that Martial creates a close parallelism between his own existence and Juvenal's; we have seen too that Martial's characterisation of life in Bilbilis is far more idealised than in the rest of the book and topped off with sexual fantasy. So it would make sense if the depiction of Juvenal were – to a point where the tangle between social and literary interaction, and the balance between respect and mockery, is perhaps indistinguishable to the reader – a fantasised version of the real Juvenal based on his literary works. The close parallel between them also points to the fact that Martial himself had often given voice to the complaints of the client in his own poetry, which he too had set amid the sweat and noise of Rome. Other aspects in the description could have a metapoetic air: Martial's wakefulness (*quicquid . . . uigilaueram*) in Rome, though characterised as lost sleep, certainly also suggests the wakefulness of poetic composition (more on this in a moment). His return to Bilbilis after many Decembers, *multos post Decembres*, could obviously simply be seen as counting the passing years by their final month,[67] but given that December is also a metonymy for the Saturnalia, the feast at which Martial seems often to have published his books, we may also have a metaliterary description of his writing career.[68] Martial proposes himself delighted to be away from the drudgery of Rome. In other words, it makes very good sense for the interpretation of this poem as a whole if it was written to celebrate the publication of Juvenal's first book, a work profoundly influenced by Martial.

[65] See previous note.
[66] A possibility acknowledged by Uden 2015: 225. For more on recitation in the period, see Roller in this volume.
[67] Cf. 3.36.7.
[68] See Canobbio 2011 ad 5.18.1, citing 4.17.4, 5.30.5, 5.84.9, 7.72.1, 10.87.7, 12.62.15.

The Metapoetic Reading Reinforced: Statius

At this point I would like to introduce another, in my view significant, intertext, which strengthens the case for a metapoetic reading. Martial describes his sleeping-in as paying himself back for thrice ten years of too little sleep, referring to his thirty-four-year sojourn in Rome (15–16):[69]

> et totum mihi nunc repono, quicquid
> ter denos uigilaueram per annos.

> And now I pay myself back in full for my wakefulness over thrice ten years.

Not only Lindsay and Patricia Watson's excellent recent commentary, but seemingly all previous scholarship misses a striking allusion to a poem completed within the previous decade, Statius' *Thebaid*. In the sphragis of the final book, Statius addresses his personified work (*Theb.* 12.810–12):

> Durabisne procul dominoque legere superstes,
> o mihi **bis senos** multum **uigilata per annos**,
> Thebai?

> Will you last into the future and be read when you're left behind by your master, O *Thebaid*, on whom I stayed long awake over twice six years?

In fact, he concludes, the *Thebaid* will survive her master, thanks to her good reputation, the support of Caesar, and the keenness of the young of Italy to learn the poem (*Theb.* 12.812–19). Martial's allusion is strongly marked lexically. Statius uses *uigilata* to refer to staying awake by night to write, a well-known theme.[70] Although they shared a number of the same patrons, Martial never names Statius, or vice versa. The relatively few treatments of the topic tend to merge the two poets' inferred personal relationship, which is imagined on limited evidence to have been poor, with the undoubted intertextual one.[71]

It is well known that Martial's engagement with epic often implicitly asserts the claims of his own genre.[72] This allusion parodies and banalises the epic poet's evocation of the sleepless toil of poetic composition with a conceit about catching up on thirty years' sleep and a financial metaphor (*repono*). In the context of the previous and following lines, one naturally interprets Martial's *uigilaueram* as a reference to a lack of sleep brought about from early rising, presumably in part to undertake the morning calls

---

[69] In fact thirty-four years (10.103.7–9).
[70] To exemplify only with *uigilo* and its cognates, Lucr. 1.142 *noctes uigilare serenas*, Ov. *Ars* 2.285, *Tr.* 2.11, Cic. *Tusc.* 4.44, Stat. *Silv.* 3.55.35.
[71] So Heuvel 1936–7, and also Henriksén 1998.
[72] See Zissos 2004 on Valerius Flaccus; Hinds 2007, esp. pp. 136–9.

that Juvenal is now undertaking; however, the use of *uigilo* might hint at
wakefulness devoted to literary composition, even without awareness of
the allusion. In that context one could also view Martial as capping Statius'
twice six years of literary toil with his own thrice ten years (whether of literary work or lost sleep or both), a common form of competitive allusion.[73]
But this poem comes in Martial's twelfth and final book – that significant number;[74] like the sphragis closing Statius' twelfth and final book,
the poem ends with a reflection on his own mortality. Can we therefore see
a hint that the letter to Juvenal, addressed to a poet of the next generation
who has taken over his subject matter, is itself a sort of sphragis on Martial's
work?[75]

Conclusion

It would be a possible interpretation of Martial's letter to Juvenal that it
was written well before Juvenal's career as a satirist had begun, and provides external confirmation of the tiresome and subservient urban lifestyle
that inspired his angry first book. By this interpretation, which accords well
with old-fashioned biographical readings of Juvenal, the poem documents
a purely social interaction, and Juvenal is portrayed as a poor client because
he was. This is possible but (as I have argued) unlikely. Not because it would
be an unfashionable argument: rather, the comparison to Martial's earlier
representations of Bilbilis (above all *Epig.* 1.49) and to the preface and other
poems in Book 12, the stylised fantasy of Martial's country existence, and
apparent metapoetic elements combine with the stark resemblance of Juvenal to his satirical creation in such a way that the poem makes much more
sense as a literary as well as just a social interaction. The unquestionable verbal intertextuality with Juvenal's first book of *Satires* is then best explained
as Martial's imitation of Juvenal, and we may follow Uden not only in the
implication that we should probably date the first book of *Satires*, or at least
parts of it, to 100 or 101, significantly earlier than was generally thought, but

---

[73] Cf. e.g. Hinds 1998: 35–47, on the 'many mouths' motif.

[74] See especially Holzberg 2002: 122–51.

[75] One further observation: Juvenal is of course as given to epic parody as Martial is, introducing
himself in the first Satire as the alternative to endless epic recitations. His own one mention of
Statius, in the seventh Satire, presents him as a pimp prostituting out his girlfriend, the *Thebaid*
(*Sat.* 7.82–7, esp. 82–3 *carmen amicae | Thebaidos*). It seems plausible (though commentaries do
not make the point, to my knowledge) that Juvenal's imagery arises from an *interpretatio praua* of
exactly the same passage of Statius (*Theb.* 12.810–12), personifying his poem as a woman who kept
him up, that Martial had had fun with in *Epig.* 12.18. Where Martial turns Statius' literary use of
uigilata into a straightforward image of lost sleep, we could infer from Juvenal that it referred to
sleepless nights of passion.

also in seeing the poem as a literary homage. I suggest that this engagement between the last book of Martial and the first of Juvenal strongly identifies the two poets: Martial's past material, from which (here at least) he happily steps back, is now Juvenal's. The baton has been passed. Without reopening the question of the twelfth book's publication, one can remark that the poem would have stood well as the last in Martial's collection.

PART II

Interactions on and off the Page

CHAPTER 8

Amicable and Hostile Exchange in the Culture of Recitation

Matthew Roller

The literary and social practice of recitation figures prominently in the works of Martial, Plutarch, Pliny, Tacitus, Juvenal and Suetonius, to name some key authors active in the period this volume covers. By 'recitation' I refer to the practice of reading out a prepared but provisional text, representing an author's literary work-in-progress, to an audience – whether an intimate gathering, or larger and more 'public' one – that will notionally provide suggestions for improvement before the author finalises and 'publishes' the work.[1] The kinds of work-in-progress attested as being recited range over virtually every literary genre: epic, lyric, elegiac, dramatic and epigrammatic poetry, as well as historiography, oratory and dialogue (at least) among prose genres.[2] As a stage of the editing and revising process in which authors and audiences confront each other directly, it seems fair to describe recitation as an arena of literary interaction par excellence. Fundamentally, recitation is a social activity, involving a group of participants

I thank the auditors who attended my recitation of this work at the 'LINTH 2' conference in Rostock, June 2014. None of them embarrassed me with frank criticism, but I inferred some critical judgments from their gestures, murmurs and silences. I then circulated a revised draft to the volume editors, Chris Whitton and Alice König, who generously offered discreet suggestions for improvement. I hope this chapter is imprinted with the values and interests of this literary community, and that it interacts appropriately with other members' contributions – as well it should, given the sociality and amicable reciprocity of the writing and editing process.

[1] By 'recitation' I mean the socio-literary practice in general; when I speak of '*a* recitation' I mean a specific event in which a particular author reads out a particular work to a particular audience. The use of the English word 'recitation' to label this activity is a scholarly convention. The Latin verb *recitare* means 'to read out to an audience from a prepared, written text'; this verb and its associated nouns *recitatio/recitator* are indeed used to refer to this literary activity (*OLD* s.v. 2). However, other lexical items may be used to label this activity: the verbs *legere* and *audire*, and the associated nouns *lector*, *auditor* and *auditorium*. Recitation may also be described or referred to without any of these lexical items appearing. Furthermore, *recitare* and *recitatio* may refer to other kinds of 'reading out', such as of laws, letters, wills, or other documents to audiences in lawcourts, assemblies, army camps, or the senate (*OLD* s.v. 1). Rarely *recitatio/recitare* refers to the reading out of a finished, published literary text, rather than a work-in-progress: Mart. 2.71.3, Suet. *Claud.* 42, cf. Gell. 18.5.1–6. For semantics see Valette-Cagnac 1997: 23–4, 111; Binder 1995: 268–70.

[2] On the genres recited see Binder 1995: 296–7.

gathered at one time and place. Each participant takes on a role – reciter or auditor – to which specific expectations about comportment attach. The verbal exchange in a recitation event, which is synchronic and collocal, imprints the resulting literary work in ways different from the imprint created by interactions of a more specifically 'textual' sort. By 'textual' interaction I mean the situation in which an author selectively appropriates, responds to and reworks elements of a completed, 'published' text that he reads – whether that text is itself synchronic and collocal (produced by the author's contemporaries and acquaintances, a dynamic much discussed in this volume)[3] or was produced at another place and time. Furthermore, since recitation involves a social actor performing before a judging audience, the overall protocols of social reciprocity and exchange govern how the participants' roles are defined and their comportment is judged. These judgments, in turn, affect the relative prestige and social standing of the participants. These social consequences of recitation are no less important, and perhaps more important, than the strictly literary consequences. My aim in this chapter is to investigate, through the lens of exchange theory, the literary and social interactions that occur in recitation, and the consequences of those interactions. I focus in particular on exchanges that are represented either as amicable or as hostile, considering the impact these divergent flavours of interaction have on the literary production and social standing of the participants.

Cooperation, Competition and Exchange

At the outset of this investigation, however, some background about recitation is required. The earliest surviving references to the practice under discussion date to the 30s BC. We hear of non-senatorial, 'professional' poets reciting their works in progress, whether in controlled (e.g. domestic) spaces for select, invited audiences, or in civic arenas for indiscriminate audiences. These poets, who typically plead poverty, present themselves as seeking economic gain no less than literary fame.[4] The first author of senatorial status to recite his own literary works is allegedly Asinius Pollio, also

---

[3] On textual interactions among contemporary authors who may or may not also have interacted socially, see Kelly, König, Mratschek and Whitton in this volume; also Gibson for a thought experiment on the relationship between social and textual interaction.

[4] Horace and other contemporary poets reciting: Hor. *Sat.* 1.4.22–5, 73–8; *Epist.* 2.1.219–23; *Ars* 438–52 (see below), 470–6. Virgil reciting: Serv. ad *Aen.* 4.323, 6.861; Gell. 6.20.1. Binder 1995: 269–75 discusses these early recitations; Markus 2000: 171–4 considers how Juvenal handles the trope of the impoverished poet reciting.

in the 30s to 20s BC.[5] Among senatorial and equestrian reciters, as we shall see, the focus is less on money and fame than on the discharging of reciprocal social obligations and achieving high standing in the community of the like-minded. Besides poetry, aristocrats also recite historiography and oratory – literary genres particularly associated with their own social class. Over the subsequent 150 years, recitations by 'professional' poets and by aristocrats composing in various genres are mentioned or described frequently enough to lend the impression that such activity is routine.[6] The era of Nerva, Trajan and Hadrian, however, furnishes our richest information about this activity by far. Not only does the Younger Pliny abundantly describe (or prescribe) the contemporary culture of recitation, but additional striking descriptions appear in Juvenal, the post-Domitianic books of Martial, and Plutarch. Furthermore, Tacitus and Suetonius, the principal historical writers of the Trajanic and Hadrianic era, provide much of our information about the practice of recitation in the Julio-Claudian and Flavian eras. While these authors do not directly describe recitation as practised in their own day, they reveal their awareness of and interest in recitation precisely by noting its prevalence and discussing its praxis in the periods about which they write. Whether the efflorescence of information about recitation, both contemporary and earlier, in the era of Nerva, Trajan and Hadrian is an artefact of the texts that happen to survive, or reflects an actual uptick in the social and literary significance of recitation in this era, is difficult to say: perhaps a bit of both.[7]

Let us begin our more focused investigation by describing some well-documented features of recitation that may, at least on their surface, appear to constitute paradoxes. The first paradox is as follows. On the one hand, those who recite their literary works to assembled audiences, and who attend recitations given by others, form a *cooperative* community characterised by a shared commitment to improving one another's works in

---

[5] Pollio: Sen. *Contr.* 4.*pr*.2 (with Dalzell 1955; Binder 1995: 272–3); Seneca actually says Pollio was 'the first of all Romans' to recite his works to an invited audience. A generation or so later are T. Labienus (Sen. *Contr.* 10.*pr*.8) and Sextilius Ena (Sen. *Suas.* 6.27; though Ena's status is uncertain).

[6] 'Professional' poets reciting in the Julio-Claudian and Flavian periods: Pers. 1.13–23 and *passim*; Petr. *Sat.* 90–3; also, numerous poems from Martial's early (Domitianic) books portray Martial himself and other poets reciting: e.g., *Epig.* 1.29, 38, 52, 63, 66, just from book 1. These poets' status is not always clear, though Martial seems to address them as social equals and rivals. Senatorial aristocrats, including some emperors, who recite in the Julio-Claudian and Flavian periods are attested at Ov. *Pont.* 3.5.37–42; Sen. *Ep.* 122.11–13; Tac. *Ann.* 4.34, 14.19, 16.4, *Dial.* 2–3, 23.2; Suet. *Tib.* 61.3, *Claud.* 41, *Nero* 10, *Dom.* 2.2, *Vita Lucani*; Plin. *Ep.* 1.13.3, 7.17.11–12. For all texts up to Pliny's day that refer to recitation, see Binder 1995: 269–96.

[7] My brief historical survey here is a modification of Roller 2011: 215. Uden 2015: 94–8 takes a different view, arguing that Pliny's engagement with recitation is a rearguard action defending an institution in decline.

progress.[8] Participants assume one of the roles that this activity makes available, and their comportment is governed by norms associated with the role they assume. Everyone agrees, that is, to observe the rules of play. And 'play', in a key sense, it is. For the literary activity of composition and recitation, at least among elites, is normally classified as *otium*, 'leisure time'. This is time not devoted to *negotia,* the civic duties and other economically or socially beneficial activities through which lofty Romans strive for pre-eminence and distinction. On the other hand, members of the recitation community also *compete* with one another: as we shall see, they strive for approbation in their reciting as well as in the works they eventually publish. Thus they are engaged in constructing hierarchies in which each participant strives to be ranked as high as possible relative to the others. This quest for social distinction is more characteristic of *negotia* than of *otium.* This, then, is the first paradox: members of the recitation community both cooperate and compete; and their activities, though 'officially' carried out under the banner of *otium*, include features that are more typical of aristocratic *negotia.*[9]

Now for the second paradox. As noted already, works presented in recitations are not finished but 'in progress', provisional and subject to change. The recitation's avowed purpose is to elicit from the audience candid feedback, in a relatively controlled and private environment, by which the author will improve his work prior to publishing it as a finished work – that is, before he releases it to be copied and circulated widely through his social network or via booksellers.[10] Yet, at the same time, some participants in these events do describe what goes on in them – obviously, for otherwise we would know nothing whatsoever about recitation as a social and literary activity. We hear, for example, how specific works are received by an audience, and how audience members and reciters comport themselves in relation to the norms associated with the roles they assume. Thus the recitation event in practice is rather less private and controlled than the ideology of provisionality would lead one to expect. Audience judgments can

---

[8] On the literary community that is both presupposed and constructed by recitation, see e.g. Gurd 2012: 105–26 (recitation is usually the province of what he calls 'genetic' readers, a community of known specialists or connoisseurs); also Dupont 1997: 52–4; Barchiesi 2004: 22–4 (and *passim*); Johnson 2010: 42–56, 73.

[9] On recitation's declared limitation (among elites) to the sphere of *otium,* and the paradox whereby it nevertheless takes on features of aristocratic *negotia,* see e.g. Valette-Cagnac 1997: 114–15; Roller 1998: 289–98 and 2011: 215–17; Johnson 2010: 44. On Plinian *otium,* see Bütler 1970: 41–57; Gibson and Morello 2012: 169–99.

[10] On provisionality, Delvigo 1990: 91–2; Dupont 1997: 48–50; Fantham 1999: 222–3; Parker 2009: 208–14; on what 'publication' (*editio*) means, see Starr 1987: 215 (and *passim*) and Johnson 2010: 52–3.

and do escape into the larger world via the reports about these events that circulate orally and in writing. Consequently, recitation manifests some of the dynamics of public performance, in which a judging audience gathers around a performer, evaluates his performance by the standard of the community's values, compares it to the performances of other contemporaries or predecessors, and then monumentalises it so that people elsewhere and at other times will know of it. In particular, recitation takes on key features of public oratory as performed in the late Republican *contio*, the law courts, and the senate of the late Republic and early Empire – all quintessential arenas of aristocratic *negotia*. To summarise, then, the second paradox is that any given recitation is both a 'private', off-the-record event produced for a restricted audience, and also a public, visible, spectacular performance that is potentially available to a broad audience extending well beyond that particular event's immediate participants.[11]

These two paradoxes are homologous – indeed, they are opposite sides of the same coin. To view reciters and their audiences as a cooperative community committed to furthering a shared literary enterprise underpins the ideology that recitations are 'private', provisional, candid and secret: everyone seeks to help everyone else improve their work, without exposing them to broader criticism or ridicule, as this community collectively pursues its literary vision. Conversely, to view the community as competitive, and intent on constructing social hierarchies, accounts for the more 'public', spectacular dimension of the recitation event: the competitive ethos causes judgments passed on works to escape the boundaries of the particular event and become more widely known. Yet we should not be surprised that recitation has these two, somewhat opposed, faces – which is to say, these paradoxes are more apparent than 'real'. If there are any universals in Roman aristocratic culture, one is surely that cooperation and competition are inextricably combined in any number of social venues. In the senate, aristocrats compete ferociously for magistracies and honours, even while the body must function more or less effectively as a whole in order to govern. In battle, aristocratic cavalrymen and commanders are part of a highly coordinated, disciplined military unit, yet seek to outstrip their peers through conspicuous displays of valour. Similar analyses could be offered for advocacy in the courts, performances in the declamation halls, and – as several contributions in this volume demonstrate – other domains of specifically literary interaction.[12] Furthermore, the tension between

[11] For this paradox, see Valette-Cagnac 1995: 13–14 and 1997: 114–15; Roller 1998: 294–6.

[12] On competition and cooperation in other literary domains, see e.g. Harries and Kelly in this volume.

competition and cooperation, besides being visible in diverse social contexts, also persists over time, albeit in ever-changing ways. Indeed it is noteworthy that recitation emerged and established itself as a new arena of competition and cooperation precisely in the Augustan and early Julio-Claudian era. Perhaps aristocrats were compensating for the reduced opportunities for competitive status-building in what had previously been the premier arenas for oratory – the public *contio*, certain *quaestiones* and other courts, and to some extent the senate. So as some traditional venues for competing in eloquence withered or took on new forms in the early Empire, Roman aristocrats constructed new competitive arenas to fill the lacuna.[13]

In the balance of this chapter I hope to shed new light on the competitive-*cum*-cooperative culture of recitation by analysing it in terms of exchange. The social norms that govern conduct in the recitation, like so many other social norms, are fundamentally matters of reciprocity. Modern exchange theory is well suited for analysing social systems that include both cooperative and competitive elements, since the theory posits mechanisms that create social bonds (i.e. cooperative, communitarian elements) that are also hierarchical (i.e. competitive). Regarding recitation, those who participate and thereby assert their membership in the recitation community incur obligations that they may be judged to have discharged appropriately or inappropriately through their very conduct as participants. The degree to which an individual participant's conduct manifests this community's norms – hence whether he engages the community in an amicable or hostile way – provides grounds for other participants to include or exclude him, or rank him higher or lower in the community's social hierarchy. Membership and standing in this community therefore depends upon the management of reciprocal obligations. In the sections to follow, I examine how these obligations are defined and managed.

Three Obligations within the Recitation Community

Marcel Mauss, the foundational figure in the modern study of exchange and reciprocity, asserted that membership in a community constituted by exchange entails a threefold obligation: the obligation to give, the obligation to receive and the obligation to reciprocate.[14] Within the recitation community, I propose that this threefold obligation takes the following

---

[13] Recitation as a 'substitute' domain of eloquence: Dupont 1997: 44–5; Osgood 2006: 536; Roller 2011: 215–19 (each in different ways).

[14] Mauss 1990a: 8–14.

form: the obligation to recite works in progress, the obligation to attend such recitations, and the obligation to provide appropriate feedback to the reciter. Let us examine the evidence for these three obligations in turn. Regarding the obligation to recite, consider a letter of Pliny (*Ep.* 2.10) in which the author gently upbraids his addressee Octavius Rufus – a senior senator, and correspondent on literary matters – for writing poems but not reciting them:[15]

> Hominem te patientem uel potius durum ac paene crudelem, qui tam insignes libros tam diu teneas! . . . (2) Quousque et tibi et nobis **inuidebis**, tibi maxima laude, nobis uoluptate? . . . Magna et iam longa exspectatio est, quam frustrari adhuc et differre non **debes** . . . (4) Dices, ut soles, 'amici mei uiderint' . . . (5) . . . sed dispice ne sit parum prouidum, sperare ex aliis quod tibi ipse non **praestes**. (6) Et de editione quidem interim ut uoles: recita saltem quo magis libeat emittere . . . (7) Imaginor enim qui concursus quae admiratio te, qui clamor quod etiam silentium maneat . . .

> You're an unyielding man, or rather stubborn and almost cruel, holding back such distinguished books for so long! (2) How long will you **begrudge** yourself the greatest praise, and us the greatest pleasure? . . . We've long harboured a great expectation, which you **ought** not still to be disappointing and putting off . . . (4) As usual, you'll say, 'But my friends will see to it [sc. after I am dead].' . . . (5) . . . but consider whether it's not short-sighted to hope from others what you will not **offer up** to yourself. (6) Regarding publication, meanwhile, do as you wish: but at least recite, to inspire yourself to publish . . . (7) In fact I picture what a gathering, what wonderment, what acclamation, even what silence awaits you . . .

Pliny overtly deploys the language of social obligation (*inuides*, *debes*, *praestes*, emboldened in the Latin text and translation) to imply that one who claims to be a poet, or is known to be composing verses, assumes an obligation to recite his work-in-progress to the community of the like-minded, and not hold it back. This community is the 'us' (*nobis*, 2) who will praise Rufus and take pleasure in his poetry, and in whom the 'expectation' of a recitation (*exspectatio*, 2) resides; it is this community that Pliny predicts will assemble, marvel, applaud and so on (*concursus*, *admiratio*, *clamor*, 7) at the longed-for recitation. Indeed, one is hardly a poet at all should one fail in the obligation to recite, as a one-couplet epigram of Martial reveals with devastating brevity: *Nil recitas et uis, Mamerce, poeta uideri: | quicquid uis esto, dummodo nil recites* ('You don't recite, Mamercus,

---

[15] In *Ep.* 1.7.5 Pliny is eager to hear Rufus' verses; *Ep.* 9.38 suggests Rufus may finally have published them. On Pliny's addressees, see in brief Birley 2000a, along with Sherwin-White's (1966) notes ad loc.; more comprehensively, the individual entries in *PIR²*.

yet you wish to be deemed a poet: be whatever you want, provided you
don't recite', *Epig.* 2.88). The first verse asserts that Mamercus' failure to
recite his poetry calls his claim to membership in the community of poets
into question – the converse of the norm articulated by Pliny, that a poet
incurs the obligation to recite. The second verse turns this logic inside out:
Martial pronounces himself content to accept Mamercus' claim to being a
poet, *provided that* Mamercus does not recite. The contradiction between
the two verses conveys the joke: for the implication is that Mamercus'
poetry is so awful that Martial will simply concede his claim to being a
poet, to avoid having to sit through a recitation.[16]

Pliny reiterates this norm, and adds other obligations incumbent on
authors, in *Epistles* 8.12. He addresses Cornelius Minicianus, a literary
equestrian from northern Italy.[17] The topic is an upcoming recitation by
Titinius Capito, another high-ranking equestrian with literary interests. I
quote the letter in full, to show the pervasiveness of the language of social
obligation, and to indicate the range of those obligations as Pliny describes
them.

> Hunc solum diem excuso: recitaturus est Titinius Capito, quem ego audire
> nescio magis **debeam** an cupiam. Vir est optimus et inter praecipua sae-
> culi ornamenta numerandus. Colit studia, studiosos amat fouet prouehit,
> multorum qui aliqua componunt portus sinus gremium, omnium exem-
> plum, ipsarum denique litterarum iam senescentium reductor ac reforma-
> tor. (2) Domum suam recitantibus **praebet**, auditoria non apud se tantum
> **benignitate mira** frequentat; mihi certe, si modo in urbe, **defuit numquam**.
> Porro tanto turpius **gratiam non referre**, quanto honestior causa **referen-
> dae**. (3) An si litibus tererer, **obstrictum** esse me crederem obeunti uadi-
> monia mea, nunc, quia mihi omne negotium omnis in studiis cura, minus
> **obligor** tanta sedulitate celebranti, in quo **obligari** ego, ne dicam solo, certe
> maxime possum? (4) Quod si illi **nullam uicem** nulla quasi **mutua officia
> deberem**, sollicitarer tamen uel ingenio hominis pulcherrimo et maximo et
> in summa seueritate dulcissimo, uel honestate materiae. Scribit exitus illus-
> trium uirorum, in his quorundam mihi carissimorum. (5) Videor ergo **fungi
> pio munere**, quorumque exsequias celebrare non licuit, horum quasi fune-
> bribus laudationibus seris quidem sed tanto magis ueris interesse. Vale.

I make apologies for this day alone: Titinius Capito is going to recite. I don't
know which is greater: my **obligation**, or my desire, to hear him. He's an

---

[16] Alternatively, the second verse may mean that a recitation of this work will expose Mamercus'
   incompetence and thereby demolish, rather than sustain, his claim to being a poet (likewise at *Epig.*
   8.20). But this interpretation seems less pointed.
[17] On Minicianus' literary interests (*studia*) cf. *Ep.* 7.22.2. He also receives letters on other topics:
   Ep. 3.9, 4.11.

outstanding man, to be counted among the leading lights of the age. He cultivates literature (*studia*); he loves, cherishes, and promotes producers of literature (*studiosi*); he is the harbour, the protection, the asylum of many who try their hand at writing; an exemplum for all; he has restored and made anew literature itself, which was long in decline. (2) He **supplies** his house to reciters, and attends readings held elsewhere with **amazing generosity**: me, at least, he's **never failed**, provided he was in town. Besides, **the better the reason for reciprocating, the more shameful it is to fail to reciprocate**. (3) If I were entangled in a lawsuit, I would feel **bound** to someone who stood bail for me: as things are, since all my effort (*negotium*) and concern is directed toward literature, am I any less **bound** to someone whose exceptionally diligent attendance gives him, if not the only **claim upon me**, certainly the greatest? (4) But even if I **owed him no return, no (so to speak) reciprocal duties**, I would still be attracted by the man's genius, which is really splendid, outstanding, and charming even when treating very serious topics; or by the dignity of his theme. He writes about the deaths of famous men, including some who were very dear to me. (5) So I see myself as **discharging a pious duty**: those whose funerals I could not attend, their funeral orations (of a sort) I may now be present for – late, to be sure, but that much the more true. Farewell.

Let us focus on the rhetoric of this letter. Pliny insists that he is obligated to attend Capito's upcoming recitation, in part because of all Capito has done for the community of reciters: he has provided his house as a venue, he turns up at all the *auditoria* (i.e. to attend recitations given by other members of the community), and in particular he has never failed to attend Pliny's recitations without good excuse. Therefore, Pliny is bound: he cannot possibly fail to reciprocate these services, and a proper return consists in attending Capito's recitation. The letter is awash with the language of gift exchange and reciprocal obligation (emboldened above): *debere, praebere, deesse, obligari, obstringi, gratiam referre, munus fungi, benignus, mutuus, officia, uices*. Such obligations, Pliny makes clear, are incurred by all members of the literary community to any particular member who is as diligent in his service to that community as Capito is. Yet Pliny also insists on his personal obligation, due to Capito's dedicated attendance at Pliny's own recitations.[18] There is also Capito's subject matter. He is reciting the deaths of famous men, some of them recently dead figures who were dear to Pliny. In this regard, to attend Capito's recitation is also to

---

[18] Pliny makes a show in his letters of holding himself strictly accountable for attending others' recitations, hence for maintaining amicable exchange relations: e.g. *Ep.* 1.13.5 *Ego prope nemini defui; erant sane pleri amici*; also 5.21.1. Yet he equally makes a show of *not* holding others strictly accountable. Thus in *Ep.* 1.13.5–6 he hopes not to appear to be reckoning up a (monetary) balance: *ne uidear, quorum recitationibus adfui, non auditor fuisse sed creditor*. See also below.

'discharge a pious duty' (*pio munere fungi*) to the memory of those to whom Pliny feels a connection.[19] Indeed, this letter itself seems to participate in the general balancing of obligations to friends and peers that Pliny herein describes. For the opening phrase, 'I make apologies for this one day', may hint that he is withdrawing from, or justifying a proposal to reschedule, some arrangement previously agreed with his addressee Minicianus. Such a prior arrangement obviously entails an obligation, but this letter explains why that obligation is necessarily trumped by a greater one to Capito, at least for the one day Capito will be reciting. Pliny's defensive claim that, at the moment, all his effort and care (*negotium, cura*) is devoted to his literary efforts (*studia*) rhetorically corroborates his overall effort in this letter to elevate the status of this particular recitation so that it can reasonably claim parity with the sorts of obligations traditionally considered more 'serious' (*negotia*).[20] Many additional texts, from Pliny, Martial and other authors, also express or imply the dual obligation that the three texts just discussed already document. Namely: within the community of producers of literature there is a concrete obligation to give recitations, and a similar obligation to attend recitations given by other members of this community.

Let me now document the third obligation within this community – the obligation to provide appropriate feedback when one is an auditor of another's recitation. To grasp what counts as 'appropriate feedback', let us examine more closely the idea that a recitation presents work-in-progress that the audience should help the author edit and improve prior to his publishing the work. The atmosphere of such recitations is deftly sketched by Pliny in a number of letters, themselves addressed to friends with literary interests who either attend recitations, interact with people who do, and/or read and comment on Pliny's 'polished' drafts subsequent to his own recitations. In *Epistles* 7.17 Pliny writes, 'I want to be praised not when I recite, but when I am read. Therefore I pass over no type of editing: first I work over what I have written; then I read it to two or three people; then I give others a version to be marked up . . . and finally I recite to a larger crowd,

---

[19] The implication is that these men were murdered under Domitian, and no proper exequies were then possible. But now, under Trajan, commemoration can finally take place, and Capito's recitation of his work *Exitus illustrium uirorum* (if that is the title) is a step in that direction. Tacitus' *Agricola* appears motivated by the same impulse (*professione pietatis*, 3.3; also *Agr.* 1–3 in general).

[20] *Ep.* 8.21.1–3 similarly parades its weighing and prioritising of obligations, with the opposite result: the claims of a client in a law court, to which Pliny was unexpectedly summoned, had to be honoured notwithstanding the recitation he had previously scheduled himself to deliver, and to which he had invited auditors.

and if you believe me, that is when I edit most keenly.'[21] In *Epistles* 8.21 he articulates more specifically the audience's role in this process of editing: 'And besides, what do your companions have to offer, if they assemble for their own amusement? It's a spoiled person, behaving like a stranger, who would rather *hear* a friend's good book than help *make* it good.'[22] The language of social proximity and distance – 'companions', 'strangers', 'friends' (*sodales, ignoti, amici*) – again asserts the normative closeness of the community of those who write, recite and attend literary recitations; and that Pliny speaks of what the auditors have to 'offer' (*praestant*) towards improving the reciter's work folds the requirement to 'offer' *something* into this community's reciprocal obligations more generally.

But what exactly should the auditors be offering? In *Epistles* 5.12, Pliny remarks that a particular recitation provided just the kind of feedback he needed: 'Intending to recite a little speech I am thinking to publish, I invited some people to keep me on my mettle – just a few, so that I would hear the truth . . . I got what I was looking for: I found people to give me the benefit of their counsel, and spotted some additional things myself to correct. I've corrected the book, which I've sent to you.'[23] This letter seems to indicate that, in Pliny's view at least, the recitation provides the opportunity for the author to receive preliminary comments and editing suggestions on new work via oral, face-to-face interaction with members of the literary community. Recitation represents an early stage of the process of refining new work, and (normatively) has a relatively 'private', cooperative character. The editing process eventually moves into a more textual form of interaction, with texts of revised work circulating among members of the community for further and perhaps final editing. This progressive, oral-to-textual form of editorial interaction – driven by a norm of reciprocity and a

---

[21] *Ep.* 7.17.7 *Nec uero ego dum recito laudari, sed dum legor cupio. Itaque nullum emendandi genus omitto. Ac primum quae scripsi mecum ipse pertracto; deinde duobus aut tribus lego; mox aliis trado adnotanda . . . nouissime pluribus recito, ac si quid mihi credis tunc acerrime emendo* (additional justifications at §§14–15). The addressee of this letter, one Celer (of uncertain identity), evidently belongs to the recitation community: he has allegedly informed Pliny that the question has arisen – on the occasion of Pliny's recitation of an oration – whether orations should be recited at all (§2). Celer therefore either attends recitations himself, or discusses them with people who do. In §14 Pliny asks Celer to edit the post-recitation revised draft of this oration.

[22] *Ep.* 8.21.5 *Et alioqui quid praestant sodales, si conueniunt uoluptatis suae causa? Delicatus ac similis ignoto est, qui amici librum bonum mauult audire quam facere.* Pliny subsequently (§6) asks his addressee, Maturus Arrianus, to read and edit a collection of poetry that Pliny has revised following recitation.

[23] *Ep.* 5.12.1–2 *Recitaturus oratiunculam quam publicare cogito, aduocaui aliquos ut uererer, paucos ut uerum audirem.* . . . (2) *Tuli quod petebam: inueni qui mihi copiam consili sui facerent, ipse praeterea quaedam emendanda adnotaui. Emendaui librum, quem misi tibi* (similarly *Ep.* 3.18.8–9, 8.21.6). Pliny's addressee, Terentius Scaurus, is otherwise unknown. But since he is called upon to edit Pliny's post-recitation revision, he evidently belongs to this literary community.

corresponding sense of obligation among members of this literary community – may extend to the finished works themselves, potentially accounting for aspects of textual interactivity analysed by other contributors to this volume (more on this in the conclusion). Returning to recitation, 'appropriate feedback' evidently consists of audience responses that aim to save the author-reciter from errors and solecisms, sharpen his expression, and the like, in the early stages of the revising and refining process. Providing such feedback is evidently as much an obligation for members of this community as the obligation to recite what one has written, and to attend recitations given by others.[24]

Pliny provides fascinating detail regarding the precise form appropriate feedback takes, along with further justification for reciting, in *Epistles* 5.3, addressed to his literary friend Titius Aristo:[25]

> (8) Itaque has recitandi causas sequor, primum quod ipse qui recitat aliquanto acrius scriptis suis auditorum reuerentia intendit; deinde quod de quibus dubitat, quasi ex consili sententia statuit. (9) Multa etiam a multis admonetur, et si non admoneatur, quid quisque sentiat perspicit ex uultu oculis nutu manu murmure silentio; quae satis apertis notis iudicium ab humanitate discernunt.

> (8) I adhere to the following reasons for reciting: first, because the reciter attends more keenly to his writing out of respect for the auditors; second, because whatever the reciter is doubtful about, he decides, as it were, according to the judgment of an advisory council (*consilium*). (9) Furthermore, he is advised on many points by many people, and if he is not advised, he discerns what each one thinks from their expression, eyes, nods, hands, murmurs or silence: by such signs they distinguish sufficiently clearly their true judgment from their polite assent.

Once again, Pliny tasks the auditors of a recitation with offering critical judgments by which the author can improve his work. Their supposed cooperation with one another and with the reciter in furthering a shared literary enterprise is neatly encapsulated in the image of the *consilium*, an advisory body, constituted to achieve just this end. Yet, in order to extract those critical judgments from his audience, the reciter must apparently be an expert in corporeal semiotics. For Pliny seems to concede that the

---

[24] In general on proper audience conduct at recitations, Binder 1995: 303–5.

[25] Better known as a jurist, Aristo evidently belongs to the community of reciters: like Celer in *Ep.* 7.17 (n. 21), Aristo has reported to Pliny (§1) that people have criticised Pliny for reciting works of a particular genre, in this case lyric poetry. Aristo's report suggests that he either attends recitations himself or talks about them with people who do. On Pliny's interactions with Aristo see Harries in this volume.

audience is not always disposed to offer bald criticism directly to the reciter; their instinctive kindness (*humanitas*) does not allow that. Instead their 'true' judgments (*iudicium*) are conveyed by their expression, gesture, and (perhaps involuntary?) vocalisations, which constitute 'sufficiently clear indications' (*notae satis apertae*). These indications are what the reciter must be able to interpret in order to improve his text.

It is instructive to compare this indirect form of criticism with the more direct form practised by the great Augustan poet Quintilius Varus, as described by Horace (*Ars poetica* 438–44). Varus minced no words when critiquing other poets' recitations: 'If you recited something to Quintilius, he used to say, "Please correct this, and this." And if you tried in vain two or three times and said you couldn't do better, he'd tell you to delete your ill-turned verses and put them back on the anvil. If you preferred to defend your fault rather than change it, he'd waste no further word or empty effort to keep you from loving, all alone without rival, yourself and your writings.' Such perfectly frank and candid criticism is evidently absent from the kind of recitation event Pliny imagines, and indeed would be considered the height of rudeness, as we shall see.

Other texts from our period also imply that the norms of recitation include providing critical feedback to the reciter but preclude 'candid' criticism. In *Epigrams* 8.76, Martial portrays a tug-of-war over precisely this matter. '"The truth please, Marcus, tell me the truth; there's nothing I'd rather hear." So you always beg and ask me, Gallicus, when you recite your books or plead a case for your clients. It's hard for me to deny you what you ask. Hear, then, something that is truer than true: you do not really want to hear the truth.' Here Gallicus, the reciter, (reasonably) seeks feedback from his audience. Martial, as auditor, cannot or will not provide the (implicitly negative) 'frank' critique he thinks is warranted; nor, he suggests, docs Gallicus really want to receive that criticism, his protestations notwithstanding. Therefore, Martial declines to ruffle the smooth surface of this relationship, at least not face-to-face. Yet we note that he is willing to expose his interchanges with Gallicus, and his implied judgment of Gallicus' poetry, to the reading audience of his published poem. Hence, he applies different social forms and norms to interactivity on the page from those he applies face-to-face (see below). A particular social dynamic, portrayed more overtly in other poems, may be at work here that explains Martial's reluctance to be candid. In *Epigrams* 10.10 Martial describes how his attempts, as a 'poor' poet, to cultivate a wealthy patron are trumped by an aristocrat who, notwithstanding his higher status, performs client services more impressively than Martial can. 'Am I to leap to my feet frequently for him [sc. the wealthy man we are cultivating] as he recites his poems? Yet you stand and at the same time put both your hands to your lips' – that is, he displays his approval more demonstratively than Martial. In this situation, the quality of the reciter's poetry is beside the point: the would-be clients praise effusively in any case, seeking to ingratiate themselves in hopes of establishing a relationship that will channel resources to them. What matters here is not the wealthy patron's recitation of his poetry and his auditors' critical evaluation of it, but the auditors' demonstrative performance of appreciation, and the wealthy patron's evaluation of his auditors' performance. The actors are in the audience, as Shadi Bartsch once put it.[26] Thus the obligation to provide 'appropriate' critical feedback in the recitation may be pre-empted by other social needs – particularly the 'poor' professional poet's alleged need to shoehorn an economically beneficial relationship into the armature of a notionally more egalitarian, aesthetic relationship among members of a literary community.

Pliny's literary circle, which includes his fellow reciters and auditors along with a fair number of his epistolary correspondents, is composed largely of senators and high-ranking equestrians. The broadly shared economic, cultural and social interests among members of the senatorial–equestrian aristocracy tend to minimise dynamics of inequality such as Martial portrays.[27] Yet even absent a social structure in which subalterns ingratiate themselves, Pliny's literary community is strikingly averse to offering overt or frank criticism of a reciter's expression, style or content. Assuredly no such criticism would be offered within the bounds of the recitation event itself, and perhaps not even via discreet subsequent commentary or correspondence. Consider *Epistles* 2.10, which we discussed earlier, in which Pliny urges Rufus to recite his poetry. He imagines the likely audience response to such outstanding verses, based on the responses his own recitations have received: 'I picture what a gathering, what wonderment, what acclamation and even what silence awaits you: for I am

---

[26] Bartsch 1994. Similarly *Epig.* 12.40, where Martial is cultivating a rich man from whom he hopes to receive substantial gifts or perhaps a bequest. 'You lie; I believe you. You recite bad poetry; I praise it. You sing, I sing (etc.).' Being agreeable, pliant, and quick to praise (no matter what) are among the strategies that those in need of resources employ when seeking to ingratiate themselves with people who can provide those resources.

[27] Age differentials may, however, produce similar effects, even within the aristocracy. In *Ep.* 6.6.6 Pliny asks a fellow senator to support the young Julius Naso's candidacy for office, noting that Naso's credentials include his diligent attendance at Pliny's recitations. Saller 1982: 122–3 speaks of aspiring younger aristocrats as 'protégés' of older, established ones, rather than as 'clients'; he reserves patronage vocabulary for relations between persons of sharply different social and economic status.

delighted by silence no less than applause when I speak or recite, provided it's a keen and focused silence that is desirous of hearing more.'[28] This vision of the polite, applauding, (at worst) sometimes silent audience – discharging its obligation to attend Rufus' recitation and provide appropriate feedback – accords with the image of the polite auditors Pliny evokes in *Epistles* 5.3, discussed above, whose *humanitas* precludes overt expression of their (negative?) *iudicium*. Elsewhere too Pliny remarks on the praise his own recitations receive, or describes the praise that he, as an auditor, bestows on other reciters during their recitations.[29] But he never shows himself, or any other member of this community, offering frank, overt criticism of the style, expression or content of recited works à la Quintilius Varus. If there is any space for critical views to be communicated within the recitation, perhaps they take the form of murmurs, nods, gestures and silences as described in *Epistles* 5.3.[30]

The three instances I have found in which Pliny overtly criticises the content or style of a recited text seem to be exceptions that prove this rule. Twice Pliny complains that his bête noire Regulus recites work with inappropriate content, and once Pliny offers mixed praise (at best) for Silius Italicus' poetry. Yet Pliny seems not to have attended Regulus' recitations, but instead heard about them from others; and he does not speak about any particular recitation by Silius, but only of Silius' general practice. Thus, while Pliny airs these criticisms to the particular addressees of his letters, and ultimately to his letters' wider readership, he never offered them directly to the reciters, either at the actual recitations (for he seems not to have attended these) nor in discreet subsequent communications.[31]

---

[28] *Ep.* 2.10.7 *Imaginor enim qui concursus quae admiratio te, qui clamor quod etiam silentium maneat; quo ego, cum dico uel recito, non minus quam clamore delector, sit modo silentium acre et intentum, et cupidum ulteriora audiendi.*

[29] *Ep.* 3.15.3–4, 3.18.8–9, 4.19.3, 4.27.1–2, 5.17.2–4, 6.17 (see below), 6.21, 9.27.

[30] At *Ep.* 7.17.11 Pliny describes how the Claudian-era senator and poet Pomponius Secundus decided from the 'silence or applause' of a large recitation audience (*ex populi uel silentio uel assensu*) whether something should be removed or retained. Here silence apparently implies disapproval, while at 2.10.7 (n. 28) it may imply enthusiasm.

[31] Criticism of the content of Regulus' recitations: *Ep.* 1.5.2–4; 4.7.1–2. Criticism of Silius' style (as revealed in his recitations): *Ep.* 3.7.5. Pliny himself receives criticism not in recitation events themselves, it seems, but via third parties who report what people are saying about his recitations. He claims to hear from his correspondents that some people questioned whether it was fitting for a senator of his stature to write and recite light poetry (*Ep.* 5.3); whether oratory should be recited at all, by Pliny or anyone else (*Ep.* 7.17; he poses the same question himself at 2.19); and that he is a poor reciter of poetry in particular (*Ep.* 9.34). Such criticism never concerns the general content, style or expression of the works being recited (a point carefully made at *Ep.* 5.3.2), but either overarching matters of propriety or very local matters of presentation.

Hostile Exchange in the Recitation Community

Pliny uses his letters as a vehicle for criticising audience members at recitations who fall short of his standards of comportment. In *Epistles* 1.13 he laments a tendency among auditors to cut corners on their obligation to attend: they delay entering the recitation hall until the reciter is well along or even nearing the end; or they leave before the end, some boldly walking out and others – who have the good grace to be embarrassed – escaping surreptitiously. Sometimes they do not show up at all, despite timely invitations and reminders. Such behaviour contrasts sharply, of course, with Pliny's own practice: he proclaims, 'To be sure, I've almost never been absent for anyone.'[32] Indirectly, Pliny is acknowledging that some people maintain an alternative calculus of exchange. They hold that their time is precious, hence they count their attendance as a favour or gift-offering to the reciter, imposing a gift-debt for which gratitude and reciprocity is owed. Such a view contrasts with Pliny's view that attending recitations is a fundamental obligation of all members of this literary community. Though Pliny here rejects the alternative calculus and criticises those who act in light of it, in another letter – *Epistles* 3.18, where he describes his own recitation of the *Panegyricus* – he makes a show of considering the value of his auditors' time. He claims to have invited his friends to come 'only if convenient' and 'if they really had time', knowing full well (he says) that it is never convenient to attend a recitation. To his delight, however, not only did his friends show up, but they insisted that he add a third day of reciting to the two days originally scheduled – not as an honour to himself, but in observance of the obligation they owe to the community of literature-lovers in general.[33] While acknowledging that the value of auditors' time is an issue, then, he boasts that his auditors in this case cleave to the communal norms and values that he himself holds.

In *Epistles* 6.17 Pliny describes another way audience members can fall short of his ideal. This letter's topic is 'a twinge of indignation' (*indignatiuncula*) Pliny felt when attending the recitation of a 'highly polished book' (*liber absolutissimus* – presumably of poetry, though Pliny does not specify the genre).[34] The cause of his annoyance is this: a few audience

---

[32] *Ep.* 1.13.2, 5 *equidem prope nemini defui.* Cf. n. 18.

[33] *Ep.* 3.18.4–5 *Cepi autem non mediocrem uoluptatem, quod hunc librum cum amicis recitare uoluissem, non per codicillos, non per libellos, sed 'si commodum' et 'si ualde uacaret' admoniti (numquam porro aut ualde uacat Romae aut commodum est audire recitantem) . . . per biduum conuenerunt . . .* [sc. *et*] *ut adicerem tertium diem exegerunt.* (5) *Mihi hunc honorem habitum putem an studiis? Studiis malo, quae prope exstincta refouentur.*

[34] For the stylish rendition of *indignatiuncula* I thank Chris Whitton. Pliny's addressee, (presumably Claudius) Restitutus, receives the letter ostensibly because he shares Pliny's respect for literature, and

members 'listened as if they were deaf and dumb: they did not open their lips or stir a hand, and didn't stand up even from being fatigued at sitting'.[35] Recall that the movement of audience members' hands, lips and bodies are key signs of their judgment of the work, which the reciter-*cum*-semiotician must be able to interpret. In withholding such signs, these auditors fail in their obligation to provide appropriate feedback to the reciter. Pliny pillories them for their comportment: 'Why such seriousness, such wisdom? Why, rather, such laziness, arrogance, lack of manners, even madness, to spend the whole day in order to give offence, and to leave as an enemy someone to whom you had come as a close friend?'[36] In the terms used in this chapter, these auditors' comportment has turned amicable exchange into hostile exchange. Instead of unifying the community around a shared literary enterprise, underpinned by the threefold obligation we have been discussing, these audience members are stirring up antagonism and hostility, turning a friend into an enemy, and fraying the community more broadly (note that they have offended Pliny), precisely in their purposeful refusal to discharge the obligation of providing appropriate feedback. They have, to be sure, shown up for the recitation, thereby fulfilling the second obligation – but their presence only makes their showy refusal to interact appropriately in their role as audience members all the more galling. Better, probably, to have failed in the second obligation and simply not to have shown up at all.

What could audience members possibly be aiming for, in engaging in such behaviour? Pliny's subsequent words are telling (*Ep.* 6.17.4):

> *Disertior ipse es? Tanto magis ne inuideris; nam qui inuidet minor est. denique siue plus siue minus siue idem praestas, lauda uel inferiorem uel superiorem uel parem: superiorem quia nisi laudandus ille non potes ipse laudari, inferiorem aut parem quia pertinet ad tuam gloriam quam maximum uideri, quem praecedis uel exaequas.*

> Are you yourself more eloquent? All the more should you not be spiteful; for the spiteful person is lesser. So whether you perform better or worse or the same, praise [sc. the reciter] whether he is inferior [sc. to you], superior, or the same: praise your superior because you cannot yourself be praised unless

---

likewise gives reciters the benefit of the doubt (§5 *quis uno te reuerentior huius operis, quis benignior aestimator?*). Hence he should understand and share Pliny's 'twinge of indignation'.

[35] *Ep.* 6.17.1–2 *Recitabatur liber absolutissimus. Hunc duo aut tres, ut sibi et paucis uidentur, diserti surdis mutisque similes audiebant. Non labra diduxerunt, non mouerunt manum, non denique assurrexerunt saltem lassitudine sedendi.*

[36] *Ep.* 6.17.3 *Quae tanta grauitas? Quae tanta sapientia? Quae immo pigritia arrogantia sinisteritas ac potius amentia, in hoc totum diem impendere ut offendas, ut inimicum relinquas ad quem tamquam amicissimum ueneris?*

he is praiseworthy; praise your inferior or equal because it matters to your own glory that a person you surpass or equal seem as great as possible.

In posing the rhetorical question 'are you more eloquent?', Pliny implicitly acknowledges – under the guise of criticising bad behaviour – that recitation can be a competitive arena governed by the logic of performance in the public eye. Specifically, he infers that the problematic audience members believe themselves superior to the reciter, are consequently expressing their disapproval, and are seeking to elevate themselves over him in the perceived hierarchy of literary achievement. The remaining audience members must weigh these competing claims to pre-eminence; hence the 'spectacularity' of what are in effect rival performances by the reciter and the disrespectful audience members. Pliny himself, as a member of that audience, is one judge of these performances; obviously he prefers that of the reciter to that of the auditors, though a few other audience members judged the other way.[37] Yet Pliny's objection to the rude auditors is not so much to the substance of their claim – for he seems willing to entertain the possibility that they are, in fact, more eloquent, or better poets – as to their strategy. According to Pliny, one comes out best in the competitive arena if one simply *praises everything*. The rising tide of praise lifts all boats, one's own in particular. Here, then, Pliny theorises the strategy we have already seen him assert as a norm and carry out in his own practice: to say or signal nothing overtly negative about the style or content of any other reciter's work. Of course, the auditors Pliny criticises here would not agree that simply praising everything is a good competitive move. For tearing down one's competitors – 'going negative' – is a tried and true strategy for elevating one's own standing in the eyes of observers external to the competition. Thus, even as Pliny asserts a norm of conduct in the recitation, he reveals that others do not abide by it; actual social interactions may be considerably messier and less pleasant than Pliny's ideal would allow. The universal praise for which Pliny argues does, however, have the advantage of maintaining the *appearance* of a cooperative and harmonious community, keeping reciter and audience on friendly terms even as it also (in Pliny's view) elevates the auditor's standing relative to the reciter. Pliny disapproves of engaging in baldly competitive, hierarchy-establishing behaviour within the recitation, but is prepared to countenance such behaviour insofar as it *appears* to be consistent with, or decently masquerades as, cooperative, all-for-one and one-for-all behaviour.

[37] *Ep.* 6.17.1 *duo aut tres, ut sibi et paucis uidentur, diserti*: here the *pauci* must be other auditors who align themselves with the rude ones (*sibi*).

Among his contemporaries, Pliny is not alone in this view. Plutarch too, in a lengthy discussion of the comportment proper to those who listen to lectures, deems it de rigueur for auditors to be polite and attentive, and to find reasons for bestowing praise notwithstanding the availability of reasons for finding fault. To be sure, significant differences separate the scenarios discussed by Plutarch and Pliny: Plutarch writes for a Greek audience, targeting youths who are new to being auditors, and he focuses in particular on the situation of listening to a philosopher, which should notionally confer moral benefit on these young auditors. Plutarch deals only tangentially with literary recitation of the Plinian sort, while Pliny never discusses or considers the pedagogical dynamic that concerns Plutarch. Nevertheless, the norms for audience comportment that these two authors assert are strikingly similar, regardless of the differences in the performance situations.[38]

An especially striking assertion of proper behavioural norms, spurred by an even more egregious violation of those norms (in Pliny's view), is described in *Epistles* 6.15. Pliny addresses Voconius Romanus, an equestrian friend with literary interests. Voconius evidently attends recitations, as Pliny does, though neither man attended the recitation under discussion in this letter. In any event, Pliny assumes that Voconius shares his views about proper audience comportment.[39] Pliny begins the letter as follows:

> Mirificae rei non interfuisti; ne ego quidem, sed me recens fabula excepit. Passennus Paulus, splendidus eques Romanus et in primis eruditus, scribit elegos. Gentilicium hoc illi: est enim municeps Properti atque etiam inter maiores suos Propertium numerat. (2) Is cum recitaret, ita coepit dicere: 'Prisce, iubes...' Ad hoc Iauolenus Priscus (aderat enim ut Paulo amicissimus): 'Ego uero non iubeo.' Cogita qui risus hominum, qui ioci.

> You weren't there for an amazing thing: neither was I, but the story was still fresh when it reached me. Passennus Paulus, an equestrian luminary who is outstandingly learned, writes elegies. This is a family tradition for him:

---

[38] Plut. *Mor.* 44a–46d (= *De recta ratione audiendi* 13–16). Arrogance of auditor who is completely undemonstrative, as if trying to make others think he could do better: 44a–b. Those who are best are also most generous with their praise: 44c. Auditor's obligation to find something to praise: 44e–45b. Proper bodily comportment for auditors: 45c. Appropriate and inappropriate expressions of approval: 45f–46c. Plutarch also considers how young auditors may be reproved for their poor deportment by the philosophers whom they have come to hear, and how they should receive such criticism (46c–d) – a dynamic Pliny does not consider, as this expressly pedagogical dynamic is foreign to his recitation community. I am grateful to Katarzyna Jaźdźewska for discussion of the similarities and differences in the audience-worlds described by Plutarch and Pliny. For more on Plutarchan pedagogy, see Uden in this volume.

[39] For Voconius' literary interests see *Ep.* 3.13, where Pliny sends him a draft of the *Panegyricus* to edit and correct, apparently prior to reciting it (*Ep.* 3.18).

for he comes from the same town as Propertius and even counts Propertius among his ancestors. (2) When he was giving a recitation, he began to speak thus: 'Priscus, you bid . . . ' At this Javolenus Priscus, who was present as a very close friend to Paulus, said, 'But I don't bid!' Imagine people's laughter and jokes.

Pliny vouches for the high quality of the poetry Paulus was reciting when he characterises him as 'outstandingly learned' (*in primis eruditus*) and reports his claims to be descended from Propertius (evidently a declaration of literary allegiance and aspiration). The opening words of Paulus' recitation, *Prisce iubes*, are hexametric, presumably the first words of an elegiac poem. Roman authors frequently claim to write at the request or with the support of a friend or patron; such a claim provides a vehicle for naming and honouring someone with whom the author wishes to affiliate himself for aesthetic or economic reasons.[40] In this case the dedicatee Priscus, far from acceding to the convention and accepting the honour of being so named, pointedly exposes the fictionality of the trope (a fictionality that everyone already recognised) and thereby openly spurns the honour, perhaps because he does not wish to be associated with or seen to be endorsing the poetry Paulus produces. The audience is amused and the reciter is mortified. In exchange terms, Priscus rejects the gift Paulus proffers in the most humiliating way, transforming amicable exchange – Priscus was present, recall, 'as a very close friend' – into hostile exchange. According to Pliny's values and norms, Priscus has failed in his obligation to provide appropriate feedback, for he has violated the tacit principle of levelling no criticism and causing the reciter no discomfort at his own event.

This passage has sparked considerable scholarly debate regarding what, if anything, Paulus did wrong to warrant such a slapdown; what kind of criticism, if any, Priscus is really levelling; and how Pliny's own commentary here shapes his readers' (and our own) understanding of these events.[41] It is clear, however, that Pliny judges Priscus to be out of line, and believes he should have known better. He writes that Priscus has a public career and gives rulings on points of civil law, making his antics at the recitation all

---

[40] So, e.g., Pliny himself does in *Ep.* 1.1.1 – the first letter in the collection – addressed to Septicius Clarus: *Frequenter hortatus es ut epistulas . . . colligerem publicaremque*; similar (and roughly contemporary) are Quint. *Ep. ad Tryphonem* 1.1.1 (*Efflagitasti cotidiano conuicio ut libros . . . emittere inciperem*) and Tac. *Dial.* 1.1 (*Saepe ex me requiris, Fabi Iuste, . . .*). These are prose texts, but the dedicatory trope is identical. On the rhetoric and ideology of this trope, see Janson's classic discussion (1964, esp. pp. 60–4); also Beck 2013: 299–300.

[41] Beck 2013: 297–300 surveys previous scholarship; also Schröder 2001.

the more remarkable.[42] That is, Pliny implies that the standards of conduct incumbent on a public figure engaged in his *negotia* are equally binding upon that figure as an auditor at a recitation. Though recitations by definition take place in the realm of *otium*, Pliny here can equate the social and political stakes for reciter and audience with the stakes of the *negotia* they perform in the civic realm.[43] Indeed, this recitation as Pliny describes it has a spectacular, competitive dynamic. The audience, by its laughter, judges that Priscus has gotten the better of Paulus, and that a hierarchy has consequently been established. Word has gotten out ('the story is fresh'), and Pliny himself further amplifies it by relating it first to Voconius and then to the broader readership of his letters. Yet Pliny rejects this audience judgment, as he also does in *Epistles* 6.17 (discussed above). He is sympathetic to the reciter, and dismisses Priscus as 'mad'.[44] How else could such comportment by an auditor, such treatment of a friend who is reciting, be understood?[45]

There is a further dimension to Pliny's criticism of Priscus. As we have seen, Pliny objects to Priscus violating the (Plinian) ideal of the recitation event as a cooperative enterprise by like-minded community members to help one another publish the best books possible. This ideal is achieved when all parties conscientiously discharge their duties to recite, attend and provide appropriate feedback – i.e. when amicable exchange prevails. Priscus, in Pliny's view, has turned the event into a competitive, hierarchy-establishing spectacle characterised by hostile exchange and the abandonment of at least one obligation, that of providing appropriate feedback. Yet Pliny, even as he avows his commitment to the ideal, and even as his rhetoric here and elsewhere places him on the side of confirming these idealising norms, is himself complicit in violating these norms. First, by

---

[42] *Ep.* 6.15.3 *Interest tamen* [sc. *Priscus*] *officiis, adhibetur consiliis atque etiam ius ciuile publice respondet. quo magis quod tunc fecit et ridiculum et notabile fuit.*

[43] For the *negotium*-like stakes recitations may take on, see above and n. 9; also *Ep.* 7.17.11 (with Roller 2011: 216–17), 8.12.3, 8.21.3. On Javolenus Priscus, his rulings on civil law, and Pliny's possible competition with him, see Harries in this volume.

[44] *Ep.* 6.15.3–4 *Est omnino Priscus dubiae sanitatis . . . interim Paulo aliena deliratio aliquantum frigoris attulit. Tam sollicite recitaturis prouidendum est . . . ut sanos adhibeant.*

[45] On aggressive, reciter-deflating interruptions by audience members, see Barchiesi 2004. Auditors can fail or transgress in their obligation to provide appropriate feedback in other ways too. Martial is preoccupied with auditors who memorise the poems he recites, and then recite them as their own (*Epig.* 1.29, especially rich in exchange language; also 1.38, 52, 53, 63, 66, 72; 10.100; 12.63). Such theft or plagiarism – taking where giving is expected – sows distrust, transforming the normatively amicable exchange that binds the recitation community together into hostile exchange that cleaves the community asunder. Spahlinger 2004 offers a social and literary analysis of the plagiarism theme in Martial; Seo 2009 discusses its exchange dynamics.

articulating these norms in his letters, and by describing how they are exemplified or violated in his own or others' comportment during recitations,
Pliny is exposing to the public eye – the readership of his letters – precisely
those exchanges and judgments that he overtly insists do not belong in the
public eye, but should be kept within the bounds of the recitation event.
That is, in the very act of describing what should be kept secret, and in
insisting on that secrecy, he betrays the secret.[46] Second, as we have also
seen, Pliny consistently fashions himself in his letters as an ideal member
of the recitation community, one who manifests in his own behaviour the
norms of amicable exchange and obligation fulfilment that he holds so
dear. Sometimes he portrays the addressees of his letters, or certain other
auditors, as equally ideal; he also chastises auditors like Priscus who fall
short of that ideal.[47] Yet precisely via this presentation of self and others in
his letters, Pliny is ranking some members of the community, including
himself, higher than others. Hence he too is playing a competitive ranking
game, judging who are better members of the community and who are
worse, and furthermore he submits his own and others' behaviour (as he
represents it) to the judgment of the readership of his letters – all in the very
act of articulating the ideal of a non-competitive, cooperative community
that keeps its dirty laundry out of the public eye. It has long been recognised
that Pliny uses his letters as a vehicle for advantageous self-fashioning, and
for presenting himself as an ideal senator, advocate, governor, administrator and so on. The letters in general are well adapted to this purpose, and
the recitation letters are no exception.[48] It is also clear that recitations could
generate 'buzz' in the social circles that cared about them, so it is unsurpris-
ing that scuttlebutt about so-and-so's latest is passed around in letters.[49] Yet
Pliny's recitation letters involve two distinctive paradoxes. Pliny undercuts
the recitation community's ideals of secrecy and candour in the very act
of articulating those ideals to the readership of the letters; and he seeks
competitive advantage for himself in the eyes of that same readership by

---

[46] An epistle, with a single 'official' addressee, may appear 'private' or 'secret' insofar as confidential
information is theoretically being transmitted to just one person. But in selecting particular letters
for inclusion in a collection to be published for a broader readership, Pliny obliterates that notional
confidentiality. I thank Alice König for her thoughts about the simultaneously private and public
faces of the published epistle.

[47] Binder 1995: 300–3; also Beck 2013: 297, 303–4 on Pliny as 'censor' of others' comportment.

[48] Marchesi 2008: 2–4 offers a brief overview of this topic, with bibliography.

[49] E.g. in *Ep.* 1.5 and 6.17 Pliny passes along gossip he has heard from others about the goings-on in
particular recitations at which he was not present himself; in *Ep.* 5.3, 7.17 and 9.34 he describes
what he has heard through the grapevine about his own recitations. At Tac. *Dial.* 2.1, the city is
abuzz about Maternus' recitation; and Martial (*Epig.* 1.29) learns via rumour (*fama refert . . .*) that
Fidentinus is plagiarising his poetry.

decrying the efforts of others to seek competitive advantage within the recitation event.

To conclude this chapter, let us examine perhaps the most audacious instance of hostile exchange within the recitation community in all of Nervan, Trajanic and Hadrianic literature. The text in question is the beginning of Juvenal's first Satire – the gambit that opens his entire satiric oeuvre. The text is as follows (*Sat.* 1.1–6):

> Semper ego auditor tantum? Numquamne reponam
> uexatus totiens rauci Theseide Cordi?
> Impune ergo mihi recitauerit ille togatas,
> hic elegos? Impune diem consumpserit ingens
> Telephus aut summi plena iam margine libri
> scriptus et in tergo necdum finitus Orestes?

> Am I only ever an auditor? Am I never to retaliate,
> having been annoyed so often by the *Theseid* of hoarse Cordus?
> Will this man recite his comedies to me unpunished,
> and that one his elegies? Will a vast *Telephus* consume the day unpunished,
> or an *Orestes* written at the top of the roll (the margins already being full)
> and also on the back, and still not completed?

The satirist introduces himself as one who has sat in the audience for many a trying recitation – listening repeatedly to an epic poem read out in a hoarse voice, and over-long tragedies that waste a whole day. Rhetorically he asks whether his fate is only ever to be an auditor. The answer, of course, is no: for now he has written some poetry himself – satire, as he subsequently indicates (1.19–21, 30) – and it is finally his turn to 'retaliate' (*reponam*) by reciting, and thereby take revenge on others for what they have inflicted on him (*impune . . . impune?*). The conceptual framework of reciprocity is clear here, and is familiar from Pliny: members of the community are obligated both to give recitations of their own work, and to attend the recitations of others. The twist, however, is that here this exchange is presented as hostile from the outset. The satirist, now at long last giving a recitation of his own work, promises to subject his auditors to an experience every bit as awful, if not worse, than those to which they subjected him. In this satirical inversion of the obligations of reciprocity, the competition is framed as a race to the bottom, with the satirist striving to outdo his auditors/rivals in creating the worst possible recitation experience. But there is more. This poem itself, of course, is one of the satires that our poet has written and is here declaring his intention to recite. We who read the text of this poem are directly addressed at various points;

yet the satirist is addressing us not so much as readers of the finished, published text (though we are that), but – in the fiction of the satirist's own self-positioning – as *auditors* attending the satirist's recitation of this poem as a work-in-progress: for so he sets himself up at the poem's beginning.[50] And since we are being addressed as auditors, it follows that *we ourselves* are precisely those bad and annoying poets who have previously recited with Juvenal in our audience, and upon whom he is now taking his revenge. As we begin to read this poem, then, we find ourselves rather uncomfortably under attack from the reciter/author/satirist for our prior transgressions against him. The textual interaction between poet and 'us' as readers is thus set up to mimic precisely the social interaction at the recitation between the reciter and 'us' as auditors. This kind of move is typical of satire, which has a way of seizing its readers by the collar, insisting that it is addressing them, and refusing to allow them to stand back or detach themselves from the polemic. I wish to stress, however, that this vertiginous opening gambit only works by presupposing that the culture of recitation involves both cooperation and competition. The 'cooperative' norm of reciprocal reciting and attendance at recitations is patently on display, albeit in a hostile mode (as befits satire); but so is the reciter's competitive desire to equal or surpass the efforts of prior reciters (now sitting in his audience) – namely, to take the crown for inflicting misery. Thus Juvenal's opening neatly displays, even as it travesties, the combination of cooperation and competition, articulated via exchange language, that we have seen to characterise the culture of recitation more generally.

Conclusions

I end with a few general points about the kinds of 'literary interaction' the culture of recitation enables and promotes in the era of Nerva, Trajan and Hadrian. First, literary works in progress are always already 'intertextual' in at least a Bakhtinian way, since any author's text necessarily, from its inception, participates in the dialogic texture of all literature: repetition, appropriation, alteration, response and so on.[51] No text, at any stage of its development, is ever free of such relations to the earlier and contemporary texts, produced at many different times and places, that constitute the

---

[50] Addresses to readers: *expectes*, 1.14 (if this verse is retained); *admittitis*, 1.21; *dices*, 1.150. On Juvenal as a reciter (as well as critic of recitations) at *Sat.* 1.1–18, and for other cultural dimensions of this passage, see Uden 2015: 25–9, 98–104.

[51] See e.g. Whitton and Langlands in this volume, whose essays adumbrate the wide range and varied intensity that intertextual engagement in this period can exhibit.

literary universe the new text enters. Nevertheless, such intertextuality is 'interactive' in a somewhat limited way. An author can 'interact' with a fixed, published text (whether its author is dead or alive) only via appropriation and response. The resultant new text may, in its turn, shape future readers' reception and understanding of the earlier texts with which it interacts, but would not normally change the actual words of those texts. Recitation, however – this is my second general point – is a form of literary interaction that is social as well as textual, involving living members of a local community. Because author and audience are both alive, present and responsive to one another, audience feedback at a recitation and at any subsequent stage of editing can trigger changes in the text under development. Thus the finished work is sure to be imprinted with the values and preferences of this community as constituted at that time and place. This imprint may take a variety of forms, which we may or may not be able to spot and distinguish from other formative forces.[52] I speculate, however, that the habits of interactivity cultivated and confirmed in the recitation and elsewhere in the editing process 'spill over' into finished works that respond to and interact with the finished texts of other contemporary authors. That is, the specifically textual forms of interactivity discussed in other chapters of this volume may themselves echo the exchange dynamic among authors and auditors promoted and sustained by the culture of recitation. Third, because the collocal, synchronic recitation community in which Pliny, Martial and other authors participate includes members of the Roman imperial ruling class (i.e. the senatorial–equestrian aristocracy centred in or focused on Rome), and because the exchange that is constitutive of recitation may, in its competitive and sometimes hostile dimension, produce social rankings and hierarchies, it seems inevitable that recitation should sometimes have political and civic consequences resembling those of the more formal *negotia* discharged by members of this ruling class – notwithstanding that this activity is (for aristocrats, at least) typically declared to take place *out* of the civic sphere in the realm of *otium*. In this respect recitation may share the social stakes of any public performance.

---

[52] At Tac. *Dial.* 3.2, Maternus' visitors expect to find him revising the text he recited the previous day to make it less offensive to the powerful, in light of the response it received in the recitation. Though fictional (or fictionalised), this exchange hints at one form such an imprint might take. Meanwhile Pliny claims, in general and in particular cases, that he and other reciters revise their work in light of feedback received at recitations or later in the editing process (*Ep.* 5.12.1–2; 7.17.7, 11; 8.21.6). But he never describes any specific revision(s) made as a result of this process.

CHAPTER 9

Images of Domitius Apollinaris in Pliny and Martial
Intertextual Discourses as Aspects of Self-Definition and Differentiation

Sigrid Mratschek

Poet and Epistolographer: Intertextuality and Self-Representation

Pictures are 'a direct shot into the brain'.[1] In discursive terms, their message is an interplay of intellect and sensory perception. Such is the case in a series of repeatedly shifting portraits of the prominent senator L. Domitius Apollinaris. Martial, a knight from the province of Hispania Tarraconensis, produced satirical snapshots of social networking with his patron Apollinaris. Pliny the Younger, a senator from northern Italy, was an 'engaged observer' of such relationships and the author of metadiscursive prose epistles *to* and *about* Apollinaris. In the interplay of intertextual discourse between these different genres, the character sketches of Apollinaris should be understood not as depictions of an empirical reality, but as self-conscious reflections of the ways in which their authors identify themselves and the world around them. In his interactions with Martial's poems and with Domitius Apollinaris as protagonist, using visions of the underworld as figures for the political atmosphere in Rome and competing to visualise the most beautiful *locus amoenus*, Pliny developed subtle performative strategies and ideas to reinvent himself as *littérateur* and politician. This chapter, then, is about some of the ways in which literary and social (or socio-literary) interactions of this triangular relationship impact dynamically on each other, on

I here express my gratitude for a wealth of stimulating ideas to Roy Gibson, who sent me a pre-publication copy of his and Ruth Morello's book, and to Chris Whitton, whose commentary on Pliny's Book 2 represents an enrichment of the entire collection of letters; also for much learnt from the relevant monographs by Ilaria Marchesi (2008) and Victoria Rimell (2008). Warm thanks for their comments are due to all who attended the Literary Interactions conference in June 2014, especially to Alice König (St Andrews) who brought her LINTH project to Rostock; also to Mme Marie-Pierre Ciric and the publishing house of Klincksieck (Paris) for kindly permitting the photograph of the inscription to be reproduced (Fig. 9.1). Translations from Martial are based on Shackleton Bailey 1993, those of Pliny on Walsh 2006.

[1] Apophthegm of the Saarbrücken behaviourist and marketing guru Werner Kroeber-Riel, cited after Gries 2006.

Fig. 9.1. Statue base of the Domitii: inscription of L. Domitius Apollinaris, Xanthos, AD 93–6. Reproduced with permission from Balland 1981, plate XII, no. 49.

and off the page: contrary to a common assumption – and of particular interest in times of regime change – they not only distort reality, but also create it.

The Focus of Networks: Domitius Apollinaris, Martial and Pliny the Younger

Our texts are silent on the protagonist's career,[2] but when studied in conjunction with new inscriptions they offer a kaleidoscope of insights into the networks of which he formed a part. A family statue gallery from the Letoon in Xanthos shows that Domitius Apollinaris had managed to upgrade his *nouitas* through alliance with the powerful figure Valerius Patruinus,[3] subsequently being promoted to the rank of imperial legate of Lycia–Pamphylia (93–6).[4] All that remains today of the gallery of six bronze statues is the 4.36-metre-long limestone base with its six inscriptions (Fig. 9.1).[5] Those honoured here, apart from Apollinaris, the ἡγεμών,

---

[2] For the periods away from Rome there are no Martial epigrams.

[3] Apollinaris had commanded two legions in the east under L. Valerius Patruinus (AD 83–9); see Syme 1991b: 588–602.

[4] Balland 1981: 103–5. His governorship (ὁ δικαιοδότης) is further documented by an inscription from Tlos honouring his son (*IGR* III, 559 = *TAM* II, 570); see Syme 1991b: 588 n. 2 and *PIR²* D 133.

[5] Balland 1981: 130 on the wall dowel-holes for the bronzes and the find-site south of the Nymphaeum.

were his second wife Valeria Vet(t)illa, his father-in-law Valerius Patruinus, a son from his first marriage called Domitius Seneca, the latter's wife,
Clodia Decmina, and a boy called Neratiolus.[6] Both Apollinaris and Pliny,
who was about ten years younger, were among the successful *homines noui*
whose careers prospered under Domitian.[7] Apollinaris' career began with
the quaestorship *c.* 77 and the praetorship *c.* 83. In contrast to Pliny, whose
political career reached its zenith only under Trajan, with the consulship
(*suff.* 100) and the governorship of Pontus–Bithynia (*c.* 110–12),[8] Apollinaris ceases to be mentioned by contemporaries as a political actor from
the point at which, aged 42, he attained a suffect consulship under Nerva
(*suff.* 97).

What links existed between these two senators? Both Pliny and Domitius Apollinaris were natives of Italia Transpadana; both were patrons of
Martial. Pliny's birthplace, Comum, was 50 miles as the crow flies from
Vercellae, birthplace of Apollinaris.[9] Pliny's contacts with Vercellae find no
mention in his letters. Little attention has been paid, so far, to the fact that
the people of Vercellae, early in the second century, honoured Pliny for his
munificence with an inscription (*CIL* v, 5667); he had it set up on his estate
near Comum only 5½ miles south-east of where it was found.[10] Pliny's
flaminate mentioned in the inscription was probably held at Vercellae.[11] It
was thus no mere coincidence that intertextual discourses in Pliny's letters
invoke Martial's poems about their mutual friend Apollinaris. As an
author himself, Pliny competed with the poet in creating portraits of
Apollinaris. Having a *patria* in common and a similar social background
in this dynamic region beyond the Po – between 69 and 103 it produced
most of the consuls and men of letters[12] – could lead, as in the case of
Pliny and Apollinaris, to solidarity and the forming of alliances, but also to
rivalry.

---

[6] On the individuals represented see Syme 1991b: 589–602.
[7] On Apollinaris (born *c.* 52 or 53) and Pliny (born *c.* 62) see Syme 1991b: 558, 563.
[8] As *legat(us) pro pr(aetore) prouinciae Pon[ti et Bithyniae pro]consulari potesta[te]* (*CIL* v, 5262 = *ILS* 2927 from Comum; cf. *CIL* xi, 5272 from Hispellum), see the reconstruction by Alföldy 1999: 221–44, commented on by Gibson and Morello 2012: 270–3.
[9] On Comum see Plin. *Ep.* 1.3.1 (*meae deliciae*) and 5.7.2 (*communis patria*). On Vercellae see below.
[10] At the beginning of the second century, as the *cursus honorum* of *CIL* v, 5667 ended with the offices of *augur* in 103 (Plin. *Ep.* 4.8.1) and of *curator aluei Tiberis* in 104–6 (*Ep.* 5.14.2); see Birley 2000a: 16. According to a hypothesis of Mommsen (*CIL* v, p. 606), the inscription was set up near Comum. The archaeological site, Cantù, belonged to Comum in antiquity; see Andermahr 1998: 384. A dedicatory inscription of a *saltuarius* to Jupiter (*CIL* v, 5702) for L. Verginius Rufus, victor over Vindex, who owned a property adjacent to Pliny's land, was discovered not far away, at Brianza (*Ep.* 2.1.8 *utrique eadem regio, municipia finitima, agri etiam possessionesque coniunctae*).
[11] Andermahr 1998: 384.   [12] Mratschek 2003: 219–41.

The Patron (*Beneficium*)

Model Roles Redefined: Doctus Apollinaris vs Plinius Anxius

Both Domitius and Pliny were linked by the social bond of *amicitia* to Martial, who would send them his books of epigrams for circulation among the high society of Rome, while also immortalising his patrons in his poems.[13] Interaction among those involved generated a complex of social relationships founded ultimately on the principle of gift-exchange specific to the social anthropology of ancient cultures.[14] Of six Martial epigrams to Apollinaris, no fewer than four were dedicatory poems.[15] All without exception were presented as an apostrophe to a gift (*munus*) – a book-roll, a choliamb, a rose, or Saturnalian verses.

Gradually, by inference from these snapshots, Apollinaris comes to acquire a more distinct profile: once the uncontested *elegantiae arbiter* of his time, *doctus Apollinaris* (4.86) moved on to become an enthusiastic advocate of Martial's miniature art (7.26). The limping iamb is Martial's witness that he himself could not love his verse more than did his dedicatee Apollinaris. An image from love elegy (*amore . . . nugarum flagret*)[16] conveys the enthusiasm with which Apollinaris responded to the first poetry volume, and is also a ploy integral to Martial's self-fashioning as a poet in great demand. Contemplating Apollinaris, amateur of the fine arts, with a taste for Attic verse, dedicatee in 89 of the first four books of Martial's epigrams (4.86), no one would guess that this was the successful *homo nouus*, recently returned from a six-year tour of duty in the east as commander of two legions under the governor P. Valerius Patruinus, the *XVI Flavia Firma* in Cappadocia and the *VI Ferrata* in Syria (83–9).[17] When Martial found him engrossed in his work and had to interrupt him in order to hand him the seventh book of epigrams, Apollinaris had only just taken up the

---

[13] Mart. 5.15.3–4 . . . *gaudet honorato sed multus nomine lector,* | *cui uictura meo munere fama datur.* On circulation 7.97.10; 13 *O quae gloria! Quam frequens amator!* | . . . *uni mitteris, omnibus legeris.* E.g. Pliny (*Ep.* 3.21.2, 4) paid Martial travelling expenses (*uiaticum*) in recognition of his verse. See White 1978: 90–2.

[14] Mauss 1990b: 157, Bourdieu 1993: 180–1, 192–3 and the current definitions in Satlow 2013: 4–11. See Roller in this volume on the language of gift-exchange in Pliny.

[15] In Book 4 (4.86), Book 7 (7.26; 7.86) and Book 11 (11.15): see Nauta 2002: 161. In the gift – still the subject of dispute – of a wreath of roses (7.89) with a poem, or as a poem, there is a further dedication; see below.

[16] Mart. 7.26.7–8 *Quanto mearum, scis, amore nugarum* | *flagret* [sc. Apollinaris]: *nec ipse plus amare te possum.* The metaphor of love's flame is from elegy, e.g. Ov. *Her.* 16.117 *ferus in molli pectore flagrat amor.*

[17] Identified by Syme 1991b: 590–1 with the Ignotus of inscription *IGR* III, 558 = *TAM* II, 569. Friedländer's (1886) dating of Dec. 88 needs revision in the light of the epigraphic evidence.

important urban post of *praefectus aerarii militaris* (92–4), preceding Pliny in this.[18] While observing all due respect for the business affairs of the new prefect of the *aerarium militare*, Martial did not neglect to point out that the recipient, as protagonist, was himself a 'part of the poetic gift'.[19]

In Martial's enigmatic rose poem (7.89), Apollinaris metamorphosed into a lover of erotic poetry, after his marriage in 92 to the wealthy Valeria Vettilla, daughter of Valerius Patruinus of Ticinum, under whom he had served in the army.[20] Attribute of the love goddess and of the Muses, the rose was also the subject of poetry.[21] With the words *i, felix rosa*, Martial despatched to his patron a garland of roses and a poem that together were to ensure Venus would continue to favour Apollinaris well into old age.[22] This quatrain, perpetuating the memory of Apollinaris festively crowned, was in a volume of poetry widely read in Italy and Gaul.[23] The sympotic setting recurred elsewhere: at night, the time 'when the rose rules', the Younger Pliny was likewise receptive to the light Muse.[24] On 17 December 96 Martial welcomed Domitius Apollinaris back from Asia Minor with a witty poem in the style of Catullus as a Saturnalian gift (11.15).[25] Humorously inverting Lucretius' hymn to Venus as mother of the Roman people (*Aeneadum genetrix*), he here has the chaste priest-king Numa Pompilius proclaim the *mentula* to be 'father to all humans', the object being to enlighten the dignified ex-legate, in the final *pointe*, about the difference between erotic poetry and lifestyle.[26]

---

[18] Pliny may have been prefect of the *aerarium militare* for 94–6 (Syme 1991b: 591, 598), but 95–7, or a shorter term, are equally possible and perhaps preferable; see the meticulous revision of Pliny's senatorial *cursus* (*CIL* v, 5262 = *ILS* 2927) by Whitton 2015a.

[19] Mart. 7.26.3 *hoc qualecumque, cuius aliqua pars ipse est.*

[20] Mart. 7.89.1–2 *I, felix rosa, mollibusque sertis | nostri cinge comas Apollinaris.* Syme's (1991b: 592) reasoning remains persuasive even without the wedding day as occasion for the poem; cf. Nauta 2002: 160–1.

[21] E.g. the hymn to the soft rose, ῥόδον τέρεινον, Anacr. fr. 55 West, trans. Campbell 1988: 230, vv. 4–10: τόδε γὰρ θεῶν ἄημα, | τόδε καὶ βροτοῖσι χάρμα, | Χάρισίν τ' ἄγαλμ' ἐν ὥραις, | πολυαν-θέων Ἐρώτων | ἀφροδίσιόν τ' ἄθυρμα. | τόδε καὶ μέλημα μύθοις | χαρίεν φυτόν τε Μουσῶν. See Rosenmeyer 1992: 88, 210–12, 222. Used as model in Rome since Gellius (kind advice from Martin West). Fitzgerald 2007: 149 too votes for the 'rose as a poem or book'.

[22] Mart. 7.89.3–4 *Quas* [sc. *comas*] *tu nectere candidas, sed olim, | sic te semper amet Venus, memento.*

[23] On the circulation in Vienne: Mart. 7.88 precedes the rose poem. See Fitzgerald 2007: 149.

[24] Mart. 10.20(19).19–20 = Plin. *Ep.* 3.21.5 *haec hora est tua* [i.e. *Musa*], *cum furit Lyaeus, | cum regnat rosa.*

[25] Mart. 11.15.11–12 *uersus . . . | Saturnalicios.* On the dating, see Syme 1991b: 598. The Saturnalia and the myth of Saturn the bringer of culture were attributed to Numa's calendar of feasts (Var. *LL* 5.64; Fest. 432.20 L). See Versnel 1993: 136–227; Rimell 2008: 140–4.

[26] Mart. 11.15.9–14 *ex qua nascimur, omnium parentem | quam sanctus Numa mentulam uocabat. | . . .* (14) *mores non habet hic meos libellus.* See Williams 2002: 165–6; Sullivan 1979: 418–32 and 1991: 115–84. The allusion to Venus was previously ignored, e.g. Lucr. 1.1 (Venus as *Aeneadum genetrix*); 2.598–9 (on *tellus, natura rerum*) . . . *ferarum et nostri genetrix . . . corporis*; Col. 3.9 *benignissima rerum omnium parens natura.*

Whereas 'the fractured, tightly sprung and metamorphic universe' of Martial's epigram corresponds to his 'unstable and nervy perception of the world' in his poetic reflections on the metropolis Rome, the heart and microcosm of a vast, complex empire,[27] the Younger Pliny, by contrast, in his collection of letters, presents a harmonious picture of the different life that was to follow under Trajan's *initia felicissimi principatus*.[28] Pliny's readers are intended to visualise the 'aesthetics of existence' as lived by the elites of Italy,[29] with their codes of behaviour and their sophisticated literary taste, and Pliny himself as an example, representing the 'good' aristocrat under 'the best' of all emperors.[30]

At the same time, Pliny represented the ideal discerning *lector studiosus* who helped ensure that Martial achieved fame during his lifetime for his short satirical poems with their punchy endings.[31] The basic principles of poetic composition employed by Martial, variation and juxtaposition,[32] were also his own. Conforming to an epistolographic principle of his own, the pen portraits of their mutual friend Domitius Apollinaris were arranged not chronologically, but in accordance with intended strategies of reception aesthetics (*uarietas*).[33] Apollinaris appears *once* in each triad of the nine books of letters,[34] and in each letter one of the three criteria crucial for a senator's social standing is placed under scrutiny: influence, effectiveness in public life, wealth. In his dual role of addressee and orator, Apollinaris provides a foil for the author's self-positioning in the form of a climax. The epistolary format enabled Pliny to present his persona as a montage of pictures selected and arranged by himself. The structure and the topic sequence are reminiscent of Martial: Pliny first shows himself in the letters (*Ep.* 2.9, AD 101) playing the subordinate role of a suppliant (*suffragator*) addressing the all-powerful patron, Apollinaris; next as owner of

[27] Rimell 2008: 4–12.
[28] Plin. *Ep.* 10.2.2. Cf. Tac. *Agr.* 3.1 *et, quamquam primo statim beatissimi saeculi ortu Nerua Caesar res olim dissociabiles miscuerit – principatum et libertatem – augeatque cotidie felicitatem temporum Nerua Traianus...* On *Felicitas* and *Securitas* in Trajan's coinage programme and in Pliny, see Seelentag 2004: 99–107.
[29] The 'aesthetics of existence' concept was developed by Foucault 2005, no. 357: 904 and 1989: 60–2 in connection with the issue of status-appropriate patterns of behaviour with particular reference to the lifestyles of antiquity, e.g. exemplary self-development by the individual.
[30] On Pliny's self-exemplification and idealisation in Book 10 by suppressing problems, see Woolf 2006: 95, 103–5; Stadter 2006: 69, 74–5; for further, different views of Book 10 see Harries and Lavan in this volume. Cf. A. König 2007: 177–205.
[31] Mart. 1.2.4–5. See Fitzgerald 2007: 73–4; Rimell 2008: 10–11.   [32] Rimell 2008: 6, 20.
[33] Plin. *Ep.* 1.1.1 *Collegi non seruato temporis ordine*, with Gibson and Morello 2012: 14, 20, 103. For the principle of *uarietas* see 9.2.2 (Ciceronian *uarietas* as unattainable exemplar), 2.5.7 (in style), 3.9.1 (in pleas), 4.14.3 and 9.22.2 (in lyric poetry), 5.6.13 (in landscape).
[34] Publication in triads, discussed by Syme 1958: 660–3 and Bodel 2015: 70–1, is not sustained: see Sherwin-White 1966: 27–41; Gibson and Morello 2012: 265–70.

a renowned villa in rivalry with Apollinaris (*Ep.* 5.6, AD 105); and at the discursive climax, finally – rather than where chronology would place it, near the beginning of the letters – the politicians Apollinaris and Pliny measure up to each other in a senatorial debate that had historically taken place in spring 97, ten years before (*Ep.* 9.13.13, *c.* 107). This is also the high point of Pliny's self-projection as a loyal supporter of Trajan and ideal senator for the new regime.[35]

In *Epistles* 2.9 Domitius Apollinaris is introduced to us as an influential patron from whom the author is soliciting a recommendation for the candidature of Erucius Clarus for the military tribunate.[36] In the year following his suffect consulship (100), Pliny held no office. This enables him to adopt an astutely self-deprecating stance for the first encounter, that of a suppliant (*anxius et inquietus*), appealing on the model of Cicero's affective strategy to the addressee's emotions,[37] and deploying the *diligeris, coleris, frequentaris* tricolon to stylise Apollinaris into *the* charismatic political leader figure whom all naturally follow.[38] Under Trajan, with Domitius Apollinaris long since politically sidelined, this strategy can hardly have failed to achieve its object.

The Politician (*Negotium*)

Visions of the Underworld: Apollinaris vs Pliny, and the Senate of Rome

Two of Martial's longer epigrams (10.12 and 10.30) feature portraits of Apollinaris, the over-stressed ex-consul of the year 97, torn between *otium* and *negotium*. Thematically they correspond to two letters of Pliny the Younger: in the private space as owner of a villa (*Ep.* 5.6, AD 105) and in the public space as a speaker in the senate (9.13.13, *c.* 107). The *Fasti Ostienses* reveal that Domitius Apollinaris took up office on 1 July 97 and relinquished it on 1 September.[39] Martial claims not to be weighed down by sorrow as he

---

[35] Whitton 2012: 359.

[36] *Ep.* 2.9.2 *meo suffragio peruenit ad ius tribunatus petendi.* Cf. *Ep.* 2.9.1 (next n.), commentary by Whitton 2013: 140–7. Cf. Birley 2004: 92 on Erucius Clarus, who rose to supreme power during Trajan's Parthian war (*suff.* 117, 146 *praefectus urbi* and *cos. ord.* II).

[37] *Ep.* 2.9.1 *Anxium me et inquietum habet petitio Sexti Eruci mei. Afficior cura et . . . quasi pro me altero patior; et alioqui meus pudor, mea existimatio, mea dignitas in discrimen adducitur . . . meo suffragio peruenit ad ius tribunatus petendi, quem nisi obtinet in senatu, uereor ne decepisse Caesarem uidear.* His models here are Cicero (*Ad fam.* 11.16–17) and Quintilian (*Inst.* 4.pr.); see Whitton 2013: 141–2 and in this volume, p. 57.

[38] Plin. *Ep.* 2.9.6 *ostende modo uelle te, nec deerunt qui, quod tu uelis, cupiant.*

[39] Vidman 1982: 45 and *AE* 1954, 220: in the pair following M. Annius Verus and L. Neratius Priscus. Syme 1991b: 588 n. 2 and Nauta 2002: 160 accordingly date the epigram to the second half of 97.

bids farewell to his friend, off to seek restoration after a gruelling summer
in the capital (10.12.1–3):

> Aemiliae gentes et Apollineas Vercellas
>   et Phaethontei qui petis arua Padi,
> ne uiuam, nisi te, Domiti, dimitto libenter . . .

> Domitius, now heading for the folk of the Aemilian Way and Apollo's Ver-
> cellae and the fields of Po, Phaethon's river, upon my oath I let you go
> gladly . . .

Here for the first and only time Martial uses the *gentilicium* Domitius for
Apollinaris, and here we learn that the latter was a native of Vercellae, where
there was an inscription dedicated to his daughter [*Domit*]*ia* [*Apolli*]*naris*
f(*ilia*) [*Fa*]*dilla* too.[40] The epithet *Apollineae* applied to Vercellae is not
sound evidence of a cult of Apollo,[41] but a subtle allusion to the *cognomen*
Apollinaris and Vercellae's poetically gifted son, who endowed his birthplace with reflected glory from the god of poetry.[42] A second epithet alludes
to Apollinaris' destination as *Phaethontei . . . arua Padi*, evoking the famous
Ovidian scene of Phaethon's headlong plunge into the Po after driving his
father's chariot too close to the burning radiance of the sun.[43] Martial's
mythological *exemplum* depicting *hybris* and death[44] and the sun metaphor
could be a coded warning to Apollinaris not to stray too near the centres of
imperial power. The nape of his neck had already been 'singed' or 'rubbed
raw' (*perusta colla*)[45] in summer 97 by the yoke of the suffect consulate, and
by the end of October, following the adoption of Trajan, a further transfer
of power was imminent. The opening poems of Book 10 (6 and 7) celebrate
Trajan's return to Rome.[46]

The imagery in which Martial clothes the imagined return of Apollinaris
to Rome and the seat of power, depicting it as a 'descent to the underworld',
Virgil's *pallida regna*, grows out of his intertextual evocation of Tibullus'

---

[40] Pais 1884, no. 899 = Roda 1985, no. 20. Alföldy 1999: 328, no. 6, corrects earlier readings.

[41] See Nauta 2002: 160 n. 50 on the slender evidence of Stat. *Silv.* 1.4.58–9.

[42] *Apollineas* (*Vercellas*) made Apollinaris' cognomen redundant, see Syme 1991b: 588. The play on
his name was repeated four centuries later by Sidonius Apollinaris; see Mathisen 1991: 29–43 and
Mratschek 2017: 317.

[43] Ov. *Met.* 2.319–26, esp. 319–20 and 323–4 *At Phaethon, rutilos flamma populante capillos,* | *uoluitur*
in praeceps . . . | *Quem procul a patria diuerso maximus orbe* | *excipit Eridanus.*

[44] Ovid (*Met.* 2.323–8) styles his description of Phaethon's fall into the Eridanus (Po) as a funerary rite,
with the river god rinsing his smoking face and nymphs interring his smouldering body in a hillock
and dedicating a funerary inscription to him. On the hybris, see the epitaph (vv. 327–8): *Hic situs*
est Phaethon, currus auriga paterni; | *quem si non tenuit, magnis tamen excidit ausis.*

[45] Mart. 10.12.5–6 *. . . ut messe uel una* | *urbano releues colla perusta iugo.* Note the stylistic device of
ambiguitas in the participle *perustus*.

[46] Rimell 2008: 203. Trajan took over the *tribunicia potestas* on 28(?) October; see Kienast 2017: 116.

pallida turba, the crowd of shades flitting by dark waters.[47] Apollinaris, 'tanned like an Ethiopian' when he first returns from his holiday in the sunlit 'upper world' of Vercellae, grows pale like death itself on merging again with the *pallida turba*, the pallid, spectral army of his urban friends in Rome.[48] Like voracious Death (*rapax mors*) in Tibullus' hypotext, the capital has robbed Apollinaris of his healthy tan and transformed him into one of the bloodless denizens of Hades with whom he now socialises.[49] Martial's radical vision of the unhealthy pallid throng is 'a metonym for and epigrammatic entombing' not only *of* the *urbs*,[50] but *in* the *urbs*.

Metaphorical use of black-and-white contrasts, borrowed by Tibullus from the war context for application to the power struggles among the senate leadership cadres, was politically loaded.[51] Visions of the underworld depicting autocratic rule generate a complex intertextual web from the Republic onward. Fearing the worst from the Caesarians, Cicero had already quoted Atticus' sarcastic description of them as *illam* νέκυιαν, that realm of the dead.[52] Like Martial's underworld vision, the imperial palace of Domitian in Pliny's *Panegyricus* is presented as a place of terror, where the emperor sought out darkness and secrecy – *tenebras semper secretumque captantem*; his pallor was contagious.[53] Tacitus singles out as the nadir of misery under Domitian the pallor of senators (*denotandis tot hominibus palloribus*) compelled to look on impotently – and under the emperor's eye – as their colleagues were condemned.[54] Through the twist in the plot,

---

[47] Tib. 1.10.37–8 *Illic percussisque genis ustoque capillo | errat ad obscuros pallida turba lacus*. Cf. Virg. *Aen.* 8.244–5 (*regna . . . | pallida*); 10.761 (*pallida Tisiphone*); *Georg.* 1.277; Cic. *Tusc.* 1.48. See André 1949: 145; Heil 2004: 78–9.

[48] Mart. 10.12.9–11 *Et uenies albis non cognoscendus amicis | liuebitque tuis pallida turba genis. | . . . | Niliaco redeas tu licet ore niger*. Note the colour display referring to the myth of Phaethon: Αἰθίοψ means 'burnt-face', i.e. Ethiopian, 'negro'. See LSJ s.v. and Balsdon 1979: 59, 217. Cf. Ov. *Met.* 2.235–6 and Plin. *Nat.* 2.189 on the sun-chariot of Phaethon that burnt the skin of the Ethiopians, turning it black. There is also the greenish discolouration of a corpse. Both were foreigners, cf. Mart. 10.12.8 (Apollinaris as *peregrinus*) and Ov. *Met.* 2.323 on the death of Phaethon (*procul a patria diuerso . . . orbe*).

[49] Mart. 10.12.11 *Sed uia quem dederit rapiet cito Roma colorem*. Cf. Tib. 1.10.33 (*atra . . . mors*); 1.3.65 (*rapax mors*).

[50] Rimell 2008: 12, 20–4. *Turba* is used fifty-nine times in Martial's corpus (ibid. 21 n. 10).

[51] On Martial as a 'political poet', see Fearnley 2003: 613–35.

[52] Cic. *Att.* 9.12(11).2 *Quam ille* [sc. *Matius*] *haec non probare mihi quidem uisus est, quam illam* νέκυιαν, *ut tu appellas, timere! . . . Vtinam in hac aliquod miseria rei publicae* πολιτικὸν *opus efficere et nauare mihi liceat!*

[53] Plin. *Pan.* 48.4 *Obseruabantur foribus horror et minae et par metus admissis et exclusis*; on Domitian, 48.4 (*femineus pallor*) and 48.5 *tenebras semper secretumque captantem, nec umquam ex solitudine sua prodeuntem, nisi ut solitudinem faceret*. See Braund 1998: 64–5 (repr. in Rees 2012a: 96–7); C. Kelly 2015: 227.

[54] Tac. *Agr.* 45.2 *Praecipua sub Domitiano miseriarum pars erat uidere et aspici, cum suspiria nostra subscriberentur, cum denotandis tot hominum palloribus sufficeret saeuus ille uultus et rubor, quo se contra*

Martial creates an anti-propempticon, hailing the departure that allowed a senator, for the space of a summer month, to see the 'upper world' once more, and parodying the happy anticipation of reunion in Rome as a return to the realm of shades, to the Orcus-dwellers in their white togas.[55] It demonstrates Martial's acute awareness of how drastically politics had been transformed.[56] Was he thinking of his own departure, now that his panegyrics to Domitian would have made him *persona non grata* with Domitian's successors? Or did he fear political purges under the new regime as previously under Augustus, when unworthy senators had been termed 'Orcus-dwellers' and expelled from the senate?[57]

Not until well on into Trajan's reign, in 106–8, were the last aftershocks of the denunciations of the Domitian era and the dark side of Nerva's rule reflected in the works of Pliny. Domitius Apollinaris was present in the senate in 97 as *consul designatus* under Nerva[58] when Pliny launched his memorable attack on Publicius Certus: in his (lost) speech *De Heluidi ultione* he had demanded revenge for the murder of the younger Helvidius, in which Certus, under Domitian, had been complicit.[59] *Maiestas* trials and factional rivalries in the senate had then brought death to no fewer than twelve men of consular rank.[60] Pliny's proud self-presentation as orator addressing the senate reveals that Apollinaris had backed the 'wrong' side.[61] Like Fabricius Veiento, three times consul (*cos.* III 83), who had

---

pudorem muniebat. On 'Martial and Tacitus on regime change', see Rimell in this volume; on the emperor as observer, Woodman 2014: 319.

[55] Compare Mart. 10.12.9 (*albis...amicis*), 1.55.14 (*urbanis albus in officiis*) and 10.19(18).4 *Eheu! Quam fatuae sunt tibi, Roma, togae!*

[56] Martial's Book 10 is presented as a second edition (10.2.1–4), 'after the death and the *damnatio memoriae* of Domitian' (Rimell 2008: 5); see also Rimell and König in this volume. This expurgated version is generally dated to the year 98 after Trajan's accession to the throne, but as with Tacitus' *Agricola* an earlier composition date under Nerva but after the adoption of Trajan, at the earliest at the end of October 97, is possible; see Syme 1958: 19; Fearnley 2003: 629. Of an anthology containing Books 10–11, the accompanying poem to Nerva (12.5) is preserved.

[57] Suet. *Aug.* 35.1 (on the *lectio senatus*) *et quidem indignissimi et post necem Caesaris per gratiam et praemium allecti, quos orciuos uulgus uocabat.* Cf. the ambiguity of Martial's *manibus* ('from my hands' and 'from the shades of the dead') in announcing Book 10 (1.2.1–2): see Rimell in this volume.

[58] Plin. *Ep.* 9.13.13 *Dicit Domitius Apollinaris, consul designatus.* Pliny's plea was delivered during the half-year from January to July 97, after Apollinaris' return and before his suffect consulship.

[59] Cf. *Ep.* 9.13.16 on the 'bloodstained flattery' (*cruenta adulatio*) of Certus. He had proposed the *sententia* of condemnation in the senate: see Sherwin-White 1966: 492. On Pliny's 'revenge', see Whitton 2012: 353–4.

[60] Suet. *Dom.* 10–11 (catalogue of those executed), esp. 10.2 *Complures senatores, in iis aliquot consulares, interemit.* Cf. 15.1, Tac. *Agr.* 45.1 (*tot consularium caedes*). But see Woodman 2014: 316 *contra* Syme 1958: 597.

[61] Sherwin-White 1966: 157 implies that a late shadow was cast on the picture of friendship (Plin. *Ep.* 2.9; 5.6).

been closely associated with Domitian's reign of terror,[62] Apollinaris had defended Publicius Certus.[63] The process of coming to terms with the past was intimately bound up with Rome's future. Pliny contrives to present the struggle between the old Domitianic order and the incoming power elite on the political stage of the senate in such a way as to show himself at the centre of the action. A friend from the ranks of the consulars took him aside and urged him to desist: Pliny had made himself 'conspicious to future emperors'.[64] He was also warned against Certus' powerful friend, whose name none dared speak, with armies in the east at his disposal: M. Cornelius Nigrinus Curiatius Maternus. Governor of Syria from 94 or 95 to 97 and hero of Domitian's Dacian wars, Cornelius Nigrinus was Trajan's rival for the imperial throne, and with the adoption of Trajan saw his political career terminated before the year was out[65] – as, evidently, did Domitius Apollinaris.

Commitment for the orphaned family of the younger Helvidius, which had its roots in the Stoic opposition,[66] and the explosiveness of the political situation *before* the election of Nerva's successor, required courage. How much courage becomes clear when Pliny stoically responded to his friend's warning during the tumultuous session of the senate with the words of Aeneas: *Omnia praecepi atque animo mecum ante peregi* ('I foresaw all this, and ran it through in my mind', Virg. *Aen.* 6.105). With his subtle allusion to the Sibyl's warning about descent into the kingdom of Death, Pliny defined not only his plea before the senate (*actio*) and its perils as his 'descent into the underworld', but along with it – as Ilaria Marchesi has persuasively shown – the entire self-aggrandising project to which his *Epistles* and his political career were devoted.[67] Pliny translated Martial's underworld metaphor into Virgilian verses with the aim of reminding the public of the time of terror endured under Domitian, while distancing

---

[62] *Ep.* 4.22.4 *Cenabat Nerua cum paucis; Veiento proximus atque etiam in sinu recumbebat.* Junius Mauricus alludes to Veiento's adaptability and his *nequitia sanguinariaeque sententiae* (4.22.5–6); cf. Juv. 4.113 (Domitian's council).

[63] *Ep.* 9.13.13 *Iam censendi tempus. Dicit Domitius Apollinaris consul designatus, dicit Fabricius Veiento . . . Omnes Certum nondum a me nominatum ut nominatum defendunt.* On Veiento, see Syme 1958: 633; Balland 1981: 118. A certain Attica and her husband Fabricius Veiento, consul for three times, dedicated an inscription to the dea Nemetona in Mainz *c.* 83 (*CIL* XIII, 7253 = *ILS* 1010).

[64] *Ep.* 9.13.10 *Notabilem te futuris principibus fecisti.*

[65] *Ep.* 9.13.11 *Nominat quendam, qui tunc ad orientem amplissimum et famosissimum exercitum non sine magnis dubiisque rumoribus obtinebat.* On identification and career (*AE* 1973, 283) see Alföldy and Halfmann 1973: 331–73, esp. pp. 361–6; cf. Griffin 2000: 90; Eck 2002a: 211–26.

[66] On Thrasea Paetus and Helvidius Priscus the Elder, see Syme 1958: 596–7, 1991b: 568–87; Penwill 2003: 347–53, 360–2.

[67] Marchesi 2008: 36–7. The allusion generated a dialogue between Book 1 and Book 9, see Hoffer 1999: 9–10; 67.

himself both from that past and from the *mali principes* of the future.[68]
The atmosphere of danger underlined Pliny's heroism in avenging Helvidius and in his fearless championing of the *optimus princeps*, Trajan. Whereas
Apollinaris, after his 'katabasis' into the centre of power, was sucked into
the *pallida turba* in Rome and became assimilated – the suffect consulship
of 97 is his last documented official position – Pliny for his part survived
unscathed, although the 'thunderbolts' of the year 93/4 under Domitian
had fallen perilously close.[69] He succeeded in declaring that at that point
his career halted, a tendentious remark that represents Pliny's prefecture of
the *aerarium militare* under Domitian as the 'longer route' to the top after
his praetorship.[70]

The process of editing his letter collection enabled Pliny to create his
own account of the evolution of his *persona*.[71] Reshaping the chronology
of events, he retrospectively stylised his first encounter with Apollinaris and
the outstanding success of his speech into a climax of the collection – and
a pivotal moment in his career (*Ep.* 9.13.23):[72] as a result Publicius Certus
was supposed to be dismissed from office – at the *aerarium Saturni* – and,
unlike his colleague there Bittius Proculus, failed to become a consul.[73]
In reality, Certus died from disease, and Bittius Proculus did not become
consul until 99, two years later.[74] By his smart move in attacking Publicius
Certus, Pliny gained the *aerarium Saturni*, which led directly to a consulship. The addressee of the letter, not coincidentally, was a highly promising
young orator, the 25-year-old Ummidius Quadratus, who revered Pliny as
rector and *magister* in the art of rhetoric.[75]

---

[68] *Ep.* 9.13.11 (on Cornelius Nigrinus) '*Esto' inquam, 'dum malis.*'

[69] *Ep.* 3.11.3 . . . *tot circa me iactis fulminibus quasi ambustus mihi quoque impendere idem exitium certis quibusdam notis augurarer.* This letter, indicating that Pliny supported the philosopher Artemidorus financially in spite of the latter's banishment from Rome, has striking structural similarities to that of the Certus affair. Whitton 2015a: 7–9, 20 distinguishes between the expulsion of the philosophers from the capital and from Italy by edict.

[70] *Pan.* 95.3–4 . . . *substiti,* (4) . . . *longius iter malui.* . . . *inuisus pessimo* [sc. *principi*] *fui.* See Whitton 2015a: 17–20; for a different view Syme 1991b: 564–5 and Sherwin-White 1966: 75, contrary to Birley 2000a: 14–15 (appointment by Nerva).

[71] Gibson and Morello 2012: 27–32, 250–1; Gibson 2015: 195–8.

[72] Gibson and Morello 2012: 28; Whitton 2012: 355–6; Gibson 2003: 245 and 254: 'Praise of the self is a key mechanism for exercising control in advance over the reception of your deeds by society.'

[73] *Ep.* 9.13.23 *obtinui tamen, quod intenderam. Nam collega Certi consulatum, successorem Certus accepit.* Pliny on Certus: '*Reddat praemium sub optimo principe, quod a pessimo accepit.*'

[74] *Ep.* 9.13.24 *sed non tamquam fortuitum, quod editis libris Certus intra paucissimos dies implicitus morbo decessit.* See Eck 1993: 449. Q. Fulvius Gillo Bittius Proculus was the stepfather of Pliny's wife.

[75] *Ep.* 6.11.2 *atque inter haec illud, quod et ipsi me ut rectorem, ut magistrum intuebantur et iis, qui audiebant, me aemulari, meis instare uestigiis uidebantur.* See Sherwin-White 1966: 362 and Syme 1968a: 84–98 (= *RP* II, 672–85) on Ummidius Quadratus Sertorius Severus, *cos. suff.* 118 under Hadrian.

An attentive reader leafing back through the collection will be able to identify an anonymous forensic speech full of pathos with the *De Heluidi ultione* mentioned in the second of Pliny's letters.[76] Pliny had composed it after the senatorial debate in the year 98, drawing on 'Cicero's palette' and portraying himself as a 'second Cicero' in his campaign against Catilina–Certus.[77] Arrianus Maturus received an advance copy and a note requesting his comments.[78] A letter to Velius Cerealis likewise referred to the plea on behalf of Helvidius, without naming a book title, and used the words *nosti metus* to reawaken old fears.[79] Pliny circulated it among friends initially, venturing only a decade later to disclose name and title of the speech and publish his plea. He revived it in Book 9 as a historical event documenting his loyalty to the persecuted family, and also, as a senator of consular rank, immortalised his self-comparison with Cicero.[80] Pliny's exhortation to continue along the path to immortality that has carried few out into the light of fame (*in lucem famamque*) after enticing many out of darkness of silence (*e tenebris et silentio*) can be read as his postscript for his friend Tacitus on the Certus affair.[81]

Martial's and Pliny's underworld scenarios thus differ structurally, even though they both play out on the political stage of the year 97. Martial, conjuring up the realm of the dead with his alternation from light to darkness, is out to create a graphic evocation of the quiveringly taut atmosphere of fear and uncertainty that gripped the Roman political scene before the adoption of Trajan. It is all the more fitting that he is rewriting his own epitaph in the virtual monument at the beginning of Book 10 (2.1–12), and that Rome has risen from the Styx under Trajan's new regime by reading on (72.10), as Victoria Rimell shows in her chapter in this volume on the 'art of survival'. In Pliny's case, by contrast, the author's voluntary descent into

---

[76] *Ep.* 1.2.1 (*librum*). See Gibson and Morello 2012: 27–8.

[77] *Ep.* 1.2.3–4 *erat enim* [sc. *materia*] *prope tota in contentione dicendi . . . Non tamen omnino Marci nostri* ληκύθους *fugimus . . .* Cf. Cic. *Att.* 1.14.3 (Rome, 13 Feb. 61 BC) on Crassus' praise for Cicero's merits due to suppression of the Catiline conspiracy: *Totum hunc locum, quem ego uarie meis orationibus . . . soleo pingere, de flamma, de ferro (nosti illas* ληκύθους*), ualde grauiter pertexui.* On the *aemulatio* of Cicero, cf. Plin. *Ep.* 1.5.12.

[78] *Ep.* 1.2.1 *Hunc* [sc. *librum*] *rogo ex consuetudine tua et legas et emendes . . .* According to Sherwin-White 1966: 30, Book 1 was edited in 98/9. Cf. the reformulation of Cicero's themes in Book 10 identified by Woolf 2006: 102–4.

[79] *Ep.* 4.21.3 (*c.* 104/5) *Nam patrem illarum* [sc. *Heluidiarum sororum*] *defunctum quoque perseuerantissime diligo, ut actione mea librisque testatum est*; *Ep.* 4.21.5, referring to the only son of the Younger Helvidius: *Nosti in amore mollitiam animi mei, nosti metus.*

[80] *Ep.* 4.21.3. Sherwin-White 1966: 40–1 dates publication of Book 9 to 106–8. On self-stylisation as 'opponent of Domitian', see Ludolph 1997: 143, 154 and 166.

[81] In the next letter, *Ep.* 9.14 *Pergamus modo itinere instituto, quod ut paucos in lucem famamque prouexit, ita multos e tenebris et silentio protulit.* Excellently interpreted by Whitton 2012: 356.

the underworld proves to be a means of establishing his authority, that of the politician and orator who has embarked on the path leading into the light of immortality.

The Owner of the Villa (*Otium*)

The Semiotics of Visualisation: Apollinaris' Formianum *vs Pliny's* Tusci

In the world of the Roman elites, no identifying mark is more revealing than their private villas. These are interrelated, reflecting the relationships of their owners, or their alterity.[82] Interminable scholarly debate over whether Pliny's metaphorically dense villa descriptions are fictive or based on real villa architecture[83] has hitherto left one specific question unaddressed: why did Pliny choose to send *his* villa description, of the *Tusci*, to Domitius Apollinaris in particular, the dedicatee also of Martial's epigram about Apollinaris' villa in Formiae? The answer is simple: Pliny (*Ep.* 5.6) has shaped his own life design and his own villa near Tifernum Tiberinum,[84] which owed its superiority to dissociation, in conscious contrast to Domitius Apollinaris' lifestyle, represented in his coastal estate (Mart. 10.30). Pliny's summer residence was not by the sea but at the foot of the Apennines, six miles above Città di Castello.[85] In this context there is no mention of the fact that Pliny the Younger had inherited the Tuscan estate from the Elder, and that the tenants on his land, mostly reserved for viticulture, were paying him an annual total of over 400,000 sesterces in rent.[86]

Literary letter writer and poet compete here to evoke this loveliest *locus amoenus*, the ekphrasis in prose competing with that in verse. This ingenious exchange between Martial and Pliny draws attention to the 'interactive' nature of literature and the poetic transformation of Pliny's epistle: being 'cultured' did not only mean being capable of reading both villa descriptions and understanding its allusions, but also responding creatively to it: author (Pliny and Martial), dedicatee (Apollinaris, Martial's 'empowered' reader) and audience (private friends and a larger reading public)

---

[82] Elsner 1998: 44; Henderson 2002: 15–20, 2004: 67, 71; Gibson and Morello 2012: 218.

[83] For this reason, I refer here just to Bergmann 1995: 406–20, with copious bibliography.

[84] On Pliny's villas as focus for his autobiographical sketch, see Whitton 2013: 219.

[85] Gibson and Morello 2012: 228–33 ('Archaeology in Tuscany/Umbria'), esp. pp. 228–9; on Pliny's trip to Tifernum Tiberinum in summer 99, Seelentag 2004: 183–97.

[86] Plin. *Ep.* 10.8.5 *locatio, cum alioqui CCCC excedat . . .* Andermahr 1998: 38, with reservations. For a contrary view: Champlin 2001: 122–3; Gibson and Morello 2012: 202–3, 223–4.

should thus be seen as standing in an active relationship to one another.[87] Pliny's villa letter of summer 105, the time of his *cura aluei Tiberis*, is our last document referring to Apollinaris as a living person. It is not only the relationship between Pliny and Apollinaris that appears in a new light as a result of these literary interactions, but also the author's persona and the design of his letter collection. Comparison focused on the process of literary transformation is instructive.

Martial's poem (10.30.1–4) begins like a hymn with an invocation of the balmy climate and charming situation of Apollinaris' villa on the shore at Formiae, a place favoured by the senator above all others for his escapes from Trajan's Rome, the 'city of Mars'.[88] Pliny's letter (5.6.1), by contrast, leads off with Apollinaris asking about the unhealthy climate affecting Pliny's summer residence near the border between Etruria and Umbria. The letter writer measures the mild climate of Formiae (*temperatae Formiae*) against the remarkable clemency (*mira clementia*) of the summers at Tifernum Tiberinum.[89] Martial's lyrical evocation of a mobile yet tranquil sea (*uiua . . . quies ponti*), the gaily painted boat impelled gently forward on the breeze (*aura*), as if by the stirring of a girl's purple fan, has its counterpart in Pliny's depiction of the *forma pulcherrima* of the landscape, which resembles a vast amphitheatre.[90] With its expanse of 'bejewelled' wild-flower meadow (*prata florida et gemmea*) set between shade-giving hills and brooks tumbling down towards the Tiber, the air always refreshed by soft breezes (*aurae*), the scene carries clear and intended overtones of the Tempe valley, the classic *locus amoenus*, as described by the author's uncle, Pliny the Elder.[91] A further intertextual allusion involving the 'Tuscan soil', said to require 'nine ploughings to tame it' into farmland, this too echoing

[87] Cf. Whitton on prose–prose intertextuality and Marchesi on the web of poetic intertexts in Pliny; see Roller on Pliny's recitations and Rimell on the reader's active involvement in Martial's epigrams, all of them in this volume.

[88] Mart. 10.30.1–4 *O temperatae dulce Formiae litus,* | *uos, cum seueri fugit oppidum Martis* | *et inquietas fessus exuit curas,* | *Apollinaris omnibus locis praefert.* On the poem, see Kreilinger 2004: 131–5; Fabbrini 2007: 117–80. The image of the Rome of general Trajan as 'city of stern Mars' evokes memories of the foundation of the 'city of Mars' (*Mauortia . . . moenia*) by Romulus in Virgil (*Aen.* 1.276–7). Cf. König in this volume on the city–country contrast.

[89] Mart. 10.30.1; cf. Plin. *Ep.* 5.6.5.

[90] Mart. 10.30.11–15; cf. Plin. *Ep.* 5.6.7–11, esp. 7 *Regionis forma pulcherrima. Imaginare amphitheatrum aliquod inmensum . . . Lata et diffusa planities montibus cingitur, montes summa sui parte procera nemora et antiqua habent.* Cf. the satirically overdrawn 'amphitheatre of Orpheus' near Pliny's town house on the Esquiline hill (Mart. 10.20(19).6–10), below.

[91] *Ep.* 5.6.11 *Prata florida et gemmea trifolium . . . alunt; cuncta enim perennibus riuis nutriuntur.* Cf. Plin. *NH* 4.31 *ultra uisum hominis attollentibus se dextra laeuaque leniter conuexis iugis, intus silua late uiridante, ac labitur Penius uiridis calculo, amoenus circa ripas gramine, canorus auium concentu.* On Pliny's appropriation of a poetic style, see Stat. *Silv.* 1.5.12 (*gemmantia*).

the *Natural history* (*Ep.* 5.6.10; *NH* 18.181), characterises the *doctus Apollinaris* as well-read.[92] Roy Gibson and Ruth Morello suggest that this detail also symbolises the interactions between the two Plinys, in the same way as the villa, which the Younger erected on a site belonging to the Elder, but to his own design, in which he incorporated the original buildings.[93]

Where Martial's villa poem seeks its effects acoustically during recitation of the choliambs by means of startling *pointes* in line-endings, Pliny creates 'a villa to behold'.[94] The words *magnam capies uoluptatem* (5.6.13) invite Apollinaris to enter, in an act of imaginative fantasy, into this classical *locus amoenus* and to allow the visually performative flow of poetic ekphrasis to make its impact on him. Pliny does not confine himself to visualising the villa for his addressee.[95] By an internal focalisation he constructs a picture within the picture, a bird's-eye view, directing Apollinaris' gaze down from the hilltop to the villa halfway down: *Neque enim terras tibi, sed formam aliquam ad eximiam pulchritudinem pictam uideberis cernere* ('You will have the impression not of gazing at the landscape, but at some painting of a scene of breathtaking beauty', *Ep.* 5.6.13).[96] In parallel with Roman painting, the focus has shifted from the gaze *in* the picture to the gaze observing the picture and observing the act of gazing.[97] Apollinaris as beholder initially stands outside the picture specially created for him, before being included – as a visitor – in a sightseeing tour through the villa complexes. This rhetorical device, blurring the distinction between description and villa, between reading and seeing, merges the descriptive act and the visual act into a single perception – a *Gesamtkunstwerk* from the pen of Pliny.[98] The *uarietas* of the landscape and the *dispositio* of the property coincide with the rhetorical requirements for the composition of his *Epistles*.[99]

---

[92] *Ep.* 5.6.10 *tantis glaebis tenacissimum solum . . . assurgit, ut nono demum sulco perdometur.* Cf. Plin. *NH* 18.181 *Spissius solum, sicut plerumque in Italia, quinto sulco seri melius est, in 1uscis uero nono.* See Gibson and Morello 2012: 224–5; a contrary view in Sherwin-White 1966: 265. Cf. Mart. 4.86.3 (*doctus . . . Apollinaris*).

[93] Plin. *Ep.* 5.6.41 *Amo enim, quae maxima ex parte ipse incohaui aut incohata percolui.* For interpretation, see Gibson and Morello 2012: 223.

[94] Chinn 2007: 265–80 and Whitton 2013: 220–1.

[95] Following rules on rhetoric from Horace (*Ars* 17) and Quintilian (*Inst.* 6.2.32; cf. 4.3.12) relating to visual effects (*enargeia, illustratio* and *perspicuitas*) used to eulogise a place.

[96] Lefèvre 2009: 232.   [97] Elsner 2007: 87.

[98] Referred to also by Barthes as 'reality effect'; see Chinn 2007: 270–1. The overall view presented has such suggestive power that Apollinaris' eyes can recover purely as a result of the depiction (n. 97), or that the reader, who 'in the letter crawls round in every corner' with Pliny, is enabled by the act of reading (*legenti*), as opposed to a physical tour of inspection (*uisenti*), to put down the letter temporarily for a rest (*Ep.* 5.6.40–41).

[99] *Ep.* 5.6.13 *ea uarietate, ea descriptione, quocumque inciderint oculi, reficientur.* See Gibson and Morello 2012: 216, 225–6.

Martial handles the idea of ekphrasis playfully (1–24), deploying ever new and limping punchlines to heighten the listeners' expectation right up to the peripeteia. He captures the carefree ease (*otium*) of the *Formianum* in two paradoxical images: fish are so abundant in the inshore waters that Apollinaris can cast for them while reclining on his couch;[100] and a medley of trained salt-water fish in fishponds obediently swim up at their master's bidding and await transfer to the day's menu.[101] Familiar with this passage, Pliny refrains from quoting it in his letter. His preference is not the subjugation of nature, but a setting created by nature: not a fish-pool (*piscina*), but an abundance of game for the table, and a swimming-pool.[102] If Formiae offers sea-angling from the couch, Pliny's alcove is as restful as a forest, but with a roof to keep the rain off.[103] To him, Martial's lines appear better suited to his villa by Lake Como, which has similarities to the sea,[104] than to the Tuscan villa.

Pliny's elaborate villa description (4–40) ends in a reflection on literary theory in which he discusses concept and length of ekphrasis (41–4), comparing his own practice with scene descriptions by renowned epic poets.[105] The well-read Apollinaris could appreciate why he invokes Homer, Virgil and Aratus as canonic models,[106] contending in accordance with the principle of *aptum* that 'what is extensive is not the letter which gives the description, but the villa which is described'.[107] The description of the shield in Homer (*Il.* 18.478–82) had stood ever since as the prototype for all subsequent ekphraseis, bringing, in Giuliani's words, 'nothing less than the world itself before the [observer's] eyes'.[108] Virgil's shield description

---

[100] Mart. 10.30.16–18 *Nec seta longo quaerit in mari praedam,* | *sed a cubili lectuloque iactatam* | *spectatus alte lineam trahit piscis.*

[101] Mart. 10.30.19–24. Negatively connoted as *aquarium* by Sullivan 1991: 159. On archaeologically documented fishponds at Formiae, see Giuliani and Guaitoli 1972: 191–219; on fish-farming, Mielsch 1997: 23–32.

[102] Mart. 10.30.21 *piscina rhombum pascit et lupos uernas.* Cf. Plin. *Ep.* 5.6.7 *Frequens ibi et uaria uenatio;* 5.6.25 *Si natare latius aut tepidius uelis, in area piscina est.* On the 'power over nature' in Martial vs Pliny's natural wonders, and *mirabilia* as 'a barometer' for reconstructing shifting cultural attitudes, see Ash in this volume.

[103] *Ep.* 5.6.39 (on the *cubiculum*) *Non secus ibi quam in nemore iaceas, imbrem tantum tamquam in nemore non sentias.*

[104] *Ep.* 9.7.4 (on his villa 'Comedy') *Ex hac ipse piscari hamumque de cubiculo ac paene etiam de lectulo ut e naucula iacere.* Reference kindly supplied by Chris Whitton (personal communication); see also Sherwin-White 1966: 486; Fabbrini 2007: 138–9.

[105] Chinn 2007: 268–70. The length breaches the epistolary principle of *breuitas.*

[106] The expression *miraris* identifies them as marvels, held in awe by observer or reader.

[107] *Ep.* 5.6.44 *non epistula quae describit, sed uilla quae describitur magna est.* On the principle of appropriateness (*aptum*), cf. Hor. *Ars* 14–23 and Quint. *Inst.* 11.1.1 (as *uirtus . . . maxime necessaria*).

[108] Giuliani 2003: 39.

(*Aen.* 8.626–731) was 'a work of art beyond reproducing in words', and to read Aratus' didactic poem on astronomy was comparable with beholding the constellations in the starry sky.[109] Pliny had endeavoured to set the whole villa before the eyes of Apollinaris.[110]

Pliny's celebrated letter about his *Tusci* (5.6) was designed as a response and a contrast piece to Martial's epigram on Apollinaris' villa in Formiae. In his *conclusio* (44–6), he refers the reader to the catalogue in Martial (10.30.5–10)[111] of ten suburban villas belonging to Apollinaris, and closes the circle by finally answering Apollinaris' opening question: *Habes causas cur ego Tuscos meos Tusculanis Tiburtinis Praenestinisque praeponam* ('now you know why I prefer my Tuscan estate to any in Tusculum or Tibur or Praeneste', *Ep.* 5.6.45; cf. 1).[112] His quotation from Martial is a clear allusion *to* and rejection *of* Apollinaris' impressive line-up of villas. Pliny uses this rhetorical device to emphasise that he prefers his own provincial retreat to the numerous and fashionable resorts of his correspondent. In his letters as a whole he modestly compares Apollinaris' ten luxurious villas with the three locations where he had villas of his own, at Tifernum Tiberinum, on Lake Como, and by the sea at Laurentum, two of which are left unmentioned here.[113]

Pliny seems to have been rather more impressed by Martial's literary technique in evoking the landscapes of the prettiest country retreats for his readers visually, in conformity with Quintilian's rules of rhetoric, as if they were tourists, conveying the illusion of beholding the view from the heights of the Sabine and Alban Hills outside Rome, southwards down the entire coastline as far as the Gulf of Baiae:[114] from the vantage point of the Tibur estate outside Rome, owned by Apollinaris' wife Valeria Vettilla (and her

---

[109] Virg. *Aen.* 8.625 *clipei non enarrabile textum.* Cf. Aratus' *Phaenomena* for connoisseurs.

[110] *Ep.* 5.6.44 *Similiter nos, ut 'parua magnis', cum totam uillam oculis tuis subicere conamur.*

[111] In addition to his favourite villa at Formiae, Apollinaris owned nine other villas south of Rome, alluded to here by Pliny (*Ep.* 5.6.45). On their location, see below.

[112] With Sherwin-White 1966: 329–30 and Balland 1981: 120, I prefer the MS reading of *Tusculanis* to the *in Tuscano* conjectured by Mommsen. The cliché of the spurned villas at Tusculum, Tibur and Praeneste (*Ep.* 5.6.45) is a witty quotation from Martial's catalogue of Apollinaris' various villas (10.30.5–10). Pliny's emphatic *ego . . . meos* establishes the contrast with Apollinaris and his villas.

[113] Apart from the *Tusci* and his *Laurentinum* (*Ep.* 2.17), Pliny owned at least three villas on Lake Como: cf. *Ep.* 9.7.1–2 (*Huius* [i.e. *lacus Larii*] *in litore plures uillae meae*) and 3.19.2 (accumulation of estates). See Andermahr 1998: 384; Sherwin-White 1966: 486.

[114] Mart. 10.30.5–10 *Non ille sanctae dulce Tibur uxoris,* | *nec Tusculanos Algidosue secessus,* | *Praeneste nec sic Antiumque miratur;* | *non blanda Circe Dardanisue Caieta* | *desiderantur, nec Marica nec Liris,* | *nec in Lucrina lota Salmacis uena.* Stat. *Silv.* 4.4.15–18 confirms that these were the restorative retreats favoured for the heat of midsummer. See Sullivan 1991: 158; Fabbrini 2007: 124–31.

father),[115] down over shade-giving oakwoods[116] towards little harbours with foundation myths reaching back to Homer and Virgil,[117] and the Lucrine Lake, celebrated like Formiae for its abundant fish and its oyster-beds.[118] Pliny adopted this hilltop perspective (*ex monte*) for the panoramic view he shares with Apollinaris, overlooking the villa complex.[119]

Nevertheless, the idyllic setting of the villa at Formiae is deceptive; the splendour proves to be worthless for its owner. Martial shatters the illusion by announcing that Rome, the city of Mars, has debarred Apollinaris from enjoying its amenities:[120] the rooms stand empty, and the place's beauty (*amoenitas loci*) is being enjoyed by others. The poem's ending and climax are an ironic *makarismos* on the servants: *O ianitores uilicique **felices**! | Dominis parantur ista, seruiunt **uobis*** ('Lucky janitors, lucky bailiffs! These delights are acquired for their owners, but it is you they serve', 10.30.28–9).[121] The beneficiaries of all this enviable luxury are not the owners but the staff. The paradox represents an inversion of the Roman social order. The real slave in this 'upside-down world' is Domitius Apollinaris, the senator, shackled by the affairs of the capital city (*negotiosis rebus urbis haerens*).[122] The epigram is neither a 'compliment' on his political activity nor a 'homage' to his wealth and lifestyle.[123] Combining the literary technique of the peripeteia and the choliambic metre, humour and playful misdirection, Martial transforms his lyrical praise for Apollinaris' dream

---

[115] Hor. *Carm.* 3.4.22–3 *seu mihi frigidum | Praeneste seu Tibur supinum.* Syme 1991b: 598 is in error when he writes that Apollinaris preferred his wife's estate at Tibur, only 20 miles from Rome, to the Formianum.

[116] Algidum (Cava dell'Aglio), 1770 feet (540 m) up in the hills, and the cool Praeneste with its terraced temple to Fortuna Primigenia, were famed for their oak forests (Hor. *Carm.* 3.23.9–10, 4.4.58; Serv. ad *Aen.* 7.678); Tusculum was known for its salubrious climate (Cic. *RP* 1.1). Algidum was at the gap, Tusculum on the outer ring of the Alban hills, Praeneste 'at the foot of the (Sabine) hills' (Cato fr. 6 Peter).

[117] Aetiologies in Mart. 10.30.8–9 (*non blanda Circe Dardanisue Caieta | . . . nec Marica nec Liris*): Circeii, where Elpenor's grave and Odysseus' drinking-cup were displayed (Plin. *NH* 15.119; Theophr. *H. plant.* 5.8.3), derives from Circe (Hom. *Od.* 10.133–574), Caieta from the wet-nurse of Aeneas and mother of the Latins (Virg. *Aen.* 7.1–2), Minturnae, at the mouth of the Liris, from the cult of the nymph and goddess Marica (*CIL* I², 2438; Hor. *Carm.* 3.17.7–8).

[118] Mart. 10.30.10 (*nec in Lucrina lota Salmacis uena*) alludes to the metamorphosis of Salmacis and Hermaphroditus in the Lucrine Lake (Ov. *Met.* 4.285–388; 15.319). On the abundance of fish, see Serv. ad *Georg.* 2.161; on the oyster cultures, Plin. *NH* 9.168.

[119] Plin. *Ep.* 5.6.13 *Magnam capies uoluptatem, si hunc regionis situm ex monte prospexeris.*

[120] Mart. 10.30.25 *Frui sed istis quando, Roma, permittis?* On Trajan's Rome as 'city of stern Mars', see above.

[121] The choliamb with its final trochee or spondee emphasises the final word in each case, *fe-lices* and *uobis.*

[122] Martial closes the loop by returning to the beginning of the poem (v. 3), where he had presented Apollinaris as 'wearied by restless cares'.

[123] Thus Nauta 2002: 161; Fabbrini 2007: 123, 132, 162, 165–6.

villa into a witty parody, challenging and entertaining both protagonist and audience through the unexpected anomalies of a *mundus inuersus*.

Intertextuality and 'Immortality': the Creation of Literary Authority

In their respective *conclusiones* (Mart. 10.30.25–30; Plin. *Ep.* 5.6.44–6), Martial's *Formianum* and Pliny's *Tusci* are seen to function as the social space for the creation of differing identities and for negotiating the Roman concept of *otium* and *negotium*. As a political metaphor, they are representative of the diverging aristocratic lifestyles of the author and the addressee, Pliny and Apollinaris.[124] In Martial's Formianum everything serves the *dolce far niente*; in complete contrast, the guided tour of Pliny's villa complex draws attention to the practical benefit (*usus a fronte*) behind the architectural show-side (*haec facies*).[125] Apollinaris' display of ostentatious affluence contrasts with the elegant restraint shown by Pliny in the design of his villa complex, aesthetically a blend of urbanism and nature.[126] Figures embedded in a triangular relationship such as Apollinaris and Marchesi's 'Regulus connection' act as catalysts for the literary interplay that mirrors the competitive ranking games performed on the changing cultural and political stage.[127]

Pliny constructed literary production (*studia*) as a life-fulfilling activity and an intellectual world as an alternative to public life (*negotium*) in Rome. His central paean to inspiration-giving leisure (*otium*) is the conceptual link between villa and composition that prompts the writing of the letter; it contrasts sharply with Martial's open parading of Apollinaris' *negotium* as politician.[128] Martial ultimately unmasks his hymn to Apollinaris' favourite villa as mere illusion;[129] but Pliny closes his villa letter with a hymn to perfect *otium*. Apollinaris' villa remains untenanted, and Apollinaris himself becomes the victim of his political ambitions; but Pliny, following literary tradition, creates his country estate as a poetic place,[130] that is to say a

---

[124] Letters always foreground first-person focalisation. On Pliny's construction of the self, see Henderson 2002: xiii n. 7, 12–14.

[125] *Ep.* 5.6.29 *Haec facies, hic usus a fronte.*

[126] Pliny's anxiety to avoid ostentation, as an offence against social norms and good taste, shows in his efforts to play down the luxury. See Hoffer 1999: 29–44; Lefèvre 2009: 233.

[127] Compare Marchesi and Roller in this volume.

[128] Whitton 2013: 220; cf. *Ep.* 2.17: the Laurentinum as 'shrine of the Muses' (μουσεῖον).

[129] Mart. 10.30.26–7 *Quot Formianos inputat dies annus | negotiosis rebus urbis haerenti?*

[130] Pliny here follows in the literary tradition of estate descriptions; cf. the famous depiction of the Sabine estate in Hor. *Epist.* 1.16. On the country estate as a place of poetic writing, see Harrison 2007b: 244–7; Schmidt 1977: 97–112; cf. Bowditch 2001: 239–46 on the construction of the *locus amoenus*, and Bergmann 1995: 420 on the villa as '*utopia* – a "no place"'.

place where the ideal life that the author commends to the addressee and the reader becomes possible: 'Leisure (*otium*) there is more profound, more rich, and therefore more carefree'.[131] Pliny prefers his *Tusci*, 150 miles from the capital, for him the ideal retreat, allowing him what Apollinaris lacked: freedom from dress conventions and from unwelcome intrusions. This was an advantage not enjoyed at his Laurentine villa, a little south of Ostia and within a day's travel from Rome.[132] His self-positioning is focused on a 'disciplined and managed *otium*' that exercises body and mind equally, qualifying Pliny as a serious writer – and making him different from Apollinaris (*Ep.* 5.6.45–6): 'All around is peace and tranquillity, which aids the healing powers of the countryside (*salubritas regionis*),' he writes; 'even the sky is clearer there, and the air more limpid. There I feel both mentally and physically at my best, for my studies exercise my mind and hunting my body.'[133]

Pliny's servants (*mei*), in contrast to those of Apollinaris, share the comforts of the villa – in the style of the ideal Roman *familia* – with the master of the house, who had been chosen as patron of Tifernum Tiberinum while he was still little more than a boy.[134] Instead of proclaiming the beatitude of the servants, the sole beneficiaries of Apollinaris' abandoned villa (*seruiunt uobis*), Pliny's letter closes with a plea to the gods: *Di modo in posterum hoc mihi gaudium, hanc gloriam loco seruent* ('I only pray that in the days to come the gods may preserve this joy for me, and this glory for the place', 5.6.46).[135] Chris Whitton[136] has pointed out that the author is here not so much celebrating his own immediate pleasure (*gaudium*) as inscribing his own immortality (*gloria*) in the cultural memory of future generations (*in posterum*); like Horace, he has erected a 'monument for eternity'.[137] This artwork, in which letter and architecture, visualisation and villa coalesce,[138] is signed (in letters cut from boxwood) with the initials of

---

[131] *Ep.* 5.6.45 *altius ibi otium et pinguius eoque securius; nulla necessitas togae, nemo accersitor ex proximo.* See Ludolph 1997: 128–9.

[132] The Tuscan villa was situated 150 miles (240 km) north-east of Rome, the Laurentinum 16.6 miles (25 km) south-west of Rome; see Champlin 2001: 125; Lefèvre 2009: 224; Syme 1991b: 580.

[133] Cf. Gibson and Morello 2012: 250: Spurinna's positive embracing of life into extreme old age supplies the role model. On *otium litteratum* as a 'social activity', see also Champlin 2001: 125–6. It is emphasised again in the closing letters (*Ep.* 9.36 and 9.40) about the Tusci.

[134] Plin. *Ep.* 5.6.46 *Mei quoque nusquam salubrius degunt*; 4.1.4 *Oppidum* [sc. *Tifernum Tiberinum*] . . . *quod me paene adhuc puerum patronum cooptauit.* On Pliny's local roots, see Champlin 2001: 122–3.

[135] Note the paronomasia of the semantically unrelated verbs *seruiunt* (Mart. 10.30.29) and *seruent* (Plin. *Ep.* 5.6.46).

[136] Whitton 2013: 219; cf. Gibson and Morello 2012: 227; Bergmann 1995: 408.

[137] Pliny evokes the thought and language of Hor. *Carm.* 3.30.1 *Exegi monumentum aere perennius.*

[138] Whitton 2013: 219 and 2015: 111 on 'architexture'; Chinn 2007 *passim*.

dominus and *artifex*.[139] Designed as a reflection *of* and response *to* Martial's topsy-turvy world, as displayed in his poem on Apollinaris' Formianum, and as a counter-image to its *dominus*, ruled by political ambitions and his slaves, Pliny finally reveals his superior identity to his correspondent, fashioning himself as the master who commands respect, because he creates and controls both his dream villa *and* the aesthetics of his art.

Visuality and intertexts, underworld visions and villa description work together in Pliny's letters to generate a meaningful web of imagery setting processes of reinterpretation in motion. They provide tools for ethical and political self-definition (e.g. in Pliny's praise for inspiration-giving *otium*), for marking himself off from his social peers (e.g. when he distances himself from the Domitian era), or for the creation of literary authority with aspirations to immortality (*gloria*) for himself as creator of his work. When spaces bring these images together so as to construct literary self-projections, the author is enabled to create a new reality for himself beyond the real world, as Pliny does in reinventing himself in the public arena as an orator of Ciceronian stature and a fearless defender of the Domitianic regime's victims,[140] in the private sphere, in accordance with the ideal senatorial lifestyle, as both *dominus* and *artifex*.

Aeternitas: the Rivalry of two Artists

For posthumous glory, too, the writer of letters and the poet vied with one another. Martial often addresses the precious reader who brings him fame during his lifetime[141] and later will confer immortality: 'Through him you will escape the sluggish waters of ungrateful Lethe and survive in the better part of yourself', prophesies the personification of Roma,[142] who is made

---

[139] *Ep.* 5.6.35 *alibi ipsa buxus interuenit in formas mille discripta, litteras interdum, quae modo nomen domini dicunt, modo artificis.* Cf. below *Ep.* 7.33.2 (Tacitus as *optimus artifex*). On the artist's signature, see Squire 2013: 370; on the 'symbolic code', Bergmann 1995: 420. Similarly, the brick stamps bear the initials CPCS, the logo of the master of the house; cf. Gibson and Morello 2012: 229.

[140] Elsewhere, too, Pliny (*Ep.* 1.5.17) presented himself as a man who had let his actions speak louder than words in the resistance to Domitian (prosecution of Arulenus Rusticus): *Haec tibi scripsi, quia aequum erat te pro amore mutuo non solum omnia mea facta dictaque, uerum etiam consilia cognoscere.* On this, see Ludolph 1997: 166. Plin. *Ep.* 3.11.3 *Atque haec feci, cum septem amicis meis aut occisis aut relegatis, occisis Senecione, Rustico, Heluidio, relegatis Maurico, Gratilla, Arria, Fannia . . .* On this, Gibson 2003: 247; Whitton 2015a: 6–9, 13–15.

[141] Mart. 1.1.2 *toto notus in orbe Martialis*; 1.1.4–5 *cui, lector studiose, quod dedisti | uiuenti decus atque sentienti.* Cf. 5.13.3 *toto legor orbe frequens*; 8.61.3 *orbe cantor et legor toto*; 6.64.6 *meos, quos nouit fama, libellos.*

[142] Mart. 10.2.7–8 *Pigra per hunc fugies ingratae flumina Lethes | et meliore tui parte superstes eris.* Note Rimell in this volume on survival strategies.

to play an instrumental role in the poet's interaction with the public and
in his skilful self-promotion. In an echo of the art of Horace being seen
as a 'monument for eternity', he constructs a morbid fantasy of a future,
inexorably ageing Rome in the midst of impressive decaying monuments,
a Rome in which his own historical present has become past, and nothing
remains save his poems, which a visitor carries away to his distant home:[143]
'These are the only monuments that do not know how to die', asserts
Martial, in an allusion to Ovid, as he contemplates quitting Rome.[144] His
poetry and his poetic identity are tied to place and space. It will not only be
Pliny's travel purse, but first and foremost his own flourishing poetic fame
(*laeta ... gloria uatis*) that he will take with him to his Spanish birthplace of
Bilbilis, proclaiming to his fellow citizens there: 'For I am your ornament,
your renown and your glory.'[145]

   'Nothing drives me more than a passionate desire for eternity', professed
Pliny the Younger.[146] He came into contact with the idea of immortality
when it fell to him at the age of 16, in the year 78, to dedicate to the *Aeternitas* of the goddess of Rome and the emperors Vespasian and Titus a temple
of the ruler cult in Comum that his biological father had built after the Year
of Four Emperors; the Flavians were the first to honour the ruling emperor
as guarantor of the cosmic permanence of the Empire.[147] Pliny himself
founded a temple for the ruler cult with a statue of Trajan in Tifernum
Tiberinum, and while governor of Pontus–Bithynia strove zealously to add
to the *aeternitas* and *gloria* of the emperor.[148] Like Martial, he declared his
literary corpus to be the sole medium that is equivalent to a monument (*hoc
uno monimento*) and can ensure immortality: 'All else is frail and fleeting as

---

[143] Mart. 8.3.5–8 *Et cum rupta situ Messalae saxa iacebunt | altaque cum Licini marmora puluis erunt, |
me tamen ora legent et secum plurimus hospes | ad patrias sedes carmina nostra feret.* This referred to
the marble tombs built for M. Valerius Messalla Corvinus (*cos.* 31), patron of Tibullus, and for C.
Iulius Licinus, Augustus' wealthy freedman, on the Via Salaria, see Mratschek 1993: 36, 268 no. 16
(Messalla); 7, 275 no. 37 (Licinus). Messalla's grave had been split by a fig tree (Mart. 10.2.9).

[144] Mart. 10.2.12 *solaque non norunt haec monumenta mori.* Ov. *Tr.* 3.3.77–8 (in exile at Tomis) *hoc satis
in titulo est. Etenim maiora libelli | et diuturna magis sunt monimenta mihi.* Cf. the web of further
allusions quoted by Rimell in this volume.

[145] Mart. 10.103.3–4 *ecquid laeta iuuat* [sc. *Augusta Bilbilis*] *uestri uos gloria uatis? | Nam decus et nomen
famaque uestra sumus.* Note the *pluralis maiestatis.* See Rimell 2008: 186 and 79, and for Martial in
Spain see also now Kelly in this volume. Cf. Plin. *Ep.* 3.21.2.

[146] *Ep.* 5.8.2 *Me autem nihil aeque ac diuturnitatis amor et cupido sollicitat, res homine dignissima.* Cf.
Cic. *Arch.* 28 (*de meo quodam amore gloriae*).

[147] Pais 1884, nos. 745–6; see Alföldy 1999: 211–19. For *Aeternitas* in the coinage, see Seelentag 2004:
464–5.

[148] *Ep.* 10.8.1–4; 4.1.5 (*templum*), with Seelentag 2004: 183–5, 191–2; *Ep.* 10.41.1 (*opera non minus aeter-
nitate tua quam gloria digna*); 10.41.5 *feres enim me ambitiosum pro tua gloria.* See Stadter 2006:
73.

men themselves, who die and are no more.'[149] Pliny, who compares the art
of the literary portrait to visual portraiture and seeks to create an undying
image (*immortalem . . . effigiem*) of himself and of his peers,[150] bequeaths
to posterity a virtual autobiography, artfully composed from the pictures
sketched in his letters. He knows that he cannot rely on his talent to guide
him along the path to immortality, but can only achieve it through hard
work, diligence and reverence for posterity.[151] And so, in protreptic vein,
he urges his readers to face life's choices resolved to strive for afterlife in the
collective memory of generations to come, just as he himself continues to
do – in interaction with Apollinaris, while yet pursuing a different path;
Seneca and Sallust are his models (*Ep.* 9.3.2):[152]

> Ac mihi nisi praemium aeternitatis ante oculos, pingue illud altumque
> otium placeat. Etenim omnes homines arbitror oportere aut immortalitatem
> suam aut mortalitatem cogitare et illos quidem contendere, eniti, hos qui-
> escere, remitti nec breuem uitam caducis laboribus fatigare . . .

> If the reward of immortality were not in prospect, my choice would be for
> a life of idle and utter leisure. Indeed, I believe that all must opt for either
> immortality or mortality. Those who choose the first must strive and strug-
> gle, while those who opt for the second must live peacefully in relaxation,
> without wearying their short-lived existence with transient toil . . .

Self-perception and the perception of others could differ sharply. Martial's
portrait of Pliny and Pliny's obituary for Martial, with the authorial 'I' reinventing himself and the other through their respective literary activities and
in line with their self-perceptions, shed light on the discourses between the
two about this literary aspiration. What greater thing can life bring than
honour and fame forever?[153] Martial had dedicated only a single poem to
Pliny, his patron. It included a witty parody depicting Pliny and his town-
house on the Esquiline Hill near the 'watery Orpheus': the audience listening raptly to the divinely inspired singer consists of the menagerie of
animals, petrified into grimacing stone figures in the nymphaeum. Pliny

---

[149] In *Ep.* 2.10.4 (to Octavius) *Habe ante oculos mortalitatem, a qua asserere te hoc uno monimento* [i.e.
his poetry] *potes; nam cetera fragilia et caduca non minus quam ipsi homines occidunt desinuntque.*
See Höschele 2010: 46–7.

[150] *Ep.* 3.10.6 (on Vestricius Cottius) *sed tamen, ut scalptorem, ut pictorem . . . admoneretis, quid
exprimere, quid emendare deberet, ita me quoque formate, regite, qui non fragilem et caducam, sed
immortalem . . . effigiem conor efficere.* See Leach 1990: 21–3; Whitton 2012: 345–6, 364 (also on the
following points).

[151] *Ep.* 9.14 *Posteris an aliqua cura nostri, nescio; nos certe meremur, ut sit aliqua, non dico ingenio (id
enim superbum), sed studio et labore et reuerentia posterorum.*

[152] Marchesi 2008: 232–6 uncovers the allusions to Seneca's *De breuitate uitae*, his *Letters to Lucilius*
and Sallust (*Cat.* 2.9; 3.1); cf. Gibson and Morello 2012: 101–2, also Pausch 2004: 60–3.

[153] *Ep.* 3.21.6 *Tametsi quid homini potest dari maius quam gloria et laus et aeternitas?*

suppressed this unwelcome caricature of his *alter ego*. In his obituary to Martial (*Ep.* 3.21.5) he chose to cite only the second half of the poem (Mart. 10.20(19).12–21), which depicted him fulfilling his favourite roles: active by day as a high-flying orator at the Centumviral Court, emulating the manner of Cicero and the *grauitas* of Cato, but by night keeping company with the Muse as consumer and producer of light neoteric verse. Thus amputated, Martial's satirical epigram became an innocuous poem of Plinian style, the witty dedication a Plinian self-portrait, the eulogy to the deceased a panegyric to the living obituarist.[154] Could this be the reason why he expressed serious doubts about the high aspirations of Martial, relative to the genre he pursued, and about Martial's 'immortality' as a poet?[155]

---

[154] As Henderson 2001: 59–73 and 2002: 47–52 has brilliantly demonstrated with reference to 'Pliny's self-immortalisation'. See also Fitzgerald's nuanced reading in this volume, pp. 110–11.

[155] *Ep.* 3.21.6 *'At non erunt aeterna, quae scripsit* [sc. *Martialis*]*!' Non erunt fortasse, ille tamen scripsit, tamquam essent futura.* For his own portrait, Pliny (*Ep.* 7.33.2) would have chosen Tacitus, 'the finest artist': *Nam, si esse nobis curae solet, ut facies nostra ab optimo quoque artifice exprimatur, nonne debemus optare, ut operibus nostris similis tui scriptor praedicatorque contingat?* Cf. Pliny's favourable judgment on the *aeternitas* of Tacitus' writings (*Ep.* 6.16.2) and *historias . . . immortales* (*Ep.* 7.33.1); see Whitton 2012 *passim*, esp. p. 347.

CHAPTER 10

Reading Frontinus in Martial's Epigrams

Alice König

Frontinus and Martial make an unlikely pair in a volume on literary interactions. Frontinus is best known today as the author of a dutiful and rather arid administrative treatise on the management of Rome's aqueduct network (the *De aquis*), a text that seems worlds apart from Martial's ludic, provocative poetry. His other surviving texts are also in the administrative/technical vein,[1] and have tended to be overlooked in (excluded from?) studies of Flavian, Nervan and Trajanic literature on the grounds, presumably, that they are hardly 'literary' enough to count.[2] Yet as one of contemporary Rome's most influential statesmen (he was awarded a rare third consulship in 100, probably in recognition of the role he had played in securing Nerva's adoption of Trajan),[3] Frontinus knew, served alongside, patronised, and even enjoyed literary leisure time with, some of the most celebrated authors of the day. His writings, on such important topics as military expertise, land management and Rome's water supply, also seem to have been reasonably well known. In fact, they occasionally became points of reference around which other authors defined some of their literary, social and political positions.

We have seen a little of Pliny's engagement with Frontinus – both statesman and author – in the introduction to this volume. Frontinus features in both the *Epistles* (4.8, 5.1 and 9.19) and the *Panegyricus* (61–2) as a social and

---

I am grateful to John Henderson, Victoria Rimell, Chris Whitton and the audience at the first Literary Interactions conference in St Andrews for their generous feedback on earlier versions of this chapter, which was written during a Leverhulme Trust Research Fellowship.

[1] A treatise on Roman land surveying, preserved in the *Corpus Agrimensorum Romanorum* (accessibly presented in Campbell 2000; see also Thulin 1913); and the *Strategemata*, a four-book collection of strategic *exempla*. Frontinus' now lost *De re militari* is known only from *Strat.* 1.pr.1.

[2] The latest overview of Flavian Rome is a case in point: Frédéric Hurlet's survey of Flavian 'sources' in Zissos 2016 (Hurlet 2016) does not even consider Frontinus as an author 'worthy of passing mention' (how it describes Quintilian), and Frontinus barely gets a look-in elsewhere in that volume, or in Boyle and Dominik 2003, let alone in more specialist readings of Flavian and Trajanic literature.

[3] Syme 1958: 16–17; Eck 2002a: 219–26. Frontinus may even have been involved in Nerva's succession (Grainger 2003: 14, 100).

political benchmark against which Pliny can measure himself and others; and some of Frontinus' writing may factor into this – even when no explicit mention of it is made – in ways that sharpen or develop the comparisons which Pliny is trying to draw. As I have argued elsewhere, Frontinus' self-presentation in the *De aquis* adds an extra dimension to the role that readers (might) see him playing in Tacitus' contemporary *Agricola* (17.2), as an alternative senatorial paradigm who bridges the divide between 'Flavian' and 'post-Domitianic' in ways that Agricola cannot.[4] And the Greek author Aelianus Tacticus identified Frontinus and his military treatises as important landmarks, both in the personal story behind his composition of a new *Tactical theory* and in a wider debate about the continuing value of Greek theory/science in a world conquered by Rome: Frontinus figures in that text (*pr.*2 and 1.2) not just as an influential patron but as the representative of a Roman military writing tradition whose inferiority to its Greek counterpart Aelian is determined to assert.[5] In his *Strategemata*, Frontinus engages in some literary interactivity with the likes of Cato the Elder and Valerius Maximus, and treats the theme of civil war (*inter alia*) in ways that invite comparison with several Flavian and post-Flavian texts (particularly Silius Italicus' *Punica*).[6] The *De aquis*, meanwhile, references (among others) Cicero, Virgil, Horace, Livy and Statius.[7] Frontinus' embeddedness in Roman literary culture should not be underestimated, in other words; indeed, it was the network of interactions – personal, social, political and literary – that can be traced between him and some of the currently better-known authors and patrons of his day that inspired this volume.[8]

This chapter is an attempt to unpick just one strand of that web – a strand that centres around the same extraordinary historical window (Nerva's transitional principate) with which several other chapters are concerned. Earlier in this volume Victoria Rimell explores the convergences and potential interplay between another pair of texts that (like the *De aquis*) were polished off and published in 97–8: Martial's tenth book of *Epigrams* (second edition) and Tacitus' *Agricola*.[9] Like the *De aquis/Epigrams* 10 duo, these two texts look very different from each other, and they are rarely read

---

[4] König 2013: 370–6.
[5] I discuss Aelian's interactions with Frontinus (and Trajan), and Arrian's follow-on interactions with Aelian (and Hadrian) in the second *Literary Interactions* volume.
[6] A. König forthcoming.   [7] Baldwin 1994: 503–4.
[8] Plutarch is also part of this web: one of his regular addressees, Sosius Senecio, was Frontinus' son-in-law. Indeed, it would have come as no surprise had Frontinus put in an appearance in the dialogue which is the subject of Roy Gibson's chapter in this volume.
[9] On the likely date of the *De aquis*, published shortly after Nerva appointed Frontinus to the post of *curator aquarum* in 97, see especially Rodgers 2004: 5–8.

in close dialogue as a result. There are correspondences, however, which make for a productive experiment in parallel reading and raise important questions about literary interactivity at the level of consumption, not just composition. My own discussion will consider some hazy topical overlaps (more interdiscursivity than intertextuality) and the role played by readers (ancient and modern) in bringing diverse texts into conversation with each other. Unlike Rimell (and Roy Gibson, in his dialogue between Pliny and Plutarch at the other end of this volume), I am not restricted only to the exploration of suggestive connections, however; I have the luxury of being able to follow up some overt interactions. My chapter particularly homes in on two occasions in *Epigrams* 10 where Frontinus is explicitly called up by Martial's pen.

In both cases, Martial appears to be invoking the (states)man, not his writings; but the two are not so easy to disentangle, as we will see, and that raises methodological as well as interpretative questions. I will argue that aspects of Frontinus' *De aquis* (almost certainly in circulation – but how widely? – when Martial was editing *Epigrams* 10) potentially lurk in the background of the verses in 10.48 and 10.58 where Frontinus is talked of, poised to invest Martial's words with extra significance. But I will also consider what is at stake when we choose to read these references to Frontinus as invitations/opportunities to bring some of his own writing alongside and into dialogue with Martial's poetry. Does cross-pollination with the *De aquis* enrich, over-egg or constrict our understanding of Martial's politics? What difference does it make to our understanding of Martial's poetics – and the wider literary culture in which he, Frontinus, Tacitus and their contemporaries were writing? Does it require us to adjust our notions of (ancient and modern) reading habits and reading communities? In what ways might it affect our responses to Frontinus and his works? And how does it contribute to our picture of literary, social and political (inter)activity more generally in 97–8? Frontinus' social and political prominence (and Martial's emphasis on that, more than on Frontinus' authorial endeavours) will prompt scrutiny of the disjunctions and overlaps between personal and textual interactions, a recurring theme of this volume.[10] The 'un-literary' nature of the *De aquis* will trigger reflections on boundaries and cross-fertilisation between conventionally 'literary' and 'less literary' genres (at the point of reception, as well as production).[11] And analysis of obscure, almost invisible, indefinite nods in

---

[10] My discussion intersects particularly with Kelly's and Mratschek's contributions.

[11] This is something which the chapters of Harries and Lavan also bring to the fore.

(inter)textual directions alongside clearer, more direct verbal echoes will feed into the wider picture which this volume is building up of the varied and complex nature of the dialogues which contemporary authors entered into with each other and their readers.

Reading Frontinus in Martial's *Epigrams* is thus an opportunity to probe many of the issues at the heart of this volume. But it is also a bid to involve Frontinus – so often marginalised – in future discussions of the literature of this period. Indeed, in unpicking the role that he and his texts sometimes played in other authors' (and their readers') responses to the world in which they were writing, I hope to show how appreciation of that role – and of those interactions – can deepen our understanding of late Flavian, Nervan and early Trajanic literary culture.

Epigrams 10.48

Nuntiat octauam Phariae sua turba iuuencae,
  et pilata redit iamque subitque cohors.
Temperat haec thermas, nimios prior hora uapores
  halat, et immodico sexta Nerone calet.
Stella, Nepos, Cani, Cerialis, Flacce, uenitis?   5
  Septem sigma capit, sex sumus, adde Lupum.
Exoneraturas uentrem mihi uilica maluas
  attulit et uarias quas habet hortus opes,
in quibus est lactuca sedens et tonsile porrum,
  nec deest ructatrix mentha nec herba salax;   10
secta coronabunt rutatos oua lacertos
  et madidum thynni de sale sumen erit.
Gustus in his; una ponetur cenula mensa:
  haedus inhumani raptus ab ore lupi,
et quae non egeant ferro structoris ofellae   15
  et faba fabrorum prototomique rudes;
pullus ad haec cenisque tribus iam perna superstes
  addetur. Saturis mitia poma dabo,
de Nomentana uinum sine faece lagona,
  quae bis Frontino consule trima fuit.   20
Accedent sine felle ioci nec mane timenda
  libertas et nil quod tacuisse uelis:
de prasino conuiua meus Scorpoque loquatur,
  nec facient quemquam pocula nostra reum.

The eighth hour is announced to the Pharian heifer by her band of devotees and with that, one javelin-wielding cohort returns to camp as another takes its place. This hour tempers the heat of the baths, the one before exhales too much steam, and the sixth burns with Neronian excess. Stella, Nepos, Canius, Cerialis, Flaccus, are you coming? The couch takes seven; we are six; add Lupus. My steward's wife has brought me mallows that unburden the stomach and sundry fruits of the garden. Among them, languid lettuce and snipped-off leeks; there is no shortage, either, of belching mint or the saucy herb; sliced eggs will garland mackerels seasoned with rue and there will be breast of sow, drenched in fishy-brine. These will serve as tastings. My little dinner will be set out in just one course: a kid snatched from the jaws of a beastly wolf, plus titbits of the kind that need no cutting up, plus workman's beans and uncultivated young greens; a chicken and ham-leftovers from three dinners past will add to the pile. When every one has had their fill, I shall offer ripe apples and a wine (with no dregs) from a Nomentan flagon which turned six years old during Frontinus' consulship.[12] Jollity (with no bitterness to it) will accompany all that; there will be none of the frank free-speaking that causes anxiety the next morning, there will be nothing said which you might wish unsaid. Let my guests talk of the Greens and of Scorpus; heaven forbid that my drinks should get anyone put on trial.

Frontinus makes his first appearance in Martial about halfway through *Epigrams* 10, that double-edged book that was first issued under Domitian in 96 and then revised and republished under Trajan at the end of 98. In 10.48 Martial reworks a familiar trope, the dinner party invitation, to assemble a group of poets and patrons for a supper of home-grown leaves, mackerel and chopped eggs, sow's udder soaked in tunny-sauce, a young goat 'snatched from the jaws of an inhuman wolf', meat morsels, workmen's beans, course young greens, a chicken and a three-day-old ham. The makeshift, muddled nature of this feast complements ideas touched upon in the preceding poem (and elsewhere), where Martial identifies components of the happy life, including 'land that is not unyielding' and a table *sine arte* ('without finesse').[13] But, as Emily Gowers has shown, the food in this poem (as in many of Martial's *Epigrams*) also serves as a metaphor for Martial's poetic style, celebrating his crude, salacious wit, the festive licence that tumbles through his books, and his penchant for surprising readers with a jumble of seeming inconsistencies.[14]

   The table set, Martial looks ahead to what he will serve his sated guests for dessert (18–20): ripe fruit (*mitia poma*) and wine without sediment from a Nomentan flagon (*de Nomentana uinum sine faece lagona*), which turned twice three years old in the year of Frontinus' consulship (*quae*

---

[12] On Heinsius' conjecture of *trima* for the *prima* of the MSS, see Housman 1907 (cited from Diggle and Goodyear 1972: 728–9). If *prima* were right, *bis* (as a substitute for *iterum*) would apply not to *trima* (as in my translation) but to *Frontino consule*, meaning (implausibly) 'a Nomentan flagon which was first bottled (?) during (or after?) Frontinus' second consulship'.

[13] Spisak 2002: 137.   [14] Gowers 1993: 245–64.

bis Frontino consule trima fuit). For most commentators, this reference to Frontinus simply helps Martial draw attention to the age of his wine.[15] I suggest, however, that Frontinus' presence in the poem raises questions about dates and dating that extend well beyond the comestible. Indeed, Martial's mention of him, like his description of the dishes that the wine will accompany, prompts reflection on the nature of Martial's poetry, and in particular upon the age – or the vintage – of the poems that make up the second edition of *Epigrams* 10.[16] In addition – if Martial's mention of Frontinus also points readers to the aqueduct treatise which Frontinus had recently been writing (as I argue it might) – it invites comparison of Martial's work with wider contemporary literary trends, and in particular one that Frontinus' own text embodies (as does Tacitus' *Agricola*): the celebration of Nervan/Trajanic reforms, indeed of a new political era – set alongside implicit acknowledgement that some of the impurities of the past continue to plague the present.[17]

Time is made to matter in the poem right from the start. The eighth hour is announced before we discover anything else; and it brings with it both closure (of the Temple of Isis, v. 1) and changeover (v. 2), as one cohort returns to camp and another comes out on duty. The next two verses elaborate on the merits of Martial's chosen hour, emphasising its relative coolness in comparison with the steamy seventh hour and scorching sixth. This helps Martial to set not just the scene but also the tone for the dinner party to which – in verse 5 – he invites his literary guests: it proclaims a preference for temperateness generally and a rejection of anything that is drainingly, or even dangerously, hot. But his weighing-up of time here does not just contribute to the construction of Martial's poetic persona: it also contains a political subtext.

The 'Nero' of verse 4 is shorthand, of course, for Nero's Baths, and re-spins Martial's clock-watching as a quick tour of the bathhouse (from temperate *tepidarium* to the steamy *laconicum* – sweat-room – and then on to the sweltering *caldarium*). Martial's glossing of *Nerone* as *immodico*

---

[15] E.g. Peachin 2004: 158.

[16] 10.48 reuses many titbits (*faba, haedus, oua, pulli, perna* etc.) from the *Xenia* (i.e. Martial's juvenilia), which also plays with the tracking/manipulation of time; cf. esp. 13.119 for another carefully weighed/aged Nomentan vintage. (I am grateful to Victoria Rimell for pointing me in this direction.)

[17] The *De aquis* opens with a eulogy of Nerva's devotion to the state and bursts with reformative zeal. The continuity of maladministration, corruption and theft is a recurring theme, however (*Aq.* 31–4, 65–7, 72–3, 75–6, 91), and the treatise closes with a warning from Frontinus to future law-flouters (*Aq.* 130). On the emphasis which Frontinus places on fraud and mismanagement, see Evans 1994: 57–8; Cuomo 2000: 193–4; Peachin 2004: 109–13 and Appendix 7. For broader readings of the treatise: DeLaine 1995; Del Chicca 1995; A. König 2007.

also inevitably evokes the emperor himself[18] – and that invites us to look for political allusions in the rest of the passage. When one does, the language of *temperantia* particularly jumps out (celebrated as a key Trajanic virtue in Pliny's *Panegyricus*, for instance).[19] In this light, the three hours that Martial foregrounds begin to resemble (perhaps) Rome's three imperial dynasties, in reverse chronological order (why count backwards like this, unless to prompt reflection on chronological trajectories?). The sixth, that smoulders with immoderate Neronian heat, conjures up the Julio-Claudians, who self-combusted in the wake of some sizzling imperial antics and a very real fire (think, too, of representations of Nero as the sun – the sixth hour was when the sun was at its height).[20] The seventh, with its excess of steam, represents the Flavians, who rose to power amid the flames of civil war and whose last incumbent had a particularly fiery reputation (for book-burning, *inter alia*).[21] And the eighth, which tempers the heat of what has gone before (and also marks the slide towards the end of the day?), embodies (perhaps) the present regime, cool and calming – at least in comparison. Quotidian time reframed as epochal time.[22]

On this basis, one might go back and make deductions from the opening pair of verses. The cult of Isis (conjured up by the Pharian heifer) seems to have been especially popular with the Flavian emperors, and connected to Domitian above all,[23] so the temple's closure (triggered by the striking of the new hour) might signal the end of Domitian's reign. The changeover of cohorts, meanwhile, perhaps evokes a handover of command at the imperial/dynastic level – although (and this is a point we will come back to) one body of men is replaced here by another of identical appearance

---

[18] Cf. e.g. *Ep.* 7.34, where Nero and his baths are explicitly compared; also Tac. *Ann.* 15.23, where Nero's reaction to the birth and death of his daughter is characterised as *immodicus*. As Gowers 1993: 256 puts it, 'Nero's baths loom over the dinner like an immoderate tyrant.'

[19] See e.g. Plin. *Pan.* 2, 10, 41, 55, 76, 79, 80, 82 (where Trajan behaves with admirable *temperantia* and *temperamentum*), and also 3, where *temperamentum* characterises the new register which the senate must adopt in addressing Trajan.

[20] Balland 2010: 88: 'L'expression *immodico . . . Nerone . . .* peut rappeler qu'au milieu de l'année 64 (où Martial arriva à Rome) les chrétiens, accusés d'être coupables de l'incendie de la Ville, brûlèrent transformés en torches vivantes; les jardins de l'empereur, au Vatican, furent ainsi symboliquement et atrocement illuminés'.

[21] Of course, Domitian was credited with restoring some of the buildings – including libraries – that burnt down during various fires (Suet. *Dom.* 5 and 20); but he was also associated with tyrannical uses of fire against opponents and writers (Suet. *Dom.* 10; Tac. *Agr.* 2).

[22] As Victoria Rimell and Chris Whitton both pointed out to me, if we read Martial's hour-by-hour scheme in vv. 3–4 (too) literally we end up with an unusually early dinner-time (2pm) – an oddity striking enough, perhaps, to make readers look closely at what Martial is up to here. While we are counting, it is worth noting the numbers at v. 6 (*sex sumus*), where Lupus (Wolf-man, who comes to gobble the kid that was snatched from the jaws of an inhuman *lupus*, v. 14) makes seven.

[23] Jones 1992: 101; Tac. *Hist.* 3.74; Suet. *Dom.* 1.2 and 5; Dio 66.24.2.

(a feature emphasised by the fact that *redit* and *subitque* share the same subject, the singular *pilata . . . cohors*). Martial's characterisation of the hour for his dinner party thus teases us with the possibility (probability?) that this epigram is not just about food, Martial-style, and its literary meaning, but also about regime change – a theme that is particularly topical, of course, for the second, revised edition of Book 10. If we choose to follow up the hints embedded in verses 1–4, we understand that the feast to which Martial's guests are invited will start at the eighth hour *in the age of Trajan*.

Age is then a recurring theme in the description of food that follows. A kid and fresh young greens (primitive, even: these *prototomi*, the first-cut leaves, are *rudes*) contrast with ripe apples and 'a ham that has already survived three dinners' (17).[24] Its placement at the end of a line (paralleling the position of *rudes* in the verse above) draws attention to the word *superstes*, which we have met once already in the book, in *Epigrams* 10.2, where Martial celebrates the likely immortality of his poetry:

> . . . quem cum mihi Roma dedisset,
> 'nil tibi quod demus maius habemus' ait.
> 'Pigra per hunc fugies ingratae flumina Lethes
> et meliore tui parte superstes eris.
> Marmora Messallae findit caprificus et audax
> dimidios Crispi mulio ridet equos:
> at chartis nec furta nocent et saecula prosunt,
> solaque non norunt haec monumenta mori.'
>   (*Epig.* 10.2.5–12)

> . . . [Reader,] when Rome gave you to me she declared: 'I have nothing greater to give you. Through him you will escape the sluggish streams of thankless Lethe and the better part of you will live on. The fig tree causes cracks in Messalla's marble and the cocky mule-driver laughs at Crispus' crumbling horses. But thefts do no harm to my volumes and the passing of centuries benefits them. These are the only monuments that do not taste death.

The comparison which Martial draws here between the fate of his poetic monuments (which will escape death) and that of physical memorials (which disintegrate over time) does not simply channel Horace *Odes* 3.30, among other texts:[25] it evokes also the destruction of statues and erasure

---

[24] On that unlucky kid: being snatched from the jaws of a wolf is proverbially unlikely (cf. Plaut. *Poen.* 776), one of many hints that we should read this dinner party as a grotesque kind of fantasy (that overwrites Catullus 13 among other models). Thanks again to Victoria Rimell for nudging me on this.

[25] Also Ovid (*Am.* 1.15.41–2, 3.15.19–20; *Met.* 15.871–9), as Rimell 2008: 68–71 and Hardie 2012: 327–9 discuss.

of inscriptions that accompanied the recent demise of Domitian[26] – and in so doing returns us to the theme of political *re*writing with which *Epigrams* 10.2 begins. For 10.2.1–4, of course, announce that what we are reading is a revision: it is a book that has been recalled (*nunc reuocauit*), trimmed back with an up-to-date file (*lima rasa recenti*), and renewed in large part (*pars noua maior erit*).

Some commentators read awkward back-tracking and anxious reposi-tioning in Martial's decision to reissue *Epigrams* 10; it has been seen as an acknowledgement that his praise of Domitian might make him unpopular with the new dynasty and an attempt to reinvent himself as a poet who will appeal to a Trajanic readership.[27] But this interpretation overlooks the obvi-ous irony inherent in his juxtaposition in 10.2 of that declaration of renewal with the claim a few lines later that his poetry cannot be destroyed (a claim which gains extra piquancy if read in dialogue with Tacitus' use of the word *superstes* at *Agr.* 3.2 and 46.4).[28] Running through his introduction to the second edition, in other words, is a tacit acknowledgement that, though cut out, the poems of his first edition still (and always will) survive. Mar-tial did not need to republish *Epigrams* 10; he had already published Book 11, whose opening few poems hail Nerva's accession,[29] and he could have left 10, as he left Books 1 to 9, to fade from view (or continue to circulate) in its original state. Arguably, his republication draws attention not to his new Trajanic identity but to the very difficulty of forging one, to the chal-lenge that faced authors who ended up straddling these two, supposedly distinct political eras. Indeed, it draws attention to Martial's (deliberate?) failure (after the tentative efforts of *Epigrams* 11) to reinvent/re-present him-self substantially. Even as it introduces a revised, Trajanic-era edition, 10.2 reminds readers that traces of the old will (always) linger amid the new.[30]

The word *superstes*, then, conjures up a political problem: for being a 'survivor' (or a 'leftover') in AD 98 is (as Tacitus' *Agricola* synchronically emphasised) a complicated position. Martial's use of the same word in 10.48 to characterise a ham might look innocuous but it calls 10.2 to mind, not least because the food at this dinner party invites readers to reflect on the

---

[26] Fitzgerald 2007: 158; Rimell 2008: 71–2; Hardie 2012: 329.

[27] E.g. Coleman 1998: 338–9, 355; Spisak 2002.

[28] On which, see Rimell's analysis earlier in this volume, pp. 77–9; also Kelly in this volume (pp. 177–8) on a Statian parallel.

[29] On the complexity of Martial's engagement with Nervan ideology in *Ep.* 11, see especially Fearnley 2003: 622–6; Rimell 2008: 162–4; and Morello in this volume.

[30] Cf. *Ep.* 12.4, where Martial draws attention to the parallel existence of different (abridged and unabridged) versions of Books 10 and 11. On the ways in which Books 10–12 complicate (or col-lapse) distinctions between Flavian past and Nervan/Trajanic present, see also Fowler 1995: 209; Henderson 2001: 81–2; Fitzgerald 2007: 158–60; Rimell 2008: 67–8; Hardie 2012: 329.

kind of poetry that Martial is writing. (Just how appetising are leftovers? Some things taste best fresh, others benefit from maturity; has Martial's meat gained in flavour – or has it deteriorated? Jarring notes in his description of the choice morsels that he is serving up make us wonder quite how palatable any of it is – and, indeed, whether any of it is quite what it seems . . .).[31] A subtext about literary recycling and the wider context of imperial *saecularisation* is thus woven into the menu of 10.48 – a subtext which Frontinus' appearance helps to bring out.

Two whole verses are devoted to Martial's description of the wine, more than for any other single item at the feast: we are meant to look closely at it. And the elaborate phrasing of verse 20 prompts us to think particularly hard about its age. *Bis* applies to *trima* (though that is not immediately obvious),[32] making the wine six years old during Frontinus' consulship. But which one? His first, in 73 (in which case the wine would have been maturing for nearly thirty years), or his second, in 98, to which the juxtaposition of *bis* with *Frontino consule* teasingly points us (in which case we are looking at a wine that is still young, perhaps even immature)?[33] The answer presumably is both (as so often in the *Epigrams*, and particularly in Martial's epoch-straddling *Epigrams* 10). Martial's (enigmatic and eye-catching) description of his wine draws attention not just to the past (the time during which the wine has been maturing) but also to the present (and to what Frontinus is up to right now).

In 98 Frontinus was not only emerging as one of Rome's leading senators: he was closely connected with both Nerva and Trajan, and may even have been viewed (not least because he was busy parading himself thus in the *De aquis*) as something of a poster boy for the new regime.[34] Allusion to his second consulship, then, places Martial's dinner party (and the epigram itself: it is one of the few in Book 10 that we can securely identify as belonging to the second edition)[35] firmly in the Trajanic 'new age' – especially if we can assume that mention of Frontinus in 98 will trigger thought of his recent role as *curator aquarum* and perhaps also the

---

[31] Why *lactuca sedens*, for instance? Or *ructatrix mentha*? Or *exoneraturas uentrem . . . maluas*, for that matter, unless to provoke some double-takes (regurgitation) and even disgust in the reader?

[32] Housman 1907: 252–3 (Diggle and Goodyear 1972: 729). See n. 12.

[33] At 10.49.3 Martial connects the youth (as well as the provenance) of a wine with poor quality: the 'leaden' Sabine wine is *modo conditum* (recently laid down).

[34] Take its opening paragraph (*Aq.* 1), for instance, where the verbal parallels which Frontinus establishes between his and Nerva's *diligentia* and *amor* for the state proclaim their shared ethos, even their partnership. The *De aquis* is – among other things – an exercise in showing that Nerva and Trajan's re-empowerment of Rome's beleaguered senatorial elite was underway and working well (A. König 2007).

[35] Peachin 2004: 157; Balland 2010: 87.

aqueduct treatise which that post inspired him to write. The phrase *sine faece* ('without dregs') in verse 19 may even reinforce a Nervan/Trajanic vibe. For it could be read as a witty allusion to Frontinus' recurring concern in the *De aquis* with purification and transparency, a concern that allies him with the new dynasty's rhetoric of reform.[36] When coupled with Frontinus' name, in other words (and thanks to the ideas which reference to his political career and possible interplay with his most recent publication together conjure up), the absence of lees in the flagon helps to give Martial's choice of wine a particularly (early) Trajanic 'flavour'.

However, verse 20 also makes it clear that the wine has been maturing during the Flavian dynasty, having been laid down some time before 98 (if not before 73). It thus crosses political eras – and in so doing embodies a message about Martial's poetry and the times in which he was writing. For, if the laxative mallow and burping mint symbolise the provocative crudity of his humour, and the hotchpotch of hors d'oeuvres (served all in one go) draws attention to the sometimes incongruous variety of his collected epigrams, the hybrid nature of the wine reminds us that the book we are reading is itself (inevitably) a Flavian–Trajanic blend. It may (like the contents of Martial's Nomentan flagon, and Frontinus' career for that matter) have taken on a new dimension with the accession of Nerva and Trajan, but its foundations were laid in the previous regime – and not even the removal of unwanted 'dross' will alter that. (Another intersection with Frontinus' *De aquis* might occur here. For all its talk of cleansing and the eradication of corruption, the treatise makes it clear that Rome's aqueducts – and Rome itself – continue to be plagued by problems that originated in previous political eras. There is continuity, not just change. Indeed, the continuity of pre-Trajanic problems is the driving force of the treatise, and – alongside the rhetoric of reform – the foundation on which Frontinus' authority is built.)[37]

It is not simply that a residue of the old lingers on in the new (despite judicious sieving), then; this Flavian vintage, that is being served at the start of Trajan's principate, reminds us that the past is often an integral basis of the present. Martial's dating of the wine in 10.48 thus returns us to a tension that we saw picked out in 10.2 between (supposed) political change and poetic continuity. Moreover, together with the closing verses of

---

[36] Frontinus spends a considerable amount of time in the *De aquis* claiming credit (which he shares strategically with the emperor) for cleansing various aqueducts of noxious sediments, weeding out corrupt water men and problems with waste, and clarifying the network's correct distribution figures: e.g. *Aq.* 9, 33–4, 64, 74–7, 89–93, 130.

[37] See above, n. 17.

the epigram (when wine leads us on to boozy talk) it also invites speculation about political continuity.

For much of 10.48, we (like Martial's guests) are transported to the sanctuary of a private home, whose detachment from public life is underlined by references to the outside world in the frame of the poem. Gowers has argued that the 'convivial licence' of Martial's dinner couch is contrasted with the 'threatened liberty' of this wider world only at the epigram's 'furthest margins', in verses 1–2 and 24.[38] But Martial's mention of Frontinus ensures that politics intrudes well before the poem (and the party) have begun to wrap up. Indeed, his evocation of AD 98 and the imperial upheavals that surrounded it overshadows the epigram's final four lines, and in so doing alerts us to the possibility that Martial's private, poetic world is not as insulated from public/political life as the poem's structure initially suggests.

Verses 21–4 discuss the kind of conversation that is likely (or ought) to accompany dinner. Martial's pronouncement that there will be 'jollity without malice' (*sine felle ioci*), 'freedom that brings no regrets the following morning' (*nec mane timenda | libertas*), and 'nothing you would wish you had kept to yourself' (*nil quod tacuisse uelis*) on one level simply reinforces the festive, light-hearted, even licentious atmosphere that his menu has established. More specifically, it references a recurring topos in satire and invective, whereby poets explore the balance between anything-goes, Lucilian-style frankness and a less acerbic self-restraint (which Juvenal – another of Martial's interactive acquaintances[39] – particularly eschews). In so doing, it pursues the ongoing analogy between Martial's dinner party and his epigrams to reinforce a claim he makes elsewhere (not altogether seriously, of course) about the (relatively) innocuous nature of his writing. But, following his reference to Frontinus and through him to the poem's immediate political context (both of which are picked up by the echo in *sine felle* of *sine faece*), this discussion of conversational/literary register may also take on a political dimension – and not a particularly reassuring one.

For, with regime change in mind, the juxtaposition of *timenda* and *libertas* and allusions to silence and self-censorship inject a troubling note. (We might even be tempted to read some correspondence – or interaction – with Tacitus and his *Agricola* in Martial's phrase *nil quod tacuisse* [*Tacuisse?*] *uelis*.)[40] Verses 21–2 may appear to promise unconstrained speech, but they surround it with a sense of anxiety and caution that not only alert us to the potential for social faux pas but also remind us of

---

[38] Gowers 1993: 256.   [39] See especially Kelly's chapter in this volume.   [40] Especially *Agr.* 2–3.

the way in which Domitian's principate was often described. The poem's final word – *reus* – even threatens to transport us not just to the law courts (where slanderous slurs might be challenged) but back to the world of informers and treason trials from which Rome, thanks to Trajan, is supposed to have escaped. Note Martial's insistence once more on the passing of time (*mane*): a wine-filled evening, followed by the cold light of day (a less positive progression, perhaps, than the passing of hours we see at the start of the epigram). For Gowers, Martial's closing injunction to his readers to talk of chariot-racing, lest drunken discourse puts anyone on trial, celebrates the fact that the guests at his dinner 'are free to discuss the circus, a subject removed from serious political slander'.[41] But it may also hint that his guests are *only* free to discuss such frivolities – that more serious topics are off the menu, because talking now, in 98, is still a potentially hazardous enterprise.[42] Some kinds of conversation (like some kinds of wine) might be the cause of sore heads in the morning.

If that reading is right, 10.48 does not follow its own advice: for, under cover of licentious, poetic frivolity, it takes the liberty of making a serious political point. Far from maintaining a distance between private and public, convivial/poetic and political, it collapses those worlds – and in the process draws attention to overlaps between eras and dynasties too. The epigram's ring composition (that political frame linking verses 1–4 with 21–4) thus takes on a potentially sinister thrust, as time threatens to become cyclical rather than progressive – and as the 'temperate' eighth hour starts to feel a little less refreshing. For in the light of the continuity that we glimpse not just in the wine and Martial's poetry but also in the politicised atmosphere that invades the epigram (and the dinner), the changeover of cohorts back in verse 2 acquires an unsettling significance, insofar as it reminds us that transition can involve repetition (remember *redit*: 'returns') as well as transformation.

Frontinus, that prominent Flavian survivor who repositioned himself so successfully under Nerva and Trajan – and whose *De aquis*, like *Epigrams* 10, marks dynastic change by publishing updated corrections (of water supply records, rather than poems) that are tangled up with older pre-Nervan material, whose errors continue to muddy the waters[43] – plays a pivotal role

---

[41] Gowers 1993: 263.
[42] Balland 2010: 88 reaches a similar conclusion. When he reissued *Epigrams* 10, Martial presumably anticipated some edgy cross-fertilisation between this and *Ep.* 11.1 (where, under Nerva, talk of racing – and Scorpus – is placed in competitive tension with the reading of Martial's 'holiday' book – *liber otiose*).
[43] See especially *Aq.* 64–76, where Frontinus brings together figures from the old (erroneous) imperial records and his own (more accurate) findings in order to underline the differences between them.

in pointing this out. For the questions which his association with the wine raises about ages, vintages and the relationship between old and new not only introduce a political note into the supposedly sheltered dinner party (and poem); they help to expose a fallacy inherent in political periodisation, and *Epigrams* 10, and indeed the *De aquis* itself: namely that, despite the efforts that emperors and authors made to advertise change, new eras (and editions) were not always so very different from what had gone before.

Indeed, at a stretch the (seasoned, or still relatively young? naturally dross-free, or artificially strained?) wine that Martial promises to serve may be read as a thought-provoking metaphor not just for Martial's own poetry but also for some of the new-era writing that others were doing around him. It depends in part on where we think the interactions between Martial and Frontinus start and stop. Does 10.48 simply conjure up Frontinus the statesman, and the political history with which he was associated? (Or not even that? Is Frontinus, after all, merely a temporal or social, not a political, co-ordinate in Martial's homely menu?) Or does the epigram also – necessarily, automatically? – gesture towards the *De aquis*? (Can mention of Frontinus in 98 avoid doing so? Are the statesman and his texts separable? Does the lack of close lexical connections matter? Is the fact that many will have been aware that Frontinus was writing this text, and beginning to circulate it, enough to trigger some kind of interactivity?) And might 10.48, through interplay with the *De aquis* and the reflections which it prompts on contemporary literary production as well as regime-change, even spark a chain-reaction of further interactions with other contemporary texts (like the *Agricola*) which were themselves busy marking and reflecting upon the start of a supposedly new (literary and political) era?

The picture which Tacitus paints at the start of the *Agricola* of trends in literary activity in changing political contexts gives the impression that authors reacted individually to what was going on around them, but not so much to each other. His authors either follow common patterns or stick their necks out on an individual basis; they do not (as he represents them) sharpen each other's ideas or agenda by corresponding or cross-referencing amongst themselves.[44] What we have seen here (and in a number of other chapters) alerts us to a more complex, intense set of interrelationships, with intertextual cross-fertilisations (on and off the page, and across different genres and reading contexts) helping collectively to interrogate and shape authors' and readers' responses to changing times – and, indeed,

---

[44] The shortage of obvious references in Tacitus' own works to contemporary authors and texts might tempt us to think that Tacitus himself eschewed such cross-fertilisations; as e.g. Whitton 2012 underlines, however, his allusive engagement with contemporaries is not to be underestimated.

subsequent readings of each other's texts (a cycle of intertextuality and interdiscursivity nuancing each other).[45]

Epigrams 10.58

By turns boisterous and melancholic, lewd and philosophical, outward-looking and introspective, the epigrams that immediately follow 10.48 baffle the reader with the variety of their styles and subjects (food and drink, death and age, glory, sex, clientship, city vs country, *negotium* vs *otium*); but they also tantalise us with faint verbal and thematic connections (for example, a shared interest in measuring, as in 10.50, 53, 55 and 57),[46] which invite us to trace patterns and subtexts across and between them, while eluding attempts to pin any firmly down. The 'safe' topic of conversation that Martial recommends for his dinner party at the end of 10.48 – the chariot-racer Scorpus – pops up twice, in 10.50 and 10.53; and his shock death not only engages with other poems in *Epigrams* 10 where mortality, achievement (especially poetic) and the value and transience of fame are debated but also reminds us – if reminder were needed – that what might seem light-hearted in Martial one moment can change in an instant and feel suddenly serious. Indeed, the death of Scorpus so soon after he has been recommended as a 'safe' topic of conversation might even signal the death – or at least the dearth – of such 'safe' topics. That possibility is complicated by the fact that he returns from the dead to speak himself in 10.53 (more time-travel, again collapsing past and present). *Epigrams* 10.59, meanwhile, returns us to the book's opening poem and revokes the suggestion given there that we pick and choose what we read (10.1: 'If I seem rather too long a book, with too late a full-stop, read a few poems only (*legito pauca*): I shall then be a little book. Quite often my small pages end with the end of a poem. Make me as short as you want me to be (*fac tibi me quam cupis ipse breuem*)'). Employing the metaphor of dining once more to talk about his poetry, Martial here demands readers with large, wide-ranging appetites, not fussy eaters who merely trifle with 'titbits' (the *ofellae* he promised in 10.48?). In so doing, he further complicates the experience of reading his epigrams. The ground shifts beneath our feet, as an approach that was approved at the start of the book is replaced halfway through by a conflicting model. By calling to mind as well as contradicting his introductory poem, 10.59

---

[45] Cf. especially Marchesi's chapter in this volume, on the way in which new meanings emerge out of the dialogue between parallel/competing *re*deployments of texts in other near-contemporary works.

[46] As Rimell 2008: 66 points out, *Epigrams* 10 particularly 'chews over the passage of time, celebrating birthdays, and debating what it is to think about and approach mortality at crucial life junctures'.

thus marks a caesura in *Epigrams* 10, which kick-starts the second half of the volume by making us look back over what (and how) we have been reading and by raising more questions than it answers about how to proceed.[47]

The distinction that Martial draws at 10.59.2 between brevity and quality might encourage us to pay particular attention to his longer poems. As it happens, 10.48 is the second-longest of the book (reason itself, perhaps, for unpicking it carefully); and the longest, 10.30, introduces a theme (the hassles of life in Rome, set against the pleasures of a country retreat) which is picked up by two other relatively long pieces – 10.51 and 10.58[48] – the second of which not only sits right next to that thought-provoking caesura but also brings us back to Frontinus.

The opening verses of 10.58 focus on place, transporting us to 'the calm retreat of coastal Anxur', where Martial revels (and puts down roots) in an idyllic sanctuary:

> Anxuris aequorei placidos, Frontine, recessus
>   et propius Baias litoreamque domum,
> et quod inhumanae cancro feruente cicadae
>   non nouere nemus, flumineosque lacus
> dum colui . . .

> When I made my home in the calm backwaters of coastal Anxur, in a seaside villa quite close to Baiae, and a grove untroubled, even at the height of summer, by inconsiderate crickets, and free-flowing ponds . . .

These verses, and especially the epigram's first two words, closely recall 10.51.7–10, where Martial similarly celebrates Anxur's 'watery' delights, inviting us to read the two poems as a pair.[49] And because 10.51 compares the charms of Anxur with the topography of Rome, where days are stolen (vv. 5–6) and men become weary and resentful (vv. 15–16), an implicit (and unfavourable) contrast with Rome is immediately triggered at the start of 10.58 too. Its evocation of temperate tranquillity is reminiscent also of the 'not stagnant water' (*nec languet aequor*), 'the living quiet of the sea' (*uiua sed quies ponti*) and the light breezes (*leni . . . uento*) of 10.30,

---

[47] In this sense, it mimics the effect of *Epigrams* 10 as a book, which Rimell 2008: 65 describes as 'a fault line in Martial's twelve-book epic tome, which teaches us to keep looking backwards and forwards, to (re)read everything differently'.

[48] At sixteen and fourteen verses long respectively, *Ep.* 10.51 and 10.58 stand out from the poems immediately surrounding them, which are all eight verses long or shorter. On city vs country in *Ep.* 10, see especially Spisak 2002: 132–4; Fearnley 2003: 630–1; Merli 2006a: 259–61.

[49] Balland 2010: 63 also notes similarities between them.

another Rome-rejecting poem.[50] But Martial's lyrical rewriting of a scene he has painted (more than once) before also draws attention to his poetic talents, which is fitting because this version of the city–country contrast concentrates particularly on the constraints, or demands, which life in Rome imposes upon poetic production.[51]

First Martial sketches his poetic ideal (vv. 5–6); and the gently moving waters and absence of harsh heat and noise that introduce it embody both the benign literary freedom that he claims to have enjoyed at Anxur (where he had leisure to cultivate the learned Muses with Frontinus: *doctas tecum celebrare uacabat | Pieridas*) and the kind of authentic, unadulterated, free-flowing, pleasant-sounding poetry that we are invited to believe he composed as a result. In Rome, by contrast, he finds himself 'tossed about in the city's depths' (*iactamur | in alto urbis*) and forced to 'waste' his life in 'fruitless toil' (*et in sterili uita labore perit*).[52] These are recognisably poetic images which underline, with deliberate irony, the ignominy of his un-poetic situation[53] – brought about in part, presumably, by his poetic fame: Martial has made it big, and is now being buffeted by the turbulent tide of his success. Verses 6–7 might be read as a subtle boast, in other words, as much as a complaint:

> nunc nos maxima Roma terit.
> Hic mihi quando dies meus est?

> now almighty Rome wears us down. In the city, when do I have a day that belongs just to me?

Crucially, it is not just any old Rome that is complained about here; it is Rome AT THIS MOMENT, as opposed to Anxur IN THE PAST. 10.30 depicts both Rome and Formiae in the present tense: Apollinaris flees, admires, desires; breezes blow, fish are caught, Rome keeps men captive, and bailiffs reap the benefit. 10.51 similarly focuses on 'now' (*iam*, v. 1): Rome may have stolen days in the past, but Faustinus is depicted (still) resisting its hazards in the present, and Anxur is as vibrant as ever. In 10.58, by contrast, the poetic retreat of Anxur is consigned to the past (*dum colui . . . uacabat*) by

---

[50] On 10.30, see also Mratschek in this volume. Martial's attitude to both city and country is fluid, of course; for Merli 2006b: 338–40 the city–countryside contrast in Book 10 is even 'more complex and less stereotypic' than in other books.

[51] Merli 2006a: 266; Spisak 2002: 138.

[52] Clientship (note the talk in v. 11 of haunting thresholds), or perhaps two-penny poetry? (In pers. comm. Rimell recently pointed out that *damna* (v. 12) is used at 13.1.3 to refer almost directly to the book of *Xenia* itself.)

[53] On this imagery (and the echoes it contains of Virg. *Aen.* 1.3 and Hor. *Epist.* 2.2), see especially Rimell 2008: 89 and 199.

the present, bruising force of 'mightiest Rome' (**nunc** *nos maxima Roma terit*). Of course, Martial's *nunc* might be making a merely seasonal point, referring to (say) October/November in no particular year, as opposed to (say) August/September when many people were away from Rome.[54] But it may also be epoch-marking in some way or another, drawing attention (for instance) to Martial's growing readership and the new demands which his popularity is making of him.[55] Michael Peachin wonders whether it is a new phase not in Martial's but in Frontinus' career that is being marked: might *nunc* allude to Frontinus' 'stressful occupation with the water supply'?[56] Given the questions which Frontinus' presence in 10.48 raises about time, age and dynasties, I would go further and see Martial's emphatic NOW as an invitation to scrutinise the trajectories of both men (at a point in the poem where the emphasis on *nos* gives way to *mihi*), against the backdrop of wider literary and political developments. In a book whose exact timing is a moot point, *nunc* invites us to look all over again at the double caesura of 96/98 which divides the Flavian past from the Trajanic present.

On one level, Frontinus functions simply as a representative patron in 10.58, through whom Martial is able to articulate some of his (timeless) frustrations with the hassles of being a client. He begins the epigram as a literary companion, immersed in Martial's poetic world, literally surrounded (on the page) by its *placidos recessus* and *doctas Pieridas*. But as the demands of Rome break in, first-person plurals become wryly poetic (while *iactamur* in v. 7 might apply to both men, *pascimus* applies to Martial alone), and the rising statesman and epigrammatist begin to go separate ways. Their history – a timeline of the evolution of their relationship – is plotted as we read, with *nunc*, as always in *Epigrams* 10, contextualised by what has come before. The epigram ends with a (defiantly poetic) avowal of Martial's devotion to Frontinus, that reunites them but also captures the gulf that has opened up between them. The trajectory that Frontinus takes within these verses inevitably evokes his wider political career, his move from the leisurely margins of public life to the very heart of Roman politics, where – under the auspices of Nerva and Trajan – he was now setting

---

[54] Thanks to Chris Whitton for emphasising this, a useful reminder that we/I need not always default to political readings. That said, seasons and (un)seasonality often feature in Martial as invitations to reflect on epochal change, poetic and political (e.g. 13.127, where the unseasonality of roses prompts political reflection; also 12.1 and 12.18, on Martial's new book/career-chapter/relationship with Rome).

[55] Cf. 11.3, where Martial is read as far afield as Britain (a counterpoint to 11.1, where no one is reading his volumes).

[56] Peachin 2004: 159.

a new blueprint for Rome's governing class. And that adds an extra dimension to the use that Martial makes of him (as an insider, who is helping Martial to define his outsider status). For in progressively distancing himself from Frontinus as the poem develops (and as time marches inexorably on, towards the present day), Martial does not simply reject the trials and tribulations of *negotium* per se; he inevitably (deliberately?) contrasts his own endeavours with the specifically Nervan/Trajanic model of *negotium* which Frontinus now (*nunc*), in 98, embodies.[57]

The closing words of the epigram perhaps underscore this. As André Balland has noted, the striking phrase *et non officiosus amo* calls to mind an earlier epigram (1.55), where Martial had previously used the language of *amare* and *officium* (again in the closing pair of verses) to round up another formulation of his avowed preference for the country/*otium* over the city/*negotium*: 'I pray that whoever has no love for me has no love for this [leisurely/rustic] life; may that kind of man live out his pallid existence in the exercise of civic duties (*urbanis officiis*).'[58] A life of *officium*, in other words, is the poor alternative to a share in Martial's interests and affections: the two are incompatible, Martial tells Fronto, a(nother) paragon of military and civic service: *clarum militiae, Fronto, togaeque decus.*[59] In 10.58, *amor* and *officium* are still in tension, but the distance between them has shrunk. Martial remains *non officiosus*, which in the first instance refers to his unconventional behaviour as a client ('I love you, albeit undutifully'), but also evokes his ongoing rejection of civic obligations (as the trajectory of the epigram and its echo of 1.55 nudges us to see: 'I love you, even though I am no fan of *officium*/officialdom'). He closes 10.58, however, by overwriting the confrontational dismissal (*non amet... non amat...*) that concludes 1.55 with an embrace (*amo*) that builds a last-minute bridge between himself and his patron after the growing differentiation of the previous verses.

Talking of bridges (or aqueducts), we might want to compare what Frontinus himself does with the concepts of *amor* and *officium* in the *De aquis*. Frontinus brings *diligentia* and *amor* into close cooperation with each other in his preface, when characterising his and Nerva's approach to Roman administration: like his emperor ('I couldn't say if he was more

---

[57] Some literary interaction with John Henderson has helped me see that the opposition between Martial and Frontinus is there from v. 1, with *Frontine* (*frons*: at the forefront, on the cusp) placed in tension with the retreating or backing-off (*recessus*) that Martial champions/embodies.

[58] Balland 2010: 108–9.

[59] Balland is so struck by the parallels between the two poems that he suggests that the Fronto of 1.55 may even be Frontinus (ibid. 108–13).

dedicated or more passionate in his attitude to the state', *nescio diligentiore an **amantiore** rei publicae imperatore*), Frontinus claims to have been roused not only to industry but also to devotion (*non ad diligentiam modo uerum ad **amorem***) when Nerva appointed him to the office of *curator aquarum* (*nunc mihi ab Nerua Augusto . . . aquarum iniunctum **officium** ad usum, Aq.* 1). He is also at pains throughout the treatise (e.g. *Aq.* 2, 77 and 130) to show that he goes above and beyond the call of duty in the exercise of his new *officium*. Frontinus may himself be engaging in some literary – not merely political – interaction in this: his passionate claims to be motivated by *amor* may be a move (conscious or subconscious) to wrest the language of love from the likes of Martial and the world of poetry and to override its now traditional isolation from definitions/representations of *negotium*. Over-interpretation? Perhaps. But who wouldn't back Martial to seize on such a detail and work it up into a topos? Martial's collocation of *officiosus* and *amo* may just be a nod towards Frontinus' rhetorical manoeu-vre. If so, it is also – crucially – a further refinement of Frontinus' attempts to unite the two concepts/worlds. Martial's happiness to profess 'devotion' (*amor*) but reluctance to act *officiose* does not simply align him with the long-standing Catullan/elegiac tradition which underpins (and is evoked by 10.58's echoes of) 1.55; it brings his career choices into competitive contrast with the model that the paradigmatic Frontinus is setting.

Martial's nostalgia for Anxur's 'riverlike lakes' (the *flumineosque lacus* of v. 4) may also feel faintly suggestive in connection with Frontinus.[60] For, in a climactic section of the *De aquis* (*Aq.* 87–93: the one bit which anyone scrolling through the text is likely to zoom in on) Frontinus foregrounds Nerva's decision to separate a river and lake, which together had been polluting much of Rome's water supply, as evidence of the transformative effect that Nerva's (and of course Frontinus') *cura* and *diligentia* were having – not just on the aqueducts themselves but on the very health of the whole city.[61] The allusion is vanishingly subtle (so elusive that some

---

[60] Balland 2010: 113 also notes this possibility.

[61] *Aq.* 87–93 represent a (welcome) pause, after lists of incorrect and correct distribution figures (which Frontinus himself acknowledges may seem 'not only dry but also confusing', *Aq.* 77) and before the text's closing discussion of the laws and practices relating to the aqueducts' maintenance; here Frontinus brings aqueduct administration into explicit dialogue with contemporary politics, in eye-catching ways. Nerva's decision to move the source of the Anio Novus so that the river can no longer muddy the lake's clear waters is foregrounded as the highlight of his celebrated reforms (which themselves, we are to understand, are emblematic of his wider approach to government); indeed, such is the impact of his separation of river and lake that a new inscription has been set up, celebrating Nerva as the aqueduct's new founder (*Aq.* 93). (On the possibility that Trajan is the emperor named in this inscription, see Rodgers 2004 ad loc.)

commentators have marvelled at Martial's failure to refer to Frontinus'
activities as *curator aquarum* anywhere in this epigram),[62] but together with
the suggestive phrasing in the final verses and the contrast that is drawn
between past and present part way through, this striking (re)coupling of
flumen and *lacus* (as part of a distinctively *previous* paradise) may hint at
a certain (jocular?) scepticism about the vision of a Rome revitalised and
refreshing – dramatically cleaned up and freer-flowing – that the *De aquis*
itself presents us with. Anxur's long-standing *aequoreus*-ness (v. 1) stands
in mute contrast to Rome's newly *aqua*[duct]-rich state.[63]

10.58 feels personal and pessimistic, at the same time as being playful
(let us not underestimate that) and perhaps parodic. Its range of moods
and meanings is extended by the fact that Martial engages with Frontinus
in more than one guise – as a sometime-poet, patron and prominent
statesman. Frontinus' presence does not make a politicised interpretation
inevitable; but signposts within the poem do point us towards that if we
choose to follow them up. Overlaps with several surrounding epigrams
have a similar effect. Given its similarities with 10.51, there has been some
debate about whether or not 10.58 was originally addressed to Faustinus –
or whether Frontinus should be taken as the recipient of both.[64] In fact, the
difference in addressee helps these epigrams to function more effectively as
a pair (and as part of a trilogy with 10.30, which in turn links them to other
cycles of epigrams within Book 10), for the change in personnel enables
Martial to develop their common themes in thought-provoking ways.[65] In
the wake of his appearance in 10.48 and the role that he may play in 10.58,
turning a comparison between past and present into an(other) opportunity to reflect on differences between political eras, Frontinus contrasts
more sharply than he might otherwise have done with Faustinus (who
contrasts also with Apollinaris in 10.30).[66] For while Faustinus belongs
firmly to Martial's literary circle and seems thoroughly committed to a

---

[62] See e.g. Baldwin 1994: 485: 'if Martial's poem is addressed to our man, he seems to have missed a
golden opportunity . . . for neatly pointed flattery by not contrasting the waters near which Frontinus takes his leisure with those to which he devotes his working days.' Cf. White 1975: 295–6
n. 41.

[63] A connoisseur might detect John Henderson's input here.

[64] On the question of 10.58's addressee, see especially White 1975: 295–6 n. 41; Baldwin 1994: 485; Nauta
2002: 55 n. 51; Peachin 2004: 158–9; Balland 2010: 108–14 (the consensus favours Frontinus). On
the possibility (generally discounted) that 10.51 may have been addressed to Frontinus, see Damon
1997: 162 n. 37; Peachin 2004: 158 n. 8.

[65] Balland 2010: 63 sees 10.58 as 'dans une large mesure une *retractatio* de x.51'.

[66] As Mratschek discusses in this volume, the focus of 10.30 – Domitius Apollinaris – was consul in 97,
and (like Frontinus) a useful coordinate for both Martial and Pliny in their respective self-portraits
(and particularly their interactive reflections on *otium/negotium*).

life of cultured leisure,[67] Frontinus figures more as an outsider (in 10.48 he is not one of the epigram's invited poet-guests, but an intrusion from public life into a private party) and as an emerging member of Rome's new governing elite (in 10.58). In conjunction/comparison with both Faustinus and Apollinaris, in other words, Frontinus adds an extra piquancy to a series of epigrams that set out Martial's (growing?) disenchantment with (?especially Nervan/Trajanic) Rome (Frontinus being a more striking Nervan/Trajanic paradigm than Apollinaris was).[68]

As with 10.48, the most controversial aspect of what I am suggesting here is that, as well as engaging with Frontinus the man (in all of his dimensions), 10.58 is also engaging with and responding to some of Frontinus' writing – to the textual Frontinus who survives to this day. (Would it be at all controversial if the text involved were not a 'technical' treatise? Should it be controversial for that reasons?)[69] It may even prompt reflection on the literary phenomenon that Frontinus' *De aquis* represents.[70] For this treatise does not just celebrate Nerva's administrative reforms (and the new scope that they might give to ambitious senators); it also asserts a harmonious and mutually beneficial relationship between writing and public/political life (one that goes beyond the easing of tensions between authors and emperors and the tentative literary revival that we see explored, for instance, in Tacitus' *Agricola*).[71] *De aquis* unites Roman (particularly Livian) historiography, imperial record-keeping, Ciceronian oratory and administrative pamphleteering in one text, in a way which forges constructive connections between literary and civic/political activity. Martial, by contrast, in plotting his (and Frontinus') journey from the learned, leisured Muses to the prosaic maelstrom of civic duty as a narrative of

---

[67] As Nauta 2002: 67 points out, Faustinus (the recipient of nineteen epigrams) 'is never praised for any kind of oratorical, political, or military activity; what does receive attention is his literary production and his life of cultured leisure at his villas'. On Faustinus' role in Martial's epigrams, see also Balland 2010: 39–91, esp. pp. 55–65.

[68] As Mratschek in this volume notes (p. 210), Apollinaris' career seems to have fizzled out with his Nervan (suffect) consulship.

[69] Ancient 'technical' and scientific writing has been re-evaluated from lots of different angles over the last couple of decades (e.g. Nicolet 1995; Meißner 1999; Formisano 2001; Asper 2007; König and Whitmarsh 2007; Fögen 2009; Taub and Doody 2009; Doody, Föllinger and Taub 2012; Formisano and van der Eijk 2017; König and Woolf 2017) and we now have a much better understanding of the internal complexities of some of these texts and their embeddedness in the literary, social and political cultures of their time.

[70] Cf. Geue's comments in this volume (pp. 376–7, 384) on 'generic turf wars' and literary interactivity.

[71] See especially *Aq.* 1–3, where Frontinus' writing is represented as (among other things) a service to the state, because of the role that it plays in teaching Frontinus what he needs to know as *curator aquarum*; also his claim (ibid.) that his other texts have been written for other people's instruction.

literary degeneration, challenges that (just as his – suspiciously? – lees-less wine in 10.48 perhaps raises questions about the artificially cleansed atmosphere of Frontinus' *De aquis*). *Epigrams* 10.58 is not just another variation on the 'Rome-makes-(good)-writing-difficult' theme, in other words, but a fascinating counterpoint to Frontinus' *De aquis* (and other texts written around the same time), which invites reflection on the diversity of contemporary literary (and not-so-literary) activity, and on the variety of stories that could be told about the relationship between literary production and the civic and political world. Like 10.48, its engagement with Frontinus (as both statesman and author) also shines a spotlight on the intricate dynamics and different levels of literary interactivity, and the role played by such interactions (not just individual textual interventions) in the digestion and evolution of contemporary discourse.

Beyond *Epigrams* 10

Martial's interaction with Frontinus does not necessarily stop there: two later epigrams (12.8 and 12.50) contain suggestive nuggets. Indeed, *Epigrams* 12.8 opens with a pair of verses that closely recall *De aquis* 88.1, where Frontinus rejoices that Rome, 'the queen and mistress of the world, who is goddess of the lands (*quae terrarum dea consistit*), and to whom there is no equal and no second (*cui par nihil et nihil secundum*), senses the care of her most devoted emperor and prince Nerva each day':

> Terrarum dea gentiumque Roma,
> cui par est nihil et nihil secundum,
> Traiani modo laeta cum futuros
> tot per saecula computaret annos,
> et fortem iuuenemque Martiumque
> in tanto duce militem uideret,
> dixit praeside gloriosa tali:
> 'Parthorum proceres ducesque Serum,
> Thraces, Sauromatae, Getae, Britanni,
> possum ostendere Caesarem; uenite.'
> (*Epig.* 12.8)

When Rome, goddess of the globe and its peoples – who has no equal, and no inferior that comes close – was joyfully counting out Trajan's future years and could see in such a great leader a brave, youthful and Mars-like soldier, she said (revelling in this splendid ruler): 'Nobles of Parthia, leaders of the Seres, Thracians, Sarmatians, Getans, Britons, I can show you a Caesar: come!'

Most commentators assume that, rather than this being a case of Martial borrowing from Frontinus (or vice versa), the phrases in question were interpolated into the *De aquis* from Martial by a later editor (the favourite candidate being the mediaeval copyist Peter the Deacon).[72] That theory is prompted by the difficulty readers tend to have in accepting that the author of a practical, administrative work might have shown some occasional poetic flair (as the scholar Justus Lipsius put it in 1598, 'the sober and learned pen of Frontinus does not approve of or like the playfulness of poets'),[73] and also by an assumption that Martial and his consumers were unlikely to be closely acquainted with a text like the *De aquis*. My readings of 10.48 and 10.58 have argued otherwise, and invite us to test out the possibility that we have here another instance either of Frontinus echoing Martial or (more likely, given the publication dates)[74] of Martial reusing a phrase from Frontinus, in the expectation, presumably, that his readers would recognise it.

Connection with Frontinus' *De aquis* potentially loads 12.8 with new layers of meaning. Standing alone, it looks ahead (optimistically: *laeta*; proudly: *gloriosa* – or crowingly, even?) near the start of Trajan's reign to what his principate may bring. In characterising him primarily as a soldier-emperor (vv. 5–6), its boast to the chieftains of Parthia, Serica and other far-flung places particularly conjures up the prospect of great military campaigns and conquests. Association with *De aquis* 88.1, however, deploys other aspects of the regime's propaganda by pointing us back to some of its founding rhetoric (Nerva's diligent and patriotic concern for civic reform, which was often contrasted with Flavian mismanagement and corruption).[75] In their allusion to the *De aquis* (if allusion it is), the epigram's opening verses thus extend the scope of our look at Trajan, not just by setting one (military) picture of him alongside a different (civic) feature of his imperial persona, but also by turning our thoughts to the origins of his principate, as well as its potential destination. 12.8's echo of (or borrowing from?) Frontinus may even prompt reflection on the very evolution of imperial imagery – and the role that texts (and interactions) themselves play in it. By transporting us from one laudatory text to another and back again, 12.8.1–2 draws attention to the power that literature and literary dialogue has, to shape (and complicate) a reader's view of the emperor.

---

[72] E.g. Rodgers 2004 ad loc.; Dederich 1839: 108–9.   [73] Lipsius 1598: 1.2.

[74] Kappelmacher 1916: 183–5; Grimal 1944: 89; González Rolán 1985: ix–x and 59–60; Nauta 2002: 55, n. 51; Peachin 2004: 156–7.

[75] Cf. Plin. *Pan.* 62.2 on the senatorial committee that Nerva had set up to look into (or at least parade the need for) financial economies (Syme 1930).

Epigrams 12.50 potentially complicates our picture of Trajan – or at least Trajanic times – further. Across Martial's corpus, poems apparently in praise of the emperor are accompanied by others that seem to muddy the waters.[76] 11.7, for instance, contrasts the days of Domitian (when the emperor's depravities could provide a handy cover for a wanton woman) with Nerva's reign ('under the emperor Nerva, you may be a Penelope', 4–5).[77] But, in pointing out that its addressee does not want to reform – Paula is still lustfully promiscuous, despite the demise of her Domitianic excuse – it draws attention to a continuity of vice that cuts against the moral change that Nerva's accession is supposed to herald.[78] *Epigrams* 12.50 is not obviously in the same category. It makes no mention of the emperor himself, or of the times in which it is set; rather, it satirises a private villa for its impractical extravagance. But in describing the sound, everywhere, of streams of water going to waste (*et pereuntis aquae fluctus ubique sonat*, 12.50.6) it uses a phrase that resembles one in that section of the *De aquis* where Frontinus celebrates the transformative impact of Nerva's 'diligent' reforms – in this instance, the fact that not even waste waters go to waste: *ne pereuntes quidem aquae otiosae sunt* (*Aq.* 88.3). Striking though that phrase is, it may be a coincidence.[79] Even so, in recalling (however deliberately/accidentally) that particular chapter of the *De aquis*, it evokes not just Frontinus' praise of Nerva but also *Epigrams* 12.8, where our view of Trajan is expanded by it. In so doing, in investing Martial's description of a rich man's property with a faint political twist, it invites comparison between Nervan/Trajanic rhetoric and the reality behind it. Indeed, like *Epigrams* 11.7, it may prompt readers to reflect on the fact that, despite the new regime's thrifty providence (and despite Frontinus' *De aquis*), private (Domitianic-style?) profligacy still persists.[80] Indeed, it may draw wry attention to the fact that Frontinus' *De aquis* has not been being read widely or carefully enough – a tongue-in-cheek recommendation to his readers, perhaps, to acquaint themselves better with (the whole of) that work (not least its final chapter, *Aq.* 130, where Frontinus promises imperial retribution to those who flout the regulations).

---

[76] A point often made: e.g. Garthwaite 1990, 1993 and 2009: 422–6; Boyle 1995b: 97–8; Fearnley 2003: 620–1; Delignon 2008: 459–62 and n. 43; Wolff 2009. Cf. Lorenz 2002 for a sceptical response.

[77] On 11.7, see Fitzgerald in this volume (pp. 122–5).

[78] Ruth Morello's chapter below (focusing on 11.5, in conjunction with Pliny 8.6) offers a particularly rich analysis of the ways in which *Epigrams* 11 gets us looking afresh at political eras and the difference between past and present.

[79] The other obvious intertext for Martial here is Ov. *Am.* 2.15.24. I hesitate to suggest that Frontinus had this in mind when penning *Aq.* 88.3 . . .

[80] Cf. Delignon 2008: 458, who is adamant that Martial does not invite readers to see public/political subtexts in epigrams about private vice.

Martial's engagement with Frontinus in 10.48 and 10.58 potentially enriches other epigrams beyond the scope of his tenth book, then, helping him to trigger various political as well as social reflections, and to sharpen his self-positioning along the way. It must also have impacted on (and not just engaged with) Frontinus' self-positioning: by cementing (not just exploiting) his reputation as a model Nervan/Trajanic statesman; but also by nuancing readers' responses to the statesman and some of his writing, by contextualising and interrogating some of the claims that the *De aquis* makes. Indeed, it may – in loose dialogue with Tacitus' *Agricola* – perform on Frontinus what Ilaria Marchesi calls an 'overdetermination of [the author] as a cultural object', with new ideas about what 'Frontinus' and his writings signify arising out of these interlocking engagements with him.[81] In the process, it underscores the embeddedness of literary (inter)activity within a wider web of personal, social, intellectual and political interactions. And it reminds us that Martial's literary interactions and interests ranged well beyond the world of verse, crossing genre boundaries – and that he expected his readers to do likewise. It also raises questions about the profile and status of Frontinus' *De aquis* and texts like it. Just how widely read was it? And how marginal or pivotal a reference-point did it (not just its author) become for other authors attempting to make sense of the times? Where in the literary scheme of things was it thought to sit? In what literary light did Frontinus, Martial and their contemporaries regard it (where does administrative writing stop and 'literature' start?), and did literary interactions play a part in determining the (inevitably fluctuating) answer to that question?[82]

The indirect nature of Martial's interactions with the *De aquis* – the absence of explicit textual allusions and his engagement with Frontinus as an acquaintance/statesman first and foremost – raises other questions. What intertextual habits did Martial anticipate/play to in his (various circles of) readers? *Do* his verses point us beyond the consul/patron to his (now celebrated) aqueduct treatise, or does the temptation to go there only arise in certain kinds of (particularly modern?) readers? Have I overdetermined 'Frontinus' as a literary coordinate?[83] And (especially given that uncertainty) how instructive/distorting is it to insist on reading *Epigrams*

---

[81] See Marchesi on Lucan 'between Martial and Pliny' in this volume, p. 352.

[82] As Chris Whitton has pointed out to me (pers. comm.), Pliny – like Martial – makes little if any reference to Frontinus (or indeed Quintilian) *as an author*, which contrasts with his approach to Tacitus; so did genre (historiography vs 'technical' writing) matter after all?

[83] Geue (below, p. 368, with reference to Marchesi and Whitton) sounds an important note of caution: 'the hint of an "actual relationship" can act as unfairly stout hermeneutic scaffolding to prop up flimsy intertextual latticework'.

10 with the *De aquis* in mind? In particular, might excessive reference to Frontinus' treatise lead to political over-interpretation? Those questions are unanswerable, but worth asking nonetheless. Indeed, that is the point of this chapter: it squeezes out the connections and possible cross-fertilisations between Martial and Frontinus, personal and textual, in order to probe some of the dynamics of literary interaction during Nerva's brief principate and the dilemmas that we face in analysing them as temporally and culturally removed readers.

CHAPTER II

Saturninus the Helmsman, Pliny and Friends
Legal and Literary Letter Collections

Jill Harries

Late in the reign of Trajan, the tenth book of Pliny's *Letters* was launched into circulation at Rome, celebrating the 'friendship' of Pliny and his emperor. The bulk of this collection covered various aspects of Pliny's controversial governorship of Bithynia, including matters of law and finance. Modern scholarly familiarity with Pliny's travails in his province has perhaps obscured the unique quality of the correspondence. The style is concise, business-like and to the point, and the frequent occurrence of paired letters, covering a single subject and consisting of questions from Pliny, arising from his governorship, and answers from Trajan, is unusual, if not unique, in the literary epistolary tradition.

As Myles Lavan shows in the following chapter, the focus on a single subject is consistent with the functioning of imperial correspondence in general. There was, however, another precedent. Pliny numbered many legal experts (*iuris periti*, *iuris consulti*) among his correspondents and would have known that several had published voluminous collections, which they entitled *Epistulae*. These consisted of requests for advice on matters of legal interpretation from their clients, paired with their learned responses. These usually brief exchanges were confined to the matter under discussion and devoid of stylistic ornamentation, in line with the conventions operative in juristic technical discourse. Nor were they merely academic, or even pedagogic, exercises. The legal opinions of eminent jurists could be cited in court cases, and were therefore of practical use both to their recipients and to other readers of the collections. Moreover, the lawyers were also players in the great game of senatorial politics; their collections, like those of Pliny, advertised their networks of clients and friends.

From Pliny's standpoint, the existence of these collections posed challenges but also opportunities for new experiments in literary interaction. Juristic literature was a technical discourse, which avoided literary pretension – yet collections of *Epistulae* were a recognised literary genre. This was a genre that Pliny had made his own, with every letter designed as a literary production. Pliny was also aware that assertions of cultural superiority reinforced political clout. The challenge posed to Pliny by the lawyers was that they represented themselves as patrons and controllers of legal knowledge – and combined their assertion of the power of knowledge with claims to be men of culture as well. This last, as we shall see, was a claim that Pliny was not prepared to concede.[1] In exploring the possibility – and it must be admitted that the connections are speculative – that Pliny engaged in competitive dialogue with the lawyers' collections and that they, in their turn (and still more speculatively, as the texts are fragmentary), accrued cultural capital by comparison and even interaction with his earlier books, we will be able to see the process feed into a wider network of social and political interaction that went to the heart – and the top – of Roman administrative culture.

With what, then, did Pliny interact in his own Book 10? No complete book of lawyer's letters survives and the overall strategy employed by their authors in their compilation must remain a mystery; we cannot therefore assess the extent of selectivity or repetition, features carefully avoided in the Plinian collection. The texts are to be found, in fragmentary and much corrupted form, in Justinian's *Digest of Roman law*, a compilation of extracts from the classical Roman jurists issued in AD 533. In the *Digest*, where material was arranged by topic, not author, the individual identities of the long-dead 'contributors' were subsumed by the overall purpose of the compilation, to serve as a teaching book and a reference book for lawyers in courtrooms. In the 1880s the German scholar Otto Lenel reassembled the juristic fragments and other testimonia to create a *Palingenesia* of legal authors, thus enabling them to be read in terms of authorial style and agendas.[2] For this reason, it is Lenel, not the *Digest*, who is the sourcebook for what follows, although *Digest* referencing will be used, in accordance with general convention.

The *Digest*'s referencing system included the titles of the works from which the extracts were drawn (e.g. Javolenus, *Epistulae* 11); this, as we shall see, is crucial for the identification of many extracts as letters in the first place. The *Digest* reveals the existence of books of *Epistulae*, by lawyers from the time of Augustus to the mid second century, when they seem to have abandoned the letter form as redundant for their purposes.[3] Many

---

[1] This chapter accepts recent arguments, discussed by Lavan in this volume (pp. 282–4), that Pliny, not his executor, was the editor of Book 10.

[2] Lenel 1889.

[3] The earliest known jurist-author of *Epistulae* is Antistius Labeo, praetor under Augustus, whose *Epistulae* (number of books uncertain) are cited at *Dig.* 41.3.30.1; cf. also Gell. *NA* 13.13.2 (correspondence

such citations from letter collections are at second hand, incorporated by later writers to demonstrate the workings of the legal tradition; these were printed by Lenel in italics. However, even those texts which purport to derive verbatim from a first- or early second-century author were reworked at various points unknown over the succeeding centuries, either by the authors themselves or at a later stage in the transmission of the text, prior to its incorporation in the *Digest*.[4] These problems with textual transmission, as we shall see, affect our ability to identify letters not explicitly referenced as such.

Saturninus the Helmsman

Lawyers provided their own window on Roman life. Our first exchange derives from the eleventh book in a collection of *Epistulae* compiled by Pliny's distinguished older contemporary, Javolenus Priscus (consul in 86):[5]

> *Anonymus/a* [we do not know the writer's name][6] *to his/her friend Priscus greetings* (*Anonymus/a Prisco suo salutem*),

> [Seius] Saturninus the chief helmsman from the British fleet left in his will an inheritance in trust to his heir-executor Valerius Maximus, the ship's captain, whom he requested to restore the inheritance to his son [Seius] Oceanus, when he had reached the age of sixteen. [Seius] Oceanus, before he reached the stated age, died; now one Mallius Seneca, who says he is the uncle of [Seius] Oceanus, is claiming these goods on the grounds of close kinship, but Maximus the ship's captain claims them for himself, because the person to whom he had been instructed to restore the property is now deceased. [I ask therefore:] Do these goods belong to Valerius Maximus the captain and heir in trust or to Mallius Seneca, who says he is the uncle of the dead boy?

> *Priscus to his friend Anonymus/a greeting* (*Priscus Anonymo/ae suo/ae salutem*):

> [I replied:] If [Seius] Oceanus, to whom the inheritance left in trust by the will of [Seius] Saturninus should have been restored when he reached the age of sixteen by Valerius Maximus, the heir in trust, then died before he had reached that term of his age, the inheritance held in trust belongs

---

between Labeo and Ateius Capito, consul AD 5). The second is Proculus (eleven or more books), who probably flourished under Nero and the Flavians and was credited in the second century with being the leader of one of Rome's two rival law schools. His precise dates (and other names) are uncertain.

4 The extent of editorial intervention by Justinian's lawyers is controversial; my view (which I believe is that of modern legal scholars in general) is that hypotheses of interpolations by the compilers should be rejected, unless there is incontrovertible evidence for their existence.

5 My suggested restorations are offered in italics and later additions bracketed.

6 For a letter by Rutilia Polla raising a query on land rights, see *Dig.* 18.1.69.

to the person to whom the rest of Oceanus' estate belongs . . . [grounds for decision are highly technical][7]

The text supplied above features some minor but significant departures from the version in the *Digest*. The most important of these, the restoration in italics of the epistolary greetings formula, not present in the text as we have it, is justified by the source reference to *Epistulae* 11 supplied by the *Digest* compilers: one characteristic of letters is that they are headed by a greeting from the sender to the recipient and there is no reason to assume that these were, in their original form, exceptional. The square bracketing of 'I asked, therefore' and 'I replied', and of the nomen Seius reflects probable modifications by later jurists, who adapted the original letter form to the Q&A format of the *quaestio*, the question-form used in problem literature; and who had a professional liking for Seius as an imaginary character (the modern lawyers' equivalent is John Doe) used for purposes of case discussion.

The exchange on Saturninus' will reflects the austerity of juristic culture. There are no literary flourishes; the relevant facts of the case and the Anonymous' options, as s/he saw them, are presented for Priscus' opinion. The use of *nunc* ('now') and the present tenses show the case is under current consideration. Priscus' opinion could be no more than advisory but, given his standing as an ex-consul, would be potentially decisive, if cited before an adjudicator. The Anonymous had, or should have had, reservations about the claims of Mallius, whose name suggests an uncle on the mother's side; despite his allegations of *proximitas*, he would have had little claim under the laws of intestate succession, which favoured claimants descended from a common male ancestor (*agnatus*). Priscus, however, simplified matters by dismissing both claims in favour of the (unknown) owner of the rest of Oceanus' property.

For lawyers, this is the end of the story. But Javolenus chose to present this exchange as an element in a dossier of correspondence, issued by a man of political as well as legal distinction. He and his fellow lawyers

---

[7] *Dig.* 36.1.48 (greetings formula not in the Latin not included) *Seius Saturninus archigubernus ex classe Britannica testamento fiduciarium reliquit heredem Valerium Maximum trierarchum, quo petit, ut filio suo Seio Oceano, cum ad annos sedecim peruenisset, hereditatem restitueret. Seius Oceanus antequam impleret annos, defunctus est; nunc Mallius Seneca, qui se auunculum Seii Oceani dicit, proximitatis nomine haec bona petit, Maximus autem trierarchus sibi se uindicat, ideo quia defunctus est is cui restituere iussus erat. [Quaero ergo] utrum haec bona ad Valerium Maximum trierarchum heredem fiduciarium pertineant an ad Mallium Senecam, qui se pueri defuncti auunculum esse dicit. [Respondi] si Seius Oceanus, cui fideicommissa hereditas ex testamento Seii Saturni, cum annos sedecim haberet, a Valerio Maximo fiduciario herede restitui debeat, priusquam praefinitum tempus aetatis impleret, decessit, fiduciaria hereditas ad eum pertinet, ad quem cetera bona Oceani pertinuerint . . .*

chose to label their collections as *Epistulae*, thus asserting their place in an established literary genre and challenging comparison with the likes of Pliny (and, previously, Cicero). On what literary grounds, therefore, can the lawyers' letter collections be viewed as akin to the *Epistulae* of Pliny?

Lawyers' Letters and the Younger Pliny

As Roy Gibson stated in his analysis of how a 'letter' should be recognised: 'often the epistolary character of an individual text is guaranteed by its place within a larger group of epistolary texts, such as a letter collection . . . The importance of the letter collection, then, to guiding the reader as to the need to read its constituent texts as letters cannot be [over]estimated.'[8] It follows that if lawyers chose to publish work as *Epistulae*, they intended to signal some kind of generic identity with other letter collections – and that the authors of other published *Epistulae* may also have interacted with them. Nor should an element of competition be ruled out. Whatever the dates of publication of Pliny's books of *Epistulae*, they postdate those of Proculus (mid to late first century AD) and Priscus, and perhaps those of Juventius Celsus as well.[9] Pliny, therefore, would have been aware of their work when publishing his own. Indeed, if they had given public readings of their work, Pliny, an habitué of such events, could well have attended them.

Lawyers' letters did not count as letters only because they were collected and labelled as such. Criteria suggested by modern scholars for what a letter should consist of include that it is a written message from one person or group to another, which must be set down in a material form and conveyed from sender to recipient, who are physically separate and distanced from each other. Its identity as a 'letter' is signalled by the inclusion of a greeting formula and it will normally be of relatively limited length.[10] Literary variants, where the letter form is also exploited for didactic purposes, include Horace's *Epistles*,[11] Seneca's *Epistulae morales* and, in the sense that his son, absent in Athens, is the addressee, though not formally greeted, Cicero's *De officiis*. A 'letter' does not require an answer, although the point of the lawyers' collections, like most of Pliny's dealings with Trajan in *Epistles* 10,

---

[8] Gibson and Morrison 2007: 15–16.
[9] Juventius Celsus the Younger was consul II in 129 but the *Letters* are an earlier work, as some were later incorporated into his *Digest*.
[10] Trapp 2003: 1; Gibson and Morrison 2007: 3–13. One problem with identifying lawyers' letters not referenced as *Epistulae* is that the greetings formula was one of the first elements to be left out.
[11] Morrison 2007: 107–31.

is that there was an exchange of question and answer. The first of the pair, who initiates the exchange, seeks information, advice or guidance. Unlike, therefore, didactic letters, which are the product of the initiating, and often sole, writer, the advantage of status is conceded by the seeker of knowledge or advice to the respondent, who is able, by helping him or her, also to confer a *beneficium*.

The lawyers' letters of the latter part of the first century AD and the first part of the second, which can be clearly identified as such, fulfil all or most of the above criteria. The parties to an exchange are named or an exchange can be inferred, the letters were (presumably) conveyed from one to the other, the formula of greeting (X to Y *salutem*) would have been standard, even when, as is usually the case, it has not survived, because of the problems of transmission to be discussed below.[12] The letters are often (though not invariably) distinguished by their brevity and, unlike the bulk of Pliny's efforts, their lack of literary pretension. Moreover, like the collections of legal *Quaestiones* and *Responsa*, associated by the legal historian F. Schulz with *Epistulae* as 'problematic literature', the letters were circulated with a view to educating readers in legal problems and their solutions, as well as enhancing the authority of the writer. They may also have had an open-ended quality; these exchanges were a conversation that could be continued indefinitely.[13] But although *Epistulae* served the same didactic purpose as did lawyers' collections of questions (*Quaestiones*) and answers (*Responsa*), the choice to publish Q&As as *Epistulae* offered a different signal to readers.[14] In other words, authors of lawyers' *Epistulae* were to be seen as, somehow, 'like' Pliny – but did Pliny want to be seen as 'like' them?

The centrality of the exchange format also affects how the two parties to a correspondence were expected to interact in terms of status. David Langslow has suggested, with reference to *epistulae* in scientific and technical literature, that 'the sender is never the less knowledgeable party' (though he may pretend to be).[15] This was the reverse of the case with lawyers. The lawyers' clients who initiated an exchange were, by definition, the less knowledgeable; they hoped to profit from the respondent's expertise. In these exchanges, therefore, the second sender, the respondent, was the expert – the same relationship that was conceded by implication to Trajan by Pliny, as governor of Bithynia, in his *Epistulae* 10. In a different

---

[12] Note the divergence from the language employed by Pliny and Trajan, with their use of *carissime* ('very dear') and *domine*, discussed by Lavan in this volume, pp. 288–94.

[13] Oikonomopoulou 2013: 129–53; Jacob 2004: 25–54.

[14] Though note Varro's confusing of genres with his *Quaestiones epistolicae*, as recorded by Aulus Gellius.

[15] Langslow 2007: 226.

category, however, were the exchanges between lawyers of equal expertise on points of technical interest: Aristo, Neratius Priscus and Iuventius Celsus exchanged questions and answers with each other for their own satisfaction and on terms of equality, as a means of clarifying their own thinking on disputed points.[16] And of course it helped to have a lawyer in the family, hence Neratius' response to a question from his brother Marcellus.[17]

Within a few decades of Pliny's death, the epistolary format had outlived its usefulness for lawyers. For a while, such collections commanded respect: Javolenus' pupil, the jurist Salvius Julianus (consul in 148), cited an opinion from the twentieth book of the *Letters* of Caecilius Africanus, who was also admired by Aulus Gellius.[18] And the last lawyer to exploit the *epistula* form, the long-lived Hadrianic and Antonine academic jurist, Pomponius, was perhaps the most inventive in his use of the genre, expanding the scope of the lawyer-letter (in at least twelve and perhaps twenty books) to cover imaginary cases and importing the occasional literary flourish, to make his text more attractive to a non-expert readership.[19]

Problems of Transmission

To label a collection as *Epistulae*, then, was to make a literary statement. But later generations of jurists prioritised the technical aspects of their discipline at the expense of such literary merit as their original authors might have claimed for themselves. The fragmentary state of juristic writing in general can be blamed on the editorial depredations of Justinian's compilers (to whom we also owe it that we have the texts at all), but, in the case of the letter collections, the material with which Justinian's people worked had already suffered significant modification in previous centuries. Later generations of lawyers, who transmitted but also discreetly revised the work of their predecessors, often for teaching as well as general advisory purposes, were not interested in the preservation of the letter form, preferring to record questions and answers on legal matters under the all-embracing and more specifically 'lawyerly' *quaestiones* (questions) or *responsa* (replies).[20] In

---

[16] *Dig.* 2.14.7.2, Aristo to Celsus; *Dig.* 19.2.19.2, Neratius to Aristo; *Dig.* 20.3.3, Aristo to Neratius.

[17] *Dig.* 33.7.12.43.

[18] *Dig.* 40.2.5: Salvius Julianus (*Dig.* 42) refers to Javolenus' practice in Africa and Syria, describing him as his *praeceptor*; *Dig.* 30.39.*pr.*, where Ulpian (*Ad Sabinum* 21) cites Julianus' citation; he had not seen the Africanus original. Also Gell. *NA* 20.1.

[19] *Dig.* 35.1.110; 40.4.61; 40.5.20 (letter as literary form, with Greek quotation about his enthusiasm for learning keeping him alive at 78 years of age).

[20] Cf. *Dig.* 46.3.94.3 (Papinian, *Quaestiones* 8), the Severan jurist Papinian's citation of a letter from one Fabius Januarius with the greeting preserved; the text is then modified with the substitution of

order to suppress the 'epistolary' character of the citation, they employed a number of devices, which are evidenced in the Saturninus letter with which we began: deletion of the greeting (X to Y *suo/ae salutem*); omission of the 'question' part of the exchange, leaving only the answer as Y replied (*respondit*) to X; and reframing the dialogue as self-referential, with the author providing both question (*quaero*, 'I ask') and answer (*respondi*, 'I replied'). In addition, the Saturninus letter may have been modified for teaching or generalist purposes by the insertion of a standard juristic imaginary family *nomen*, Seius (although the non-juristic *cognomina* Saturninus and Oceanus, and Mallius Seneca, survived intact). As David Langslow has commented, with reference to dedicatory letters on scientific and technical literature, 'a letter can become anything by trimming in the process of transmission. This has off-putting implications for one setting out to collect a corpus of letters on a given subject.'[21]

Problems of revision by the original author and then successor jurists abound. P. Juventius Celsus provides salutary examples of how the existence of a consultation initiated and responded to by letter can be identified, even when the formal greeting has been edited out. As reported by Ulpian in the second decade of the third century, Celsus commented on contracts with minors 'not inappropriately' in two places, the eleventh book of *Epistulae* and the second of his *Digesta*.[22] The two are the same: Celsus had incorporated his earlier *Epistulae* into his *Digesta* and modified the format accordingly. The initiator of the consultation was the praetor Flavius Respectus, whose question is supplied in Ulpian's paraphrase; then 'Celsus said to Respectus' – and the *responsum* is duly supplied. But at no point are greeting formulae used; they have been deleted as irrelevant to the main purpose, the statement of the point of law.

Ulpian provides further illustration of the processes of adaptation, with reference to two cases, both recorded in Celsus, *Digesta* 7, but lacking explicit reference to his *Epistulae*. Here the indicator of an epistolary exchange, namely the presence of real names involved with real, rather than hypothetical or general, cases, is one that must be used with care; there were means of 'responding' other than by letter. The first case does mention a letter: in a paraphrase, Ulpian states that Celsus dealt with a problem

---

fictitious names Titius and Gaius Seius for the originals and the fiction of the jurist asking (*quaero*) and answering (*respondi*) in the first person.

[21] Langslow 2007: 212. See also Schulz 1946: 224 'many of the *responsa* in our collections may thus have been given by letter, although the epistolary form has been expunged'.

[22] *Dig.* 4.4.3.1 (Ulpian, *On the edict* 11) *Vnde non ineleganter Celsus Epistularum libro undecimo et Digestorum secundo tractat, ex facto a Flauio Respecto praetore consultus . . . Celsus igitur Respecto dixit . . .*

concerning partnership, with reference to a letter from Cornelius Felix, suggesting that in the original text, Celsus drew on his *Epistulae* collection.[23]
Secondly, on mandate, Celsus, as reported by Ulpian, stated that he had
offered a *responsum* to one Aurelius Quietus, who had experienced a problem with his personal physician, concerning unauthorised building in his
gardens at Ravenna. Although reference to the letter form is lacking, the
case is brought by a named individual with a personal and specific problem; Celsus' *Digesta* plays down the original prompt, which was probably
a letter from Quietus, originally preserved and published as such in Celsus'
Epistulae, along with Celsus' reply.[24]

It may be helpful to list various modes of epistolary survival, using
Proculus, who may not have survived till Nerva's reign but was the author
of eleven books of letters (at least) directly cited by the *Digest*, Javolenus
Priscus and, again, the versatile Celsus. The Justinianic *Epistulae* referencing of Proculus and Priscus (showing that, whatever they seem now, these
texts were letters once) allows some certainty as to the modes of modification employed, although not, for certain, their date or their extent. In
citations from Javolenus' fourteen books of *Epistulae*, the letter form has
almost entirely disappeared and is identifiable only from the reference.

The vicissitudes, therefore, of the survival of the lawyers' letters may be
categorised (as lawyers loved to do) in ascending order of modification, as
follows:

1.   The primary text in the *Epistulae* exchange would have contained
     the greetings formulae from both, a question in the first letter and
     an answer in the second. Closest to the originals, therefore, are texts
     where greetings are preserved from one or both parties, although there
     may be other evidence of interference.[25] A few lawyers' letters sur-
     vived with their greetings formulae intact. The Flavian lawyer Proculus
     exchanges greetings with clients or friends named as Nepos, Licinnius
     Lucusta and Atilicinus;[26] and, perhaps the last lawyer to publish *Epis-
     tulae*, the Hadrianic academic jurist, Pomponius, recorded a salutation
     from one Junius Diophantus and his own response – 'I instructed him'

---

[23] *Dig.* 17.2.58.*pr.* and 1 (Ulpian, *On the edict* 31) *Tractatum ita est apud Celsum libro septimo Digestorum
ad epistulam Corneli Felicis.*

[24] *Dig.* 17.1.16 *Ait Celsus . . . hoc respondisse se, cum Aurelius Quietus hospiti suo medico . . . in hortis eius
quos Rauennae habebat . . .*

[25] *Dig.* 23.4.17 *Atilicinus Proculo suo salutem . . . respondit* (move from greetings form to third-person
reply form).

[26] *Dig.* 50.16.125 *Nepos Proculo suo salutem; Dig.* 23.3.67 *Proculus Nepoti suo salutem* (on a different
case); *Dig.* 31.48 *Licinius Lucusta Proculo suo salutem . . . Proculus Lucustae suo salutem; Dig.* 23.4.17
Atilicinus Proculo suo salutem . . . Proculus respondit [sic].

(*didici*).[27] Other exchanges, involving Aristo's friend Neratius Priscus, are described in terms of *responsa*, but can be identified as *Epistulae* from the referencing by Ulpian as an intermediary, or by Justinian.[28]

2. No greeting survives (this applies to all following categories) but the text retains the use of first and second person, individuals and places are named, and the case is specific. On an appeal against the inappropriate construction by a named individual, Hiberus, of plumbing for baths against a party wall, Proculus is asked both for his opinion, which he supplies with a citation from an earlier jurist and creative use of analogy, and for his personal intervention with Hiberus: 'I therefore ask that you should speak with Hiberus to prevent him doing this unlawful thing.'[29] Proculus, therefore, was required to do more than provide advice; as a patron of his (unnamed) correspondent, he was expected to intervene actively and use his *auctoritas* on his client's behalf to protect his interests. Another anonymous enquiry concerned a land purchase by a named person, Rutilia Polla.[30] This consisted of a lake, the Sabatensis Angularis, and a band of land ten feet wide around it: what happened if the lake 'expanded'? Could she have an extra ten feet in addition to the submerged land? (The answer was no.) The text as we have it appears to be an enquiry on behalf of Rutilia, perhaps by her agent, but it is possible that the original letter, prior to textual tampering, may have originated with Rutilia herself.

3. The case was originally specific and not hypothetical but the names have been wholly or partially edited out (along with the greetings, as usual) to make the text of general application. Celsus' *Digesta*, as we have seen, contained letters from his published *Epistulae* collection reworked as general cases. One such was the will of 'a certain person' (*quidam*), which left an unspecified sum of money to a real place, the *res publica* of the Graviscani, for supervision of repairs to the town's road connecting it with the Via Aurelia. The 'question was' (*quaesitum est*) whether the will was valid, as no sum was specified. 'Iuventius Celsus replied' that the amount could be assessed in terms of what the job required, unless this was incompatible with the size of the *testatrix*' estate, in which case the amount could be assessed by a judge. The

---

[27] *Dig.* 4.4.50 *Iunius Diophantus Pomponio suo salutem.*

[28] *Dig.* 19.2.19.2 *Est epistula Nerati ad Aristonem*; on farm tools, the subject of the correspondence, see also Plin. *Ep.* 3.19.7. Both *Dig.* 33.7.12.35 *Neratius Rufino respondit* and *Dig.* 33.7.12.43 *Neratius Marcello fratri respondit* are ascribed by Ulpian (*Ad Sabinum* 20) to Neratius, *Epistulae* 4. On various Neratii Prisci, see Syme 1957; Camodeca 2007.

[29] *Dig.* 8.2.13 *Qua de re uolo cum Hibero loquaris, ne rem illicitam faciat.*

[30] *Dig.* 18.1.69.

key word is *testatrix*. Although at some point a redactor of the text substituted the gender-neutral *quidam* (rather than *quaedam*) for the name of the Anonyma at the start of the extract, his failure to follow through by substituting *testator* for *testatrix* allows us, still, to perceive a real woman patron of her community generously, if erratically, at work.[31] And the *testatrix* is unlikely to be the only female, information on whose gender has been removed from the record by the substitution of the all-purpose *quidam*; the involvement of women, therefore, in the creation of case law may be seriously understated in the sources.

4.   The opinion and the question are framed in hypothetical, general terms, signalled by the use of standard fictitious names, such as Titius/a, Seius/a. (This device allowed the creation of numerous family relationships, with legal implications; thus Titius could be married to Seia (but not Titia, who would be his daughter, paternal aunt or niece); Seia's father would be Seius but her mother might be Maevia, with a brother called Maevius married to a lady called Attia and so on. Titius, Seius or Maevius may also have owned slaves called Damas or Sticho.) In these documents, there is no named questioner or greeting. The letter form, the author of the question and all details of the names and people involved have been deleted or reworked in general terms.

5.   An opinion is offered in 'response' to a question. There were a variety of forms, already discussed, of question and answer and who is represented as posing the question. An exchange in Proculus, *Epistulae* 2 discussed a possibly hypothetical question from a now anonymous correspondent. 'I ask' what happens if a wild boar falls into a trap, which 'you' have set for that purpose, but 'I' released him and carried him off. Is he 'yours'? Did 'I' steal him? And if 'I' then released him in a wood, what action (lawsuit) could you use against 'me'? 'He' (Proculus) responded that the answer depended on the circumstances, such as whether the land where the trap was set was public or private, 'my' land or another's, did 'I' have permission to set the trap and so on, although Proculus' general conclusion was that if 'I' have caught and secured the boar he is my property and so 'I' can sue. The switch from

---

[31] *Dig.* 31.30. Possibly two stages of intervention (at least) here. Lenel opined that the reference to the size of the estate and referral to a judge was a later interpolation, ascribed to Tribonian. If this was a later gloss (but not necessarily Justinianic), the use of *testatrix* must pre-date the modification of the woman's name (or *quaedam*) to *quidam*, as the gender of the benefactress would not otherwise be ascertainable from the main text. Compare Paul's revision of his *Decreta* as *Sententiae* (early third century AD): in *Decreta* 1 (*Dig.* 37.14.24) Camilla Pia appeals from Hermogenes (the judge), but as reworked in the *Sententiae* (*Dig.* 10.2.41), the case is general, 'a certain woman had appealed from a judge' (*quaedam mulier ab iudice appellauerat*).

the first person ('I ask') to the third person ('he answered') signifies minor textual corruption. The identity of the original questioner has been subsumed by the lawyers' imperative to focus on the case, rather than the form of the original text.

6. An opinion survives in isolation and there is no evidence that it derives from a letter, other than the book reference. For example, Priscus ruled on a status case concerning a named individual, Statius Primus; his decision was extracted, without the question or supporting material, from his *Epistulae* 12.[32]

Such were the hazards confronting the survival of lawyers' letters and their transmission to posterity. Aside from Justinian's agenda of systematisation, which consigned texts not included in the *Digest* to official oblivion, it was lawyers themselves who subverted the integrity of their *Epistulae* as a distinctive genre. At the time of their publication, the authors of lawyers' *Epistulae* were engaged in an exercise of self-promotion; not only were their learning and authority on display but also the extent of their friendships and the social importance of the problems on which they were consulted. Those who cited the contents of *Epistulae* later, however, were interested, not in the political or social prestige of individual jurists, but in the vitality of the legal tradition as a professional discipline. While some later adaptors respected the wording of the texts transmitted to them, there was no obligation on them to do so. Greetings formulae disappeared; the recording of the names of those whose letters had raised questions became a matter of chance; the context in which a *responsum* was issued was excluded as irrelevant. Even the character of legal *Epistulae* as a two-way exchange was subverted; in the last decades, in which collections of lawyers' letters could be advertised as a distinct genre, Pomponius' letters discuss hypothetical cases for which no initial epistolary prompt was required.[33]

It follows that, due to the problems of textual transmission, the general criteria outlined above for identifying 'letters' require modification. Texts deriving from collections referenced in Justinian's *Digest* as *Epistulae* were letters once but may no longer look like letters at all (i.e. they may lack greetings formulae, the name of the initiating party; they may also be quoted in paraphrase by a later author, who describes his source as an *epistula*). The text must, still, be a written message conveyed from sender to

---

[32] *Dig.* 28.5.66. Statius had claimed a *hereditas*, but was not entitled to it, because he had not been instituted as *heres*; it did not help that he had received a legacy or been charged with the care of a freedman. If the will did not manumit him, he was still a slave.

[33] *Dig.* 35.1.10 (Titius); 40.4.61 (Stichus); both are imaginary characters used as types in legal argument. For Pomponius' other law letters, see *Dig.* 40.5.20; 4.4.50.

recipient and the two must be physically separated; in addition, there must be evidence of an exchange between the named initiator of the consultation and the respondent. The case under discussion in its original form must have been specific, involving named individuals and/or locations, but may no longer appear to be so.

Behind these often dry documents can be seen the contested realities of people's lives. Acts of patronage are reflected in the legal world; the Anonyma *testatrix* seeks to help her fellow townsmen, the Graviscani, with their road, but omits a crucial detail; the concerned neighbour of the obtrusive bathhouse seeks both personal and patronal help from his 'friend' Proculus. Residence in town or Italian countryside each had their trials. In Minturnae, in a real case referred to Pliny's friend Aristo, tenants of an apartment over a cheese shop complained of nuisance from the fumes exuded from the floor below – to what effect is not known.[34] In hunting country, land does not advertise to the huntsman its legal status (public or private) or ownership; who then owned the wild boar in the trap which was let go in the wood (a question also of potential interest to a modern animal rights activist)? And what of contrasting perspectives on a lake view? When Pliny looked at a beautiful lakeside house, he thought of delightful villas and local stories of floating islands, all consigned to elegant letters;[35] Rutilia Polla or her agent worried about how much she owned of a lake shore.

Pliny and the Lawyers

What did Pliny make of contemporary *iuris periti*? Two authors of letter collections, both senatorial heavyweights, do not emerge as congenial types. The relationship with Javolenus Priscus (*Epistulae* edited in up to fourteen books), who had prospered under Domitian as the holder of a number of provincial posts, and continued to flourish in the new era of Nerva and Trajan, was distant, perhaps intentionally so. On a formal level, Pliny recommended a client to Priscus' notice[36] but, in a separate letter to the same client, Voconius Romanus, he recounted an abrasive intervention from Priscus at a poetry reading; despite Priscus' acknowledged distinction

---

[34] *Dig.* 8.5.8.5. This is recorded as a *responsum*, but the detail suggests a real case, perhaps originally submitted to Aristo by letter.

[35] Plin. *Ep.* 8.20 (Lake Vadimon, discussed by Ash in this volume); 9.7 (two Plinian villas on Lake Como).

[36] *Ep.* 2.13, although Pliny unhelpfully addresses a number of Prisci in his letters. For the identity of this Priscus see Sherwin-White 1966: 173–5; for Neratius Priscus as the preferred addressee, see Whitton 2013: 193–4.

in matters of law, when it came to a literary soirée, he fell short of the conduct expected of a cultivated man.[37] The same sense of muted disapproval
is present in Pliny's account of contentious senatorial proceedings concerning an extortion trial which involved an unseemly altercation between one
Licinius Nepos and a praetor, who was none other than the younger P.
Juventius Celsus (consul II in 129).[38] Priscus certainly and possibly Celsus
would be the competition for Pliny *Epistulae* 10.

Perhaps Pliny preferred jurists he could patronise. He regularly consulted
a far less politically distinguished jurist, the *eques* Titius Aristo, an unassuming character, who exchanged letters with two fellow jurists, but is not
known to have issued a collection of *Epistulae* under his own name.[39] Pliny's
preference for Aristo is in line with his general liking for men of talent but
relatively humble status, who had yet to make a name for themselves.[40]
Despite their lack of a senatorial career profile, Titius Aristo and his associate Neratius Priscus (*Epistulae* in four books) both had influence; they
were members of Trajan's *consilium* and provided him with legal advice.[41]
But Aristo, unlike the competitive senatorial aristocrats, such as Javolenus
Priscus and Celsus, was a self-effacing type, and thus in need (or so Pliny
imagined) of a testimonial to enhance his public profile.[42] Aristo is nowhere
cited as an author of *Epistulae*, but a response in a letter of his to Neratius
Priscus (who did publish a letter collection) was cited later, and a number of
responsa to named individuals are included in the *Digest*, which could derive
from *Epistulae*. One in particular, to Cerellius Vitalis, preserved in Ulpian,
addresses a real case, concerning a nuisance caused in a specific locality outside Rome, and thus resembles other consultations likely to have used the
letter form.[43]

The Aristo of Pliny's *Letters* is a literary construct, as well as a real person
(for a parallel, see Sigrid Mratschek in this volume). In a letter expressing

---

[37] *Ep.* 6.15 on the public recitation by an *eques*, Passennus Paulus, of his elegiac verses (also considered
by Roller in this volume). Pliny's take on Javolenus was that he was, in Sherwin-White's phrase,
'rather odd' (*dubiae sanitatis*), but nonetheless an illustrious administrator and imperial adviser,
who gave responses on the *ius ciuile* in a public capacity (*publice*). On the influence of Horace and
Propertius on Passennus' poetry, see *Ep.* 9.22.

[38] *Ep.* 6.5 on the disputed right of a former governor of Bithynia, threatened with prosecution under
the extortion law, to call witnesses in his defence.

[39] *Ep.* 5.3 and 8.14 are addressed to Aristo; see *Ep.* 1.22 to Catilius Severus for Aristo's health and
character sketch. Aristo did correspond with Neratius Priscus and Celsus; his letters, however, may
have been preserved in their collections, rather than independently.

[40] Sherwin-White 1966: 136, on Catilius Severus, Septicius Clarus and Pompeius Falco.

[41] *Dig.* 37.12.5 (Papinian's *Quaestiones*) *Diuus Traianus . . . consilio Nerati Prisci et Aristonis . . .*

[42] *Ep.* 1.22.

[43] *Dig.* 8.5.8.5 *Aristo Cerellio Vitali respondit.* Cf. *Dig.* 2.14.7.2 *eleganter Aristo Celso respondit.*

concern over Aristo's health, Pliny exploited the occasion to create a literary word-portrait of a man who was not only a friend but also, for these purposes, an idealised stereotype. Pliny's construction of the 'good jurist', of which Aristo was an exemplar, shows him not as a narrow specialist but as a virtuous man, a learned polymath and philosopher.[44] Aristo, wrote Pliny, had no equal in moral character and wisdom; he was an expert in literature and literary culture in general (*bonae artes*), as well as history. He had wide experience of private and public law and was always on hand to give detailed consideration to any obscure point bothering Pliny. His learning was placed at the service of his legal clients generously but he avoided ostentation, did not frequent the forum or gymnasia as more high-profile careerists did and preferred the simple life.[45] Because of his possession of the four cardinal virtues, goodness, duty, justice and courage, he was more truly a philosopher than many who vaunted themselves as such.

The 'good jurist', then, was a man of broad culture. But Aristo was also vulnerable. The apolitical *eques* was out of step with the performance culture of his age, being more retiring and therefore liable to be overlooked; he could not expect to impose himself on the spectacle culture that was Roman public life.[46] Pliny was well aware that there were set ways of being nice about his friends and that the choice of qualities and attributes mattered. Pliny therefore fashions a representation of a jurist which implicitly counteracts the downsides of the juristic stereotype as pedantic and obscurantist, a type memorably created in Cicero's attack on Servius Sulpicius Rufus in the *Pro Murena* in 63 BC.[47] Aristo is acquitted of the narrowness which could attach to the figure of the lawyer through the emphasis placed on the breadth of his culture and the nobility of his character. He is portrayed as socially useful, a man who helps his friends and clients as all good patrons must. But jurists *qua* jurists worked behind the scenes; it was advocates, like Pliny himself, who often exploited jurists' specialist knowledge to acquire celebrity status for themselves through public pleading in famous cases. Still, Pliny insisted, there was much to be said for the quiet life: the publicity-averse Aristo avoids showing off because his integrity and simplicity of life reflect the values of an earlier, less self-seeking age.[48]

[44] *Ep.* 1.22. The addressee was L. Catilius Severus Iulianus Claudius Reginus, consul in 110 and 120, prefect of Rome under Hadrian in 137–8. See Sherwin-White 1966: 136–8.
[45] For show-offs, see Plin. *Ep.* 1.10.6 (Euphrates) and 2.3 (Isaeus).
[46] For jurists as failed advocates, see Quint. *Inst.* 12.3.9 *Quod si plerique desperata facultate agendi ad discendum ius declinauerunt . . .*
[47] Cic. *Mur.* 22–8.
[48] Sherwin-White 1966: 69 observes that Pliny preferred the socially less eminent Aristo to the more powerful senatorial jurists of the time, notably Javolenus Priscus and Neratius Priscus.

For Pliny, it was axiomatic that the authors of the lawyers' letters were – or should be – also men of broad culture (as Priscus, by implication, was not). Sensitive as he was to the approbation of audiences of his public readings, Pliny worried when he heard that Aristo had criticised him for acting in a manner inappropriate for a senator by giving recitations of his poetry to a wider audience; his list of precedents justifying his behaviour (all by then deceased) is a measure of his respect for Aristo's erudition, as well as his desire for approval.[49] But more significant is Pliny's consultation of Aristo in 105, concerning a senatorial vote on the fate of the freedmen of the (allegedly) murdered Afranius Dexter. Here his choice of recipient was influenced by Aristo's connection with the most austere champion of the relevant legislation: as Tacitus would record, Aristo's mentor, C. Cassius Longinus (suffect consul AD 30), had in AD 61 insisted on rigorous enforcement of the SC Silanianum, which condemned to death all members of the household of a murdered man who were under the same roof (in this case, over four hundred lives, including those of women and children).[50]

Pliny's letters offer an idealised image of what a good *iuris peritus* should be: a master of many disciplines, not one, efficient at his work as a legal consultant, unassertive but true to the values of philosophy (a claim also made by authors of technical treatises in other fields). The reverse type was the narrow specialist, the man who lacked the broad culture of the truly civilised individual, liable to turn awkward in senatorial debates or to disrupt literary occasions with inappropriately thuggish behaviour. Pliny, then, would not have been impressed by lawyer-letter collections, which, though useful as collections of practical knowledge, embodied precisely those narrowly specialist attitudes, to which he, as a man of broad and enlightened culture, would object. Could he, as a recognised master of the literary letter do better? *Epistulae* 10 suggests that he could.

Pliny, *Letters* 10 and Lawyers' *Epistulae*

Pliny *Letters* 10 stands apart from his previous nine books of letters. Although the Q&A format of his exchanges with Trajan on problems with the Bithynians echoes the format of the lawyers' exchanges, the main purpose was to document the author's friendship with his emperor. The first fourteen letters, which signal the overall character of the book, concern matters of patronage which arose prior to Pliny's departure for his province

---

[49] *Ep.* 5.3; see Morello 2007: 176–7.   [50] Whitton 2010; Harries 2013a.

in *c.* 110. Book 10, therefore, did not advertise itself as being directly in competition with the lawyers, because the relationship with the emperor was obviously more important – and gave Pliny an immediate advantage over the competition. There was therefore an element of occlusion; the lawyers were not immediately or obviously targeted. However, the overall format of the Bithynia section of Pliny's *Epistulae* 10 reflects the habitual practice of paired questions and answers employed in contemporaneous exchanges between lawyers and their colleagues or clients, which, if not unique to lawyers, was certainly a distinctive feature of their compilations.

Pliny's tenth book therefore, while containing features characteristic of administrative correspondence in general (see Lavan in this volume), could also have invited comparison with the lawyers' letters, and, as might be expected, would highlight a set of differences, all of which worked to Pliny's advantage. With Pliny's arrival, after some health problems, in his province, the paired letters between governor and emperor dominate the correspondence in a manner no jurist's exchange with clients could hope to match. The point was further reinforced by the roles ascribed to each: Pliny, the questioner, takes the role of the client; Trajan, the respondent, lays down the law.

Moreover, the law itself took on a more complex identity. In Bithynia, the Roman law of the jurists was reduced to the status of one legal system among many and Pliny, unlike the Rome-based jurists, had to negotiate the conflicting demands of competing legal systems. In line with a system devised by Pompey for his settlement of the province in 63 BC, many Bithynians lived under local laws, and relatively few exchanges related directly to legal questions concerning the Roman *ius ciuile*. Through decisions of governors and judges, which reflect the crucial but largely undocumented expansion of Roman legal usage in the non-Roman provinces,[51] the lines between local and Roman rules and conventions were increasingly blurred. There was, for example, growing confusion as to the applicability of pontifical law in the provinces. Could a temple be removed to accommodate a new forum at Nicomedia?[52] Pliny's worry was that the terms of the dedication rendered the ground on which it stood 'sacred'. The reply from Trajan, or a legal adviser, reflects the concise style of the Rome-based jurist: 'the land of a non-Roman city is not legally capable of being dedicated as can take place under our law', a hard line that would be contradicted a few decades later by the jurist Gaius' statement that consecrated

---

[51] *Ep.* 10.68 *secundum exemplum proconsulum*. See Harries 2013b: 45–62.
[52] *Ep.* 10.49, reply at 10.50. Cf. *Ep.* 10.70–1, a more rigorous questioning of the fate of a temple to Claudius at Prusa.

provincial land, while not technically *sacrum*, would be regarded 'as if sacred.'[53]

Pliny had therefore to decide, with Trajan's help, not only on interpretation of law, but which law to follow. As was the case in legal discourse generally, the citation of authoritative texts and precedents was important but Pliny faced the extra problem of deciding on the applicability to Bithynia of previous judgments issued for other provinces. For example, when the status of foundlings and foster-children was at issue, Pliny had heard read out letters from Vespasian to the Lacedaemonians, from Titus to them and to the Achaeans, and from Domitian to the two proconsuls of Achaea, but none applied directly to Bithynia.[54] Equally vexatious was the interplay between the laws of the free cities, which were distinct from the Roman system and inconvenient proconsular precedents. On the question raised by Pliny of which creditor had prior claim for the recovery of money owed from contracts of hire and sale, and the previous practice of proconsuls in favouring the rights of the cities over private claimants, Trajan, or his jurist, produced a characteristically terse jurist's response: the legal rights of the cities can be determined only by reference to their own laws and the emperor has no right to overrule them.[55]

Emperors were the ultimate source of law. Because they generated, usually, a decisive outcome, Pliny's exchanges with Trajan diverged from the conventions of juristic discourse, in which questions could always have alternative answers, and could be asked again of other people ad infinitum. Trajan's decisions, recorded by Pliny for literary posterity, had already leaped off the page into human lives; when the community of Nicaea claimed the estates of citizens who had died intestate, contrary to the principles of Roman law, which supported the rights of agnate relatives to inherit, two named imperial procurators were co-opted onto Pliny's council of advisers to help sort out the dispute.[56] Trajan's jurists advised but they were nameless; emperors (and their friends) decided.

It was perhaps ironic that some of the emperor's replies, for example on consecrated land or the status of local law, may have been authored in Trajan's name by an anonymous juristic adviser.[57] This shadowy third

---

[53] *Solum peregrinae ciuitatis capax non sit dedicationis quae fit nostro iure.* By contrast, Gaius *Inst.* 2.5–7a defines the situation more flexibly a few decades later: ground is sacred only if consecrated by the authority of the Roman people, so in the provinces such ground is not strictly *sacrum* but '*pro sacro habetur*'.

[54] *Ep.* 10.65.3.   [55] *Ep.* 10.108–9.

[56] *Ep.* 10.84. The two procurators were Viridius Gemellinus and Trajan's freedman Epimachus.

[57] For the 'prosy clerk' in charge of routine replies, see Sherwin-White 1966: 615 on *Ep.* 10.30, 32, 78, 117, 119. For Pliny's preference for a definitive general imperial ruling over *exempla*, individual precedents, see *Ep.* 10.65.2 *quia nihil inueniebam aut proprium aut uniuersale quod ad Bithynos referretur, consulendum te existimaui . . . neque putaui posse me . . . exemplis esse contentum.*

party in the correspondence, however, unlike the lawyers with their published collections, had no public identity, and thus no means of challenging
Pliny's profile as the confidant of emperors. Pliny, in reality, may have been
the recipient of replies from a number of officials acting in Trajan's name,
including legal opinions authored by the very jurists with whom he aimed
to compete. But only Trajan is visible, a constant support to his consci-
entious, albeit beleaguered, governor. This correspondence was thus both
business exchange and literary artefact.

Conclusion

The lawyers' letters, now largely lost, have their own value for the student
of ancient Roman life and letters. Though they survive now only in fragmentary form and were subjected to the vicissitudes of textual corruption,
accidental or deliberate, they provide a window on the lost worlds of the
Roman litigant and the problems he or she confronted, as property owner,
builder, city representative or as the flat-dweller harassed by inconsiderate
neighbours. The political and social eminence of the lawyer-authors would
have ensured a readership among their contemporaries for their collections,
with the hope that they would inform generations of lawyers thereafter.

In labelling their collections as *Letters*, such lawyers as Proculus, Javolenus, Celsus and Pomponius also asserted their claim to be regarded, in
some sense, as literary men; their published case-law *Epistulae* were a signi-
fier of their status in the cultured world of Pliny and friends. Nor were there
obvious reasons to disregard their collections as contributions to the established epistolary literary genre. Experiments in *Epistulae* as poetic, satiric or
didactic, authored by such literary eminences as Horace and Seneca, had
demonstrated the potential diversity of the uses to which 'letters' could be
put. The jurists, in effect, proposed that collections of legal opinions in letter form, which certainly counted as technical literature, should also bear
literary comparison with the likes of Pliny (and Cicero).

Reading between the lines, Pliny may have viewed this project with dis-
favour. Two lawyers, known to be authors of *Epistulae*, he seems to have
disliked. Moreover, his celebration of Aristo's breadth of culture contained
an implied criticism of the narrow specialist; such people could not count
as members of a cultured elite – and, we may infer, nor could their assem-
blages of legal opinions in the form of letters count as 'literature'. In *Epistulae* 10, after an initial demonstration of his status as imperial *amicus*, Pliny
showed the lawyers how exchanges of 'question and answer' should be conducted. By drawing on his formidable literary reputation, Pliny offered an

epistolary collection which the jurists, with their technical limitations, and noted, if not notorious, for their dry style, could not hope to match. And Pliny further undermined the competition by making the subject of his gubernatorial exchanges – with Trajan, no less – a record, not merely of legal questions and disputes of uncertain outcome, but of the exercise of ultimate power.

In this contest over what a 'letter' or a 'letter collection' should be, Pliny emerged the winner. Despite the jurists' attempt to acquire the status accorded the authors of literary collections of *Epistulae*, Pliny's insistence that *Letters* were more than simply a record of correspondence would prevail. He, therefore, is widely read by students of the ancient world, while the readership of the letters of Priscus, Celsus and company consists now, as it did then, of legal specialists. However, while Pliny would have been happy to see at least some of the lawyers' *Epistulae* consigned to literary oblivion, their writings are nonetheless a significant commentary on the world of Pliny himself and an important coordinate in our study of literary cross-fertilisation. The correspondences (and differences) between the lawyers' letters and Pliny's Book 10 remind us that literary interactions occurred in all sorts of directions, between material that originated in very different contexts, and with ramifications that reached well beyond the literary sphere. Indeed, without the lawyers to act as both precedent and provocation, Pliny *Letters* 10 might never have existed at all.

CHAPTER 12

Pliny Epistles *10 and Imperial Correspondence*
The Empire of Letters

Myles Lavan

The comfortable world of scholarship on Book 10 of Pliny's *Letters* was rocked to its foundations by three iconoclastic papers published independently by Greg Woolf, Philip Stadter and Carlos Noreña in 2006 and 2007. In different but mutually supporting ways, these papers sought to extend to Book 10 the accumulated insights of two decades of work on the literary ambition and sophistication of the first nine books of the *Letters*.[1] Where the correspondence with Trajan had previously been treated as a book apart – an archive of real letters rather than a work of literature – Woolf, Stadter and Noreña all argued that it was in fact an artfully crafted text with its own particular project (which they each described slightly differently). This chapter takes stock of their arguments by recontextualising Book 10 within the small but not insignificant corpus of imperial correspondence transmitted by inscriptions, papyri and juristic compilations.[2] Although I am convinced by their critique of the conventional 'archive' model of Book 10, I take issue with their suggestion that the individual letters have clearly been subjected to a process of stylisation analogous to, though different from, that to be observed in the letters of Books 1–9. I will show that nothing in their form or content distinguishes the letters in Book 10 from other examples of correspondence between emperors and Roman administrators in the provinces (though this does in itself invalidate their other arguments).[3]

Thanks to Roy Gibson, Jill Harries, Alice König, Chris Whitton and Greg Woolf for comments and suggestions.

[1] Marchesi 2008, Gibson and Morello 2012 and Whitton 2013 epitomise the new approach to Books 1–9.

[2] Because the comparanda are almost exclusively letters between the emperor and office-holders in the provinces, the chapter focuses on the Bithynian letters (*Ep.* 10.15–121) rather than the fourteen earlier letters that open the book.

[3] My project has obvious parallels with Coleman 2012, which similarly juxtaposes Book 10 with non-literary letters (and argues that they exemplify the 'bureaucratic language' of the Roman Empire), but it will become clear that I depart from Coleman in my understanding of the sociology of the

My larger goal is to shift attention from the letters in Book 10 to the wider phenomenon of imperial correspondence that they exemplify. The subtitle, 'empire of letters', gestures towards the centrality of correspondence in the Roman Empire. Communication by letter was one of the most important technologies of empire in the pre-industrial world.[4] This was already obvious to contemporaries: Aelius Aristides praised Rome for the fact that the emperor could 'stay where he is and manage the entire civilised world by letters, which arrive almost as soon as they are written, as if they were carried by winged messengers'.[5] Fergus Millar has shown that the surprising intensity of Pliny's correspondence with Trajan in Book 10 is consistent with what we learn about imperial letters from juristic sources and he rightly underlines the significance of these letters for the government of the Empire: 'government at a distance, by means of letters, was simply the standard mechanism through which the empire worked'.[6] My aim in this chapter is to show that the importance of this correspondence extended far beyond the functional dimensions of sharing information and enabling decision-making across long distances. In a world where members of the office-holding elite were often separated by vast distances for long periods of time, regular correspondence was essential to building and maintaining the emperor's personal ties to the aristocratic friends and slave and freed dependents on whom the administration of the Empire depended. Replicated across hundreds of individual relationships and repeated year after year, the conventions of this correspondence must have played a crucial role – only dimly visible to us – in structuring relations between the *princeps* and the various strata of the imperial elite. It was also an important space in which the ruling elite reaffirmed shared beliefs about the justice, good judgment and above all the *humanitas* of Roman administration. All imperial correspondence deserves to be read with the same attention to rhetoric and ideology that Woolf, Stadter and Noreña apply to Book 10.

This chapter also reflects on two profound questions that Book 10 raises about the relationship between literary and non-literary texts. Like the juristic letter collections discussed by Jill Harries in the last chapter, Book 10

imperial elite, which I see as being in many respects patrimonial rather than bureaucratic in character, and hence on the utility of an ahistorical model of 'bureaucratic' language. It will also emerge that, although I differ from Woolf, Stadter and Noreña in their assessment of the stylisation of the individual letters (and their identification of the editor), my view of Book 10 remains much closer to theirs than to the traditional archive model as restated by Coleman (esp. pp. 233–4).

[4] The papers in Radner 2014 locate Roman imperial correspondence in a long tradition of imperial practice.

[5] *Or.* 26.33, trans. Oliver 1953.

[6] Millar 2000, aptly subtitled 'government by correspondence'. See further Millar 1977: 313–41; Arcaria 2000; Meyer-Zwiffelhoffer 2003: 278–89; Hurlet 2006: 202–301.

problematises the very distinction between the literary and the non-literary. What happens when ordinary letters are selected, arranged and published as a unit in a reading culture in which the letter book was well established as a literary form? I will suggest that the literary letter book is constructed as much by its readers as by the letter writer. Perhaps more importantly, situating Book 10 in the context of the meagre remains of the wider corpus of imperial correspondence provides an opportunity to reflect on the ways in which our assessment of the political and social importance of literary texts can be distorted by the fact that we have such a restricted view of the discursive context in which they originally circulated. It is all too easy, I will argue, to exaggerate the significance of the individual literary texts that survive relative to the vastly larger corpus of ephemeral texts and other discourse that do not.

The Literary Turn in Reading Book 10

Though Woolf, Stadter and Noreña differ in their approach and focus, there is a striking convergence in their conclusions: all three insist that Book 10 was the product of careful design. According to Stadter, it was 'composed . . . for political and literary purposes', *'carefully edited . . .* for the same audience as the rest of Pliny's letters and following many of the same principles'.[7] Book 10, writes Woolf, is 'not a collection of confidential despatches from the Euxine front', but 'an *artfully constructed* image of the good aristocrat in his province, and of the best of emperors in Rome'.[8] For Noreña, the friendship between Pliny and Trajan as presented in Book 10 is *'artfully constructed'* and mutually beneficial: Pliny's aim was 'to fashion himself . . . as something more than just another bureaucrat'; Trajan too benefitted from the advertisement of the civility of his relations with a senator.[9]

The three papers highlight the evidence of selection and arrangement in the collection as we have it: Pliny's requests have been paired with Trajan's responses, though the latter must have been received much later; there are several references to letters which do not appear in the collection and have apparently been omitted; the published letters largely avoid repetition of subject matter, which suggests some selection in the pursuit of variety; they avoid uncomfortable subjects such as conflicts or disagreements within the Roman administration, though these are unlikely to have been absent from

---

[7] Stadter 2006: 61, 62–3 (emphasis in this and the following quotations mine).
[8] Woolf 2006: 103.   [9] Noreña 2007: 261, 246, 252.

Pliny's governorship; the final two letters are particularly effective as a closural device, revisiting the blurring of public and private that characterises the first letters and counterbalancing Pliny's journey from Rome to Bithynia at the beginning of the Bithynia letters. All three scholars also go out on a limb to argue that the editor was none other than Pliny himself, noting variously the absence of positive evidence for the prevailing assumption that Pliny died in Bithynia, the parallels with the editorial principles of Books 1–9, the continuity in the project of self-fashioning and Pliny's track record as an innovator in the realm of public self-presentation.

These papers have unquestionably revitalised the reading of Book 10 and usefully problematised ancient historians' all too comfortable assumptions about its value as evidence for Roman provincial administration. I am wholly convinced by the critique of the 'archive' paradigm. We can no longer assume that Book 10 contains all the letters between Pliny and Trajan or even that it is a representative sample of the subjects on which they corresponded. As for the identity of the editor, Woolf, Stadter and Noreña have again usefully called into question the conventional assumption that Book 10 was published posthumously. That said, I remain inclined towards the established view. The closing letters about Pliny's wife's journey to Italy following her grandfather's death (*Ep.* 10.120–1), for all their merits as a closural device, seem to me to tell against the provocative hypothesis that Pliny was the editor. Their very appositeness as a counterbalance to the letters about Pliny's journey from Rome that open the Bithynian sequence (10.15–18) seems to highlight their role as substitutes for any letters about Pliny's own departure from the province, drawing attention to the absence, while the reference to a death might be read as an allusion to Pliny's own. But these are no more than hints. The question must remain open.

Where I do take issue with the three papers is the impression they give that the individual letters have obviously been reworked in the service of the editor's larger project. The position has been articulated most clearly by Greg Woolf, who writes that 'Book 10 is much more similar to the other books than has been acknowledged . . . its relationship to actual correspondence is just as remote.' 'Why,' he asks, 'are [the letters] so easily comprehensible? Why do no replies refer to more than one subject? Why do Pliny and Trajan always emerge so well?'[10] Stadter similarly claims that the letters have been edited to restrict their content to a single subject and suggests more vaguely that Pliny has 'redirected emphases to attract and inform

---

[10] Woolf 2006: 97; the argument for the 'artificiality' of the letters is reiterated in his recent reprise of the subject, Woolf 2015: 133.

his larger audience'. He argues that the letters have been crafted to 'place the relation between Trajan and Pliny in an atmosphere of friendship and respect' – notably by means of the warm style of address with which Trajan greets Pliny (*mi Secunde carissime*) – and to demonstrate Trajan's paternalistic care for provincials.[11] Noreña in contrast insists that the letters of Book 10 are very different from those of Books 1–9, that they are primarily functional rather than literary in character and that they are representative of Roman administrative practice.[12] But he too suggests that the modes of address used by Pliny and Trajan (*carissime* and *domine*) are unusual.[13]

These observations suggest that the letters of Pliny and Trajan are clearly artificial (Woolf and Stadter) or at least idiosyncratic (Noreña) in their form and/or content. This has important implications for readers of Book 10 insofar as it opens the door to readings of some or all of the letters as fictional. All three papers explicitly reject this hypothesis.[14] Taken together, however, they imply a degree of obvious artificiality which – if left uncorrected – would positively invite such a reading. In the next section, I show that the key features that have been represented as anomalous – the restriction of each letter to a single subject and the modes of address used by Trajan and Pliny respectively – are in fact typical of imperial correspondence preserved in other contexts. Of course realism does not prove authenticity, so this is no proof that they have not been edited – or even that they are not outright fictions. But it does relieve the growing pressure in that direction. There is also a risk that the new readings of Book 10 will detract from a proper appreciation of the importance of the wider body of imperial correspondence insofar as they suggest that some of the book's most interesting features – the construction of intimacy between emperor and senator and the idealisation of their partnership in just and beneficial government – are part of its particular literary or political project. In the final section, I will show that everyday correspondence was just as invested in those constructions.

Some Formal Features of Imperial Correspondence

Almost all of the once massive body of correspondence between emperors and provincial governors, imperial procurators and other administrators in the provinces has been lost. But the letters in Book 10 are not the only exceptions. Several imperial letters to governors and procurators survive

---

[11] Stadter 2006: 67, 70.   [12] Noreña 2007: 239.   [13] Noreña 2007: 247–50, 252–4.
[14] Woolf 2006: 93–4 (cf. Woolf 2015: 135, 144); Stadter 2006: 69, 75; Noreña 2007: 239.

in copies on stone or on papyrus.[15] Dozens more have been preserved by the jurists, because they contained a decision on a relevant matter of law.[16] Although the surviving corpus is tiny compared to the original volume of correspondence and the chronological distribution is very uneven (with hardly any examples from the first century), enough letters survive to show that the correspondence between Trajan and Pliny is not obviously anomalous in form or content.

Accessibility

One supposed anomaly of the letters of Book 10 is their accessibility. 'Each letter, with few exceptions,' notes Stadter, 'is concerned with only one subject . . . This restriction of content is surprising, considering the difficulty and expense of sending letters.' He contrasts Cicero's letters from Cilicia, which normally cover numerous subjects, and notes the similarity to the letters of Books 1–9, which tend to have the same unity of focus.[17] Woolf writes: 'If they were really not intended for publication, why are they so easily comprehensible (by contrast with Cicero's actual correspondence from Cilicia which, like most real letters, presumes a good deal of shared information between correspondents)? Like the letters in Book 9 and unlike Cicero's private correspondence, each letter in Book 10 has a unity of theme.'[18] The tendency to focus on a single topic and

---

[15] There is no good corpus of imperial letters to governors and other officials preserved on inscriptions or papyrus, though many can be found in Oliver 1989 and the appendix to Hurlet 2006. Examples up to the death of Septimius Severus: letter of Caesar to a legate in Asia (*AE* 2009, 1429); letter of Domitian to a prefect of Egypt (*CEL* no. 85); letter of Hadrian to a governor of Asia (*MAMA* IX, pp. xxxvi–xxxvii); letter of Hadrian to a prefect of Egypt (Oliver 1989, no. 70); letters of Marcus Aurelius and Lucius Verus and then Marcus and Commodus to two governors of Mauretania Tingitana (*AE* 1971, 534); letter of Marcus Aurelius to a procurator in Gaul (*AE* 1962, 183); letter of Marcus and Commodus to (probably) a governor of Lycia and Pamphylia (*SEG* 48, 1582); letters of Septimius Severus and Caracalla to a governor and also to a procurator of Moesia Inferior (*CIL* III, 12509). We also have two letters of Domitian and one of Nerva transmitted in one of Pliny's letters to Trajan (*Ep.* 10.58.4, 6 and 8).

[16] Letters transmitted by the jurists are presented most accessibly in Gualandi's compilation of imperial constitutions (the technical term for a ruling by the emperor) discussed by the jurists, where verbatim quotations are distinguished typographically from paraphrase and commentary (Gualandi 1963). The jurists sometimes identify a constitution explicitly as an *epistula*, but they more often use the looser term *rescriptum* or the verb *rescribere*. In the usage of the jurists, 'rescripts' encompass not just letters to officials and other important persons and communities, but also subscripts (*subscriptiones*) to private petitions (*libelli*) – a different genre and a different audience (a certain example: *Coll. Leg.* 3.3.5–6). On the taxonomy of imperial pronouncements, see Millar 1977: 203–59 and Oliver 1989: 1–24. Burton 2002: 274–6 gives a very conservative list of responses specifically to provincial governors, not all of them preserved verbatim. There are other examples where the context indicates the response is to a governor or other officials.

[17] Stadter 2006: 66.   [18] Woolf 2006: 97.

to provide contextual information that might be left tacit are certainly features of the stylisation of the letter form in Books 1–9. But a degree of accessibility that would be anomalous in ordinary correspondence seems to have been the norm in correspondence on administrative matters. Like the letters of Pliny and Trajan in Book 10, those preserved in the jurists or on inscriptions or papyri normally limit themselves to a single or at most a few related topics and briefly recapitulate the context before stating their decision – making them quite transparent even to readers who were not party to previous correspondence.

The letters that survive are almost exclusively short and limited to a single subject. Of course we need to reckon with the possibility of excerption. The texts we possess were transmitted by interested parties – the individuals or communities who inscribed them on monuments, the individuals who kept papyrus copies for their own use, and the jurists who quoted them to illustrate the law. It is at least an *a priori* possibility that they excerpted the material relevant to them from longer letters that also dealt with other matters. But the evidence weighs against this hypothesis. The small minority of letters that are transmitted in their entirety, complete with salutation and valediction, conform to the norm of brevity and clarity.[19] The same is true of texts that are explicitly labelled a 'copy' (*exemplum, exemplar, antigraphos*) of an imperial letter.[20] *Exemplum* is the legal term for a copy of a document and there was a convention of distinguishing between a 'copy' of and an 'extract from' (*caput ex, kephalaion ek, meros*) an imperial pronouncement.[21]

The only exception to the single-subject norm known to me is the unusually long response of Marcus Aurelius and Lucius Verus to M. Ulpius Apuleius Eurycles, *logistes* (financial superintendent) of the *gerousia* at Athens (Oliver 1989, no. 170) – not a provincial governor, but still an official

---

[19] Letters preserved complete with salutation and valediction: Caesar to a legate in Asia (*SEG* 59, 1479, lines 14ff.); Marcus Aurelius to Domitius Marsianus (*AE* 1962, 183); Caracalla to an Aurelius M[–]us whose cognomen has been erased, possibly an imperial procurator (*SEG* 50, 1187); an unknown emperor to Clodius Secundus, apparently a man of rank, perhaps an imperially appointed curator (*AE* 1949, 24).

[20] Copies introduced as *exemplum epistulae*: Hadrian to Avidius Quietus (*MAMA* IX, pp. 36–7; note also the similarly labelled and equally brief letters of Quietus to Hesperus and Hesperus' response); Marcus Aurelius and Lucius Verus to Coiedius Maximus (*AE* 1971, 534); Marcus Aurelius to Domitius Marsianus (*AE* 1962, 183); Marcus and Commodus to Vallius Maximianus (*AE* 1971, 534); Septimius Severus and Caracalla to Heraclitus (*ILS* 423).

[21] See *TLL* s.v. *exemplum* (1349.39–1350.12) and *caput* (424.81–425.60). For examples, see Anastasiadis and Souris 2000 s.v. *antigraphos* and *kephalaion*.

appointed by the Roman state.[22] The letter runs to more than sixty lines and covers three distinct topics: statues of previous emperors that had been found in storage, a case involving a public slave who had collected monies owed to the *gerousia* without authorisation and the problem of other debts outstanding to the *gerousia*. That said, all three issues had evidently arisen in the single letter of Eurycles to which the imperial letter was a reply and in each case the emperors take the time to recapitulate the situation as presented by Eurycles before announcing their decision. This is very common in the surviving letters, which often preface a decision with a mini-narrative of the circumstances to which it applies (further examples can be found in the next section). This tends to make imperial responses intelligible even in the absence of the original request for advice.

This economy of focus and provision of contextual information, features which would be otiose and impractical in purely personal letters, were functional in the context of Roman administrative practice. We know that the letters of emperors, governors and other officials were often forwarded to other interested parties for information, action or decision and were often kept for future reference, both in official archives in Rome and the provinces and by private individuals. Trajan sent Pliny a copy of a response to the prefect of the Pontic shore (*Ep.* 10.22) and Septimius Severus and Caracalla similarly forwarded a copy of their letter to a procurator to the provincial governor (*CIL* III, 12509). Copies were even sent to persons outside the Roman administration or displayed in public. A provincial governor wrote to the city of Aizanoi, enclosing copies of a letter he had received from Hadrian, another he had sent to an imperial procurator and the procurator's response (*MAMA* IX, pp. xxxvi–xxxvii); copies of all four texts were inscribed on the wall of the Temple of Zeus. A letter that Hadrian wrote to the prefect of Egypt was posted publicly in a legionary camp on the emperor's instructions; a papyrus copy was found in the Fayuum (Oliver 1989, no. 70). When Septimius Severus and Caracalla wrote to the provincial procurator confirming some fiscal immunities claimed by the city of Tyras, they sent a copy of that letter to the provincial governor to notify him of the decision. He in turn sent copies of both letters to Tyras, where they were later inscribed, together with the governor's covering letter, to create a monumental record of the privilege (*CIL* III, 12059). Pliny mentions

---

[22] Even more complex is a text of Marcus Aurelius ruling on a large and diverse body of disputes at Athens (Oliver 1989, no. 184), but it is not a response to a governor. It is probably an edict rather than a letter (so Oliver) and certainly directed at the Athenians, as the emperor's explanation for his use of Greek at the end makes clear.

Bithynians who had private copies of letters of emperors to governors –
and not just of their own province – as well as letters to cities and imperial
edicts.[23] Provincials sought out and preserved these texts because they
expected the emperor's words to offer them leverage over Roman officials
in the future.[24]

Given the expectation that such letters might circulate beyond their
immediate correspondence context, it made eminent sense to restrict their
scope and to make them as intelligible as possible as stand-alone documents. As for the costs of sending correspondence across the vast spaces of
the Empire, there was nothing to prevent officials from bundling a number
of letters on different topics. In any case, the Roman state, like its imperial predecessors, had developed the human and material infrastructure to
regularly move documents between the provinces and Rome.[25] It was able
and willing to bear the significant costs involved – or rather, it displaced
them onto the individual cities of the Empire. These were among the most
resented impositions of the Roman state, presumably because of the lack
of predictability and openness to abuse.[26] The correspondence of Roman
officials was thus relieved of much of the need for economy that applied to
all private correspondence in the ancient world. In short, Pliny's exchange
with Trajan does look very different from Cicero's correspondence with
his friends, but the frequency of correspondence, the narrow scope of each
letter and the generous provision of context all seem to be entirely characteristic of correspondence on administrative matters, and not a sign of
literary stylisation.

Trajan Addressing Pliny

Trajan addresses Pliny in the vocative in twenty of fifty-one letters, variously
using the forms *mi Secunde carissime* (14 times), *Secunde carissime* (5 times)
and *mi Secunde* (once).[27] Both Stadter and Noreña suggest that this is
unusual. Stadter highlights Trajan's frequent use of the greeting *mi Secunde
carissime*, which he describes as 'a warm greeting which goes beyond the
purely official and administrative'. He notes that *carissime* is very rare in

---

[23] See *Ep.* 10.58, 65 (letters to two governors of Achaea) and 72.
[24] See especially Ando 2000, ch. 4.
[25] See Kolb 2000 on travel by diploma and Radner 2014 on communication as a technology of empire.
    Millar 2000 highlights the surprising volume of correspondence with the emperor ('the constant
    flow of messages, complaints and documents') given the long time lag in communication, the cost
    of travelling vast distances and the added complexity that emperors and governors were normally
    on the move.
[26] Mitchell 1976; Millar 1986: 304–5 (= Millar 2004: 382–3).   [27] Coleman 2012: 198.

Cicero's letters and contrasts the use of the 'less committal' *mi Maxime* in a letter of Domitian reproduced by Pliny (*Ep.* 10.58.6).[28] Noreña similarly observes that *carissime* was 'not a typical form of address from an emperor to a subordinate' and that 'use of the cognomen alone was standard practice'.

But the forms of address used in Book 10 are easily paralleled in the corpus of imperial letters. To my knowledge, there are ten surviving letters which address their recipient in the vocative. A bare cognomen occurs only once. The other nine instances append *mi* and/or *carissime* in a familiar style that exactly parallels the forms of Book 10, with five examples of the *Secunde carissime* type, three of the *mi Secunde* type and one of the *mi Secunde carissime* type.[29] It is worth emphasising that the addition of *mi* is, like *carissime*, a mark of familiarity.[30] On this evidence, the most one could say is that the compound form *mi Secunde carissime*, which accounts for three-quarters of the addresses in Book 10 but only one of eight in the comparanda, might express greater intimacy than a bare *carissime*. But the difference is one of degree, not kind. The only other pattern that emerges from the data is a concentration of the *Secunde carissime* form in the second century. The only two first-century letters, both by Domitian, use the *mi Secunde* form. In contrast, five of six letters from the latter half of the second century use *Secunde carissime*; another uses *mi Secunde carissime*. In between, two letters of Hadrian use the bare vocative and *mi Secunde* forms. This might suggest the hypothesis that the form (*mi*) *Secunde carissime* displaced *mi Secunde* as the standard mode in which an emperor addressed senators (and equestrians) sometime between Domitian and Antoninus Pius. One could further speculate that the change post-dated the publication of Book 10, that Trajan's use of *carissime* was therefore unusual at the time and that it perhaps canonised a new style which became the norm in the second century. But the sample of surviving letters is too small, and too heavily skewed towards the second century, to support such an elaborate argument. The only conclusion we can draw with any confidence is that *carissime* was a common – indeed the most common – mode by which emperors addressed senators in letters.

[28] Stadter 2006: 70.
[29] Plain vocative (once): *Taurine* (Hadrian at *Coll. Leg.* 1.11.3). *Secunde carissime* type (5 times): *Gemine carissime* (Antoninus Pius at *Dig.* 48.6.6), *Saxa carissime* (Marcus and Verus at *Dig.* 48.18.1.27), *Piso carissime* (Commodus at *Dig.* 29.5.2), *Lepide carissime* (Unknown at *ILS* 6090), *Iuliane carissime* (Severus Alexander at *Dig.* 31.87.3). *Mi Secunde* type (3 times): *mi Maxime* (Domitian at *CEL* no. 85, writing to an equestrian prefect), *mi Maxime* (Domitian at Plin. *Ep.* 10.58.6), Ῥάμμιέ μου, presumably a translation of *mi Rammie* (Hadrian in Oliver 1989, no. 70, writing to an equestrian prefect; the first line establishes that the Greek text is a translation). *Mi Secunde carissime* type (once): *mi Marsiane karissime mihi* (Marcus Aurelius at *AE* 1962, 183, writing to an equestrian procurator).
[30] On the addition of *mi* as a mark or profession of intimacy, see Dickey 2002: 215–16.

Pliny Addressing Trajan

A vocative address appears in all but five of Pliny's sixty-three letters to Trajan (notably more often than in Trajan's replies and evidently a mark of respect in its own right). The address is almost always *domine*, with eighty-two examples across fifty-six letters. The only exceptions are five instances of *imperator* with various epithets (*optime, sanctissime, indulgentissime*) in the opening series of letters that pre-date Pliny's governorship. Pliny's regular use of *domine* has surprised many readers in the light of his assertion in the *Panegyricus* that under Trajan 'we do not speak of a master, but a father' (*non de domino, sed de parente loquimur, Pan.* 2.3).[31] But the vocative *domine* is well attested as an epistolary address in a wide range of social contexts and most commentators have glossed Pliny's use of it as a conventional and respectful but not obsequious form of address.[32] Carlos Noreña has proposed a very different interpretation. Arguing that *domine* is out of place in public correspondence with an emperor, but typical of private correspondence with a family member, he suggests that it was a central pillar of Pliny's artful self-presentation as the emperor's intimate.[33]

An immediate problem with contextualising Pliny's usage is the paucity of examples of letters written *to* emperors. I know of only two other examples, both addressed to Hadrian.[34] They both include a vocative address, like most of Pliny's letters. One is a letter of a proconsul of Baetica, who addresses the emperor as *optime imperator*, exactly as Pliny does in the pre-Bithynian epistles.[35] The other is a letter of Trajan's widow Plotina. She addresses Hadrian as *domine*.[36] Since Plotina was Hadrian's adoptive mother, this is consistent with Noreña's thesis that *domine* was used by kin – but does not prove that it was not also used by senators. *Domine* was certainly a conventional mode in which senators addressed emperors both in letters and in person by the middle of the century. In a transcript from a hearing before Marcus Aurelius, a senatorial *aduocatus fisci* addresses him as *domine imperator*.[37] Similarly, Fronto regularly addresses not just Marcus

---

[31] See also *Pan.* 7.6, 45.3, 55.7.

[32] Sherwin-White 1966: 557; Williams 1990: 18; Adams 1995: 119; Dickey 2002: 96; Coleman 2012: 194.

[33] Noreña 2007: 247–50. He accepts Dickey's argument that the address use of the vocative *domine* had by the early second century diverged from the referential use of other cases, but argues that this did not apply to the emperor: '*dominus* [though it is specifically the vocative *domine* that is at issue] was objectionable when applied to the emperor in public contexts' (p. 250). But this depends on privileging Suetonius' testimony that Augustus objected to the address use of *domine* as evidence for the Trajanic period over the *prima facie* evidence of Pliny's letters that *domine* was in fact acceptable.

[34] We also have a handful of petitions addressed to emperors by ordinary provincials, but they are not comparable.

[35] Letter of Taurinus Egnatius, excerpted at *Coll. Leg.* 1.11.2. Also discussed by Millar 1977: 329.

[36] Oliver 1989, no. 73.   [37] *Dig.* 28.4.3.

Aurelius, with whom he was particularly intimate, but also Lucius Verus and Antoninus Pius as *domine* in his correspondence.

Our understanding of Pliny's choice of address is complicated by the fact that it stands at the nexus of two related but distinct developments, which are now visible only in broad outline – the increasing use of *dominus* as a respectful title at all levels of imperial society and the growing comfort of both emperors and subjects of all ranks with the use of *dominus* as an imperial title. The most familiar aspect of the first development is the proliferation of the vocative *domine*.[38] The early stages are somewhat obscure, but it is clear that it was well established by the mid first century AD, perhaps through the generalisation of a usage previously confined to family members.[39] According to Seneca, *domine* was a polite way of greeting someone whose name you had forgotten (*Ep.* 3.1). It features in both Petronius and Martial. By the early second century, it is the most common mode of address in the Latin letters from Vindolanda and Egypt.[40] It had wide currency, often used by inferiors (especially when asking favours), but also employed by peers and even social superiors, as in a letter to a collegium of *fabri* in Narbo by their patron (who addresses his clients as *domini optimi et karissimi mihi*, *CIL* XII, 4393, AD 149). The social context of a correspondence is therefore underdetermined by the use of *domine* alone, though the degree of reciprocity can be more revealing (as in Book 10). Eleanor Dickey must be right that the address use of *domine* acquired some semantic autonomy from other uses of *dominus*, even if the compartmentalisation cannot have been as complete as she suggests. The semantics of *dominus* are further complicated by several other related but less well-documented practices such as appending *dominus meus* to the name of a family member or close acquaintance when referring to them (first attested of family members in the first century AD, used of peers and dependants by the second),[41] adding *domino/ae* to kinship terms (*marito, coniugi, fratri, sorori, filio* etc.)

---

[38] Dickey 2002: 77–99; also Bang 1921.

[39] Dickey 2002 suggests a three-stage development, with *domine* originating in 'private amatory language' in the second century BC, becoming an address used within the family by the late first century BC, and expanding into a generalised polite address in the late first century BC and early first century AD. But the early evidence for the erotic use is almost all in elegy and cannot be abstracted from the *seruitium amoris* trope in which it is embedded. Even the evidence for early familial use is thin, though Suet. *Aug.* 53 does seem to imply that it was to be expected that Augustus' sons and grandsons would address him and each other as *domine*.

[40] Adams 1995: 118–19 on the Vindolanda tablets; Dickey 2002: 89–91.

[41] Family: Seneca of his brother (*domini mei Gallionis*, *Ep.* 104.1). Superior/peer: the Trajanic senator P. Dasumius of his fellow senator Julius Ursus Servianus (*Vrsi Seruiani domini mei*, *ILS* 8379a). Dependant: a tutor of his *pupillus* (*Publium Sempronium dominum meum*, *Dig.* 32.37.2). See further *TLL* s.v. *dominus* 1925.19–52 (Kapp).

in epitaphs for family members[42] and adding the dative *domino* to the name of the addressee in the salutation of letters.[43]

Intertwined with the proliferation of *domine* and other forms in social intercourse outside the household is the increasing use of *dominus* to refer to the emperor, a long-term trend complicated by the idiosyncrasies of individual reigns.[44] Augustus had suppressed all efforts to call him *dominus*, even by his kin (apparently conflating address and referential uses).[45] By the late second century emperors were regularly addressed as *domine* and styled *dominus* (*noster*) by civilians, soldiers, imperial procurators and even senators.[46] This sea change in political discourse supplied the terminology for Mommsen's thesis of a transition from *Prinzipat* to *Dominat*.[47] Pliny's use of *domine* is one of several signs that it was already under way by the time of Trajan. Part of the explanation for this departure from the Augustan norm must be semantic divergence of the address use of *domine* from the lexeme *dominus*, as Eleanor Dickey has argued. But the link to the sphere of chattel slavery was always there to be recuperated (as Martial clearly shows, e.g. in 1.81), so the fact that Pliny and presumably others addressed Trajan as *domine* shows that he was less scrupulous than Augustus about stamping out any hint of a masterly style, despite Pliny's claims in the *Panegyricus*. One could compare the Egyptian recruit who refers to Trajan as *imperator dominus noster* in a letter to the prefect of Egypt (*CEL* no. 149, AD 113–17), which suggests that the title was current at least in the army. The impulse to style the emperor *dominus* seems to have come as much from below as from above (note the theatre audiences who hailed Augustus and Domitian as *domini* and the tendency of Greeks to style the emperor *kurios* from the beginning of the principate), and had been encouraged by Gaius, Nero and Domitian. Trajan did not – and presumably could not – return to Augustan purism.

---

[42] Bang 1921: 87–8.

[43] *CEL* nos. 141–2 and 147 (the first two to a father, the last to a patron). Fronto's letters to Antoninus Pius, Marcus Aurelius and Lucius Verus include 51 examples of *domino meo* in the salutation.

[44] Mommsen 1887–8: 18–22; Béranger 1953: 62–8; Noreña 2011b: 283–97; Lavan 2013a: 143–5.

[45] Suet. *Aug.* 53 and Dio 55.12.2. He was followed in this by Tiberius (Tac. *Ann.* 2.87; Suet. *Tib.* 27; Dio 57.8.2). In all these cases, the language used suggests that the stricture extended to the address use of *domine*. But this is the last firm evidence for the suppression of *domine* (Tac. *Ann.* 12.11.2 is often cited to suggest a similar prohibition by Claudius, but it is far too vague to bear this interpretation), so the address use of *domine* may have become established at any time in the later first century.

[46] The earliest examples of the use by senators are in a letter of Fronto (*dominus noster, Ad amicos* 1.14), a letter by the pontifex Velius Fidus to a colleague (*dominus noster, ILS* 8380) and a statue base dedicated by the legate of Numidia (*dominus imperator, AE* 1968, 585) – all from the reign of Antoninus Pius.

[47] Mommsen 1887–8: 18–22.

It remains hard for us to fully understand the connotations of Pliny's *domine*. Usage was changing, presumably with some social and geographic variation. The semantics of *dominus* probably also depended on both form and context. There may well have been a difference between the address use of *domine* in a letter and the referential use of another case in an *acclamatio* in the theatre, such as the acclamations of Domitian to which Suetonius took objection (*domino et dominae feliciter!*, Suet. *Dom.* 13.1). Despite this residual uncertainty, neither the evidence for the use of *domine* as a common epistolary address nor that for its use specifically to emperors gives grounds to suppose that it was anomalous for a senatorial legate to address the emperor as *domine* in the early second century.

Further evidence that it was in fact conventional can be found in a dossier of letters inscribed on the wall of the temple of Zeus at Aizanoi in Phrygia concerning rents due on land belonging to the temple (*MAMA* IX, pp. xxxvi–xxxvii). The inscription preserves the text of a Greek letter of the provincial governor Avidius Quietus to the city of Aizanoi followed by copies of three Latin letters that had been forwarded by Quietus: one of Hadrian to Quietus, one of Quietus to the imperial procurator Hesperus and finally Hesperus' reply to Quietus. Quietus was proconsul of Asia in AD 125–6, only fifteen years after Pliny's governorship in Bithynia (and was probably the son of Pliny's homonymous correspondent).[48] It is unfortunate that the dossier does not include Quietus' original letter to Hadrian and that Hadrian does not use any vocative in his letter to Quietus. But the remaining two letters are nonetheless instructive. Quietus addresses Hesperus in precisely the style that Trajan most often uses to Pliny: *mi Hespere carissime*. Hesperus in turn addresses Quietus as *domine*, just as Pliny normally addresses Trajan. The relationship between the two men is not entirely clear. As proconsul of Asia, Avidius Quietus was a senator of consular rank. Hesperus' identity and status are more problematic. He is identified in Quietus' letter to Aizanoi as a *procurator Augusti*. The 'patrimonial' procurator for the province of Asia, responsible for overseeing the emperor's properties in the public province, was normally an equestrian. But he had other procurators answering to him, so Hesperus may have been a subordinate procurator, perhaps a freedman, based near Aizanoi.[49]

---

[48] *PIR*² A 1409 and 1410.

[49] Procurator of Asia: Millar 1977: 329. Subordinate based in Aizanoi or Synnada and probably a freedman: Laffi 1971: 41–2 and Christol and Drew-Bear 2005 (identifying him with the freedman procurator HESPER[–] named on an undated fragmentary block of Phrygian marble found at Lepcis Magna and thus as the *procurator Phrygiae*, a post attested from the reign of Hadrian with responsibility for imperial possessions in that region, including the marble quarries at Dokimeion).

In any case Hesperus was not formally subordinate to Quietus, because the provincial procurator answered directly to the emperor, but Quietus was clearly the social superior. This is compelling evidence that the asymmetry of Trajan's *carissime* and Pliny's *domine* in Book 10 is in fact entirely typical of correspondence within the socially stratified imperial elite that governed the Empire.

Friendship, Partnership and Good Government

If the letters of Book 10 are not as anomalous or idiosyncratic as has been suggested, one important corollary is that everyday imperial correspondence shared many of their most interesting features. The letters of Book 10 certainly idealise both the relationship between emperor and governor and that between Romans rulers and provincial subjects. But neither feature is peculiar to Book 10 – or even to the rule of Trajan. Even in ordinary correspondence, emperors sought to convey affection and respect for the officials to whom they were writing and regularly idealised the workings of provincial government.

As I have already indicated, imperial letters to governors and other officials regularly use familiar forms of address. A bare cognomen is the rare exception. Emperors normally add an affectionate *mi* or *carissime*, just as Trajan does to Pliny. It is certainly not a Trajanic innovation, since the earliest examples are letters of Domitian.[50] Nor is the courtesy exclusive to senators: equestrians receive the same tokens of intimacy.[51] It is notable that the few letters that are preserved complete with the original *salutatio* show that emperors often inserted the familiar *suo* after the recipient's name.[52] A letter of Marcus Aurelius appointing the equestrian Domitius Marsianus to the post of patrimonial procurator in Narbonensis nicely shows that affectionate friendship was the normal register for imperial correspondence even with officials of lower rank:[53]

---

[50] Plin. *Ep.* 10.58.4 (Domitian to Lappius Maximus: *mi Maxime*) and *CEL* no. 85 = *P. Berlin* 8334 (Domitian to L. Laberius Maximus: *mi Maxime*).

[51] *CEL* no. 85 (Domitian to a prefect of Egypt: *mi Maxime*); Oliver 1989, no. 70 (Hadrian to a prefect of Egypt: Ῥάμμιέ μου, translated from Latin); *AE* 1962, 183 (Marcus Aurelius to a patrimonial procurator of Narbonensis: *mi Marsiane karissime mihi*; the warmest address among the surviving letters is bestowed on the man of lowest rank).

[52] *AE* 1947, 44 (Augustus to a man of rank, possibly a *curator rei publicae*); *SEG* 48, 1582 (letter of Marcus and Commodus, probably to a governor of Lycia and Pamphylia); *AE* 1962, 183 (Marcus Aurelius to a patrimonial procurator of Narbonensis).

[53] *AE* 1962, 183. The text of the letter is appended to the dedicatory inscription on the base of an equestrian statue erected in his honour in Bulla Regia.

Exemplum codicillorum

Caesar Antoninus Aug(ustus) Domitio Marsiano suo salut(em).

Ad ducenariae procurationis splendorem iamdudum te prouehere studens utor opportunitate quae nunc [o]btegit. Succede igitur Mario Pudenti
tanta cum spe perpetui fauoris mei, quantam conscientiam retinueris inno-
centiae diligentiae experientiae.

Vale mi Marsiane karissime mihi.

Copy of the letter of appointment

Caesar Antoninus Augustus to his friend Domitius Marsianus, greetings.

Having long desired to elevate you to the distinction of a procurator-
ship of two hundred thousand sesterces, I take the opportunity which now
presents itself. Take therefore the place of Marius Pudens, with confidence
that my continued favour will match your continued consciousness of your
integrity, diligence and experience.

Farewell my dearest Marsianus.

Note the familiar forms *suo* in the salutation and *mi . . . karissime mihi* in
the valediction, the profession of personal investment in the candidate's
success (*prouehere studens*) and the promise of continued favour (*fauor*).
It is also worth noting that emperors regularly style governors and other
administrators 'my friend the proconsul' etc. when writing to other parties,
for example in the many letters they sent to cities.[54] All this is characteristic of the fact that the administration of the early Empire retained
many features that sociologists would label patrimonial.[55] There were no
impersonal 'bureaucrats' in the Roman Empire; all office-holders were
(and were expected to be) fixed within a web of patronage that bound
them in personal relationships to superiors, peers, subordinates and those
whom they administered. Correspondence played a key role in creating
and continually renewing that web.

The letters of Book 10 give the impression of a virtuous partnership
between emperor and governor, both dedicated to just and beneficial
governance. Book 10 presents 'the very best of the imperial system,' as
Stadter puts it, 'illustrating the many ways in which emperor and governor
attempted to rule the provinces justly and honestly'.[56] One key mechanism by which this effect is achieved is the regularity with which Trajan
commends Pliny's actions and decisions. This too seems to be entirely

---

[54] See e.g. the letters indexed in Anastasiadis and Souris 2000 s.v. *philos*, with numerous examples of
senatorial and equestrian governors. For a lower-ranking equestrian, see the letter of Vespasian to
Sabora (*CIL* x, 8038): *Otacilium Sagittam amicum et procuratorem meum.*
[55] Saller 1982; Eich 2005; Bang and Turner 2015.   [56] Stadter 2006: 68

typical of imperial correspondence. Confirming the decision of the governor of Baetica to exile a young man for accidentally causing the death of
another young man, Hadrian endorses his judgment: 'You rightly (*recte*)
moderated the punishment of Marius Evaristus to fit the measure of the
fault. For even in the case of more serious offences, it matters whether they
were committed knowingly or by accident.'[57] He confirms the proposal of
a governor of Lugdunensis in a case of disputed *tutela* in the same terms:
'In my opinion you would rightly (*recte*) prevent this deceit [by ruling as
you propose].'[58] Marcus Aurelius similarly opens a fragmentary response
to Claudius Etoneus, probably a governor of Lycia and Pamphylia, by
commending the actions he has reported: 'You acted rightly . . .' (ὀρθῶς
ἐποίησα[ς . . .] – presumably a translation of Latin *recte fecisti*).[59] Two of
Trajan's letters to Pliny open in exactly the same way, with the emperor
commending Pliny for having acted 'rightly'.[60]

In ordinary letters, as in Book 10, emperors regularly take the time to
explain their decisions, often representing them as conforming to universal
norms of justice. Domitian's instructions (*mandata*) for the procurator of
Syria, Claudius Athenodorus, included a section on preventing abuse of the
requisitioning system. A Greek translation was published in the province,
presumably by the procurator. Domitian's instructions are grounded in an
appeal to justice: current abuses are 'most unjust' (ἀδικώτατον); 'it is just
(δίκαιον) to assist the provinces in their exhaustion'.[61] *Humanitas* figures
particularly prominently.[62] Hadrian justifies a reform of the regime for letting public contracts on the grounds that the existing system is altogether
inhumanus.[63] In a letter to the prefect of Egypt, he announces an improvement in the inheritance rights of children born to legionaries during their
term of service and describing this as a 'more humane' interpretation of the
law.[64] A particularly revealing example is a response by the co-emperors
Marcus Aurelius and Lucius Verus to Voconius Saxa, probably the governor of Africa in AD 161–2. Saxa had tried a case in which a slave had
confessed to being party to a murder but was suspected of having invented
the story in order to escape from his master's power. Saxa first condemned
him based on his own confession and then had him tortured to test his
claims about his accomplices. When torture 'confirmed' that he had made

---

[57] *Coll. Leg.* 1.11.3.   [58] *Dig.* 27.1.15.16.

[59] *SEG* 48, 1582, line 1. Cf. also line 5: ἦν δὲ εἰκός σε φροντίσαι καὶ τῶν σειτωνικ.[ῶν χρημάτων(?)].

[60] 10.16 and 28. Cf. *merito* opening 10.115, 117 and 121.

[61] Oliver 1989, no. 40, lines 19 and 21–2.

[62] See further Bauman 1980, esp. pp. 173–9, 182–201; 1996: 152–6.   [63] *Dig.* 49.14.3.6.

[64] Oliver 1989, no. 70 (φιλανθρωπότερ[ο]ν ἑρμηνεύω). As the first line of the papyrus makes clear, this
is a Greek translation of a Latin letter. The original almost certainly used some form of *humanus*.

up the story, the governor wrote to the co-emperors seeking permission to annul his earlier verdict and instead have the slave sold to another master. Their reply, preserved in Ulpian, opened by commending him for his *humanitas*:[65]

> Extat epistula Diuorum Fratrum ad Voconium Saxam . . . cuius uerba haec sunt: 'Prudenter et egregia ratione humanitatis, Saxa carissime, Primitiuum seruum, qui homicidium in se confingere metu ad dominum reuertendi suspectus esset, perseuerantem falsa demonstratione damnasti quaesiturus de consciis, quos aeque habere se commentitus fuerat, ut ad certiorem ipsius de se confessionem peruenires. Nec frustra fuit tam prudens consilium tuum, cum in tormentis constiterit neque illos ei conscios fuisse et ipsum de se temere commentum. Potes itaque decreti gratiam facere et eum per officium distrahi iubere, condicione addita, ne umquam in potestatem domini reuertatur, quem pretio recepto certum habemus libenter tali seruo cariturum.'

> There is a letter of the Divine Brothers to Voconius Saxa . . . These are its words: 'You acted judiciously and with a fine regard for *humanitas*, my dear Saxa, in condemning the slave Primitivus, who was suspected of having invented a charge of murder against himself out of fear of being returned to his master, with a view to interrogating him about the accomplices whom he had also falsely claimed to have had, in order to get a more credible confession about himself. Your judicious plan was not in vain, since torture established both that he had no accomplices and that he had recklessly lied about himself. You may therefore annul your verdict and command him to be sold by your staff, with the proviso that he never be returned to the ownership of his master. We are certain that [the master] will be glad to be deprived of a slave of that sort, once he has been paid his value.'

Saxa's proposal was relatively enlightened, in that he wanted to acquit a criminal who had confessed his own guilt (Ulpian quotes the rescript to confirm the principle that confessions should not always be believed) and he had no choice but to torture the slave, since a Roman court could not normally admit evidence from a slave except under torture.[66] But it is nonetheless striking that the grammar of the sentence ascribes the *humanitas* specifically to the decision to condemn and interrogate under torture (*damnasti quaesiturus*) – though it obviously also qualifies the purpose clause that comes at the end of the sentence ('in order to get a more credible confession about himself'). That judicial torture could be seen as part of an act of *humanitas* reveals much about the flexibility of *humanitas* and the acceptance of torture in Roman culture. What matters for present

---

[65] *Dig.* 48.18.1.27 (Ulpian *De off. procons.* 8), also discussed by Bradley 1994: 169.
[66] Buckland 1908: 87.

purposes is the fact that the emperors do not just give their approval but also recapitulate the situation as Saxa had presented it in his letter, providing a mini-narrative which constructs the governor's decision, now approved by the emperors, as an expression of Roman *prudentia* and *humanitas*. Note also the familiar *Saxa carissime*. The resulting impression of partnership in good government is entirely familiar from Book 10.

We should not rush to an instrumentalist reading which sees this idealising rhetoric as being directed at provincials. Although some letters to governors did find their way into the hands of ordinary provincials – and not just through the publication of Pliny's letters – the primary audience was always the imperial elite.[67] The vision of humane and just government seems to have been as much for their own benefit as for their provincial subjects. This is entirely characteristic of ideology in the profound sense, insofar as it distorts the vision of the dominant as much as – if not more than – that of the subaltern. Describing the torture of a slave as an act of *humanitas* is a characteristically ideological misrecognition. The men who administered the Empire – and profited most from its operations – were understandably eager to see their actions as conforming to their own exacting moral standards.

It bears pointing out that none of the features I have noted are distinctively Trajanic. The small number and uneven chronological distribution of surviving letters severely restricts the opportunities for diachronic analysis, but the overwhelming impression is one of continuity of tone and language. One possible exception is the rhetoric of the new era, idealising the Trajanic present in explicit or implicit contrast to a vilified Domitianic past. This is familiar from early Trajanic texts such as Tacitus' *Agricola* and Pliny's *Panegyricus*, and also pervades Book 10.[68] It extended to ordinary correspondence. In a letter to Didius Secundus (probably a provincial governor) about the treatment of the property of persons sent into exile, Trajan takes the opportunity to denigrate Domitian and idealise the new regime:[69]

> Caput ex rescripto diui Traiani ad Didium Secundum: 'Scio relegatorum bona auaritia superiorum temporum fisco uindicata. Sed aliud clementiae meae conuenit, qui inter cetera, quibus †innocentiam rationum mearum temporum†, hoc quoque remisi exemplum.'

> Section from a rescript of the Divine Trajan to Didius Secundus: 'I know that the property of relegated [i.e. exiled] persons has, through the greed of

---

[67] So also Woolf 2006: 104.   [68] *Ep.* 10.1.2, 3a.2, 12, 23, 55 and 97.
[69] *Dig.* 48.22.1 (Pomponius 1 *Ad Sab.*).

recent times, been claimed for the fisc. But a different approach befits my clemency. I concede this too as another example by which <I maintain> the innocence of the accounts in my times.'

The text of the penultimate clause as transmitted by the Littera Florentina is obviously problematic. The conventional explanation is that a verb (such as *tueor*) has been omitted and *meorum* was corrupted to agree with *rationum*, as translated here.[70] A reference to 'my times' (*meorum temporum*) would balance the *superiorum temporum* in the first clause and echo a similar claim in one Pliny's letters: forcing citizens to accept loans from their cities 'is not in accordance with the justice of our times' (*non est ex iustitia nostrorum temporum*).[71] However the textual problem is resolved, Trajan's letter clearly contrasted present virtue with past vice. Even in everyday correspondence, a response to a query on a fiscal matter could be an opportunity to reiterate the new regime's claim to be a break from the past.

Conclusion

Recontextualising Book 10 within the once massive, but now largely lost, corpus of imperial correspondence serves to illustrate the danger of exaggerating its political importance. Work on Latin literature is increasingly dominated by political and sociological readings. These have much to recommend them, since literary texts certainly work in the world. But it is all too easy to exaggerate the political significance of an individual literary work (or even literature as a social practice) compared to broader textual practices such as correspondence (to say nothing of the spoken discourse). This is especially true when literary texts survive severed from the wider discursive context in which they originally circulated, as is the case for the Roman world, where the vast majority of ephemeral texts has been lost. In different ways, Woolf, Stadter and Noreña all credit Book 10 with a special importance as a vehicle of imperial self-representation. Yet enough other imperial letters survive to show that the broader practice of correspondence must have been more important than the publication of Book 10 for most of the projects they discuss, whether idealising the relationship between emperor and senators or asserting the justice of Roman rule in the provinces.

---

[70] For a range of conjectures, see the apparatus to Mommsen 1868–70 (printing the transmitted text, while suggesting *temperaui* as a correction to *temporum*); Bonfante et al. 1918–31 (printing <*tueor*>); and Mommsen and Kruger 1963 (printing the transmitted text).

[71] *Ep.* 10.55. Cf. *nec nostri saeculi est* at 10.97.2.

All emperors maintained at least the fiction of personal relations with the individual members of the senatorial and equestrian elite. This is entirely in keeping with what we know about the role of patronage in Roman society. Given the amount of time that senators, office-holding equestrians and increasingly emperors spent in the provinces, they must have been heavily dependent on letters as a supplement to face-to-face contact – just as Peter White has so brilliantly illustrated for the senatorial elite of Cicero's time.[72] Looked at collectively as a discursive formation, this correspondence must have been a key medium through which relations between the *princeps* and the various strata of the imperial elite – the senatorial and equestrian orders and presumably also the emperor's own *familia* (though we have no surviving correspondence with imperial freedmen or slaves) – were continually renegotiated.

As for any wider provincial audience that may have read Book 10, it would certainly not have been their only insight into imperial correspondence and its rhetoric of good government. The Roman state invested heavily in claims to rule for the benefit of its subjects and in ensuring that those claims reached their eyes and ears.[73] The most important medium was imperial and praesidial pronouncements addressed directly to provincial audiences. We know that emperors and governors regularly wrote letters to the individual cities of the Empire and often addressed larger audience – groups of cities, provinces and even the whole Empire – through edicts.[74] These were often read aloud in public and published in a prominent place. We also know that the audience was listening because so many individuals and communities chose to copy those letters and edicts and sometimes inscribed them on monuments.[75] Book 10 would not even have given them a unique insight into the 'private' communication between emperors and governors. The epigraphic and papyrological records prove that even these letters often found their way into the hands of ordinary provincials.

Where does this leave Book 10? My goal has not been to deny that we can read Book 10 as idealising Roman provincial administration or as constructing an intimate friendship between emperor and senator, but rather to show that there is nothing special about Pliny's letters in either respect. Those operations seem to be characteristic of imperial correspondence in general. One could speculate about the effect of selection – the ways in which the particular mix of subjects in Book 10 might not be representative

---

[72] White 2010.   [73] Ando 2000, esp. ch. 4.
[74] For the surviving texts and their rhetoric, see Lavan 2013b, ch. 5.   [75] Ando 2000: 109–10.

of the wider body of correspondence that readers would have encountered in other contexts – but it is hard to press such a reading very far given our limited grasp of that larger correspondence.[76] It would probably be more fruitful to stop trying to analyse Book 10 as the vehicle of a particular political project, because it is hard to imagine a political reading of Book 10 that could not be better predicated of imperial correspondence in general. In a recent return to the subject, Greg Woolf proposes moving beyond instrumental readings, noting that all three of the revisionist papers 'tended to privilege political and therefore contemporary concerns' and 'have not done enough to take it seriously as literature'.[77] One does not have to accept Woolf's arguments that the individual letters of Book 10 are as stylised as those of Books 1–9 in order to follow his injunction to read them as literature. The 'literary' is an effect produced as much by the reader as by the text. I remain convinced that the closest analogue for the relation in which the individual letters of Book 10 stand to the practice of correspondence is the Ciceronian letter corpus rather than the earlier books of Pliny's letters (because the letters are not obviously the product of literary stylisation, as those of Books 1–9 are). But Mary Beard has already shown in a ground-breaking paper that the editorial work of selecting and arranging Cicero's letters created meaningful structures at the level of the book and invited new modes of reading that were attentive to those structures.[78] In the meantime, Pliny's first nine books had assimilated the letter book even closer to the model of the Augustan poetry book. When Book 10 was edited and published as a supplement or appendix to Books 1–9, it circulated in a reading culture whose expectations had been shaped by those earlier collections. The question to ask is how a *doctus lector* – one with an eye for 'the frames, sequences, juxtapositions, symmetries' created within a book and a taste for 'the *delectatio* of discovery (and of foiled expectations)' – would read Book 10.[79] Woolf's latest paper explores some of the possibilities. All this is largely independent of how much editing has gone into the individual letters and the collection as a whole – or indeed who the editor was. The key question is how we read it.

[76] Woolf 2006: 99–103 suggests some plausible contrasts.
[77] Woolf 2015: 136–7.   [78] Beard 2002.   [79] Whitton 2013: 12.

CHAPTER 13

Traditional Exempla *and Nerva's New Modernity*
Making Fabricius Take the Cash

Ruth Morello

How a culture handles marvels is always revealing, and Roman culture regularly opened a world of marvels for the contemplation and wonder of all. As Rhiannon Ash demonstrates in this volume, post-Domitianic writers make exotic wonders such as savage beasts from unknown climes 'safe' either by consigning them to the Empire's exotic margins, or by stage-managing them at home in the arena, under the emperor's controlling gaze. Rome had its own domestic wonders, however, in the form of its great exemplary individuals, stories about whom were transmitted through successive generations as didactic clichés, neatly packaged in retellable story patterns. These depended for their effectiveness not only upon the memorability of the feats they recorded, but also upon the familiarity generated by repeated contemplation and by the creative application of the tales in each new situation. Roman *exempla*, then, formed an extraordinary mental archive of clichés of wonder that could fade or mutate into vigorous new life in each new generation.

This chapter investigates the reworking of such exemplary material in two short Nervan/Trajanic texts: Martial *Epigrams* 11.5 and Pliny *Epistles* 8.6. Both are about republican *exempla*, although they differ in genre and in mode: Martial's epigram seems to offer playful panegyric about a new emperor's effect upon the *summi uiri* of Rome's republican past, while Pliny's letter briefly adduces republican *exempla* to attack the memory of an imperial freedman and to deplore his effect upon the contemporary senate. What unites them, however, is a treatment of *exempla* in counterfactual terms to explore human responses to power, a phenomenon that seems to gain ground in the period between Julius Caesar and Trajan, in both satirical and panegyrical modes and across multiple genres. Although Rebecca Langlands in the next chapter rightly emphasises the potential healing and uniting force of the familiar and repeatable 'story grammar' that underpins exemplary tales, this chapter explores a more Saturnalian approach in which pre-imperial *exempla* are inverted or even voided in the

302

counterfactual game that seems to speak of a modernity characterised by its disconnection from the past.

Book II was Martial's first post-Domitianic publication (probably appearing in December 96), and although its initial poem is not addressed to the new emperor, the rest of the opening sequence clearly marks it as Nerva's book; he appears as ruler of the Saturnalia in II.2, as Augustus restored in II.3, as consul under the protection of Julian/Trojan deities in II.4, and as a *princeps* who (unlike his predecessor) provides no easy cover for marital infidelities in II.6.[1] The book's frequent obscenity suggests renewed freedom and gaiety under Nerva, an atmosphere enhanced by the Saturnalian themes of (e.g.) poems 2, 6 and 15. A return to the Augustan Golden Age is also implicit in echoes of Ovid in the opening poems. The representation of the emperor as a new Augustus is, by now, conventional in accession panegyric, but Martial's own counterfactual potential to compete with his predecessors as an 'Augustan' poet is also in play.[2] In II.2 the image of a centurion reading Martial's works in the Getic frosts offers a potentially uneasy allusion to Ovid's exile poetry (one which nevertheless marks how far we have come since exiled Ovid longed to escape those frosts and bring his verses home).[3] II.3, with its implied *recusatio* of imperial epic, already begins to establish a counterfactual mode for the book, as Martial suggests he might have done even better if he could have enjoyed the patronage of a new Maecenas.[4]

II.5, however, takes us to pre-Augustan times, as the poet imagines summoning up a 'catalogue' of republican heroes (including the leaders in the Republic's final struggles) in an epigrammatic *nekuia*, in order to observe their responses to the new emperor:

> Tanta tibi est recti reuerentia, Caesar, et aequi
>   quanta Numae fuerat: sed Numa pauper erat.
> Ardua res haec est, opibus non tradere mores
>   et, cum tot Croesos uiceris, esse Numam.
> Si redeant ueteres, ingentia nomina, patres,   5
>   Elysium liceat si uacuare nemus,
> te colet inuictus pro libertate Camillus,
>   aurum Fabricius te tribuente uolet;

---

[1] On II.6 (and Martial's 'plain speaking' throughout Book II) see Fitzgerald in this volume.
[2] See Gunderson 2014: 132–3; Lowrie 2007: 102–8; cf. Kraus 2005: 186.
[3] Fitzgerald 2007: 189–90. On Martial's Ovid, cf. Geyssen 1999; Rimell 2008: 165–8; Hinds 2007. On the political quality of the opening poems of the book, see Fearnley 2003: 622.
[4] 'If Maecenas were alive now' is a recurring counterfactual for Martial: 1.107; 8.56; II.3, 12.4. See Saller 1983.

te duce gaudebit Brutus, tibi Sulla cruentus
    imperium tradet, cum positurus erit;   10
et te priuato cum Caesare Magnus amabit,
    donabit totas et tibi Crassus opes.
Ipse quoque infernis reuocatus Ditis ab umbris
    Si Cato reddatur, Caesarianus erit.

Your reverence for right and justice, Caesar, is as great as was Numa's, but
Numa was poor. This is a difficult thing, not to sacrifice *mores* to wealth, and
to be Numa when you have exceeded many a Croesus. If the ancient fathers,
mighty names, were to return, were it allowed to empty the Elysian grove,
Camillus, unconquered in liberty's defence, will pay court to you, Fabricius
will accept the gold if you give it, Brutus will rejoice in your leadership, to
you bloodstained Sulla will hand over his imperium when he is about to lay
it down; and Magnus along with Caesar (the private citizen) will love you
and Crassus will bestow on you all his wealth. Cato, too, himself, were he to
be restored, called back from the nether shades of Dis, will be caesarian.[5]

We might read 11.5 as the Nervan epigrammatist's answer to the Forum of
Augustus, or, alternatively, as homage to Horace *Odes* 1.12.33–44 (*Romulum
post hos prius an quietum | Pompili regnum memorem*, 'Should I first men-
tion Romulus after these, or the peaceful reign of Pompilius?', 33–4), where
another exemplary catalogue illustrates, in an elaborate priamel, the ethical norms now matched and exceeded by a Caesarian honorand who brings
the new *quietum . . . regnum*. Such positive readings of 11.5 abound. Nauta,
for example, takes its exemplary catalogue as an assertion of Nerva's republican spirit, 'mirroring the official ideology', while Nordh regards it as a
parade of 'waxworks skilfully arranged around the image of the emperor'.[6]
For such readers, the ghosts of the exemplary dead here enthusiastically
acknowledge Nerva's superlative rectitude and the modest forbearance of
his rule.

   Two factors should give us pause. First: an ethically normative use of
republican *exempla* is uncharacteristic of Martial's own voice; indeed, as
we shall see, he routinely ascribes such rhetoric to a *tristis turba* of hirsute
hypocrites. That is not to say that Martial never uses exemplary comparanda in panegyric – examples in praise of Domitian include 7.5, 8.4 and 9.93,
and echoes of such material appear in Martial's praise of Nerva elsewhere.[7]
However, his praise of Domitian more commonly deploys comparison with

---

[5] The translations in this chapter are partly adapted from the Loeb editions of Shackleton Bailey 1993
   (Martial) and Radice 1969 (Pliny).
[6] Nauta 2002: 437; Nordh 1954: 231. Cf. Kay 1985: 68; O'Connor 1998: 193; Gowing 2005: 105; Rimell
   2008: 162.
[7] Nauta 2002: 436–7.

divinities and demigods (particularly, in Book 9, Hercules), rather than a sustained exemplary *Heldenschau* of republican mortals.[8]

Secondly, the ethical principles the exemplary figures usually represent are shattered by the disturbingly uncharacteristic behaviour ascribed to them in 11.5; the *exempla* are further problematised by Martial's unorthodox handling of a classic rhetorical trope in which the speaker summons republican *exempla* from the dead. In oratorical contexts, the frightening solemnity of such rhetorical necromancy fitted the grand mode, and it was frequently used by Cicero to exert pressure on the living to behave properly.[9] Memorable examples include the ghost of Appius Claudius summoned to castigate Clodia in *Pro Caelio* 33–4, the 'thought experiment' that restores Clodius to life in *Pro Milone* 79, the conjuring-up of the elder Malleolus in *II Verrines* 1.94, of the Metelli in *Pro Sestio* 130, and of Marius and other famous destroyers of Gauls in *Pro Fonteio* 36, or the suggestion that Manlius and other criminally-minded Sullan colonists should call up their great patron (*Cat.* 2.20). It is a means of speaking 'home truths' to the living, of bearing witness to crimes, and of reaffirming traditional (often familial) virtue, but it is not, one would think, an epigrammatic mode: it needs strong lungs (*ualentiorum haec laterum sunt, Orator* 85) and a big occasion. Above all, these 'ghosts', good or bad, represent fixed traits: the re-vivified Clodius of the *Pro Milone* will be exactly what he was in life and the point is precisely that he could not change. Instead, it is the living who will adapt to emulate or improve upon models of the past.

Martial's version of the summons to the exemplary dead becomes a necromantic cartoon, as he empties out the Elysian grove (*Elysium liceat si uacuare nemus*, 6).[10] Furthermore, his ghosts do not enact 'restored behaviour' by re-performing the values for which they traditionally stand; rather, they affirm that in view of Nerva's existence they will no longer be the men they once were.[11] In doing this, Martial sabotages the normal mechanisms of exemplarity; *exempla* have been well conceptualised as

---

[8] Garthwaite 1993. On Hercules, see Henriksén 2012: xxviii–xxx and ad 9.64, 65, 101. Cf. Stat. *Silv.* 4.2.50–1; 4.3.155–7. In *Epig.* 9.65 we do find a playful counterfactual in Domitianic panegyric (*si tibi tunc isti uultus habitusque fuissent . . . tu iussisses Eurysthea*); cf. *Epig.* 9.103 (Paris might have returned home with Castor and Pollux instead of Helen, had they been as beautiful as Hierus and Asylus).

[9] On the grandeur of invoking the dead, see Cic. *Top.* 45, *Brut.* 322, *Or.* 85. On the motif *ab inferis excitare*, see Dufallo 2007, esp. pp. 13–35; Steel 2013: 151–9; cf. Panayotakis 2010: 300–3 on theatrical traditions of 'necromancy'.

[10] For the most famous epic version of this image, cf. the dead pouring out of Erebus in Hom. *Od.* 11.36–43.

[11] The term is originally employed by the theatre anthropologist Richard Schechner (1985), but has been applied by Dufallo 2007: 75, in particular, to instances of exemplary prosopopoeia in the late Republican and Augustan periods.

ethical models perfectly balanced between singularity and repeatability,[12] but Martial's exemplary figures are undermined on both counts, as they cede to Nerva and thus not only cease to be marvels but simultaneously lose their value as didactic clichés.

Making *exempla* change so radically is Martial's innovation, and to illustrate the shock of this, I suggest an experiment in counterfactual literary history. In the *Pro Caelio*, Cicero's Appius Claudius Caecus is the model of Claudian excellence against which his descendant's actions are to be judged, as Cicero imagines him asking Clodia, 'did I break up the treaty with Pyrrhus so that you could make shameful amorous bargains?' Now imagine a 'lost' poem by Catullus or Calvus in which Appius returns from the dead only to offer Clodia some of Pyrrhus' wealth in return for sexual favours (after all, we all know those Clodii kept it in the family . . .). This is nonsense, of course, but it works well enough as a version of Martial's *jeu d'esprit* in 11.5. If *exempla* transmit models of behaviour from an older world, Martial seems to be jamming transmission, not least by selecting two of the most intransigently virtuous *exempla* available, namely Cato and Fabricius Luscinus, to be transformed into unrecognisably venal 'wets' by the beneficent influence of the new emperor.[13]

My second text, Pliny *Epistles* 8.6, offers a briefer (but equally overblown and unexpected) list of *exempla*, this time contrasting honours awarded to conquering generals of the past for their role in expanding Roman might with the immeasurably greater ones showered upon Claudius' imperial freedman, Pallas, as reward for services performed as a civil servant in AD 52:

> Conferant se misceantque, non dico illi ueteres, Africani Achaici Numantini, sed hi proximi Marii Sullae Pompei -- nolo progredi longius --: infra Pallantis laudes iacebunt. (*Ep.* 8.6.2)

> Let -- I will not say the Africani and Achaici and Numantini of old -- but these most recent Marii, Sullas, Pompeys (I will go no further) join together and intermingle, and they will fall short of the praise accorded to Pallas.

No necromancy here, but once again a catalogue of great republicans is eclipsed by a single figure. Pliny's *exempla* illuminate the absurdity and venality of the modern imperial world, a fawning senate's poor grasp of reality and of traditional values, and even the despairing sense of

---

[12] Lowrie 2008: 177; for more on the dual ontology of *exempla*, see also Langlands 2015 and Roller 2015.

[13] Cf. Ash in this volume (p. 131) on the 'corrosive impact of interaction with Romans' implied in some of Martial's *Liber spectaculorum*, and on the emperor's 'oppressive' insistence that wild animals develop an *ingenium mitius* (*Sp.* 12.5–6).

contemporaries that the honours for Pallas must have been some kind of joke on the senate's part (*dicerem urbanos, si senatum deceret urbanitas*, 8.6.3).

Both writers' *exempla* are presented as counterfactual thought experiments (let us empty out the underworld and imagine what the dead would think of Nerva ~ imagine piling up the praise of all these men and see how it would be eclipsed by Pallas' honours). Each text engages to some degree with the expectations generated by a traditional exemplary catalogue and the stock figures who typically populate it. Both are laden with irony, as Rome's greatest men are lined up as foils to two very different moderns, one a new emperor and the other an easy target from a previous generation.

Republican *Exempla* under Imperial Rule

Gowing's influential studies have demonstrated that republican *exempla* gradually lost symbolic force during the course of the first century AD, and that the early imperial period, in particular, is marked by shifts in attitudes to the depiction of traditional *exempla* in literature and in public architecture.[14] Cicero's hortatory or apotreptic use of *exempla* gave way under Augustus to the deployment of *exempla* as contextualising tools to depict the renewal of past virtues by today's Great Man; Augustus himself was said to have wished viewers to compare his own performance with those of the great men whose statues stood in his new forum.[15] In imperial authors, republican *exempla* acquire a stock laudatory function in addresses to autocratic rulers, particularly at the moment of accession; in Pliny's *Panegyricus*, for example, Trajan is portrayed not only as a 'type' of the old Roman (*uident enim Romanum ducem unum ex illis ueteribus et priscis, Pan.* 13.5) but as having surpassed traditional *exempla* to become his own rival and *exemplum* (*sine aemulo* [*ac*] *sine exemplo secum certare, Pan.* 13.5).[16] The distance travelled since the Republic is also expressed as an awareness that special pressures in the contemporary world contribute to the excellence of the new *exemplum*; it is so much harder, after all, to embody old-fashioned virtue when one lacks the inspirational atmosphere of the days of Fabricius, Scipio or Camillus (*Pan.* 13.4):

[14] Gowing 2005 and 2009. Dufallo 2007 also argues for a change in this period in the handling of the *ab inferis excitare* motif.

[15] Suet. *Aug.* 31.5; cf. *RG* 8.5. See Gunderson 2014: 135–6.

[16] Gowing 2005: 123. The mode is set by Cic. *Marc.* 5 (a passage reworked more than once in Plin. *Pan.* 13–14), in which no previous Roman generals are mentioned by name, but all are swept up into a single group outclassed by Caesar himself.

> Hac mihi admiratione dignus imperator <uix> uideretur, si inter Fabri-
> cios et Scipiones et Camillos talis esset; tunc enim illum imitationis ardor
> semperque melior aliquis accenderet.

> A general would scarcely seem worthy of this degree of admiration if he
> had lived among Fabricii and Scipios and Camilli; for in those days a desire
> for emulation and the constant presence of a better rival could set a man
> on fire.

These are the sorts of things *exempla* are meant to do: an encomiast can
measure the latest great man against the best standards and find either that
he matches them, or that he sets an entirely new standard for himself and
others to follow.

This is not to say that the traditional exemplary tale was dead. The
literature of *exempla* was still plentiful; the deaths of each generation's great
men acquired their own exemplary status, and biographical traditions
were laboratories both for making new *exempla* and for restoring old
ones. Similarly, *exempla* masquerade as a technical resource for orators
or military men: we might think of Frontinus' collection of stratagems,
or of Valerius Maximus' collection of exemplary tales, both of which
were ostensibly designed as user-friendly sourcebooks, but which also
implicitly raise difficult questions about the value of pre-imperial *exempla*
in an imperial world.[17] Above all, however, they were still tools of the
trade in the rhetorical schools, and Quintilian expects the orator to store
vast numbers of these figures in his mind for quasi-didactic deployment
(*Inst.* 12.2.30):

> An fortitudinem, iustitiam, fidem, continentiam, frugalitatem, contemp-
> tum doloris ac mortis melius alii docebunt quam Fabricii, Curii, Reguli,
> Decii, Mucii aliique innumerabiles?[18]

> Take heroism, righteousness, trustworthiness, self-discipline, frugality, con-
> tempt for pain and for death. Who will better teach these lessons than Fabri-
> ciuses, Curiuses, Reguluses, Deciuses, Muciuses and countless others?

Such figures are, as Mayer notes, 'the small change of the exemplary
tradition'.[19] They were also, of course, done to death. Even the move

---

[17] On the complexities of these re-presentations of exemplary traditions, see especially König 2017 on
Frontinus, and Langlands 2008 and 2011 on Valerius Maximus.
[18] In a familiar move, the great individuals become pluralised types in a catalogue of names; see Henderson 2011: 153, 163; Habinek 2000: 277.
[19] Mayer 1991: 133. Fabricius (alongside Curius) appears regularly in Senecan catalogues of *exempla*.

Martial makes in building towards a Catonian climax in 11.5 has itself long been hackneyed:

> 'Decantatae,' inquis, 'in omnibus scholis fabulae istae sunt; iam mihi, cum ad contemnendam mortem uentum fuerit, Catonem narrabis.' (Sen. *Ep.* 24.6)

> Those tales are played to death in all the schools; any minute now, when we've got to the 'death should be scorned' schtick, you'll be telling me about Cato.

So Martial 11.5 is a riotous play upon the forms of a cliché. Pliny, in rather different fashion, offers a more modest but still remarkably teleologically driven mini-catalogue of such traditions.

However, neither epigram nor epistolography seems a natural haven for classic republican *exempla*. Cicero uses them far less frequently in letters than in speeches or other works; the same is true in Seneca, who, although generous with *exempla* in his dialogues, keeps them to an efficient minimum in letters.[20] Even Pliny – never one to worry about appearing a bit of a prig – tends to avoid them.[21] *Exempla* seem, perhaps, too formal for the genre.

As for Martial, our modern, urban, disrespectful poet likes to distance himself from such material (although, as we shall see, there is an unusual concentration of significant republican *exempla* in Book 11).[22] Martial's *exempla* are typically spoken by pontificating hypocrites, and implicitly teach the reader not to imitate people who spout *exempla*.[23] Take the depilated pretty boy of 9.27 who habitually invokes the bearded *maiores*,[24] but uses his 'Catonian tongue' for 'unspeakable' sexual acts (*pudet fari | Catoniana, Chreste, quod facis lingua*, 14):[25]

---

[20] See Armisen-Marchetti's response to Mayer (Mayer 1991: 174).

[21] Although he is happy to report a compliment paid to him (by Nerva), about the *exemplum simile antiquis* that he himself has provided (*Ep.* 7.33). On Plinian exemplarity (including his marked preference for contemporary *exempla* rather than traditional republican ones), see Gazich 2003; Méthy 2003. On Pliny's habit of constructing himself as a model, see Whitton 2013: 9.

[22] For an emperor's book distinguished by a concentration of poems centred upon a single motif, cf. Garthwaite 1993: 85 on the theme of hypocrisy in 'Domitian's' Book 9.

[23] Cf. *Epig.* 4.11, where Antonius Saturninus likes to associate himself with Mark Antony; Lorenz 2002: 138–9.

[24] For hairy *exempla*, cf. *Epig.* 9.47.1–2. On lack of body hair as a mark of the effeminate *cinaedus*, see Kay 1985: 164.

[25] See Greenwood 1998: 244–5; Powell 2010. For an old-fashioned appearance and a fondness for *exempla* as hypocritical covers for inadequacy, cf. *Epig.* 1.24; 5.51; Quint. *Inst.* 12.3.12; Juv. *Sat.* 2.3 (*qui Curios simulant et Bacchanalia uiuunt*); contrast Sall. *Cat.* 54.6 on Cato's preference for being (rather than merely seeming) good.

> Curios, Camillos, Quintios, Numas, Ancos,
> et quicquid umquam legimus pilosorum
> loqueris sonasque grandibus minax uerbis,
> et cum theatris saeculoque rixaris.
>
> (*Epig.* 9.27.6–9)

> You prate of Curiuses, Camilli, Quinctii, Numas, Ancuses, and of all the
> bristly philosophers we have ever read of, and you vociferate in loud and
> threatening words, and quarrel with the theatres and the age.[26]

In 7.58, Galla's dossier of ex-husbands is depressingly full of *cinaedi*, and
our speaker first advises her to seek instead a rough, hairy chap who never
shuts up about the Curii and the Fabii – and then corrects himself: *sed
habet tristis quoque turba cinaedos. Tristis turba* is the key phrase here; this
is the misery squad of bores, hypocrites and strident critics – the readers,
in other words, who shouldn't be reading Martial in the first place.

In the case of the lawyer of 6.59, *exempla* highlight an absurd inability
to respond appropriately to unglamorous reality.

> Tu Cannas Mithridaticumque bellum
> et periuria Punici furoris
> et Sullas Mariosque Muciosque
> magna uoce sonas manuque tota.
> Iam dic, Postume, de tribus capellis.
>
> (*Epig.* 6.19.5–9)

> You, with a mighty voice and every gesture you know, make the court
> ring with Cannae, and the Mithridatic War, and insensate Punic perjuries,
> and Sullas and Mariuses and Muciuses. Now mention, Postumus, my three
> goats.

Such lofty rhetoric might have suited a grand (republican?) case about public violence, murder or poisoning, but makes a lawyer foolishly ineffective
when the client just wants his neighbour brought to book for small-scale
goat-rustling.

Elsewhere, both Numa and Brutus become markers of boastful absurdity: we find *consule . . . Bruto natus/natam* as exaggerated shorthand for
'old' (10.39.1; 11.44.1). Martial's addressee in 3.62.1 claims that he drinks a
vintage from the days of Numa (*sub rege Numa condita uina bibis*). There
is no moral exemplarity here, and the drinker's implied claim to connois-
seurship is destroyed by the nonsensical exaggeration – a wine of so many
centuries in age would be undrinkable were it even available.

---

[26] See Henriksén 2012: 118. The plurals that imply endless repetition in 9.27.6 and 1.24.3 are also
distancing and belittling strategies.

So when in 11.5 Martial wades into exemplary shallows, speaking in his own voice, and piling up his *exempla* into an apparently panegyrical catalogue, he breaks from his usual practice. Nevertheless, the wider context of Book 11 suggests a possible shift in his agenda: although 11.5 remains an extreme case, republican or kingly *exempla* are more common in (Nerva's) Book 11 than in any earlier book, and the poet's attention returns frequently to the contrast between past and present.[27] The opening poems focus in particular upon a selection of *exempla* that link both the mid-republican past and the Augustan swerve with the naughtiness of Martial's modern world (Fabricius' daughter and stern Cato in 11.2, Augustus and Maecenas in 11.3, Aeneas – and Nerva as himself the best *exemplum* – in 11.4, and as the crowning piece of this opening mini-cycle the blizzard of *exempla* we've seen in 11.5).

Two of Martial's stock figures of earlier books appear with particular frequency in Book 11. Fabricius, who is reimagined as taking the famous bribe in 11.5, was earlier the model of old-fashioned virtue who might nevertheless have enjoyed Martial's *lasciuos libellos* (7.68.4), and a helplessly laughing spectator at Latinus' mimes (9.28.4).[28] In 11.16, he becomes the strait-laced template for the imagined reader (a useless one, since he can't resist Martial's wanton verses), and in 11.2 he is the simple farmer whose daughter is forbidden (along with Cato) to read Martial's book. Cato himself acquires programmatic significance from the very beginning of Martial's work as the exemplary version of Catullus' *seueriores*.[29] In the opening preface, he is the archetype of the misfit in Martial's audience who will have to leave or adapt: *Non intret Cato theatrum meum, aut si intrauerit, spectet* ('Let Cato not enter my theatre – or, if he does, let him watch', 1.*pr.*).[30]

Like Fabricius, Cato appears with particular frequency in Book 11 – as the unwelcome reader (along with Fabricius' daughter and some forbidding Sabine ladies, respectively) in 11.2 and 11.15, and as the model for a disapproving freedman in 11.39. Moreover, he already stars in counterfactuals in at least three other instances in Martial before he turns *Caesarianus*

---

[27] On the republican (and Augustan) flavour of Book 11, see Rimell 2008, esp. p. 162, together with the judiciously sceptical response of Lorenz 2010: 25.

[28] Cf. *Epig.* 10.73.3, where Fabricius is imagined as too fond of simplicity to wear the fine toga recently presented to Martial by a friend.

[29] See Lorenz 2002: 142. Other Cato epigrams include 2.89 (*exemplum* for drunkenness); 5.51 (the character who parades books and scribes, but can't offer a simple greeting in Latin or in Greek). On Cato as impediment to enjoyment, see Citroni 1975: 11. Pliny embraces his own status as the 'Cato' figure in the verse of Martial (*Ep.* 3.21) and of Sentius Augurinus (*Ep.* 4.27); cf. *Ep.* 2.17.24 (Pliny stays away from Saturnalia celebrations), and *Ep.* 8.7 (he spends Saturnalia reading Tacitus!).

[30] Fitzgerald 2007: 71–3. Cf. *Epig.* 6.64 on the critic of Martial's verse who lacks the moral authority of a Fabius or a Curius.

in 11.5. Two poems of Book 1 are about the modern possibility of being a better sort of Cato: in 1.8 a sensible modern man can be Cato (or indeed Thrasea) without the dramatic suicide (*hunc uolo, laudari qui sine morte potest*, 1.8.6), while in 1.78 one can commit suicide without being Caesar's enemy (*Hanc mortem fatis magni praeferre Catonis | fama potest. Huius Caesar amicus erat*, 1.78.9–10).[31] In both poems the message is 'be as Cato was, but don't do as Cato did'. In 9.28 Cato is also among the exemplary figures who could be 'turned' into something different from what they were by Latinus (*Latinus | ille ego sum, plausus deliciaeque tuae, | qui spectatorem potui fecisse Catonem, | soluere qui Curios Fabriciosque graues*, 9.28.1–4).[32]

Book 11 also offers other nonsensical versions of the appeal to a hallowed past. 11.15, for example, crowns one (rejected) *exemplum* with an (absurd) better one, by urging readers to speak of the penis in the good plain Latin of Numa:

> nec per circuitus loquatur illam,
> ex qua nascimur, omnium parentem
> quam sanctus Numa mentulam uocabat.
> (*Epig.* 11.15.8–10)

> and let [my book] by no roundabout phrase speak of that from which we are born, the parent of all, which hallowed Numa called the penis.

Martial's exhortation is framed in quasi-Lucretian terms: no reader of the *De rerum natura* could read *illam, ex qua nascimur, omnium parentem* without anticipating praise of *alma Venus*, but Martial's readers should know better. Martial's invocation of venerable authority ('holy Numa') before the bathetic punchline (*mentulam uocabat*) suggests that his blunt word has the best and most moral precedents, but this comic appeal to the (a?) history of language is as hollow as the appeal to Numa to validate claims about the vintage of the wine in 3.62.1.

The *mentula* is the hero(ine), as it were, of 11.16 too; here, however, we see Martial taking advantage of his appeal to Numa in 11.15 to play further counterfactual games with *exempla*, as he imagines the sexually arousing effect of his poems upon readers who model themselves upon even the most moral figures of the Roman past (*sis grauior Curio Fabricioque licet*, 'though you may be more strait-laced than Curius and Fabricius', 11.15.6). A girl from Patavium (i.e. a Livian girl, steeped in moral *exempla*?) will

---

[31] See Fitzgerald 2007: 81–3. A further modern improvement upon Catonian suicide is offered in *Epig.* 6.32, on the death of Otho.

[32] On the pairing of 9.27 and 9.28, partly by means of the *exempla uirtutis* around which the two epigrams are built, see Henriksén 2012: xxxiii.

find herself inflamed by them, and even Lucretia (another Livian girl . . .) will seek secret titillation from them behind Brutus' back. So it seems that Martial's verse has the same power as Nerva's virtues to change exemplary figures.[33]

In the light of all this, a reading of 11.5 as a priamel in praise of Nerva starts to look less convincing. Closer reading suggests rather that Martial is engaging creatively – and destructively – with the normal workings of exemplarity, and his counterfactual necromancy has shattering consequences for the whole of imperial history before the winter of 96. So let us turn once again to 11.5.

Undoing History

In Roller's schema, exemplarity functions in a four-step process, beginning with the original remarkable deed, which is soon evaluated and praised, then subsequently commemorated and monumentalised, and in successive generations re-commemorated and re-evaluated for each new era's changing circumstances.[34] This is a cyclical process, but in 11.5 Martial disrupts that cyclical exemplarity by adapting and distorting a more linear teleological design familiar from Virgil's *Heldenschau*. The *nekuia* of 11.5, while subtly recalling Odysseus' encounter with the dead in *Odyssey* 11,[35] offers an epigrammatic version of the 'Parade of Heroes' in *Aeneid* 6, featuring not only Numa (*Aen.* 6.809–12), but also Camillus (taking over the Virgilian Brutus' role as the man who acts *pro libertate*),[36] Brutus himself, Caesar and Pompey (on good terms, as they are in Virgil's Underworld, *Aen.* 6.832–5), as well as Fabricius (*paruoque potentem | Fabricium*, *Aen.* 6.843–4). Martial's adjustments to the template are important: Virgil populated the underworld with future heroes of Rome (culminating with Augustus), whom Anchises shows to his son as inspiration; by contrast, Martial evacuates Rome's past worthies from hell, in order to make them irrelevant and uninspiring in the face of the new 'special one'.[37]

---

[33] Inversion of tradition is a typical move for Martial: see e.g. *Epig.* 11.104 on the disappointingly modest wife, with Watson 2005.

[34] Roller 2009: 216–17; cf. Roller 2004: 1–7.

[35] Should we think of Achilles' wish in the Homeric scene that he had made a different choice in life? See Holzberg 2004/5: 220 on the coincidence of book number, suggesting that *Epig.* 11.5 stands for the encounter with the Underworld that must precede Martial's 'Odyssean' Spanish *nostos*.

[36] Mart. *Epig.* 11.5.7 ~ Virg. *Aen.* 6.821.

[37] Martial's scenario may owe something to mime: see Panayotakis 2008: 196 on the performances of Virgil's underworld scene in the theatre that are suggested by Augustine *Serm.* 241.5 (= *PL* 38, 1135–6): 'it seems that the ghosts of deceased Romans somehow participated in the plot'.

The epigram's opening offers a playful *adynaton* that comments on the impossibility (implicit in *ardua*, 11.5.3) of retaining *mores* under pressure of wealth (vv. 1–4).

> Tanta tibi est recti reuerentia, Caesar, et aequi
>   quanta Numae fuerat: sed Numa pauper erat.
> Ardua res haec est, opibus non tradere mores
>   et, cum tot Croesos uiceris, esse Numam.

Had no more than the first four lines survived, we would have thought this a panegyrical *nuga* about Nerva's paradoxical virtue amid riches.[38] Subsequent *exempla* play upon the wealth/poverty theme. Two of them, Fabricius and Camillus, both won fame for abjuring financial deals with foreign invaders, while a more recent (and less admirable) plutocrat, Crassus, completes this financial sequence. All three, however, now prove the general truth that it is difficult (i.e. impossible) not to give up one's *mores* in the face of extraordinary wealth, as we see Fabricius finally taking the gold, Camillus paying homage, and even grasping Crassus giving up his fortune to Nerva.[39] Crassus' presence here suggests that it is not only the positive *exempla* who abandon their natures for Nerva – *any* dominant characteristic, good or bad, is simply reversed by Nerva's existence, in an epigram that now looks like an astonishingly thorough exploration of Saturnalian upheaval.[40]

In keeping with the celebration of a new emperor's accession, a further motif emerges: freedom restored in the smooth transfer of power to a worthy ruler. Several of Martial's republican *exempla* belong to 'civil war' narratives and they draw force from a common interest in how power is transferred and transmitted.[41] With this theme comes the further paradox that dominates the rest of the poem: Rome's greatest symbols of freedom and tyranny alike will abandon their positions in the face of the new leader

---

[38] I owe this point to Andrew Morrison. The familiar link between poverty and goodness appears in the declamatory tradition with particular reference to some of our *exempla* in 11.5 (e.g. Sen. *Contr.* 2.1.8: a poor man's son who refuses the opportunity to be adopted by a rich man who has disinherited his own sons expresses gratitude for the poverty that enables him to live blamelessly, adducing familiar *exempla* in support: Croesus, Crassus, Tubero and Fabricius). On the special value of such figures to the moralist, see Mayer 1991: 165. NB in Book 11, poverty and old-fashioned severity as paired concepts are rejected in poems 2, 3 and 5, and to some extent in 4.

[39] Crassus exemplifies *auaritia* in Val. Max. 9.4.1, and this vice dominates the opening of Plutarch's *Life of Crassus*. Cf. Cic. *Fin.* 2.75, 3.22; Sen. *Contr.* 2.1.7; 5.1; 5.7; 7.2.7; Sen. *NQ* 5.18.10.

[40] NB Dolansky 2011: 495 on the Saturnalia, when 'normative codes of behaviour were reversed'.

[41] On this template see Breed, Damon and Rossi 2010: 3–21. Camillus might seem an odd figure in this context, although in some ancient sources he too is associated with Concord and with the sharing and extension of power (as the man who vowed a temple of Concordia after a particularly difficult episode in the history of the struggle of the orders): Plut. *Cam.* 42.3–4; Momigliano 1942; Farrell 2013.

who has finally joined freedom to the principate (*res olim dissociabiles*, in Tacitus' words).[42] This is edgy, potentially risky comic writing, reflecting and outrageously enacting the struggles already found in the exemplary tradition in its effort to accommodate the effects of Roman civil wars. Valerius Maximus, for example, explicitly marks out civil war themes as disturbingly unwelcome in exemplary texts (3.3.2), while Frontinus returns repeatedly to tales of civil war in his 'disconcerting, disorienting miscellany of episodes', in which foreign wars and internecine conflict are presented in a turbulently repetitive exploration of disharmony.[43]

In Martial, the change to the *exempla* is not necessarily positive, and the whole situation seems even more odd when one tries to find Nerva's implicit place within these refashioned exemplary narratives. The emperor is from the start an impossible blend of opposites. He matches the modest-living Numa in justice and moderation, for example,[44] but also beats Croesus for wealth (and will be further enriched by the counterfactual acquisition of Crassus' wealth too). One might expect to see him outclass Numa, Fabricius, Curius, Pompey and Caesar *in the very qualities they exemplified* but in the cases of the two most intransigently consistent virtuous *exempla*, he appears in Martial's counterfactual history on the 'wrong side', as the Pyrrhus who *succeeds* in his bribery (*te tribuente*) of Fabricius' imagined ghost and the Caesar who (finally) wins over the Cato who was the symbol of resistance to (both) Caesarism and epigram.[45]

Fabricius was characterised in a colourful tradition by his honourable aversion to bribery (and his rejection of bribes offered, variously, by Pyrrhus, Pyrrhus' doctor and Samnite enemies), his resistance to the allure of great (even kingly) power, his personal poverty, contempt for Epicurean pleasure, and stern insistence that others live by proper standards of frugality: as Buszard observes, 'he is not virtuous despite his poverty; his poverty reflects and enhances his virtue'. He is accorded extraordinary prominence in Plutarch's *Life of Pyrrhus*, as the model Roman statesman.[46] He is also

---

[42] Tac. *Agr.* 3.1.

[43] See A. König forthcoming. The dangers of writing about Cato during the empire are famously explored in the *Dialogus*; on the difficulties of interpreting Cato's significance in that work, see van den Berg 2014, esp. pp. 124–57; cf. Bartsch 1994: 101–25.

[44] On a special association of Numa with Nerva in Martial, see Henriksén 2012: 118.

[45] On Martial's verse as allowing a variety of incompatible, possibly uncomfortable perspectives, while still remaining light-hearted, see Garthwaite 1993: 94; cf. Lorenz 2002: 142 on Martial's persona as that of a 'naïve Figur, die eine komische Panegyrik vorträgt'. On the 'porous boundary' between praise and mockery, see Garthwaite 2009: 427.

[46] Plut. *Pyrrhus* 20–21.4; also Cic. *Cael.* 39 (poverty and resistance to pleasure), *Off.* 3.86; Hor. *Carm.* 1.12.40–4; Val. Max. 4.3.6; Col. *RR* 1.pr.13–14; Sen. *Ep.* 120.6; Quint. *Inst.* 12.2.30; Gell. *NA* 4.8.7; Flor. 1.13.21; Tac. *Ann.* 2.88. On Fabricius, see Buszard 2005, esp. pp. 482–6; Vigourt 2001;

remembered for a counterfactual assertion of his own, in which he claimed that if Pyrrhus' own people were to know Fabricius, they would prefer him to Pyrrhus as their ruler.[47] For Quintilian, Fabricius was an *exemplum* unusable in any context other than a praise of principled poverty.[48] This is, then, a most unexpected character to abandon his *mores* in the face of extraordinary wealth and power, and yet in this new world he will not only take the bribe but want it (*uolet*). Martial's epigram is an adynaton from start to finish, in which even the most stable and reassuring material from the past is now reconsidered and changed by its imagined interaction with the modern world.[49]

Just to enhance the bizarre 'Alice in Wonderland' feel, the changes in the *exempla* are expressed in an unexpected shift from the 'future less vivid' construction, with its quasi-counterfactual present subjunctive (*redeant*), to the simple future indicative that is conjured into existence by the poet's thought experiment: if we WERE TO summon all our great men from the dead, they WILL behave in front of Nerva as they never did in life. It is conceivable that the influence of Virgilian prophecies and the *Heldenschau* of *Aeneid* 6 is to be felt in the apodosis in each imagined situation.[50] At all events, in Martial's epigram, those who stood for freedom (one way or another) WILL simply abandon that principle: Camillus, who fought for liberty, WILL cultivate Nerva; Brutus WILL rejoice in this Caesar's rule; Sulla WILL change his decision to return power to its normal channels; Caesar and Pompey, who could not acknowledge any leader, WILL now do so; and even their colleague Crassus (the most modern Croesus among Martial's *exempla*) WILL cede his financial power. Cato, the ultimate symbol of republican freedom, crowns this foray into the world of the impossible by embracing the Caesarism that has (before *this* Caesar) been synonymous with the loss of freedom. That the climax (and epigrammatic 'point') of the poem is that Cato WILL BE a Caesarian (*Caesarianus erit*) acknowledges that our impossible, imaginary situation WILL call forth new reality; this is the crucial shift of outlook that guarantees the permanence for Caesarism that

---

Berrendonner 2001 (on removal of Rufinus from senate for possession of excessive silverware, cf. Flor. 1.13.21); Tac. *Ann.* 2.88 (Fabricius still a 'live' *exemplum* for Tiberius).

[47] Plut. *Pyrrh.* 20–1; *Apophthegmata* 194–5.

[48] Quint. *Inst.* 7.2.38: Fabricius could not feature in a defence of theft on the grounds of poverty and need.

[49] This mode is found in other epigrams that praise the emperor (e.g. *Epig.* 1.6 an *adynaton* of nature).

[50] Think of such passages as Virg. *Aen.* 1.292–3 (*cana Fides et Vesta, Remo cum fratre Quirinus | iura dabunt*). The future tenses in Anchises' prophetic speech to Aeneas in Book 6 (in which, after all, he too implores Caesar to give up his attempt to gain supreme power) are in the background here too. For the definitively 'imperial' future tense, see Ash in this volume on Mart. *Sp.* 1.7–8, and compare also the future *optabit* in Lucan 10.154 (discussed below).

could no longer exist for Fabricius, Sulla or Brutus. The poem shifts, then, from today's Caesarian rectitude (*tanta tibi est recti reuerentia, Caesar*), to an exemplary past (*Numa pauper erat*) that is now erased by the greater achievement of a new Caesar, and points finally to the certainty of a future that will itself also eradicate and undo the past (*colet, uolet, gaudebit, tradet, amabit, donabit,* CAESARIANVS ERIT).[51] Despite the illusory Catonian teleology in the catalogue, we begin and end with (this) Caesar, who also negates every bit of history in between. The parallel themes of money and freedom/succession work together in a counterfactual study of the flow of *more* power and money to Nerva, who already beats all Croesuses. Moreover, as each exemplary figure gives up the thing that makes him distinctive, there is no ethical reassessment of his original deed in each instance: it is simply an unnecessary act in a world where Nerva exists, and so can be imaginatively and counterfactually excised from history.

Martial's radical exploitation of the counterfactual mode in this poem positions us at multiple renewal points in history simultaneously, as he 'undoes' not only imperial history (by omitting it entirely from his catalogue: not even Augustus is called upon here to approve the new successor) but the memory of republican history, too, sweeping away the triumviral wranglings of the 60s–40s BC and the dictatorship of the 80s, and imaginatively suggesting a new 'regal' period under the Just King Numa/Nerva, when the most unbending opponents of kings and tyrants willingly support the newcomer and *all* our civil wars never happened. That the 'quiet' Nerva's avatar is the peaceful Numa (also often depicted as elderly, like Nerva), who was the first to *take over* power in the new Rome after the turbulence of Romulus' foundation, only re-emphasises that this Saturnalian *jeu d'esprit* is marking a turning point in history, allowing us to heal civil discord and forget the violent death of a ruler.[52] The most recent 'transfer of power' is elided in this fantasy tale in which one is never quite sure where one is on the historical timeline, and the new emperor is not, after all, the old man who came to power after a murderous end to the previous regime, but the virtuous man of destiny, formed by nature to be a natural recipient of power willingly handed on. So far, then, this epigram does indeed work as a creatively bizarre panegyric.

---

[51] As Alice König reminds me, this is significant in the light of Martial's publication of a new version of Book 10 of the *Epigrams*.

[52] Numa is the archetypal 'wise successor'; Martial's audience might well read the Numa in this poem in light of the Numa in Virgil's Underworld (who follows in the sequence of Anchises' speech not only after Romulus but also after Augustus): Virg. *Aen.* 6.809–12. Dufallo 2007: 119: 'the importance of Numa's achievement in bringing peace to early Rome appears, as a consequence, to lie first and foremost in its capacity to recall the possibility of peace to the subjects of Augustus'.

Change and the Imperial Counterfactual

This is not, of course, the first attempt at a counterfactual treatment of classic republican *exempla* in the imperial period – nor, indeed, is it the only uncomfortable counterfactual thought experiment associated with Nerva in our surviving texts. Pliny gives us a curious anecdote about a dinner at Nerva's house (*Ep.* 4.22.4–6).[53] Conversation turns to the memory of Catullus Messalinus, a man of positively Juvenalian disrepute, and one of Domitian's two most notorious informers (the other one is reclining beside Nerva at this very party). Nerva asks, 'What would have happened to him if he had survived until today?' Mauricus replies, 'He would have been here, dining with us.' It is easy to read this anecdote as showing off the ruefully self-aware wit of Mauricus, but it is also precisely this kind of 'what if' question that is naturally asked at a period like the one immediately after Domitian's assassination. Syme, indeed, suggested that what is on show here is a sly gambit on Nerva's part, a provocative question from a subtle and canny survivor that elicits exactly the answer he is looking for and shuts down a potentially uncomfortable conversation. At all events, Martial 11.5, although seemingly a most unusual production in itself, may have been well addressed to an emperor who, as a poet in the lighter genres himself *and* (if we follow Syme) a master of the exemplary counterfactual, would be sympathetic to such literary endeavour.[54]

The counterfactual (as a 'contrary to fact in present time' construction) is built into the use of *exempla*, since the underlying question of so many appeals to *exempla* is 'what would X do if he were here now?'[55] However, the counterfactual mode acquires new life during the imperial period, thanks to the increasing prominence of declamation, which regularly required its practitioners to turn historical or mythological events topsy-turvy and to ask counterfactual questions which echo the rhetorical moves of Martial 11.5.[56] Famous showpieces on republican topics asked, 'Should Cicero beg Antony for his life?' (Sen. *Suas.* 6) or 'Should Cicero burn his writings in exchange for guarantees of safety from Antony?' (*Suas.* 7); the speaker might adduce arguments from character suggesting that Cicero (being the man he was) would never do this (e.g. *Suas.* 6.14).[57] It is not difficult, then

[53] On the importance of such social contexts as occasions for the extratextual renegotiation and re-mediation of exemplary material, see Langlands in this volume.
[54] Syme 1958: 5–6; cf. Plin. *Ep.* 7.33 (above). For Nerva as Tibullan poet, see Martial 8.70, 9.26; cf. Plin. *Ep.* 5.3.5.
[55] Cf. the quasi-historical thought experiment ('contrary to fact in past time') in Livy 9.17–19: 'what would have happened if Alexander had invaded Italy?'
[56] See van der Poel 2009.   [57] See Roller 1997: 124.

(although I know of no specific surviving instance), to imagine a declamatory exercise entitled 'should Fabricius take Pyrrhus' cash?'

The undoing of the past is further implied in any *suasoria* in which a long-dead republican is addressed; even such texts as the pseudo-Sallustian 'Letters to Caesar' imply that history might have been different if only the speaker had been able to advise and persuade Caesar better than his real contemporaries had. Cicero's *Pro Marcello* 17 ascribes to Caesar himself the wish that he could bring back civil war casualties from the dead – an 'undoing' of history in this first 'imperial' panegyric that is later reflected in Pliny's speech for Trajan (*infectumque reddere quicquid fieri non oportuerit, Pan.* 80.3). Although rewriting darker events of the past, as a kind of healing escapism, is not quite the same as the radical undoing of the great exemplary acts that Martial embarks upon, it is clearly part of the trend towards the counterfactual that we are tracing in this chapter.

Other versions of the phenomenon posit an 'ethical' time travel *back* to the past, as they ask how the men of today would be if they could be transported back to better times; a famous instance is the assurance in the *Dialogus* that just living in the past *would have* made today's men into good orators.[58] Conversely, in Livy's account of Cato's speech against the repeal of the Lex Oppia, Cato contrasts the virtue of the relatively recent past with the likely greed of contemporary women, who (if transported back in time) would have stood in the streets to take the gifts of Pyrrhus' ambassador, Cineas (34.4.11).[59]

There is also, of course, a further theatrical context in which the counterfactual was a routine element – one with which Martial himself was very familiar – namely the re-enactment of familiar tales (including Roman 'historical myths') as thrillingly novel punishments for criminals. In this extratextual setting (frequently retextualised by Martial) the most cliché *exempla* become wonders again, as they fascinate and horrify a new age of spectators, while simultaneously being contained and devalued by being played out in the arena. The classic 'miracle' (*tam saeua miracula*, 1.21.3) of Mucius Scaevola burning his own hand, for example, is downgraded in 8.30 to 'Caesarian' sport:

---

[58] Tac. *Dial.* 41.5; see Gowing 2005: 116–17 on the argument that men like Cicero are no longer needed and that the republican past is no longer relevant to today; cf. Mayer 2001: 215 on Hor. *Sat.* 1.10.68 (asserting that the rough Lucilius would change his ways if he were brought into life in the modern world). For the cliché that it was easier to live an exemplary life in the old days, see (e.g.) Sen. *Contr.* 2.1.18 (*facile est, ubi non noueris diuitias, esse pauperem*); Plin. *Pan.* 13.4 (discussed above).

[59] See Chaplin 2000: 97–105. Here the imagined failure to live up to the *exemplum* is the classic symptom of moral decline; in Martial, however, overturning the *exempla* is the symptom of *mores* retained.

> Qui nunc Caesareae lusus spectatur harenae,
>   temporibus Bruti gloria summa fuit.
>
>   (*Epig.* 8.30.1–2)

The entertainment now viewed in Caesar's arena was the summit of glory
in Brutus' days.

Martial's return to this scene in 10.25 completes the familiar move, as
Martial insists (as he did in regard to Cato's suicide) that there are better
decisions to make, and that a truly brave man would simply refuse to
endure such torture and accept instead an inglorious death. In any theatrical re-enactment, of course, there was always a risk of an unscripted
reversal of the usual story: one might think, for example, of the bear that
eats 'Orpheus' in *Spectacula* 21.[60]

   In the literary tradition, other poetic counterfactuals perform mock-
rebellions against the ethical dominance of the past. Ovid's cheeky rejection
of stern *exempla*, for example, has most to do with how much he himself
refuses to conform to them (and welcomes new interpretations in which
they conform to his requirements). In the *Ars amatoria*, he asserts that he
prefers the *cultus* of the modern day to the simplicity of the old days (*Prisca
iuuent alios; ego me nunc denique natum | gratulor: haec aetas moribus apta
meis*, 3.121–2), while elsewhere making light of one of the most familiar stories from Rome's earliest days, the rape of the Sabine women; once again,
the counterfactual mode (with an apodosis expressed in the future tense)
is the vehicle (*Ars* 1.131–2):

> Romule, militibus scisti dare commoda solus:
>   haec mihi si dederis commoda, miles ero.

> Romulus, you alone knew how to give perks to your soldiers: if you give
> such perks to me, *I'll* be a soldier.

Later literary counterfactual treatments of exemplary figures, however,
begin to imagine the effect of more modern environments on past individuals; from the pressure exerted *by* the past in traditional ethical exemplary
contexts we move to the pressure *on* the past and the surprise effects
that can be achieved by exploring the counterfactual. When Lucan, for
example, shows us Caesar luxuriating at Cleopatra's banquet, noting the
folly of parading extraordinary wealth to such a man, his meditation
depends for its full effect upon a counterfactual, as he imagines the

---

[60] See Coleman 1990: 62 (cf. ibid. 71 on staged naval battles that could go either way). On Martial's
    Scaevola epigrams, see Fitzgerald 2007: 57–67.

temptations Egyptian splendours would have exerted upon even the most high-principled of the Republic's greatest paupers, Fabricius, Curius and Cincinnatus (*BC* 10.149–54):

> Non sit licet ille nefando
> Marte paratus opes mundi quaesisse ruina;
> pone duces priscos et nomina pauperis aeui,
> Fabricios Curiosque graues, hic ille recumbat
> sordidus Etruscis abductus consul aratris:
> optabit patriae talem duxisse triumphum.

> Even if it were not Caesar, in his impious warfare greedy to get wealth by the havoc of a world – place here the ancient leaders whose names adorn an age of poverty, Fabricii and stern Curiuses, or let the consul, summoned unwashed from his plough in Etruria, take his place at this table, and he will pray to celebrate for his country a triumph as splendid.

Here again we find Fabricius and his kind abandoning their indifference to wealth under the pressure of extraordinary opulence (albeit with their country's glory in mind rather than their own), while this Caesar remains unchanged and unchanging (albeit only in his persistent viciousness).[61] In Book 3, we have already seen Lucan surveying a catalogue of historical moments at which Rome's treasury was enriched, as Caesar breaks down its doors and removes the gold that the Gauls left behind when they were chased from Rome by Camillus, the wealth brought back by Pompey and Cato – and the wealth that Fabricius refused to take from a king (*quo te Fabricius regi non uendidit auro*, 3.160).[62] Once again, history is undone – here in a more straightforwardly sinister way – by the first of the imperial Caesars.[63] This passage now forces us to reread Pompey's speech in Book 7 with a more cynical eye, and to re-evaluate the misguided counterfactual that Lucan ascribes to him (*BC* 7.358–60):

> Si Curios his fata darent reducesque Camillos
> temporibus Deciosque caput fatale uouentis,
> hinc starent.

> If the fates restored the Curiuses, and returned to our age the Camilli and the Decii who devoted their lives to death, they would stand on our side.

---

[61] See Lintott 2010: 258. For Caesar as a cunning dissimulator at Egyptian feasts, cf. Frontin. *Strat.* 1.1.5.

[62] Cf. *BC* 7.358–9.

[63] Cf. the punchline at *BC* 3.168: *pauperiorque fuit tunc primum Caesare Roma* ('then for the first time Rome was poorer than a Caesar'). Cf. *Epig.* 12.15.3–5 on how the new emperor put Domitian's treasures on public display in temples (before then, *omnes cum Ioue pauperes eramus*).

Pompey assumes here that traditional *exempla* can still work as they always did, and that great men would oppose Caesarism in their imagined returns to life; by contrast, Lucan's nuanced counterfactual in Book 10 sketches the degree to which they would become more like Caesar himself.

For counterfactual panegyric, we can turn to Statius *Silvae* 1.1, in praise of Domitian's giant equestrian statue, which already makes some of the same moves as Martial 11.5.[64] In an extended series of counterfactual propositions, the poet manipulates an array of *exempla* from the past, drawing upon the physical qualities of the statue and the historical or mythical associations of its environment to highlight the degree to which it (and, by extension, the emperor himself) towers above all forerunners. This horse, Statius says, is so much bigger than epic's Wooden Horse that Troy simply *could not have* held it, *even if* her walls had been pulled apart.[65] There is a Virgilian 'reality' here: we are expected to remember Aeneas' account (*Aen.* 2.235–9) of the partial demolition of Troy's wall and the joyful efforts of boys and maidens to pull the Horse into the doomed city. Statius, however, builds his images from this Virgilian 'reality' to an impossible climax that demolishes even the traditional narrative of Hector's death as it imagines Aeneas and Hector together trying to pull the beast into the city (*ipse nec Aeneas nec magnus duceret Hector!*). In the real Roman cityscape, Domitian's horse *is* in position in the Forum, where it intimidates and surpasses all other 'horses' in the vicinity: Castor's horse, Cyllarus, is terrified in the temple nearby (*Silv.* 1.1.53–4), and the new arrival dwarfs Julius Caesar's appropriation of the equestrian statue of Alexander in the nearby Forum of Caesar. Finally, even Marcus Curtius, who famously performed a *devotio* by riding his horse into a chasm to pacify the gods, lifts his head from the lake named in his honour to acknowledge Domitian's superiority as an equestrian.[66] A counterfactual that substitutes Domitian for Curtius rewrites the tale of Curtius' sacrifice too (*Silv.* 1.1.81–3):

> 'Quod si nostra tulissent
> saecula, temptasses me non audente profundo
> ire lacu, sed Roma tuas tenuisset habenas.'

> 'But if our age had borne you, you would have ventured to plunge into the lake's depths, though I dared not; but Rome would have held your reins.'

---

[64] Parallel noted already by Nauta 2002: 437.

[65] The Virgilian horse is suggested already by the speculation that Pallas could have contributed to its making (*Silv.* 1.1.5–6 *an te Palladiae . . . effinxere manus* ~ Virg. *Aen.* 2.15 *diuina Palladis arte*). On such echoes of the *Aeneid*, see (e.g.) Geyssen 1996: 48–56.

[66] Livy 7.6.1–6; D.H. 14.11.20–1; Val. Max. 5.6.2; Cass. Dio fr. 30.2 ~ Zonar. 7.25; Varro *LL* 5.148–50.

The original Curtius plunged into the chasm because of an oracle requiring Rome to sacrifice her most valuable resource (*quo plurimum populus Romanus posset*, Livy 7.6.1); his courage *would have been* surpassed by this new horseman in the Forum (i.e. Domitian), who *is*, nevertheless, too valuable to sacrifice and would have been prevented from plunging to his death. The emperor's superiority is expressed, then, in terms of his capacity to change the story and to 'undo' the *exemplum*.

Most revealing for our purposes is the interaction between the memory of the Caesarian and Augustan period and the Domitianic horse, since Statius exploits the Caesarian environment of the statue to construct a much briefer and more focused Caesarian version of the counterfactuals we have seen in Martial 11.5. In both cases, the 'punchline' is Cato's conversion to Caesarism: *te signa ferente | et minor in leges gener et Cato Caesaris iret* ('with you as standard-bearer, both his son-in-law – the "lesser man" – and Cato would march according to Caesar's laws', *Silvae* 1.1.27–8). Once again the past acknowledges the superiority of the present, as Domitian surpasses Caesar in clemency, and (in the poetic counterfactual, at least) eradicates the need for the historical civil war: Magnus becomes *minor* and even Cato (by now the climax of all Caesarian 'priamels'?) accepts this new Caesar.[67]

We can, then, read Martial 11.5 as a reworking, in his book for the new emperor, of a literary predecessor's panegyric of the old one. More broadly, both works participate in a much wider interdiscursivity, as they manipulate exemplary figures and story-patterns that had become embedded in the wider cultural discourse about the relevance of traditional virtues to the new imperial world. The counterfactual, it seems, develops partly as a response to Caesarian power, and by December 96 is already becoming a distinctive modern mode of playful panegyric and satire alike in the post-Julian world.

Bathetic Teleology and the Counterfactual Catalogue

But now finally we turn to Pliny, and look from a different perspective at some of the themes that have emerged from the study of Martial. Once again, we find a rare appearance of republican *exempla* in a genre where they are not usually most at home, namely the list of republican greats in *Epistles* 8.6 that acts as comparandum for the absurd celebration of Pallas

---

[67] Dewar 1998: 73. On the Forum Romanum of the post-Augustan period as a 'unified monumental precinct proclaiming the glory of the Julian house', see Dewar 1998: 69–70. On another possible reference to Domitian's equestrian statue in Book 11, see Nauta 2002: 438 on *Epig.* 11.21.

that Pliny documents. This time the exemplary catalogue is deployed in hyperbolic condemnation, but the counterfactual mode is again the delivery mechanism for quasi-comic exploration of the absurdities of power.[68]

Epistles 8.6 is the second of Pliny's letters on this subject. In *Epistles* 7.29, Pliny has read the inscription in honour of Pallas, Claudius' notorious freedman (and former slave of Antonia Minor), recording the award of praetorian insignia voted for him in 52, together with the substantial sum which Pallas turned down (*huic senatus ob fidem pietatemque erga patronos ornamenta praetoria decreuit et sestertium centies quinquagies, cuius honore contentus fuit*, 7.29.2).[69] The honour paid to Pallas is farcically inappropriate (*mimica et inepta*), and the inscription is evidence of Pallas' misguided attempt to pose as an *exemplum* of self-restraint (*ausus est . . . etiam ut moderationis exemplum posteris prodere*, 7.29.3). Pliny's addressee, Montanus, is expected to hover between laughter, outrage and disbelief (*Ridebis, deinde indignaberis, deinde ridebis, si legeris, quod nisi legeris non potes credere*, 7.29.1).

In the much longer *Epistles* 8.6, Pliny repeats the inscription verbatim and then reveals that he has made a historian's effort to seek out the senate's original honorific decree – which eclipses the inscription in absurdity (*Postea mihi uisum est pretium operae ipsum senatus consultum quaerere. Inueni tam copiosum et effusum, ut ille superbissimus titulus modicus atque etiam demissus uideretur*, 8.6.2). The letter responds to the decree section by section, exploring the panegyric elements of the decree as evidence for the senate's degeneracy. Pliny does not adduce Fabricius here (and I am not, indeed, arguing for any direct relationship between Pliny's letter and Martial 11.5). However, once again, a 'modest' refusal to accept a cash gift is a key feature of the story, and, as *Epistles* 7.29 established, it is part of the absurdity that a freedman who was richer than Crassus posed as an *exemplum* of moderation on the very grounds that he refused to add yet more to his already swollen bank account. Moreover, the letter becomes a detailed study of misplaced panegyric offered by the senate to a low-status recipient for comparatively unglamorous service to the state – such effusiveness, Pliny says, might suggest borders extended and armies rescued (*prolatos imperi fines, redditos exercitus rei publicae credas*, 8.6.6).

To add to the topsy-turvy quality of the whole affair, it seems that the emperor intervened to beg Pallas to accept the money; *this* emperor (unlike

---

[68] On Pliny's two Pallas letters, see Leach 2013.

[69] Pliny here makes no mention of Pallas', extraordinary wealth, but his uncle made much of it (Plin. *NH* 33.134). Pallas was among the freedmen who became richer than Crassus (cf. Tac. *Ann.* 12.53).

Martial's Nerva in his counterfactual encounter with Fabricius) was unsuccessful, and he eventually instructed the senate to withdraw the monetary award. Pliny dwells upon the inversion of the relative status of freedman on the one hand and emperor and senate on the other, as the ruler obeys the public commands of the servant (*Imaginare Caesarem liberti precibus uel potius imperio coram senatu obtemperantem*, 8.6.12) and the servile senate offers praetorian insignia to a slave (*mitto quod Pallanti seruo praetoria ornamenta offeruntur – quippe offeruntur a seruis*, 8.6.3). This inversion of the status of all parties is a public and political version of the temporary social upheaval of the Saturnalia.[70]

Pliny's commentary on the decree's text begins with the list of *exempla*. There is no suggestion, however, that such *exempla* featured in the senate's decree, and the effects achieved by inserting them into the narrative are Pliny's own. The exemplary figures are not summoned from the dead, but they are given agency in 'gathering themselves and mixing themselves together' (*conferant se misceantque*) as the foil to Pallas. The brief catalogue is expressed in two parts, of three names each; in keeping with Pliny's observation in *Epistles* 8.6.6, all the names are those of Rome's greatest commanders. Pliny begins with the heroes of the middle Republic who are represented only by 'territorial' *cognomina* won by expansion into new provinces (including Greece) or by the annihilation of old enemies (*illi ueteres Africani, Achaici, Numantini*); we move on to men with more prosaically familial names (all with disturbing associations) who exemplify the disturbing threat of outstanding individuals and personal ambition for power (*hi proximi Marii, Sullae, Pompeii*).[71] The generalising plurals both suggest that the list could be far longer than it is, and downplay the great individuals themselves, who are now subsumed into the collective and eclipsed by the unimpressive Greek name of the honorand.

Furthermore, Pliny's climactic *recusatio* (*nolo progredi longius*) suggests an implicit test for the reader; if this short set of *exempla* has already felt like a potted history of how power and ambition has shifted over the generations, then to finish the sequence brings us right up to date in the

---

[70] The implicit presence of the Saturnalian motif is enhanced for Pliny's sequential readers by the juxtaposition of this letter with *Ep.* 8.7, in which Pliny writes to Tacitus that he is (metaphorically?) extending his Saturnalia holiday. On 'Saturnalian' effects created by letter juxtaposition in Pliny Book 8, see Morello 2015: 160–2.

[71] *Proximi* here can be read as merely in contrast with *ueteres*, or as part of a collapsing of time (comparable with that which we have seen in Mart. 11.5). From the perspective of someone observing the senate's behaviour under Claudius, of course, Pompey, at least (if not, perhaps, Marius or Sulla), could still seem part of relatively recent history, but by the time of Trajan, referring to any of these three as *proximi* requires a certain sleight of hand, and suggests that one of the natural ways to deal with republican *exempla* is to elide the decades of imperial rule.

imperial world. The teleological drive of Pliny's catalogue (as, ultimately, of Martial's) is towards Caesarism and one-man rule. Surely the next hero in this chronological sequence is Julius Caesar (and, indeed, every subsequent Caesar)? Pliny, however, changes teleological direction, as it were, as the real *telos* turns out to be the Greek slave Pallas, in a context in which we have been led to expect the more usual Caesarian punchline. And although Pliny self-consciously avoids explicitly including Caesar among the 'foils' in Pallas' priamel, the senate, it seems, is implicitly less discreet (and more willing to 'go further'), since the plaque recording the honours paid to Pallas by the decree is affixed in the most public place possible: the base of Julius Caesar's statue.[72] The symbolism of this location for Pallas' inscription is striking. If the equestrian statue of Domitian in the Forum is an 'equine cuckoo' in a Caesarian nest, to use Dewar's vivid image, then Pliny has converted the scenario to bathos: here the interloper is not Statius' aggressive imperial equine but an absurdly unworthy subordinate whose Greek name is incongruously recorded on Caesar's own statue base.[73]

The counterfactual mode here supports Pliny's implicit message. Once again, the subjunctives and the imagined piling-up of *exempla* to demonstrate the successive debasement of panegyrical commemoration suggest the despair about modernity that is characteristic of the period. Once again, the apodosis in the 'future less vivid' construction is a future indicative (a much more natural one, since we are not in the world of *adynata* here, and Pliny is merely predicting the inevitable result of his thought experiment: *infra Pallantis laudes **iacebunt***). Moreover, Pliny's exemplary contrast between modern honorand and *Heldenschau* initially encourages the reader to accept the validity of the old *exempla* as a starkly hyperbolical contrast between the virtue of the senatorial military men of olden times, worthy recipients of the praise of their peers, and the modern inadequacy of senate and honorand alike. As the brief catalogue progresses, however, we realise its more sinister teleological force: these *exempla* are not just 'mixed up together' as the foil to Pallas, but rather they also sketch the degeneration of the *exempla* themselves as Rome heads towards Caesarism.

The use of a counterfactual construction not for panegyric purposes, but to sharpen an attack on the senate's failure to uphold its own traditional values, recalls a Ciceronian text that is illuminating here. In *II Verrines*, Cicero appeals to the senate to consider its own reputation (*splendor uester facit ut peccare sine summo rei publicae detrimento ac periculo non possitis*,

---

[72] Plin. *NH* 34.18 gives us our only other piece of information about this statue, also in a context of honours accepted by the recipient: *Caesar quidem dictator loricatam sibi dicari in foro suo passus est.*

[73] Dewar 1998.

1.22); in this instance, of course, this is to be expressed by taking action against Verres, whose crimes are set in a quasi-historical context by Cicero's counterfactual 'mixing up together' of all past misdeeds (which will then be eclipsed by Verres' wickedness):

> Quis est in populo Romano qui hoc non ex priore actione abstulerit, omnium ante damnatorum scelera, furta, flagitia, si unum in locum conferantur, uix cum huius parua parte aequari conferrique posse? (*II Verr.* 1.21)[74]

> Is there one single Roman who has not come away from the first hearing convinced of this, that if we could gather together in one the crimes and robberies and wicked deeds of every man found guilty in the past, they could hardly be held equal or comparable to the tithe of what this man has done?

In *Epistles* 8.6 Pliny is drawing upon an analogous 'prosecutorial' ethos, and he enhances the political shaming of the senate by the addition of specific exemplary names from the past.

Epistles 8.6 trumps 7.29 by shifting the focus from the absurd self-promotion of an imperial freedman in his own inscription, to yet more disgraceful tributes paid by both senate and emperor (*Inueni tam copiosum et effusum, ut ille superbissimus titulus modicus atque etiam demissus uideretur*, 8.6); not only is the panegyric that is the target of Pliny's attack more effusive, but the practitioners of it are (or should be) much greater men. The most recent players in the story (the Claudian senate and the emperor himself) are merely the logical endpoint of a decline that was implicit in the catalogue. The inflationary process, in which the inscription is eclipsed by the decree and the freedman's self-praise is swept aside in favour of the shameful fawning of the ruling classes (and 7.29 is outdone by 8.6), works alongside the extreme *deflationary* process in the teleology of the exemplary catalogue.

Pliny plays upon the comic aspects of the situation, not only asking Montanus to laugh with him at Pallas' self-importance, but suggesting that one might see the decree's text as a self-aware satirical joke – if it is not merely evidence of the senate's wretched condition (*Vrbanos qui illa censuerunt putem an miseros? Dicerem urbanos, si senatum deceret urbanitas*). The decree then becomes, on one reading, a Catullan game, one in which the state's representatives of *seueritas* turn to *urbanitas* – but all this is so unthinkable that Pliny retreats to counterfactual subjunctives.

Here Pallas' attempt to create an *exemplum* is disgracefully assisted by the senate, and the failure of the attempt is illuminated by Pliny's addition

---

[74] Cf., in eulogising mode, Cic. *Phil.* 9.10: *omnes ex omni aetate qui in hac ciuitate intellegentiam iuris habuerunt, si unum in locum conferantur, cum Ser. Sulpicio non sint comparandi.*

of 'real' *exempla* expressed in counterfactual terms. This exploration of exemplarity is well situated, moreover, in a book in which the next letter of comparable length and weight, *Epistles* 8.14, explores the consequences of the failure of exemplarity in the generations of senators immediately preceding Pliny's, as young senators could no longer learn proper senatorial behaviour from their fathers, but could only witness the mute servility of those who should have been their models (*Ep.* 8.14.2):

> Priorum temporum seruitus ut aliarum optimarum artium, sic etiam iuris senatori obliuionem quandam et ignorantiam induxit.

> The slavery of earlier times caused a certain forgetfulness and ignorance, both of the other high arts and also of senatorial law.

Both the republican *exempla* of 8.6 and the paternal models that were missing in 8.14 have failed Pliny's generation, and 8.6 offers a savagely comic exploration of that phenomenon. The man who had no training by example in how to be a senator reports in 8.6 an instance of senatorial behaviour from just before his own times, and points up its absurdity by reference to counterfactual *exempla*.

Conclusion

The texts we have looked at play upon different sorts of humour to be generated by the exemplary situations they build, employing counterfactuals to explore the ways in which *exempla* don't quite work any more. The counterfactual mode, with its persistent cynicism about the stability and value of exemplary virtue, becomes an important marker of modernity, as new manipulations of the cultural expectations on which Rome's sometimes rather leaden exemplary traditions rested imply a disconnection from the past, particularly the republican past. More seriously, of course, all this mirrors a collapse in the exemplary system when we get an individual who doesn't fit the traditional mould. Even as early as the *Pro Marcello*, the Caesar who eclipses all previous *exempla* becomes, by implication, the last *exemplum* standing, competing only with himself. Counterfactuals become increasingly common in the imperial period, in times when nothing seems quite real anyway; they are applied in different ways and to different degrees, but always with an eye to enhancing the comically satirical possibilities of an exemplary catalogue when it is recast in counterfactual terms. The counterfactual mode works as a party game (perfect for the Saturnalia, when every social convention has already been turned on its head with impunity), to trigger laughter in the readers and addressees of Pliny's letter and Martial's epigram alike, but the game only works by subverting the wider cultural expectations of a readership steeped in the clichés of the exemplary traditions.

The beginning of Martial's Book 11 suggests a return to a restored Augustan era – a better one for everyone, this time, including our poet, whose work attests to the fact that he's done better than Ovid, and can be a Virgil as well when he needs to. Martial offers a disrupted and disruptive Saturnalian view of history's confrontation with modernity, as he pits the traditional expectations of cyclical exemplarity against the teleological drive of the Virgilian *Heldenschau* (here taken to a paradoxical conclusion). The final stage of Roller's schema of exemplarity might normally include bringing new elements to the fore, or adjusting the details of an original *exemplum* to make the exemplary narrative contribute more powerfully to a new catalogue of great men – itself a kind of library of ethical actions and decisions.[75] The only new category that Martial designs here is the group of *exempla* who give up the deeds and characteristics that made them exemplary in the first place; he undoes the very first stage of Roller's schema and thereby hamstrings the exemplary project from the outset. In this book of 'returns' (to the golden Augustan era, to Caesarian peace, to freedom and joyous obscenity, to Saturnalian revelry) 11.5 imagines a situation in which there is really nothing to return to except the joke itself. Martial composes a *Heldenschau* that echoes a persistent theme in his handling of exemplary figures: that they can (and should) be 'turned' to suit today's *mores* and Martial's poetic requirements. But funnily enough, whatever historical stuff did or did not happen, there is a punchline, and that punchline is still a Caesar – another one.

---

[75] On the power and effect of exemplary catalogues, see now Roller 2015.

CHAPTER 14

Extratextuality
Literary Interactions with Oral Culture and Exemplary Ethics
Rebecca Langlands

Writing in the early second century AD, Suetonius and Tacitus tell their own versions of the same striking exemplary anecdote about an episode that they claim took place decades earlier, amidst the turmoil of AD 69, during the civil wars that unfolded between the death of Galba on 15 January and the death of Vitellius in mid December. Tacitus relates the story in his *Histories* (Tac. *Hist.* 3.54) and Suetonius relates it in his biography of the short-reigning emperor Otho (Suet. *Otho* 10).[1] It is the edifying, troubling story of a brave and loyal soldier who falls on his sword for the sake of truth, as a means of sending an emphatic message to his emperor; this soldier sacrifices his own life in order to convince his leader of the veracity of the report that he has just delivered – namely that they have just suffered a crippling defeat at the hands of the enemy. In both Tacitus' and Suetonius' versions the soldier's words and action subsequently rouse (*excitus, concitatum*) his leader into action himself.[2] However, the versions of the story are also markedly different, since each author places this story at a different moment in the so-called Year of the Four Emperors: for Suetonius it happens in the spring of 69, for Tacitus in the December of that year. Moreover, the story unfolds in opposing camps: in Suetonius' account the emperor in question is Otho; in Tacitus' account it is Vitellius.

In his account of the Year of the Four Emperors, Kenneth Wellesley describes Tacitus' version of this arresting tale as 'a remarkable – and perhaps true – story',[3] and indeed both authors go to some lengths to

---

[1] Versions of the story also occur in Plutarch's biography of Otho (*Otho* 15), and Cassius Dio 62.11, both in the context of Otho's defeat and suicide, and both told with slightly different emphasis from the accounts in Tacitus and Suetonius, as evidence of the loyalty of the soldiers towards Otho.

[2] Tac. *Hist.* 3.55.1 *Vitellius ut e somno excitus Iulium Priscum et Alfenum Varum cum quattuordecim praetoriis cohortibus et omnibus equitum alis obsidere Appenninum iubet* ('Vitellius, as if awakened from sleep, ordered Julius Priscus and Alfenus Varus with fourteen praetorian cohorts and all the cavalry to block off the Apennines'); Suet. *Otho* 10: *tunc ad despiciendam uitam . . . concitatum* ('then he was spurred on to despise life').

[3] Wellesley 2000: 161.

establish the episode's authenticity (Suetonius has heard the story from an eye-witness; Tacitus associates it with a named individual, Julius Agrestis). Yet, from the perspective of an ancient historian attempting to reconstruct the events of 69, it is hard not to feel that the appearance of more or less the same story in two different camps might somewhat undermine the veracity of the tale: surely they can't both be true . . . ? In her brief discussion of the passage in Tacitus' *Histories*, Rhiannon Ash makes sensible alternative suggestions: 'Tacitus may have transferred the story from an Othonian to a Vitellian context, or at least chosen to anchor a floating anecdote here.'[4] I will argue that if we take into consideration the dynamics of 'extratextuality' – that is to say, on the analogy of 'intertextuality', allusion to a referent that is not in textual form, that reaches beyond intertextuality – we may accept both these suggestions simultaneously, and I suggest that to do so will enrich our understanding of these texts. The concept of the 'floating anecdote' is a useful one. It enables us to grasp easily the idea of a story that can 'move' within the historical framework from one place to another, as this story seems to do. The phrase also evokes a story's existence outside the text, a medium where such movement and mutation is more possible – within the oral dimension of cultural memory that complements the textual. One aim of this chapter is to establish what it means for something to be a floating anecdote, what its specific qualities might be as a mode of thinking about the past, and how it has the capacity, despite its 'floating' quality, nonetheless to seem 'true', and to function perfectly well as a realistic detail within the historiographical tradition, as a real incident that really happened. In its exploration of the dynamic dialogue between extratextual discourses and textual production and consumption, my discussion will thus complement and extend a number of other reflections in this volume on the relationship between on-the-page and off-the-page interactivity.[5]

This chapter will also establish that the anecdote's appearance in these texts testifies to a particular post-Flavian moment to which the story belongs and from which it emerges. While the texts themselves claim that the story belongs to 69, we will see that as much as anything it represents a particularly post-Domitianic remembering of 69 that serves an important cultural purpose for the era in which Suetonius and Tacitus were writing. One of the things that marks out and characterises the post-Flavian period which is the focus of this volume is its own sense of coming 'after' and

---

[4] Ash 1999: 120.
[5] See the chapters by Ash, Buckley, König, Rimell, Roche and Roller in this volume.

having to pick up the pieces, re-establish connections that have been ruptured, between present and exemplary past, for instance, or between good
deeds and rewards. This was a period during which the Romans drew on
the familiar and resilient structures of exemplary ethics in order to remember recent history in such a way as to make new, salutary sense of the trau-
matic events of the previous generations. The practice reflects the deep
commitment of Roman writers of the era to exemplary ethics (despite their
sense that its connections have been ruptured by recent events) and their
faith in its ability to regenerate virtue through storytelling. In the works
of writers such as Pliny, Suetonius and Tacitus the emphasis is less on the
traditional republican *exempla*, and more on the minting of new *exempla*
fit for the imperial age and its moral uncertainties.[6]

The structures of exemplary ethics helped to give shape to cultural memory of the events of recent decades, influencing both what was remembered about the civil war, and how it was remembered, in the sense that
recent scholars of cultural memory use the term 'remembering' or 'remembering', to describe not merely the recall of things that have happened,
but the active creation of meaningful past, and the performance of one's
own present in relation to the past.[7] In their deployments of this anecdote
Suetonius and Tacitus, each in his own way, contribute to this cultural
move. This story is configured in both texts as a new *exemplum* for a new
era, and represents a cultural strategy for making sense of a recent period of
significant trauma marked by civil conflict and leadership crisis, by reworking traditional Roman ethical scenarios. The central act of the sacrifice of a
person's own life for the greater good is of course one of the most prevalent
motifs of Roman *exempla* right through the tradition, and it is repeated
again and again in the famous tales celebrated by the Romans; it is also
specifically manifested in the traditional idea of *devotio*, whereby the noble
leader pledges his own life for the success of the army.[8] The structures of
these ideas are woven into the accounts of Suetonius and Tacitus even as
they are also subverted in their narratives, for here the self-sacrifice is not
of the leader himself, but of one of his soldiers, and his action throws the
moral weakness of the leader into high relief. In this post-Flavian variant
of the scenario we find an ordinary soldier taking command of a situation when his emperor proves incapable of doing so, standing firm against
the accusations of the masses, and with his steadfast loyalty and integrity

---

[6] On this see Langlands 2014a, with further references.
[7] For a helpful articulation of this idea see the introduction to Erll and Rigney 2009, esp. pp. 1–2; see
    also Taylor 2003; Rigney 2008.
[8] See Edwards 2012 for a discussion of the way Tacitus reworks the motif of *devotio* in *Histories* 3.

providing a quiet moral centre amid a maelstrom of political instability and capriciousness.

***

In Suetonius' biography, as in Plutarch's, this anecdote appears as part of his account of the unexpectedly heroic death of Otho, and it also represents an unusual moment of moral optimism and redemption within a series of imperial biographies notable for their bleak moral outlook. By and large Suetonius paints a picture of a world where bad things happen to good people and vice versa, and there is no connection between the way you behave and what happens to you in life. Being virtuous is never shown to pay, and attempts to do good very often come to nothing or even backfire.[9] Here, however, in the description of Otho's death, we have, finally, a moment of redemption, for traditional Roman exemplary ethics as well as for the individual. This is personal redemption for Otho, who is transformed by his response to the act of the unnamed soldier from a second Nero into a man who is able to die the noblest of deaths. This exemplary deed of a common soldier inspires Otho to his own act of heroism, and in the subsequent scene the emperor takes his own life, calmly and courageously in the manner of a Catonian Stoic, as unlike the cowardly Nero (who demands *exempla* and cannot imitate them) as it is possible to be.[10] The episode also marks a moment in Suetonius' work of redemption for exemplary ethics, in that the story represents (at last) the perfect functioning of exemplarity, whereby the virtue and deed of one person inspires and enables the virtue of another, both through emulation of the virtues and of the deed itself.[11]

In April 69, Otho's army has been defeated at Bedriacum by Vitellius' troops, and a soldier arrives to bring him news of the defeat (so that he will surrender); the messenger is not believed, and so, to prove the truth of his announcement, he kills himself before Otho's eyes. Not only does this convince the emperor, but it also directs his next and final moves in two respects: first it convinces him of the virtue of his men, which leads him to want to spare them further suffering in civil war, and second it provides him with a model of swift and courageous death which he is quick to take up:

---

[9] As I have argued recently in the case of Suetonius' life of Augustus (Langlands 2014b).

[10] Suet. *Nero* 49.3; Suet. *Otho* 10.2–11.2; on these death narratives, see Edwards 2007: 36–9, 159–60.

[11] For Suetonius' tendency to represent the failure of exemplarity, see Gunderson 2014; Langlands 2014b; for emulation at the heart of Roman exemplary ethics, see Langlands forthcoming.

> ...tunc ad despiciendam uitam exemplo manipularis militis concitatum, qui cum cladem exercitus nuntiaret nec cuiquam fidem faceret ac nunc mendaci nunc timoris, quasi fugisset ex acie, argueretur, gladio ante pedes eius incubuerit. Hoc uiso proclamasse eum aiebat non amplius se in periculum talis tamque bene meritos coniecturum. (Suet. *Otho* 10)

> ...then he was spurred on to despise life by the example of a common soldier: when this man had announced the defeat of the army, and no one would believe him, and he was accused first of lying and then of cowardice as if he had fled from the battlefield, he fell upon his sword at Otho's feet. [My father] used to say that at this sight Otho declared that he would no longer endanger the lives of such men who were so well deserving.

The story is also lent historical authenticity by Suetonius' claim that it is one of a number of titbits about Otho related to him (often) by his own father, who served in this war himself: *Interfuit huic bello pater meus Suetonius Laetus, tertiae decimae legionis tribunus angusticlauius. Is mox referre crebro solebat...* ('My father, Suetonius Laetus, fought in this war, an equestrian tribune of the Thirteenth Legion. Later he often used to relate that...', *Otho* 10). This Suetonian authentication makes it all the more notable that in Tacitus' *Histories* the story appears in an entirely different historical context. Here it is part of the story, several months later, of the downfall of the appalling Vitellius, and adds to this emperor's characterisation as a man who is unable to face the reality of his situation after his own defeat at Cremona, and is willing to repress any attempts to reveal the truth. In his variant of the story, Tacitus brings out similar ethical issues around the themes of loyalty and truth as does Suetonius. However, rather than associating the tale with the characterisation and transformation of Otho, as Suetonius and Plutarch do, Tacitus uses it to emphasise the utter uselessness of Vitellius as leader and emperor, his cowardice and his inability to take action. In Tacitus' version the context is this: it is late in 69, Vitellius' forces have been obliterated, the devastating sack of Cremona has been fatal to his cause, but he is refusing to accept the reality of the situation. Here the self-killing hero of the story is the centurion Julius Agrestis, a figure of loyalty and steadfastness, who must find a way to convince him of the hopelessness of the situation so that the fighting can end. He persuades Vitellius to allow him to visit the enemy's camp and the battlefield to ascertain the situation. On his return, just as in Suetonius' version, the emperor refuses to believe his bad news, and accuses him of being corrupt just as Suetonius' soldier is accused of lies and cowardice; once again the messenger must prove the truth of his announcement by taking his own life:

Agrestis ad Vitellium remeauit abnuentique uera esse quae afferret atque
ultro corruptum arguenti 'quandoquidem' inquit 'magno documento opus
est, nec alius iam tibi aut uitae aut mortis meae usus, dabo cui credas.' Atque
ita digressus uoluntaria morte dicta firmauit. (Tac. *Hist.* 3.54)

Agrestis travelled back to Vitellius, and when the latter refused to accept
the truth of the news he brought and even accused him of bribery, he said:
'Since a weighty proof is needed, and you now have no further use for either
my life or my death, I will give you something you can believe.' And taking
his leave he confirmed his words by killing himself.

There is no mistaking the similarities in plot and key elements in the
episodes related in these two passages, and there is clearly a close relationship between them that cannot be merely coincidental. We might choose
to approach this similarity in terms of intertextuality: perhaps one author
drew upon the other, or – as scholars often posit in such cases – both drew
on a common earlier written source. A comparison which puts the passages
of Suetonius and Tacitus in direct relation to one another is certainly illuminating, and later in this chapter I shall suggest that Tacitus is expecting
his readers to be aware of the alternative, Othonian variant when we read
his Vitellian variant; the nuances of Tacitus' text can best be appreciated if
we read it in the context of alternative variations, and the critical approach
of intertextuality is useful here. However, to view this allusiveness purely
in terms of textual versions of the story would be to miss a great deal; the
references are extratextual as well as intertextual.

Both Suetonius and Tacitus make clear that the extratextual dimension
of the anecdote is significant. Both authors indicate in their deployment
of the anecdote that they are drawing on a rich contemporary oral culture
in which such stories circulate as a rather particular medium of cultural
memory and exemplary ethics. In the absence of mass media such as radio,
television and the internet, people from all strata of society made sense of
current and past events through face-to-face conversations, usually incorporating narrativisation. Tacitus describes this practice at *Histories* 3.54, in
the passage immediately preceding his relation of our anecdote; the usual
oral circulation of information about events has been suppressed by Vitellius, resulting only in the proliferation of tales that are horrific rather than
true: *prohibiti per ciuitatem sermones, eoque plures ac, si liceret, uere narraturi,
quia uetabantur, atrociora uulgauerant* ('conversations among the townfolk
were forbidden, so they proliferated; if they had been allowed, they would
have given truthful reports, but because they were prohibited, more horrific accounts had been disseminated'). An important medium of this kind

of *uulgata* cultural memory was the easily memorable and pointed story that has the qualities of what folklorists call a 'tellable tale' (such as a fairy-tale, urban myth or ghost story), of being easily recalled and appropriated by new authors for new tellings.[12] It is helpful to think of such exemplary anecdotes generically as constituting a 'medium' (in the sense that this term is used in studies of cultural memory, to describe the means of commem-oration and communication of shared cultural memory and ethical ideas) and that this medium (unusually) can be found both in textual and non-textual form, and is distinct from the literary medium to which the *Histo-ries* and the *Lives* belong. This medium, the exemplary anecdote, is marked by concision of narrative, 'tellability', retellability and moral charge, and a tendency to reproduce and adapt familiar cultural schemata or culturally recognised scenarios that give shape and meaning to personal and cultural memories; all these qualities enable its stories to be handled in a particular way and perform particular cultural functions.[13] They possess the narrative features that have been identified by researchers in the field of cognitive psychology as enabling stories to be easily remembered and repeated, cir-culated in oral form, and adapted for new circumstances; they are light on specific historical details and on complexity, but highly engaging in their ethical significance, with 'story grammars' that seem to say something of broad relevance about the human condition.[14] To expand the metaphor of the 'floating tale', such a 'retellable tale' can 'float', because it is light and portable, easily memorised and repeatable. Anecdotes of this kind are regularly integrated into literary texts, where they are usually presented in such a way as to retain their moral and exemplary impact. This poten-tial impact is enhanced for readers when a text self-consciously marks this integration of exemplary material within itself as a moment of interme-diality, making it clear that the literary work is hoping to mobilise the special qualities of another medium that has a separate existence outside the text.[15] This is what Suetonius and Tacitus do in relation to this story: they do not simply integrate the narrative itself within their works, but also evoke a whole interpretative framework of exemplary ethics through their

---

[12] On these aspects of modern urban myths, see Brunvand 1983; for further elaboration of the concept of 'retellability' in the context of Roman exemplary ethics, see Langlands forthcoming.

[13] On cultural scenarios and schemata as recurrent narrative motifs that convey important values within cultures and also help to structure the way that individuals living within cultures under-stand and experience their own lives, see Taylor 2003.

[14] See e.g. Rubin 1995; Thornborrow and Coates 2005.

[15] I am drawing here on ideas about intermediality articulated in Dinter 2013a, who discusses interme-dial allusions to ecphrasis within epic poetry; I attempt to identify an analogous dynamic at work when it comes to references to *exempla* in Latin prose literature.

overt allusions to the extratextual culture from which it comes. This framework, significantly, brings with it the operation of a different kind of truth, beyond the historical, which also enables the historical to resonate beyond itself.

Markers of this intermediality can be found both in their rendering of the anecdote itself and in the text that surrounds it. Not only is the story itself rendered in both cases with the formal structure and scope of an *exemplum* (a concise narrative with a clear moral import), but both Tacitus and Suetonius include in their texts exemplary markers, signalling that they are alluding to this extratextual practice that operates beyond the text itself, and makes reference to something outside it. Most explicitly, Suetonius calls the soldier's deed an *exemplum* and, in addition, in the ensuing narrative we see its moral exemplarity operationalised, as Otho responds to the soldier's death as an *exemplum*, by being inspired by it to aspire to virtue himself and then by imitating the courage and commitment of the soldier in his own subsequent behaviour. Tacitus' framing of this episode within the interpretative framework of moral exemplarity is more formal and literary. The anecdote is introduced with a recognisably exemplary rubric: *Notabili constantia centurio Iulius Agrestis . . .* ('With remarkable constancy, the centurion Julius Agrestis . . .', *Hist.* 3.54). The phrase *notabili constantia* with which Tacitus marks the beginning of this episode constitutes precisely the kind of introductory rubric that we find introducing exemplary anecdotes, for instance in Valerius Maximus' collection *Facta et dicta memorabilia*, as well as in philosophical and rhetorical texts that deploy *exempla* in argument, such as consolations, treatises, panegyric and legal speeches, specifying the virtue to be enacted and calling attention to the outstanding nature of the deed. It is a reference to the recognised exemplary form, headlining the virtue which is about to be exemplified.[16] With this concise pair of words Tacitus signals that we are about to encounter the sort of signal virtue that is worthy to be commemorated in the form of *exemplum*; an exemplary tale is about to be embedded here within this historiographical text. This headline phrase is immediately followed by the name of the protagonist in the nominative case, another common feature of *exempla* cited in texts. Then, at the end of the story Tacitus rounds off the tale with the kind of moral summary again familiar from Valerius Maximus, which confirms for the reader the moral lesson that they are intended to take away, spelling out the specific virtues to be found in the deed: 'Some

---

[16] See Guerrini 1981 on the conventional structure of a rhetorical *exemplum*, ABC (introduction–narrative–conclusion).

people say that he was killed on the orders of Vitellius, and record his loyalty and *constantia*' (*Quidam iussu Vitelli interfectum, de fide constantiaque eadem tradidere, Hist.* 3.54).[17] In addition, by mentioning in this context the uncertainty about the real circumstances of Agrestis' death, Tacitus also emphasises here the way that exemplary truth trumps historical truth. That is to say, the more broadly applicable moral truth about humanity takes priority in exemplary cultural memory – and, perhaps, in historiography too, at times – over the truth about what actually happened on one specific given occasion.

Furthermore, both authors embed the story in their text at a point where there is emphasis upon the oral circulation of stories and its cultural function in making sense of experience and recent events through telling stories about the past. Suetonius explicitly frames this anecdote as emerging from a culture of the oral tradition of retellable tales. The story is introduced as being part of his father's own memory of that difficult period, handed down to Suetonius himself orally over the years:

> Interfuit huic bello pater meus Suetonius Laetus, tertiae decimae legionis tribunus angusticlauius. Is mox referre crebro solebat, Othonem etiam priuatum usque adeo detestatum ciuilia arma, ut memorante quodam inter epulas de Cassi Brutique exitu cohorruerit; nec concursurum cum Galba fuisse, nisi confideret sine bello rem transigi posse; tunc ad despiciendam uitam exemplo manipularis militis concitatum . . . (*Otho* 10)

> My father, Suetonius Laetus, fought in this war, an equestrian tribune of the Thirteenth Legion. Later he often used to relate that Otho, even as a private individual, so hated civil war that he shuddered when during a dinner party the deaths of Cassius and Brutus were mentioned; and that he would not have challenged Galba if he had not been confident that the matter could be settled without any war; and then that he was also spurred on to despise life by the example of a common soldier . . .

This is more than a straightforward citation of sources;[18] rather, Suetonius' account suggests that from the first this anecdote was formulated and formed as a particular kind of cultural artefact – a retellable moral tale that strives to make sense of historical figures and events. It may well be the case that Suetonius' father was present when a soldier in Otho's army

---

[17] Other places in the *Histories* where Tacitus embeds references to the exemplary in his narrative and analysis include *Hist.* 1.3.1, 1.15–16, 1.50, 1.71, 2.13, 2.64, 3.51, 4.42, 4.58–9, 4.67. See also Hunink 2004 on Tacitus' deployment of *exempla* in the *Histories*.

[18] However, it does plug into a privileging of 'autopsy' as a historical methodology that seems to be flourishing in Latin literature of this period, drawing, of course, on a long tradition in Greek historiography; cf. Tac. *Hist.* 4.18, *Ann.* 3.16; Plin. *Ep.* 6.16.

killed himself and that he saw this very incident unfold, and personally related what he had seen to his son, and that the version in Suetonius' text can be traced directly to its source, a real event. However, even in this case the correlation between event and text is not exact; Suetonius Laetus was mediating the event through his shaping of it into a memorable, repeatable, orally transmitted narrative.[19] As he represents the incident in this passage, Suetonius makes this mediation very clear. First he emphasises the oral transmission of the tale itself; it is told in reported speech, introduced by the phrase *is mox referre crebro solebat*. The imperfect tense here makes clear that telling such stories about Otho's army is not merely a one-off testimony, a single report, but rather an ongoing (family) tradition of retelling one's memories of those days – explicitly as a means of characterising the key historical figures and explaining important events; the *mox* also emphasises the lapse of time between the event itself and later working of it into a story. Furthermore, to strengthen this allusion to the extratextual oral tradition of exemplary storytelling, Suetonius also incorporates into the transmitted memory itself another reference to oral memory, in a kind of *mise en abyme*: the 'remembering' and retelling of the deaths of Cassius and Brutus in the context of a banquet, which Otho couldn't bear to hear (*memorante quodam inter epulas de Cassi Brutique exitu*). This is an allusion to another conventional setting for the oral circulation of stories in ancient Rome: storytelling during festivities and banquets, and the tradition of relating the deaths of famous figures from history (to which of course this anecdote itself now belongs as part of Otho's death narrative).[20] What we see here is an explicit, multi-layered allusion in one medium – the textual medium of biography – to another medium – that of the oral tradition of 'retellable' stories – a separate ancient medium with its own particular take on the past. This intermedial allusion brings to Suetonius' account a sense of its embeddedness in a cultural tradition that integrates the textual and non-textual transmission of exemplary tales, and reminds us that each is simultaneously reliant on the other.

Tacitus' description of an urgent and widespread oral tradition, with its potential to generate unhelpfully alarmist versions of events, has been cited above, and it immediately precedes his relation of our anecdote, drawing the attention of readers to the presence and impact of such stories within Roman society. There is also another technique used in this section of the

---

[19] On the concept of mediation and re-mediation in cultural memory, see Erll and Rigney 2009.

[20] The deaths of Brutus and Cassius have particular resonance for the account of Otho's own death that follows shortly: both killed themselves after defeat amid the confusion of civil war, Cassius unaware of Brutus' victory; thanks to John Henderson for this point.

Histories to evoke the embeddedness of his anecdote in oral tradition: he interweaves our anecdote with another familiar 'floating anecdote' of antiquity, a generic tale which I shall label 'Impressing the Captured Spy', and which has a long and visible literary pedigree. Tacitus' manipulation of this established scenario within these same pages of *Histories* 3 provides an illuminating comparison with his treatment of the 'Loyal Soldier' scenario that is the focus of this chapter. It demonstrates his expectation that these powerful yet flexible stories will be familiar to his Roman readers, and it shows how such cultural scenarios can become part of the historiographical record repeatedly and in different places, yet without eroding their plausibility.

The 'Impressing the Captured Spy' scenario not only appears in historical and exemplary works but also finds its way into handbooks of military strategies, oscillating in the surviving textual tradition between the forms of a historically situated narrative and a generally applicable diplomatic technique.[21] At the core of this anecdote/strategy is the idea that it can pay to intimidate an enemy spy with a confident, open display of your strength and resources; if you happen to capture a spy who has infiltrated your encampment, instead of torturing them and putting them to death, as might be your first instinct, you should show them all round your camp – willingly revealing to them the secrets that they have been trying to obtain by stealth. You should show off to them your lovely sharp weapons, your stores of grain, your men engaged in their rigorous military training, and then send them back to their own leader to report on all of this and to communicate what a formidable enemy you are. In the surviving ancient historiographical tradition this strategy is instantiated in a whole series of different historical settings: Herodotus describes Xerxes as using this ruse with Greek spies in Book 7; in Livy (Book 30) it is Scipio who shows Hannibal's spies around his camp, and succeeds in intimidating him so much that Hannibal decides not to fight the Romans but to try to negotiate instead; Frontinus tells the same story about the Roman general Laevinus and Pyrrhus as an example of military strategy. This, then, is another retellable tale that finds itself repeated in a variety of specific historical settings, but also constitutes a trope that is more broadly applicable to military strategy. The case of this transferable tale, with its roots clearly so far back in Greek history, usefully conveys a sense of how these kinds of stories can appear so naturally in different historical settings. First and

---

[21] This combination of specific and general is a defining feature of *exempla*; see further Lowrie and Lüdemann 2015b; Langlands 2015.

foremost, they are culturally important 'plots' or cultural schemata which convey some sort of broader truth about the world. Their embeddedness in any particular historical setting is only secondary to this primary function, in that it lends the story a local flavour and a sense of authenticity.

Naturally Tacitus adapts this familiar scenario to new Tacitean ends, giving it a new twist, which works best precisely when his readers are already familiar with the established story-grammar structure. In this new context of the anarchy of 69, the tried and tested ruse does not work at all, because Vitellius is such an obstinate fool, determined not to face up to his situation. In Tacitus' version of events, the plot is repeated numerous times to no avail; Vitellius keeps sending spies to the Flavian camps, they keep getting captured by the enemy, proudly shown round the Flavian camp, and sent back to Vitellius to let him know that his situation is hopeless; but he refuses to allow this information to take effect.

> At Vitellius fractis apud Cremonam rebus nuntios cladis occultans stulta dissimulatione remedia potius malorum quam mala differebat. Quippe confitenti consultantique supererant spes uiresque: cum e contrario laeta omnia fingeret, falsis ingrauescebat. Mirum apud ipsum de bello silentium; prohibiti per ciuitatem sermones, eoque plures ac, si liceret, uere narraturi, quia uetabantur, atrociora uulgauerant. Nec duces hostium augendae famae deerant, captos Vitelli exploratores circumductosque, ut robora uictoris exercitus noscerent, remittendo; quos omnis Vitellius secreto percontatus interfici iussit. (*Hist.* 3.54)

> However, Vitellius, when his forces had been smashed at Cremona, hid the news of the disaster and with foolish dissimulation delayed the remedy for misfortunes rather than the misfortunes themselves. There would have been hope and resources for a man prepared to confide and consult; but when, on the contrary, he pretended that everything was going well, his lies made everything worse. There was an extraordinary silence regarding the war in his presence. Conversations among the townsfolk were forbidden, so they proliferated; if they had been allowed, they would have given truthful reports, but because they were prohibited, more horrific accounts had been disseminated. And the enemy generals did not fail to increase the rumours, by capturing Vitellius' spies and taking them around the camp, so that they could see the strength of the victorious army, and then sending them back. Every one of these men Vitellius interrogated in secret and then ordered to be killed.

Over and again his spies keep returning to his camp to tell him what they have seen and he absolutely refuses to act upon this. He interrogates each one of them, kills him so he cannot reveal the dire situation to anyone else, and then he just carries on as usual. It seems that nothing can get through to him. It is in the context of this desperate situation that Julius Agrestis, our hero, steps in, motivated, it seems, to force his commander to face up to the truth. He has already tried every other means of persuading him, as Tacitus puts it, *ad uirtutem* 'in the direction of virtue', or, as we might say: 'to man up'. He now concludes that the only way that he can bring home the truth to Vitellius is to sacrifice his own life.

Tacitus' account can clearly be read as drawing on influential literary works such as those of Herodotus and Livy, but the scenarios he reproduces also transcend specific texts because they are not just individual stories told in the works of these famous authors, but more broadly are fundamental cultural scripts or schemata which are part of Greco-Roman culture, and which not only shape the literary representation of the past, but even serve to shape the way people experience and make sense of their own lives. We can imagine that such scenarios also informed the way that those both on the battlefield and within the city shaped the tales they disseminated about recent events so as to make events meaningful and understandable. This helps us to see how such exemplary anecdotes can become part of the historical record without losing their special attributes. As with a reusable military strategy, there is no need to pin the stories once and for all to a single historical setting; they can be repeated again and again. Indeed, this repeatability is part of an *exemplum*'s function: to encode a useful kind of behaviour that might be repeated and adapted for other circumstances.[22] Viewed in this light there is no need to feel uncomfortable about the idea that Julius Agrestis might, in December, have deployed a similar persuasive practice to that deployed by Otho's soldier back in April, just as Antonius, general in the Flavian camp, might have deployed the same military stratagem which, according to the literary tradition, had been used by such figures as Xerxes and Pyrrhus before him. It was a bold technique that suited that desperate year of 69.[23] The story of 'Impressing the Enemy Spy' has its own truth as a diplomatic principle, rendered into historiographical reality by generations of ancient historians, whether or not it ultimately derives from a real, historical event. Just so, our anecdote has its own moral truth and Tacitus concludes his story by saying precisely this about it: we are not sure on the details, but what really matters here – and what we can all agree on – is its moral impact: 'Some people say that he was killed on

[22] On iterativity as a feature of *exempla*, see Lyons 1989: 8–15; Langlands 2008: 4.
[23] See also Chaplin 2013 on way that the ancient Romans really did imitate *exempla* in their behaviour and in their self-representation, reinforcing the sense of repeated patterns in Roman culture and historiography.

the orders of Vitellius, and record his loyalty and *constantia* (*Quidam iussu Vitelli interfectum, de fide constantiaque eadem tradidere*).[24]

***

In comparing their versions, I have shown that both Suetonius and Tacitus give the same story its own particular settings and details that tie it into the wider projects of their works. However, the core story also works independently of these and has its own logic and thematic significance, which is generated with reference to the familiar plots and motifs of the Roman *exempla* tradition. This core schema addresses, among others, the themes of loyalty and trust and of the difficulty of knowing the truth about a situation. These are issues that also speak to particular anxieties relating to this particular period of political and military instability in Rome. How can loyalty be expressed in a context of deep suspicion and frequent betrayal and changing of sides? The story reflects anxieties about the inadequacy of leaders in this period and the way that their subordinates – just ordinary men in the army – have to take the initiative and direct events themselves in the absence of effective leadership. At its heart is the challenge – perennial, but especially poignant during the chaos of civil war, and especially relevant after the Domitianic culture of *delatores*[25] – of gathering reliable intelligence: who can you trust and how can you gather reliable information about the enemy? This is a military issue that can easily translate into the wider anxieties of politics and private life. Above all this story is about the desire of these subordinates to end the war and bring about peace; in the accounts of both Suetonius and Tacitus the men who kill themselves are trying to persuade their respective leaders to surrender and end the fighting.

In order to elucidate the distinction that I am drawing between the textual medium of historiography and the largely oral medium of the 'tellable' exemplary tale, and to enrich my interpretation of this ancient anecdote, I want briefly to consider an analogous modern example. This is an anecdote that one hundred years later constitutes an important way that the First World War is commemorated within twenty-first-century British culture. Like our ancient Roman anecdote this is a story that belongs to an

---

[24] In the context of historiography, details matter because they add realism and plausibility, but here Tacitus is alluding to a different tradition – one that is multivocal and democratic, rather than coming from a single author. In this medium of exemplarity (which moves easily between text and orality), details may differ from variant to variant, but what remains constant – and what is really important and at the heart of the thing – is the moral charge and value of the story.

[25] On the anxieties generated by the culture of informers in this period, see Uden 2015: 24–50.

informal and unauthorised medium of cultural memory, rather than a public monument instituted by a civic council, for instance. It is the story of the 'Christmas truce', which relates that on Christmas Day 1914 troops fighting on the front line on both sides of the war decided to call a truce, and the German and Allied soldiers played football against one another in no man's land. This is a story that I have heard many times in my life, although I cannot recall where or when I first came across it; it is generally well known in modern British culture. Significantly, its authority comes not from a written source, but from its status as common knowledge, shared by members of our community. Whether or not this episode finds its way into modern written historiography, its power comes precisely from its oral medium: it is memorable, retellable, it belongs to us all, we don't need to be a historian or to have consulted any sources in order to be able to retell this tale confidently next time it seems relevant in the pub. It is qualitatively different from historiography, and represents another and different way of making sense of the past. Indeed, it is not only that it does not require reliable sources, but sources might actually detract from its power as a story.[26] What kind of source material could adequately support this Christmas truce idea? An official account, whether from a military report or from a historian, would risk looking like propaganda; we would want to know what the author's investment in the idea was. Similarly, the testimony of hundreds of letters home from soldiers describing the occasion would be fascinating material, but would fragment the story by focalising it through individuals; this would risk complicating our emotional understanding of the episode, when the very point of it is that it celebrates their, and by extension our, togetherness and shared experience.

It is true that some people, understandably, read this story as being primarily about the futility of war, and it is indeed heart-rending to think of those young men, compelled to fight against one another by the decisions of their leaders, when they would have so much preferred to be playing football with one another in the park. However, I think this is also a story that is seeking to make sense of the past specifically in relation to our present day; like all cultural memory, it presents itself as unbroken connection to past while actually being a meaningful performance in and for the present.[27] In the present day what the story allows us to share with one another is the notion of a mutual and perennial commitment to peace by the ordinary people, regardless of nationality. Left to our own devices,

---

[26] On the positive value of not citing authoritative sources for a story discussed in the context of Roman *exempla* and intertextuality, see Welch 2013.

[27] See n. 7.

peace is what we Europeans, whatever our nationality, wanted all along, this story affirms. Reinforcing this sense of inevitable European together-ness are the shared cultural rituals of communal bonding which the story celebrates: Christmas and football. Moreover, for many people in Europe today, Christmas celebrations and football matches are precisely the kind of communal events during which people gather with family and friends, share stories like this, and remind themselves of their common humanity (and in the context of shared history and cultural practices of Britain and Germany, especially Christmas, where traditions such as the Christmas tree were imported into British culture from Germany in the generation prior to the First World War).

For members of British culture in the twenty-first century, the story of the Christmas truce of 1914 celebrates the endurance, through the worst of times, of the shared humanity of the ordinary people, who never really wanted to go to war at all, but were swept up in the plans of the people in power. A similar message is encoded in these passages from Suetonius and Tacitus, and in the 'floating anecdote' on which I believe they both drew. In essence it can be read as the story of how ordinary folk can be decent, brave and loyal even when their leaders fail them and everything has descended into chaos. Suetonius uses this story as a sudden and unexpected beacon of hope that the broken connections of exemplarity and virtue may be repaired. However, in its complexity, Tacitus' account may go even further towards a conveying a message of healing for his own day, making use of the repeatability of this story in order to enrich his poignant message of loyalty and courage in the face of anarchy and failure of leadership; like the Christmas truce, his story establishes an enduring commitment to peace on *both* sides of the civil war. For I would argue that Tacitus is not so much transposing the story from one historical setting to another, as repeating a familiar story-grammar that he can take for granted is common knowledge among his readers, and repeating it in a significantly new setting. Tacitus' location of the story in the context of Vitellius' camp is a knowing echo of the familiar Othonian version that we find in Suetonius' account and in the other ancient sources, and is to be read against that well-known extratextual alternative that was common knowledge in his day.[28] By creating a new ver-sion of the story that unfolds in the opposing camp, making the emperor in question not Otho but Otho's enemy Vitellius, Tacitus can make the point that these virtues of loyalty, courage, constancy and the desire to end

[28] It does not matter too much for my argument whether Suetonius' account preceded Tacitus', since the latter need not be alluding directly to Suetonius' version, but can be seen as engaging with that variant in its extratextual form.

the fighting were to be found among the ordinary men on both sides of the war. Even in these dark days of civil war and confusion, there was an enduring commitment from the Roman people (under whichever incompetent, villainous leader they may have found themselves) to peace, and – most importantly of all for Tacitus and for his contemporaries – to Truth, and to communicating the truth in such a way that it is believed.[29]

Conclusion

I hope to have demonstrated that an awareness of the important extratextual tradition of exemplary ethics and cultural memory (to which exemplary tales belong) can help us better appreciate the allusions to episodes in recent history in the works of Suetonius and Tacitus. The literary texts engage with this extratextual allusive field, drawing on and adapting its familiar motifs and schemata in order to address the urgent need to make sense of the events of the civil war for their own post-Flavian era. Exemplary ethics was both a textual and an extratextual cultural practice, where texts worked together with more ephemeral media such as conversations, jokes and after-dinner storytelling to maintain and keep what I describe elsewhere as 'sites of exemplarity' alive as constituents of evolving cultural memory.[30] Particular exemplary tales, themselves always evolving over time, reproduced and adapted the key cultural schemata which helped to shape the way that members of Roman culture made sense of their own experience. Here, at the start of a new post-Flavian era, we can see how those long-cherished schemata of military tactics, leadership and heroic self-killing are newly redeployed in cultural memory generally, beyond their recurrence in particularly textual form, but are also knowingly integrated by Tacitus and Suetonius into their particular literary accounts of 69, as a means to begin to heal (or seal) the traumas of a civil war.

---

[29] Cf. Edwards 2007: 142–3 for the suggestion of a parallel between Agrestis and the position of Tacitus himself. But John Henderson (following Haynes 2003) responds to my optimistic reading: 'most important for Tacitus is that "Truth" is swamped in the Make-Believe that makes the only true account of civil war a tale of suicidal futility'.

[30] On sites of exemplarity, see Langlands forthcoming.

PART III

Into the Silence
The Limits of Interaction

CHAPTER 15

The Regulus Connection
Displacing Lucan between Martial and Pliny

Ilaria Marchesi

This chapter investigates the possible reasons for the inverse matrix of presence of Lucan in two coeval and proximate bodies of work: Martial's *Epigrams* and Pliny's *Epistles*.

My argument stems from the presence of a double paradox, affecting both the Pliny–Martial relationship and the internal cohesion of Martial's corpus. The first paradox consists in the fact that Lucan does not appear anywhere in Pliny, though the author of the *Epistles* is not shy in admitting his sympathy for the families of some of the martyrs in the ranks of the Stoic opposition to Nero, fallen during the purges in which Lucan was eliminated. Conversely, Martial not only claimed geographical and cultural allegiance to Lucan in one of his poems (*Epigrams* 1.61), but he also produced a series of birthday-poems on Lucan (to which add Statius, *Silvae* 2.7) and dedicated them to the executed poet's widow (7.21–3). While in the first instance one may see perhaps a politically and socially neutral act – even if, by reasons of geography, Martial lists Lucan in the company of other dissidents, the two Senecas (1.61.7–8) – the birthday poems are definitely less timid in making ethical and political considerations part of the praise of Lucan, openly blaming Nero's cruelty for the poet's death.

In Pliny's case, the ostracism he reserves for Lucan extends to both the literary and prosopographical levels in his collection. Just as there is no mention of Lucan, even in the context of the letters detailing the dangers he had faced for his Stoic sympathies during the years of Domitian's purges, so too Lucan's epic poem apparently plays no part in the rich web of poetic intertexts that the *Epistles* mobilise. A single pointed allusion to the *Bellum ciuile* (about which see below) has been detected in Pliny's otherwise richly polyphonic text. The double absence is somewhat surprising, since Pliny constructed Neronian and Domitianic times as strongly connected by

A preliminary version of this chapter was presented at the conference 'Literary Interactions under Nerva, Trajan and Hadrian II', organised by Chris Whitton at Rostock in June 2014. Many thanks to him and to the entire audience for their valuable comments and the collegial discussion afterwards.

both the recursivity of the persecutions and the genealogical continuities in the ranks of the opposition that suffered them – and Lucan had, after all, been eliminated during the purges following a senatorial conspiracy. In both ages, Pliny suggests, Rome had witnessed the persecutions of the same kind of anti-tyrannical subjects; from age to age, moreover, it was the same families that provided the resistance with new members.[1] No matter how real the dangers into which Pliny may have run while in office during the last years of the 'bad' emperor's rule, when he came under the attacks of informers and a dossier in his name was opened and even reached the emperor's desk (*Ep.* 3.11, 7.27), the *Epistles* make a significant effort at situating their author on the heroic side of the senatorial resistance to the autocratic rule of every new despot.[2] Pliny's association with the women – widows or offspring – of the senatorial opposition is a crucial aspect of the authorial portrait he constructs in such texts as *Epistles* 3.16 and 9.13, dedicated to his relationships with Arria the Elder and her daughter. Continuities and recursivity are what Pliny predicates on the side of the persecutors as well. The most relevant case in point is Regulus, whose crimes Pliny memorably describes as no less grave, but perhaps more covert under Domitian than under Nero, as he remarks in *Epistles* 1.5.1, the first in the nine-letter cycle to deal directly with his antagonist: *sub quo non minora flagitia commiserat quam sub Nerone sed tectiora* ('under whom his crimes had been no less grave than under Nero, but more covert').[3]

Based on our current sense of Lucan's work, conversely, it appears paradoxical that a poet such as Martial could also write poems in praise and memory of the author of an anti-tyrannical work. There is apparently nothing in Martial's poetry that may be constructed as openly oppositional to power – and there is very little that may indicate more covert resistance, at least in the choice of official sponsors for the rapidly accumulating installments of his collection.[4] Not only did Martial unfailingly dedicate to the latest autocrat in power his most recent poetic output; he also chose as one of his patrons Regulus, the same long-term *delator* that Pliny had taken as

---

[1] On the issue of recursivity, see the synthesis in Griffin 2002: 171ff. For the transmission through feminine lineage of the senatorial opposition to which Pliny protests a long-standing association, see Carlon 2009: 21ff.

[2] Reactions range from scepticism, following Syme (*passim*), to full endorsement. See Gibson and Morello 2012: 35, to which one may add now Winsbury 2013 as militant in Pliny's support.

[3] On the presence and internal articulation of the Regulus cycle in Pliny's *Epistles,* see most recently Gibson and Morello 2012: 68–73.

[4] On doublespeak as a locus for power negotiations potentially infiltrating Neronian and Domitianic public discourses, see Bartsch 1994: 63–97. For the advocation of a subversive reading in the *Epigrams,* see Boyle 1995b: 94–100 and Garthwaite 1998: 157–72. Spisak 1999 remains useful in pointing to the normative force attached to Pliny and Martial's panegyrical works.

the embodiment of the recursive continuity between Nero's and Domitian's ages.

Martial's Regulus is not simply one of the potential elements helping to articulate Pliny's distancing of Martial (evidenced by his *exitus* letter for him, *Ep.* 3.21). The presence of Regulus as a patron and addressee in the *Epigrams* triggers a further and perhaps deeper ideological and literary short circuit, in which I see the second paradoxical aspect in the interconnected body of evidence I analyse in this chapter. With an apparent internal contradiction, Martial uses the work of an apparently anti-Neronian author as the literary vehicle of a positive epideictic moment for Regulus, by redeploying some charged language from the *Bellum ciuile* proem in poems dedicated to him (1.12 and 1.82). As we will see in detail below, in a moment of encomiastic frenzy for Regulus, who had just escaped the collapse of a building, Martial recycles some of the language Lucan had used in his panegyrical dedication to Nero and in the portrayal of the physical and metaphysical causes of the collapse of the Republic (*BC* 1.67–82 and *passim* in the opening gambit of the poem). This intertextual connection may not have gone unnoticed, and may have actually contributed to – as in '(partly) motivated' – Pliny's ostracising silence on Lucan.

By studying the pulviscular cloud of allusions that forms at the core of the triangular relationship of Pliny and Martial to and through Lucan (and around Regulus), this chapter reaches two related conclusions. The first is that a reason for the different treatment of Lucan in Martial and Pliny may be found in the chronological succession of their interventions, a chronology that determines textual reception, in terms of the literary and sociopolitical meaning of their texts. Pliny composes and publishes his *Epistles* after Martial's *Epigrams* had already used Lucan and his text and, in so doing, had provided an interpretation against which any new interpretation would have to be measured. The literary transaction between the *Epigrams* and the *Epistles* hinges on the pre-orienting of interpretation that Martial's poem caused both in a potential reader of Lucan, such as Pliny, and in the readers whom Pliny may have envisioned for his own work.[5] When, in the only instance of direct interaction with Lucan in his collection, he alludes unmistakably to a line in the *Bellum ciuile* (*Ep.* 1.23.1, considered below), Pliny does so by taking into account and responding to Martial's treatment of that text in his Regulus epigrams. What is more,

---

[5] On the complex renegotiations necessary for works of the 96–8 biennium to establish themselves in the new political and cultural climate (and on the ultimate instability of meaning they thus acquire with readers), see Rimell's study of the second edition of *Epigrams* 10 in conjunction with Tacitus' *Agricola* in this volume.

he does so with cultural, as much as political and social, issues in mind, pointing to the larger, extra-literary value of this kind of literary interaction. The dialogue between the two collections produces an overdetermination of Lucan as a cultural object: the meaning of his text arises from and consists in its being disputed between competing literary redeployments.[6] In this light, we are able to appreciate one effect of literary interactions: the emergence in particular texts of sociopolitical connotations that pre-orient interpretation and delimit the range of their possible readings at a given moment in time. As two intersecting collections of re-edited and reassembled occasional material in whose stratified formation time (in the sense of *the passing* of time) has played a significant role, the collections of Pliny and Martial provide a good testing ground for exploring the phenomenology of literary composition as a process rather than in its sole final products.[7]

A second, incidental conclusion is also put forward in this chapter, which has to do with the tone that may be assigned to Lucan's proem by Martial. The reapplication of the language from the (pro-Neronian?) poem by an (anti-Neronian?) author to a Neronian and post-Neronian friend of the emperors (no question marks about Regulus' position are necessary) seems to go hand in hand with the presence of decidedly pro-Lucan poems in the same corpus. As we have seen, the same book in which we read of the *porticus* incident, treated in allusively Lucanian terms, also contains a clear poetic endorsement of Lucan's value as a poet (1.61). More pointedly, Book 7 of the *Epigrams* contains the triptych of eulogising poems about Lucan's birthday (7.21–3) along with compositions addressed to Regulus and calling into question his role as patron. Yet there seems to be no sign that their collocation with those inspired by and dedicated to Regulus in the eventual collection may have been felt in any way inappropriate.

With this evidence in focus, my chapter attempts to reassess (and of course leave open) the question of adjudicating the ultimate tone of Lucan's proem, by trying to gauge the reactions of some of its chronologically close readers and reusers. The fact that Martial uses material from that passage in apparently straightforward praise of one of Nero's associates strongly suggests that such a 'straight', non-subversive reading of the proem to the *Bellum ciuile* was indeed possible. This does not mean that we *must* read that text straight, or that this was the only possible reading of the poem at

---

[6] For a similarly subtle (but differently articulated) interaction, see Mratschek's chapter in this volume, which carefully maps the mutual relations and strategic self-positioning of Pliny, Martial and Domitius Apollinaris, both in- and outside their texts.

[7] On a phenomenological approach to reading Pliny's literary corpus as a book *in fieri* and the process–product semiotic tension embedded at its core, see Gibson 2015.

the time. It only means that it was not impossible to read Lucan's praise of Nero contained in the poem as a serious encomium, if this is what Martial does for the benefit of his patron, and that this 'straight' reading was enough to make it unlikely that Pliny could reuse Lucan's text free from biases. The issue of how to read earlier imperial panegyric proves to be no archaeological concern for Pliny, and his interaction with Martial and his reuse of Lucan and with Lucan by way of Martial suggests how high the sociopolitical stakes of such literary interactions could be in the present.

Reverse Positioning

As we move to a closer reading of the texts at hand, a first clarification is in order, addressing what I mean by 'presence' and 'absence' of Lucan from Pliny's and Martial's collections. With Lucan's absence from Pliny's corpus, I mean two things. First, the non-existent part that Lucan's poem seems to play in the web of poetic intertexts which the *Epistles* mobilise. Pliny, as I have tried to suggest in the past, is an author whose prose warmly welcomes poetic intertexts. To my knowledge, however, there is practically no trace of Lucan as a target of poetic allusion.[8] For this absence it would not be difficult to provide an immediate rationale, based on the letter of the absent text. It is easy to think, for instance, that the *Bellum ciuile* may have appeared to start on such a pro-Nero note that it was made inappropriate for reuse in any anti-tyrannical context such as Pliny's triumphantly post-Domitianic collection, no matter the chronological distance. And yet, Lucan's praise of Nero in the prologue to that work has not always been taken as straightforwardly as this argument may demand. In view of the rest of the poem, in which Caesarism (if not Caesar himself) is openly and unmistakably attacked, the seriousness of Lucan's dedication to Nero has been called into question.

However, Lucan is also absent from Pliny's *Epistles* on a second level. If it is difficult to decide how Lucan's poem could be construed (as pro- or

---

[8] On the web of poetic allusions developed in Pliny's *Epistles*, see Marchesi 2008. One single instance of citation and in the context of a clear-cut rebuttal is rather little. The only accredited tangency between Pliny and Lucan is a rephrasing, at *Ep.* 1.23.1, of Cato's pessimistic conclusion about the destiny of *Libertas* in the civil war (*BC* 2.303, in the expression *inanem umbram*). The connection has been labelled a 'possible echo' in Hoffer 1999: 197 (following Guillemin 1929: 119); for a possible interpretation of this intertextual *hapax*, see below. Trisoglio flagged a second Lucanian intertext in his commentary to the phrase *concordiae discordiam* in *Ep.* 8.14.13, presented as an analogue to *BC* 1.98 *concordia discors*. An alternative or supplementary target of allusion could be Ov. *Met.* 1.433 *discors concordia*, or, even more proverbially, Hor. *Epist.* 1.12.9 *concordia discors*, both relevant parallels kindly indicated to me by Chris Whitton. As we are about to see, Pliny is no stranger to this particular kind of triangulation.

anti-Neronian, or even neither), Pliny also maintains a somewhat counter-intuitive silence on the author of the *Bellum ciuile*. After all, no matter how pro-Neronian the prologue to the poem may have been, Lucan did indeed become a victim of the emperor's repressive counterstrike – and, in so doing, he might be seen as validating the anti-Caesarian side of his poem. Of course, the absence of any mention of this martyr of Nero, even in the context of letters which are more Stoically coloured and which allude to Pliny's own Stoic allegiances during the difficult years of Domitian's purges, may be similarly explained. In the *vita* tradition, Lucan's demise was hardly exemplary of Stoic virtue. In the way he moved from conspiring to testify-ing against innocents or from bragging about the tyrant's impending killing to begging for his own life, he violated all rules of the Stoic code of conduct. Suetonius' *vita* speaks clearly of Lucan's early and boisterous involvement in the Pisonian opposition to Nero and his eventual cowardly attempts to save his life by implicating other conspirators – including his own mother:

> Facile enim confessus et ad humillimas deuolutus preces matrem quoque innoxiam inter socios nominauit, sperans impietatem sibi apud parricidam principem profuturam.

> For he was easily forced to a confession, descended to the most abject entreaties, and even named his own mother among the guilty parties, although she was innocent, in hopes that this lack of filial devotion would win him favour with a parricidal prince.[9]

Lucan was no Thrasea Paetus, nor was he credited with the firmness Pliny emphasises for Paetus' wife in the same circumstances (*Epistles* 3.16 and 9.13). Author and poem may thus be similarly condemned to joint *damnatio memoriae* in Pliny – though for opposing reasons: the poem may be left out of the poetic substratum of Pliny's *Epistles* because excessively pro-imperial (at least in its opening gambit), and the author may be banned from their prosopographical horizon because insufficiently anti-tyrannical (in his opposition to Nero's rule).

This reciprocal construction of value of text and author, however, comes close to becoming a double standard, especially when we pair the silent treatment imposed on Lucan with the presence of Lucan in Martial's *Epigrams*. With Lucan's presence, I mean two distinct but perhaps not unrelated elements, in both cases most explicitly, if allusively, connected to Regulus. Regulus is not a minor figure for Martial's *Epigrams,* since quite a few laudatory poems take him as their object, and he even appears among

---

[9] Translation from Rolfe 1914.

the dedicatees of Book 2.[10] Regulus is no minor figure in Pliny's *Epistles* either. Incidentally (but also significantly), he is the only truly negative character in the richly populated universe of the collection – a person, perhaps the only person in the collection, whom Pliny methodically and unrelentingly attacks. The attitudes of the two authors can hardly be more different: for Pliny, Regulus is the epitome of a sociopolitical return of the repressed, a historically unrevisable 'Vergangenheit, die nicht vergehen will' ('past that does not want to pass'). From this peculiar role with which he is invested stem the trenchant labels Pliny attaches to Regulus as *omnium bipedum nequissimum* ('most wicked of all two-footed creatures', *Ep.* 1.15.14) and, most technically, *uir malus dicendi imperitus* ('a bad man unskilled in speaking', *Ep.* 4.7.5).

Pliny's adversary in the Centumviral court makes his triumphal entrance into Martial's collection of epigrams in the context of his own miraculous surviving the collapse of a portico in a suburban villa.[11] Martial twice mentions the accident from which Regulus, favoured by the gods, escaped unscathed (*Epig.* 1.12 and 1.82):

> Haec quae puluere dissipata multo
> longas porticus explicat ruinas,
> en quanto iacet absoluta casu!
> Tectis nam modo Regulus sub illis
> gestatus fuerat recesseratque,   5
> **uicta est pondere cum suo repente**,
> et, postquam domino nihil timebat,
> securo **ruit** incruenta damno.
> Tantae, Regule, post metum querelae
> **quis curam neget esse te deorum**,   10
> propter quem fuit innocens ruina?
>   (*Epig.* 1.82)

This portico which, scattered in clouds of dust, spreads long ruins over the ground, see from what mischief it lies absolved! For under that roof Regulus had just been driven and had got out of the way, when it was suddenly overcome by its own weight, and since it had no fear for its lord, crashed harmless and without blood. Regulus, after fear of such heavy complaining

---

[10] The Regulus cycle in Martial involves the following epigrams: 1.12 and 1.82 (on the *porticus* incident, about which see *infra*); 1.111 (on his learning and *pietas*), 2.74 (on his ability to secure acquittal of the guilty), 2.93 (as surprise dedicatee of Book 2, but not of 1); 4.16 (on his proverbial acquittal powers); 5.10 (on post-mortem fame), 5.21 (on his authority in matters of mnemotechnics); 5.28 (as a paragon of oratory); 5.63 (in the same role for poetic style); 6.38 (as father of a promising son); 6.64 (on his appreciation of Martial's poetry); 7.16 (on the former patronage of the poet); 7.31 (on his wealth, as opposed to the poet's indigence).

[11] On the nature, purpose, and construction details of this building, see Eden 1990.

is past, who would deny that you are under divine protection, for whose sake ruin caused no harm?[12]

In both epigrams, Martial appears to redeploy some of this charged enco-miastic language, noting that the *porticus* under which Regulus has just passed *uicta est **pondere . . . suo repente*** ('was suddenly overcome by its own weight', 6) and collapsed harmlessly, once it knew it was not going to harm its owner (*innocens ruina*, 11). The language Martial uses here reactivates retrospectively another passage earlier in his first book, an epigram on the same theme, in which we read that the arch *subito **collapsa ruit, cum mole sub illa** | gestatus biiugis Regulus esset equis* ('suddenly it fell in ruin when, under that mighty mass, Regulus had just been driven in his two-horse carriage', *Epig.* 1.12.7–8):

> Itur ad Herculei gelidas qua Tiburis arces
> 　　canaque sulphureis Albula fumat aquis,
> rura nemusque sacrum dilectaque iugera Musis
> 　　signat uicina quartus ab urbe lapis.
> Hic rudis aestiuas praestabat porticus umbras, 　　　　　　　5
> 　　heu quam paene **nouum** porticus ausa **nefas**!
> **nam subito collapsa ruit, cum mole sub illa**
> 　　**gestatus biiugis Regulus esset equis**.
> Nimirum timuit nostras Fortuna querelas,
> 　　quae par tam magnae non erat inuidiae. 　　　　　　　　10
> Nunc et **damna iuuant**; sunt ipsa pericula tanti:
> 　　**stantia non poterant tecta probare deos**.
> 　　　　　　　　　　　　　　　　　　　　　(*Epig.* 1.12)

Where the road runs to the heights of cool Tibur, sacred to Hercules, and milky-hued Albula steams with its sulphureous waters, the fourth milestone from the neighbouring city marks a farm and sacred grove, acres dear to the Muses. Here a rustic portico secured a summer shade; alas, how nearly did that portico dare a crime unheard of! For suddenly it fell in ruin when, under that mighty mass, Regulus had just been driven in his two-horse carriage. Assuredly Fortune had fear of our complaints; she could not brave odium so great. Now even losses please; dangers themselves bring repayment: a stand-ing roof could not have proved that there are gods.

In both cases, the allusive redeployment of some charged language that can be traced back to the proem of the *Bellum ciuile* brings Lucan to the forefront. After concluding the panegyrical dedication to Nero, in moving into the historical and aetiological section of the proem, Lucan remarked,

---

[12] Translations of Martial adapted from Ker 1968.

à propos of the fall of the Republic, that the destruction of the old order
followed from the laws of political physics – the impossibility of the body
politic to continue to exist forever unperturbed. In particular, the Republic
was brought down by *nimio . . . graues sub pondere lapsus | nec se Roma ferens*
('the grievous collapse of excessive weight, and Rome unable to support her
own greatness', *BC* 1.71–2). He reinforced this notion by adding the sententious conclusion *in se magna ruunt* ('great things come crashing down
upon themselves', *BC* 1.81). On account of the dissemination of potential
echoes, the passage deserves extended quotation:

> Fert animus causas tantarum expromere rerum,
> immensumque aperitur opus, quid in arma furentem
> impulerit populum, quid pacem excusserit orbi.
> Inuida fatorum series **summisque negatum**   70
> **stare diu nimioque graues sub pondere lapsus**
> **nec se Roma ferens** . . .
> **In se magna ruunt**: laetis hunc numina rebus   81
> crescendi posuere modum.
>
> (*BC* 1.67–72, 81–2)

> My mind moves me to set forth the causes of these great events. Huge is the
> task that opens before me – to show what cause drove peace from the earth
> and forced a frenzied nation to take up arms. It was the chain of jealous
> fate, and the speedy fall which no eminence can escape; it was the grievous
> collapse of excessive weight, and Rome unable to support her own great-
> ness . . . Great things come crashing down upon themselves – such is the
> limit of growth ordained by heaven for success.[13]

The connections perhaps run even deeper, since in both cases Martial reinforces the cosmic dimensions of this exercise in epigrammatic *parua si
licet* rhetoric with the adoption of the appropriate language for ruinous
collapses and their physical and metaphysical causes. The parallel lexical
choices are telling: Martial has *nefas* (1.12.6), *fortuna* (1.12.9), *ruina* (1.82.2),
casus (1.82.3) and *deus* (1.12.12, 1.82.10). It is the same level of diction that
Lucan deployed throughout the proem of his epic: *nefas* (*BC* 1.6, incidentally in the same line as in Martial's epigram, and 1.37); *fortuna* (1.84); *fatum*
(1.33, 1.42, 1.70); *ruunt* (1.70) and *ruina* (1.150); *deus* (1.35 and 1.62). Martial's over-inflated flattery is particularly evident in the morals that the epigrams draw from the episode. The first poem claims not only that the gods
were on Regulus' side, but also that a proof that gods actually exist may be
found in the favour they have shown to him on that occasion or, perhaps,

---

[13] Translation adapted from Duff 1928.

that the building *needed* to collapse to show as much: *stantia non poterant tecta probare deos* ('a standing roof could not have proved that there are gods', 1.12.12). The second epigram, at the other end of the book, revisits the same facts and returns to the same celebratory tone, concluding once again that no scepticism is now allowed about the gods' favouring Regulus: *quis curam neget esse te deorum, | propter quem fuit innocens ruina?* ('who would deny that you are under divine protection, for whose sake ruin caused no harm?', 1.82.10–11). Lucan's impossible rehabilitation of the *nefas* of civil war by way of the mercantile metaphor *hac mercede* indicating Nero's coming to power relied on the same paradox of a 'harmless' collapse (*innocens ruina*) or 'appreciated' loss (*damna placent*):

> Iam nihil, o superi, querimur; scelera ipsa nefasque
> hac mercede placent.
>
> > (*BC* 1.37–8)

> We, gods, complain no more: even such crimes and such guilt are not too high a price to pay when this is the return.

The delicate allusion to Lucan – and Lucan's potentially ambiguous proem – is particularly intriguing. We seem to be called to witness the reuse of the language from an apparently pro-Neronian poem (the proem of the *Bellum ciuile*) penned by an apparently anti-Neronian author (Lucan), addressed to a Neronian and post-Neronian friend of emperors (Regulus). Of course, my characterisation of poem and poet as pro- or anti-Nero respectively is based on the hypothesis advanced above to account for Lucan's (and his poem's) absence from Pliny's *Epistles*. Question marks would, in truth, be necessary for each of them, in order for my argument not to be read as circular. On the other hand, if we can trust Pliny's trenchant judgment, no question marks are needed to nuance our assessment of Regulus' position. At any rate, beyond helping to stabilise Regulus' value in the literary equation we are studying, Pliny is also useful for possibly confirming that the trope of a collapsing building is particularly apt for Regulus, and for responding to his social standing.

Some charged language which *Epistles* 1.5 uses for Regulus' political and social capital suggests as much:

> Nec me praeterit esse Regulum δυσκαθαίρετον: est enim locuples, factiosus, curatur a multis, timetur a pluribus. (*Ep.* 1.5.15)

> Nor am I forgetting that Regulus is 'hard to knock down': he is rich, well connected, valued by many and feared by even more.

In the context of heightened intertextual awareness that these texts apparently create, even the standard tag Pliny used in the same letter, *deos adesse* ('the gods helped me', 1.5.5), responds to and retrospectively reactivates Martial's repeated attestations of the presence of the gods in the Regulus *porticus* affair.[14]

This double order of presence for Lucan in association with Regulus, one should not forget, seems to go hand-in-hand with the presence of decidedly pro-Lucan poems in the same corpus. The same book in which we read of the Regulus *porticus* incident also contains a clear poetic endorsement of Lucan's value as a poet (1.61). More pointedly, however, Book 7 of the *Epigrams* contains the triptych of eulogising poems about Lucan's birthday (7.21–3), composed for the poet's widow, which are definitely less timid in making ethical and political considerations part of the praise of Lucan. Yet there seems to be no sign that their collocation with those inspired by and dedicated to Regulus in the eventual collection may have been felt in any way inappropriate. The star of this patron of Martial has not yet set, as Book 7 still has poems addressed to Regulus in the role of potential (if no longer actual) patron of the poet.[15]

It may also be useful to contemplate a possible counterargument at this point: namely, that Martial's Lucanian winks are in turn liable to be read ironically, at least to a certain point. It is not impossible, that is, that Martial is ultimately content, given the fallout he may have had with his patron Regulus later in his career, for readers to catch the retrospective irony of the allusions. Once Regulus can no longer be counted among Martial's protective deities, in other words, the tone in which his praise was formulated may undergo a new interpretation as well. Just as Lucan's praise of Nero might have been reread and reinterpreted *ex post facto* as ironic, the same option may be open for Martial's homage to Regulus. This kind of value shift may have taken place, incidentally, before the actual waning of Regulus' social and political prestige, still lively according to Pliny between 92 (the most likely date of publication for *Epigrams* 7) and 97 (when he openly attacks Regulus with *Epistles* 1.5). However, even if a post-decline ironic reading of Martial's homage will eventually become possible, what should we make of Pliny's silence on Lucan? If Martial's allusions were

---

[14] On the destabilising effect of reading Martial's in Pliny's text, see Henderson 2001; for a refocusing on the narrower context of the *porticus* fall, see Marchesi 2013. On possible alternative resonances in the rare Greek adjective Pliny applies to Regulus (connected to *hairein* 'to catch') as relevant for the Pliny–Tacitus dialogue on oratory, see the keen observations developed in Whitton 2012: 357.

[15] 'It is of interest that Martial never mentions him after Book 7 but gives no hint as to why' (Williams 2004 on *Epig.* 2.74.2).

eventually readable as double-edged, wouldn't that possible ironic reading re-establish Lucan's proem as a viable vehicle of satire and tyrant debunking? Pliny does not seem to avail himself of that subversive reading of Lucan at any point. Quite the contrary: nothing in his corpus suggests that the paradox of Lucan's absence is in any way mitigated by the passing of time or the taming of political tides.

The paradoxical quality of the situation just described, it is just as important to remember, derives solely from the formulation that has been given here of the relative positioning of the actors involved in the literary negotiation. No ancient or modern reader has apparently been perturbed by Lucan's inverse matrix of presence in and absence from collections by authors who seem to have entertained opposed sympathies, if not militated on opposed political and ethical fronts.[16] The paradox is modestly proposed, then, as a heuristic move and an openly provisional point. It is a point of origin for an argument on a literary interaction; it most definitely is not a point of arrival of the configurations of literary and political reception that it assumes. What it may be particularly useful for, in sum, is in the way it helps us acknowledge that Lucan is a particularly unstable element in the system – in particular, in his position vis-à-vis Nero in the poem's opening dedication. A point to which it is time to move.

Value Assessment

Our reading of the opposed behaviour in regard to Lucan (in connection with the similarly opposed relation both works display to Regulus) brings us to the question of adjudicating on the ultimate tone of Lucan's proem and its relation with both the rest of the poem and the biographical material traditionally associated with its author – a relation so problematic and conflictual that it has engendered the label for the *Bellum ciuile* of a poem at war with itself.[17] The task should be undertaken with great care. Assessing the tone and meaning of a piece of literature from a distance – a long distance – is at the same time impossibly difficult and critically dangerous. Not unlike *intentio auctoris*, authorially intended tone is just as unrecoverable as is authorially intended meaning, and no neo-positivist approach can

---

[16] That Martial's personal patronage connections would set him in different circles from Pliny has long been suggested. See White 1975 and Pitcher 1999, esp. p. 560. The social dimensions of their activities as writers extend beyond the rituals of patronage and public performance to reach the subtle grain of the poetic and rhetorical diction.

[17] For the label, see Masters 1992, 73. *Loci classici* of the critical debate on the nature and tone of Lucan's proem are Grimal 1960; Ahl 1976; Dewar 1994; Bartsch 1997 (also 2005); Narducci 2002; Casali 2011 (esp. pp. 83–92).

compensate for that. The situation of the text at hand is fraught with ambiguities and tensions, and the interplay and cross-purpose working of the questions I have raised along the way about the distribution of pro- or anti-Neronian labels from the (perhaps opposed) points of view of Pliny and Martial tries to respond to the dimmed, nuanced, chiaroscuro light that it seems necessary to adopt in tackling the issue of the value of Lucan's text.

If it is difficult, even impossible, to assess now the tone of Lucan's proem, moving the hermeneutic operation back in time to try and assess how that text was, or may have been read, in the generation alive during its composition (Lucan died in AD 65; Martial was born in 40, Pliny in 61/2) is just as difficult. It is, however, an exercise that may produce some hermeneutic gain. When one focuses on how Pliny and Martial appear to read it, two elements emerge from that chronological sectioning of the proem's reception history. First, it appears that the text was indeed divisive from the start, and that it was liable to appear in contexts fraught with ambiguity; second, some of the associations each side of the debate was making to that text are indeed recoverable. The semantic accretions and incrustations that had developed around Lucan's proem can actually be read as more than just an index of his relation to Nero.

In other words, Martial's vocal treatment of Lucan may in fact tell us something about the reception of his text. The first element emerging from the kind of presence Lucan has in the *Epigrams* is that it is both textual and biographical. There are both epigrams establishing what we now call an 'allusive' connection with Lucan's text and epigrams that insist on the biographical circumstances of the author: the *genius loci* and the personal genius in the birthday poems – of the author. This circumstance seems to suggest that using the *vitae* to orient the reading of the proem is, after all, a historically defensible procedure. Text and man are mutually inclusive and mutually implicating, even when they are at odds no less now than in Martial's days. Of course, this kind of biographical implication in the interpretation process is not intended as a renewed form of biographism. What is at stake is not the production of the text but the circumstances of reception.[18] From the start, in the case of Lucan and his poem, readers of one were forced (or decided) to be mindful of the other. For Lucan's poem the act of interpretation apparently took place at the intersection of the textual data and the biographical circumstances attached to its author – an intersection that the readers were called upon to produce.

---

[18] For similar caveats and disclaimers in the study of Martial's interaction with Juvenal, see Kelly's chapter in this volume, esp. pp. 161–4.

Interpretive acts relied (and still do) on the mutual positioning of author and reader around and across a text, and authorially projected reader and reader-constructed author are functions of the same interpretive act. The textual/literary/historical mythologeme [*Lucan] has some essential bearing on the textual/literary/historical interpretation of the texts associated to him. And this, in turn, means that any 'fact' about the cultural reception of that mythologeme may tell us something about what his texts may have been made to mean.

The second element that emerges from Martial's allusions and dedications to Lucan is that in this case it may be possible to disprove a negative prejudice about the proem of his epic. By taking place in connection with Regulus, the redeployment of Lucan's text shows that it was not impossible for the text of the dedication to Nero to be read in earnest. To be sure, that does not mean that only this reading was possible, to the exclusion of any other, more subversive one; it only means that a non-parodic reading did fall within the spectrum of possibility. In turn, this notion has a corollary of potential interest for Pliny: the time in which intertextual connections happen and the context in which they are made are significant. The fact that Pliny writes and publishes his collected epistles after Martial has written and published his encomia of Regulus via Lucan is not idle. Martial's acts of literary deference pre-orient the interpretation of the text they reuse (and of the authorial figure behind it). The possibility that the proem may be reused, with no apparent irony, in the serious praise of a Neronian agent, then, predetermines the sociopolitical interpretation of that text. Being available for more than one interpretation does not make a text neutral; it only makes it complex.

The attacks that Pliny reserves for Regulus appear to be the external counterpart of Martial's behaviour – and they may have something to do with Lucan as well. The correct positioning of such literary works as the *Bellum ciuile* vis-à-vis the power of the autocrats ruling Rome is a vital issue for Pliny's cultural project: as already hinted above, in the *Epistles* Neronian and Domitianic times are constructed as a notional continuity. More importantly, for Pliny the two tyrannical ages are also mediated by (if not united in) the figure of Regulus, whose crimes he pointedly describes, in the opening salvo against his adversary, as no less grave, but only perhaps more covert under Domitian than under Nero (*Ep.* 1.5.1). The connection of the two ages goes beyond the realm of the ideal (and the shifts of ideological construction) to become a biographically embodied continuity. If Pliny reserves an unusual amount of bile for his treatment of this character, it may be in part due to the double role that Regulus is made to serve, as the foil for the ideal society predicated on the present (what Trajan's reign has overcome) and as the object of a practical character assassination necessary for that present to distance itself from the past (what Trajan's rule needs to excise in order to gain coherence). In sum, if Regulus is the wholesale signpost for the age of the *delatores* to whose name Pliny apparently insists on returning, by contrast the silence his *Epistles* maintain on Lucan is more evident. The damning of Lucan's memory – achieved by surgical indifference – is balanced by the insistent and negative memorialisation of Regulus.

In *Epistles* 1.5, in sum, Pliny appears as having come to Regulus later than Martial and, in a way, too late, when a marked association of that character with Lucan material has already been established – and that material had been given a decidedly positive spin. In this sense, one may argue, Lucan's absence from Pliny's corpus may find an additional motivation in the way he positions his text with regard to Martial's handling of Lucan. Not only can Lucan's proem be read as an unabashedly pro-Neronian moment (as Martial suggests by redeploying it for Regulus and thus provisionally but markedly stabilising its tone), but it is also the way in which Martial has occupied Lucan as a subject of encomiastic poetry that makes it difficult for Pliny to tread in the wake of that poetry. Pliny's silence could thus be more the effect of a polarisation imposed by Martial than the consequence of a literary inclination – a reaction more than a free choice.

Paradox of Presence

Drawing towards our conclusion, it is time to revisit the single, indirect but unmistakable, reference to Lucan that has been at times attributed to Pliny. Having explored the interconnected webs of allusions linking Pliny and Martial in their opposed treatments of Lucan, we are perhaps in a better position to appreciate some of the complexities of the act. In setting up the rhetorical terms of his short defence of the dignity of the tribunate, Pliny writes:

> Consulis an existimem te in tribunatu causas agere debere. Plurimum refert, quid esse tribunatum putes, inanem umbram et sine honore nomen an potestatem sacrosanctam, et quam in ordinem cogi ut a nullo ita ne a se quidem deceat. (*Ep.* 1.23.1)

> You want to know whether I think you should keep practising in the law courts while holding the office of tribune. Much depends on what you believe the tribunate to be, an empty shadow and a mere title, or an inviolable authority which should not be called in question by anyone, not even by the holder himself.

The allusion is a clear and pointed one. In the *Bellum ciuile*, Lucan had Cato state in his final deliberation to join the war, though reluctantly: *tuumque | nomen, Libertas, et inanem persequar umbram* ('and I shall follow your name, Freedom, and your empty shadow', *BC* 2.303). Pliny reuses the three charged terms *nomen, inanis* and *umbra* as the discarded alternative in a clearly marked opposition referring to the dignity of the office he too once held. If Lucan can make his Cato so disheartened, Pliny appears to want none of it, and mounts the best defence he can for one of the institutions that Lucan had deemed lost, once and for all, with the outbreak of civil war. In so doing, and in doing it (perhaps) in the pulviscular context we have explored thus far, however, Pliny also evokes a third text in which the tag *inanis umbra* we associate with Lucan is just as prominently displayed, but also intersects with themes of rhetorical virulence and building collapse. These three elements are found in a compact passage from Ovid's *Tristia* (3.11.21–5):

> In causa facili cuiuis licet esse diserto,
>   et minimae uires frangere quassa ualent.
> Subruere est arces et stantia moenia uirtus:
>   quamlibet ignaui praecipitata premunt.
> Non sum ego quod fueram. Quid inanem proteris umbram?

> Anyone can be eloquent when the brief is easy, and the least strength shatters what's already broken. It's brave to take citadels and standing walls: any coward can crush what's already down. I am not what I was. Why trample an empty shadow?

While evoking, only to discard it immediately, Lucan's poem and his certainly pessimistic (if not perverse) depiction of Cato, Pliny also seems to remind his advice-seeking friend Falco of a subtler antecedent – a context that provides him with a different perspective and makes the question on which he is inviting deliberation multifaceted. The activation of the diverging intertext suggests an alternative authorial self-positioning as well. Practising law while in office does not simply amount to denouncing the utter futility of the office one holds, as Lucan's paradoxical Cato suffices to prove. Considering one's office an empty shadow also seems to bring into focus the dangers of practising a vicious kind of oratory, the kind that tramples the fallen. The metaphors we read in Ovid suggest that this is the kind of oratory of someone who is most pointedly 'not Pliny'. Having reached the end of Book 1 of his *Epistles*, and having read the epigrams Martial had dedicated to the falling-down of buildings around Regulus, we have some fairly clear idea of who this not-Pliny figure may be. After all, while Martial, via Lucan, was evoking the collapse of a building for his patron, Pliny still insists, via the same Lucan (now complicated by Ovid), on the strength of the post-Domitianic Regulus and on his ability to withstand any attempt to topple him. Attacking him is tantamount to a virtuous overcoming of *stantia moenia,* not the easy victory achieved by the *ignauus,* who treads on the ruins once the walls have been levelled.

What should we say, in conclusion, about the literary interactions across these texts? The essential point my chapter has tried to make is that, in the case of *Lucan as an object of literary and political contention, Martial and Pliny's diverging citational strategies have proved to be not only a matter of rhetorical and poetic practices, but also the vehicle for political and social concerns. Even when necessarily understood as fully textual and literary objects, Martial, Pliny and Lucan are not figures whose existence can be evaluated solely in the realm of literature. The catalytic effect that Regulus appears to have on the intertextual dynamic suggests that any production of meaning in canonical texts takes place in the immediacy of social and political tensions of the present and contributes to determining its cultural geography of power. Also, by bringing into focus the dynamics of allusion to Lucan in Martial and Pliny, we have been able to glimpse how the policies and politics of literary production and interpretation force readers to engage in a peculiar kind of dynamic semiosis, not unlike what takes place in the back and forth of a dialogue. As in a dialogue meaning is formed progressively, with every new exchange at once determining the direction of the conversation and reinterpreting the whole set of utterances that has come before, so too in these collections the value of individual pieces accrues in time. As happens in the flow of an oral exchange, but perhaps more radically in this particular type of engaged literature, every new exchange between works that position themselves in such relationships also has to take into account the more cogently non-retractable and non-editable context of the published collection of which it becomes an integral part. These contexts are, in turn, in a dialectic relationship with the social, political and cultural environment in which and for which they are produced. For contemporary and ancient readers alike, the result of literary interactions is the need to negotiate with particular phenomenological care the process of meaning formation and not just its eventual outcomes.

CHAPTER 16

Forgetting the Juvenalien in Our Midst
Literary Amnesia in the Satires

Tom Geue

We critics usually want to see our authors talking with one another. And if they happen to look the other way, committed to riding out the cringe of reciprocal snubbing, we have ways of making them talk.[1] Intertextuality – at least its current form in mainstream Latin studies – is one such way of forcing the conversation. The reader-response slant of this intertextuality[2] empowers the critic as host to make use of many gestures, from the minute verbal echo to the macrocosmic structural parallel, to shoehorn even the most autistic of authors into meaningful 'interaction'. And yet, as many of this volume's contributions caution, the toolkit for these acts of socio-textual engineering has been assembled from the texts of a very different time, and a very different Rome.[3] In addition, the model of a coterie gluing itself together through adhesive allusivity works well for the interactions seen in our grand document of the age, Pliny's correspondence; but it gets on less well in the darker corners of the Nervan–Trajanic–Hadrianic network. This chapter will worry about what we do with one mute partygoer stewing in his own isolation, the one who fails to say much to or about anyone important, and fails to have anything much said to or about him: that silent assassin of post-Domitianic life, the satirist Juvenal.

Juvenal presents a problem for tracking literary interactions. The founding pose of his first Satire (1–18) is that of an audience member standing up to be counted after years passively enduring a stagnant (where Pliny might say flourishing) literary scene: no more. Juvenal's first act as mayor of his own making is to retract himself from the society of letters trending around him: a society of one-way traffic jammed between booming

Thanks to the editors and conference participants for talking with me, and making this project such an interactive pleasure.
[1] Cf. Gibson in this volume, whose fictional dialogue is a nice way of sublimating this desire for interaction.
[2] Hinds 1998: 10, 47–51 notably privileges (or at least raises to equality) the reader as agent in the intertextual transaction.
[3] See e.g. Uden (this volume), pp. 387–8; also König and Whitton's Introduction, p. 12.

soliloquisers and studiously ignored audiences. And, if our speculative dates[4] hold true enough, that society took its revenge by genteel neglect of his roaring protestations. Save Martial (probably/perhaps),[5] no contemporary names Juvenal or alludes to the *Satires*. When it comes to the self-appointed nub of the arbiters of taste, i.e. Pliny and his teammate Tacitus, the silence is especially deafening.[6] They take no notice; Juvenal shrugs it off, for he wants nothing to do with the living, and only wants to get at them via the dead (*Sat.* 1.170–1). So: is this more mutual indifference than literary interaction?

Some scholars have thought as much. Highet stretched subtle intertextual clues to breaking point to freeze a nice solid layer of ice between Pliny and Juvenal, the men themselves.[7] Freudenburg's more recent attempt at reading the Juvenal, Pliny, Tacitus triangle shifts the claim from the social to the literary sphere, but still makes much of Juvenalian hostility: certain early satires come across as parodies to knock the wind out of a huffing, puffing 'indignation industry' (i.e. Pliny and Tacitus).[8] In this chapter, I shall probe how far we can take this idea of Juvenal the disaffected alien at odds with the Plinian *Zeitgeist* of association, interaction, reciprocity, connectedness; how our satirist might corrode the social seal of the *Epistles*, which ceaselessly slog away at building prosopographical community. I shall apply a key metaphor cluster from Latin studies – memory, and its dark side, oblivion – to see where (if anywhere) the conventional lexicon of intertextuality might get us at the Juvenalian end of days, a long trek from the Augustan poets. The diffuseness and obliquity of allusion in Juvenal may well be part of the blunted point, a favourite technique in a brand of satire that stubbornly *refuses* to point, brand or name anyone or anything

---

[4] Publication dates for the works treated in this chapter are notoriously fuzzy, and that is part of the interactive entertainment. For Juvenal (the star of my second-rate show), I follow broadly the contours of Syme 1979 and Courtney 1980, but take Uden 2015's redating very seriously; suffice to say the *Satires* were being trotted out somewhere between the posts of *c.* 100 and *c.* 130.

[5] Though see Kelly in this volume. Ash (also this volume) puts late Juvenal together with Martial only through their common funnelling of *mirabilia* discourse; this interaction is diachronic, indirect, but no less interesting for it. Uden (this volume) shows Juvenalian interaction through introversion in a nice juxtaposition of pseudo-Plutarch, Quintilian and Juvenal 14.

[6] The notion of Tacitus and Pliny as united front is itself a Plinian effect; for the complex relationship between them (sometimes itself modelled as a one-way conversation), see Whitton 2012, and Marchesi 2008: 97–206. On the broader relationship between Juvenal and Tacitus through satiric 'tone', see Keane 2012.

[7] Highet 1954: 292–4. Syme 1979 finds the silence unremarkable: multiple literary circles can, and always did, spin along in tandem (p. 255).

[8] For Freudenburg 2001's reading of Juvenal against team Pliny–Tacitus, see pp. 209–77, esp. pp. 234–42.

in the vicinity of contemporaneity.⁹ But before we commit, let us limber up with a bracing trot around some methodological pitfalls.

Firstly, we (a thinly disguised I) could afford to be a little more up-front about the relationship between social and literary networking, and how the elevation of the former (in a fundamentally historicist discipline such as Classics) can often draw lines around, and in some cases outright determine, our response to the latter. By this I mean that, even in our post-biographical heyday of sophisticated, sceptical and suspicious criticism, the hint of an 'actual relationship' can act as unfairly stout hermeneutic scaffolding to prop up flimsy intertextual latticework.¹⁰ We (think we) know that Pliny and Tacitus got along swimmingly, so the suite of metaphors used to frame their points of contact is swung positively: homage, wink, nudge, nod, play; just lads and banter, yeah? But could that dominant background story of social intimacy actually blind us to moments of greater (textual, biographical?) hostility? The same goes for dates, although these are excitingly tough to nail in our period: the sense of real-time priority or posteriority always makes us look in certain ways, for certain things (and directions of reference 'making more sense' in turn often ground arguments for dating). In this chapter, my version of the Tacitus–Juvenal and Pliny–Juvenal relationships couldn't quite be misted up by flicking through real social calendars, because we have no (erm . . . textual) evidence for Juvenal skirting the same scene. I like to think that my vision of the relationships, then, is based on a more dependable sense of aesthetic and generic incompatibility; a noble virtue made of necessity. And yet I shudder to think what I would do if Pliny had mentioned Juvenal favourably in his correspondence, just once. The dependable earth (not to mention the sinkhole-ridden moral high ground) would move. Such is the power of literature to produce a light of extratextual reality, which it then casts back over itself. That hermeneutic circle is a vicious one, much as we try to be virtuous with it.

The next issue, set for recurrence *ad nauseam*, is that of genre. This can of worms springs open immediately as soon as Juvenal enters the interaction – and other chapters in this volume run up against the same problem.¹¹

⁹ On Juvenal's timelessness, see Uden 2015: 13 and *passim*; on his vague targeting as an encouragement to the audience to make the final strike, pp. 24–50.

¹⁰ Cf. Marchesi in this volume (e.g. pp. 360–2) on how we orient Martial and Pliny vis-à-vis Lucan, which usually depends on what caricaturised political positions we ascribe to all three. Whitton (this volume), p. 49 notes the scale of variation in the Pliny–Quintilian relationship, and how difficult it is to band diverse intertextual moments into a sealed, solid 'interaction'.

¹¹ See Buckley (this volume).

It is often difficult to 'prove' intertextual activity through the old trump card, the substantive verbal echo, when scanning the prose–verse interface; it is also possible that we pernickety scholars set far too much store by these minor details, and overestimate the 'ideal reader' as enhanced cyborg versions of ourselves.[12] Nevertheless, sustained lexical pokes and brushes are a means whereby authors pin themselves to other specific authors, and for that reason, we should note their absence as much as unpick their presence.[13] And that brings me to the next point: the kinds of interactions we are monitoring here are not simply the monogamous relationships favoured by intertextuality studies in Latin (Pliny and Tacitus, Pliny and Martial, Virgil and Horace etc.); nor are they the less faithful three-or-more-way flirtations of 'window-reference'[14] type intertextuality. Rather, we are plotting bigger attractive/repulsive energies working at the level of genre as well as individual texts, which amount to no less than a spirited confrontation over the right way to write the real. Juvenalian satire is a perfect instance of this, and the question is tied to debates about what satire and its close companion parody are really after in the end. Some examples: when Juvenal sounds off against blustering epic at the beginning of Satire 1, is he puncturing the genre itself, or does the whole stand for a particularly offensive part (namely, say, Valerius Flaccus)?[15] Does Satire 4 pick on the general mode of panegyric poetry – or does it swipe at Statius and his shameless *De bello Germanico*?[16] The question of target (general vs particular, particular through general, general through particular?) is a monotonous one for satire scholars, but it should be kept somewhere accessible at all times for the discussion below, in which we must flip agnostically between calling Pliny and Tacitus, or their genres, or their worldviews, the palimpsestic/holographic butt of the joke.

The next problem grows from this, and looms even larger: the old chestnut of what to do with 'conspicuous absence', and how to dodge the trap

---

[12] See Whitton (this volume), pp. 40–1. On interaction without lexical repetition, see Uden (this volume), pp. 386–7.

[13] This is less controversial when presence draws attention to absence (such as with Marchesi 2013's reading of the relationship between Pliny and Martial); this article argues that we can look to absences full stop, even when we miss all-out authorising markers (such as named mention of the author in question somewhere else in the text). See also Marchesi's chapter in this volume.

[14] Thomas 1986: 188.

[15] Henderson 1999: 260–4 tracks *Sat.* 1's opening salute to Valerius Flaccus, but also allows oscillation between general and specific, e.g. p. 262: 'The shades tortured by Aeacus' (vv. 9f.) points away from Valerius and toward the epic katabasis in general.'

[16] Santorelli 2012: 9–13 follows tradition and reads *Sat.* 4 as targeted parody of *DBG*, Uden 2011: 123 goes for general caricature of panegyric.

of tendentiousness and/or intellectual dishonesty in making absences a little more conspicuous than they perhaps should be. One of the purposes of
this volume is to find new ways of mapping all the rich varieties of interaction coursing through our period; and the volume shows that these are
richer and more varied than once thought. But does this hum of interactive background noise authorise us to do something meaningful with
gaps in interaction – with silences, absences, polite or polemic ignoring? I
would say yes – and intertextuality studies had better get used to counting
the benefits. Several chapters in this volume do wonders with deliberate
omissions and heads buried in sand.[17] Ours is a period of remembering,
associating and aligning; but it is also one of hardcore oblivion, of wip-
ing certain slates clean.[18] It is an age when the avalanche of cultural and
economic interactions in the Roman Empire means digging in the self to
the pointed blanking of the other.[19] This chapter, then, belongs amid the
genial company testing what happens when interactions fail to happen: in
my case, how more aggressive acts of neglect, rewriting and erasure can be
considered, paradoxically and against the grain, as priceless forms of interaction in themselves.

Selective Memory

This chapter began thought-life as a vague desire to stir the pot: what would
happen if we applied some of the standard tropes of Conte–Hindsian allusion – memory and recognition in particular[20] – to a completely inappropriate text, in a completely inappropriate fashion? The tropes were
made for verse–verse intertextuality; I am interested in prose–verse. Memory and recognition naturally lend themselves to vertical/diachronic intertextuality (e.g. Lucan channelling Virgil), because, well, it is difficult to
get so worked up about 'remembering' or 'recognising' what you heard
at last month's recitation; I am interested in the horizontal/synchronic

---

[17] Marchesi (cf. Marchesi 2013), Rimell, Uden in this volume.

[18] The balance is nicely encapsulated in the famous formulation of Tac. *Agr.* 2.3: *memoriam quoque
     ipsam cum uoce perdidissemus, si tam in nostra potestate esset obliuisci quam tacere.* See Rimell (this
     volume) on the complex relationship between remembering and forgetting in the *Agricola* (and
     Martial *Ep.* 10). Juvenal is deeply infused with the post-Domitianic spirit of *damnatio memoriae*; cf.
     the crowd's treatment of Sejanus in *Sat.* 10, for which see Freudenburg 2001: 11–13.

[19] On which phenomenon see Uden in this volume, and Uden's (2015: 203–15) excellent reading of
     Sat. 15 (he mentions the growing discourse of local identity on p. 208, among other places).

[20] For various tropes of self-annotation, see Hinds 1998: 1–16. For memory, see Hinds 1998: 3–4 (via
     Conte 1986: 57–69); for recognition, Hinds 1998: 8–10 (via Narducci 1973).

version, i.e. 'remembering' the very recent literary past (a sure sign of short-term memory gone awry). I was also intent on testing a suspicion I had always harboured about the obverse of memory: could one also operate an anti-allusion[21] by troping a moment not in terms of remembering, but in terms of forgetting?

Believe it or not, the search turned up two cases in Juvenal where the systems of memory(/oblivion) and intertextuality touch. The first is about the politics of the memorandum: what *should* be mentioned (cf. *memorare* below) and recalled in the written record. I'm talking about the now disproportionately famous reference to Otho's mirror and the 'Annals and fresh History' in which it should have been treated (at least in Juvenal's book (of Tacitus?)). This verse has borne on its slim shoulders the heavy weight of dating: it has been slapped back and forth as one of the only possible *termini post quem* in *Satires* Book 1,[22] depending on whether one takes it as a reference to Tacitus in particular, or historiography in general (that issue again). In what follows, I bravely slink from leaning either way; rather, I want to press what Otho's mirror and its non-inclusion in previous history tell us about Juvenalian satire's avowedly more capacious hard drive, and how all of this (if obliquely) gets at Pliny's epistolographic habit of supplementing Tacitean history with anecdotal titbits. The second example (*Sat.* 10.229 and surrounds, after Pliny *Ep.* 8.18) is perhaps less well known, but certainly on the map of Juvenalian intertextuality (noted by Syme, again on a quest for chronology).[23] This instance is an even richer case of allusion mingled with marker tropes; but here the relevant nexus is of dementia, amnesia and non-recognition. I shall argue that the nod to Pliny works in tandem with a nearby eruption of intra-authorial intertextuality (back to *Sat.* 1) to test how much and how far our 'ideal' reader remembers; and if they do remember, to make sure that the next step is to forget Pliny and his naïve ethic of a world pulled back from the brink. Juvenal upends the Plinian target text, and effaces the Plinian *Weltanschauung in nuce* – there will be no last minute happy endings emerging from this blighted interaction. So satire tries to dispose of its main generic rival for anecdotage (letters) via a timely bout of radical forgetfulness.

---

[21] For the notion of the anti-allusion in Lucretius – a glancing reference to an author or genre, for the sole purpose of rejection – see Cowan 2013. He explicitly distinguishes it from antiphrastic allusion (p. 125): 'Anti-allusion excludes the source text and even denies its status as source text, or as bearing any significance at all.'

[22] Syme 1979: 262 basically represents the old orthodoxy, which has stuck hard; for the revisionist position and early dating, see Uden 2015: 219–26, and now Kelly in this volume.

[23] Syme 1979: 253–5.

Mirroring History's Addenda

Our first 'interaction' looks more like narcissistic navel-gazing. Halfway through Satire 2, the one about the aristocratic *cinaedus* who acts like a Cato, Juvenal lights on a particularly offensive type of mirror-brandishing pathic. The toilette of this gentleman reminds Juvenal of how Otho used to admire himself looking all nice and armed before battle action. The episode is marked as a supplement to other, less adequate historical accounts of Otho doing the rounds in Rome. This is not quite counterfactual history, but corrective history, gerundival history. Juvenal focuses on what *should* have been 'there' (i.e. the part that history glosses over):

> Ille tenet speculum, pathici gestamen Othonis,
> Actoris Aurunci spolium, quo se ille uidebat
> armatum, cum iam tolli uexilla iuberet.
> Res memoranda nouis annalibus atque recenti
> historia, speculum ciuilis sarcina belli.
> Nimirum summi ducis est occidere Galbam
> et curare cutem, summi constantia ciuis
> Bebriaci campis solium affectare Palati
> et pressum in faciem digitis extendere panem,
> quod nec in Assyrio pharetrata Sameramis orbe
> maesta nec Actiaca fecit Cleopatra carina.
>
> (*Sat.* 2.99–109)[24]

> Another holds a mirror, the accessory of pathic Otho, 'spoils of Auruncan Actor', in which he used to check himself out when he'd put on his armour, while ordering the battle standards to be raised. It's an episode worth a mention in recent annals and modern history, that a mirror was part of the kit for civil warfare. Well, I guess it's the mark of a supreme general to slaughter Galba while pampering his skin, the courage of the highest citizen on the battlefields of Bebriacum to claim the Palatine throne while plastering his face with a mask of dough. Quivered Sameramis in her Assyrian city did no such thing, nor did Cleopatra weeping in her ship at Actium.[25]

The question raised above is: where is *there*? Which new annals and recent history are we revising here? The received wisdom once was that this just had to be a dig at Tacitus. Mention of *historia*, Galba and Otho in the same breath – come on, a no-brainer![26] The tag was used to push Book 1

---

[24] Latin follows the Oxford Classical Texts.
[25] Translations are adapted (imperfectly remembered) from Braund 2004.
[26] E.g. Keane 2012: 412 on this moment as an 'implicit reproach' to Tacitus for giving too balanced a portrayal of Otho.

definitively beyond the publication of *Histories* 1[27] – and that seemed as good as we could get. Recent histories have been positively revisionary, however: Uden has argued convincingly[28] that this need not strictly refer to Tacitus, hence helping to shunt Book 1 back a few years to a political context in which it makes more sense (AD 100/1). While I cannot help bending with the wind here, I also wonder whether we can't have our date cake and eat some too. If we accept an early second-century ambit for Book 1, perhaps we could read this creative act of supplementation not just as an allusion (albeit to something *not* there) in the conventional sense, but rather a kind of premature editorial intervention into a gestating, still crystallising text.[29] By this I mean that, if word was circulating that Tacitus was already working on *Histories*, and if very early drafts of the text were floating round alongside recitation sneak-previews and general hype, Juvenal's memorandum could be a bid to fill out and top Tacitus' Otho narrative before it even set. Such a move would be an interesting instance of preemptive 'corrective' allusion: a process enabled by the porous filters and lengthy drip-feedback loops of recitation, revision and publication that was literary culture in contemporary Rome.[30] Even if this is necessarily speculative, the possibilities of interaction fan out into a vertiginous, epicyclic complexity. The typical temporalities of intertextuality go wild when we let texts do their thing as motile *processes* rather than box them to languish as static outcomes.[31]

So a pointed glare at Tacitus is still conceivable, but perhaps neither necessary nor sufficient to give us something good to interact with. If Otho's mirror were mentioned in Tacitus, this could be the place where we might see in the mirror a nice self-reflexive marker: Juvenal 'reflecting' or 'echoing' Tacitus right back at him, or using the mirror preemptively to distort his Otho-in-the-making. But instead, Juvenal makes us look in that mirror only to find nothing there; he tricks us with the ultimate optical a/i-llusion. If the mirror only performs a fraction of the work my Hindsian Mr Hyde wants it to here, perhaps we can inch a little further by paying attention to

---

[27] Tacitus was thought to be at work on *Histories* by AD 106, from Pliny's Vesuvius letters (*Ep.* 6.16 and 6.20) – see, for example, Damon 2003: 4–5. Ash 2007: 2 n. 9 revives the position of Syme 1958: 119–20: publication could have been in instalments, with rounds of recitations.

[28] See n. 22.

[29] Syme 1958: 119 thinks Tacitus could have begun his 'serious researches' as early as AD 98. We are in murky waters here, as we should be; we would do well to abandon the notion of crisp publication dates and one-way directions of influence (as if it were ever straightforward to establish them, even in our glorious information age!).

[30] On which see Dupont 1997; Gurd 2012; Johnson 2010.

[31] Cf. Whitton 2012: 350; Marchesi (this volume), p. 352.

the original object of interest: memory. Juvenal boils down the task of historiography with a historiographically inflected tag: *res memoranda*.[32] 'Recollection', of course, isn't just a metaphor of intertext: it is the very job that Roman historiography liked to see itself (in the mirror) *doing*. That which 'ought to be recalled', then, is the plume of historiography on that Year of the Four Emperors (in which Tacitus' contribution was/is/will be but the latest instalment). This is a flash of charged generic interaction whereby Juvenal makes a big claim for totalising *satura*: not just better than epic at seeing the world as it is,[33] but better than history at remembering it as it was – a true reflection!

Juvenal's satiric history is crafted to wow in a few ways here.[34] The claim to know more than historiography is especially impressive given the genre's standing in the Juvenalian satire of the near future. Satire 7 gives us a glimpse of what history means to Juvenal[35] – a bloated stack of papers whose volume could only be surpassed by satire itself:

> Vester porro labor fecundior, historiarum
> scriptores? Perit hic plus temporis atque olei plus.
> Nullo quippe modo millensima pagina surgit
> omnibus et crescit multa damnosa papyro;
> sic ingens rerum numerus iubet atque operum lex.
> Quae tamen inde seges? Terrae quis fructus apertae?
> Quis dabit historico quantum daret acta legenti?
>
> (*Sat.* 7.98–104)

So is your work more profitable, you writers of history? This process swallows yet more time and midnight oil. With no limit for any of them, the

---

[32] *Memorare* and relatives are fundamental to Tacitean (as to most) historiography: cf. *Hist.* 1.1 *Initium mihi operis Seruius Galba iterum Titus Vinius consules erunt. Nam post conditam urbem octingentos et uiginti prioris aeui annos multi auctores rettulerunt, dum res populi Romani memorabantur pari eloquentia ac libertate*... Then *Ann.* 1.1 *Sed ueteris populi Romani prospera uel aduersa claris scriptoribus memorata sunt*; cf. also the memory language of *Dial.* 1.3 *Ita non ingenio, sed memoria et recordatione opus est, ut quae a praestantissimis uiris et excogitata subtiliter et dicta grauiter accepi, cum singuli diuersas sed probabilis causas afferrent, dum formam sui quisque et animi et ingeni redderent, isdem nunc numeris isdemque rationibus persequar, seruato ordine disputationis.* And already *Agr.* 1.2 *Sed apud priores ut agere digna memoratu pronum magisque in aperto erat, ita celeberrimus quisque ingenio ad prodendam uirtutis memoriam sine gratia aut ambitione bonae tantum conscientiae pretio ducebantur.* But don't forget *Agr.* 2.3: *Memoriam quoque ipsam cum uoce perdidissemus, si tam in nostra potestate esset obliuisci quam tacere.* One might say memory is one of *the* Tacitean themes, threading the most prominent positions of every single one of his works.

[33] Juvenal's relationship with epic is an old hand of scholarship: see Connors 2005; Freudenburg 2005a; Jones 2007. Syme 1979: 265 also understands Juvenal's relationship with historiography here through the analogy of his relationship with epic.

[34] For more on history in Juvenal's satire, see Keane 2012: 406–9.

[35] Keane 2012: 411 limits the applicability of this passage to Tacitus in particular, taken as it is with impoverished, jobbing writers; but the statement about the *operum lex* still stands.

thousandth page swells and grows, bankrupting you with papyrus outlay; so
the huge number of facts and the law of the genre lay it down. But what's
the yield from it? What's the fruit of the earth you've ploughed? Who'll give
a historian as much as he'd give to some newsreader?

The massive stock of facts dictates a whole lot of wasted paper; such are
the rules of the game. If the most salient feature of historiography is its
comprehensiveness, we come back to Juvenal's historical supplement with
a jaw dropped even lower: somehow our weighty satirist has managed to
expand the genre that was already at maximum capacity, by definition, by
law. Though there be infinite *res* for history to incorporate, one thing it
cannot do is include the juicy, trivial details; satire, on the other hand, is
free to chew over this bread and butter, as well as modulate upwards as high
as you care to climb.[36] This kind of interaction is a megalomaniac version
of the apparently more modest supplementary strategies of epistolography
(see below) and biography; if Satire 2 fell just a few years down the line,
it would be hard to resist seeing this as a simultaneous poke at the Suetonian Otho forming in the wake of the Tacitean one. For he too missed the
mirror.

But Juvenal does far more to vaunt the capacity of satiric history here.
Not only does he parade satire's remarkable knack for capturing the world
in efficient bursts of synecdoche (a mirror image is representative gear for
civil war, where opponents are really facing 'themselves'): the way he tells
this 'story' is also a showpiece for what satire can do. And that is to rewrite
history so that big events are shaken out of their causal and chronological straitjackets, and interspersed with a raft of trivia to break any lin-
gering sense of narrative progression. Galba's death comes first (and it is
suggested, against the grain, that this is the direct handiwork of Otho himself, mirror in one hand, bloody sword in the other); then (or simultaneously) comes Otho's manicure; suddenly we lurch forward to Bedriacum,
Otho's last stand; then comes the lunge at the Palatine (*solium affectare
Palati*, 2.106), which seems to skip to that last stand against Vitellius at
Bedriacum, while at the same time maintaining a strange sense of 'beginning' (*affectare* usually refers to the initial stages of a campaign, the striv-
ing/aspiring phase – as if Bedriacum (vs Vitellius) were the same moment
as the first shot at the throne (vs Galba)). So Juvenal wreaks havoc with
due historical process, mixing up cosmetics and conquests.[37] Through the

---

[36] On the 'universal inclusiveness' of Juvenalian satire, see Jones 2007: 18–19; he also mentions (if
curtly) Juvenal's relationship with historiography (pp. 18–19, 123).

[37] As is good and proper when dealing with civil war; Bedriacum in the background of the mirror
perhaps also shunts us forward to the second battle of 69 fought there.

rapid-fire references to Sameramis and Cleopatra, he also shows how much
history satire – with its penchant for cramming in comparables only to have
them outdone – can get through in a few lines of verse. Eastern queens,
both legendary and historical, rub shoulders with the western queen of AD
69. Satire's hyperactive rolling through *exemplum* after *exemplum*, with no
respect for causality, chronology or corollary, makes for the most extensive
history of all.[38]

This, then, is how satire 'recalls': it scratches in and fills up the details
absent from the more official historical record. In that sense, it closely
(pre-?)mimes a trick often pulled by Pliny in his letters to Tacitus. The
following could be a good example of an interaction that doesn't rest on
verbal echo, but plugs in via its similarity of 'pose', 'gesture', 'move':

> Auguror, nec me fallit augurium, historias tuas immortales futuras; quo
> magis illis (ingenue fatebor) inseri cupio. Nam si esse nobis curae solet ut
> facies nostra ab optimo quoque artifice exprimatur, nonne debemus optare,
> ut operibus nostris similis tui scriptor praedicatorque contingat? Demon-
> stro ergo, quamquam diligentiam tuam fugere non possit, cum sit in pub-
> licis actis, demonstro tamen quo magis credas, iucundum mihi futurum
> si factum meum, cuius gratia periculo creuit, tuo ingenio tuo testimonio
> ornaueris. (*Ep.* 7.33.1–3)

> I augur that your histories will be immortal, and the augury won't be wrong.
> That's why (I freely admit) I'm desperate to be included in them. If we usu-
> ally make sure that none but the best artist takes our portraits, why shouldn't
> we want our deeds to fall to a writer and publicist like yourself? So here is an
> account of an incident which can hardly have escaped your thorough eye,
> since it was in the official records; but I am sending it nonetheless so that
> you may be more assured of my pleasure if this episode of mine, which accu-
> mulated acclaim from the risks attending it, is embellished by the testimony
> of your genius.[39]

Pliny's famous humble request for his own inclusion in Tacitus' *Histories*
is a more genteel example of the same 'supplementing' strategy we have
seen in Satire 2 – the big difference being that here, the author himself
wants to be written in (*inseri cupio*). I shall make more of this key split
between the Plinian/Juvenalian approaches to writing the self below. From
a Juvenalian point of view, Pliny becomes the vain Otho admiring his own
desired reflection in the Tacitean mirror. But, importantly, this is also a
site of generic abrasion and sparking, where Pliny points out the limits of

---

[38] Cf. interestingly König 2017's parallel arguments about Frontinus' stretching and straining of historiography and epic in the *Strategemata*.
[39] Pliny translations again misremembered from Radice 1969.

historiography, and shows off the 'spontaneous', episodic, anecdotal capabilities of the letter form. The Vesuvius letters are up to something similar: even if Pliny frames that material as of little interest to Tacitus, as somehow 'beneath' history, he is simultaneously snickering at history's reluctance to get its hands so sooty.[40] Pliny's polite plea for treatment under the historical agenda's 'any other business' is also – like Juvenal's correction – a sortie in a campaign of generic imperialism: I can move into and landscape your turf, but you have to keep off mine.

The question still bugs: how can we model such an interaction? If we were still lazily reclined on the deceptive *terra firma* of pre-Uden, I would probably push to read the passage of Juvenal as a strike at both Tacitean history and the Plinian tic of wanting to supplement Tacitean history (with himself). As indeed I did in the original conference paper on which this chapter is based. But the interaction has rubbed off on me. Now that *Satires* Book 1 could fare just as well before the time of *Histories* 1–2 and *Epistles* 7, I am hesitant to insist on a traditionally direct triangulation where the scathing satirist punctures the serious litterati. And perhaps this is a godsend. It allows us to see that an 'interaction' can take place through parallel responses to a fundamental literary crux of the age: what is the best form to 'remember' things in text? Is historiography, the tried and tested repository of *memoria*, the best/only way? Or can different forms remember differently, remember more and remember better? In some ways historiography is a much greater threat to Juvenalian satire than epic or tragedy, because it carries the weight of the document, the true reflection; we could speak similarly of its strained overlap with verisimilar letter writing. I have tried to stress, then, that this flash of 'memory' in Juvenal is nowhere near a 'mere' trope of intertextuality, but a grappling with a *Zeitgeist*: how you record, what you record, what forms tell more of the whole story. This interaction is a tussle of genres, all bidding for the best memory and biggest database – and no need for a verbal echo to seal the deal.

Forgetting Happy Endings

So we've run over the stakes of the memory game; now to look into a case of deliberate memory *loss*. My second family of examples will relieve classical intertextualists in so far as the chronology and direction are much clearer: it's generally agreed that Juvenal 10 appeared somewhere around

---

[40] See *Ep.* 6.20.20, and Marchesi 2008: 171–89 on the relationship between historiography and epistolography in *Ep.* 6.16 and 6.20; according to her, *Ep.* 6.20 'is allegedly not *historia*, but offers itself as such' (p. 188).

120, a long way removed from the Trajanic *floruit* of Pliny *Epistles* 8.18.[41]
But it will again cause squirming because – even with a litany of contextual and thematic similarities to bolster the connection – there is precious little verbal correspondence on which to fall back. In this case, I want to claim a little more vociferously that this lack of *direct* reference is part of the dynamics of the interaction. In these two passages that deal with senescence ended right and ended wrong respectively, it is in Juvenal's interests to forget – and make the reader forget – that Pliny ever happened.[42]

Pliny *Epistles* 8.18 deals with the last will and testament of Domitius Tullus, a man split fifty-fifty between negative and positive exemplarity: in life he actively courted the attention of legacy-hunters, but at the last hurdle he made good by gifting everything to his adopted niece and grandchildren. For a while he looked like a willing victim of *captatio*, but managed to keep it in the family in the end. Towards the end of the letter, Pliny tests the lower limits of epistolary gentility by rendering a grim picture of Domitius on his nursing home deathbed, a man completely dependent and incapacitated:

> Quippe omnibus membris extortus et fractus, tantas opes solis oculis obibat, ac ne in lectulo quidem nisi ab aliis mouebatur; quin etiam (foedum miserandumque dictu) dentes lauandos fricandosque praebebat. Auditum frequenter ex ipso, cum quereretur de contumeliis debilitatis suae, digitos se seruorum suorum cotidie lingere. Viuebat tamen et uiuere uolebat, sustentante maxime uxore, quae culpam incohati matrimoni in gloriam perseuerantia uerterat. (*Ep.* 8.18.9–10)

> Crippled and deformed in every limb, he could only go over his vast wealth with his eyes, and could not even turn in bed except through outside help. He also had to have his teeth cleaned and brushed for him – a disgusting and pitiful detail – and when complaining about the humiliations of his deformity was often heard to say that every day he licked the fingers of his slaves. Yet he went on living, and kept his will to live, helped chiefly by his wife, whose devoted care turned the former criticism of her marriage into a lasting honour.

Domitius' slaves now perform his most basic bodily functions for him, including the embarrassing task of popping food into his mouth; the old man barely has enough life in him to joke that he was licking the fingers of

---

[41] Sherwin-White 1966: 38–9 estimates a 'book-date' for Book 8 of around AD 107–8, although *Ep.* 8.18 is elegantly stripped of temporal markers: 'There are no close indications of time' (p. 468).

[42] For other prosopographical connections and allusive overlap between Juvenal and Pliny, see Whitton 2013: 34–5. He scrapes together no antipathy from the allusions themselves (p. 35 n. 203), though this chapter begs to differ in the case of *Ep.* 8.18/*Sat.* 10; and we might ponder whether to do something similar with Juvenal's blow-out of a Plinian unequal dinner party (*Sat.* 5 and *Ep.* 2.6) – although the dating (did I mention that already?) gets complicated.

the hands that fed him. The Juvenalian response to this degraded geriatric was first noticed by Syme,[43] who pointed to the striking image of taking food from someone else's fingers – one vivid detail in *Sat.* 10's morbid catalogue of old-age horrors:

> Ille umero, hic lumbis, hic coxa debilis; ambos
> perdidit ille oculos et luscis inuidet; **huius**
> **pallida labra cibum accipiunt digitis alienis**,
> ipse ad conspectum cenae diducere rictum
> suetus hiat tantum ceu pullus hirundinis, ad quem
> ore uolat pleno mater ieiuna. Sed omni
> membrorum damno maior dementia, **quae nec**
> **nomina seruorum nec uoltum agnoscit amici**
> cum quo praeterita cenauit nocte, nec illos
> quos genuit, quos eduxit. Nam codice saeuo
> heredes uetat esse suos, bona tota feruntur
> ad Phialen; tantum artificis ualet halitus oris,
> quod steterat multis in carcere fornicis annis.
>
> (*Sat.* 10.227–39)

Old man A is crippled in his shoulder, B in the groin, C in the hip. The loss of both eyes makes this man jealous of one-eyed men. **That man takes food in his bloodless lips from someone else's fingers**. He used to split his jaws wide at the sight of dinner but now just gapes like a swallow's chick when his fasting mother flies to him with her mouth full. But worse than any physical decline is the dementia. **It doesn't remember the names of slaves or recognise the face of a friend** who dined with him the previous evening or the children he fathered and raised himself. You see, in a cruel will, he keeps his own children from becoming his heirs and leaves everything to Phiale. That's the power of the breath of her skilful mouth, which was for sale for many years in the brothel's den.

If we wanted to cast this as a troped, targeted and downright rubber-stamped allusion, we certainly could (and I shall): the very concept of 'taking food from someone else's fingers' hints at a process of incorporating outside material which, within satire's bodily systems and along its alimentary canals,[44] must already be suspicious. The context is also too similar to ignore. Two old men on their last legs, both harried by legacy-hunters; one resists the temptation and passes his wealth to his family as he should, the other melts in the prostitute's mouth and forgets his rightful biological heirs. What I am really driving at here, however, is the curious combination of taking a Plinian image, inverting his example, and topping it all with glazed non-recognition (*nec . . . agnoscit*). This is the dark

---

[43] Syme 1979: 253–5.
[44] Gowers 1993: 109–219 is always seminal on the metapoetics of food in satire.

side of allusion-as-recognition. Not the old woman at the end of Lucan 1 who recognises Pompey's trunk, and models the reader recognising Priam's trunk underneath,[45] but an old man who fails to recognise anything: literary past and literary future, the whole damn legacy. Crippled with dementia, he has to forget. Here the reader gets invited to obliterate the Plinian example, yield to the experienced mouth of the Juvenalian, and indulge in pure self-destructive pleasure; no last-ditch redemption at the end of days.

The paradox of course is that we need to recognise in order not to recognise, remember in order to forget.[46] To be sure, few readers today have the memory of a Syme to call on to realise that they should be forgetting something. But this section of Juvenal 10 has another precious moment of recall embedded within the frame of amnesia, a moment so easy to recognise that I wonder how far Juvenal is baiting the reader's 'memory', and satirising our own mental exercise of recollection-through-reading.[47] I might even say he is dramatising his own dementia alongside the reader's recall, forgetting himself even as we try to remember.

The breadcrumbs are first laid earlier in the long mini-treatise on old age which makes up a quarter of Satire 10. If we flashback to that forgotten recent past, we see that the old man is not only characterised by his inability to recognise, but to be recognised. We couldn't identify this old man even if we tried; we couldn't say if it was Domitius Tullus or not, for they all look the same to us:

> Deformem et taetrum ante omnia uultum
> dissimilemque sui, deformem pro cute pellem
> pendentisque genas et talis aspice rugas
> quales, umbriferos ubi pandit Thabraca saltus,
> in uetula scalpit iam mater simia bucca.
> Plurima sunt iuuenum discrimina, pulchrior ille
> hoc atque †ille† alio, multum hic robustior illo:
> una senum facies, cum uoce trementia membra
> et iam leue caput madidique infantia nasi;
> frangendus misero gingiua panis inermi.
> (*Sat.* 10.191–200)

Above all get a load of that face, ugly and hideous and unrecognisable, and the ugly hide where the skin should be, and the floppy jowls and such

---

[45] Lucan *BC* 1.686, Conte's flagship troping of allusion as recognition (see Hinds 1998: 8–10; cf. n. 20).

[46] Cf. Cowan 2013's version of this problem (pp. 129–30).

[47] Cf. Galen's invited reader, deftly moving their way around all sorts of cross-referencing and recollection (Johnson 2010: 83–4 – thanks to Alice König for the suggestion!). Cf. Rimell (this volume), p. 69 on the ring-compositional structures of *Agricola* and *Epigrams* 10, another way of thematising memory through reading. We might also bring in Quintilian 10.1.19–20, a passage hooking together reading, memory – and literature as food/reading as digestion.

wrinkles as the mother ape scratches on her cheek where Thabraca spreads its shady groves. Young men have a lot of differences between them: this one's more handsome than that one, and that one more handsome than another; this one is much more strapping than that one; but old men have one common face: their limbs tremble along with their voice, their head is now smooth, they're a kid with a runny nose; the poor sod's bread has to be chewed with unarmed gums.

The squint to individuate wrinkles the reader into the position of recogniser. Perhaps *una senum facies* already lays down the gauntlet: the topos of old age looks the same in every author, Pliny among them, and it will be difficult to spot the difference. Immediately after this, we have the first case of the old man's chronic forgetfulness:

> Nam coitus iam longa obliuio, uel si
> coneris, iacet exiguus cum ramice neruus
> et, quamuis tota palpetur nocte, iacebit.
> (*Sat.* 10.204–6)

Sex is now a long-forgotten memory, and if you were to try him, his little muscle just lies there with its blood vessel, and will continue just to lie there, even if you manipulate it the whole night.

Primed as we are with the themes of non-recognition and oblivion, I hope the next step in the working won't jar too much. For when Juvenal tries to capture the host of ailments circling round the old man a few lines later, the issues of recognition, memory, similarity and identity come through loud and clear at the level of poetic practice:

> Praeterea minimus gelido iam in corpore sanguis
> febre calet sola, circumsilit agmine facto
> morborum omne genus, quorum si nomina quaeras,
> promptius expediam quot amauerit Oppia moechos,
> quot Themison aegros autumno occiderit uno,
> quot Basilus socios, quot circumscripserit Hirrus
> pupillos, quot longa uiros exorbeat uno
> Maura die, quot discipulos inclinet Hamillus;
> percurram citius quot uillas possideat nunc
> quo tondente grauis iuueni mihi barba sonabat.
> (*Sat.* 10.217–26)

More to the point, the trickle of blood in his already frozen body warms up only with fever, and the whole bunch of dieases dances around him in formation. If you asked their names, I would sooner set out how many lovers Oppia has had, how many sick people Themison finished off in a single autumn, how many associates Basilus ripped off, how many wards Hirrus did the same to, how many men the lanky Maura sucks off in one day, how many students Hamillus lays; I would speed more rapidly through how many villas he possesses, the guy at whose bladework my heavy beard used to rasp as a young man.

Many have pegged this passage as a strange lapse into nostalgia. The OTT Juvenal of Satire 1 is back, and the intra-authorial intertextuality is marked beyond doubt by the perfect rehashing of a whole hexameter, the famous autobiographical mid-point in that asphyxiating twelve-verse sentence of Satire 1.19–30: *quo tondente grauis iuueni mihi barba sonabat* (1.25). Interestingly, this is a memory of a memory: a throwback to a time when Juvenal was already remembering the same beard rasping, the same barber shaving. Can we hear this line's repetition in a section that makes the old man deaf (209–16); or can we see it in a context making him blind (227)? Is this slip of repetition an intentional (uh-oh!) self-reference, or is it the work of an old satirist[48] who won't list the names of the diseases because he can't, just as the old man stricken with Alzheimer's can't remember the names of his slaves (234)? Juvenal perhaps plants this low-hanging fruit to get us in the mood for recollection, so that we remember to forget or forget to remember Pliny's Domitius a few lines later. Thus, in the same textual neighbourhood where Juvenal crosses out Pliny, he also appears to forget himself.

I have attempted to chalk up how two forms of intertextuality – inter and intra-authorial[49] – here work not on the expected plane of memory, but on that of wholesale memory loss. This is an acrimonious interaction indeed, and well worthy of a satirist: Juvenal takes an image from Pliny's fingers, then up-ends the protagonist's fate to avert Pliny's vapid happy ending. Whereas Pliny saves the elite Roman male from himself, preserves the backbone and hope of Rome for another generation, Juvenal sells the toothless old codger to the youngest and most accomplished sucker. Pliny resolves a crisis point into an affirmation and continuity of the status quo; Juvenal diverts the precious legacy away from the legitimate heirs and into the dead-end of Phiale the oral artisan's gob-pocket. The contrast in worldview could barely be starker. Throughout the episode, thematic seeding of oblivion, deafness, blindness, non-recognition, as well as a bold recycling of a memory of a memory, livens us up to the complex interaction. This Hadrianic satire urges us to forget that brief blooming of hope under Pliny's Trajan; remember that it's as bad as it's ever been, and of course probably worse (*quo tondente . . .* – still shaving after all these years); and forget about

---

[48] All that we know of Juvenal's body is that its beard was once maintained by a plucky barber; and that it is old and wrinkled (*Sat.* 11.203). Try picking that in a line-up.

[49] For more on intra-authorial intertextuality in Juvenal, see Gold 2012.

the future, for Rome is old, and the Greek prostitute is running off with the inheritance in her mouth.

Keeping to Himself

There is one more general point to be made on the Juvenal–Pliny interaction, and this time it is about the very idea of 'interaction' within the two authors. The English word smacks of the social, and translates dangerously naturally to literature: authors meet, greet, converse in person as in texts, and the interpersonal and intertextual worlds cross, collide, stand in and speak for each other. This is Pliny to a T. His letters are quasi-autobiographical pieces that, more often than not, *place* him in society. He names names; he talks to specific people; he works with A in the forum for or against B; he mourns the loss of X; he sees the famous Y speak in Rome; he gives a gift to town Z.[50] In short, Pliny is embedded in the Rome he writes. His letters are social documents working to create bonds, and the selves bound by those bonds. Just as letters – those targeted vessels of communication – are wont to do. They like to interact.

Juvenal is in the other corner, and a corner so dark we barely know where it is. His satires are defiantly anti-autobiographical. He refuses to name names.[51] His poems tend to take the form of tiring tirades at their most monologic; they give the finger to the Plinian ideals of polite aristocratic exchange and indulgent reciprocity. Satire 10 is a prime example: this solipsistic soliloquy addresses no one in particular. It is true that some of the satires (especially the later ones) talk to an addressee. But this addressee either disappears as soon as he is invoked (cf. Umbricius forgetting his audience of one in *Sat.* 3,[52] or Fuscinus fading immediately behind the clouds in 14);[53] or they are there only to become part of the skewering process (e.g. Persicus in 11).[54] Juvenalian satire obstinately opts out of any such thing as 'interaction'. The satirist tries his best not to be present in the poems he writes, let alone the society he writes about.[55]

---

[50] Whitton (this volume) plays on the geometry with his clever triangular beast (QPT). Studying such interactions perhaps inevitably takes us back to school mathematics, as we are ever looking to compass nicely bounded literary 'circles'.

[51] Cf. n. 9.

[52] *Sat.* 3.60; see Braund 1996's note ad loc., and her essay there on *Sat.* 3.

[53] Cf. Ferguson 1979 ad *Sat.* 14.1 (and note the metaphor!): 'the name appears only in the first line: the person addressed is as dark as his name, and Juvenal promptly forgets him for the general reader'.

[54] Cf. Geue 2017.

[55] For this phenomenon of the 'invisible' satirist, see Uden 2015, and again Geue 2017.

This is where Juvenal and Pliny really don't get on: the idea of an authorial self actively interacting with, even shaping, a functioning society; the idea of writing as an integral and integrating part of a social process rather than a voice booming in the wilderness.[56] But these vastly different approaches to the individual in society don't necessarily mean these authors have nothing to say to each other, even across the chasm. On the contrary: this is a true interaction, and an interaction so important because it gives us two roughly contemporary visions of what literary interaction might (not) be. For a fuller cross-section, we should audit the grumpy recluse as well as, alongside, the breezy socialite at whom he growls.

Forget It

This chapter has tried its darnedest to convince that intertextuality studies can sometimes afford to forget about verbal correspondence and targeted one-to-one relations.[57] The first example showed how useful it can be to play noncommittal on the old question of general/specific target. Even if we retreat from claiming a direct relationship to Tacitus, we can still project interesting interactive patterns at the level of generic turf wars. The second case was admittedly a more 'classical' author vs author contretemps. We saw how an (anti-)allusion can function to crowd out, discredit and erase another text; how the tropes of forgetting and non-recognition can paradoxically invoke an 'original' only to have it obliterated. In that case, our ideal reader had better sit up and take notice, lest she be the old sod caught out with chronic amnesia.

If intertextual readings can still help farm the pickings of our embarrassingly rich period, they need to accommodate better the various forms of interaction which float free of the prized verbal echo: silences, absences, erasures; woollier dynamics where the precise participants are unnamed, the precise relationships unspecified, the precise coordinates unverifiable. There is nothing better than a scrupulously vague satirist to get these nebulous conversations flowing – from which he will, of course, promptly slide away.

---

[56] For literary revision as a key motif and zone of social cohesion in Pliny, see Gurd 2012: 105–26.
[57] Though not (necessarily) that it *should*: Whitton (this volume) makes a good case for servicing the older intertextual 'nodes' still coming on strong in our period, especially those linking prose authors.

CHAPTER 17

Childhood Education and the Boundaries
of Interaction
[Plutarch], Quintilian, Juvenal

James Uden

In the sprawling empire of the second century, when Roman and Greek identities were increasingly subject to redefinition and challenge, the child became a symbol of imagined stability. The child of the French Revolution, according to one writer, was 'a blank slate on which the future could be inscribed', and the child of the Industrial Revolution was 'the playful master of a material world he turns into his toy' (Higgonet 2009: 90, 91). The virtuous Greek or Roman child of the second century, by contrast, embodied not the future but the past, symbolising a fantasy of continuity, not change. Many of the period's prominent authors were concerned with the transmission of traditional Greek and Roman ideas to the young. Plutarch devotes a great deal of time to demonstrating the importance of early childhood education in the *De audiendis poetis* and the *Parallel lives*, and presumably also in the now-lost *On the wet-nurse* (Lamprias catalogue, no. 114).[1] A civic interest in education is evident in the letter of Pliny on the endowment of a school (*Ep.* 4.13.3–10) and reflected in the quasi-paternal and pedagogical role he assumes throughout his letters.[2] If the *Achilleid* of Statius, written under Domitian, suggests that the irrepressible hero could not be turned from his violence by his education on Scyros, then the *Kingship orations* of Dio Chrysostom, written under Trajan, argue more positively for the importance of *paideia* in curbing native passions. Both Greek and Latin authors in the late first and early second century became intensely interested, at this most cosmopolitan period in the Empire's history, in the preservation of traditional values. It is the closeness of imperial interaction that forces authors to reflect upon the ways in

I would like to thank every member of the Literary Interactions project, and especially Alice König and Chris Whitton, for their advice, inspiration and encouragement. My thanks also to audiences at Union College, Universität Rostock, and Boston University, who offered comments on this chapter at various stages of development.
[1] Bradley 1999; Duff 2008; Xenophontos 2015.   [2] Bernstein 2008.

which individual and separate cultural traditions might be preserved. In these elite texts, education is presented less often as a practical training for the 'real world' of Empire than as a parochial sort of cultural defence mechanism. The educated child – vulnerable to influence, liable to be misled – is made to embody the precarious continuity of tradition itself.

To this period also belong three of the most extensive discussions of childhood education to survive between Plato and late antiquity: the anonymous treatise *De liberis educandis*, preserved with Plutarch's works; the first book of the *Institutio oratoria* by the teacher of rhetoric, Quintilian; and the fourteenth Satire of Juvenal, which begins with a long attack on the miseducation of Roman youth.[3] In this chapter, I argue that these texts are characterised by concerns about regulating Greco-Roman cultural interaction. While Quintilian advocates the Roman child's firm control over both Greek and Roman language and culture, both the Plutarchan author and Juvenal construct highly artificial and exaggeratedly insular visions of childhood education, which attempt to restrict the influence of 'foreign' culture on the worldview of the child. Moreover, all three texts expand in various ways on the agricultural imagery already present in the Greco-Roman pedagogical tradition, in order to present the child as a symbolic space which can be administered, cultivated, bounded and controlled. In this chapter I also use the relationship *between* these texts as a means of exploring the dynamics of literary interaction in the late first and early second century. Juvenal's fourteenth Satire, to an extent that has not previously been appreciated, has a close intertextual relationship with Quintilian's first book, enlarging upon a strand of satire already evident in the *Institutio oratoria*. The relationship between Satire 14 and the *De liberis educandis*, though, is better analysed as a case of literary 'interaction'. No clear verbal parallels appear – nor should we expect them to do so, given each text's ideological investment in projecting a sense of isolation from other cultural groups. Rather, both respond to cultural proximity in the second-century Empire in strikingly similar ways, using childhood education as a means to express an anxiously anachronistic vision of Greek or Roman identity. The politics of

---

[3] Quintilian's work was completed soon before his death in (perhaps) 96: Kaster 1995: 334. Juvenal's fifth book of *Satires* was published soon after 127: Courtney 1980: 2. The dating of the Plutarchan treatise is more speculative. Perceived failings in style and argument have led scholars since Muretus to deny its authenticity, but its many similarities with the genuine works suggest that it is closely related to their milieu, as either 'an unrevised work [of Plutarch] or an auditor's copy of his lecture or an enthusiast's composition in the mode of Plutarch' (Bloomer 2011: 220 n. 12). Swain 2013: 376–7 remarks that the author's comments on breastfeeding and pederasty 'situate him in the later first to early second century'. For the three works, I cite the texts of Babbitt 1927, Winterbottom 1970 and Clausen 1992.

textual interaction between the three treatises exemplifies their pedagogical principles.

As will be evident, then, this chapter aims to use some of the flexibility and breadth of interaction as a critical term. If intertextuality makes a web out of texts, joining them together at points of explicit lexical correspondence, then interaction can encompass texts that, for lack of such lexical correspondence, seem to fall through the strands. At the conferences from which this volume originates, interaction became a rubric that encompassed a wide variety of critical approaches (cultural memory, world literature, statistical approaches to literary analysis). Many of these approaches seek to move, in the phrasing of Rebecca Langlands, 'beyond intertextuality', at least in the form in which it has been typically conceived by Latin literary scholars.[4] They focus instead on how texts seem to act, how they mobilise similar tropes and ideas in response to shared cultural and political stimuli. Interaction on this model is a dynamic process, made possible by the exchange of ideas in recitations, by the oral culture of anecdotes and *exempla*, by the circulation of texts between literary centres and throughout the Empire, by the resources of a shared fund of 'classical' knowledge, and by translation and constant adaptation. Once texts are viewed against this wider field of literary activity, the silences between Latin and Greek works, and the commonalities they do not acknowledge, become a variety of interaction potentially as significant as explicit allusion.[5] Interaction therefore does not supplant intertextual analysis; rather, it presents textual correspondence as one aspect of a broader and largely extratextual exchange of images and ideas, and shows how direct verbal hits can elucidate meaningful misses. Pseudo-Plutarch and Juvenal seem unrelated. But they interact, not only because they demonstrate dependence upon a common tradition of pedagogical language and imagery, but because each constructs a parochial vision of a child's education in defensive awareness of the proximity of other cultural groups with competing histories and identities within the Empire.

This very insularity highlights another benefit of interaction as a critical rubric for our period. The sophisticated analyses of intertextuality that were developed in the 1990s but still largely set the agenda for Latin literary studies centred primarily upon the poetic culture of the late Republican and Augustan period, when authors were eager, at a crucial point in the development of Roman literary identity, to construct lines of filiation with Greek culture and with each other. Studies of Latin poetic intertextuality

---

[4] For the 'dynamics of "extratextuality"' among works of our period, see Langlands (this volume), p. 331.
[5] See Geue, Marchesi and Rimell in this volume.

drew an ever-tighter net around our already (by the standards of other disciplines) small corpus of Roman texts, focusing on a milieu in which the Roman writers themselves were very much oriented towards connectivity. But the much more diffuse and heterogeneous literary culture of the second century is different, and not merely because of the predominance of prose. An itinerant Greek sophist, a Christian apologist in Asia Minor and a Latin poet in Spain all may draw from a shared pool of language and ideas from previous Greek and Roman literature. Yet to measure the knowledge each group had of each other merely by seeking allusions between their texts would belie the fact that such groups frequently responded to their proximity by projecting a sense of isolation. (Hence, rather than asking whether imperial Greek authors read Latin literature, we should perhaps ask why they would admit having done so.) The three texts on childhood education by pseudo-Plutarch, Quintilian and Juvenal are an especially valuable guide to this complex literary world, since these authors are most explicit about the principles of exclusion – the fantasy of erecting cultural boundaries – that shape and regulate literary interaction under Nerva, Trajan and Hadrian. In their description of education as cultural curatorship, the boundaries of interaction are theorised and exemplified.

[Plutarch]

The *De liberis educandis* ('On raising children') begins with conception, gives advice on the care of the baby and selection of a wet-nurse, paedagogue and teachers, and examines various aspects of the child's moral and rhetorical training. It also belongs to a wider body of Greek and Latin texts in the imperial period that proclaim the importance of bold and unfettered speech, before curtailing their own speech or warning of its dangers. In the work's opening chapter, the author praises the virtue of 'free speech' (παρρησία, 1b), which the author says is a privilege of noble birth. Later, in Plutarchan mould, he praises those who combine philosophy and politics (8a). Yet despite warnings about parasites and flatterers and advice about modest and proper behaviour, we get no glimpse in the text of the child actually speaking to anyone outside the household or fulfilling any kind of social role. Instead, we hear more about the dangers of speech: the child should be kept away from 'encomiastic nonsense' (πανηγυρικῶν λήρων, 6a), and the author specifically cautions that children should not be encouraged to speak extemporaneously in front of crowds (6b–d, the particular skill of the sophists). At another point, the author says that readiness of speech should be used only in certain situations and with caution, as if it were a 'drug' (6e). Then he praises at remarkable length the virtues of silence; 'timely silence is wise and better than all speech', he concludes (10e). As Joy Connolly (2001: 355) observes in her reading of the work, such famous speakers as Socrates, Demosthenes and Pericles are all praised for moments when they chose not to say anything. The child of this treatise is urged to accept the importance and nobility of free public speech, but then safely insulated from any opportunity to undertake such speech himself.[6]

The text's cultural ideal, *paideia*, 'literary culture', has a timeless transcendence. It alone is said to be 'immortal and divine' (5e), and impregnable to outside forces like tyranny and war (5f–6a). But the corollary to that vision is that the education the treatise offers is deliberately distanced from the social and political world around it. A child's mind, it urges, should be a 'treasury of culture' (παιδείας . . . ταμιεῖον, 9e); the aim is not so much for the child to perform the precepts of the past, but to store and preserve them.[7] The author cites an eclectic array of philosophers in support of his ideas: Plato most often, but also Socrates, Crates, Diogenes, Bion, Pythagoras and Aristippus, with allusions to Aristotle and Xenophon as well. The pedagogical instructions are issued against a dense background of literary allusion.[8] The author subtly alludes to imperial recastings of Odysseus as philosopher when he compares students' sampling of the *enkuklios paideia* to 'sailing to visit many cities'; by contrast, to study philosophy, he says, is to 'live in the best city' (7d).[9] Many of the situations imagined by the text seem to reflect less the actual dynamics of any household in the second-century Empire, and more the world of New Comedy. The author warns that the badly educated son will keep company with parasites and waste his patrimony freeing courtesans (5b); he contrasts the harsh father with the lenient father (13e), in the manner of the *Adelphoe*; and he says that sons should learn proper behaviour by observing their fathers' lives as if looking in a mirror, a classic New Comic motif (14a).[10] Education is presented in deliberately timeless terms, as taking place within the world of Greek literature and history, rather than in the real political territory of the second-century Roman world.

---

[6] All three texts considered here focus specifically on the education of children who are socially elite and male.

[7] Cf. LSJ s.v. ταμιεῖον: the word acquires the broad sense of 'storeroom' in imperial Greek, but the classical meaning of 'treasury' persists, and it is used of the Roman *aerarium* by Polybius (3.26.1) and Plutarch (*Cat. min.* 16.2).

[8] On the mutual influence between literature and technical texts in antiquity – the distinction would have seemed far less clear to Roman audiences – see König in this volume. Berry 1958 and Bourke 2014 emphasise the eclecticism of the work's allusions to philosophers.

[9] On Odysseus as philosopher, see Montiglio 2011: 124–47.

[10] Fantham 1972: 68–9. On comic allusions in the *De liberis educandis*; see Bloomer 2011: 62.

Yet the treatise develops its own metaphorical notion of territory in its frequent association between education and the cultivation of land. The agricultural metaphor was already very common in ancient discussions of pedagogy. Werner Jaeger traced it back to the fifth-century sophists, and it is present in Cicero and Seneca, among other authors.[11] But nowhere in Greek or Roman literature is the metaphor more developed – and almost obsessively repeated – than it is here. The author formulates it early on: 'natural ability is like the soil, the teacher is the farmer, and the verbal instructions and teachings are like the seed' (2b). The child of promising talent who is not taught correctly is like a good piece of land that goes to waste (2e). Wise teaching is like the stake that farmers set beside young plants (4c). Books of philosophy are likened to farmer's tools (8b). Encouraging students is likened to watering plants (9b). The treatise as a whole, like so many works of imperial Greek literature, seems 'atopic' (to appropriate a term from John Moles' analysis of Dio Chrysostom), conspicuously lacking in references that ground it in a particular place and time, preferring instead to draw its themes and characters from the world of the past.[12] Yet at least at a figurative level, the insistence with which the author likens agriculture to education transforms the students into a kind of place. Cultivating these children ensures that one sort of Greek territory remains amid the ubiquity of Roman power, even if it is only the spiritual territory of tradition, of learning, of cultural sensibilities, planted and preserved in the minds of Greek children.

The insularity of the educational model offered in the *De liberis educandis* reflects the fact that, for the Greek child of the Roman Empire, opportunities for genuine political leadership of the Classical kind had been foreclosed.[13] But rather than describing these realities explicitly, the treatise constantly presents its own insularity in combative terms as a form of protection from pollution by non-Greeks. So, the author warns that the child's slaves should be Greek so that the child is not 'contaminated by foreigners' (4a), and warns that paedagogues should not be 'prisoners-of-war or foreigners' (4a). When it comes to the women who will breastfeed and nurse the baby, the author says that they 'should, first of all, be Greek women in respect to their characters' (πρῶτον μὲν τοῖς ἤθεσιν Ἑλληνίδας, 3e). The non-elite women who were employed in Roman and Greek

---

[11] Jaeger 1939: 312–13; Morgan 1998: 256–60, citing Cic. *Leg.* 1.46 and Sen. *Ep.* 34.1.

[12] Moles 2005: 126. Cf. Uden 2015: 51–85 on a comparable placelessness in Juvenal.

[13] See Plut. *Praec. ger. reip.* 813c–f, with Swain 1996: 165–9. At 814a of that treatise, Plutarch compares the dissident magistrates of Greek cities under Roman rule to naughty children; their cultural adulthood is replaced by an enforced infancy.

households to breastfeed assume a surprisingly prominent role in Latin and Greek literary culture of the second century, as symbols, within a cosmopolitan empire, of the earliest points of transmission of cultural influence.[14] The Greek physician of the Hadrianic period, Soranus, also advises in his gynecological treatise that the wet-nurse should be Greek, so that 'the baby nursed by her will become accustomed to the best language' (διαλέκτῳ, 2.19.15). From the Roman perspective, the character of Vipstanus Messalla in Tacitus' *Dialogus* complains that 'nowadays, once the baby is born, he is entrusted to some little Greek slave', and her idle speech corrupts the child's mind, so susceptible is the child to first impressions (29). Favorinus, in a Hadrianic-era speech (Gell. 12.1.5–23), rails at length against the unnatural way that strangers wean our noble children, since the milk of foreign women (*barbarae nationis*) corrupts the nobility of the child's mind – yet just who is 'foreign' here is hard to tell, since the speech was given in Greek but preserved in Latin, and perhaps, slyly, the capacity of the speech to appeal to the prejudices of both cultures at once is precisely the point. In the case of pseudo-Plutarch, the formulation 'Greek in respect of character' suggests that ethnicity is less important to the *De liberis educandis* than the transmission of Greek cultural values.[15] The learned Hellene within the Roman Empire must remain, in short, a 'treasury of culture', a storehouse of transcendent *paideia* amid the earthly treasuries of the Roman state. The child is projected as the object and symbol of this ideal.

Quintilian

The ideological orientation of the first book of Quintilian's *Institutio oratoria* is in many ways the precise opposite of the *De liberis educandis*. Here, in contrast to the insularity of the Greek work, Quintilian describes the training of the Roman child in terms of worldly control and administration, and advocates mastery over both Greek and Latin. The teacher's own rhetorical performance in the *Institutio oratoria* travels consistently along both tracks, offering Latin and Greek terminology in tandem, drawing many of his ideas from Greek authors and appealing explicitly to the Greek ideal of the *enkuklios paideia* (1.10.1).[16] Earlier Roman notions

---

[14] See Bradley 1991: 13–36 on the lives of nurses in Rome, and Holford-Strevens 2003: 114 n. 80 on the array of texts on nursing in the first and second centuries.

[15] For Hellenism as a cultural rather than an ethnic designation in this period, see Whitmarsh 2001: 116–29.

[16] Cousin 1936. Eshleman 2012: 186 remarks on the uniqueness of Quintilian's bicultural history of rhetorical theory. On the importance of Greek *paideia* in Quintilian, see also Jones 2015, who argues convincingly for commonalities between Roman and Greek educational ideals in the period.

of the 'poverty of the Latin language' (Lucretius) or of a Rome captivated by Greek captives (Horace) are in Quintilian recast in more reciprocal terms of cultural exchange. 'We use obviously Greek words when we have none of our own,' he says, 'just as they sometimes borrow words from us' (1.5.58). Discussing his preference for the Greek term *rhetorike* over the Latin *oratoria*, he says that Latin words do not always express fully the sense of Greek concepts, just as Greek words often fail to express the full meaning of Roman concepts (2.14.1). 'When we study Latin literature (*litterae*),' he asks, 'should we not look back to Greek literature?' (1.12.6). Significantly, this mastery over two languages is conceived in the spatial terms of agriculture. To study only one language, Quintilian says, would be like asking a farmer not to cultivate fields and vines and olives and fruit trees at the same time (1.12.7; cf. 2.19.2). The Roman is encouraged to think expansively; he should cultivate more than one crop.

Quintilian puts particular emphasis on the need for bilingual childhood education.[17] He too deals with the selection of the baby's nurse, and says, first of all, that she should speak correctly (1.1.4), without specifying (as Soranus did) which language she should speak. But later he says that the Roman child should begin with Greek. 'I prefer that the boy begin with speaking Greek,' he says, 'since, whether we like it or not, he will drink in Latin, which is in use by a majority [of those around him]' (1.1.13). In other words, Greek and Latin should be taught at the same time, with the teachers' focus on Greek, and Latin absorbed through the child's broader environment. Nonetheless, Greek should not be pursued to excess, or 'obsessively' (*superstitiose*, 1.1.13), such that the boy only ends up speaking Greek. This, he remarks, 'is the way of many', but it leads to certain cognitive difficulties: the child's mouth will not be trained to pronounce the Latin words correctly, Greek idioms will stick in his mind, and he will speak Greek as a matter of habit. Latin-language learning, Quintilian says, 'ought to follow soon after Greek, then quickly proceed at equal pace' (1.1.14). The distinction Quintilian draws here, between what is now known as 'simultaneous' and 'sequential' second-language acquisition, is still debated by educational psychologists, with modern studies tending towards the developmental advantages of simultaneous second-language acquisition in early infancy.[18]

Quintilian's focus on education being undertaken in and for the public sphere is nowhere more evident than in his lengthy critique of the

---

[17] See Adams 2003: 9–14 on texts describing this elite, voluntary bilingualism among Romans. As he cautions, though, prescriptive texts such as that of Quintilian can give us no 'real idea of the proportion of educated Romans who were fluent Greek speakers' (at p. 13).

[18] Tabors 1997.

contemporary fashion for home schooling, an explicit rejection of an insular model of education. 'Let the future orator,' he says, 'who must live in the throng of the crowd and the glare of the state, become accustomed already from his youth not to shirk at other people, nor to grow pale in a life of solitariness and, as it were, of shadows' (1.2.18). Instead, Quintilian says that the child should be sent to the 'crowd of the schools' (*frequentiae scholarum*), and in order to stress the importance of socialisation at these schools, he describes them as miniature versions of adult Roman society.[19] They are places where lasting *amicitiae* are forged (1.2.20), where the child will be praised and castigated (1.2.21), and where he will develop ambition, 'frequently a cause of virtues' (*frequenter ... causa uirtutum*, 1.2.22). Quintilian relates how, in his own school, the teacher would rank the boys on speaking ability every month and publicise the rankings, so that students were motivated by the honour of being at the top of the ladder. This inner *ambitio* to be celebrated by one's peers, he says, provided more motivation than teachers, paedagogues or parents ever could. This competition, too, is expressed in agricultural terms. In the *De liberis educandis*, the teacher establishing sound principles for his students is likened to the farmer setting a stake beside a growing plant (4c). The students' training is measured against something artificial, immutable, fixed – an unchanging and timeless standard drawn from the cultural repository of the Greek past. In Quintilian, in his jostling schools of ambitious children aspiring to a world of Roman power, students progress by ambitiously competing against one another, 'just,' he says, 'as vines progress to the top of a tree by first taking hold of lower branches' (1.2.26). The lived reality of Roman relationships is embedded within Quintilian's school, which is already a location for social climbing.

Quintilian must also refute the concerns of contemporary parents that schools breed bad morals. He responds by arguing that it is we parents who corrupt our children, not anyone at school. With a sense of immediacy and invective flair, he exclaims: 'If only we ourselves did not ruin our children's morals! We at once soften them as infants with luxuries' (*Vtinam liberorum nostrorum mores non ipsi perderemus! Infantiam statim deliciis soluimus*, 1.2.6). Quintilian's authorial voice suddenly has all the outrage and hyperbole of Roman satire.[20] He describes children of wealthy houses

---

[19] The point is well made by Bloomer 2011: 94.
[20] On invective in Quintilian, see Dozier 2015: 345–6, who cites as other examples *Inst.* 1.10.31, 8.*pr.*25–6, 8.3.6–11, 12.1.6 and 12.10.73–6. For connections with Roman satire, see Seel 1977: 113–33 on Quintilian and Persius, and Dozier 2014: 75–6, who advocates a mode of reading the *Institutio oratoria* indebted to scholarly accounts of the persona in Roman verse satire.

crawling around on purple, trained to distinguish crimson (**co**ccum) from vermilion (**con**chylium), even before they are able to pronounce these phonetically and semantically similar words (1.2.6). The home is the real moral danger zone. 'We train their palate,' he says in a pithy *sententia*, 'before we train their speech' (*ante palatum eorum quam os instituimus*, 1.2.7). Although in his first chapter he described parents teaching their children the rudiments of education, the same domestic space is now viewed through the lens of satire. Children at home 'see our mistresses, our male slave lovers (*concubinos*);[21] every dinner party is raucous with obscene songs; they witness things it is shameful to say' (1.2.8). Habit becomes 'nature' (*natura*, 1.2.8), one of the key words of the treatise. Excluding perhaps the emphasis on the first-person plural (it is 'we' who do wrong), Quintilian here seems to have struck upon Juvenal's trademark tone before Juvenal ever published a line. Some thirty years later, when the satirist himself wrote Satire 14 on the same theme, he did not miss the cue.

Juvenal

'The greatest reverence is owed to the child' (*maxima debetur puero reuer-entia*, 14.47), proclaims the speaker of the fourteenth Satire, a surprisingly positive maxim for a poet who typically speaks in negatives. It caught the eye of Highet, for whom it represented evidence of Juvenal's love of children, an affection so 'genuine that it forces its way into his poetry against his will'.[22] But rather than seeing the line as an irruption of per-sonal feeling, Mayor had already recognised in it a parallel to Quintilian.[23] In *Institutio oratoria* 11.1.60–8 Quintilian describes the tact and delicacy required of the orator when pleading suits initiated by sons against their parents, or parents against their children. The deference shown to different family members will be 'more or less,' he says, 'according to the reverence owed to each person' (*magis autem aut minus ut cuique personae **debetur reuerentia***, 11.1.66). Yet, as Mayor does not note, the maxim also evokes the *Institutio oratoria* in a far broader sense, recalling the innovative focus in the first book on the child as the subject of training and on children's sus-ceptibility to early moral corruption. Juvenal expands on satirical elements already present in Quintilian's work.[24] The rhetor's outburst of invective

---

[21] Williams 2010: 32.
[22] Highet 1954: 145; similarly on the apparent affection for children in the *Satires*, Highet 1949: 255; Wiesen 1963: 469; Colton 1979; Jenkyns 1982: 195–7.
[23] Mayor 1881: 296, also citing Plato *Leg.* 729b–c.
[24] Colson 1924: 25 recognised a 'general resemblance' between *Inst.* 1.2.6–8 and *Sat.* 14.1–83, but the suggestion has not been pursued; Anderson 1961 does not consider *Sat.* 14. Evidence of close reading

against home schooling is grossly enlarged in the fourteenth Satire, which, in its unequal sections of parents' corrupting influence (1–106) and the evils of greed (107–331), traces a familiar link between childhood education and the moral outlook of the adult Roman citizen. The poem's correspondences to Quintilianic language and ideas, though, are put to emphatically un-Quintilianic purpose. Juvenal garishly paints Roman domestic life as a seedbed of vice, while at the same time imagining the father as the only effective teacher, and restricting instruction to the home. The paradoxical fourteenth Satire thus creates a pedagogical dead-end: the student can only truly be taught in the very place he is most likely to be led astray.[25] These very contradictions reflect a far broader imperial anxiety. How can pure and traditional Roman (or Greek) ideals be transmitted to the young, if education involves becoming part of a world that is inextricably Greco-Roman? Like the author of the *De liberis educandis*, Juvenal responds by creating an insular and xenophobic vision of teaching; and the tension between an idealised, bounded vision of cultural education and the reality of a heterogeneous, cosmopolitan world is on especially clear display.

Satire 14 begins with a sentence that recalls Quintilian's complaint that parents transmit vice to their children. The satiric voice tells Fuscinus that many sordid practices will 'cling' (*haesuram*) to a man's reputation, practices that are 'shown and handed to children by their . . . parents!' (*quae monstrant ipsi pueris traduntque parentes*, 3). The postponement of the word *parentes* to the final position of this opening sentence is obviously aimed to shock. But for readers of Quintilian it must have been a shock of recognition as much as disapproval, since he too had warned in the opening of his work of the tenaciousness of a child's earliest influences, which 'cling' to the child (*haerent*, 1.1.5), especially if they are bad. As the poem continues, Satire 14 expands upon Quintilian's earlier emphasis on imitation, nature and the susceptibility of the young to corruption by their environment. Quintilian argued against the pedagogical advice of contemporaries and forebears by advocating that education should begin before the age of seven (1.1.15–9, and see Laes 2011: 96 on the age of seven in the ancient world as a common 'boundary between early and late childhood'); the speaker of Satire 14 echoes Quintilian's warning and says that influences received

---

of the *Institutio oratoria* by Juvenal has recently been stressed by Gellérfi 2013a, 2013b, though in general scholars have been reluctant to imagine it as an object of allusion (see Whitton in this volume). Keane 2007: 36 notes the similarities between the fourteenth Satire and the *De liberis educandis*.

[25] Geue 2012: 162–74 is excellent on the satirist's paradoxical emphasis in this poem on the impossibility of satiric teaching.

before the age of seven will be determinative of the child's personality (10–14). Domestic *exempla*, both texts agree, have particular force on the young. 'Such is nature's law: more swiftly do familial examples of vice corrupt us', the satirist writes; so we must take care that 'our children do not follow our bad behaviour'.[26] Just as Quintilian affirms the teachability of all children, remarking that the genuinely 'unable to be taught' (*indociles*, 1.1.2) are as rare as prodigies, the speaker of Satire 14 says emphatically that 'we all are able to be taught (*dociles*) to imitate' – in an enjambed satiric twist – 'depraved and crooked practices' (40–1).[27] He declares that the house of a father should be kept clear of 'what it is foul to say and to see', of prostitutes and the songs of parasites (44–6; cf. Quintilian's mistresses, dinner parties and *pudenda dictu* at 1.2.8). This new emphasis on the paramount importance of childhood education is pointedly dissonant with prior points in Juvenal's poems. So, in a passage of Satire 7, the satirist had attributed adult success not to education, but to astrology: 'what makes the difference is the star-sign that greets you, as you begin to utter your first wails'.[28] Satire 14 delivers the opposite message. 'It will make an enormous difference which skills and ethics you institute in your children' (*Plurimum enim intererit quibus artibus et quibus hunc tu | moribus instituas*, 73–4), the speaker says, alluding to the mission of Quintilian's work, and perhaps also, in the verb (*instituas*), to its title.[29]

Juvenal of course expands on vice in a way quite alien to Quintilian. His children, who are polluted by gambling, adultery and even murder, belong to a far grimmer textual world. Yet if Quintilian's text pervasively described pedagogical flaws in moral terms, Juvenal's Quintilianic Satire insistently describes moral flaws as perverted pedagogy. One boy has 'learned' (*didicit*, 9) to gourmandise, with his wastrel father 'demonstrating' (*monstrante*, 10) how to do it. Rutilus, who takes sadistic pleasure in whipping slaves, does not 'give instruction' in gentleness of spirit (*praecipit*, 16), but rather 'teaches' cruelty (*docet*, 18). For Larga's daughter, naming her mother's

---

[26] *Sat.* 14.31–2, 39–40. On the imagery of *natura* in *Sat.* 14, see Corn 1992. The satirist's use of the self-incriminating first-person plural in these passages – far from his typical mode – reflects Quintilian's usage in his own satiric broadsides against parental influence ('*we* have taught them; it is from *us* they hear such things', 1.2.7).

[27] Only here does Juvenal use *docilis* in its core, pedagogical sense; it appears elsewhere only in the Oxford fragment, in its rarer, poetic sense of 'expert' (O26).

[28] *Sat.* 7.194–6 *Distat enim quae | sidera te excipient modo primos incipientem | edere uagitus.* These lines occur in a passage describing Quintilian himself (7.186–214), and may well allude to him too: *ita futurus eloquentissimus edidit aliquando uagitum et loqui primum incerta uoce temptauit* (*Inst.* 1.1.21).

[29] The title appears to be given as *De institutione oratoria* in the prefatory letter to Trypho (Kennedy 1969: 31, 143). Juvenal's heavily elided line 73 is itself enormous and barely contained by its metre – because it recalls a prose treatise?

many lovers offers training not only in adultery but in counting: 'she was never able to name them so quickly, or list them off at such a pace, that she didn't need to draw breath thirteen times' (26–8). Now, while her mother dictates to her, she fills up her tiny wax tablets with letters to her own lover (29–30). As the poem zeroes in on *auaritia* as its cardinal fault, the emphasis is again on teaching:

> Et pater ergo animi felices credit auaros
> qui miratur opes, qui nulla exempla beati
> pauperis esse putat; iuuenes hortatur ut illa
> ire uia pergant et eidem incumbere sectae.
> Sunt quaedam uitiorum elementa, his protinus illos
> imbuit et cogit minimas ediscere sordes;
> mox acquirendi docet insatiabile uotum.
>
> (*Sat.* 14.119–25)

And so the father who marvels at wealth, who thinks that there are no *exempla* of a happy poor man, believes that the greedy are happy in spirit. He encourages the young to continue down his path, and to devote themselves to the same way of life. Vices have certain basic elements. He impresses these upon them from the beginning, and forces them to learn by heart the basest trivialities. Before long, he teaches them an insatiable will for gain.

The cluster of pedagogical vocabulary (*exempla ... elementa ... imbuit ... ediscere ... docet*) underlines the intellectual poverty of the lesson. In the *Institutio oratoria*, the teacher begins with the most basic rudiments (*elementa*), and then the student memorises (*ediscere*) edifying portions of text.[30] As the child learns, the teacher gives encouragement, 'imbuing' students with his own values.[31] Eventually the student's own ethical sense develops as a mirror of his teacher. In Juvenal, the young, initially unwilling (*inuiti*, 108), develop their own will (*uotum*, 125) for vice through the bad example and sinister encouragement of their parents. One father forces his son to memorise a crassly mercantile, limply prosaic *sententia*, apparently of his own devising: *unde habeas quaerit nemo, sed oportet habere* ('no one cares where it came from, but have it you ought').[32] 'You're teaching (*doces*, 237) them to rob and swindle and gain wealth by all crooked means', the satirist accuses. Another father has 'taught' (*praecepit*, 227) his child the love

---

[30] Cf. *Inst.* 1.1.35–6 on the young child memorising edifying *sententiae*, and 2.7.2–4 on the value for more advanced students of committing to memory texts from orators and historians. Quintilian particularly criticises the practice 'which fathers especially demand' (*quod quidem maxime patres exigunt*) of forcing sons to memorise and declaim their own compositions (2.7.1).

[31] Cf. *Inst.* 1.1.20: the child should be 'questioned and praised, and should also take joy sometimes in his achievement'. The teacher 'imbues': 1.1.5 (*imbuas*), 1.1.9 (*imbuit*).

[32] *Sat.* 14.207. For *oportet* as prosaic, see Axelson 1945: 13–14.

of money, but his progeny will turn against him: the 'disciple lion will roar loudly and do away with its trembling trainer [or 'teacher', *magistrum*] in its cage' (246–7). The nightmarish descriptions of vice deliberately invert scenes and ideas from Quintilian's *Institutio oratoria*, while at the same time fulfilling the satiric potential of that earlier text's warnings of the dangers of miseducation.

Juvenal also expands upon the agricultural imagery integral to the ancient discourse of pedagogy, though his satiric focus, predictably, is on the mismanagement and destruction of land rather than its healthful cultivation. There is an agricultural allusion at line 215, when the satirist says that 'we must be sparing with children' (*parcendum est teneris*), a phrase long recognised as an allusion to a passage in the *Georgics* in which Virgil is advising restraint in the pruning of tender young plants (2.362–70; cf. *parcendum teneris*, 363).[33] More broadly, though, Satire 14 is replete with images of Romans immorally and irresponsibly cultivating land, and although these passages primarily indict his contemporaries for *auaritia*, it is not surprising, in light of the metaphors of ancient pedagogical discourse, that the poem's bad educators are also its bad cultivators. One figure compulsively buys up his neighbours' cornfields, vineyards and olive plantations, and if a neighbour refuses to sell, he destroys his crops at night out of spite (141–60). It is hard, the satirist says, to express 'how much land goes on sale because of damage' (151). To these amoral landowners the satirist contrasts a figure from Italy's idealised rustic past, who tells his children that luxurious purple clothing tempts people to vice and crime (187–8). Consistent with the pervasive metaphor, this idealised old father and teacher is also a good cultivator, and the other half of his lesson concerns the divine injunction for responsible care of the land (179–84). There is perhaps a subtle and incriminating logic to the poem's union of the Quintilianic theme of childhood education with that of greed, given Quintilian's own reputation for amassing wealth.[34] In Juvenal's seventh Satire, this wealth is represented, too, in terms of land ownership (188–9): 'how, then, does Quintilian own so much grazing land?' The origin of that wealth in teaching suggests a wicked satiric turn on the pedagogical metaphor of agriculture. The successful teacher can amass land instead of merely cultivating it.

---

[33] Quintilian (2.4.11) alludes to the same passage in the *Georgics* when he warns teachers not to be overly harsh in criticising students in their care.

[34] It may be overstated to call Quintilian's wealth a 'commonplace' (Anderson 1961: 10), but he certainly enjoyed unusual success. He is said by Jerome to have held the annual salary of 100,000 sesterces established by Vespasian: Kaster 1995: 335. Mart. *Epig.* 2.90, addressed to Quintilian, contrasts the simple life with that of the man of wealth and ambition – not Quintilian explicitly, though it is hard to ignore the hint.

The emphases in Juvenal's fourteenth Satire reflect a deep intertextual engagement with Quintilian's treatise on oratory, but the ideological orientation of Juvenal's poem is sharply opposed to that work's bicultural focus and its emphasis on Roman children's mastery of both Latin and Greek. When Quintilian inveighs against the corruption of children by their parents, and attacks the perverted education in luxury they receive in the home, he does so specifically to advocate that children ought therefore to be educated *outside* the home, in schools. Juvenal omits this vital conclusion to Quintilian's argument. There is no mention of classes or schools in Satire 14. This is a significant contrast to a section in an earlier poem of Juvenal, which is, precisely, a lengthy description of students in a class (7.150–77).[35] Instead, the satirist deprecates the ability of anyone except parents – particularly, the father – to influence the morals of their children. Father and son play the roles that should, according to Quintilian, be played by professional teachers, and they are described as *magister* and *discipulus* (212–3) and *magister* and *alumnus* (246–7). Juvenal offers just as airtight and cloistered a vision of the educative process as the *De liberis educandis*, though here the parochialism is Roman, not Greek. Indeed, there is a specific rejection of Greek philosophy in the poem. The satiric voice says that the moral instruction of 'a thousand bearded teachers' (12) – that is, philosophers – will be useless once a child has been raised in a corrupting environment. He cites Diogenes (308–14), Epicurus (319) and Socrates (320), dismissively concluding that 'Nature and philosophy always say the same thing' (*numquam aliud Natura, aliud sapientia dicit*, 321). Another section of the poem attacks a Jewish father, whose impropriety lies only in his perceived threat to the sanctity of Roman tradition: he teaches his children, in the satirist's anxious hyperbole, to 'despise the laws of Rome and learn by heart Jewish law' (100–1). Arthur Walzer argues that Quintilian aimed in the *Institutio oratoria* to fold moral philosophy into his programme of rhetorical education, thereby limiting the cultural authority of philosophers and other intellectuals in Domitianic Rome, and creating a programme of ethical and rhetorical training that was deliberately self-contained.[36] Juvenal's Hadrianic satire goes further and restricts the influence of *anyone* on the young, except for the very people whose moral corruption the poem decries: their parents.

---

[35] As Colson 1924: 30 notes, Juvenal (at *Sat.* 7.151) and Quintilian are the only two extant authors to use *classis* in this sense of 'class' (*TLL* s.v. *classis* III.B.1).

[36] Walzer 2006. Note especially the remarkable passage at *Inst.* 1.pr.14–15, attacking the prominence of (presumably Greek) philosophers in Rome, and suggesting that the true 'lovers of wisdom' in the Empire are Roman administrators.

This claustrophobic, circular poem offers no explicit educational programme. Rather, it offers a monstrous satiric expansion of anxieties about education in the period, directing its hostility in particular towards non-Romans. As a result, Roman tradition itself emerges from the satire as itself something embattled, precarious, mired in the past. The satirist dutifully trots out the old characters, the old ideals: the Catonian image of father as teacher (189), the citizen 'useful to his fatherland' in peace and war (71–2), the rustic hardihood of early Rome (161–5). One son is urged to 'raze Moorish hovels and Brigantine forts', asserting the ideals of Roman imperialism (196–7). 'You could see a Catiline in any people,' the satirist assures us, but 'you won't see a Brutus or a Cato anywhere else' (41–3). Even the citations of Quintilian and the revival of his Latin voice can be seen as attempts to buttress the Romanness of the satirist's self-presentation. The *rhetor* becomes not only a source but an icon, a symbol for Roman culture and rhetoric blown up to well over life-size. The poem is remarkable also for its repetitions of the satirist's *own* voice, in a curious attempt at self-authorisation.[37] When the satirist asks at the end of the poem whether he has 'filled the lap' of the greedy man with his escalating amounts of expected wealth (327), he echoes the question he had asked in the very first of the *Satires* nearly thirty years earlier (1.87–8): 'when did the lap of *auaritia* ever stretch wider?'[38] An entire line at the conclusion of Satire 10 is repeated verbatim at the end of Satire 14 (10.365 = 14.315).[39] For Stein 1970: 36, the invective on greed in Satire 14 aims to 'unify' and 'vitalise' the 'commonplace topics of satire' into one 'complete and coherent statement'. It is more that, once Juvenal has fashioned a pedagogical dystopia in which genuine moral instruction is impossible, the needle gets stuck in the groove. The circularity of the satire and its insular self-repetitions reflect the solipsistic attempt to produce virtuous Romans while shielding them from the actual, multicultural world of Rome. The author of the *De liberis educandis* urges that children should preserve the *paideia* of the past and hides the contemporary political world from view. Juvenal's poem is equally parochial, its vision of education equally timeless. In the paradoxical desire to live the past in the present, Quintilianic pedagogy becomes its own impossible ideal.

---

[37] Corn 1992: 311, 319–21; Geue 2012: 171–2. On the poem's repetitiveness, cf. Keane 2015: 184: the satirist is 'straddling the line between a valued elder and an insufferable drone'.

[38] On the date of Juvenal's first book, see Uden 2015: 219–26 and Kelly in this volume.

[39] Other repetitions: the satirist's promise (14.256–64) that real life will prove more entertaining than any theatrical entertainment recalls Democritus at the Circus in *Sat.* 10.36–50; the description of merchants' sea-voyages (14.275–83) rehearses the same event from *Sat.* 12.17–82.

Boundaries

We make a community out of writers as soon as we have read them. It seems natural, then, to project that shared experience back onto the writers themselves, and some chronological coincidences readily give rise to intense, imagined scenes of interaction. We might think of Shakespeare and Cervantes for example,[40] or Goethe and Byron, or Dickens and Dostoevsky. In the next and final chapter of this book, Roy Gibson discusses just such a pairing – Plutarch and Pliny – as an examination of this readerly urge to see authors interact. Yet the texts in this chapter demonstrate that literary figures of the early second century had their own heightened awareness of cultural proximity to one another. These authors were peculiarly self-conscious about the boundaries of interaction, which they imagined in fully spatial terms. The child of their texts is represented as a delimited territory of cultural influence. Whatever the exact chronological relationship between the *De liberis educandis* and Juvenal's fourteenth Satire, it is clear from the pedagogical politics of both works that we should not seek direct allusion between Latin and Greek; each is invested in an artificially isolated vision of Greek or Roman culture. Equally, Juvenal's intertextual expansion of his Latin predecessor Quintilian reflects the poem's emphasis on Roman education, even to the point of perverting the rhetor's vision by restricting teaching to the Roman home. The relationship between these texts involves a complex negotiation between allusion and silence, conducted against the interactivity of Empire itself. What can a child do in a world of such immensity, heterogeneity and change? Look back.

---

[40] Their meeting is the subject of Anthony Burgess' short story, 'A Meeting in Valladolid': Burgess 1989: 3–21.

CHAPTER 18

Pliny and Plutarch's Practical Ethics
A Newly Rediscovered Dialogue

Roy Gibson

A Newly Rediscovered 'Dialogue'

As has been widely publicised elsewhere, a fragment of the opening chapters of a Latin text unknown to modernity has recently been rediscovered in the monasteries of San Millán de la Cogolla in northern Spain, where it lay undetected amidst excerpts from the *Natural history* of the Elder Pliny in a manuscript itself previously recorded as lost. The text purports to record a dialogue which took place in Rome during the reign of Domitian involving three persons all certainly dead by the early 120s, namely Plutarch, Pliny the Younger and Plutarch's main Roman patron, Sosius Senecio.[1] A first English translation with commentary is offered below.

The text is attributed to Minicius Fundanus, consul of 107 and proconsul of Asia *c.* 122–3;[2] but it cannot be authenticated with complete certainty, since both lexical choice and various mannerisms of style are compatible with the prose style of a later era. It is possible that the dialogue is at root a work of plausible but ultimately imaginative fiction, in the mould of, for example, the *Dialogus de oratoribus* of Tacitus.[3] Both the 'author' and the rediscovered work's main characters were emerging figures on the stage of Domitianic Rome, and would go on to have distinguished political or literary careers under Nerva and Trajan. But we have no independent evidence that they all four were personally acquainted, much less that three of them engaged in an extended dialogue which a fourth recorded for posterity many years later. Indeed, the echoing silence that Pliny and Plutarch maintain about one another in their extant

Warm thanks for help and advice are offered to Alice König and Chris Whitton, also to John Henderson, Lieve Van Hoof and audiences in St Andrews and Manchester. All dates are AD.
[1] On Senecio, see below and n. 32.   [2] On Fundanus, see below and n. 28.
[3] For an instance of direct allusion to the Tacitean work, see n. 31; for the absence of Tacitus himself from the work, see n. 35.

works is a void that the rediscovered dialogue was perhaps invented to fill.[4]

It is true that Plutarch's circle of Roman senatorial friends is dominated by northern Italians and *noui homines* (like Pliny himself), and that the works of the pair reveal up to seven shared friends and acquaintances.[5] It is clear, in particular, that both Plutarch and Pliny were personal friends of Fundanus and Senecio.[6] But, unless we insist that those who could have known one another *must* have been acquainted, these shared friendships may still have left Pliny and Plutarch unfamiliar with one another.[7] We *can* bring the pair tantalisingly close together on the basis of Pliny's assertion that, during the reign of Domitian, he appeared in court 'on behalf of Arrionilla, the wife of Timon, at the request of Arulenus Rusticus'.[8] Plutarch himself had a brother called Timon, and knew, or at least had met, Arulenus Rusticus.[9] It may well be that Plutarch's relatives were involved in legal action at Rome during his own probable visit there in Domitian's reign *c.* 92, and that Pliny acted in their defence.[10] The connection could be drawn tighter, in fact, if the otherwise unattested name Arrionilla were to be replaced by Aristylla – who is mentioned as the addressee of a series of letters written by Plutarch's own wife, Timoxena,

---

[4] Plutarch's silence about Pliny, at least in the surviving works, must be viewed in the context of the former's silence even about such distinguished Greek contemporaries as Dio of Prusa and Epictetus (Jones 1971: 34–6; cf. nn. 25, 70 below). For the silence, in turn, of all contemporary Roman authors about Plutarch (including Suetonius and Tacitus alongside Pliny), see Jones 1971: 61–2. It has sometimes been conjectured that in his lives of Galba and Otho, Plutarch drew on the histories of the Elder Pliny; but the issue has never been definitively settled (Syme 1958: 674–6; Damon 2003: 22–30). For other silences, exclusions and interactions between broadly contemporary texts, see Geue, Rimell and Uden in this volume; for neglected intertextuality, see Whitton in this volume.

[5] See Jones 1971: 48–64, noting Julius Secundus (himself a character in the *Dialogus* of Tacitus), Arulenus Rusticus (who is mentioned in the newly rediscovered text), the Avidii Nigrini elder and younger, Avidius Quietus, and the already mentioned Sosius Senecio and Minicius Fundanus; cf. Stadter 2015: 8–9 and 21–44 on Plutarch's Roman friends more generally. On Secundus, Rusticus, Quietus and the Nigrini, see further nn. 28, 34, 64.

[6] See nn. 28, 32.

[7] Cf. Swain 2000b: 41, 'One of the demerits of prosopography is the pressure to put individuals in productive relationships.'

[8] *Ep.* 1.5.5 *Aderam Arrionillae Timonis uxori, rogatu Aruleni Rustici; Regulus contra. Nitebamur nos in parte causae sententia Metti Modesti optimi uiri: is tunc in exsilio erat, a Domitiano relegatus.*

[9] On this meeting, which is referred to in the rediscovered dialogue, see immediately below, and n. 35.

[10] The suggestion was first made in 1869 by R. Volkmann, but soon struck from the record by Wilamowitz-Moellendorff 1889 (and subsequently ignored by Sherwin-White in his standard commentary on Pliny). It is tentatively revived by Jones 1971: 24–5. On the date of Plutarch's visit to Rome, see n. 18.

in the course of the *Marriage precepts*.[11] But ultimately the evidence here amounts to conjecture built upon speculation.

At any rate, the rediscovered dialogue no doubt owes its preservation amongst excerpts from the *Natural history* in part to the 'coalescence' of the two Plinii that was increasingly commonplace in later antiquity and the Middle Ages;[12] perhaps in part also to the name Minicius Fundanus. As governor of Asia in the 120s, Fundanus received a rescript from Hadrian affirming that Christians should only be put on trial for specified charges of criminal activity: a probable restatement of the position found in the rescript received by Pliny from Trajan on the same matter at *Epistles* 10.97. Transmitted by both Justin Martyr and Eusebius,[13] the rescript may have served to raise the name Minicius Fundanus to sufficient notoriety for a Christian copyist to think it worth transmitting at least an excerpt.

Historical Context for the 'Dialogue'

The work is entitled *C. Minici Fundani Dialogus de Graecorum et Romanorum moribus*, which, to judge from the surviving contents, must signify 'Dialogue on the ethical habits of the Greeks and Romans'.[14] It is addressed to none other than Suetonius Tranquillus, who, like the historical Minicius Fundanus, also outlived Plutarch, Senecio and Pliny – albeit only to be exiled from the imperial court *c.* 122. In essence the dialogue, after some customary preliminaries, allows discussion of the relative merits of upper-class Greek and Roman modes of life, with a strongly ethical colouring. Suetonius, of course, is a suitable addressee. Protégé of Pliny,[15] possibly inspired by Plutarch's *Lives* to write his own imperial biographies,[16] and the author of works on both Greek and Roman games and on *Rome and its customs and manners*,[17] the bilingual Suetonius would be bound to take an interest in Fundanus' work.

The historical context for the dialogue is a significant moment in the 90s. As the rediscovered work appears to confirm, Plutarch was in Rome

---

[11] *Mor.* 145a. Arionilla has been connected with Arria, the wife of Thrasea Paetus, although that would require the spelling Arrianilla; see Syme 1968b: 146 (= *RP* II 712), also Sherwin-White 1966: 97. The conjecture of Aristylla for Arionilla was first made by Volkmann (previous note).

[12] Stout 1955; cf. Cameron 2016.

[13] Justin *Apol.* 1.68; Euseb. *Hist. Eccl.* 4.9.1–3; Syme 1991b: 617–18; Minni 2007.

[14] Cf. the description of the *Nicomachean ethics* at Cic. *Fin.* 5.12 *Aristotelem et eius filium Nicomachum, cuius accurate scripti de moribus libri . . .* ('Aristotle and his son Nicomachus, whose carefully written books *de moribus . . .*').

[15] See n. 30.   [16] Jones 1971: 62.   [17] Wallace-Hadrill 1983: 43–9.

in the period 92–3, when he was in his middle to late forties. There he attracted the Stoic senator Arulenus Rusticus as a member of the audience for one of his lectures, during Rusticus' own consulship in the last months of 92.[18] Within a year or so of his consulship, Rusticus was executed in an unexpected Domitianic purge of the 'Stoic opposition' that also swallowed up the senators Herennius Senecio and Helvidius the Younger and saw the exile of numerous others.[19] In the wake of the executions and expulsions of these persons, who often claimed adherence to philosophical ideals, Domitian appears to have expelled philosophers first from Rome and then later from Italy – as if to underline the pernicious influence of Greek philosophy. Plutarch, who knew the exiled Junius Mauricus (brother of Arulenus Rusticus) well enough to mention him favourably in a work perhaps published before 93, could have been under pressure to leave Rome during these events.[20]

The *Dialogus de moribus* takes place during Rusticus' consulship. Throughout the trials and expulsions which followed in the next two years, Plutarch could count on the protection of his young 'patron' Q. Sosius Senecio, who was perhaps of praetorian rank around this time and in some favour with Domitian.[21] Senecio appears as Plutarch's host and interlocutor in the rediscovered work, but Plutarch's main interlocutor here is Senecio's coeval, the Younger Pliny. The latter was tribune in either 91 or 92, and at the time of dialogue either had already been designated praetor for 93, or would soon be so designated for service in 94.[22] The purported recorder of the dialogue, Minicius Fundanus, shared with Pliny a Transpadane origin, and would attain the praetorship perhaps half a decade after the date of the dialogue. Fundanus was a few years younger than his countryman, and perhaps two decades junior to Plutarch. Syme hailed him as 'the most distinctive character in the whole [of Pliny's]

---

[18] The date of the visit had been conjectured by Jones 1971: 22–3, 51 (on the basis of Plut. *Mor.* 522d–e and 632a and epigraphical evidence): it is doubted by some (e.g. Russell 2001a: 7) and accepted by others (e.g. Stadter 2015: 37–8, who dates a meal with Senecio in Rome to this period).

[19] For a clear narrative of events, see Carlon 2009: 27–34; for connections between members of the 'Stoic opposition', see Syme 1991b: 568–87; and for the Helvidii elder and younger, see Birley 2000a: 61, also n. 34 below. The dating of the Domitianic treason trials and expulsions, and Pliny's career in relation to them, have been newly re-evaluated by Whitton 2015a: I follow his evaluations here and in what follows.

[20] Jones 1971: 24–5; cf. Plut. *Galba* 8.8 for the favourable reference to Junius Mauricus. See also Jones 1971: 36–8 on the involvement of Philostratus' Apollonius of Tyana in these events (another contemporary figure unmentioned by Plutarch).

[21] Jones 1970: 102 and 1971: 25. On Senecio as dedicatee of Plutarchan works, and his later career as twice consul under Trajan, see n. 32.

[22] See Whitton 2015a for an authoritative survey of the tangled evidence for Pliny's career before his consulship of 100. Praetors were designated a year in advance of their service; see n. 46.

correspondence, not excepting Cornelius Tacitus',[23] largely on some details supplied by Pliny and the characterisation which emerges from Plutarch's ethical works. In *On the control of anger* he is made to give an account of how he was cured from a tendency towards anger, while at the opening of *On tranquillity* he is pictured writing a characteristically peremptory letter to a mutual friend (*Mor.* 464e). But any such tendencies are suppressed in the rediscovered work, where Fundanus is apparently quite as self-effacing as is Tacitus in the *Dialogus de oratoribus*.

As for the characterisation of others, Pliny appears in the dialogue much as he appears in his own *Epistles* – somewhat conventional and rather serious, but ready to talk candidly about himself and his personal affairs, albeit in a way that is not lacking in self-satisfaction. As for Plutarch, *his* character appears closer to that reflected in Plutarchan epistolary treatises, where moralising pronouncements are standard, than in the dialogues, where technical discussion seasoned by the moralising aside is the preferred mode.[24] It should not surprise us that Plutarch, although a foreigner and outsider, is willing to criticise a young star of senate and courtroom such as Pliny on his home ground. An anecdote told in the treatise *On brotherly love* suggests that he did not fear to speak forthrightly to members of the Roman elite.[25] Plutarch also appears somewhat long-winded – perhaps an accurate reflection of someone who wrote so much and all but confessed his own loquacity in an essay *On talkativeness*.[26]

The Text

Fundanus writes, of course, in Latin; but he omits to tell us whether the 'original' conversation took place in Greek or in Latin. Presumably, any actual dialogue of this type involving Plutarch and his circle in Rome would have been conducted in Greek, since Plutarch himself tells us that

---

[23] Syme 1991b: 619. On Fundanus' origins and career, see n. 28.

[24] On Plutarchan self-effacement in (e.g.) the *Table talk*, where the author is at pains to emphasise that he is a partaking in a communal endeavour, see König 2011; cf. J. König 2007 on the character of the *Sympotic questions*.

[25] At *Mor.* 479e a self-styled philosopher who refused to treat his brother with familial consideration finds himself on the receiving end of some frank criticism more familiar from the school of Epicurus. For frankness of speech in Plutarch's ethical treatises, see van Meirvenne 2002. However, such liberality of address is hardly to be compared to the dressing-down that their contemporary Epictetus gives to a well-connected Roman at *Disc.* 2.14. For important differences between Epictetus' radical criticisms of society's 'normal' values and Plutarch's tendency to accept the ambitions and social values of his readers (but desire to give them a philosophical inflection), see Van Hoof 2010, esp. pp. 20–1, 28–9, 55–6, 94–5, 167, also Bowie 2002: 47–50.

[26] *Mor.* 511d, with Van Hoof 2010: 173–4.

he had little time to practise his Latin during his travels to Rome and Italy – although he is surely exaggerating when he states that his mastery of the language belongs to a later phase of life.[27] The translation of the text which I offer here is deliberately literal, and makes no attempt to smooth out the rather formal nature of the original.

C. MINICI FVNDANI[28]
DIALOGVS DE GRAECORVM ET ROMANORVM MORIBVS[29]

1.1 You have often asked me, Tranquillus Suetonius,[30] about Greek customs and habits, and how these compare with Roman customs and habits. I would scarcely dare to reply to your query and take up such a weighty investigation – running the risk that we think ill of our own practices or those of the Greeks – if I had to offer my own opinion rather than that of eloquent and learned men, whom I heard treating this very question some years ago.[31] **1.2** So, what is needed is not talent but rather my memory and powers of recall. I must now repeat, with the same divisions and arguments – keeping to the course of the discussion – those eloquent reflections which I heard, powerfully expressed, from men of great eminence, each of whom advanced different but plausible arguments, thereby displaying the idiosyncrasies of his individual talent and character.

2 Our friend Sosius Senecio[32] was acting as host to Plutarch, who had come to Rome at the invitation of that highly distinguished man to offer lectures

---

[27] Plut. *Demosth.* 2.2. For Plutarch's knowledge of Latin, see Jones 1971: 76–7, 81–7; Van Hoof 2010: 91 nn. 33–4; Stadter 2015: 130–48; J. König forthcoming, with further references.

[28] **C. MINICI FVNDANI**: perhaps from Ticinum in the Transpadana, Fundanus would become praetor *c.* 97 under Nerva and consul under Trajan in 107 (prior to holding the highly prestigious proconsulship mentioned earlier). He is the main speaker in Plutarch's *On the control of anger* and is mentioned at the start of *On tranquillity* (*Mor.* 464e–f: Jones 1966: 61–3); see above for his characterisation there. Fundanus is also mentioned or addressed in five letters of Pliny (1.9, 4.15, 5.16, 6.6 and 7.12). Letter 6.6 requests Fundanus' support for a young candidate, Julius Naso, whose father Julius Secundus (see n. 5 above) may also have been known to Plutarch (*Otho* 9.3); cf. Jones 1971: 22, 50, also 1968: 283–7. On Fundanus, see further Jones 1971: 57–8; Syme 1991b: 603–19; Bodel 1995.

[29] **MORIBVS**: for the title, see Cic. *Fin.* 5.12 (quoted above).

[30] **Tranquille Suetoni**: Pliny sustains a relationship of personal and literary patronage with Suetonius throughout his letters; see *Ep.* 1.18, 1.24, 3.8, 5.10, 9.34, 10.94–5. On Suetonius and his relationship with Pliny, see further Syme 1981; Wallace-Hadrill 1983: 4–5, 26–38, 162–71; Hoffer 1999: 211–25; Henderson 2002: 24–6; Méthy 2009; Lefèvre 2009: 160–8; Gibson 2014. For Suetonius' interest in Greek and Roman customs and his possible literary relationship with Plutarch, see above. For the affectation of reversing *nomen* and *cognomen*, see Mayer 2001: 88 on Tac. *Dial.* 1.1 *Iuste Fabi*.

[31] **Frequenter ex me requiris . . . audiui**: cf. Tac. *Dial.* 1.1–2 *Saepe ex me requiris . . . audiui*. The closeness of much of 1.1–3.1 to the opening chapters of the *Dialogus* of Tacitus is remarkable. On the shared conventions of the two prefaces, see Janson 1964: 60–4; van den Berg 2014: 17–25, 63–5.

[32] **Sosius Senecio**: Senecio's *patria* has long been disputed, although Jones 1971: 103 argues vigorously for an eastern origin. Plutarch may have met Senecio in Achaea during the latter's quaestorship in the mid to late 80s, and makes him dedicatee not only of the *Parellel lives*, but also of *Table talk*

and give advice to their friends.[33] It was the day after Plutarch had delivered a public lecture, during which Arulenus Rusticus,[34] who was consul
at that time, had received a personal message from Caesar, who was then
on campaign. Since the message was delivered in person by a soldier, and
the audience had fallen silent, Plutarch paused that Rusticus might read
the letter. But that outstanding man refused and would not break the seal
until Plutarch had finished his lecture and the audience had dispersed. On
account of this incident everyone admired the dignity of Rusticus, but some
warned him not to provoke Caesar further.[35]

3.1 Senecio, recognising my desire to renew friendship[36] with Plutarch, had
invited me to converse with them in his house. As it chanced, on that same
day, he received a visit from Plinius Secundus. Of all three men I was a

and *On progress in virtue*. Senecio likely played a key role in the adoption of Trajan by Nerva (Eck
2002a: 220–1) and was twice *consul ordinarius* under Trajan (99, 107), serving with distinction in
both of that emperor's Dacian campaigns. He receives two letters from Pliny (*Ep.* 1.13, 4.4) – who
is acquainted both with Senecio's father-in-law, Julius Frontinus (*Ep.* 4.8.3, 5.1.5, 9.19), and with his
son-in-law, Pompeius Falco (*Ep.* 1.23, 4.27, 7.22, 9.15). On Senecio, see further Jones 1970: 100–4
and 1971: 54–7, Birley 2000a: 90 s.v., Stadter 2015: 36–40.

[33] **amicis**: for the probable purposes of Plutarch's visits to Rome (including those of ambassador), see
Jones 1971: 20–1, 63. Making visits to Rome to offer advice to friends coheres with the purpose of
Plutarch's late ethical works, which are designed 'not to communicate the eternal truths of philosophy to mankind, but to offer help to a particular group of human beings who find themselves in
a specific social and historical situation' (Van Hoof 2010: 25–6); cf. Van Hoof 2014 for a succinct
overview of Plutarch's 'practical ethics'.

[34] **Arulenus Rusticus**: the career of the Stoic senator Junius Arulenus Rusticus had been long retarded
(he had been praetor as long ago as 69), perhaps because of his association with Thrasea Paetus. The latter was a 'Stoic' critic of the regime executed by Nero in 66, whom Rusticus had
tried to aid as tribune in that year and whose biography Rusticus would write (Tac. *Agr.* 2.1).
In this biography Rusticus appears also to have praised Helvidius Priscus the Elder (Suet. *Dom.*
10.3) – a son-in-law of Paetus – who had been executed by Vespasian *c.* 74 for persistent abuse
and lack of respect (Suet. *Vesp.* 15). That Domitian was willing to countenance – and Rusticus willing to accept – a consulship in 92 might seem to indicate a willingness on both sides
to move forward. But for his death in the next year or so in Domitian's 'purge', see above on
'Historical context for the dialogue'. Pliny makes a fuss of his connections with Rusticus and his
brother, Junius Mauricus, throughout his correspondence: *Ep.* 1.5, 1.14, 2.18, 3.11.3, 4.22.3ff., 5.1.8,
6.14.

[35] **. . . lacesseret**: an anecdote previously known only from Plutarch's *On meddlesomeness* (*Mor.* 522d–
e), although Plutarch omits the detail about Rusticus' consulship and the warning not to provoke
Caesar. (For the rarity of such contemporary illustrations in Plutarch's ethical works, see Van Hoof
2010: 192–3.) Domitian himself was absent from Rome between May and December 92, on campaign against the Sarmatae and Suebi. Also absent from the city (and the dialogue) is Cornelius
Tacitus, then abroad on a lengthy posting, perhaps a legionary command (Tac. *Agr.* 45.5; Birley
2000b: 234–5; Woodman 2014: 6).

[36] **amicitiam**: Plutarch appears to have visited Rome a couple of times prior to 92 (Jones 1971: 21–
2): it was here rather than in Greece that Fundanus must have met him (Syme 1991b: 618–19).
Inscriptional evidence may indicate that Senecio's house was on the Caelian (Jones 1970: 101); Pliny's
house was on the nearby Esquiline (*Ep.* 3.21.5).

keen listener and I had often conversed separately with each on literary matters and on the best way for a man to order his own affairs. When Pliny entered the chamber of Senecio[37] (for in those days it was not deemed wise to discourse more openly), he found us there engaged in conversation with Plutarch about the conduct of Rusticus on the previous day. Plutarch gave it as his opinion that when a messenger arrived from somewhere or other, we ought not to rush up or even rise to our feet. And if a friend says, 'I have something new to tell you', it would be better for us to reply, 'I should prefer that you had something useful or profitable.'[38] **3.2** After listening for some time to our dialogue about the necessity of welcoming the profitable rather than the new, Pliny interjected. 'So far as literary activities are concerned,' he declared, 'it befits us to offer a welcome to the new, since, unlike others, I do not disparage the intellects of our own time, nor do I believe that nature, as if wearied and exhausted, no longer produces anything worthy of admiration.'[39] Plutarch answered that he took little interest in the new *rhetores*, and that so long as he had Homer, Hesiod and Euripides, there seemed no reason to give attention to such living men as Capito of Pergamum or Antiphon of Athens; rather, it became a man to devote himself to study of philosophy, and to the teachings of Plato above all.[40] In reply, Pliny

---

[37] **cubiculum Senecionis**: whereas Cicero's dialogues are often set out of doors in country estates (Mayer 2001: 91), this conversation evidently takes place in Rome and in a part of the house considered private; cf. the similar setting of the *Dialogus* of Tacitus in the *cubiculum Materni*, on the day after the latter has potentially offered offence to the imperial house (Tac. *Dial.* 3.1). For the *cubiculum* as a place 'for conducting serious (often confidential) business and for learned discussion and display among close associates', see van den Berg 2014: 20 n. 8.

[38] **... utile uel salutare**: cf. Plut. *Mor.* 522d: Rusticus is praised straight afterwards for his exemplarity in avoiding this sort of 'meddlesomeness' or 'curiosity' (the subject of Plutarch's own essay).

[39] **... nihil iam laudabile parere**: cf. Plin. *Ep.* 6.21.1 (with Gibson forthcoming ad loc.), where Pliny himself is making an empathetic allusion to Aper's defence of literary modernity at Tac. *Dial.* 15.1 and 22.1 in defiance of the authorial literary pessimism expressed at *Dial.* 1.1. For all his rather old-fashioned ethics (see below), Pliny is a decided literary modernist and gives sustained publicity in his letters to the productions of his contemporaries (unlike Cicero, who in his correspondence largely dwells on the great literature of the past); cf. e.g. *Ep.* 1.3, 1.13, 1.16, 2.10, 3.15, 3.21, 4.3, 4.18, 4.20, 4.27, 5.10, 5.15, 5.17, 6.15 etc.; Gibson 2014: 211–15.

[40] **... praeceptis Platonis**: on Plutarch and middle Platonism, see Dillon 2014. In his surviving work, Plutarch shows remarkably little interest in epideictic rhetoric, despite its place at the centre of the contemporary Greek cultural revival, as witnessed in the career of his contemporary Dio of Prusa, and later at Rome in Pliny's Syrian friend Isaeus (*Ep* 2.3 with Whitton 2013: 89–102); cf. Schmitz 2014 on Plutarch's relative detachment from the beginnings of the 'Second Sophistic'. Likewise, little attention is given to contemporary poetry, including the attested tragedian (Antiphon) and epic and lyric poet (Capito) mentioned here; instead, Plutarch focuses on (Platonic) philosophy. For a survey of Plutarch's attitudes, see Bowie 2002, 2014; also Van Hoof 2010: 21–2; J. König forthcoming. Even in his essay *How to study poetry*, where Plutarch sets out for the young a programme of classical poetry, '[he] is, essentially, spelling out the first, pre-philosophical, stage of Platonic education' (Zadorojnyi 2002: 303). Presumably Plutarch will have taken little interest in the quite different educational work of Quintilian (where the aim is to produce *oratores*), or even in Tacitus' *Dialogus de oratoribus*.

maintained the superiority of the traditional ways of our ancestors,[41] who had little need of philosophers.[42]

4.1 Senecio at this point intervened and called a halt to our enquiries. He requested that, since we had two such distinguished advocates for the ancestral customs and practices of Greeks and Romans, we hear them debate the merits of the manner in which both peoples conducted themselves in public and ordered their personal affairs. Pliny replied that he had had little leisure either to reflect more fully on the matter or to treat the subject now as it deserved, encumbered as he was with many duties. 'But surely,'[43] said Plutarch, 'men talk either for their own sake, or because they need something, or to benefit their hearers, or because they seek to ingratiate themselves with each other by seasoning with the salt of conversation the pastime or business in which they happen to be engaged. Perhaps it is the case that our conversation now might benefit either you or perhaps our audience, above all our mutual friend Fundanus.' 'No doubt you are correct,' answered Pliny. **4.2** 'So then, Secundus,'[44] said Plutarch, 'is it not incumbent upon you to help your friends and to look to your domestic affairs? Certainly, it becomes a man to maintain his patrimony and to offer help to those in need of aid.' To this Pliny rejoined, 'Fresh duties are continually superimposed on my longstanding ones before the earlier ones are discharged. With all these chains and fetters a great column of activities extends further every day.[45]

---

[41] **...maiorum**: there is a trace here of traditional Roman hostility to Hellenic *mores*. This is evidently not an attitude shared by Senecio or Fundanus: they are openly associated with Plutarch in his published works. But, in the *Epistles*, Pliny's broader attitudes to contemporary Hellenes are complex and resist easy summary. There is an evident continuing affection for the friends of high birth and culture acquired while on service in Syria as a young military tribune (see n. 42). Yet among the hundred or so correspondents to receive letters from Pliny, only two can be identified as certainly from the eastern Mediterranean: Catilius Severus (1.22, 3.13, 9.22) from the Roman colony of Apamea in Bithynia and Cornutus Tertullus (7.21, 7.31) from Perge in Pamphylia (*contra* Syme 1985a: 355 (= *RP* v 473) on the complete omission of eastern senators as correspondents). The activities of Greeks against their governors in Rome's courts are treated by Pliny (*Ep.* 4.9, 5.20, 6.5, 6.13, 6.31), while the inhabitants of Pontus–Bithynia are stripped by Pliny as their governor of distinguishing Hellenic features (Woolf 2006). Yet Pliny displays none of the outright hostility of the Elder Pliny, whose attitudes particularly to Greek doctors are notorious (*NH* 24.4–6, 26.11, 29.13–28); cf. Nutton 1986 and more generally Beagon 2005: 50–1; Doody 2011: 124–6.

[42] **philosophis**: Pliny later presents himself as willing to take the advice of a perhaps more socially distinguished philosopher, namely the well-connected Syrian Euphrates, at *Ep.* 1.10.9–10, where the latter puts forward the view (reassuring to a Roman) that the just conduct of public and legal affairs is 'in fact the most noble part of philosophy' (*esse hanc philosophiae et quidem pulcherrimam partem*). For the greater social prestige of Syria, as opposed to the backwaters of old Greece, see Jones 1971: 46, 61; for Pliny's extensive connections with Syria, where he had undertaken a military tribunate *c.* 82 (and met another philosopher alongside Euphrates: the similarly well-connected Artemidorus of 3.11), see Birley 2000a: 7 (= Birley 2016: 57–8). The Elder Pliny's attitudes to philosophy are more thoroughly ambivalent; see Griffin 2007.

[43] **At uero . . .** : cf. Plut. *On talkativeness* 514e–f.

[44] **Secunde**: Plutarch adheres to the practice, observable in Pliny's letters, that the latter was referred to as 'Plinius', but addressed directly as 'Secunde'; see Birley 2000a: 23–4, 79.

[45] **... maius in dies occupationum agmen extenditur**: cf. Plin. *Ep.* 2.8.3.

For I am greatly tried by my official tasks,[46] and at the beck and call of my friends.[47] Occasionally I study[48] – to be able to do which, not occasionally, but exclusively and uninterruptedly, would be, I dare not say a more proper, but certainly a happier thing.[49] Furthermore, the farms inherited from my mother are treating me badly, although they delight me as coming from my mother.[50] Their produce has been swept off by the hail,[51] while in those properties inherited from my uncle there is the pressing necessity of letting the farms, a very disagreeable one, so rare is it to find suitable tenants.'[52]

5.1 'It seems to me,' said Plutarch, 'that the man who declared that "he who would be tranquil in his mind must not engage in many affairs, either private or public" makes our tranquillity very expensive if it is bought at the price of inactivity. In idleness, softness and the betrayal of friends, family and country there is assuredly no relief for the soul from disturbances and distress.[53] Yet there are indeed some pursuits which cannot by their very nature exist together, but rather are by nature opposed to one another. Training in rhetoric and applying oneself to studying, for example, require a quiet life and leisure, while political powers and friendships with kings cannot succeed without hard work and the full occupation of one's time.[54]

---

[46] **. . . distringor officio**: cf. Plin. *Ep.* 1.10.9, 7.15.1. It was not known whether Pliny was tribune of the plebs in 91 or the following year (Whitton 2015a); but this statement suggests a date of 92 – confirmed later at 8.1 (see n. 71). If Pliny was praetor in 94 (rather than 93), then his campaign for that post would perhaps also be taking place at this time in late 92, and would not come to an end till early January 93 (according to the timetable for elections constructed by Talbert 1984: 204–7) – unless Pliny was going forward as *candidatus Caesaris*, and thus effectively assured of election (Sherwin-White 1966: 157).

[47] **. . . amicis deseruio**: cf. Plin. *Ep.* 7.15.1. Since Pliny insists that he gave up his role as an advocate in his year as tribune (*Ep.* 1.23), the reference here may be to the kinds of mundane elite business of which he complains to Fundanus in *Ep.* 1.9, i.e. weddings, betrothals, investitures and witnessing of wills, not to mention the duty of reading the literary efforts of friends or attending their readings (e.g. 1.13 (to Senecio), 3.15). The following year (93) would bring two significant cases for Pliny: the prosecution of Baebius Massa (*Ep.* 7.33), which would presage the purge of Rusticus and associates, and perhaps the defence (at Rusticus' request) of the wife of Plutarch's brother (see nn. 8 11).

[48] **Studeo interdum**: cf. Plin. *Ep.* 7.15.1. The major outputs of both Pliny (*Epistles, Panegyricus*, assorted verse) and Plutarch belong to the period after the assassination of Domitian; see Jones 1966 for Plutarch. Nevertheless, the first letter proper of Pliny's collection closes with the assertion that 'several reasons prompt my need to publish, above all the fact that the works which I have already issued are said to be in men's hands' (*Ep.* 1.2.6 *edendum autem ex pluribus causis, maxime quod libelli quos emisimus dicuntur in manibus esse*). No doubt Pliny had already published some of his forensic oratory.

[49] **. . . non audeo dicere rectius, certe beatius erat**: cf. Plin. *Ep.* 7.15.1.

[50] **. . . me praedia materna parum commode tractant, delectant tamen ut materna**: cf. Plin. *Ep.* 2.15.2, where the reference is evidently to estates held in the vicinity of Pliny's hometown of Comum. The property inherited from the Elder Pliny (mentioned later) includes the 'Tuscan' estates (see Gibson and Morello 2012: 200–33 on Pliny's estates).

[51] **. . . grandine excussi**: cf. Plin. *Ep.* 4.6.1.

[52] **. . . adeo rarum est inuenire idoneos conductores**: cf. Plin. *Ep.* 7.30.3.

[53] **. . . motibus atque perturbationibus**: cf. Plut. *Mor.* 465c.

[54] **. . . sine labore et molestia**: cf. Plut. *Mor.* 472b.

Accordingly, if you have failed in canvass for an office,[55] you will be able to live in the country and look after your own affairs. Or if you have been repulsed in wooing the friendship of some great man, your life will be free from danger and trouble.'[56] **5.2** 'Our laws,' replied Pliny, 'allow leisure to the elderly, but demand that we devote our early and middle life to our country. This tranquillity of mind you recommend belongs rather to that part of life we may properly call our own, after we have devoted ourselves to the service of the state.'[57] 'So then,' said Plutarch, 'are we not to manage our impulses, as sailors do their sails, to correspond to our capacity? Is not self-love to blame, which makes men insatiably desirous of engaging in everything and eager to be first and victorious in everything?'[58]

6.1 'Opinions differ,' replied Pliny, 'but my idea of the truly happy man is of one who enjoys the anticipation of a good and lasting reputation. Were my own eyes not fixed on the reward of immortality, I could be happy in an easy life of complete retirement; for everyone, I think, must choose between two considerations: that fame is immortal or man is mortal. The former will lead him to a life of toil and effort, the latter will teach him to relax quietly and not wear out his short existence with vain endeavours.'[59] **6.2** 'In any case,' continued Pliny, 'it is not self-love, but a proper desire for renown which incites men to contend and exert themselves,[60] both in the holding of

---

[55] **... honores**: cf. Plut. *Mor.* 467d. If, as suggested earlier in n. 47, Pliny was campaigning for the post of praetor at this time, then Plutarch appears to be implying (rather sharply) that failure in this suit will be a solution to Pliny's problems and complaints: he can now at least return to managing his estates properly or apply himself to study more effectively. More broadly, Plutarch is clearly creating a contrast between the spread of activities of which Pliny complains, and his own advice that we must focus on those activities which naturally complement one another. Did Fundanus and Senecio take Plutarch's advice *en route* to their consulships, or did they too suffer from the over-extension (apparently) evident in Pliny's *Epistles*?

[56] **... sine metu, sine periculo**: cf. Plut. *Mor.* 467d.

[57] **... nos ipsi rei publicae satis fecimus**: cf. Plin. *Ep.* 4.23.3–4. Nevertheless, Pliny hails his own villas as oases of temporary tranquillity for himself; cf. esp. *Ep.* 1.9 (to Fundanus), 2.17.20–4, 5.6.45–6, 9.36, also 6.14.

[58] **... et omnes superare**: cf. Plut. *Mor.* 471d. Underlying the exchange here is a growing divergence between the viewpoints of a 'provincial' philosopher and a metropolitan orator whose aim is to emulate Cicero's success in high office, literature and law courts. This difference is crystallised in the contrast between Pliny's *Panegyricus* (where he speaks as consul directly to Trajan, with the desire of influencing his behaviour) and Plutarch's *Parallel lives*, which offer a strongly ethical focus on 'the lives of men long dead, none of whom had lived under the Empire' (Stadter 2002: 229).

[59] **... nec breuem uitam caducis laboribus fatigare**: cf. Plin. *Ep.* 9.3.1–2. Pliny insists on a polarity between a life of complete exertion vs uninterrupted *otium* (one implicitly refused at Plut. *Mor.* 785e–f), whereas Plutarch had advised rather that one concentrate on pursuits which productively cohere with one another.

[60] **... contendere eniti**: a position developed further later. It is clear from the *Epistles* that, for Pliny, correctness of thought and behaviour is largely determined by the collective opinion of his society: the individual has value only when subject to the scrutiny and approval of the community (Riggsby 1998: 77–83; cf. Whitton and Gibson 2016: 33–5). In this regard Pliny may have appeared a little old-fashioned even in his own day, since it had apparently become fashionable amongst sections of the elite for individuals – inspired by Stoic or Epicurean philosophy – to practise intense self-scrutiny

offices, in their literary studies, and in taking up cases likely to bring fame. In my case, family precedent is an additional incentive to undertaking all these tasks.[61] My uncle, who was also my father by adoption, both held offices, advised the emperor, and was the author of many and enduring works.[62] Instead of imitating sailors, ought we not to model ourselves after those men who seek immortality in their studies by turning their hand now to one, now to another type of literature? If we cannot ultimately succeed in one pursuit, it may be that we will succeed in another.[63] At any rate, for me at least, this tranquillity of mind of which you speak is not to be bought at the price of obscurity.'

7.1 'You aver, Secundus,' said Plutarch, 'that those cases ought to be taken up which are likely to bring fame. But our mutual friend, Avidius Quietus,[64] frequently quotes a dictum of Thrasea,[65] who was in the habit of laying it down that the cases to be undertaken were these: those of friends, those which could find no advocate, and those which pertained to example. The case of friends needs no explanation. Why such as could find no advocate? Because in these the fearlessness as well as the kindliness of him who pleads them would be most strongly shown. Why those pertaining to example? Because it would make a difference whether a good or a bad one were exhibited.'[66] **7.2** 'To these categories of causes,' replied Pliny, 'though perhaps rather presumptuously, I must yet add such as are distinguished and conspicuous. For it is fair at times to plead the cause of glory and fame – in other words, one's own cause.'[67] 'So, then,' said Plutarch, 'we must suppose

with the aim of correcting and improving the self, without thought of the community or its greater good (or so Foucault 1986 argued; cf. Edwards 1997 on the letters of Seneca). For the different view of Plutarch, see n. 68.

[61] **Me uero ad haec impellit domesticum quoque exemplum**: cf. Plin. *Ep.* 5.8.4–5.

[62] **... plurima opera et mansura condidit**: cf. Plin. *Ep.* 3.5.9, 6.16.2–3, where Pliny outlines the series of offices held by the Elder Pliny (culminating in the command of the Misene fleet during the eruption of Vesuvius), his role as adviser to Vespasian, and the series of historical, biographical and encyclopedic works authored by him. It is a characteristically Roman reflex to turn to familial exemplarity in establishing ethical conduct.

[63] **... aliud insigniter facere possimus**: cf. Plin. *Ep.* 9.29.1.

[64] Avidius Quietus: north Italian, consul in 93, and later supporter of Pliny's failed attempt in 96 or 97 to prosecute a 'collaborator' in the death of Helvidius the Younger in 93/4 (*Ep.* 9.13.15: see above nn. 19, 34 for the two Helvidii), Quietus was the addressee of Plutarch's *On the delay of divine vengeance* and – with his brother Avidius Nigrinus (cited by Pliny at *Ep.* 10.65.3, 66.2; cf. Nigrinus' son at *Ep.* 5.13.6, 5.20.6, 7.6) – of *On brotherly love*. On the connections of the Avidii with Plutarch, see further Jones 1971: 51–4.

[65] **Thraseae**: Clodius Thrasea Paetus' authorship of this dictum, and its frequent quotation by Quietus, is confirmed by Plin. *Ep.* 6.29.1. Thrasea was consul in 56, leader of the 'Stoic opposition' under Nero, and later subject of a biography which would precipitate the execution of its author, Arulenus Rusticus; see n. 34. Like Pliny, Plutarch had connections with the supporters of Thrasea (Jones 1971: 24, 51–3); but Pliny soon distances himself from Thrasea's philosophical rigidity (see n. 67).

[66] **... quia plurimum referret, bonum an malum induceretur**: cf. Plin. *Ep.* 6.29.1–2.

[67] **... id est suam causam**: Pliny's revision of the dictum of Thrasea in this fashion is confirmed at Plin. *Ep.* 6.29.3. Sherwin-White 1966: 389 suggested that Pliny there misunderstands 'the principle

that glory and honour are the chief end of virtue?[68] The man whose goodness is complete and perfect will have no need at all of glory, except so far as
glory gives him access to achievement by reason of the confidence men have
in him; but a man who is still young and is fond of honours may be allowed
to plume and exalt himself somewhat even upon glory, provided that glory
is the outcome of noble deeds. But excess is everywhere harmful, and in the
case of men who cherish political ambitions, it is deadly; for it sweeps them
away into manifest folly and madness as they grasp after great power, when
they refuse to regard what is honourable as glorious, but consider that what
is glorious is good.'[69]

8.1 At that moment Cocceius Nerva[70] was heard in the entrance hallway,
asking where Plutarch might be, and bidding the slaves of Senecio to bring
him to the philosopher. Nerva was brought in by the attendants, and having
greeted everyone, learned that our friends Pliny and Plutarch had been
discussing glory and virtue. Nerva immediately began speaking in praise
of Pliny, and declared that Pliny was now satisfying the demands of both

---

of Thrasea, who deliberately excluded such cases unless they were covered by his definition in other
respects'. But Pliny is in fact distancing himself from such a doctrinaire philosopher as Thrasea: core
Roman values such as civil *gloria* and *fama* must take precedence over philosophical principle; cf.
Agricola on how 'in early life he was inclined to drink more deeply of philosophy than is permitted
to a Roman and a senator' (Tac. *Agr.* 4.3, with Woodman 2014: 100–1 for context).

[68] **. . . uirtutis**: like Pliny, Plutarch – as a Platonist – shows little taste for the 'turn inwards' found in
contemporary Epicurean and Stoic philosophy (see above n. 60; cf. Opsomer 2014 and Kechagia-
Ovseiko 2014 on Plutarch's broader attitudes to Stoicism and Epicureanism). But his views on virtue
and glory are distinctively different from Pliny's. In his ethical treatises, 'Plutarch makes use of the
reader's sensitivity to the opinion others have of him in order to persuade him to adopt a more
philosophical attitude' (Van Hoof 2010: 55, citing e.g. Plut. *Mor.* 125c). The value of honour is
conceded, but what is honourable is subjected to redefinition: philosophy is Plutarch's proposed
new way of gaining glory (Van Hoof 2010: 56).

[69] **. . . esse bonum**: cf. Plut. *Agis* 2.1–2. In his ethical treatises, Plutarch concedes to *philotimia* a
role in motivating virtuous action in the young (*Mor.* 451b–452d), but denounces love of honour as inappropriate in the mature or elderly (*Mor.* 793d). This theoretical position is consistent with the ambivalent attitude to *philotimia* demonstrated in the *Parallel lives*; see Duff
1999: 83–7, and cf. Stadter 2002: 231 on attitudes to ambition in the *Parallel lives* and Pliny's
Panegyricus.

[70] **Cocceius Nerua**: destined to be emperor within four years of the dramatic date of this dialogue,
Nerva had not long before received his second ordinary consulship, in 90 from Domitian, perhaps
for his loyalty during the revolt in Germany of Saturninus in 89. On Nerva's ancestry and career
prior to accession in 96, see Grainger 2003: 28–31 (who notes, p. 63, that Nerva would find Senecio
close to seditious in the succession crisis of 97). Nerva's entrance here to visit Plutarch is another
reminder of a Greek about whom Plutarch himself is silent: Dio of Prusa (see n. 4). The latter
describes Nerva as an 'old friend' (*Or.* 45.2) and may have received Roman citizenship through the
offices of Nerva, to judge from his likely full name Titus Flavius Cocceianus Dio – although the
matter is disputed (Jones 1978: 6–7; Salmeri 2000: 66–7 n. 67, 89 n. 176). Dio was himself absent
from Rome in the 90s: he had been in exile since the early years of Domitian's reign, and would
only be recalled upon the accession of Nerva (Jones 1978: 45–55). Pliny would encounter Dio briefly
during his tenure as governor of Pontus–Bithynia (*Ep.* 10.81–2), within the context of a legal dispute
in Prusa; but is likewise silent in other respects about him.

honour and virtue by scrupulously refusing to practise in the law courts while holding the office of tribune[71] . . .

At this point, the *Dialogus de moribus* breaks off. What else Plutarch and Pliny went on to discuss must remain a matter of speculation, although the extant works of both suggest that there was much for them to disagree about – ranging from decorous conduct in a lecture hall,[72] through flattery of self and others,[73] to patronage of one's home community,[74] and the Roman conduct of affairs in Greek provinces.[75] In particular, Nerva's open praise of Pliny – something he would soon repeat following Pliny's conduct in the deadly trial of Baebius Massa in the following year or so (*Ep.* 7.33.9–10)[76] – might well have introduced a topic related to honour and virtue, i.e. praise from another vs self-praise. Pliny's letters are notable for their author's readiness to praise his own actions in front of correspondents. But Plutarch devotes a separate treatise to the subject, which ultimately registers significant disagreement with his Roman counterpart (*Mor.* 539a–547f). For Pliny, personal glory often remains an end in itself, just at it had done for his beloved Cicero over a century before.[77]

A Rhetoric of the Roman Fake

In Richard Ellmann's classic biography of James Joyce, some highly intriguing pieces of information take up no more than four sentences in a work of

---

[71] **. . . in tribunatu causas agere**: in *Ep.* 1.23 Pliny outlines to Pompeius Falco (son-in-law of Senecio) the reasons behind his refusal to practise law during his year as tribune of the plebs.

[72] Contrast Plut. *Mor.* 44d, 45f–46a with Plin. *Ep.* 5.18, 6.17 (see the introduction of Gibson forthcoming).

[73] See Fitzgerald in this volume, p. 109, on Plutarchan powers of discernment vs Plinian eyes-wide-open self-deception; cf. Whitmarsh 2006a for Plutarch on flattery and friendship.

[74] Plutarch, like Dio of Prusa and many others of his class, strongly preferred involvement with the local politics of his hometown (Chaeronea in Plutarch's case) and region over a career in the senate or imperial administration (even at a time when the elite of the eastern Mediterranean was making significant progress on the *cursus honorum*); see Salmeri 2000: 59–63 (on those who stayed) and Madsen 2009: 59–81 (on those left). Pliny, by contrast, is involved with the affairs of Comum largely from afar and seems rarely to have gone there as an adult, despite the prominence given to his hometown in the *Epistles* (Champlin 2001).

[75] In the *Political precepts* (*Mor.* 798a–825f), Plutarch advises that local Greek affairs be conducted in such a way as to minimise Roman involvement (e.g. 814e–f, 815a); but Pliny proves himself a strongly interventionist governor (*Ep.* 10.17a.3, 10.18.2–3, 10.31.2, 4–5, 10.47, 10.48.1, with Talbert 1980); cf. Stadter 2015: 179–87 on Plin. *Ep.* 10 and Plutarchan conceptions of imperial virtue. On Plutarch's political philosophy more generally, see Pelling 2014.

[76] For the context, see Sherwin-White 1966: 447, 766.

[77] See Gibson 2003, comparing and contrasting (in particular) Plin. *Ep.* 7.33.8–9 and Plut. *Mor.* 546d–e; *Ep.* 3.11.1 and *Mor.* 547b–c; *Ep.* 3.11.2–3 and *Mor.* 544d; *Ep.* 1.18, 2.11, 3.4, 3.9 etc. and *Mor.* 513d–e; and *Ep.* 1.16 and *Mor.* 542c–d. On Plutarchan self-effacement more broadly, see König 2011.

almost 900 densely packed pages. Writing of Joyce's time in Zurich during the First World War, Ellmann declares:[78]

> The atmosphere of literary experimentation braced Joyce for *Ulysses*. In 1915 at the Café Voltaire in the old city, the surrealist movement was fomented by Tristan Tzara, Hans Arp, and others, and this group, with which Joyce was sometimes mistakenly identified, was to move on like him to Paris after the war. There was political excitement, too. In the Café Odeon, where Joyce frequently went, Lenin was a constant customer, and on one occasion, it is said, they met.

In a footnote reference,[79] Ellmann gives his source for this arresting nugget of alleged intelligence about Joyce and Lenin: 'Interview with Signora Vela Bliznakoff Pulitzer, 1954, by Lucy von Hibler'. The Bliznakoff sisters were daughters of a Bulgarian consul, and pupils of Joyce during his time in Zurich. Ellmann tells us that they were 'handsome young women', and relates a story about Nora Barnacle's use of them to influence Joyce: 'Nora asked [Vela Bliznakoff] to speak to him about [the matter], thinking her pretty face might have an influence.'[80] (The outcome was a signal success, from Nora's point of view.) Did Joyce and Lenin ever actually meet before the latter's departure from Zurich in March 1917, rather little remarked at the time, in the notorious 'sealed car' bound for Moscow and revolution? Or was Joyce merely trying to impress Vela Bliznakoff once it had become clear who this Lenin had become?

The playwright Tom Stoppard is a close reader of Ellmann's work, calling it a 'superb biography, whose companionship was not the least pleasure in the writing of *Travesties*'.[81] Stoppard refers here to his play, first performed in 1974, in which an historical associate of James Joyce, one Henry Carr, reminisces, rather unreliably, in old age about life in Zurich during the war. These reminiscences, resting ultimately on the foundation of the four sentences from Ellmann quoted earlier, bring together on stage Joyce, Lenin and the Dadaist Tristan Tzara – whom Joyce may also have met or not met.[82] Particularly effective, and hilarious, is Stoppard's integration of Lenin's own written words into the dialogue and monologues given to the character of Lenin in the play,[83] alongside the surrealist contributions of Tzara and the extravagant word play and wit

---

[78] Ellmann 1982: 409.   [79] Ibid. 781 n. 10.   [80] Ibid. 396–7.

[81] Stoppard 1975: 11. For a survey of the play and its themes, see Hunter 2000: 105–54.

[82] Ellmann 1982: 409 (cited earlier); cf. ibid. 563 (the work of Tzara and Joyce appeared in the same 1924 issue of *Transatlantic Review*).

[83] Stoppard 1975: 15 'Nearly everything spoken by Lenin and [his wife] Nadezhda Krupskaya herein comes from his Collected Writings and from her *Memories of Lenin*'.

of Joyce's speeches.[84] Ground-breakers in their separate fields, the three alarmingly self-confident men are shown to have much to disagree about in the fields of art, patriotism, politics and war.

Stoppard points a way forward for dealing with historical characters from different cultures with divergent points of view who really ought to have met, but for whose actual encounter there is only slim or contestable evidence. The possible meeting between Joyce and Lenin in the Café Odeon in Zurich before March 1917 is the equivalent (*si parua licet . . .*) of the possible defence by Pliny of the wife of Plutarch's brother during Plutarch's probable visit to Rome in 92–3. We can get the two sets of characters into the same room – very nearly almost, but not quite certainly. So why not invent a meeting, using the characters' own separately and individually published writings for dialogue, as Stoppard does again with A. E. Housman and, among others, Oscar Wilde in *The Invention of Love*?[85]

Getting Plutarch and Pliny into the same room has proved a little less fun than bringing together Joyce, Lenin and Tzara. And not only because the author of this chapter is not Tom Stoppard. But it has at least allowed us to cast aside the millstone that hangs around the neck of all comparative studies of significant figures who ought to have met, but may never have done so. Within the fictional encounter offered earlier, in fact, around 70 per cent of the text is made up from original texts by Pliny, Plutarch and Tacitus.[86] Almost all of the actual quoted words of Pliny and Plutarch are direct or, less often, slightly modified translations of the letters of the former and treatises and dialogues of the latter.[87] In Pliny's case, the relative ease with which his letters can be made to 'talk' to Plutarch's dialogues goes some way to affirming the relevance and potency of the dictum attributed to the ancient editor of Aristotle's correspondence, that a letter should be 'one of the two sides of a dialogue' (Demetr. *Eloc.* 223). The parallel between

---

[84] Stoppard grafts the whole onto an outline provided by Oscar Wilde's *The Importance of Being Earnest*; see Hunter 2000: 111–24.

[85] Stoppard 1997.

[86] Due acknowledgement is made of the translations of Church and Brodribb 1877 for Tacitus' *Dialogus*; Lewis 1879 for Pliny; and the Loeb Classical Library volumes of Perrin 1921, Fowler 1936 and Hembold 1939 for Plutarch.

[87] A majority of Latin lemmata cited in the 'commentary' are either directly lifted from Pliny's *Epistles* (occasionally slightly modified) or are offered as translations of an original Plutarchan text. Where a lemma is immediately followed by 'cf. Plin./Plut.', this indicates that the text in the dialogue on which commentary is being offered is (largely) a translation of the original source text indicated. Note that no contextual or interpretative data have been invented (as such) either in the commentary or in the introductory sections. However, some 'facts' in the text do reflect modern interpretations of ancient data, such as the assumption that the Plutarchan anecdote about Rusticus takes place during the latter's consulship. In addition, liberties to date Pliny's tribunate to 92 (rather than 91) and praetorship to 94 (rather than 93) have been taken.

dialogue and the epistolary genre is strengthened, rather than diminished, if account is taken of the particular character of much ancient dialogue. Putting extracts from Pliny and Plutarch side by side results in the almost automatic replication of a known feature of ancient dialogue, where participants tend to talk past each other or to develop their own points without full reference to the viewpoints of other speakers. No doubt, in life, the same could have happened in any actual encounter between Plutarch, the opinionated Hellene, and Pliny, the high-handed Roman. Several chapters in this volume bear testimony to the prickly egos and cultural sensitivities that lie behind the silences, omissions and exclusions inflicted by contemporary texts on each other.

The ultimate aim of the experiment has been to assess what Pliny and Plutarch do actually have to say to, and against, one another – but in a format that avoids dry analysis of what is, to modern tastes, already arid subject matter. As such I offer fictional dialogues, in all seriousness, as a potential new methodology for engaging the imagination and the intellect in otherwise conceptually difficult or aesthetically challenging subject areas.

My experiment stands at the confluence of several streams of thought, ancient and modern. Irene Peirano's monograph, *The rhetoric of the Roman fake* (2012), has sought to rehabilitate an entire class of pseudonymous and inauthentic Latin texts such as the *Appendix Vergiliana*, *Panegyricus Messallae* and *Consolatio ad Liviam*. She persuasively argues that these works were written so as to fill in or account for missing or under-documented moments and events in the biographies of Virgil, Tibullus and Ovid. As a result, these texts have become open to being read as important moments in the ancient reception of major poets, and so may shed old suspicions of artistic deficiency. Perhaps we might view ourselves, with due modesty, as late inheritors of this ancient tradition?

The ancient invention of texts to plug biographical gaps was not confined to such prestigious cultural artifacts as Virgil's juvenilia. Ancient letter collections contain spurious letters inserted alongside genuine epistles to supplement a theme or bridge a chronological rupture.[88] Letter collections were also invented wholesale and attached to the names of famous historical and literary figures, some with an evident apologetic or explanatory purpose related to a feature of the broader biographical tradition of that figure.[89] In one notorious case a correspondence forged between two fourth-century figures, the Christian bishop Basil of Caeserea

---

[88] Hodkinson 2007: 287.
[89] Morrison 2014; cf. Rosenmeyer 2001: 193–233 on the pseudonymous epistolographic tradition more broadly.

and the pagan rhetorician Libanius of Antioch, contains extensive quotations from the genuine correspondence of the same two figures and other epistolographers.[90] The desire to put into contact two figures whom the forger wished *had* been in dialogue is evident also in the spurious ancient correspondence between Seneca and St Paul,[91] as well as in works which do not pretend to authenticity, such as Lucian's *Dialogues of the dead*, which in turn influenced Erasmus and later European culture;[92] or a mime attested by Cicero which brought together in conversation at a banquet Euripides and Menander as well as Socrates and Epicurus.[93]

In the modern world, suggestive experiments have of course been conducted in the historical novel,[94] but experimental biography, in particular, has much to offer. One recent example, *John Aubrey: my own life* (2015) by Ruth Scurr, takes as its subject a seventeenth-century English antiquary. Aubrey's life is written in the form of a fictional diary – the subject did not leave one himself – where the entries are made up largely of Aubrey's own words.[95] In essence it is a cento of Aubrey's own voluminous writings, where his original text is repurposed as autobiography.[96] The diary is not an ancient form. But there clearly remains much scope to compose new letters and dialogues for ancient figures based closely, as in Scurr's exemplar, on surviving authentic writings. The results will need more than usually careful evaluation and interpretation from the reader, not to mention some good background knowledge.[97] But the result may be imaginative engagement with subjects and material otherwise prone to undeserved neglect. In the present instance, the particular value of putting Plutarch into extended fictional dialogue with Pliny has been to prompt further reflection on the dynamics of the off- and on-the-page interactions that the rest of this volume has been trying to unpick. Many early imperial authors, like Pliny and

---

[90] Van Hoof 2016.

[91] See Furst, Fuhrer, Siegert and Walter 2006 on this correspondence.   [92] See Relihan 1987.

[93] Jerome *Ep.* 52.8.3 = Cicero *Pro Gallio* fr. 4, with Cain 2013: 202–3 ad loc.; also Panayotakis 1995: 55–66. The author of the mime is usually identified as Publilius Syrus or Laberius. On the broader tradition of the faking and forging of ancient literature, see Martínez 2011 and 2014.

[94] In *Memoirs of Hadrian* (1955), M. Yourcenar has the emperor show familiarity with Pliny and stay with Plutarch at home in Chaeronea. The iniquities of historical fiction in general, and Yourcenar in particular, are the subject of Syme 1991a.

[95] Cf. Scurr 2015: 12–13: 'In constructing Aubrey's diary, I have used as many as possible of his own words. It is a diary based on the historical evidence; a diary that shows him living vividly, day by day, month by month, year by year, but with necessary gaps when nothing is known about where he was or what he was doing. I have not invented scenes or relationships for him as a novelist would.' For an early assessment of the advantages for biography of the adopted form, see S. Kelly 2015.

[96] Cf. also Houghton 2007, where a letter to Boccaccio is invented for Petrarch in order to explore his views on Ennius in connection with the epic poem *Africa*.

[97] For an unauthenticated meeting between the novelists Dickens and Dostoevsky which was later co-opted into the biographical tradition (with damaging effects), see Naiman 2013.

Plutarch, avoid explicit mention of significant contemporaries or elders; yet their works have much to talk about between themselves. Standard models of intertextuality developed and used within classics for the study of (e.g.) poetry and historiography do not readily allow these conversations to develop. Fictional dialogue is a new way to break the impasse.

Conclusion

What, finally, does this 'dialogue' between the letters of Pliny and the treatises of Plutarch do for our understanding of the two men and their works? In all the contrasts between Pliny and Plutarch we can glimpse the differences between senatorial orator and provincial philosopher, Roman traditional *mores* and Greek ethics, and, more dimly, between western comfort with hierarchies and patronage and an eastern preference for an emphasis on elite equality and *homonoia*. Yet Pliny and Plutarch have much in common: this much is clear from the time and energy that they devote to essentially the same issues. Greek and Roman may ignore one another in 'life', but their texts understand one another, even where they disagree. Plutarch, for example, is emphatic that certain activities – such as the simultaneous pursuit of a political career and a life of study and the maintenance of one's estates – are inconsistent with one another, precisely because he grasps that senators like Pliny are prone to claiming they can do it all, in their pursuit of the perfect imperial career.[98] This is in part a tribute to the time that Plutarch spent in Italy and his engagement with Roman affairs over a lifetime. His contemporary Dio of Prusa showed a distinctly less firm grasp of the role of senators and the inner workings of Roman power structures.[99] The attitudes of Pliny and Plutarch to issues small (proper conduct in the lecture hall), personal (praise of self and others, patronage of one's hometown) and political (Roman government of Greece) may differ, sometimes markedly.[100] But there is substantial agreement that *these* are the issues which need to be aired for the benefit of self and others.

One of the purposes of forgeries of ancient texts is often to reveal or confirm connections and bonds. The correspondence of Seneca and St Paul appears to have been written in late antiquity to confirm what many saw

---

[98] See nn. 46–63.

[99] It is evident from Dio's writings that he had no interest in Latin culture, and his knowledge of Roman political institutions may have matched his lack of concern with their operation: Dio's vision of empire was based on the Hellenistic practice of a monarch recruiting *philoi* or advisers from amongst the elite of his territories; his *Kingship orations* make no mention of senators or even *equites*. On Dio here, see Salmeri 2000: 89–91.

[100] See nn. 72–5.

as an instinctive sympathy between certain aspects of Christianity and Stoicism. The relationship of Pliny and Plutarch is ultimately more adversarial: hence the choice of the *Dialogus* of Tacitus, with its contrasting views on contemporary oratory, as the framework for the present 'dialogue' between the published works of the pair. One apparently trivial difference between the pair marks the profoundest gulf. Plutarch's lack of interest in contemporary literature might seem a matter of mere personal taste when compared with Pliny's decidedly modernist enthusiasms for the oratory, poetry and history produced by his Roman correspondents and the epideictic rhetoric of his Greek friends from Syria. After all, Cicero, Pliny's revered exemplar, evinced little interest in the literary productions of *his* contemporaries. But any interest that Plutarch shows in poetry is largely invested in the idea that the classics of Greek verse might function as a preparation for immersion in philosophy. For Pliny, oratory and poetry are a highway to current repute and future fame.[101] The attitudes of the pair to contemporary literary production encapsulate their differing views of the roles of honour, glory, and philosophical virtue in the conduct of their lives.[102] Fundanus and Senecio were apparently attracted to the idea that Plutarch's version of Platonic philosophy version might frame and regulate aspects of their lives. Pliny evidently was not: personal honour and the prospect of glory remained as his lodestars. In the old quarrel between rhetoric and philosophy, current since Plato's *Gorgias*, Pliny the courtroom orator stands by default on the side of rhetoric, with its emphasis on influence and reputation, not to mention the gaining of prestige in the spheres of politics and law. For Plutarch, philosophy was the superior cultural model: a message of some urgency amidst the first stirrings of the 'Second Sophistic'.[103]

---

[101] For the attitudes of the pair to literature, including contemporary literature, see nn. 39–40.

[102] See nn. 66–69.

[103] Yet Pliny could find at least one Greek philosopher to tell him that his public life in Rome was a form of philosophy: see n. 42 on *Ep.* 1.10.9–19: the just conduct of public and legal affairs is 'in fact the most noble part of philosophy'. On the scope and cultural status of 'philosophy' in the age of Pliny and Plutrach, see Trapp 2014; cf. Schmitz 2014 on Plutarch's attitude to the epideictic rhetoricians of his day. On Plutarch's place in the competition between philosophy and rhetoric, see Van Hoof 2014: 146.

ENVOI/VENIO

John Henderson

...nuntius a Spurinna: 'Venio ad te.' 'Immo ego ad te.' Coimus in
porticum Liviae, cum alter ad alterum tenderemus...

(Plin. Ep. 1.5.9)

...message from Spurinna: 'Coming over to you.' 'No – me to you.'
We met up under Livia's Colonnade, each heading for the other...

The Introduction's mention of 'bookending' to tie up the eds.' masterful
prospectus for their ingressive volume neatly finesses any 'envoi'. All the
same, reading through the essays *seriatim* underscores the dynamic trajectory latent within the ensemble, from the baseline of shake-up reïnven-
tion of Flavian–Ulpian intertextuality (Part I) through inspection of the
always precarious borderlands between literature and its contextualisation
in the extended field of textual pragmatics, power contestation and cultural discourse, whether specifically encrypted in authored show-writing
or out there in general social patterns and memes of communication (Part
II), into 'the silence' of o-pen-ended interactivity within the literary fold
that obliviates the embeddedness in the surrounding 'world' of each other's
circulation and impact on readers (Part III).

The book moves from reminding us of scholarship *qua* collective enterprise to produce and install a shareable 'textualterity' – our capacity to re-
situate and so re-charge the reception of our classic texts, one at a time and
in their so-easily naturalised clusters, by genre, period, pecking order, or
problematic. (That this is already a vaulting ambition is shown by Whitton's fierce endeavour to get *literary* prose intertextuality on the same plat-
form as is routine with verse – *before* we go on to problematise this, *pari
passu*, with the challenge of interaction beyond intertextuality.) Put Martial 10 and Tacitus *Agricola* (Rimell) together to share their moment, and
wonder how-and-why that collocation took so long. Leap past Trajan from
Valerius Flaccus to the north-eastern frontier of Tacitus' later *Annals* (Buckley), and suddenly – behold! – urgent geopolitics in myth-history rear up in

the faces of grand imperial strategy. Reader-critics (can) *make* these interactions 'happen' (p. 85, with p. 72 n. 33). We know how adequately protracted reigns (a decade plus?) can plausibly house an era, how power texts mean or are set to shape an ambience, how regime change, most particularly in the case of autocracy, induces and manifests in a written outburst of acclamation/occlusion/revisionism as part of ongoing 'changing of the guard', often masking 're-shuffle'. New faces appear, perhaps mostly on the same heads, and each honeymoon period overdoes its own significance, durability and mission to self-delude. Confronting the duo of Pliny and Tacitus *Dialogus* with their drive to repudiate their Flavian guru serves to reflate the ascendancy of Quintilian's directive to rhetorical success, which is to say, his bid to ordain terms for effectiveness 'in public life' at Rome (Whitton). Pliny re-intricates himself with Martial by standing proud, wobbling into self-delation (Fitzgerald). Suetonius' run past his dozen preceding Caesars in a row chimes with but deflates the exceptionalism of the one-and-only Trajan of Pliny's hymnic *Panegyricus* (Roche).

These projects can all slip into the envelope of intertextually founded intrication such as progressively finds, promotes, and works with, an overarching configuration, or foregrounding background, or tonic chord (only find a metaphor): as if pre-determined/-programmed to put finger on pulse, find the heart of, laparoscope, another 'Augustan', 'Neronian', 'Flavian', *Zeitgeist* to articulate and enlarge Lat. Lit. I see, however, a dagger before me: the scandal that adjudication between Flavian and Ulpian may founder before it starts – on the tightly argued objection that our archpoet of Trajan-into-Hadrianic Romespeak may prove to be a thoroughly misplaced shoulder-rubber of Martial (Kelly, esp. pp. 175–6). No wonder, in that provocative case, that the early Flavian *Spectacula* of said Martial can comfortably share their sensationalist-bent mindset with Pliny the self-appointing stylist of Trajanic serenity and . . . late Juvenal, off slipping into journo hyping at world's end Egypt: I give you, from (precisely datelined) Hadrian's haunts, interclan cannibalism! (Ash) So does our handle on literary history *bear* plotting on a period map, however provisional? (This has repeatedly been the dumping ground of insecurely datable orphan texts – Petronius, Calpurnius, [Vergiliana] . . . in the first vacant p/lot?)

Should we extrapolate from the Domitian wake and Trajanic marriage that the *Age of the Younger Pliny* more than documents: sponsors and advocates, to register a Roman World? (E.g. Devillers 2015.) If so, then what of the late Trajan-into-Hadrian scene, way beyond Pliny's reach? Is our *LINTHiaka* necessarily open-ended because we have so little to work with in negotiating between change and morphing when deathbed adoption

supplants imperial fostering and complex affinal adumbration as indefin-
able frame for splicing or seasoning continuity with Trajan with ingredients of would-be Trajan imitation – a second pick of the 'best' candidate,
minus dynastic prejudgment? (Would this be especially like or particularly
unlike the shiftless contortions in the succeeding succession narratives?)
But a project that demands our involvement now, *because* (for instance) we
do have *something* to go on, at least, when Juvenal 7 *seems* to greet a new
deal for writers with post-anointment palace patronage, and not before
time (suggesting that literature was ²still₂ centripetal round a suitably sta-
tioned Caesar, a scheme no longer operative by the Severans: Whitmarsh
2007); which is to say, we *do* have the pre-determined obligation to press
the discipline-hardened tradition of terminating the classical syllabus with
the great writers Juvenal and Tacitus plus their lamentably vital minion
Suetonius for any raison d'être that may be lurking beneath its many-times
discredited and discarded notice of intent to quit. (The Lat. Lit watershed –
'The proper place to stop is Suetonius' – never held, as for instance when
the *OLD* let Apuleius sneak into the cards, together with odd bits of sanc-
tified 'Later' Latin: John Henderson 2010: esp. pp. 148–53, quote from ed.
Souter at 149. But, then again, it never let go, either.)

Where once both satire and (satirical) history/biography coiled back into
their retro subject matter, so that Tacitus and Juvenal became prime 'Flavian' texts, even disappearing the less than fortunate epics and epigrams
that so doomed the dynasty's image (just when Roman conquest, triumph,
and architecture raised such palpably Roman *grandeur*, from [Domitian's]
Arch of Titus on, through [Hadrian's] Column and Forum of Trajan, to
anchor, for the UK, in That Wall), while the *De uita Caesarum* and *Annales*
time-slipped right back to the ranks of honorary 'Julio-Claudians'. We go
back, now, knowing full well that 'Antonine', 'Severan', let alone 'Tetrar-
chic' and 'Constantinian', Roman Worlds are a-shaping, gelled, even; and,
still more obtrusive, the alternative 'Flavian'-through-to-Hadrianic Roman
World of Dio Chrysostom (Jones 1978) heralds the onset of that laughably
misnominalised empire of Roman texts in Greek, 'The Second Sophistic',
underlines the double-whammy for Antiquity iconised in the shift from
Herculean Imperator Trajan in his breastplate bashing the borders clean
through (Parthia) to India, to the bearded Grand Tourist Hadrian, retreating from the conquests with his gaggle of Hellenophile apparatchicks, to all
appearances Becoming Greek on a thoroughgoing trip of Graecising round
a globalised Roman World. In *that* perspective, the ²closure₂ effected by the
deafening execration of dead Domitian dumps Trajan into a deep limbo,
relieved by Pliny's elevation to prime status as emperor *panegyrist* and by

repeat attempts to bunch, as [scarcely] adoptive and 'good', the run from Trajan through Marcus Aurelius; whereas Hadrian gets to lead off 'the next' dozen Caesars (in Marius Maximus' collection; opening the *SHA*), and so heads the drive heading past GraecoRoman philosophising into Christian Latin, Late Antiquity, and —

Is there a continuity for the writing, not just the subject matter, of Juvenal and Tacitus? We can bring to bear data on literary production in that *Age of Pliny*, the Trajanic decade: as a business between court, elite lifestyle, empire acculturation, letters – and we mean *letters* – were ideally placed to place themselves as where what/who matters was starred, ordained, validated: *mobilising* politeness techniques, for real impact (Roller), for careering (Mratschek); modelling for the administration itself, *its* executive language, its ruling/s, its marshalling of textuality as showroom, courtroom, headroom for government (König, Harries, Lavan); devising, exemplifying, and promoting updated protocols for best practice in interactivity (Morello). And . . . over-achieving, lest we forget, by dis/avowing reliance on the social archive of story-patterns and axiological samples that feed the establishment intercom and constantly provide terms at once for regulated immersion in, so purchase on, civil life writ large and for fastidious abjection of, so shored up boundaries against, the un-, the non-, the infra- . . . literary (Langlands). And in particular we can expand our search for interactivity from its Trajanic engine-room of Pliny's *Epistles* by following exemplary demonstrations within their compass.

The Introduction chose from Pliny's books' end for the eds.' rich demonstration of the potential for resonance way in and beyond the 'strict' literariness of these staged missives (*Ep.* 9.19) – beyond what has been felicitously dubbed 'the snakepit of intertextuality' (Soerink 2013). They mean Latinists to go back to where they started, if not to the pre-Hinds, pre-Genette, wilds (say) of the Bloomian 'Map of Misreading' (but resistance to 'revolutionary ratios', esp. 'daemonisation', inescapably binds author-readers to the undreaded 'apophrades', as the Introduction reveals in all its clarity), then at least/at the most perceptible, to encompass what the critical model of citationality must work to discount. Here, among the new discoveries capped by the limit case of the imaginary (Gibson), the volume captures the 'inter' (alia) activated by interactivity spurned, erased, ignored, redundant – and *forgot*.

I go back, very briskly indeed (lunch calls; it's Friday; I should be . . . –), to where Pliny gets going, bringing bugbear Regulus into the wreckoning (*Ep.* 1.5: work out from my epigraph snippet. I *can* do this because, quite apart from Marchesi's clarification in this volume of how anxiously featuring and/or disappearing dominant influence can equate, crossover, meld, Hoffer 2016's now canonised chapter/Oxidised essay on this master epistle is now as accessible as it is inspirationally detailed and literarily-theoretically exemplary. A long envoi you do *not* need). In this letter, Pliny buries where you are not to miss, but to learn to find, how a regular new brand of Kultchur invests the present by disinvesting its past, unlearns Quintilian/gets back to Cicero, faces up to/down self-betrayal by inventing 'neutral ground' on which to level with us, and so forth: above all, Pliny interacts by refusing to interact with his alter ego demon, he wouldn't let any poor go-between obligate him by bringing home Regulus' plea for a done deal. No: 'You're coming to me, I'm coming to you.' We meet but we don't meet, as the adventitious intermediary's intermediary models the one-sided merging of epistolary characters in the mimetic embrace of their letter: the textual simulation of coming together through the report of direct speech most precisely stages its 'impossibility' in presenting the shifters 'I/you-here-now' against their deferral situation of 'You *through proxy*/I *through proxy-not* here-*not* now'. Here, beneath the colonnade built to obliviate the shameful imperial agent (Vedius Pollio) under a temple of Concord (Ovid *Fasti* 6.637–48), we show/know how to inter Regulus. The letter goes on to make play of citing Regulus and makes itself available for citation, too – for the new improved Trajanic model of civil interaction; this regulation epistoliterarity mimes for author-implied reader relations, too – but is here to get *out*, to press the claim to its actual readers' reactions, meet us part-way, on ground of his choosing. For (the likes of) us, he's always (always already) a coming thing, never to be caught out in entrapment or caught in by the system that obliges social actors, neither ducking nor per-forming, but (just *like* Literature: unregularised) coming and going, up for approval.

And this volume is indeed fundamentally *ingressive*, too: 'only just begun'. To the NTH degree. It's ²no² coincidence that 'the Antipodes'' finest arrive in the out-turn to dispense with the verbal trousers, and bring us the Trajanic–Hadrianic scene through figuration of its globalising poet (Geue on Juvenal) and its self-imaging through pedagogic programming worldwide (Uden on post-Quintilianic education between [Plutarch] and Juvenal). And there is generated a retroactive multiplier effect, too, ampli-fying the lessons on offer across the ensemble of essays suggesting scope for active intercomparison-and-contrast within and beyond our inter-nalised methodologies for 'close reading' founded on the word – verbatim. If Juve-nal models for you-won't-catch-me-those-ways writing coming...from nowhere, proffering feints to get lost in the outback – well, this mode generalises as we find Hadrianic culture o-pening into second-century culture preliminarily defined as 'draw[ing] from a shared pool of language and ideas from previous Greek and Roman literature . . . yet . . . frequently respond[ing] to their proximity by *projecting a sense of isolation*' (Uden, p. 388). Right on cue, 'literary interaction' working with the recessive materials we have for Late Trajanic-into-Hadrianic Latin writing that has pretensions to speak for and boss their world, turns out at the death to support both a new twist to (invaginating) traditional authoriality and (in the most positive characterisation the volume formulates for its 'period') the drive towards increasingly culture-centred, even 'extratextual', enquiry. (We await the LINTH collective's next publication, set to start from *here* abouts.)

References

Adamietz, J. (1986) 'Quintilians *Institutio oratoria*', *ANRW* II.32.4, 2226–71.

Adamik, T. (1976) 'Pliny and Martial', *Annales Universitatis Scientiarum Budapestensis Sect. Class.* 4, 63–72.

Adams, J. N. (1982) *The Latin sexual vocabulary*, Baltimore.

    (1995) 'The language of the Vindolanda writing tablets: an interim report', *JRS* 85, 86–134.

    (2003) *Bilingualism and the Latin language*, Cambridge.

Ahl, F. M. (1976) *Lucan: an introduction*, Ithaca, NY.

    (1984) 'The rider and the horse: politics and power in Roman poetry from Horace to Statius', *ANRW* II.32.1, 78–110.

Alberte González, A. (1993) '*Dialogus de oratoribus* versus *Institutio oratoria*', *Minerva* 7, 255–67.

Alföldy, G. (1999) *Städte, Eliten und Gesellschaft in der Gallia Cisalpina: Epigraphisch-historische Untersuchungen*, Stuttgart.

Alföldy, G. and H. Halfmann (1973) 'M. Cornelius Nigrinus Curiatius Maternus, General Domitians und Rivale Trajans', *Chiron* 3, 331–73.

Alfonsi, L. (1962) 'Pliniana', *Aevum* 36, 171.

Allen, G. (2000) *Intertextuality*, London.

Alston, R. (1996) 'Conquest by text: Juvenal and Plutarch on Egypt' in J. Webster and N. Cooper, eds., *Roman imperialism: post-colonial perspectives* (Leicester), 99–109.

Anastasiadis, V. I. and G. A. Souris (2000) *An index to Roman imperial constitutions from Greek inscriptions and papyri: 27 BC to 284 AD*, Berlin.

Andermahr, A. M. (1998) *Totus in praediis: Senatorischer Grundbesitz in Italien in der frühen und hohen Kaiserzeit*, Bonn.

Anderson, W. S. (1961) 'Juvenal and Quintilian', *YCS* 17, 1–91. Reprinted in W. S. Anderson, *Essays on Roman satire* (Princeton, 1982), 396–486.

    (1970) '*Lascivia* vs. *ira*: Martial and Juvenal', *CSCA* 3, 1–34. Reprinted in W. S. Anderson, *Essays on Roman satire* (Princeton, 1982), 362–95.

    (1988) 'Juvenal Satire 15: cannibals and culture' in A. J. Boyle, ed., *The imperial muse: Ramus essays on Roman literature of the Empire. To Juvenal through Ovid* (Berwick, Victoria), 203–14.

Ando, C. (2000) *Imperial ideology and provincial loyalty in the Roman Empire*, Berkeley.

André, J.-M. (1949) *Étude sur les termes du couleur dans la langue latine*, Paris.

(1993) 'Hadrien littérateur et protecteur des lettres', *ANRW* 11.34.1, 583–611.

Arcaria, F. (2000) *'Referre ad principem': contributo allo studio delle 'epistulae' imperiali in età classica*, Milan.

Ash, R. (1999) *Ordering anarchy: armies and leaders in Tacitus'* Histories, Ann Arbor.

(2002) 'Epic encounters? Ancient historical battle narrative and the epic tradition', in D. S. Levene and D. P. Nelis, eds., *Clio and the poets: Augustan poetry and the traditions of ancient historiography* (Leiden), 253–73.

(2003) *'Aliud est enim epistulam, aliud historiam . . . scribere* (*Epistles* 6.16.22): Pliny the historian?' in Gibson and Morello 2003, 211–62.

(2007) *Tacitus: Histories book II*, Cambridge.

(2009) 'Fission and fusion: shifting Roman identities in the *Histories*' in Woodman 2009a, 85–99.

(2010) 'The great escape: Tacitus on the mutiny of the Usipi (*Agricola* 28)' in Kraus, Marincola and Pelling 2010, 275–93.

Asper, M. (2007) *Griechische Wissenschaftstexte: Formen, Funktionen, Differenzierungsgeschichten*, Stuttgart.

Asso, P., ed. (2011) *Brill's companion to Lucan*, Leiden.

Atherton, C., ed. (1998) *Monsters and monstrosity in Greek and Roman culture*, Bari.

Augoustakis, A., ed. (2013) *Ritual and religion in Flavian epic*, Oxford.

ed. (2014) *Flavian poetry and its Greek past*, Leiden.

Austin, R. G. (1939) 'The epilogue to the *Agricola*', *CR* 53, 116–17.

(1948) *Quintiliani Institutionis oratoriae liber XII*, Oxford.

Axelson, B. (1945) *Unpoetische Wörter: Ein Beitrag zur Kenntnis der lateinischen Dichtersprache*, Lund.

Babbitt, F. C. (1927) *Plutarch: Moralia*, vol. 1, Cambridge, MA.

Baier, T. ed. (2001) *Valerius Flaccus* Argonautica *Buch VI: Einleitung und Kommentar*, Munich.

(2003) 'Κτῆμα oder ἀγώνισμα: Plinius über historischen und rhetorischen Stil (*Epist.* 5, 8)' in Castagna and Lefèvre 2003, 69–81.

Baldwin, B. (1994) 'Notes on the *De aquis* of Frontinus' in C. Deroux, ed., *Studies in Latin literature and Roman history*, VII (Brussels), 484–506.

(1995) 'The composition of Pliny's *Natural history*', *SO* 70, 72–81.

Balland, A. (1981) 'La famille de L. Domitius Apollinaris' in A. Balland, ed., *Fouilles de Xanthos*, vol. VII: *Inscriptions d'époque imperiale du Létôon* (Paris), 103–20.

(2010) *Essai sur la société des épigrammes de Martial*, Paris.

Balsdon, J. P. V. D. (1979) *Romans and aliens*, Chapel Hill, NC.

Bang, M. (1921) 'Über den Gebrauch der Anrede domine im gemeinen Leben' in L. Friedländer, *Darstellungen aus der Sittengeschichte Roms*, 9th and 10th edn (Leipzig), IV, 82–8.

Bang, P. F. and K. Turner (2015) 'Kingship and elite formation' in W. Scheidel, ed., *State power in ancient China and Rome* (Oxford), 11–38.

Baraz, Y. and C. van den Berg, eds. (2013) *Intertextuality* (= *AJP* 134.1), Baltimore.

Barchiesi, A. (1997) 'Otto punti su una mappa dei naufragi', *MD* 39, 209–26.

(2001) 'Some points on a map of shipwrecks' in A. Barchiesi, *Speaking volumes: narrative and intertext in Ovid and other Latin poets* (London), 141–54.

(2004) 'Quando Virgilio era un moderno: una delle più antiche recite delle *Georgiche*, e il contesto di una spiritosaggine', *MD* 52, 21–8.

Barnes, T. D. (1986) 'The significance of Tacitus' *Dialogus de oratoribus*', *HSCP* 90, 225–44.

Bartsch, S. (1994) *Actors in the audience: theatricality and doublespeak from Nero to Hadrian*, Cambridge, MA.

(1997) *Ideology in cold blood: a reading of Lucan's* Civil War, Cambridge, MA.

(2005) 'Lucan' in J. M. Foley, ed., *A companion to ancient epic* (Oxford), 492–502.

(2012) 'Praise and doublespeak: Tacitus' *Dialogus*' in R. Ash, ed., *Oxford readings in Tacitus* (Oxford), 119–54 (updated version of Bartsch 1994, 101–25).

Barwick, K. (1954) *Der Dialogus de oratoribus des Tacitus: Motive und Zeit seiner Entstehung*, Berlin.

Bastomsky, S. (1985) 'The not-so-perfect man: some ambiguities in Tacitus' picture of Agricola', *Latomus* 44, 388–93.

Bauman, R. A. (1980) 'The "Leges iudiciorum publicorum" and their interpretation in the Republic, principate and later Empire', *ANRW* II.13, 103–233.

(1996) *Crime and punishment in ancient Rome*, London.

Beagon, M. (2005) *The Elder Pliny on the human animal:* Natural history *book 7*, Oxford.

(2009) 'Ordering Wonderland: Ovid's Pythagoras and the Augustan vision' in Hardie 2009, 288–309.

Beard, M. (2002) 'Ciceronian correspondences: making a book out of letters' in T. P. Wiseman, ed., *Classics in progress* (Oxford), 103–44.

Beck, J.-W. (1998) *Germania–Agricola: Zwei Kapitel zu Tacitus' zwei kleinen Schriften*, Hildesheim.

(2013) '*Pro captu lectoris habent sua fata . . .* – Plinius und der Eklat epist. 6,15', *Hermes* 141, 294–308.

Beck, M., ed. (2014) *A companion to Plutarch*, Malden, MA.

Bennett, J. (2001) *Trajan: optimus princeps*, 2nd edn, London.

Béranger, J. (1953) *Recherches sur l'aspect idéologique du principat*, Basel.

Bergmann, B. (1995) 'Visualizing Pliny's villas', *JRA* 8, 406–20. Also in Gibson and Whitton 2016, 201–24.

Bernstein, N. W. (2008) 'Each man's father served as his teacher: constructing relatedness in Pliny's letters', *CA* 27, 203–30.

(2013) '*Romanas veluti saevissima cum legiones Tisiphone regesque movet*: Valerius Flaccus' *Argonautica* and the Flavian era' in M. A. J. Heerink and G. Manuwald, eds., *Brill's companion to Valerius Flaccus* (Leiden), 154–69.

Berrendonner, C. (2001) 'La formation de la tradition sur M. Curius Dentatus et C. Fabricius Luscinus: un homme nouveau peut-il être un grand homme?' in Coudry and Spaeth 2001, 97–116.

Berriman, A. and M. Todd (2001) 'A very Roman coup: the hidden war of imperial succession, AD 96–8', *Historia* 50, 312–31.

Berry, E. G. (1958) 'The *De liberis educandis* of pseudo-Plutarch', *HSCP* 63, 387–99.

Billig, M. (1999) *Freudian repression: conversation creating the unconscious*, Cambridge.

Binder, G. (1995) 'Öffentliche Autorenlesungen. Zur Kommunikation zwischen römischen Autoren und ihrem Publikum' in G. Binder and K. Ehrlich, eds., *Kommunikation durch Zeichen und Wort* (Trier), 265–332.

Birley, A. R. (1997) *Hadrian: the restless emperor*, London.

    (2000a) *Onomasticon to the Younger Pliny: Letters and Panegyric*, Munich and Leipzig.

    (2000b) 'The life and death of Cornelius Tacitus', *Historia* 49, 230–47.

    (2004) *Marcus Aurelius: a biography*, 2nd edn, London.

    (2016) 'Pliny's family, Pliny's career' in Gibson and Whitton 2016, 51–66.

Bloomer, W. M. (2011) *The school of Rome: Latin studies and the origins of liberal education*, Berkeley.

Blum, J. (2015) 'The language of uncertainty: genre, tradition, and literary *imagines* in the *Argonautica* of Valerius Flaccus', unpublished PhD dissertation, Yale University.

Boatwright, M. T. (2000) *Hadrian and the cities of the Roman Empire*, Princeton.

Boccuto, G. (1990) 'Sulle idee retoriche di Plinio il Giovane' in *La fortuna e opere di Plinio il Giovane. Atti del convegno internazionale di studi* (Città di Castello/San Giustino), 111–37.

    (1991) 'Plinio *Ep.* VII, 9, 11. Un affermazione letteraria in distici elegiaci', *A&R* 36, 26–36.

Bodel, J. (1995) 'Minicia Marcella: taken before her time', *AJP* 116, 453–60.

    (2015) 'The publication of Pliny's letters' in Marchesi 2015a, 13–109.

Bonfante, P., C. Fadda, C. Ferrini, S. Riccobono and V. Scialoja, eds. (1918–31) *Digesta Iustiniani Augusti*, Milan.

Bourdieu, P. (1993) *Sozialer Sinn. Kritik der theoretischen Vernunft* (trans. of *Le sens pratique*, Paris 1980), Frankfurt am Main.

Bourke, G. F. (2014) 'How to create the ideal son: the unhidden curriculum in pseudo-Plutarch *On the training of children*', *Educational Philosophy and Theory* 46, 1174–86.

Bowditch, P. (2001) *Horace and the gift economy of patronage*, Berkeley.

Bowersock, G. (1993) 'Tacitus and the province of Asia' in Luce and Woodman 1993, 1–10.

Bowie, E. (1990) 'Greek poetry in the Antonine age' in Russell 1990a, 53–90.

    (2002) 'Plutarch and literary activity in Achaea: AD 107–117' in Stadter and Van der Stockt 2002, 41–56.

    (2013) 'Libraries for the Caesars' in König, Oikonomopoulou and Woolf 2013, 237–60.

    (2014) 'Poetry and education' in Beck 2014, 177–90.

Bowie, M. N. R. (1989) 'Martial book XII: a commentary', unpublished DPhil dissertation, Oxford University.

Boyle, A. J., ed. (1995a) *Roman literature and ideology: Ramus essays for J. P. Sullivan*, Bendigo, Victoria.

(1995b) 'Martialis redivivus: evaluating the unexpected classic', *Ramus* 24, 82–101. Also in Boyle 1995a, 250–69.

(2003) 'Introduction: reading Flavian Rome' in Boyle and Dominik 2003, 1–67.

Boyle, A. J and W. J. Dominik, eds. (2003) *Flavian Rome: culture, image, text*, Leiden.

Bradley, K. R. (1991) *Discovering the Roman family: studies in Roman social history*, New York.

(1994) *Slavery and society at Rome*, Cambridge.

(1999) 'Images of childhood: the evidence of Plutarch' in S. B. Pomeroy, ed., *Plutarch's advice to the bride and groom, and a consolation to his wife* (New York), 183–96.

Bramble, J. C. (1982) 'Martial and Juvenal' in E. J. Kenney, ed., *The Cambridge history of classical literature* (Cambridge), II, 597–623.

Braund, D. (2013) 'Apollo in arms: Nero at the frontier' in Buckley and Dinter 2013, 83–101.

Braund, S. M. (1996) *Juvenal: Satires book I*, Cambridge.

(1988) *Beyond anger: a study of Juvenal's third book of* Satires, Cambridge.

(1998) 'Praise and protreptic in early imperial panegyric: Cicero, Seneca, Pliny' in M. Whitby, ed., *The propaganda of power: the role of panegyric in late antiquity* (Leiden), 53–76. Reprinted in Rees 2012a, 85–108.

(2004) *Juvenal and Persius*, Cambridge, MA.

(2006) 'A tale of two cities: Statius, Thebes and Rome', *Phoenix* 60, 259–73.

Breed, B. W., C. Damon and A. Rossi, eds. (2010) *Citizens of discord: Rome and its civil wars*, Oxford.

Brink, C. O. (1989) 'Quintilian's *De causis corruptae eloquentiae* and Tacitus' *Dialogus de oratoribus*', *CQ* 39, 472–503.

(1993) 'History in the *Dialogus de oratoribus* and Tacitus the historian: a new approach to an old source', *Hermes* 121, 335–49

(1994) 'Can Tacitus' *Dialogus* be dated?', *HSCP* 96, 251–80.

Broughton, T. R. S. (1950) *The magistrates of the Roman Republic*, vol. I, New York.

Bruère, R. T. (1954) 'Tacitus and Pliny's *Panegyricus*', *CP* 49, 161–79.

Brunvand, J. (1983) *The vanishing hitchhiker: American urban legends and their meanings*, New York.

Buckland, W. W. (1908) *The Roman law of slavery: the condition of the slave in private law from Augustus to Justinian*, Cambridge.

Buckley, E. (2010) 'War-epic for a new era: Valerius Flaccus' *Argonautica*' in Kramer and Reitz 2010, 431–55.

Buckley, E. and M. T. Dinter, eds. (2013) *A companion to the Neronian age*, Malden, MA.

Buongiovanni, C. (2012) *Gli epigrammata longa del decimo libro di Marziale*, Pisa.

Burck, E. (1971) *Vom römischen Manierismus: Von der Dichtung der frühen römischen Kaiserzeit*, Darmstadt.

(1981) 'Epische Bestattungsszenen. Ein literarhistorischer Vergleich' in E. Lefèvre, ed., *Vom Menschenbild in der römischen Literatur. II* (Heidelberg), 429–87.

Burgess, A. (1989) *The devil's mode*, New York.

Burton, G. P. (2002) 'The Roman imperial state (AD 14–235): evidence and reality', *Chiron* 32, 249–80.

Buszard, B. (2005) 'The decline of Roman statesmanship in Plutarch's *Pyrrhus–Marius*', *CQ* 55, 481–97.

Bütler, H.-P. (1970) *Die geistige Welt des jüngeren Plinius*, Heidelberg.

Buttrey, T. V. (2007) 'Domitian, the rhinoceros, and the date of Martial's *Liber de Spectaculis*', *JRS* 97, 101–12.

Cain, A. (2013) *Jerome and the monastic clergy: a commentary on Letter 52 to Nepotian*, Leiden.

Cambier, G. (1969) 'Recherches chronologiques sur l'oeuvre et la vie de Valerius Flaccus' in J. Bibauw, ed., *Hommages à M. Renard* (Brussels), 1, 191–228.

Cameron, A. D. E. (2010) *The last pagans of Rome*, New York.
(2016) 'The fate of Pliny's *Letters* in the late Empire' in Gibson and Whitton 2016, 463–81.

Camodeca, G. (2007) 'Il giurista L. Neratius Priscus *cos. suff.* 97: nuovi dati su carriera e famiglia', *Studia et documenta historiae et iuris* 73, 291–311.

Campbell, B. (2000) *The writings of the Roman land surveyors*, London.

Campbell, D. A. (1988) *Greek lyric*, vol. II: *Anacreon, Anacreontea, choral lyric from Olympus to Alcman*, Cambridge, MA.

Canobbio, A. (2011) *M. Valerii Martialis Epigrammaton liber quintus*, Naples.

Carlon, J. M. (2009) *Pliny's women: constructing virtue and creating identity in the Roman world*, Cambridge.

Carratello, U. (1981) *M. Valerii Martialis Epigrammaton liber quintus. Introduzione e testo critico*, Rome.

Caruth, C., ed. (1995) *Trauma. Explorations in memory*, Baltimore.

Casali, S. (2011) 'The *Bellum civile* as an anti-*Aeneid*' in Asso 2011, 81–110.

Castagna, L. and E. Lefèvre, eds. (2003) *Plinius der Jüngere und seine Zeit*, Munich and Leipzig.

Cataneus, I. M. (G. M. Cattaneo) (1506) *C. Plinii Caecilii Secundi Epistolarum libri novem . . . cum enarrationibus*, Milan.

Champlin, E. (1991) *Final judgments: duty and emotion in Roman wills, 200 BC – AD 250*, Berkeley.
(2001) 'Pliny's other country' in M. Peachin, ed., *Aspects of friendship in the Graeco-Roman world* (= *JRA* Suppl. 42) (Portsmouth, RI), 121–8. Reprinted with addendum in Gibson and Whitton 2016, 107–20.

Chaplin, J. (2000) *Livy's exemplary history*, Oxford.
(2013) 'Alluding to reality: towards a typology of historiographical intertextuality', *Histos* working papers 2013.01.

Chapman, H. (2009) 'Josephus' in Feldherr 2009, 319–31.

Chinn, C. M. (2007) 'Before your very eyes: Pliny *Epistulae* 5.6 and the ancient theory of ekphrasis', *CP* 102, 265–80.

Christol, M. and T. Drew–Bear (2005) 'De Lepcis Magna à Aizanoi: Hesperus procurateur de Phrygie et l'administration des carrières de marbre' in J. Desmulliez and C. Hoët-van Cauwenberghe, eds., *Le monde romain à travers l'épigraphie: méthodes et pratiques* (Villeneuve-d'Ascq), 189–216.

Church, A. J. and W. J. Brodribb (1877) *The Agricola and Germany of Tacitus; and the Dialogue on oratory*, London.

Citroni, M. (1975) *M. Valerii Martialis Epigrammaton liber primus*, Florence.

Cizek, A. N. (1994) *Imitatio et tractatio. Die literarisch-rhetorischen Grundlagen der Nachahmung in Antike und Mittelalter*, Tübingen.

Clarke, K. (2001) 'An island nation: re-reading Tacitus' *Agricola*', *JRS* 91, 94–112.

(2015) 'Putting up pyramids, characterizing kings' in R. Ash, J. M. Mossman and F. Titchener, eds., *Fame and infamy: essays for Christopher Pelling on characterization in Greek and Roman biography and historiography* (Oxford), 37–51.

Clausen, W. V. (1992) *A. Persi Flacci et D. Iuni Iuvenalis Saturae*, 2nd edn, Oxford.

Clauss, J. J. (1997) '"Domestici hostes": the Nausicaa in Medea, the Catiline in Hannibal', *MD* 39, 165–85.

Clayton, J. and E. Rothstein (1991) 'Figures in the corpus: theories of influence and intertextuality' in J. Clayton and E. Rothstein, eds., *Influence and intertextuality in literary history* (Madison, WI), 3–36.

Coarelli, F. (2000) *The column of Trajan*, Rome.

Coffee, N. (2009) *The commerce of war: exchange and social order in Latin epic*, Chicago.

Coleman, K. M. (1990) 'Fatal charades: Roman executions staged as mythological enactments', *JRS* 80, 44–73.

(1998) 'Martial Book 8 and the politics of AD 93', *PLLS* 10, 337–57.

(2000) 'Latin literature after AD 96: change or continuity?', *AJAH* 15, 19–39.

(2006) *Martial: Liber spectaculorum*, Oxford.

(2012) 'Bureaucratic language in the correspondence between Pliny and Trajan', *TAPA* 142, 189–238.

Coleridge, S. T. (1817) *Biographia literaria, or, Biographical sketches of my literary life and opinions*, 2 vols., London.

Collins, A. W. (2009) 'The palace revolution: the assassination of Domitian and the accession of Nerva', *Phoenix* 63, 73–106.

Colson, F. H. (1924) *M. Fabii Quintiliani Institutionis oratoriae liber 1*, Cambridge.

Colton, R. E. (1979) 'Children in Juvenal and Martial', *CB* 56, 1–3.

(1991) *Juvenal's use of Martial's epigrams: a study of literary influence*, Amsterdam.

Connolly, J. (2001) 'Problems of the past in imperial Greek education' in Y. L. Too, ed., *Education in Greek and Roman antiquity* (Leiden), 339–72.

Connors, C. (2005) 'Epic allusion in Roman satire' in Freudenburg 2005b, 123–45.

Conte, G. B. (1974) *Memoria dei poeti e sistema letterario. Catullo, Virgilio, Ovidio, Lucano*, Turin.

(1986) *The rhetoric of imitation: genre and poetic memory in Virgil and other Latin poets* (trans. and ed. C. Segal), Ithaca, NY.

(1994) *Latin literature: a history* (trans. J. B. Solodow; rev. D. Fowler and G. W. Most), Baltimore.

Corn, A. M. (1992) '"Thus nature ordains": Juvenal's fourteenth Satire', *ICS* 17, 309–22.

Cornell, T. J. (2013) 'The citing authorities. 4.2 Individual sources: Suetonius' in T. J. Cornell, ed., *The fragments of the Roman historians* (Oxford), 1, 125–9.

Cortius, G. (G. Kortte) and P. D. Longolius (1734) *Caii Plinii Caecilii Secundi Epistolarum libros decem cum notis selectis . . .*, Amsterdam.

Coudry, M. and T. Spaeth, eds. (2001) *L'invention des grands hommes de la Rome antique*, Paris.

Courtney, E. (1980) *A commentary on the Satires of Juvenal*, London.

Cousin, J. (1936) *Études sur Quintilien*, vol. II: *Vocabulaire grec de la terminologie rhétorique dans l'Institution oratoire*, Paris.

Cova, P. V. (1966) *La critica letteraria di Plinio il Giovane*, Brescia.

(1975) 'Contributo allo studio della lettera pliniana sulla storia', *RCCM* 17, 117–39.

(2003) 'Plinio il Giovane contro Quintiliano' in Castagna and Lefèvre 2003, 83–94.

Cowan, B. (2013) 'Fear and loathing in Lucretius: latent tragedy and anti-allusion in *DRN* 3' in T. D. Papanghelis, S. J. Harrison and S. Frangoulidis, eds., *Generic interfaces in Latin literature: encounters, interactions and transformations* (Berlin), 113–34.

Craca, C. (2011) *Dalla Spagna. Gli epigrammi 1–33 del XII libro di Marziale*, Bari.

Cugusi, P. (2003) 'Qualche riflessione sulle idee retoriche di Plinio il Giovane: *Epistulae* 1,20 e 9,26' in Castagna and Lefèvre 2003, 95–122.

Cuomo, S. (2000) 'Divide and rule: Frontinus and Roman land-surveying', *SHPS* 31, 189–202.

Curchin, L. A. (2003) 'Whose hair wants cutting in Martial 12.18?', *RM* 146, 222–4.

Dalzell, A. (1955) 'C. Asinius Pollio and the early history of public recitation at Rome', *Hermathena* 86, 20–8.

Damon, C. (1997) *The mask of a parasite: a pathology of Roman patronage*, Ann Arbor.

(2003) *Tacitus: Histories book I*, Cambridge.

(2010) 'Déjà vu or déjà lu? History as intertext', *PLLS* 14, 375–88.

Damschen, G. and A. Heil, eds. (2010) *Marcus Valerius Martialis. Epigrammaton liber decimus / Das zehnte Epigrammbuch. Text, Übersetzung, Interpretationen*, Frankfurt am Main.

Darwall-Smith, R. H. (1996) *Emperors and architecture: a study of Flavian Rome*, Brussels.

de Blois, L. (1986) 'The Εἰς Βασιλέα of ps.-Aristides', *GRBS* 27, 279–88.

Dederich, A. (1839) 'Bruchstücke aus dem Leben des Sex. Julius Frontinus', *Zeitschrift für die Alterthumswissenschaft* 6, 833–55 and 1077–94.

DeLaine, J. (1995) '"De aquis suis"? The "commentarius" of Frontinus' in Nicolet 1995, 117–45.

Del Chicca, F. (1995) 'Struttura e composizione del "De aquae ductu" di Frontino', *Orpheus* 16, 41–58.

Delignon, B. (2008) 'Pourquoi commencer et comment finir? Contraintes et libertés poétiques et politiques dans la satire de Juvénal et dans l'épigramme de Martial' in B. Bureau and C. Nicolas, eds., *Commencer et finir. Débuts et fins dans les littératures grecque, latine et néolatine* (Paris), ii, 445–64.

Delvigo, M. L. (1990) '*L'emendatio* del filologo, del critico, dell'autore: tre modi di correggere il testo?', *MD* 24, 71–110.

Derrida, J. (1976) *Of grammatology* (trans. G. C. Spivak), Baltimore.

(1978) *Writing and difference* (trans. A. Bass), London.

Devillers, O., ed. (2015) *Autour de Pline le Jeune: en hommage à Nicole Méthy*, Bordeaux.

Dewar, M. (1994) 'Laying it on with a trowel: the proem to Lucan and related texts', *CQ* 44, 199–211.

(1998) 'The equine cuckoo: Statius' *Ecus maximus Domitiani imperatoris* and the Flavian forum' in J. J. L. Smolenaars, H.-J. van Dam and R. Nauta, eds., *The poetry of Statius* (Leiden), 65–83.

Dickey, E. (2002) *Latin forms of address: from Plautus to Apuleius*, Oxford.

Dienel, R. (1915) 'Quintilian und der Rednerdialog des Tacitus', *WS* 37, 239–71.

Diggle, J. and F. R. D. Goodyear, eds. (1972) *The classical papers of A. E. Housman*, vol. ii: *1897–1914*, Cambridge.

Dillon, J. (2014) 'Plutarch and Platonism' in Beck 2014, 61–72.

Dinter, M. T. (2013a) 'Intermediality in Latin epic' in H. Lovatt and C. Vout, eds., *Epic visions: visuality in Greek and Latin epic and its reception* (Cambridge), 122–38.

(2013b) 'The Neronian (literary) renaissance' in Buckley and Dinter 2013, 1–14.

Dix, T. K. (1996) 'Pliny's library at Comum', *Libraries and Culture* 31, 85–102.

Dix, T. K and G. W. Houston (2006) 'Public libraries in the city of Rome from the Augustan age to the time of Diocletian', *MÉFRA* 118, 671–717.

Dolansky, F. (2011). 'Celebrating the Saturnalia: religious ritual and Roman domestic life' in B. Rawson, ed., *A companion to families in the Greek and Roman worlds* (Malden, MA), 488–503.

Dolç, M. (1953) *Hispania y Marcial*, Barcelona.

Dominik, W. J. (1994) *The mythic voice of Statius: power and politics in the* Thebaid, Leiden.

(2007) 'Tacitus and Pliny on oratory' in W. J. Dominik and J. Hall, eds., *A companion to Roman rhetoric* (Malden, MA), 323–38.

Dominik, W. J., J. Garthwaite and P. A. Roche, eds. (2009) *Writing politics in imperial Rome*, Leiden.

Doody, A. (2011) 'The science and aesthetics of names in the *Natural history*' in R. K. Gibson and R. Morello, eds., *Pliny the Elder: themes and contexts* (Leiden), 187–205.

Doody, A., S. Föllinger and L. Taub (2012) *Structures and strategies in ancient Greek and Roman technical writing* = *Studies in History and Philosophy of Science*, special issue 43.2.

Döpp, S. 1985. 'Cicero-Rezeption bei Quintilian am Beispiel von inst. orat. 12,2,23–26', *WS* 98, 159–71.

Doulamis, K., ed. (2011) *Echoing narratives: studies of intertextuality in Greek and Roman prose fiction*, Groningen.

Dozier, C. (2014) 'Quintilian's *ratio discendi* (*Institutio* 12.8) and the rhetorical dimension of the *Institutio oratoria*', *Arethusa* 47, 71–88.

(2015) 'Innovative invective: strength and weakness in Horace's *Epodes* and Quintilian's *Institutio oratoria*', *AJP* 136, 313–52.

Dufallo, B. (2007) *The ghosts of the past: Latin literature, the dead, and Rome's transition to a principate*, Ohio.

Duff, J. D. (1928) *Lucan: the Civil war (Pharsalia)*, Cambridge, MA.

Duff, T. E. (1999) *Plutarch's Lives: exploring virtue and vice*, Oxford.

(2008) 'Models of education in Plutarch', *JHS* 128, 1–26.

Dupont, F. (1997) '*Recitatio* and the space of public discourse' in T. Habinek and A. Schiesaro, eds., *The Roman cultural revolution* (Cambridge), 44–59.

Durry, M. (1938) *Pline le Jeune. Panégyrique de Trajan*, Paris.

Eck, W. (1980) 'Epigraphische Untersuchungen zu Konsuln und Senatoren des 1.–3. Jh. n. Chr.', *ZPE* 37, 31–68.

(1982) 'Die Gestalt Frontins in ihrer politischen und sozialen Umwelt' in *Wasserversorgung im antiken Rom. I: Sextus Iulius Frontinus, curator aquarum* (Munich), 47–62.

(1993) 'Ein Militärdiplom trajanischer Zeit', *Kölner Jahrbuch* 26, 445–50.

(2002a) 'An emperor is made: senatorial politics and Trajan's adoption by Nerva in 97' in G. Clark and T. Rajak, eds., *Philosophy and power in the Graeco-Roman world: essays in honour of Miriam Griffin* (Oxford), 211–26.

(2002b) 'Verginius II.1. L.V. Rufus', *Der Neue Pauly* 12/2 (Stuttgart), 63–4.

Eden, P. T. (1990) 'Problems in Martial III', *Mnemosyne* 43, 160–4.

Edmunds, L. (2001) *Intertextuality and the reading of Roman poetry*, Baltimore.

Edwards, C. (1997) 'Self-scrutiny and self-transformation in Seneca's *Letters*', *G&R* 44, 23–38. Reprinted in J. G. Fitch, ed., *Seneca* (Oxford Readings in Classical Studies) (Oxford, 2008), 84–101.

(2007) *Death in ancient Rome*, Cambridge.

Edwards, R. (2008) 'Hunting for boars with Tacitus and Pliny', *CA* 27, 35–58.

(2012) '*Devotio*, disease, and *remedia* in the *Histories*' in Pagán 2012b, 237–59.

Ehlers, W.-W. (1980) *Gai Valeri Flacci Argonauticon libri octo*, Leipzig.

Eich, P. (2005) *Zur Metamorphose des politischen Systems in der römischen Kaiserzeit. Die Entstehung einer 'personalen Bürokratie' im langen dritten Jahrhundert*, Berlin.

Elliott, J. (2015) 'The epic vantage-point: Roman historiographical allusion reconsidered', *Histos* 9, 277–311.

Ellmann, R. (1982) *James Joyce*, rev. edn, Oxford.

Elsner, J. (1998) *Imperial Rome and Christian triumph*, Oxford.

(2003) 'Iconoclasm and the preservation of memory' in R. S. Nelson and M. Olin, eds., *Monuments and memory, made and unmade* (Chicago), 209–31.

(2007) *Roman eyes: visuality and subjectivity in art and text*, Princeton.

Epplett, C. (2001) 'The capture of animals by the Roman military', *G&R* 48, 210–22.

Erll, A. (2009) 'Remembering across time, space and cultures: premediation, remediation and the "Indian mutiny"', in Erll and Rigney 2009, 109–38.

Erll, A. and A. Rigney, eds. (2009) *Mediation, remediation, and the dynamics of cultural memory*, Berlin.

Eshleman, K. (2012) *The social world of intellectuals in the Roman Empire: sophists, philosophers and Christians*, Cambridge.

Evans, H. B. (1994) *Water distribution in ancient Rome: the evidence of Frontinus*, Ann Arbor.

Evans, R. (2003a) 'Searching for paradise: landscape, utopia, and Rome', *Arethusa* 36, 285–307.

(2003b) 'Containment and corruption: the discourse of Flavian Empire', in Boyle and Dominik 2003, 255–76.

Fabbrini, D. (2007) *Il migliore dei mondi possibili. Gli epigrammi ecfrastici di Marziale per amici e protettori*, Florence.

Fantham, E. (1972) *Comparative studies in republican Latin imagery*, Toronto.

(1990) '*Nymphas . . . e navibus esse*: decorum and poetic fiction in *Aeneid* 9.77–122 and 10.215–59', *CP* 85, 102–18.

(1999) 'Two levels of orality in the genesis of Pliny's *Panegyricus*' in E. A. Mackay, ed., *Signs of orality: the oral tradition and its influence in the Greek and Roman world* (Leiden), 221–37.

Farrell, J. (2013) 'Camillus in Ovid's *Fasti*' in J. Farrell and D. P. Nelis, eds., *Augustan poetry and the Roman Republic* (Oxford), 57–88.

Fearnley, H. (2003) 'Reading the imperial revolution: Martial, *Epigrams* 10' in Boyle and Dominik 2003, 613–35.

Fedeli, P. (1989) 'Il "Panegirico" di Plinio nella critica moderna', *ANRW* ii.33.1, 387–514.

Feeney, D. C. (1991) *The gods in epic: poets and critics of the classical tradition*, Oxford.

Fein, S. (1994) *Die Beziehungen der Kaiser Trajan und Hadrian zu den litterati*, Stuttgart.

Feldherr, A., ed. (2009) *The Cambridge companion to the Roman historians*, Cambridge.

(2013) 'Free spirits: Sallust and the citation of Catiline', *AJP* 134: 49–66.

Ferguson, J. (1979) *Juvenal: the Satires*, Basingstoke.

Ferrill, A. (1965) 'Otho, Vitellius and the propaganda of Vespasian', *CJ* 60, 267–9.

Finkelpearl, E. D. (1998) *Metamorphosis of language in Apuleius: a study of allusion in the novel*, Ann Arbor.

Fitzgerald, W. (2007) *Martial: the world of epigram*, Chicago.

Flower, H. I. (2006) *The art of forgetting: disgrace and oblivion in Roman political culture*, Chapel Hill, NC.

Fögen, T. (2009) *Wissen, Kommunikation und Selbstdarstellung: Zur Struktur und Charakteristik römischer Fachtexte der frühen Kaiserzeit*, Munich.

Formisano, M. (2001) *Tecnica e scrittura: le letterature tecnico-scientifiche nello spazio letterario tardolatino*, Rome.

Formisano, M. and P. van der Eijk, eds. (2017) *Knowledge, text and practice in ancient technical writing*, Cambridge.

Foucault, M. (1986) *The care of the self. The history of sexuality*, vol. III (trans. R. Hurley, from *Le souci de soi*, Paris, 1984), New York.

   (1989) *Die Sorge um sich. Sexualität und Wahrheit* 3 (trans. U. Raulff and W. Seitter, from *Le souci de soi*, Paris, 1984), Frankfurt.

   (2005) *Dits et écrits. Schriften*, vol. IV: *1980–1988* (trans. M. Bischoff et al., from *Dits et écrits 4, 1980–1988*, Paris 1994), Frankfurt.

Fowler, D. P. (1995) 'Martial and the book' in Boyle 1995a, 199–226. Also in *Ramus* 24, 31–58.

   (1997) 'On the shoulders of giants: intertextuality and classical studies', *MD* 39, 13–34. Also in D. P. Fowler, *Roman constructions: readings in postmodern Latin* (Oxford, 2000), 115–37.

Fowler, H. N. (1936) *Plutarch: Moralia*, vol. X, Cambridge, MA.

Fraenkel, E. (1964) *Kleine Beiträge II*, Rome.

Freudenburg, K. (2001) *Satires of Rome: threatening poses from Lucilius to Juvenal*, Cambridge.

   (2005a) 'Making epic silver: the alchemy of imperial satire' in M. Paschalis, ed., *Roman and Greek imperial epic* (Rethymnon), 77–89.

   ed. (2005b) *The Cambridge companion to Roman satire*, Cambridge.

Friedländer, L. (1886) *M. Valerii Martialis Epigrammaton libri. Mit erklärenden Anmerkungen*, Leipzig.

   (1895) *D. Iunii Iuvenalis Saturarum libri V. Mit erklärenden Anmerkungen*, Leipzig.

Fucecchi, M. (2006) *Una guerra in Colchide. Valerio Flacco, Argonautiche 6,1–426*, Pisa.

Fürst, A., T. Fuhrer, F. Siegert and P. Walter, eds. (2006) *Der apokryphe Briefwechsel zwischen Seneca und Paulus*, Tübingen.

Galán Vioque, G. (2002) *Martial, Book VII: a commentary*, Leiden.

Galimberti, A. (2016) 'The emperor Domitian' in Zissos 2016, 92–108.

Garthwaite, J. (1990) 'Martial, Book 6, on Domitian's moral censorship', *Prudentia* 22, 13–22.

   (1993) 'The panegyrics of Domitian in Martial Book 9', *Ramus* 22, 78–102.

   (1998) 'Putting a price on praise: Martial's debate with Domitian in Book 5' in Grewing 1998, 157–72.

   (2009) '*Ludimus innocui*: interpreting Martial's imperial epigrams' in Dominik, Garthwaite and Roche 2009, 405–27.

Gazich, R. (2003) 'Retorica dell'esemplarità nelle lettere di Plinio' in Castagna and Lefèvre 2003, 123–41.

Geisthardt, J. M. (2015) *Zwischen Princeps und Res Publica: Tacitus, Plinius und die senatorische Selbstdarstellung in der Hohen Kaiserzeit*, Stuttgart.

Gellérfi, G. (2013a) 'Quintilian's influence on Juvenal's Satire 1', *Acta Antiqua Academiae Scientiarum Hungaricae* 53, 165–71.

   (2013b) 'The *Institutes of oratory* as inspiration and source for Juvenal', *Graeco-Latina Brunensia* 18, 85–93.

Gesner, J. M. (1738) *M. Fabii Quinctiliani De institutione oratoria libri duodecim*, 2 vols., Göttingen.

Geue, T. A. (2012) 'Satirist without qualities: Juvenal and the poetics of anonymity', unpublished PhD dissertation, Cambridge University.

(2017) *Juvenal and the poetics of anonymity*, Cambridge.

Geyssen, J. (1996) *Imperial panegyric in Statius: a literary commentary on* Silvae *1.1*, New York.

(1999) 'Sending a book to the Palatine: Martial 1.70 and Ovid', *Mnemosyne* 52, 718–38.

Gibson, B. J. (2010) 'Causation in post-Augustan epic' in Miller and Woodman 2010, 29–48.

(2011) 'Contemporary contexts' in Roche 2011, 104–24.

Gibson, R. K. (2003) 'Pliny and the art of (in)offensive self-praise' in Gibson and Morello 2003, 235–54.

(2013) 'Reading the letters of Sidonius by the book' in van Waarden and Kelly 2013, 195–219.

(2014) 'Suetonius and the *uiri illustres* of Pliny the Younger' in Power and Gibson 2014, 199–230.

(2015) 'Not dark yet: reading to the end of the nine-book collection' in Marchesi 2015a, 185–222.

(forthcoming) *Pliny the Younger: Epistles book VI*, Cambridge.

Gibson, R. K. and R. Morello, eds. (2003) *Re-imagining Pliny the Younger* (= *Arethusa* 36.2), Baltimore

(2012) *Reading the letters of Pliny the Younger: an introduction*, Cambridge.

Gibson, R. K. and A. D. Morrison (2007) 'What is a letter?' in Morello and Morrison 2007, 1–16.

Gibson, R. K. and C. L. Whitton, eds. (2016) *The* Epistles *of Pliny* (Oxford Readings in Classical Studies), Oxford.

Gierig, G. E. (1800–2) *C. Plinii Caecilii Secundi Epistolarum libri decem*, 2 vols., Leipzig.

Giua, M. A., ed. (2007) *Ripensando Tacito (e Ronald Syme): storia e storiografia*, Pisa.

Giuliani, C. F. and M. Guaitoli (1972) 'Il Ninfeo Minore della Villa detta di Cicerone a Formia', *MDAI(R)* 79, 191–219.

Giuliani, L. (2003) *Bild und Mythos. Geschichte der Bilderzählung in der griechischen Kunst*, Munich.

Gold, B. K. (2012) 'Juvenal: the idea of the book' in S. Braund and J. Osgood, eds., *A companion to Persius and Juvenal* (Malden, MA), 97–112.

Goldberg, S. M. (1999) 'Appreciating Aper: the defence of modernity in Tacitus' *Dialogus de oratoribus*', *CQ* 49, 224–37

González Rolán, T. (1985) *Los acueductos de Roma*, Madrid.

Goodyear, F. R. D. (1981) *The Annals of Tacitus*, vol. ii: *Annals 1.55–81 and Annals 2*, Cambridge.

Gowers, E. (1993) *The loaded table: representations of food in Roman literature*, Oxford.

Gowing, A. M. (2005) *Empire and memory: the representation of the Roman Republic in imperial culture*, Cambridge.

(2009) 'The Roman *exempla* tradition in imperial Greek historiography: the case of Camillus' in Feldherr 2009, 332–47.

Grainger, J. D. (2003) *Nerva and the Roman succession crisis of AD 96–99*, London.

Greenwood, M. A. P. (1998) 'Talking flamingos and the sins of the tongue: the ambiguous use of *lingua* in Martial', *CP* 93, 241–6.

Grewing, F., ed. (1998) *Toto notus in orbe: Perspektiven der Martial-Interpretation*, Stuttgart.

Gries, R. 2006. 'Sammelrezension: SPIEGEL-Titelbilder' (review of S. Aust and S. Kiefer, eds., *Die Kunst des SPIEGEL: Titel-Illustrationen aus fünf Jahrzehnten*, Kempen 2004, and of H.-D. Schütt and O. Schwarzkopf, eds., *Die SPIEGEL-Titelbilder 1947–1999*, Berlin 2000), *H-Soz-Kult* 28.3.06.

Griffin, M. T. (1999) 'Pliny and Tacitus', *SCI* 18, 139–58. Reprinted in Gibson and Whitton 2016, 355–77.

(2000) 'Nerva to Hadrian' in A. K. Bowman, P. Garnsey and D. Rathbone, eds., *The Cambridge ancient history*, vol. XI: *The High Empire, AD 70–192*, 2nd edn (Cambridge), 84–132.

(2002) *Nero: the end of a dynasty*, New York.

(2007) 'The Elder Pliny on philosophers' in E. Bispham, G. Rowe and E. Matthews, eds., *Vita vigilia est: essays in honour of Barbara Levick* (London), 85–102.

Grimal, P. (1944) *Les aqueducs de la ville de Rome, Frontin*, Paris.

(1960) 'L'éloge de Néron au début de la Pharsale est-il ironique?', *RÉL* 38, 296–305.

Grosso, F. (1954) 'Aspetti della politica orientale di Domiziano', *Epigraphica* 16, 117–79.

Gruenwald, E. (1883) *Quae ratio intercedere videatur inter Quintiliani institutionem oratoriam et Taciti dialogum*, Berlin.

Gualandi, G. (1963) *Legislazione imperiale e giurisprudenza*, 2 vols., Milan.

Gudeman, A. (1914) *Tacitus. Dialogus de oratoribus*, 2nd edn, Leipzig.

Guerrini, R. (1981) *Studi su Valerio Massimo*, Pisa.

Guillemin, A.-M. (1929) *Pline et la vie littéraire de son temps*, Paris.

Gunderson, E. (2014) 'E.g. Augustus: *exemplum* in the *Augustus* and *Tiberius*' in Power and Gibson 2014, 130–45.

Güngerich, R. (1951) 'Der *Dialogus* des Tacitus und Quintilians *Institutio oratoria*', *CP* 46, 159–64. Reprinted in V. Pöschl, ed., *Tacitus* (Darmstadt, 1969), 349–60.

(1955) Review of Barwick 1954 and of E. Paratore, *Ancora del 'Dialogus de oratoribus'* (1954), *Gnomon* 27, 439–43.

(1980) *Kommentar zum Dialogus des Tacitus* (ed. H. Heubner), Göttingen.

Gurd, S. (2012) *Work in progress: literary revision as social performance in ancient Rome*, Oxford.

Habinek, T. (2000) 'Seneca's renown: *gloria*, *claritudo* and the replication of the Roman elite', *CA* 19, 264–303.

Halfmann, H. (1979) *Die Senatoren aus dem östlichen Teil des Imperium Romanum bis zum Ende des 2. Jh. n. Chr.*, Göttingen.

Hannestad, N. (1986) *Roman art and imperial policy*, Aarhus.

Hardie, A. (1997–8) 'Juvenal, Domitian, and the accession of Hadrian (*Satire* 4)', *BICS* 42, 117–44.

Hardie, P. R. (1994) *Virgil: Aeneid book IX*, Cambridge.

   ed. (2009) *Paradox and the marvellous in Augustan literature and culture*, Oxford.

   (2010) 'Crowds and leaders in imperial historiography and in epic' in Miller and Woodman 2010, 11–17.

   (2012) *Rumour and renown: representations of Fama in western literature*, Cambridge.

Harries, J. (2013a) 'The senatus consultum Silanianum: court decisions and judicial severity in the early Roman Empire' in P. du Plessis, ed., *New frontiers: law and society in the Roman world* (Edinburgh), 51–70.

   (2013b) 'Roman law from city state to world empire' in J. Duindam, J. Harries, C. Humfress and N. Hurvitz, eds., *Law and empire: ideas, practices, actors* (Leiden), 45–62.

Harrison, S. J. (2007a) 'Town and country' in S. J. Harrison, ed., *The Cambridge companion to Horace* (Cambridge), 235–47.

   (2007b) 'From man to book: the closure of Tacitus' *Agricola*' in Heyworth, Fowler and Harrison 2007, 310–19.

   (2013) *Framing the ass: literary form in Apuleius'* Metamorphoses, Oxford.

Hass-von Reitzenstein, U. (1970) *Beiträge zur gattungsgeschichtlichen Interpretation des Dialogus 'de oratoribus'*, Cologne.

Häußler, R. (1986) 'Aktuelle Probleme der Dialogus-Rezeption: Echtheitserweise und Lückenumfang. Eine Zwischenbilanz', *Philologus* 130, 69–95.

Haynes, H. (2003) *The history of make-believe: Tacitus on imperial Rome*, Berkeley.

Hedrick, C. W., Jr (2000) *History and silence: the purge and rehabilitation of memory in late antiquity*, Austin, TX.

Heil, A. (2004) 'Epigramm 12: Wahre Freundschaft' in Damschen and Heil 2010, 77–9.

Heldmann, K. (1980) 'Dekadenz und literarischer Fortschritt bei Quintilian und bei Tacitus. Ein Beitrag zum römischen Klassizismus', *Poetica* 12, 1–12.

Hembold, W. C. (1939) *Plutarch: Moralia*, vol. VI, Cambridge, MA.

Henderson, Jeffrey (2010) 'The *Satyrica* and the Greek novel: revisions and some open questions', *IJCT* 17, 483–96.

Henderson, John (1991) 'Statius' *Thebaid*: form pre-made', *PCPS* 37, 30–79. Revised version in J. Henderson, *Fighting for Rome* (Oxford, 1998), 212–54.

   (1995) 'Pump up the volume: Juvenal, *Satires* 1.1–21', *PCPS* 41, 101–37. Revised version in J. Henderson, *Writing down Rome* (Oxford, 1999), 249–73.

   (2001) 'On Pliny on Martial on Pliny on anon . . . (*Epistles* 3.21/*Epigrams* 10.19)', *Ramus* 30, 56–87.

   (2002) *Pliny's statue: the* Letters, *self-portraiture and classical art*, Exeter.

   (2004) *Morals and villas in Seneca's* Letters: *places to dwell*, Cambridge.

(2010) 'AI-ZYTHUM: DOMIMINA NUSTIO ILLUMEA, or out with the O.L.D. (1931–82)' in C. Stray, ed., *Classical dictionaries: past, present and future* (London), 138–75.

(2011) 'Down the Pan: historical exemplarity in the *Panegyricus*' in Roche 2011, 142–74.

Henriksén, C. (1998) 'Martial und Statius' in Grewing 1998, 77–117.

(2012) *A commentary on Martial, Epigrams Book 9*, Oxford.

Hershkowitz, D. (1998) *Valerius Flaccus' Argonautica: abbreviated voyages in silver Latin epic*, Oxford.

Heuvel, H. (1936–7) 'De inimicitiarum, quae inter Martialem et Statium fuisse dicuntur, indiciis', *Mnemosyne* 4, 299–330.

Heyworth, S. J., P. G. Fowler and S. J. Harrison, eds. (2007) *Classical constructions: papers in memory of Don Fowler, classicist and Epicurean*, Oxford.

Higgonet, M. R. (2009) 'Modernism and childhood: violence and renovation', *The Comparatist* 33, 86–108.

Highet, G. (1949) 'The philosophy of Juvenal', *TAPA* 80, 254–70.

(1954) *Juvenal the satirist: a study*, Oxford.

Hinds, S. (1998) *Allusion and intertext: the dynamics of appropriation in Roman poetry*, Cambridge.

(2007) 'Martial's Ovid/Ovid's Martial', *JRS* 97, 113–54.

Hine, H. H. (2010) *Lucius Annaeus Seneca:* Natural questions, Chicago.

Hodkinson, O. (2007) 'Better than speech: some advantages of the letter in the Second Sophistic' in Morello and Morrison 2007, 283–300.

Hoffer, S. E. (1999) *The anxieties of Pliny the Younger*, Atlanta, GA.

(2016) 'Models of senators and emperors: Regulus, the bad senator (*Epistles* 1.5)' in Gibson and Whitton 2016, 289–331.

Holford-Strevens, L. (2003) *Aulus Gellius: an Antonine scholar and his achievement*, 2nd edn, Oxford.

Hollis, A. S. (1994) 'Statius' young Parthian king (*Thebaid* 8.286–93)', *G&R* 41, 205–12.

Holzberg, N. (2002) *Martial und das antike Epigramm*, Stuttgart.

(2004/5) 'Martial, the book and Ovid', *Hermathena* 177/8, 209–24.

Höschele, R. (2010) *Die blütenlesende Muse: Poetik und Textualität antiker Epigrammsammlungen*, Tübingen.

Houghton, L. B. T. (2007) 'A letter from Petrarch' in W. Fitzgerald and E. Gowers, eds., *Ennius perennis: the* Annals *and beyond* (Cambridge), 145–58.

Housman, A. E. (1907) 'Corrections and explanations of Martial', *Journal of Philology* 30, 229–65.

Howell, P. (1980) *A commentary on book one of the Epigrams of Martial*, London.

(1998) 'Martial's return to Spain' in Grewing 1998, 173–86.

Hueber, F. and V. M. Strocka (1975) 'Die Bibliothek des Celsus: Eine Prachtfassade in Ephesos und das Problem ihrer Wiederaufrichtung', *Antike Welt* 6.4, 3–14.

Hunink, V. (2004) '"SOLACIA MALI": examples of virtue in Tacitus' "Historiae"' in G. Partoens, G. Roskam and T. van Houdt, eds., *Virtutis imago: studies on the conceptualisation and transformation of an ancient ideal* (Leuven), 173–86.

Hunter, J. (2000) *Tom Stoppard: Rosencrantz and Guildenstern are dead, Jumpers, Travesties, Arcadia*, London.

Hurlet, F. (2006) *Le proconsul et le prince d'Auguste à Dioclétien*, Bordeaux.

(2016) 'Sources and evidence' in Zissos 2016, 17–39.

Hutchinson, G. O. (2011) 'Politics and the sublime in the *Panegyricus*' in Roche 2011, 125–41.

(2013) *Greek to Latin: frameworks and contexts for intertextuality*, Oxford.

Jacob, C. (2004) 'Questions sur les questions: archéologie d'une pratique intellectuelle et d'une forme discursive' in A. Voglers and C. Zamagni, eds., *Erotapokriseis: early Christian question and answer literature in context* (Leuven), 25–54.

Jacobs, J. (2010) 'From Sallust to Silius Italicus: *metus hostilis* and the fall of Rome in the *Punica*' in Miller and Woodman 2010, 123–39.

Jaeger, W. (1939) *Paideia: the ideas of Greek culture*, vol. 1 (trans. G. Highet), New York.

James, P. (2000) 'The language of dissent' in J. Huskinson, ed., *Experiencing Rome: culture, identity and power in the Roman Empire* (London), 277–303.

Janson, T. (1964) *Latin prose prefaces: studies in literary conventions*, Stockholm.

Jeffreys, R. L. (1987) 'The *infirmitas* of Messalla Corvinus', *Latomus* 46, 196–8.

Jenkyns, R. (1982) *Three classical poets: Sappho, Catullus and Juvenal*, London.

Johnson, W. A. (2010) *Readers and reading culture in the High Roman Empire: a study of elite communities*, Oxford.

(2013a) 'Libraries and reading culture in the High Empire' in König, Oikonomopoulou and Woolf 2013, 347–63.

(2013b) 'Pliny *Epistle* 9.36 and Demosthenes' cave', *CW* 106, 665–8.

Johnson, W. A. and H. N. Parker, eds. (2009) *Ancient literacies: the culture of reading in Greece and Rome*, Oxford.

Jones, B. F. (2015) 'The sophistic Roman: education and status in Quintilian, Tacitus and Pliny', unpublished PhD dissertation, University of Washington.

Jones, B. W. (1984) *The emperor Titus*, London.

(1992) *The emperor Domitian*, London.

(1996) *Suetonius: Domitian*, Bristol.

Jones, C. P. (1966) 'Towards a chronology of Plutarch's works', *JRS* 56, 61–74.

(1968) 'Iulius Naso and Iulius Secundus', *HSCP* 72, 279–88.

(1970) 'Sura and Senecio', *JRS* 60, 98–104.

(1971) *Plutarch and Rome*, Oxford.

(1972) 'Aelius Aristides, ΕΙΣ ΒΑΣΙΛΕΑ', *JRS* 62, 134–52.

(1978) *The Roman world of Dio Chrysostom*, Cambridge, MA.

Jones, F. (2007) *Juvenal and the satiric genre*, London.

Joseph, T. A. (2010) '*Ac rursus nova laborum facies*: Tacitus' repetitions of Virgil's wars at *Histories* 3.26–34' in Miller and Woodman 2010, 155–69.

(2012) *Tacitus the epic successor: Virgil, Lucan, and the narrative of civil war in the Histories*, Leiden.

Kappelmacher, A. (1916) 'Frontin in Martials Epigrammen', *WS* 38, 181–5.

Kapust, D. J. (2011) *Republicanism, rhetoric and Roman political thought*, Cambridge.

Kaster, R. A. (1995) *C. Suetonius Tranquillus: De grammaticis et rhetoribus*, Oxford.

Kay, N. M. (1985) *Martial book XI: a commentary*, London.

Keane, C. (2007) 'Philosophy into satire: the program of Juvenal's fifth book', *AJP* 128, 27–57.

(2012) 'Historian and satirist: Tacitus and Juvenal' in Pagán 2012b, 403–27.

(2015) *Juvenal and the satiric emotions*, New York.

Kechagia-Ovseiko, E. (2014) 'Plutarch and Epicureanism' in Beck 2014, 104–20.

Keeline, T. (2013) 'The literary and stylistic qualities of a Plinian letter: a commentary on Plin. *Ep.* 7.9', *HSCP* 107, 189–224.

Keitel, E. (1984) 'Principate and civil war in the *Annals* of Tacitus', *AJP* 105, 306–25.

Kelly, C. (2015) 'Pliny and Pacatus: past and present in imperial panegyric' in J. Wienand, ed., *Contested monarchy: integrating the Roman Empire in the fourth century AD* (Oxford), 215–38.

Kelly, G. (2008) *Ammianus Marcellinus: the allusive historian*, Cambridge.

Kelly, S. (2015) Review of Scurr 2015, *TLS* 27.02.15, 3–4.

Kemezis, A. (2014) *Greek narratives of the Roman Empire under the Severans: Cassius Dio, Philostratus and Herodian*, Cambridge.

(2016) 'Flavian Greek literature' in Zissos 2016, 450–6.

Kennedy, G. (1969) *Quintilian*, New York.

Ker, W. C. A. (1968) *Martial: Epigrams*, rev. edn, 3 vols., Cambridge, MA.

Kienast, D., W. Eck and M. Heil (2017) *Römische Kaisertabelle: Grundzüge einer römischen Kaiserchronologie*, 6th edn, Darmstadt.

Kleiner, D. E. E. (1992) *Roman sculpture*, New Haven, CT.

Kleywegt, A. J. (2005) *Valerius Flaccus*, Argonautica*, book I*, Leiden.

Klodt, C. (2015) 'Das Grabmal des Verginius Rufus (Plinius, epist. 2,1, 6,10 und 9,19)', *Gymnasium* 122, 339–87.

Köhnken, A. (1973) 'Das Problem der Ironie bei Tacitus', *MH* 30, 32–50.

Kolb, A. (2000) *Transport und Nachrichtentransfer im römischen Reich*, Berlin.

König, A. R. (2007) 'Knowledge and power in Frontinus' *On aqueducts*' in J. König and Whitmarsh 2007, 177–205.

(2013) 'Frontinus' cameo role in Tacitus' *Agricola*', *CQ* 63, 361–76.

(2017) 'Conflicting models of authority and expertise in Frontinus' *Strategemata*' in J. König and G. D. Woolf, eds., *Authority and expertise in ancient scientific culture* (Cambridge), 153–81.

(forthcoming) 'Reading civil war in Frontinus' *Strategemata*: a case-study for Flavian literary studies' in L. Ginsberg and D. Krasne, eds., *After 69 CE: writing civil war in Flavian Rome* (Berlin).

König, J. (2007) 'Fragmentation and coherence in Plutarch's *Sympotic questions*' in König and Whitmarsh 2007, 43–68.

(2011) 'Self-promotion and self-effacement in Plutarch's *Table talk*' in F. Klotz and K. Oikonomopoulou, eds., *The philosopher's banquet: Plutarch's* Table talk *in the intellectual culture of the Roman Empire* (Oxford), 179–203.

(forthcoming) 'Representations of intellectual community in Plutarch, Pliny the Younger and Aulus Gellius' in A. Andurand and C. Bonnet, eds., *La République 'gréco-romaine' des lettres: construction des réseaux savants et circulation des savoirs dans l'Empire romain*.

König, J., K. Oikonomopoulou and G. D. Woolf, eds. (2013) *Ancient libraries*, Cambridge.

König, J. and T. J. G. Whitmarsh, eds. (2007) *Ordering knowledge in the Roman Empire*, Cambridge.

König, J. and G. D. Woolf, eds. (2017) *Authority and expertise in ancient scientific culture*, Cambridge.

Kramer, N. and C. Reitz, eds. (2010) *Tradition und Erneuerung: Mediale Strategien in der Zeit der Flavier*, Berlin.

Kraus, C. S. (2005). 'From *exempla* to *exemplar*? Writing history around the emperor in imperial Rome' in J. Edmondson, S. Mason and J. Rives, eds. *Flavius Josephus and Flavian Rome* (Oxford), 181–200.

Kraus, C. S., J. Marincola and C. Pelling, eds. (2010) *Ancient historiography and its contexts: studies in honour of A. J. Woodman*, Oxford.

Kreilinger, U. (2004) 'Epigramm 30: Traumvilla mit Pferdefuß' in Damschen and Heil 2010, 131–5.

Kuhn, A. B. (2015) 'The dynamics of social status and prestige in Pliny, Juvenal and Martial' in A. B. Kuhn, ed., *Social status and prestige in the Graeco-Roman world* (Stuttgart), 9–28.

Laes, C. (2011) *Children in the Roman Empire: outsiders within*, Cambridge.

Laffi, U. (1971) 'I terreni del tempio di Zeus ad Aizanoi', *Athenaeum*, 49, 3–53.

Laird, A. (2007) 'The true nature of the *Satyricon*?' in M. Paschalis, S. Frangoulidis, S. Harrison and M. Zimmerman, eds., *The Greek and the Roman novel: parallel readings* (Groningen), 151–67.

Lana, I. (1973) *La teorizzazione della collaborazione degli intellettuali con il potere politico in Quintiliano*, Institutio oratoria, *libro XII*, Turin.

Lange, A. G. (1832) 'Dialogus de oratoribus Tacito vindicatus' in K. Jacob, ed., *Vermischte Schriften und Reden* (orig. 1811) (Leipzig), 3–14.

Langlands, R. (2008) '"Reading for the moral" in Valerius Maximus: the case of *severitas*', *CCJ* 54, 160–87.

(2011) 'Roman *exempla* and situation ethics: Valerius Maximus and Cicero *de Officiis*', *JRS* 101, 1–23.

(2014a) 'Pliny's "role models of both sexes": gender and exemplarity in the *Letters*', *Eugesta* 4, 214–37.

(2014b) 'Exemplary influences and Augustus' pernicious moral legacy' in Power and Gibson 2014, 111–29.

(2015) 'Roman exemplarity: mediating between general and particular' in Lowrie and Lüdemann 2015a, 68–80.

(forthcoming) *Exemplary ethics in ancient Rome*, Cambridge.

Langslow, D. (2007) 'The *epistula* in ancient scientific and technical literature, with special reference to medicine' in Morello and Morrison 2007, 211–34.

Larmour, D. H. J. (2016) *The arena of satire: Juvenal's search for Rome*, Norman, OK.

Lauletta, M. (1998) *L'intreccio degli stili in Tacito: intertestualità prosa-poesia nella letteratura storiografica*, Naples.

Lavan, M. (2011) 'Slavishness in Britain and Rome in Tacitus' *Agricola*', *CQ* 61, 294–305.

(2013a) 'Florus and Dio on the enslavement of the provinces', *CCJ* 59, 125–51.

(2013b) *Slaves to Rome: paradigms of empire in Roman culture*, Cambridge.

(2015) 'The new green-and-yellow of *Agricola*' (review of Woodman 2014), *Histos* 9, xxxix–xlv.

Leach, E. W. (1990) 'The politics of self-representation: Pliny's *Letters* and Roman portrait sculpture', *CA* 9, 14–39.

(2013) 'Pliny's epistolary re-inscription: writing the tombs of Verginius Rufus and Pallas the Claudian *a rationibus*', *Syllecta Classica* 24, 125–44.

Lefèvre, E. (1971) *Das Prooemium der Argonautica des Valerius Flaccus: Ein Beitrag zur Typik epischer Prooemien der römischen Kaiserzeit*, Wiesbaden.

(2009) *Vom Römertum zum Ästhetizismus: Studien zu den Briefen des jüngeren Plinius*, Berlin.

Leigh, M. (2007) 'Epic and historiography at Rome' in J. Marincola, ed., *A companion to Greek and Roman historiography* (Malden, MA), 11, 483–92.

Lenel, O. (1889) *Palingenesia iuris civilis*. Leipzig.

Levene, D. S. (2010) *Livy on the Hannibalic war*, Oxford.

Levick, B. (1999) *Vespasian*, London.

Lewis, J. D. (1879) *The Letters of the Younger Pliny*, London.

Liberman, G. (1997–2002) *Valerius Flaccus. Argonautiques*, 2 vols., Paris.

Liebeschuetz, H. J. W. G. (1979) *Continuity and change in Roman religion*, Oxford.

Lintott, A. (2010) 'Lucan and the history of the civil war' in C. Tesoriero, ed., *Lucan* (Oxford Readings in Classical Studies) (Oxford), 239–68. Originally published in *CQ* 21 (1971), 488–505.

Lipsius, J. (1598) *Admiranda sive De magnitudine romana libri quattuor*, Antwerp.

Lorenz, S. (2002) *Erotik und Panegyrik. Martials epigrammatische Kaiser*, Tübingen.

(2004) 'Waterscape with black and white: epigrams, cycles, and webs in Martial's *Epigrammaton liber quartus*', *AJP* 125, 255–78.

(2010) Review of Rimell 2008, *Gnomon* 82, 22–5.

(2014) 'Martial und Quintilian (Epigr. 2,90)', *Gymnasium* 121, 45–67.

Lowrie, M. (2007) 'Making an *exemplum* of yourself: Cicero and Augustus' in Heyworth, Fowler and Harrison 2007, 91–112.

(2008) 'Cornelia's exemplum: form and ideology in Propertius 4.11' in G. Liveley and P. Salzmann-Mitchell, eds., *Latin elegy and narratology: fragments of story* (Ohio), 165–79.

Lowrie, M. and S. Lüdemann, eds. (2015a) *Exemplarity and singularity: thinking through particulars in philosophy, literature and law*, London.

(2015b) 'Introduction' in Lowrie and Lüdemann 2015a, 1–15.

Luce, T. J. (1993) 'Reading and response in Tacitus' *Dialogus*', in Luce and Woodman 1993, 11–38.

Luce, T. J. and A. J. Woodman, eds. (1993) *Tacitus and the Tacitean tradition*, Princeton.

Ludolph, M. (1997) *Epistolographie und Selbstdarstellung: Untersuchungen zu den 'Paradebriefen' Plinius des Jüngeren*, Tübingen.

Lyons, J. D. (1989) *Exemplum: the rhetoric of example in early modern France and Italy*, Princeton.

Macrae, D. (2015) '*Invitus invitam*: a window allusion in Suetonius' *Titus*', *CQ* 65, 415–18.

Madsen, J. M. (2009) *Eager to be Roman: Greek response to Roman rule in Pontus and Bithynia*, London.

Malloch, S. J. V. (2013) *The Annals of Tacitus. Book 11*, Cambridge.

(2015) 'Frontinus and Domitian: the politics of the *Strategemata*', *Chiron* 45, 77–100.

Maltby, R. (2008) 'Verbal and thematic links between poems and books in Martial', *PLLS* 13, 255–68.

Manolaraki, E. (2008) 'Political and rhetorical seascapes in Pliny's *Panegyricus*', *CP* 103, 347–94.

Manolaraki, E. and A. Augoustakis (2012) 'Silius Italicus and Tacitus on the tragic hero: the case of Germanicus' in Pagán 2012b, 386–400.

Manuwald, G. (2007) *Cicero, Philippics 3–9: edited with introduction, translation and commentary*, 2 vols., Berlin.

Manuwald, G. and A. Voigt, eds. (2013) *Flavian epic interactions*, Berlin.

Marchesi, I. (2008) *The art of Pliny's Letters: a poetics of allusion in the private correspondence*, Cambridge.

(2013) 'Silenced intertext: Pliny on Martial on Pliny (on Regulus)', in Baraz and van den Berg 2013, 101–18.

ed. (2015a) *Pliny the book-maker: betting on posterity in the Epistles*, Oxford.

(2015b) 'Uncluttered spaces, unlittered texts: Pliny's villas as editorial places' in Marchesi 2015a, 223–51.

Marks, R. (2005) *From Republic to Empire. Scipio Africanus in the* Punica *of Silius Italicus*, Frankfurt.

Markus, D. (2000) 'Performing the book: the recital of epic in first-century CE Rome', *CA* 19, 138–79.

Martínez, J., ed. (2011) *Fakes and forgers of classical literature*, Madrid.

ed. (2014) *Fakes and forgers of classical literature: Ergo decipiatur!*, Leiden.

Mason, S. (2016a) 'Josephus as a Roman historian' in H. H. Chapman and Z. Rodgers, eds., *A companion to Josephus* (Malden, MA), 89–107.

(2016b) *A history of the Jewish War: AD 66–74*, Cambridge.

Masters, J. (1992) *Poetry and civil war in Lucan's* Bellum civile, Cambridge.

Mastrorosa, I. G. (2010) 'La pratica dell'oratoria giudiziaria nell'alto impero: Quintiliano e Plinio il Giovane' in P. Galand, F. Hallyn, C. Lévy and W. Verbaal, eds., *Quintilien ancien et moderne* (Turnhout), 125–52.

Mathisen, R. W. (1991) *Studies in the history, literature and society of late antiquity*, Amsterdam.

(2013) 'Dating the letters of Sidonius' in van Waarden and Kelly 2013, 221–48.

Mauss, M. (1990a) *The gift: the form and reason for exchange in archaic societies* (trans. W. D. Halls, from *Essai sur le don*, Paris 1925), London.

(1990b) *Die Gabe: Form und Funktion des Austauschs in archaischen Gesellschaften* (trans. E. Moldenhauer, from *Essai sur le don*, Paris 1925), Frankfurt am Main.

Mayer, R. G. (1991) 'Roman historical exempla in Seneca' in P. Grimal, ed., *Sénèque et la prose latine* (Geneva), 141–69.

(2001) *Tacitus: Dialogus de oratoribus*, Cambridge.

Mayor, J. E. B. (1881) *Thirteen satires of Juvenal*, 3rd edn, London.

McDonald, I. R. (1970) 'The Flavian epic poets as political and social critics', unpublished PhD dissertation, University of North Carolina at Chapel Hill.

McGing, B. C. (1982) 'Synkrisis in Tacitus' *Agricola*', *Hermathena* 132, 15–25.

McGuire, D. T. (1997) *Acts of silence: civil war, tyranny, and suicide in the Flavian epics*, Hildesheim.

McNelis, C. (2007) *Statius'* Thebaid *and the poetics of civil war*, Cambridge.

Meißner, B. (1999) *Die technologische Fachliteratur der Antike: Struktur, Überlieferung und Wirkung technischen Wissens in der Antike (ca. 400 v. Chr. – ca. 500 n. Chr.)*, Berlin.

Merli, E. (2006a) 'Identity and irony: Martial's tenth book, Horace, and the tradition of Roman satire' in Nauta, van Dam and Smolenaars 2006, 257–70.

(2006b) 'Martial between Rome and Bilbilis' in R. Rosen and I. Sluiter, eds., *City, countryside and the spatial organisation of value in classical antiquity* (Leiden), 327–47.

Merrill, E. (1903) *Selected letters of the Younger Pliny*, London.

Méthy, N. (2003) '*Ad exemplar antiquitatis*: les grandes figures du passé dans la correspondance de Pline le Jeune', *REL* 81, 200–14.

(2007) *Les lettres de Pline le Jeune. Une représentation de l'homme*, Paris.

(2009) 'Suétone vu par un contemporain: les débuts de l'historien dans la correspondance de Pline le Jeune', *Gerión* 27, 219–29.

Meyer-Zwiffelhoffer, E. (2003) Πολιτικῶς ἄρχειν: *Zum Regierungsstil der senatorischen Statthalter in den kaiserzeitlichen griechischen Provinzen*, Stuttgart.

ní Mheallaigh, K. (2014) *Reading fiction with Lucian: fakes, freaks and hyperreality*, Cambridge.

Mielsch, H. (1997) *Die römische Villa: Architektur und Lebensform*, 2nd edn, Munich.

Millar, F. (1977) *The emperor in the Roman world (31 BC – AD 337)*, London.

(1986) 'Italy and the Roman Empire: Augustus to Constantine', *Phoenix* 40, 295–318.

(2000) 'Trajan: government by correspondence' in J. Gonzales, ed., *Trajano emperador de Roma* (Madrid), 363–88. Reprinted in Millar 2004, 23–46, and in Gibson and Whitton 2016, 419–41.

(2004) *Rome, the Greek world and the east*, vol. II: *Government, society and culture in the Roman Empire*, Chapel Hill, NC.

Miller, J. F. and A. J. Woodman, eds. (2010) *Latin historiography and poetry in the early Empire: generic interactions*, Leiden.

Minni, D. P. (2007) 'The rescript of Hadrian' in S. Parvis and P. Foster, eds., *Justin Martyr and his worlds* (Minneapolis), 38–52.

Mitchell, S. (1976) 'Requisitioned transport in the Roman Empire: a new inscription from Pisidia', *JRS* 66, 106–31.

Moles, J. (1990) 'The *Kingship orations* of Dio Chrysostom', *PLLS* 6, 297–375.

(2005) 'The thirteenth Oration of Dio Chrysostom: complexity and simplicity, rhetoric and moralism, literature and life', *JHS* 125, 113–38.

Momigliano, A. (1942) 'Camillus and concord', *CQ* 36, 111–20.

Mommsen, T. (1868–70) *Digesta. Editio maior*, 2 vols., Berlin.

(1887–8) *Römisches Staatsrecht*, 3rd edn, 3 vols., Leipzig.

Mommsen, T. and P. Kruger (1963) *Corpus iuris civilis. I. Institutiones, Digesta*, 13th edn, Berlin.

Montiglio, S. (2011) *From villain to hero: Odysseus in ancient thought*, Ann Arbor.

Morello, R. (2007) 'Confidence, *inuidia* and Pliny's epistolary curriculum' in Morello and Morrison 2007, 169–90.

(2015) 'Pliny book 8: two viewpoints and the pedestrian reader' in Marchesi 2015a, 144–84.

Morello, R. and A. D. Morrison, eds. (2007) *Ancient letters: classical and late antique epistolography*, Oxford

Morford, M. P. O. (1992) '*Iubes esse liberos*: Pliny's *Panegyricus* and liberty', *AJP* 113, 575–93.

Morgan, K. (1977) *Ovid's art of imitation: Propertius in the* Amores, Leiden.

Morgan, T. (1998) *Literate education in the Hellenistic and Roman worlds*, Cambridge.

Morrison, A. D. (2014) 'Pamela and Plato: ancient and modern epistolary narrative' in D. Cairns and R. Scodel, eds., *Defining Greek narrative* (Edinburgh), 298–313.

(2007) 'Didacticism and epistolarity in Horace's *Epistles*', in Morello and Morrison 2007, 107–31.

Mratschek, S. (1984) '*Est enim ille flos Italiae*: Literatur und Gesellschaft in der Transpadana', *Athenaeum* 62, 154–89.

(1993) *Divites et praepotentes: Reichtum und soziale Stellung in der Literatur der Prinzipatszeit*, Stuttgart.

(2003) '*Illa nostra Italia*: Plinius und die Wiedergeburt der Literatur in der Transpadana' in Castagna and Lefèvre 2003, 219–41.

(2017) 'The letter collection of Sidonius Apollinaris' in C. Sogno, B. K. Storin and E. J. Watts, eds., *Late antique letter collections: a critical introduction and reference guide* (Oakland, CA), 309–36.

Murgia, C. W. (1980) 'The date of Tacitus' *Dialogus*', *HSCP* 84, 89–125.

(1985) 'Pliny's letters and the *Dialogus*', *HSCP* 89, 171–206.

Murphy, T. (2004) *Pliny the Elder's Natural history: the Empire in the encyclopedia*, Oxford.

Mynors, R. A. B. (1963) *C. Plini Caecili Secundi Epistularum libri decem*, Oxford (corrected reprint 1968).

Naiman, E. (2013) 'When Dickens met Dostoevsky', *TLS* 10.04.13.

Nappa, C. (2010) 'The unfortunate marriage of Gaius Silius: Tacitus and Juvenal on the fall of Messalina' in Miller and Woodman 2010, 189–204.

Narducci, E. (1973) 'Il tronco di Pompeio', *Maia* 25, 317–25.

(2002) *Lucano: un'epica contro l'impero*, Rome.

Nasrallah, L. S. (2010) *Christian responses to Roman art and architecture: the second-century church amid the spaces of Empire*, Cambridge.

Nauta, R. R. (2002) *Poetry for patrons: literary communication in the age of Domitian*, Leiden.

Nauta, R. R., H.-J. van Dam and J. J. L. Smolenaars, eds. (2006) *Flavian poetry*, Leiden.

Neger, M. (2012) *Martials Dichtergedichte: Das Epigramm als Medium der poetischen Selbstreflexion*, Tübingen.

(2015) 'Pliny's Martial and Martial's Pliny: the intertextual dialogue between the *Letters* and the *Epigrams*' in Devillers 2015, 131–44.

Neudecker, R. (2004) 'Aspekte öffentlicher Bibliotheken in der Kaiserzeit' in B. Borg, ed., *Paideia: the world of the Second Sophistic* (Berlin), 293–313.

(2013) 'Archives, books and sacred space in Rome' in König, Oikonomopoulou and Woolf 2013, 312–31.

Newmyer, S. T. (2003) 'Paws to reflect: ancients and moderns on the religious sensibilities of animals', *QUCC* 75, 111–29.

Nicholls, M. (2010) '*Bibliotheca Latina Graecaque*: on the possible division of Roman public libraries by language' in Perrin 2010, 11–21.

(2013) 'Roman libraries as public buildings in the cities of the Empire' in König, Oikonomopoulou and Woolf 2013, 261–76.

Nicolet, C., ed. (1995) *Les littératures techniques dans l'antiquité romaine: statut, public et destination, tradition*, Geneva.

Nisbet, G. (2003) *Greek epigram in the Roman Empire: Martial's forgotten rivals*, Oxford.

(1988) 'Notes on the text and interpretation of Juvenal', *BICS* Suppl. 51, 86–110.

Nisbet, R. G. M. and M. Hubbard (1978) *A commentary on Horace* Odes*, book II*, Oxford.

Nishimura-Jensen, J. (2000) 'Unstable geographies: the moving landscape in Apollonius' *Argonautica* and Callimachus' *Hymn to Delos*', *TAPA* 130, 287–317.

Nordh, A. (1954) 'Historical *exempla* in Martial', *Eranos* 52, 224–38.

Noreña, C. F. (2007) 'The social economy of Pliny's correspondence with Trajan', *AJP* 128, 239–78.

(2011a) 'Self-fashioning in the *Panegyricus*', in Roche 2011, 29–44.

(2011b) *Imperial ideals in the Roman west: representation, circulation, power*, Cambridge.

Nutton, V. (1986) 'The perils of patriotism. Pliny and Roman medicine' in R. French and F. Greenaway, eds., *Science in the early Roman Empire. Pliny the Elder, his sources and influence* (London), 30–58.

Oakley, S. P. (2005) *A commentary on Livy books VI–X*, vol. III, Oxford.

Obermayer, H. P. (1998) *Martial und der Diskurs über männliche 'Homosexualität' in der Literatur der frühen Kaiserzeit*, Tübingen.

O'Connor, E. (1998) 'Martial the moral jester: Priapic motifs and the restoration of order in the *Epigrams*' in Grewing 1998, 187–204.

O'Gorman, E. (1993) 'No place like Rome: identity and difference in the *Germania* of Tacitus', *Ramus* 22, 135–54.

(2014) 'Intertextuality, ideology and truth: re-reading Kristeva through Roman historiography', *Histos* Working Papers 2014.01.

Oikonomopoulou, K. (2013) 'Plutarch's corpus of *Quaestiones* in the tradition of imperial Greek encyclopaedism' in J. König and G. D. Woolf, eds., *Encyclopaedism from antiquity to the Renaissance* (Cambridge), 129–53.

Oliver, J. H. (1953) *The ruling power: a study of the Roman Empire in the second century after Christ through the Roman Oration of Aelius Aristides*, Philadelphia.

(1989) *Greek constitutions of early Roman emperors from inscriptions and papyri*, Philadelphia.

Opsomer, J. (2014) 'Plutarch and the Stoics' in Beck 2014, 88–103.

Orr, M. (2003) *Intertextuality: debates and contexts*, Cambridge.

Osgood, J. (2006) 'Eloquence under the triumvirs', *AJP* 127, 525–51.

Otte, J. P. (1992) '*Sanguis Iovis et Neptunia proles*: justice and the family in Valerius Flaccus' *Argonautica*', unpublished PhD dissertation, New York University.

Otto, A. (1890) *Die Sprichwörter und sprichwörtlichen Redensarten der Römer*, Leipzig.

Packer, J. (1995) 'Forum Traiani' in E. M. Steinby, ed., *Lexicon Topographicum Urbis Romae*, vol. II: *D–G* (Rome), 348–56.

(2001) *The Forum of Trajan in Rome: a study of the monuments in brief*, Berkeley.

Pagán, V. E. (2012a) *Conspiracy theory in Latin literature*, Austin, TX.

(2012b) *A companion to Tacitus*, Malden, MA.

Pais, H. (1884, published 1888) *Corporis inscriptionum Latinarum supplementa Italica. Fasc. I: Additamenta ad vol. 5 Galliae Cisalpinae*, Rome.

Panayotakis, C. (1995) *Theatrum Arbitri: theatrical elements in the Satyrica of Petronius*, Leiden.

(2008) 'Virgil on the popular stage' in E. Hall and R. Wyles, eds., *New directions in ancient pantomime* (Oxford), 185–97.

(2010) *Decimus Laberius. The fragments*, Cambridge.

Parker, H. N. (2009) 'Books and reading Latin poetry' in Johnson and Parker 2009, 186–229.

Pasoli, E. (1974) 'L'Epigramma 12,18 di Marziale e la cronologia dell'attività poetica di Giovenale' in L. Barbesi, ed., *Scritti in onore di C. Vassalini* (Verona), 347–55.

Paul, G. M. (1993) 'The presentation of Titus in the *Jewish War* of Josephus: two aspects', *Phoenix* 47, 56–66.

Pausch, D. (2004) *Biographie und Bildungskultur: Personendarstellungen bei Plinius dem Jüngeren, Gellius und Sueton*, Berlin.

Pavlovskis, Z. (1973) *Man in an artificial landscape: the marvels of civilization in imperial Roman literature*, Leiden.

Peachin, M. (2004) *Frontinus and the curae of the curator aquarum*, Stuttgart.

Peirano, I. (2012) *The rhetoric of the Roman fake: Latin pseudepigrapha in context*, Cambridge.

Pelling, C. (2009) 'The first biographers: Plutarch and Suetonius' in M. Griffin, ed., *A companion to Julius Caesar* (Malden, MA), 252–66.

(2013) 'Intertextuality, plausibility, and interpretation', *Histos* 7, 1–20.

(2014) 'Political philosophy' in Beck 2014, 149–62.

Penwill, J. L. (2003) 'Expelling the mind: politics and philosophy in Flavian Rome' in Boyle and Dominik 2003, 345–68.

Perrin, B. (1921) *Plutarch: Lives*, vol. x, Cambridge, MA.

Perrin, Y., ed. (2010) *Neronia VIII. Bibliothèques, livres et culture écrite dans l'empire romain de César à Hadrien*, Brussels.

Peterson, W. (1891) *M. Fabi Quintiliani Institutionis oratoriae liber decimus*, Oxford.

Petrain, D. (2013) 'Visual supplementation and metonymy in the Roman public library' in König, Oikonomopoulou and Woolf 2013, 332–46.

Pfister, M. (1985) 'Konzepte der Intertextualität' in U. Broich and M. Pfister, eds., *Intertextualität: Formen, Funktionen, anglistische Fallstudien* (Tübingen), 1–30.

Phiddian, R. (1995) *Swift's parody*, Cambridge.

Picone, G. (1978) *L'eloquenza di Plinio: teoria e prassi*, Palermo.

Pitcher, R. A. (1999) 'The hole in the hypothesis: Pliny and Martial reconsidered', *Mnemosyne* 52, 554–61.

Platthy, J. (1968) *Sources on the earliest Greek libraries with the testimonia*, Amsterdam.

Plaza, M. (2006) *The function of humour in Roman verse satire: laughing and lying*, Oxford.

Poiss, T. (2001) 'Horaz als Erotiker betrachtet: Überlegungen zu carm. 2, 8 und carm. 3, 9', *WS* 114, 251–66.

Powell, J. G. (2010) 'Juvenal and the *delatores*' in Kraus, Marincola and Pelling 2010, 222–44.

Power, T. (2007) 'Priam and Pompey in Suetonius' *Galba*', *CQ* 57, 792–6.

(2010) 'Pliny, *Letters* 5.10 and the literary career of Suetonius', *JRS* 100, 140–62.

(2012) 'Pyrrhus and Priam in Suetonius' *Tiberius*', *CQ* 62, 430–3.

(2014) 'Suetonius' Tacitus', *JRS* 104, 205–25.

Power, T. and R. K. Gibson, eds. (2014) *Suetonius the biographer: studies in Roman lives*, Oxford.

Preiswerk, R. (1934) 'Zeitgeschichtliches bei Valerius Flaccus', *Philologus* 43, 433–42.

Quint, D. (1993) *Epic and empire: politics and generic form from Virgil to Milton*, Princeton.

Rackham, H. (1938) *Pliny the Elder: Natural history*, 10 vols., Cambridge, MA.

Radice, B. (1969) *Pliny the Younger: Letters and Panegyricus*, 2 vols., Cambridge, MA.

Radicke, J. (2004) *Lucans poetische Technik. Studien zum historischen Epos*, Leiden.

Radner, K., ed. (2014) *State correspondence in the ancient world: from New Kingdom Egypt to the Roman Empire*, Oxford.

Ramage, E. S. (1989) 'Juvenal and the establishment: denigration of predecessor in the *Satires*', *ANRW* II.33.1, 640–707.

Reed, J. D. (2011) 'The *Bellum civile* as a Roman epic', in Asso 2011, 21–31.

Rees, R. (2001) 'To be and not to be: Pliny's paradoxical Trajan', *BICS* 45, 149–68.

(2011) 'Afterwords of praise' in Roche 2011, 175–88.

ed. (2012a) *Latin panegyric* (Oxford Readings in Classical Studies), Oxford.

(2012b) 'The modern history of Latin panegyric', in Rees 2012a, 3–48.

Reiff, A. (1959) *Interpretatio, imitatio, aemulatio: Begriff und Vorstellung literarischer Abhängigkeit bei den Römern*, Cologne.

Reinhardt, T. and M. Winterbottom (2006) *Quintilian:* Institutio oratoria *book 2*, Oxford.

Relihan, J. C. (1987) 'Vainglorious Menippus in Lucian's *Dialogues of the dead*', *ICS* 12, 185–206

Riggsby, A. M. (1995) 'Pliny on Cicero and oratory: self-fashioning in the public eye', *AJP* 116, 123–35.

(1998) 'Self and community in the Younger Pliny', *Arethusa* 31, 75–97. Reprinted in Gibson and Whitton 2016, 225–45.

Rigney, A. (2008) 'The dynamics of remembrance: texts between monumentality and morphing' in A. Erll and A. Nünning, eds., *Cultural memory studies: an international and interdisciplinary handbook* (Berlin), 345–53.

Rimell, V. (2008) *Martial's Rome: empire and the ideology of epigram*, Cambridge.

Río Torres-Murciano, A. (2006) 'Farsalia en la Cólquide. Acerca de dos símiles lucaneos en el libro VI de las *Argonáuticas* de Valerio Flaco', *Emerita* 74, 201–16.

Ripoll, F. (1998) *La morale héroïque dans les épopées latines d'époque flavienne: tradition et innovation*, Louvain.

Roche, P. A. (2002) 'The public image of Trajan's family', *CP* 97, 41–60.

(2003) 'The execution of L. Salvius Otho Cocceianus', *CQ* 53, 319–22.

ed. (2011) *Pliny's praise: the* Panegyricus *in the Roman world*, Cambridge.

Roda, S. (1985) *Iscrizioni latine di Vercelli*, Turin.

Rodgers, R. (2004) *Frontinus: De aquaeductu urbis Romae*, Cambridge.

Rolfe, J. C. (1914) *Suetonius*, 2 vols., Cambridge, MA.

Roller, M. (1997) '*Color*-blindness: Cicero's death, declamation and the production of history', *CP* 92, 109–30.

(1998) 'Pliny's Catullus: the politics of literary appropriation', *TAPA* 128, 265–304.

(2004) 'Exemplarity in Roman culture: the cases of Horatius Cocles and Cloelia', *CP* 99, 1–56.

(2009) 'The exemplary past in Roman historiography and culture' in Feldherr 2009, 214–30.

(2011) '"To whom am I speaking?" The changing venues of competitive eloquence in the early Empire' in W. Blösel and K.-J. Hölkeskamp, eds., *Von der militia equestris zur militia urbana. Prominenzrollen und Karrierefelder im antiken Rom* (Stuttgart), 197–221.

(2015) 'Between unique and typical: Senecan *exempla* in a list' in Lowrie and Lüdemann 2015a, 81–95.

Roman, L. (2010) 'Martial and the city of Rome', *JRS* 100, 88–117.

Romano, D. (1987) '*Sic me iuvat vivere*. Genesi e significato di Marziale XII 18' in S. Boldrini, ed. *Filologia e forme letterarie. Studi offerti a Francesco della Corte* (Urbino), IV, 25–9.

Rosati, G. (2009) '*Latrator Anubis*: alien divinities in Augustan Rome, and how to tame monsters through aetiology' in Hardie 2009, 268–87.

Rosenmeyer, P. A. (1992) *The poetics of imitation: Anacreon and the Anacreontic tradition*, Cambridge.

(2001) *Ancient epistolary fictions: the letter in Greek literature*, Cambridge.

Rossi, A. (2004) *Contexts of war: manipulation of genre in Virgilian battle narrative*, Ann Arbor.

Rosso, E. (2009) 'Le thème de la *Res publica restituta* dans le monnayage de Vespasien: pérennité du "modèle augustéen" entre citations, réinterprétations et dévoiements' in F. Hurlet and B. Mineo, eds., *Le principat d'Auguste: réalités et représentations du pouvoir autour de la* Res publica restituta (Rennes), 209–42.

Roth, U. (2016) 'Liberating the *Cena*', *CQ* 66, 614–34.

Rubin, D. C. (1995) *Memory in oral traditions: the cognitive psychology of epic, ballads, and counting-out rhymes*, Oxford.

Rudich, V. (1997) *Dissidence and literature under Nero: the price of rhetoricization*, New York.

Russell, D. A. (1979) 'De imitatione' in West and Woodman 1979, 1–16.

ed. (1990a) *Antonine literature*, Oxford.

(1990b) 'Introduction: Greek and Latin in Antonine literature' in Russell 1990a, 1–18.

(2001a) *Plutarch*, 2nd edn, London.

(2001b) *Quintilian: The orator's education*, 5 vols., Cambridge, MA.

Rutledge, S. H. (2009) 'Reading the prince: textual politics in Tacitus and Pliny' in Dominik, Garthwaite and Roche 2009, 429–46.

Ryan, F. X. (1998) *Rank and participation in the republican senate*, Stuttgart.

Sailor, D. (2004) 'Becoming Tacitus: significance and inconsequentiality in the prologue of *Agricola*', *CA* 23, 139–77.

(2008) *Writing and empire in Tacitus*, Cambridge.

(2012) '*Agricola*' in Pagán 2012b, 23–44.

Salemme, C. (1976) *Marziale e la 'poetica' degli oggetti*, Naples.

Saller, R. P. (1982) *Personal patronage under the early Empire*, Cambridge.

(1983) 'Martial on patronage and literature', *CQ* 33, 246–57.

(2000) 'Domitian and his successors: methodological traps in assessing emperors', *AJAH* 15, 4–18.

Salmeri, G. (2000) 'Dio, Rome, and the civic life of Asia Minor' in Swain 2000a, 53–92.

Santorelli, B. (2012) *Giovenale, Satira IV: introduzione, traduzione e commento*, Berlin.

Satlow, M. L., ed. (2013) *The gift in antiquity*, Chichester.

Sauron, G. (2010) 'La bibliothèque de Celsus à Éphèse: étude de sémantique architecturale et décorative' in Perrin 2010, 374–85.

Saylor, C. (1982) 'Overlooking Lake Vadimon: Pliny on tourism (*Epist.* 8.20)', *CP* 104, 216–20.

Schechner, R. (1985) *Between theatre and anthropology*, Philadelphia.

Schenk, P. (1999a) 'Formen von Intertextualität im Briefkorpus des jüngeren Plinius', *Philologus* 143, 114–34.

(1999b) *Studien zur poetischen Kunst des Valerius Flaccus. Beobachtungen zur Ausgestaltung des Kriegsthemas in den Argonautica*, Munich.

(2016) 'Forms of intertextuality in the *Epistles* of Pliny the Younger' in Gibson and Whitton 2016, 332–54.

Schepens, G. and K. Delcroix (1996) 'Ancient paradoxography: origin, evolution, production, and reception' in O. Pecere and A. Stramaglia, eds., *La letteratura di consumo nel mondo greco-latino* (Cassino), 375–460.

Scherf, J. (2001) *Untersuchungen zur Buchgestaltung Martials*, Munich.

Schmidt, E. A. (1977) 'Das horazische Sabinum als Dichterlandschaft', *AA* 23, 97–112.

Schmitz, T. A. (2014) 'Plutarch and the Second Sophistic' in Beck 2014, 32–42.

Schöffel, C. (2002) *Martial, Buch 8*, Stuttgart.

Schröder, B.-J. (2001) 'Literaturkritik oder Fauxpas? Zu Plin. epist. 6,15', *Gymnasium* 108, 241–7.

Schulz, F. (1946) *History of Roman legal science*, Oxford.

Schwarte, K. H. (1979) 'Trajans Regierungsbeginn und der *Agricola* des Tacitus', *Bonner Jahrbücher* 179, 139–75.

Scott, J. (1990) *Domination and the arts of resistance: hidden transcripts*, New Haven.

Scott-Baumann, A. (2011) *Ricoeur and the hermeneutics of suspicion*, London.

Scurr, R. (2015) *John Aubrey: My own life*, London.

Seel, O. (1977) *Quintilian, oder Die Kunst des Redens und Schweigens*, Stuttgart.

Seelentag, G. (2004) *Taten und Tugenden Trajans. Herrschaftsdarstellung im Principat*, Stuttgart.

Seo, J. M. (2009) 'Plagiarism and poetic identity in Martial', *AJP* 130, 567–93.

Serafini, A. (1947) *Il libro di Marziale. Epigrammi*, Turin.

Shackleton Bailey, D. R. (1993) *Martial: Epigrams*, 3 vols., Cambridge, MA.

Shero, L. R. (1933) 'The Vadimonian lake and floating islands of equatorial Africa', *Classical Weekly* 27, 51–2.

Sherwin-White, A. N. (1966) *The letters of Pliny: a historical and social commentary*, Oxford.

Shreeves, E. (1978) 'Landscape, topography and geographical notation in the *Argonautica* of Valerius Flaccus', unpublished PhD dissertation, University of North Carolina at Chapel Hill.

Sijpesteijn, P. J. (1969) 'A new document concerning Hadrian's visit to Egypt', *ZPE* 18, 109–18.

(1991) 'Another document concerning Hadrian's visit to Egypt', *ZPE* 89, 89–90.

Singleton, D. (1983) 'Juvenal's fifteenth Satire: a reading', *G&R* 30, 198–207.

Smelik, K. A. D. and E. A. Hemelrijk (1984) '"Who knows not what monsters demented Egypt worships?" Opinions on Egyptian animal worship in antiquity as part of the ancient conception of Egypt', *ANRW* II.17.4, 1852–2000.

Smiraglia, P. (1955) 'Il *Dialogo*. Cronologie e rapporti con l'insegnamento di Quintiliano', *AFLN* 5, 159–89.

Smith, S. H. (2002) 'Tacitus' *Agricola*: representing imperial Rome', unpublished PhD dissertation, University of Birmingham.

Soerink, J. (2013) 'Statius, Silius Italicus and the snake pit of intertextuality' in G. Manuwald and A. Voigt, eds., *Flavian epic interactions* (Berlin), 361–78.

Spahlinger, L. (2004) '*Quem recitas, meus est, o Fidentine, libellus*. Martials Fidentinus-Zyklus und das Problem des Plagiats', *Hermes* 132, 472–94.

Spisak, A. L. (1999) 'Martial on Domitian: a socio-anthropological perspective', *CB* 75, 69–83.

(2002) 'The pastoral ideal in Martial, Book 10', *CW* 95, 127–41.

Squire, M. (2013) 'Ars in their "I"s: authority and authorship in Graeco-Roman visual culture' in A. Marmodoro and J. Hill, eds., *The author's voice in classical and late antiquity* (Oxford), 357–414.

Stadter, P. A. (1980) *Arrian of Nicomedia*, Chapel Hill, NC.

(2002) 'Plutarch and Trajanic ideology' in Stadter and van der Stockt 2002, 227–42.

(2006) 'Pliny and the ideology of empire: the correspondence with Trajan', *Prometheus* 32, 61–76.

(2015) *Plutarch and his Roman readers*, Cambridge.

Stadter, P. A. and L. Van der Stockt, eds. (2002) *Sage and emperor: Plutarch, Greek intellectuals and Roman power in the time of Trajan (98–117 AD)*, Leuven.

Starr, R. J. (1987) 'The circulation of literary texts in the Roman world', *CQ* 37, 213–23.

Steel, C. (2013) 'Pompeius, Helvius Mancia and the politics of public debate' in C. Steel and H. van der Blom, eds., *Community and communication: oratory and politics in republican Rome* (Oxford), 151–9.

Stein, J. P. (1970) 'The unity and scope of Juvenal's fourteenth Satire', *CP* 65, 34–6.

Stertz, S. A. (1993) '*Semper in omnibus varius*: the emperor Hadrian and intellectuals', *ANRW* II.34.1, 612–28.

Stoppard, T. (1975) *Travesties*, London.

(1997) *The invention of love*, London.

Stout, S. E. (1955) 'The coalescence of the two Plinys', *TAPA* 86, 250–5.

Stover, T. (2012) *Epic and empire in Vespasianic Rome: a new reading of Valerius Flaccus'* Argonautica, Oxford.

(forthcoming) '*Nulla fides, nulli super Hercule fletus*? Shifting loyalties in the *Argonautica* of Valerius Flaccus'.

Stramaglia, A. (1999) *Res inauditae, incredulae: storie di fantasmi nel mondo greco-latino*, Bari.

Sullivan, J. P. (1979) 'Martial's sexual attitudes', *Philologus* 123, 418–32.

(1991) *Martial – the unexpected classic: a literary and historical study*, Cambridge.

Sullivan, J. P and A. J. Boyle (1996) *Martial in English*, Harmondsworth.

Swain, S. (1989) 'Favorinus and Hadrian', *ZPE* 79, 150–8.

(1996) *Hellenism and empire: language, classicism, and power in the Greek world, AD 50–250*, Oxford.

ed. (2000a) *Dio Chrysostom: politics, letters and philosophy*, Oxford.

(2000b) 'Reception and interpretation' in Swain 2000a, 13–52.

(2013) *Economy, family, and society from Rome to Islam: a critical edition, English translation, and study of Bryson's* Management of the estate, Cambridge.

Swain, S., S. J. Harrison and J. Elsner, eds. (2007) *Severan culture*, Cambridge.

Syme, R. (1929) 'The *Argonautica* of Valerius Flaccus', *CQ* 23, 129–37.

(1930) 'Imperial finances under Domitian, Nerva and Trajan', *JRS* 20, 55–70 = *RP* I, 1–17.

(1957) 'The jurist Neratius Priscus', *Hermes* 85, 480–93 = *RP* I, 339–52.

(1958) *Tacitus*, 2 vols., Oxford.

(1968a) 'The Ummidii', *Historia* 17, 72–105 = *RP* II, 659–93.

(1968b) 'People in Pliny', *JRS* 58, 135–51 = *RP* II, 694–723.

(1979) 'Juvenal, Pliny, Tacitus', *AJP* 100, 250–78 = *RP* III, 1135–57.

(1980) 'Biographers of the Caesars', *Museum Helveticum* 37, 104–28 = *RP* III, 1251–75.

(1981) 'The travels of Suetonius Tranquillus', *Hermes* 109, 105–17 = *RP* III, 1337–49.

(1982a) *Greeks invading the Roman government*, Brookline, MA = *RP* IV, 1–20.

(1982b) 'The career of Arrian', *HSCP* 86, 181–211 = *RP* IV, 21–49.

(1983) 'Domitian: the last years', *Chiron* 13, 121–46 = *RP* IV, 252–77.

(1984) 'Hadrian and the senate', *Athenaeum* 52, 31–60 = *RP* IV, 295–324.

(1985a) 'Correspondents of Pliny', *Historia* 34, 324–59 = *RP* V, 440–77.

(1985b) 'Hadrian as philhellene. Neglected aspects' in J. Straub, ed., *Bonner Historia-Augusta-Colloquium 1982/1983* (Bonn), 341–62 = *RP* V, 546–62.

(1991a) 'Fictional history old and new: Hadrian', *RP* VI, 157–81.

(1991b) *Roman papers*, vol. VII (ed. A. R. Birley), Oxford.

Tabors, P. O. (1997) *One child, two languages: a guide for early childhood educators of children learning English as a second language*, Baltimore.

Talbert, R. J. A. (1980) 'Pliny the Younger as governor of Bithynia–Pontus' in C. Deroux, ed., *Studies in Latin literature and Roman history*, II (Brussels), 412–35.

(1984) *The senate of imperial Rome*, Princeton.

(1988) 'Commodus as diplomat in an extract from the *acta senatus*', *ZPE* 71, 137–47.

Taub, L. C. and A. Doody, eds. (2009) *Authorial voices in Greco-Roman technical writing*, Trier.

Taylor, D. (2003) *The archive and the repertoire: performing cultural memory in the Americas*, Durham, NC.

Thomas, R. F. (1986) 'Virgil's *Georgics* and the art of reference', *HSCP* 90, 171–98.

Thornborrow, J. and J. Coates, eds. (2005) *The sociolinguistics of narrative*, Amsterdam.

Thulin, C. (1913) *Corpus agrimensorum Romanorum I.1*, Leipzig (repr. Stuttgart 1971).

Timpe, B. (2007) 'L'insurrezione dei Batavi nell'interpretazione di Tacito' in Giua 2007, 201–20.

Toohey, P. (1993) 'Jason, Pallas and Domitian in Valerius Flaccus' *Argonautica*', *ICS* 18, 191–201.

Townend, G. B. (1959) 'The date of composition of Suetonius' *Caesares*', *CQ* 9, 285–93.

Tränkle, H. (1996) 'Exegetisches zu Martial', *WS* 109, 133–44.

Trapp, M. B. (2003) *Greek and Latin letters: an anthology with translation*, Cambridge.

    (2014) 'The role of philosophy and philosophers in the imperial period' in Beck 2014, 43–57.

Trisoglio, F. (1972) 'Le idee politiche di Plinio il Giovane e di Dione Crisostomo', *Il Pensiero Politico* 5, 3–43.

    (1973) *Opere di Plinio Cecilio Secondo*, 2 vols., Turin.

Tucci, P. L. (2013) 'Flavian libraries in the city of Rome' in König, Oikonomopoulou and Woolf 2013, 277–311.

Turner, A. (2007) 'Frontinus and Domitian: *laus principis* in the *Strategemata*', *HSCP* 103, 423–49.

Uden, J. (2011) 'The invisibility of Juvenal', unpublished PhD dissertation, Columbia University.

    (2015) *The invisible satirist: Juvenal and second-century Rome*, Oxford.

Ussani, V., Jr (1955) *Studio su Valerio Flacco*, Rome.

Valette-Cagnac, E. (1995) 'La *recitatio*, écriture orale' in F. Dupont, ed., *Paroles romaines* (Nancy), 9–23.

    (1997) *La lecture à Rome: rites et pratiques*, Paris.

van den Berg, C. S. (2014) *The world of Tacitus' Dialogus de oratoribus: aesthetics and empire in ancient Rome*, Cambridge.

van der Poel, M. (2009) 'The use of *exempla* in Roman declamation', *Rhetorica* 27, 332–53.

Van Hoof, L. (2010) *Plutarch's practical ethics: the social dynamics of philosophy*, Oxford.

    (2014) 'Practical ethics' in Beck 2014, 135–48.

    (2016) 'Falsification as a protreptic to truth: the force of the forged epistolary exchange between Basil and Libanius' in P. Gemeinhardt, L. Van Hoof and P. van Nuffelen, eds., *Education and religion in late antiquity* (Abingdon), 116–30.

van Meirvenne, B. (2002) 'Plutarch on the healing power of (a tricky) *parrhesia*' in Stadter and van der Stockt 2002, 141–60.

van Waarden, J. and G. Kelly, eds. (2013) *New approaches to Sidonius Apollinaris*, Leuven.

Varner, E. (2004) *Mutilation and transformation:* damnatio memoriae *and Roman imperial portraiture*, Leiden.

Versnel, H. S. (1993) *Inconsistencies in Greek and Roman religion*, vol. II: *Transition and reversal in myth and ritual*, 2nd edn, Leiden.

Vidman, L. (1982) *Fasti Ostienses*, 2nd edn, Prague.

Vigourt, A. (2001) 'M'. Curius Dentatus et C. Fabricius Luscinus: les grands hommes ne sont pas exceptionnels' in Coudry and Spaeth 2001, 117–29.

Völker, T. and D. Rohmann (2011) '*Praenomen Petronii*: the date and authorship of the *Satyricon* reconsidered', *CQ* 61, 660–76.

Volkmann, R. (1869) *Leben, Schriften und Philosophie des Plutarch von Chaeronea*, 2 vols., Berlin.

Vout, C. (2005) 'Antinous, archaeology and history', *JRS* 95, 80–96.

Wallace-Hadrill, A. (1983) *Suetonius: a scholar and his Caesars*, London.

Walsh, P. G. (2006) *Pliny the Younger, complete Letters*, Oxford.

Walzer, A. (2006) 'Moral philosophy and rhetoric in the *Institutes*: Quintilian on honor and expediency', *Rhetoric Society Quarterly* 36, 263–81.

Wardle, D. (2014) *Suetonius:* Life of Augustus, Oxford.

Waters, K. H. (1969) 'Traianus Domitiani continuator', *AJP* 90, 385–404.

Watson, L. C. (2003) *A commentary on Horace's* Epodes, Oxford.

Watson, L. C. and P. A. Watson, eds. (2003) *Martial: select epigrams*, Cambridge. eds. (2014), *Juvenal: Satire 6*, Cambridge.

Watson, P. A. (2005) '*Non tristis torus et tamen pudicus*: the sexuality of the *matrona* in Martial', *Mnemosyne* 58, 62–87.

Welch, T. (2013) 'Was Valerius Maximus a hack?' in Baraz and van den Berg 2013, 67–82.

Wellesley, K. (2000) *The Year of the Four Emperors*, 3rd edn, London.

West, D., and A. J. Woodman, eds. (1979) *Creative imitation and Latin literature*, Cambridge.

White, P. (1975) 'The friends of Martial, Statius and Pliny, and the dispersal of patronage', *HSCP* 79, 265–300.

(1978) '*Amicitia* and the profession of poetry in early imperial Rome', *JRS* 68, 74–92.

(2009) 'Bookshops in the literary culture of Rome' in Johnson and Parker 2009, 268–87.

(2010) *Cicero in letters: epistolary relations of the late Republic*, Oxford.

Whitmarsh, T. J. G. (2001) *Greek literature and the Roman Empire: the politics of imitation*, Oxford.

(2006a) 'The sincerest form of imitation: Plutarch on flattery' in D. Konstan and S. Saïd, eds., *Greeks on Greekness: viewing the Greek past under the Roman Empire* (Cambridge), 93–111.

(2006b) '"This in-between book": language, politics and genre in the *Agricola*' in B. McGing and J. Mossman, eds., *The limits of ancient biography* (Swansea), 305–33.

(2007) 'Prose literature and the Severan dynasty' in Swain, Harrison and Elsner 2007, 29–51.

(2013) *Beyond the Second Sophistic: adventures in Greek postclassicism*, Berkeley.

Whitton, C. L. (2008) Review of Giua 2007, *BMCR* 2008.09.53.

(2010) 'Pliny, *Epistles* 8.14: slavery, senate and the *Agricola*', *JRS* 100, 118–39.

(2012) '"Let us tread our path together": Tacitus and the Younger Pliny' in Pagán 2012b, 345–68.

(2013) *Pliny the Younger: Epistles book II*, Cambridge.

(2015a) 'Pliny's progress: on a troublesome Domitianic career', *Chiron* 45, 1–22.

(2015b) 'Grand designs: unrolling *Epistles* 2' in Marchesi 2015a, 109–43.

(2015c) 'Pliny on the precipice (*Ep.*, 9.26)' in Devillers 2015, 217–36.

(forthcoming a) 'Biography and praise in Trajanic Rome: Tacitus' *Agricola* and Pliny's *Panegyricus*' in K. de Temmerman, ed., *Oxford handbook of ancient biography* (Oxford).

(forthcoming b) *Pliny's* Epistles *and the arts of imitation: Quintilian in brief.*

Whitton, C. L. and R. K. Gibson (2016) 'Readers and readings of Pliny's *Epistles*' in Gibson and Whitton 2016, 1–46.

Wiesen, D. (1963) 'Juvenal's moral character, an introduction', *Latomus* 22, 440–71.

Wijsman, H. J. W. (1996) *Valerius Flaccus,* Argonautica, *book V: a commentary*, Leiden.

(2000) *Valerius Flaccus,* Argonautica, *book VI: a commentary*, Leiden.

Wilamowitz-Moellendorff, U. von (1889) *Commentariolum grammaticum* III, Göttingen = *Kleine Schriften* IV (Berlin, 1962), 619–59.

Wilkes J. J. (1983) 'Romans, Dacians and Sarmatians in the first and early second centuries' in B. Hartley and J. Wacher, eds., *Rome and her northern provinces: papers presented to S. Frere . . .* (Gloucester), 255–89.

Williams, C. A. (2002) '*Sit nequior omnibus libellis*: text, poet, and reader in the *Epigrams* of Martial', *Philologus* 146, 150–71.

ed. (2004) *Martial: Epigrams book 2*, Oxford.

(2010) *Roman homosexuality*, 2nd edn, Oxford.

Williams, Wes (2011) *Monsters and their meanings in early modern culture: mighty magic*, Oxford.

Williams, Wynne (1990) *Pliny: correspondence with Trajan from Bithynia (*Epistles X*)*, Warminster.

Wills, J. (1996) *Repetition in Latin poetry: figures of allusion*, Oxford.

Wilson, M. (2003) 'After the silence: Tacitus, Suetonius, Juvenal' in Boyle and Dominik 2003, 523–42.

Winsbury, R. (2013) *Pliny the Younger: a life in Roman letters*, London.

Winterbottom, M. (1964) 'Quintilian and the *vir bonus*', *JRS* 54, 90–7.

(1970) *M. Fabi Quintiliani Institutionis oratoriae libri duodecim*, Oxford.

(1984) *The Minor declamations ascribed to Quintilian*, Berlin.

Wiseman, T. P. (2015) *The Roman audience: classical literature as social history*, Oxford.

Wolff, E. (2003) *Pline le Jeune, ou le refus du pessimisme*, Rennes.

(2009) 'Ambiguïtés de Martial' in B. Delignon and Y. Roman, eds., *Le poète irrévérencieux: modèles hellénistiques et réalités romaines* (Paris), 267–75.

Woodman, A. J. (1997) 'Tacitus' in C. S. Kraus and A. J. Woodman, *Latin historians* (Greece & Rome New Surveys in the Classics) (Oxford), 88–118.

(1998) *Tacitus reviewed*, Oxford.

ed. (2009a) *The Cambridge companion to Tacitus*, Cambridge.

(2009b) 'Tacitus and the contemporary scene' in Woodman 2009a, 31–43.

(2012) *From poetry to history: selected papers*, Oxford.

(2014) *Tacitus: Agricola*. With C. S. Kraus, Cambridge.

Woodman, A. J. and R. H. Martin (1996) *The Annals of Tacitus book 3*, Cambridge.

Woolf, G. D. (1998) *Becoming Roman: the origins of provincial civilization in Gaul*, Cambridge.

(2006) 'Pliny's province' in T. Bekker-Nielsen, ed., *Rome and the Black Sea region: domination, Romanisation, resistance* (Aarhus), 93–108. Reprinted in Gibson and Whitton 2016, 442–60.

(2015) 'Pliny/Trajan and the poetics of empire', *CP* 110, 132–51.

Woytek, E. (2006) 'Der Panegyricus des Plinius. Sein Verhältnis zum Dialogus und den Historiae des Tacitus und seine absolute Datierung', *WS* 119, 115–56.

Xenophontos, S. (2015) 'Plutarch' in W. M. Bloomer, ed., *A companion to ancient education* (Malden, MA), 335–46.

Yourcenar, M. (1955) *Memoirs of Hadrian* (trans. of *Mémoires d'Hadrien*, Paris 1951), London.

Zadorojnyi, A. (2002) 'Safe drugs for the good boys: Platonism and pedagogy in Plutarch's *De audiendis poetis*' in Stadter and van der Stockt 2002, 297–314.

(2013) 'Libraries and *paideia* in the Second Sophistic: Plutarch and Galen' in König, Oikonomopoulou and Woolf 2013, 377–400.

Zissos, A. (2004) 'Navigating genres: Martial 7.19 and the *Argonautica* of Valerius Flaccus', *CJ* 94, 405–22.

(2006) 'Sailing and sea storm in Valerius Flaccus (*Arg.* 1.574–642): the rhetoric of inundation' in Nauta, van Dam and Smolenaars 2006, 79–95.

(2008) *Valerius Flaccus' Argonautica, book 1: a commentary*, Oxford.

(2009) 'Navigating power: Valerius Flaccus' *Argonautica*' in Dominik, Garthwaite and Roche 2009, 351–66.

ed. (2016) *A companion to the Flavian age of Rome*, Malden, MA.

Žižek, S. (1997) 'With or without passion: what's wrong with fundamentalism? – Part 1', www.lacan.com/zizpassion.htm.

Zwierlein, O. (1997) 'Die chronische Unpäßlichkeit des Messalla Corvinus', *Hermes* 125, 85–91.

Index Locorum

General Index

Printed in Great Britain
by Amazon

77301067R00281